URBAN
PROBLEMS:
PSYCHOLOGICAL
INQUIRIES

URBAN PROBLEMS: PSYCHOLOGICAL INQUIRIES

readings and text

edited by

Neil C. Kalt and Sheldon S. Zalkind
Baruch College, City University of New York

with a Foreword by
Timothy W. Costello

New York · Oxford University Press · 1976

Foreword

In 1960 Baritz concluded his angry but thoughtfully powerful book, *The Servants of Power,* by stating:

> Over the years through hundreds and hundreds of experiments, social scientists have come close to a true science of behavior. They are now beginning to learn how to control conduct. Put this power—genuine, stark, irrevocable power—into the hands of America's managers and the work that social scientists have done, and will do, assumes implications vaster and more fearful than anything previously hinted.

This book, rather than placing social science knowledge in the hands of industrial managers, seeks to place it in the hands of urbanists, who can then use it to help solve America's most desperate problems—those directly faced by the poor and otherwise disadvantaged and excluded who have been concentrated in misery in the large cities of our country. Accordingly, Baritz's fears about the power of social science research in one direction can perhaps be converted into strong hopes about the usefulness of that knowledge, when it is differently directed, for solving some of society's large problems—racism, poverty, inadequate housing and education, violence, and the effect of congested and polluted environments on the functioning and happiness of people.

During the past quarter of a century, while America's large cities were moving inexorably toward crisis, sociologists have been organizing their research into the perspectives of an urban sociology; few psychologists have done so. This book sets a pattern for psychologists and others to lend the power of their insights to those who now and in the future will have the responsibility for making decisions affecting millions of their fellow citizens. It also makes useful reading for others who, while not directly responsible, will, with their votes and their taxes, have to support major efforts to solve overwhelmingly complex problems. One can hope, too, that the book will help produce a long overdue shift in research support from the problems of defense, space exploration, and corporate success to the much more difficult problems of people living together in congested cities with little money, high unemployment, inadequate housing, meager education, and a great deal of anger.

As one who in the past has had the opportunity of working as Deputy Mayor—City Administrator on the problems of New York City, I can certainly vouch for the value of research-based information to guide policy decisions in almost every aspect of municipal government. I can also agree with the authors' selection of problem areas. The problems examined continue to puzzle even the most sophisticated of urbanists. The authors have provided a representative survey of research findings in each of eight of the most troublesome areas of urban life. They purport to offer no easy solutions, nor are they often able to present any final conclusions. They do offer, through their introductory reviews and the research reports presented, more guidance on human behavior than has up to now been readily available to urban policy makers and their technicians.

Timothy W. Costello
President, Adelphi University

Loren Baritz. *The Servants of Power.* Middletown, Conn.: Wesleyan University Press, 1960.

Preface

American cities seem to be caught in a web of increasingly intractable problems. For example, large numbers of city dwellers are poor. Blacks continue to have less access to educational, employment, and housing opportunities than do whites. Many people live in dwellings that are badly in need of repair. A distressingly large proportion of lower-class children are not getting an adequate education. The individual and social costs of drug use are considerable. Numerous crimes against people and property are committed. And the quality of many urban environments continues to decline.

Although these problems cannot be ameliorated without an infusion of large sums of money, money provides no guarantee that the strategies and tactics chosen will work. Instead, the utility of different strategies will probably depend on how well we understand each problem and the ways in which the several problems interact, and how carefully those strategies are designed and carried out. Toward that end, there is much that psychological research can tell us. For example, does long-term compensatory education improve the schoolwork of lower-class children? How does the design of low-income public housing affect the attitudes and behavior of the residents? Who participates in riots, and why?

In an attempt to pull together the psychological theories and research findings that shed light on these problems, we have chosen a sizable number of articles, placed them in appropriately labeled categories, and introduced each category with a selective overview of the literature. We are grateful to the authors and publishers for granting permission to reprint these articles. The choice of articles was guided by several considerations. First, we wanted to present the most pertinent theories and research findings on each problem. As a result, we selected a mix of original research and of literature reviews. Second, we felt that an understanding of urban problems requires a research strategy whose major tactic is the field study. The articles we have chosen reflect this bias, although laboratory research is not excluded. Third, our choices were influenced by the recency as well as the quality of the research. Fourth, we felt it was important to draw upon the research findings in a wide range of sources. Accordingly, we looked at portions of the psychological, sociological, educational, criminological, and ecological literatures. Though these are diverse sources, each of the articles we have chosen is concerned with psychological variables as antecedents, mediators, and/or consequents.

The articles are organized into the following categories: prejudice and racism, poverty, housing, education, drug use, crime, ghetto riots, and effects of the urban environment. In an attempt to provide a framework for the articles that examine each problem and to bring to the reader's attention theoretical positions and research findings that are not covered by the articles, we have prefaced each area with a selective review of the theory and research in that area. Taken together, these reviews and reports suggest that a variety of strategies can lessen the severity of many urban problems.

Although the readings and reviews shed considerable light, the approach we have taken has imposed limitations on our ability to examine the different problems and proposed solutions. When we could not locate any psychological research on an issue, we commented very little or not at all on that issue. Consequently, we have said little or nothing about certain important questions that have been the subject of much speculation and controversy: for example, the factors that motivate people who repeatedly commit serious crimes.

We hope that the book will help to inform many of the people who will eventually deal with the problems that confront cities. We hope, too, that the people who currently formulate policy and make the decisions that determine the directions in which cities move also find the data and their implications useful.

New York   N.C.K.
February 1976   S.S.Z.

Contents

3 HOUSING

4 EDUCATION

5 DRUG USE

6 CRIME

7 GHETTO RIOTS

8 EFFECTS OF THE URBAN ENVIRONMENT

1

PREJUDICE
AND RACISM

Introduction

Prejudice and racism continue to exist at cultural, institutional, and individual levels (Jones, 1972), despite the steps that blacks have taken toward achieving equality in this country. At the cultural level, racism appears to be sustained by a belief in the superiority of white traditions, values, language, and philosophy; and by white control of institutions, with the result that the lives of blacks are tied to standards that reflect white beliefs. For example, intelligence tests whose language and content deviate considerably from the vernacular and experience of many lower-class black children are used to assess the intelligence of those children (Sigelman, 1972); measures of standard English are used to determine the linguistic ability of blacks who speak black English vernacular—the dialect spoken by many black youths who live in inner-city ghettos (Baratz, 1969); and middle-class definitions of psychopathology are used to label as deviant the responses of lower-class blacks to poverty (Allen, 1970). At the institutional level, racial inequities are produced by laws, customs, and practices that appear to result from cultural assumptions, individual prejudice, and the acceptance of norms. For example, black high school students are usually placed in commercial or general, as opposed to academic programs (Stein, 1971), and blacks consistently earn less than whites at the same educational and occupational levels (T. Cook, 1970). At the individual level, prejudice and discrimination seem to be due primarily to the socializing influences of racist institutional practices. For example, discriminatory educational and employment practices have resulted in a disproportionately large number of unemployed or underemployed blacks. As a result, many whites may feel or believe that blacks are not ambitious and industrious, and may, both as individuals and as members of institutions, act in ways that are consistent with those beliefs. In an attempt to move toward an understanding of cultural, institutional,

3

and individual racism, let us examine research findings that shed light on some of the forms that racism takes at each of these levels.[1]

CULTURAL RACISM

The cognitive complexity of the language people speak is one apparent indicator of the nature of their culture. In an attempt to determine the relationship between race and linguistic development, Deutsch (1965) administered 52 measures of linguistic skills to 127 first-graders and 165 fifth-graders.[2] Each group contained equivalent numbers of black and white lower- and middle-class children. The findings indicate that black first-graders had significantly lower scores than white first-graders on six measures and higher scores on two measures. There were no differences on the remaining 44 measures. Among fifth graders, blacks had lower scores on 17 tests—most were designed to measure abstract and categorical use of language—and higher scores on one test. Based on these findings, Deutsch argued that the linguistic skills of black children become increasingly deficient as they advance through the primary grades. In a study of inner-city black and white elementary school students, Entwisle and Greenberger (1969) noted that "the data from kindergarten children unselected on IQ suggest that the typical inner-city black child is probably rather far behind the typical white child in linguistic development at the time of school entrance" (p. 248). They also noted that the responses of black and white first- and third-graders matched on IQ suggest that there are "large differences in semantic structures between white and black disadvantaged children" (p. 248).

While Deutsch (1965) and Entwisle and Greenberger (1969) proposed that the difference between the scores of white and black children was due to a linguistic deficit among the black children, there appear to be more plausible interpretations of the data. One, diverse subcultural groups may interpret the testing situation differently—the setting, the instructions, and the task—and may be differentially motivated to perform effectively (Labov, 1970). For example, black fifth-graders may have obtained relatively low scores because they were alienated by four years of school and/or because there was little apparent overlap between their nonschool experiences and the content of the tests. Cole and Bruner (1971, reading 1.1) examined this argument and the research findings and concluded that "cultural differences reside more in differences in the situa-

---

1. The attitudes and behaviors of whites toward blacks have been the subject of a great many investigations. Clearly, several readings cannot possibly represent the findings of those investigations. However, we feel that several readings can provide major points of reference in an examination of a portion of the literature. Toward that end, this review and the articles that follow focus on some of the dynamics of cultural, institutional, and individual racism—reflecting our belief that an under-

standing of racism requires an understanding of attitudes and behaviors at each of these interacting levels. Although groups other than blacks—for example, Indians, Jews, and Puerto Ricans—have been discriminated against, we have limited our review to black-white relations because of the profound impact they have had on this country.
2. Deutsch also examined the relationship between social class and linguistic development.

tions to which different cultural groups apply their skills than to differences in the skills possessed by the groups in question" (p. 874). Two, extensive observation of black preadolescents and adolescents led Labov (1972) to conclude that the language spoken by many inner-city black youths "is a separate system, closely related to standard English but set apart from the surrounding white dialects by a number of persistent and systematic differences" (p. 237). In other words, black English vernacular "differs from other dialects in regular and rule-governed ways, so that it has equivalent ways of expressing the same logical content" (p. 238). Labov's findings suggest that many inner-city blacks are linguistically different rather than deficient. Accordingly, it seems plausible to argue that Entwisle and Greenberger (1969) called a difference a deficit, and that the relatively poor performance of black fifth-graders observed by Deutsch (1965) may have been due, in part, to the failure of the schools to respond constructively to the linguistic difference between whites and many blacks.

A second apparent indicator of a group's culture is the stability of its families. Based on comparative data on illegitimacy rates, unemployment rates, female-headed families, delinquency, and crime, Moynihan (1965) argued that the lower-class black family is increasingly disorganized and a major cause of pathology in the black community. However, a critical examination of the validity of measures of illegitimacy rates and the reasons for those rates, of comparative percentages of black and white female-headed families when family income is controlled for, and of comparative unemployment rates and their implications led TenHouten (1970, reading 1.2) to conclude that "the evidence for deterioration of the black family . . . does not support the conclusion drawn from it" (p. 155). Rather, the data suggest that family disorganization is tied far more closely to class than to race. For example, while the difference between the proportions of black families and white families in urban areas that are headed by a female is considerable (33% versus 8%), comparison of black and white families whose annual incomes are under $3,000 indicates that the percentages of female-headed homes are 47 and 38, respectively. Among black and white families with annual incomes of $3,000 or more, the proportions are 8% and 4% (TenHouten, 1970). Thus, income is a far more powerful correlate of family separation than race. Similarly, "part of the instability of unemployment behavior for blacks derives from the fact that they are more apt to be lower-class than whites. When social class is controlled, much of the race difference in employment behavior is removed" (TenHouten, 1970, p. 155). One plausible explanation of the difference that remains is the job discrimination that has been directed toward blacks.

The data, then, imply that lower-class families, black and white, are affected adversely by their highly unfavorable positions in the labor market. The data also imply that a disproportionately large number of blacks occupy those positions because of racist institutional practices; for example, black children have been treated less favorably than white children in school settings (Beeghley & Butler, 1974; Rubovits & Maehr, 1973, reading 1.3; Stein, 1971), blacks have been treated less favorably than whites by police officers and judges (Chiricos, Jackson, & Waldo, 1972; Ferdinand & Luchterhand, 1970; Goldman, 1963; Piliavin & Briar, 1964, reading 1.4), and blacks have rarely been hired for white-collar positions by many large corporations (Eidson, 1968).

INSTITUTIONAL RACISM

The relatively poor scholastic performance of black children has, in part, been attributed to the attitudes and behaviors of white teachers toward those children (e.g., Ryan, 1971; Stein, 1971). In a partial test of this hypothesis, Rubovits and Maehr (1973, reading 1.3) tried to find out if the race and labeled ability of students influence teacher-student interaction. The teachers were 66 white female undergraduates enrolled in a teacher-training course. The students were 264 seventh and eighth graders who were selected randomly within levels of ability. Two white and two black students from the same ability level were randomly assigned to each teacher, who was given a lesson plan and a seating chart that contained each student's first name, IQ score, and a label indicating whether the student had been selected from the school's gifted program or from the regular track. Actually, one black and one white student were randomly assigned high IQs and the label "gifted." The other two students were given average IQs and the label "nongifted." The presence of each student's IQ and track was justified by explaining that this information could help the teacher to deal more effectively with each student during the session, which lasted 40 minutes.

The results indicate that teachers gave the statements made by black children less attention, less praise, and more criticism than the statements of white children. They also indicate that the statements of "gifted" black children were given the least attention, the least praise, and the most criticism. "Gifted" white children, on the other hand, received the most attention and the most praise. Teachers also chose the "gifted" white child most frequently as the most liked student, the brightest student, and the leader of the class. While the generalizability of the findings may be limited by the use of one 40-minute class, four seventh and eighth graders per class, and inexperienced female teachers, the findings identify some of the ways in which teachers may discriminate against black students, and suggest some of the reasons why blacks get lower grades than whites.

In an attempt to find out if teachers in actual classrooms respond less favorably to black children than to white children, Byalick and Bersoff (1974) observed 30 white and 30 black elementary school teachers in 15 southern schools. The results indicate that white teachers gave black males more praise and encouragement than white males. They also indicate that black females and white females received similar amounts of positive reinforcement. While the findings imply that white teachers did not discriminate against black children, three factors suggest that these behaviors may not be representative. One, the teachers who participated were volunteers. Unfortunately, Byalick and Bersoff did not tell us how many teachers chose not to volunteer. Two, the teachers knew they were being observed. Three, teachers were only observed for 30 minutes. During this period, black teachers gave white males more praise and encouragement than black males, though there was no difference in the amounts of reinforcement accorded white females and black females. Accordingly, it seems likely that white teachers, rather than disregarding each child's race, tried to avoid favoring white males, while black teachers tried to avoid favoring black males.

In a study that tried to shed light on the formation and impact of teacher expectations, Rist (1970) observed a class of black children during their first two and a half years of school (Rist was unable to observe the class during the first grade, though he was able to interview the teacher). The school was staffed by blacks and was located in a low-income black neighborhood. At the beginning of the school year, the teacher used information about each child's family, talks with other teachers, and meetings with children and their parents to evaluate each child's chances of doing well. During the second week of the term, the teacher used these evaluations to assign her pupils to a group she termed "fast learners" or to two groups that she labeled "slow learners." Rist noted that the parents of the "fast learners" had more formal education and higher incomes than the parents of "slow learners," and that "fast learners" were more likely than "slow learners" to dress neatly, speak passable standard English, and live with both parents. During the year, the teacher spent more time teaching and gave more attention to "fast learners" than "slow learners." As a result, "fast learners" were able to complete the required amount of reading-, writing-, and arithmetic-readiness material while "slow learners" were not. At the end of kindergarten, the children were given an intelligence test. The difference between the scores of "fast learners" and "slow learners" was not significant, though "fast learners," on the average, did get slightly higher scores. As first graders, 18 of these children were in the same class. Since the new teacher assigned children to ability groups on the basis of the amount of readiness material they completed in kindergarten, 17 of the 18 children were assigned to the same ability groups that they were members of the year before. At the end of the first grade, children in the highest ability group had the highest reading test scores while children in the lowest ability group had the lowest scores. As second graders, 10 of the 18 children were placed in the same class, where they were assigned to ability groups primarily on the basis of these reading test scores. During the first semester, each group was given different books to read, and reading was a group rather than an individual enterprise. In other words, the teacher did not allow any of the children to read at their own pace. As a result, "no matter how well a child in the lower reading groups might have read, he was destined to remain in the same reading group" (Rist, 1970, p. 435). A "slow learner," then, "had no option but to continue to be a slow learner, regardless of performance or potential" (p. 435). While Rist observed only one group of children, his observations imply that the nonintellectual features of many lower-class black children may generate unfavorable teacher expectancies, which in turn cause teachers to behave in ways that affect adversely the scholastic performance of these children.

While the results of these studies are not conclusive, they provide clues as to how teachers may behave in discriminatory ways. That the discrimination may be unintended does not diminish the short- or long-term damage that may be done to the victims.

The decisions that police officers and judges make about the fate of apprehended individuals can have serious consequences. For example, arrests may result in fewer and less desirable educational and employment opportunities and in chronic harassment by law enforcement personnel (Piliavin & Briar, 1964, reading 1.4). Accordingly, the way police officers and judges act toward blacks has serious implications for the welfare of the black community.

While this issue has not received a great deal of empirical attention, the studies that have been done imply that blacks and whites receive equal treatment in some cities (e.g., Black & Reiss, 1970; Terry, 1967; McEachern & Bauzer, 1964) and unequal treatment in others (e.g., Chiricos, Jackson, & Waldo, 1972; Ferdinand & Luchterhand, 1970; Piliavin & Briar, 1964, reading 1.4). In a study of the conditions that influence police actions toward juveniles, Piliavin and Briar (1964, reading 1.4) found that a disproportionately large number of blacks were "stopped and interrogated by patrolmen—often even in the absence of evidence that an offense had been committed—and usually were given more severe dispositions (than whites) for the same violations" (p. 212). The data imply that the selective apprehension and disposition of blacks were due to the prejudices of individual officers and to the way those officers interpreted the behavior of many apprehended blacks. In other words, these juveniles acted in ways—uncooperative, disrespectful, and without remorse—that police officers considered characteristic of confirmed delinquents. The findings, then, suggest that "the official delinquent . . . is a product of a social judgment, in this case a judgment made by the police. He is a delinquent because someone in authority has defined him as one, often on the basis of the public face he has presented to officials rather than of the kind of offense he has committed" (p. 214). A study in a small industrial city (Ferdinand & Luchterhand, 1970) provides some additional support for the hypothesis that race is a determinant of the disposition of juvenile offenders. The results indicate that a disproportionately large number of black first offenders, compared to white first offenders, were labeled as delinquent and referred to the juvenile court, even though the severity of the offenses allegedly committed by blacks and whites did not differ. However, race did not appear to affect police disposition of cases when there were repeated offenses, and black first offenders were not given harsher sentences than white first offenders by the juvenile court. Chiricos, Jackson, and Waldo (1972) analyzed 2,419 consecutive felony cases that were adjudicated in Florida courts during 1969–70. The results indicate that 41% of the black defendants and 28% of the white defendants were found guilty. The results also indicate that:

> ... regardless of which social or legal characteristic is introduced as a control on the original relationship between race and adjudication status, blacks are invariably adjudicated guilty more often than whites. That is, white defendants are spared the stigma of felony adjudication more often than blacks at *every* level of age or education, for *every* type of offense, attorney, plea, or court, and regardless of the extent of the defendant's prior criminal record. [p.557]

While many police officers and judges treat blacks and whites equally, the results of these studies imply that a sizable number of others do not. They also imply that prejudicial attitudes and the demeanor of many black juveniles may be important determinants of discriminatory police behavior.

INDIVIDUAL RACISM

Although survey data suggest that prejudice toward blacks has declined during the past few decades (Greeley & Sheatsley, 1971), some recent studies indicate that many blacks continue to be treated in discriminatory ways (Brannon, Cyphers, Hesse, Hesselbart, Keane, Schuman, Viccaro, & Wright, 1973; DeFriese & Ford, 1969; Dertke, Penner, & Ulrich, 1974; Gaertner, 1973; Silverman, 1974; Silverman & Cochrane, 1972).[3] The findings, though fragmentary, also suggest that prejudiced attitudes and perceived social pressure may be determinants of these discriminatory behaviors.[4] Using the responses of 87 incoming white male freshmen to questions about their attitudes and values, Silverman (1974) created and sent descriptions of eight prospective freshmen to each of the 87 subjects.

3. We are referring to the behavior of individuals as private citizens, rather than as employees of organizations or institutions.
4. A sizable number of studies suggest that attitudes are fairly weak predictors of racial discrimination (e.g., Wicker, 1969). However, Sigall and Page (1971) found that the real attitudes of many subjects were apparently less egalitarian than the attitudes they reported. While discriminatory behavior is probably determined by an assortment of factors, it seems likely that attitudes may be one important factor in a number of situations.

These fictitious freshmen were described as white or black, expressed the same or different attitudes as each subject, and revealed the same or different values. Subjects in the experimental group were asked to rate each of the people described, and were told that their ratings would determine their roommate assignments for the fall semester. Students in the control group were told that the people described were incoming freshmen at another school, and were asked to rate these people as if they were really choosing a roommate. Several weeks later, students in both groups were asked to indicate how their parents, best friends, and students at the college would feel about them if they roomed with a black student. The results indicate that subjects evaluated whites more favorably than blacks only when they thought their ratings would determine their roommates, that similarity of beliefs was an important determinant of ratings in both groups, and that the relationship between perceived social pressure and racial discrimination was considerable when subjects thought they were choosing their roommates and modest when they did not.

In a city where open housing had become a controversial issue, DeFriese and Ford (1969) asked a sample of 405 residents of white middle-class communities to sign one of two documents: a petition supporting open housing or a petition opposing open housing. Respondents were also asked to complete a questionnaire designed to measure their attitudes toward blacks; to indicate where they felt their immediate families, close relatives, close friends, neighbors, and fellow workers stood on the question of open housing; and to estimate the degree of consensus among the members of each reference group. The findings indicate that 29% signed the petition opposing open housing, 6% signed the petition supporting open housing, and 65% refused to sign either petition. The findings also indicate that people who expressed prejudiced attitudes, who thought their reference groups opposed open housing, and who felt there was considerable agreement within each group were most likely to sign the petition opposing open housing.

In an attempt to separate the measurement of attitudes and beliefs from the measurement of racial discrimination, Brannon et al. (1973) interviewed a probability sample of 640 white adults in the Detroit metropolitan area. Respondents were asked a variety of questions about open housing and other issues. Three months later, graduate students posing as members of a concerned citizens group presented the same respondents with either a petition supporting "owner's rights" or a petition supporting open housing. Respondents who signed were also asked if they would permit their names to appear in newspaper ads containing the petition. Brannon et al. found that 82% expressed attitudes favoring "owner's rights," that 16% expressed attitudes favoring open housing, and that these attitudes were strong predictors of petition signing behavior. Brannon et al. also found that respondents who favored "owner's rights" and who were asked to sign the petition supporting "owner's rights" were especially likely to allow their names to appear in newspaper ads when they thought problems were likely to arise if black families moved into their neighborhoods.

The blacks who were discriminated against in these studies (Brannon *et al.,* 1973; DeFriese & Ford, 1969; Silverman, 1974) were always unseen; that is, the college freshmen were not actually confronted with prospective black room-mates, and the homeowners were not facing black families who wanted to purchase their homes. While the people who discriminated may have behaved differently in face-to-face situations, insights into this type of discrimination are important, since many discriminatory acts originate in the absence of the victims; for example, the person who tells real estate brokers to show his house to white families only, and the person who persuades the members of his community to oppose busing because he doesn't want his children to attend school with blacks. Accordingly, the results of these studies may suggest ways of reducing an insidious form of racism.

In an elaborate study designed to find out if unintended contact between a prejudiced white and a black would produce favorable changes in attitudes and behavior, S. W. Cook (1970, 1971) hired prejudiced white females (degree of prejudice was determined earlier in an ostensibly unrelated situation) to work two hours a day for one month. Each subject was assigned to work with a white and a black female who were confederates of the experimenter. Within this context, Cook created several conditions designed to maximize the likelihood that the subjects' attitudes and behavior toward the black confederate would change. One, the black female talked about herself in ways that enabled the subject to get to know her as an individual. Two, status was equalized by giving each worker equal responsibility and authority and by rotating assignments. Three, the social norms encouraged the acceptance of blacks as equals. Four, the job required the subject and the black confederate to work together and assist each other, and the workers received a bonus if the group did well. Five, the black confederate was personable, able, ambitious, and self-respecting. The black confederate also talked about the unpleasant experiences that she had as a result of racial discrimination. The results indicate that the subjects' behavior toward the black confederate became considerably more favorable during the course of the project and that significantly more experimental subjects than controls displayed a favorable shift in attitudes toward blacks. In a recent study of housewives in public housing projects, Ford (1973, reading 1.5) reported similar findings; that is, he found that the amount of contact between white and black housewives was strongly related to the attitudes of white housewives toward blacks.

While these findings suggest that interracial contact can reduce prejudicial attitudes and discriminatory behaviors, many black-white encounters are not characterized by the conditions that maximize the possibility of change. More-over, it seems likely that these conditions will not occur often enough to appreciably reduce individual prejudice and discrimination until there are institutional changes that increase considerably the educational, job, and housing opportunities available to blacks.

SOME IMPLICATIONS FOR CHANGE[5]

The results of psychological research have a number of implications for increasing the opportunities available to many blacks. Several strategies designed to produce change in urban schools have led to considerable gains in the academic performance of economically disadvantaged black children. For example, classes characterized by considerable contact between teachers and individual children, an emphasis on learning how to learn by mastering underlying concepts and principles, and an abiding interest in the social-emotional development of each child resulted in greater academic gains than traditionally organized classes (Abelson, Zigler, & DeBlasi, 1974, reading 4.1). Open classroom instruction and the systematic use of praise and token reinforcement had more favorable effects on academic achievement than traditional classroom instruction (Rollins, McCandless, Thompson, & Brassell, 1974, reading 4.2). And computer-assisted instruction resulted in enduring gains in reading ability (Atkinson, 1974).

Several studies of white teachers' evaluations of black English vernacular suggest that black children who speak standard English are able to compete more effectively in school than black children who speak black English vernacular. For example, white teachers who listened to the taped speech of black and white lower-class children rated the black children less favorably on a number of attributes (Williams, 1970). White teachers who heard the taped answers of middle-class white or lower-class black ninth-graders to typical school questions gave the white students' answers higher grades, even though the answers given by both groups of students were identical (Crowl & MacGinitie, 1974). And 65% of the white teachers in several Alabama schools said they had difficulty understanding children who spoke black English vernacular, while 50% felt that these children were not as intelligent as children who spoke standard English (Blodgett & Cooper, 1973). If these teachers were responding to differences in speech rather than to differences in race, their responses imply that prospective and actual teachers of lower-class black children need to learn that black English vernacular is a somewhat different, though not inferior, linguistic system. They also imply that teachers are more responsive to black children when those children can speak standard English. Unfortunately, many schools are failing to teach many lower-class blacks standard English. In an attempt to develop tech-

5. Although we have only considered strategies that are implied by the results of psychological research, we would be remiss if we did not note that the passage and vigorous enforcement of anti-discrimination laws is probably the most useful strategy for increasing the opportunities available to blacks. We should also note that anti-discrimination legislation changes behavior, which in turn may generate favorable changes in the attitudes of whites toward blacks.

niques that might remedy this situation, Leaverton (1972, reading 4.3) used black English vernacular to help a class of economically disadvantaged black first-graders make the transition to standard English. The results suggest that carefully designed bi-dialectal programs may increase the ability of many lower-class black children to read and to speak standard English. Extensive field observations of inner-city black preadolescents and adolescents (Labov, 1972) suggest that a conflict between school values and street values also contributes to the failure of the schools to teach many lower-class blacks standard English. In other words, "teachers in the city schools have little ability to reward or punish members of the street culture or to motivate learning by any means" (p. 252). In an attempt to resolve this conflict, Labov proposed that a young black male who has high school level reading skills act as a cultural intermediary in the classroom by participating in the following ways: "Acquaint the teacher with the specific interests of members of the class and help design reading materials centering on these interests . . . Provide effective rewards and punishments that will motivate members of street culture for whom normal school sanctions are irrelevant . . . Lead group discussion on topics of immediate concern to members of the class . . . Maintain contact with boys outside of school, on the streets, and help organize extracurricular activities" (p. 254).

In an attempt to improve relations between the police and black citizens, a number of programs have been developed. Evaluations of some of these programs (Eisenberg, 1973; Solomon & Visser, 1973) suggest that carefully designed training and the creation of police-citizen dialogues may be one way to reduce discriminatory police behavior toward blacks. For example, Eisenberg (1973) found that policemen who participated in a series of discussions with black and white residents, compared to policemen who did not participate, displayed more favorable changes in their attitudes toward the black people in their districts. While the results of these studies are encouraging, their implications need to be tempered by the understandable failure of the research to determine systematically the behavioral effects of the programs.

Studies of the relationship between organizational conditions and retention of the hard-core unemployed (Goodman, Salipante, & Paransky, 1973, reading 2.5) contain several implications for increasing the job opportunities of chronically unemployed lower-class blacks. The findings indicate that retention of the hard-core unemployed was related to the perceived support given by one's supervisor, knowing what one's work routine would be like, work that was not boring, level of pay, and realistic expectations held by the company.

The results of the New Jersey graduated work incentive experiment (Kershaw & Skidmore, 1974, reading 2.4) imply that a guaranteed annual income would also be a useful strategy. The findings indicate that the employment rates, hours worked per week, and earnings per week of the married male heads of households in the experimental and control groups did not differ. In other words, a guaranteed annual income did not encourage male heads of households to drop out of the labor force. While additional research needs to be carried out before an adequate assessment of a guaranteed annual income can be made, these findings suggest that it would have the intended effects, and would not become a subsidy for not working.

REFERENCES

Abelson, W., Zigler, E., & DeBlasi, C. Effects of a four-year follow through program on economically disadvantaged children. *Journal of Educational Psychology*, 1974, *66*, 756–771.

Allen, V. Personality factors in poverty. In V. Allen (Ed.), *Psychological factors in poverty*. Chicago: Markham, 1970, pp. 242–266.

Atkinson, R. Teaching children to read using a computer. *American Psychologist*, 1974, *29*, 169–178.

Baratz, J. A bi-dialectal task for determining language proficiency in economically disadvantaged Negro children. *Child Development*, 1969, *40*, 889–901.

Beeghley, L., & Butler, E. The consequences of intelligence testing in the public schools before and after desegregation. *Social Problems*, 1974, *21*, 740–754.

Black, D., & Reiss, Jr., A. Police control of juveniles. *American Sociological Review*, 1970, *35*, 63–77.

Blodgett, E., & Cooper, E. Attitudes of elementary teachers toward black dialect. *Journal of Communication Disorders*, 1973, *6*, 121–133.

Brannon, R., Cyphers, G., Hesse, S., Hesselbart, S., Keane, R., Schuman, H., Viccaro, T., & Wright, D. Attitude and action: A field experiment joined to a general population survey. *American Sociological Review*, 1973, *38*, 625–636.

Byalick, R., & Bersoff, D. Reinforcement practices of black and white teachers in integrated classrooms. *Journal of Educational Psychology*, 1974, *66*, 473–480.

Chiricos, T., Jackson, P., & Waldo, G. Inequality in the imposition of a criminal label. *Social Problems*, 1972, *19*, 533–572.

Cole, M., & Bruner, J. Cultural differences and inferences about psychological processes. *American Psychologist*, 1971, *26*, 867–876.

Cook, S. W. Motives in a conceptual analysis of attitude-related behavior. In W. Arnold & D. Levine (Eds.), *Nebraska symposium on motivation, 1969*. Lincoln, Nebraska: University of Nebraska Press, 1970, pp. 179–231.

Cook, S. W. The effect of unintended racial contact upon racial interaction and attitude change. Final report, Project No. 5–1320, Contract No. OEC-4-7-051320–0273. Washington, D.C.: U.S. Office of Education, Bureau of Research, August, 1971.

Cook, T. Benign neglect: Minimum feasible understanding. *Social Problems*, 1970, *18*, 145–152.

Crowl, T., & MacGinitie, W. The influence of students' speech characteristics on teachers' evaluations of oral answers. *Journal of Educational Psychology*, 1974, *66*, 304–308.

DeFriese, G., & Ford, W. Verbal attitudes, overt acts, and the influence of social constraint in interracial behavior. *Social Problems*, 1969, *16*, 493–505.

Dertke, M., Penner, L., & Ulrich, K. Observer's reporting of shoplifting as a function of thief's race and sex. *Journal of Social Psychology*, 1974, *94*, 213–221.

Deutsch, M. The role of social class in language development and cognition. *American Journal of Orthopsychiatry*, 1965, *35*, 78–88.

Eidson, B. Major employers and their manpower practices. In P. Rossi, R. Berk, D. Boesel, B. Eidson, & W. Groves, *Between black and white: The faces of American institutions in the ghetto*. Supplemental studies for the National Advisory Commission on Civil Disorders. Washington, D.C.: Government Printing Office, 1968, pp. 115–123.

Eisenberg, T. Project Pace: An attempt to reduce police-community conflict. In J.

Snibbe & H. Snibbe (Eds.), *The urban policeman in transition.* Springfield, Ill.: Thomas, 1973, pp. 139–167.

Entwisle, D., & Greenberger, E. Racial differences in the language of grade school children. *Sociology of Education,* 1969, *42,* 238–250.

Ferdinand, T., & Luchterhand, E. Inner-city youth, the police, the juvenile court, and justice. *Social Problems,* 170, *17,* 510–527.

Ford, W. S. Interracial public housing in a border city: Another look at the contact hypothesis. *American Journal of Sociology,* 1973, *78,* 1426–1447.

Gaertner, S. Helping behavior and racial discrimination among liberals and conservatives. *Journal of Personality and Social Psychology,* 1973, *25,* 335–341.

Goldman, N. *The differential selection of juvenile offenders for court appearance.* New York: National Council on Crime and Delinquency, 1963.

Goodman, P., Salipante, P., & Paransky, H. Hiring, training, and retaining the hard-core unemployed: A selected review. *Journal of Applied Psychology,* 1973, *58,* 23–33.

Greeley, A., & Sheatsley, P. Attitudes toward integration. *Scientific American,* 1971, *225* (6), 13–19.

Jones, J. M. *Prejudice and racism.* Reading, Mass.: Addison-Wesley, 1972.

Kershaw, D., & Skidmore, F. *The New Jersey graduated work incentive experiment.* Princeton, N.J.: Mathematica, 1974.

Labov, W. The logical nonstandard English. In F. Williams (Ed.), *Language and poverty.* Chicago: Markham, 1970.

Labov, W. *Language in the inner city.* Philadelphia: Univeristy of Pennsylvania Press, 1972.

Leaverton, L. Nonstandard speech patterns. In H. Walberg & A. Kopan (Eds.), *Rethinking urban education.* San Francisco: Jossey-Bass, 1972.

McEachern, A., & Bauzer, R. Factors related to disposition in juvenile police contacts. In M. Klein & B. Myeroff (Eds.), *Juvenile gangs in context.* Los Angeles: University of Southern California, Youth Studies Center, 1964, pp. 192–210.

Mendelsohn, R. Police-community relations: A need in search of police support. *American Behavioral Scientist,* 1970, *13,* 745–760.

Moynihan, D. *The Negro family: The case for national action.* Washington, D.C.: U.S. Department of Labor, Office of Policy Planning and Research, 1965.

Peabody, Jr., M. Housing allowances. *The New Republic,* 1974, *170* (10), 20–23.

Piliavin, I., & Briar, S. Police encounters with juveniles. *American Journal of Sociology,* 1964, *70,* 206–214.

Rist, R. Student social class and teacher expectations: The self-fulfilling prophecy in ghetto education. *Harvard Educational Review,* 1970, *40,* 411–451.

Rollins, H. McCandless, B., Thompson, M., & Brassell, W. Project success experiment: An extended application of contingency management in inner-city schools. *Journal of Educational Psychology,* 1974, *66,* 167–178.

Rubovits, P., & Maehr, M. Pygmalion black and white. *Journal of Personality and Social Psychology,* 1973, *25,* 210–218.

Ryan, W. *Blaming the victim.* New York: Random House, 1971.

Sigall, H., & Page, R. Current stereotypes: A little fading, a little faking. *Journal of Personality and Social Psychology,* 1971, *18,* 247–255.

Sigelman, C. Social-class and ethnic differences in language development. In L. Wrightsman, *Social psychology in the seventies.* Monterey, California: Brooks/Cole, 1972, pp. 227–254.

Silverman, B. Consequences, racial discrimination, and the principle of belief congruence. *Journal of Personality and Social Psychology,* 1974, *29,* 497–508.

Silverman, B., & Cochrane, R. Effect of the social context on the principle of belief congruence. *Journal of Personality and Social Psychology,* 1972, *22,* 259–268.

Solomon, L., & Visser, K. Evaluation report of a police-community relations leadership training program. In J. Snibbe & H. Snibbe (Eds.), *The urban policeman in transition.* Springfield, Ill.: Thomas, 1973, pp. 168–186.

Stein, A. Strategies of failure. *Harvard Educational Review,* 1971, *41,* 158–204.

TenHouten, W. The black family: Myth and reality. *Psychiatry,* 1970, *33,* 145–173.

Terry, R. Discrimination in the handling of juvenile offenders by social control agencies. *Journal of Research in Crime and Delinquency,* 1967, *4,* 218–230.

Tilly, C., & Feagin, J. Boston's experiment with rent subsidies. *Journal of the American Institute of Planners,* 1970, *36,* 323–329.

Wicker, A. Attitudes versus actions: The relationship of verbal and overt behavioral responses to attitude objects. *Journal of Social Issues,* 1969, *25* (4), 41–78.

Williams, F. Psychological correlates of speech characteristics: On sounding "disadvantaged." *Journal of Speech and Hearing Research,* 1970, *13,* 472–488.

Cultural Differences and Inferences About Psychological Processes

MICHAEL COLE and JEROME S. BRUNER

DEFICIT INTERPRETATION

Perhaps the most prevalent view of the source of ethnic and social class differences in intellectual performance is what might be summed up under the label "the deficit hypothesis." It can be stated briefly, without risk of gross exaggeration. It rests on the assumption that a community under conditions of poverty (for it is the poor who are the focus of attention, and a disproportionate number of the poor are members of minority ethnic groups) is a disorganized community, and this disorganization expresses itself in various forms of deficit. One widely agreed-upon source of deficit is mothering; the child of poverty is assumed to lack adequate parental attention. Given the illegitimacy rate in the urban ghetto, the most conspicuous "deficit" is a missing father and, consequently, a missing father model. The mother is away at work or, in any case, less involved with raising her children than she should be by white middle-class standards. There is said to be less regularity, less mutuality in interaction with her. There are said to be specialized deficits in interaction as well—less guidance in goal seeking from the parents (Schoggen, 1969), less emphasis upon means and ends in maternal instruction (Hess & Shipman, 1965), or less positive and more negative reinforcement (Bee, Van Egeren, Streissgurth, Nyman, & Leckie, 1969; Smilansky, 1968).

More particularly, the deficit hypothesis has been applied to the symbolic and linguistic environment of the growing child. His linguistic community as portrayed in the early work of Basil Bernstein (1961), for example, is characterized by a restricted code, dealing more in the stereotype of interaction than in language that explains and elaborates upon social and material events. The games that are played by poor children and to which they are exposed are less strategy bound than those of more advantaged children (Eifermann, 1968); their homes are said to have a more confused noise background, permitting less opportunity for figure-ground information (Klaus & Gray, 1968); and the certainty of the environment is sufficiently reduced so that children have difficulty in delaying reinforcement (Mischel, 1966) or in accepting verbal reinforcement instead of the real article (Zigler & Butterfield, 1968).

The theory of intervention that grew from this view was the idea of "early stimulation," modeled on a conception of supplying nutriment for those with a protein deficiency or avitaminosis. The nature of the needed early stimulation was never explained systematically, save in rare cases (Smilansky, 1968), but it variously took the form of practice in using abstractions (Blank & Solomon, 1969), in having dialogue where the referent objects were not present, as through the use of telephones (Deutsch, 1967; John & Goldstein, 1964), or in providing secure mothering by substitution (Caldwell et al., 1970; Klaus & Gray, 1968).

A primary result of these various deficits was believed to express itself in the lowered test scores and academic performance among children from poverty backgrounds. The issue was most often left moot as to whether or not this lowered test performance was easily reversible, but the standard reference was to a monograph by Bloom (1964) indicating that cognitive performance on a battery of tests, given to poor and middle-class children, yielded the result that nearly 80% of the variance in intellectual performance was accounted for by age 3.

DIFFERENCE INTERPRETATION

Such data seem to compel the conclusion that as a consequence of various factors arising from minority group status (factors affecting motivation, linguistic ability, goal orientation, hereditary proclivities to learn in certain ways—the particular mix of factors depends on the writer), minority group children suffer intellectual deficits when compared with their "more advantaged" peers.

In this section, we review a body of data and theory that controverts this contention, casts doubt on the conclusion that a deficit exists in minority group children, and even raises doubts as to whether any nonsuperficial *differences* exist among different cultural groups.

There are two long-standing precedents for the view that different groups (defined in

terms of cultural, linguistic, and ethnic criteria) do not differ intellectually from each other in any important way.[1] First, there is the anthropological "doctrine of psychic unity" (Kroeber, 1948) which, on the basis of the "run of total experience," is said to warrant the assumption of intellectual equality as a sufficient approximation to the truth. This view is compatible with current linguistic anthropological theorizing, which concentrates on describing the way in which different cultural/linguistic groups categorize familiar areas of experience (Tyler, 1970). By this view, different conclusions about the world are the result of arbitrary and different, but equally logical, ways of cutting up the world of experience. From this perspective, descriptions of the "disorganization" of minorities would be highly suspect, this suspicion arising in connection with questions like, Disorganized from whose point of view?

Anthropological critiques of psychological experimentation have never carried much weight with psychologists, nor have anthropologists been very impressed with conclusions from psychological tests. We have hypothesized elsewhere (Cole, Gay, Glick, & Sharp, 1971) that their mutual indifference stems in part from a difference in opinion about the inferences that are warranted from testing and experimentation, and in part because the anthropologist relies mainly on data that the psychologist completely fails to consider: the mundane social life of the people he studies. As we shall see, these issues carry over into our criticism of the "deficit" theory of cultural deprivation.

A second tradition that calls into question culturally determined group difference in

---

1. It is assumed here that it is permissible to speak of minority group or poverty group "culture" using as our criterion Lévi-Strauss' (1963) definition: "What is called 'culture' is a fragment of humanity which, from the point of view of the research at hand . . . presents significant discontinuities in relation to the rest of humanity [p. 295]." We do not intend to enter into arguments over the existence or nature of a "culture of poverty," although such an idea seems implicit in the view of most deficit theorists.

intelligence is the linguist's assertion that languages do not differ in their degree of development (Greenberg, 1963), buttressed by the transformationalist's caution that one cannot attribute to people a cognitive capacity that is less than is required to produce the complex rule-governed activity called language (Chomsky, 1966).

Although Chomskian linguistics has had a profound effect on psychological theories of language and cognitive development in recent years, psychological views of language still are considered hopelessly inadequate by working linguists. This criticism applies not only to psycholinguistic theory but to the actual description of linguistic performance on which theory is based. Needless to say, the accusation of misunderstanding at the descriptive level leads to accusations of absurdity at the theoretical level.

A third tradition that leads to rejection of the deficit theory has many sources in recent social sciences. This view holds that even when attempts have been made to provide reasonable anthropological and linguistic foundations, the conclusions about cognitive capacity from psychological experiments are unfounded because the performance produced represents a complex interaction of the formal characteristics of the experiment and the social/environmental context that determines the subject's interpretation of the situation in which it occurs. The need for "situation-bound" interpretations of experiments is emphasized in such diverse sources as sociology (Goffman, 1964), psychology (Brunswik, 1958), and psycholinguistics (Cazden, 1970). This is an important issue, which we will return to once illustrations of the "antideficit" view have been explored.

Perhaps the most coherent denial of the deficit position, coupled with compelling illustrations of the resourcefulness of the supposedly deprived and incompetent person, is contained in Labov's attack on the concept of "linguistic deprivation" and its accompanying assumption of cognitive incapacity (Labov, 1970).

It is not possible here to review all of Labov's evidence. Rather, we have abstracted what we take to be the major points in his attack.

1. *An assertion of the functional equality of all languages.* This assertion is applied specifically to his analysis of nonstandard Negro English, which has been the object of his study for several years. Labov provided a series of examples where young blacks who would be assessed as linguistically retarded and academically hopeless by standard test procedures enter conversations in a way that leaves little doubt that they can speak perfectly adequately and produce very clever arguments in the process.

2. *An assertion of the psychologist's ignorance of language in general and nonstandard dialects in particular.* Labov's particular target is Carl Bereiter (Bereiter & Englemann, 1966) whose remedial teaching technique is partly rationalized in terms of the *inability* of young black children to use language either as an effective tool of communication or thinking. Part of Labov's attack is aimed at misinterpretations of such phrases as *"They mine,"* which Labov analyzed in terms of rules of contraction, but which Bereiter made the mistake of referring to as a "series of badly connected words [Labov, 1970, p. 171]." This "psychologist's deficit" has a clear remedy. It is roughly equivalent to the anthropological caveat that the psychologist has to know more about the people he studies.

3. *The inadequacy of present experimentation.* More serious criticism of the psychologist's interpretation of "language deprivation" and, by extension, his whole concept of "cultural deprivation" is contained in the following, rather extensive quote:

this and the preceeding section are designed to convince the reader that the controlled experiments that have been offered in evidence [of Negro lack of competence] are misleading. The only thing that is controlled is the superficial form of the stimulus. All children are asked, "What do you think of capital punishment?" or "Tell me everything you can about this." But the speaker's interpretation of these requests, and the action he believes is appropriate in response is completely uncontrolled. One can view these test stimuli as requests for information, commands for action, or meaningless sequences of words. . . . With human subjects it is absurd to believe that identical stimuli are obtained by asking everyone the same question. Since the crucial intervening variables of interpretation and motivation are uncontrolled, most of the literature on verbal deprivation tells us nothing of the capacities of children [Labov, 1970, p. 171].

Here Labov is attacking the experimental method as usually applied to the problem of subcultural differences in cognitive capacity. We can abstract several assertions from this key passage: (a) Formal experimental equivalence of operations does not insure de facto equivalence of experimental treatments; (b) different subcultural groups are predisposed to interpret the experimental stimuli (situations) differently; (c) different subcultural groups are motivated by different concerns relevant to the experimental task; (d) in view of the inadequacies of experimentation, inferences about lack of competence among black children are unwarranted.

These criticisms, when combined with linguistic misinterpretation, constitute Labov's attack on the deficit theory of cultural deprivation and represent the rationale underlying his demonstrations of competence where its lack had previously been inferred.

One example of Labov's approach is to conduct a rather standard interview of the type often used for assessment of language competence. The situation is designed to be minimally threatening; the interviewer is a neighborhood figure, and black. Yet, the black 8-year-old interviewee's behavior is monosyllabic. He is a candidate for the diagnosis of linguistically and culturally deprived.

But this diagnosis is very much situation dependent. For at a later time, this same interviewer goes to the boy's apartment, brings one of the boy's friends with him, lies down on the floor, and produces some potato chips. He then begins talking about clearly taboo subjects in dialect. Under these circumstances, the mute interviewee becomes an excited participant in the general conversation.

In similar examples, Labov demonstrated powerful reasoning and debating skills in a school dropout and nonlogical verbosity in an acceptable, "normal" black who has mastered the forms of standard English. Labov's conclusion is that the usual assessment situations, including IQ and reading tests, elicit deliberate, defensive behavior on the part of the child who has realistic expectations that to talk openly is to expose oneself to insult and harm. As a consequence, such situations *cannot* measure the child's competence. Labov went even further to assert that far from being verbally deprived, the typical ghetto child is

bathed in verbal stimulation from morning to night. We see many speech events which depend upon the competitive exhibition of verbal skills—sounding, singing, toasts, rifting, louding—a whole range of activities in which the individual gains status through the use of language. . . . We see no connection between the verbal skill in the speech events characteristic of the street culture and success in the school room [Labov, 1970, p. 163].

Labov is not the only linguist to offer such a critique of current theories of cultural deprivation (see, e.g., Stewart, 1970). However, Labov's criticism raises larger issues concerning the logic of comparative research designs of which the work in cultural/linguistic deprivation is only a part. It is to this general question that we now turn.

COMPETENCE AND PERFORMANCE IN PSYCHOLOGICAL RESEARCH

The major thrusts of Labov's argument, that situational factors are important components of psychological experiments and that it is difficult if not impossible to infer competence directly from performance, are not new ideas to psychologists. Indeed, a concern with the relation between *psychological processes* on the one hand and *situational factors* on the other has long been a kind of shadow issue in psychology, surfacing most often in the context of comparative research.

It is this question that underlies the oft-berated question, What do IQ tests measure? and has been prominent in attacks on Jensen's (1969) argument that group differences in IQ test performance are reflective of innate differences in capacity.

Kagan (1969), for example, pointed to the work of Palmer, who regularly delays testing until the child is relaxed and has established rapport with the tester. Jensen (1969, p. 100) himself reported that significant differences in test performance can be caused by differential adaptation to the test situation.

Hertzig, Birch, Thomas, and Mendez (1968) made a direct study of social class/ethnic differences in response to the test situation and demonstrated stable differences in situational responses that were correlated with test performance and were present even when measured IQ was equivalent for subgroups chosen from the major comparison groups.

Concern with the particular *content* of tests and experiments as they relate to inferences about cognitive capacity occurs within the same context. The search for a "culture-free" IQ test has emphasized the use of universally familiar material, and various investigators have found that significant differences in performance can be related to the content of the experimental materials. Price-Williams (1961), for example, demonstrated earlier acquisition of conservation concepts in Nigerian children using traditional instead of imported stimulus materials, and Gay and Cole (1967) made a similar point with respect to Liberian classification behavior and learning.

Contemporary psychology's awareness of the task and situation-specific determinants of performance is reflected in a recent article

by Kagan and Kogan (1970). In a section of their paper titled "The Significance of Public Performance," they are concerned with the fact that "differences in quality of style of public performance, although striking, may be misleading indices of competence [p. 1322]."

Although such misgivings abound, they have not yet crystallized into a coherent program of research and theory nor have the implications of accepting the need to incorporate an analysis of situations in addition to traditional experimental manipulations been fully appreciated.

EXTENDED IDEA OF COMPETENCE

Labov and others have argued forcefully that we cannot distinguish on the basis of traditional experimental approaches between the underlying competence of those who have had a poor opportunity to participate in a particular culture and those who have had a good opportunity, between those who have not had their share of wealth and respect and those who have. The crux of the argument, when applied to the problem of "cultural deprivation," is that those groups ordinarily diagnosed as culturally deprived have the same underlying competence as those in the mainstream of the dominant culture, *the differences in performance being accounted for by the situations and contexts in which the competence is expressed.* To put the matter most rigorously, one can find a corresponding situation in which the member of the "out culture," the victim of poverty, can perform on the basis of a given competence in a fashion equal to or superior to the standard achieved by a member of the dominant culture.

A prosaic example taken from the work of Gay and Cole (1967) concerns the ability to make estimates of volume. The case in question is to estimate the number of cups of rice in each of several bowls. Comparisons of "rice-estimation accuracy" were made among several groups of subjects, including nonliterate Kpelle rice farmers from North

Central Liberia and Yale sophomores. The rice farmers manifested significantly greater accuracy than the Yale students, the difference increasing with the amount of rice presented for estimation. In many other situations, measurement skills are found to be superior among educated subjects in the Gay and Cole study. Just as Kpelle superiority at making rice estimates is clearly not a universal manifestation of their superior underlying competence, the superiority of Yale students in, for example, distance judgments is no basis for inferring that their competence is superior.

We think the existence of demonstrations such as those presented by Labov has been salutary in forcing closer examination of testing situations used for comparing the children of poverty with their more advantaged peers. And, as the illustration from Gay and Cole suggests, the argument may have quite general implications. Obviously, it is not sufficient to use a simple equivalence-of-test procedure to make inferences about the competence of the two groups being compared. In fact, a "two-groups" design is almost useless for making any important inferences in cross-cultural research, as Campbell (1961) has suggested. From a logical view, however, the conclusion of equal cognitive competence in those who are not members of the prestige culture and those who are its beneficiaries is often equally unwarranted. While it is very proper to criticize the logic of assuming that poor performance implies lack of competence, the contention that poor performance is of *no* relevance to a theory of cognitive development and to a theory of cultural differences in cognitive development also seems an oversimplification.

Assuming that we can find test situations in which comparably good performance can be elicited from the groups being contrasted, there is plainly an issue having to do with the range and nature of the situations in which performance for any two groups can be found to be equal.

We have noted Labov's conclusion that the usual assessment of linguistic competence in the black child elicits deliberate defensive behavior and that he can respond effectively in familiar nonthreatening surroundings. It may be, however (this possibility is discussed in Bruner, 1970), that he is unable to utilize language of a decentered type, taken out of the context of social interaction, used in an abstract way to deal with hypothetical possibilities and to spell out hypothetical plans (see also Gladwin, 1970). If such were the case, we could not dismiss the question of different kinds of language usage by saying simply that decontextualized talk is not part of the natural milieu of the black child in the urban ghetto. If it should turn out to be the case that mastery of the culture depends on one's capacity to perform well on the basis of competence one has stored up, and to perform well in particular settings and in particular ways, then plainly the question of differences in the way language enters the problem-solving process cannot be dismissed. It has been argued, for example, by Bernstein (1970) that it is in the nature of the very social life of the urban ghetto that there develops a kind of particularism in which communication usually takes place only along concrete personal lines. The ghetto child, who by training is likely to use an idiosyncratic mode of communication, may become locked into the life of his own cultural group, and his migration into other groups consequently becomes the more difficult. Bernstein made clear in his most recent work that this is not a question of capacity but, rather, a matter of what he calls "orientation." Nevertheless, it may very well be that a ghetto dweller's language training unfits him for taking jobs in the power- and prestige-endowing pursuits of middle-class culture. If such is the case, then the issue of representativeness of the situations to which he can apply his competence becomes something more than a matter of test procedure.

A major difficulty with this line of speculation is that at present we have almost no knowledge of the day-to-day representativeness of different situations and the behaviors that are seen as appropriate to them by different cultural groups. For example, the idea that language use must be considered outside of social interactions in order to qualify as abstract, as involving "cognition," is almost certainly a psychologist's fiction. The work of contemporary sociologists and ethnolinguists (Garfinkle, 1967; Hymes, 1966; Schegloff, 1968) seems conclusively to demonstrate the presence of complex contingent thinking in situations that are all too often characterized by psychologists as consisting of syncretic, affective interactions. Until we have better knowledge of the cognitive components that are part of social interactions (the same applies to many spheres of activity), speculations about the role of language in cognition will have to remain speculations.

In fact, it is extraordinarily difficult to know, save in a most superficial way, on the basis of our present knowledge of society, what is the nature of situations that permit control and utilization of the resources of a culture by one of its members and what the cognitive skills are that are demanded of one who would use these resources. It may very well be that the very definition of a subculture could be put into the spirit of Lévi-Strauss' (1963) definition of a culture:

What is called a subculture is a fragment of a culture which from the point of view of the research at hand presents significant discontinuities in relation to the rest of that culture with respect to access to its major amplifying tools.

By an amplifying tool is meant a technological feature, be it soft or hard, that permits control by the individual of resources, prestige, and deference within the culture. An example of a middle-class cultural amplifier that operates to increase the thought processes of those who employ it is the discipline loosely referred to as "mathematics." To employ mathematical techniques requires the cultivation of certain skills of reasoning, even certain styles of deploying one's thought processes. If one were able to culti-

vate the strategies and styles relevant to the employment of mathematics, then that range of technology is open to one's use. If one does not cultivate mathematical skills, the result is "functional incompetence," an inability to use this kind of technology. Whether or not compensatory techniques can then correct "functional incompetence" is an important, but unexplored, question.

Any particular aspect of the technology requires certain skills for its successful use. These skills, as we have already noted, must also be deployable in the range of situations where they are useful. Even if a child could carry out the planning necessary for the most technically demanding kind of activity, he must not do so if he has been trained with the expectancy that the exercise of such a skill will be punished or will, in any event, lead to some unforeseen difficulty. Consequently, the chances that the individual will work up his capacities for performance in the given domain are diminished. As a result, although the individual can be shown to have competence in some sphere involving the utilization of the skill, he will not be able to express that competence in the relevant kind of context. In an absolute sense, he is any man's equal, but in everyday encounters, he is not up to the task.

The principle cuts both ways with respect to cultural differences. Verbal skills are important cultural "amplifiers" among Labov's subjects; as many middle-class school administrators have discovered, the ghetto resident skilled in verbal exchanges is a more than formidable opponent in the battle for control of school curriculum and resources. In like manner, the Harlem youth on the street who cannot cope with the verbal battles described by Labov is failing to express competence in a context relevant to the ghetto.

These considerations impress us with the need to clarify our notion of what the competencies are that underlie effective performance. There has been an implicit, but very general, tendency in psychology to speak as if the organism is an information-processing machine with a fixed set of routines. The number and organization of these routines might differ as a function of age, genetic makeup, or environmental factors, but for any given machine, the input to the machine is processed uniformly by the routines (structures, skills) of the organism.

Quite recently, psychologists have started to face up to the difficulties of assuming "all things are equal" for different groups of people (concern has focused on difference in age, but the same logic applies to any group comparisons). The study of situational effects on performance has forced a reevaluation of traditional theoretical inferences about competence. This new concern with the interpretation of psychological experiments is quite apparent in recent attempts to cope with data inconsistent with Piaget's theory of cognitive development. For example, Flavell and Wohlwill (1969) sought to distinguish between two kinds of competence: First, there are "the rules, structures, or 'mental operations' embodied in the task and . . . [second, there are] the actual mechanisms required for processing the input and output [p. 98]." The second factor is assumed to be task specific and is the presumed explanation for such facts as the "horizontal decalages" in which the same principle appears for different materials at different ages. The *performance* progression through various stages is presumably a reflection of increases in both kinds of competence, since both are assumed to increase with age.

The same general concern is voiced by Mehler and Bever (1968). They ask,

How can we decide if a developmental change or behavioral difference among adults is really due to a difference in a structural rule, to a difference in the form of the expressive processes or a difference in their quantitative capacity [p. 278]?

Their own work traces the expression of particular rules in behavior and the way the effect of knowing a rule ("having a competence") interacts with dependence on differ-

ent aspects of the input to produce "non-linear trends" in the development of conservation-like performance.

Broadening psychological theory to include rules for applying cognitive skills, as well as statements about the skills themselves, seems absolutely necessary.

However, the extensions contemplated may well not be sufficient to meet all of Labov's objections to inferences about "linguistic deprivation." In both the position expressed by Flavell and Wohlwill and by Mehler and Bever, "competence" is seen as dependent on situational factors and seems to be a slowly changing process that might well be governed by the same factors that lead to increases in the power of the structural rules or competence, in the older sense of the word. Yet in Labov's example, the problem is considerably more ephemeral; Labov gives the impression that the subjects were engaged in rational problem solving and that they had complete control over their behavior. He is claiming, in effect, that they are successfully coping with *their* problem; it simply is not the problem the experimenter had in mind, so the experimenter claims lack of competence as a result of his own ignorance.

Acceptance of Labov's criticisms, and we think they should be accepted, requires not only a broadening of our idea of competence, but a vast enrichment of our approach to experimentation.

NECESSITY OF A COMPARATIVE PSYCHOLOGY OF COGNITION

If we accept the idea that situational factors are often important determinants of psychological performance, and if we also accept the idea that different cultural groups are likely to respond differently to any given situation, there seems to be no reasonable alternative to psychological experimentation that bases its inferences on data from comparisons of both experimental and situational variations.

In short, we are contending that Brunswik's (1958) call for "representative design" and an analysis of the "ecological significance" of stimulation is a prerequisite to research on ethnic and social class differences in particular, and to any research where the groups to be compared are thought to differ with respect to the process under investigation prior to application of the experimental treatments.

Exhortations to the effect that college sophomores with nonsense syllables and white rats in boxes are not sufficient objects for the development of a general psychological theory have produced, thus far, only minor changes in the behavior of psychologists. The present situations seem to *require* a change.

An illustration from some recent cross-cultural research serves as an illustration of one approach that goes beyond the usual two-group design to explore the situational nature of psychological performance.

Cole et al. (1971, p. 4) used the free-recall technique to study cultural differences in memory. The initial studies presented subjects with a list of 20 words divided into four familiar, easily distinguishable categories. Subjects were read the list of words and asked to recall them. The procedure was repeated five times for each subject. A wide variety of subject populations was studied in this way; Liberian rice farmers and school children were the focus of concern, but comparison with groups in the United States was also made.

Three factors of the Kpelle rice farmers' performance were remarkable in these first studies: (*a*) The number recalled was relatively small (9–11 items per list); (*b*) there was no evidence of semantic or other organization of the material; (*c*) there was little or no increase in the number recalled with successive trials.

Better recall, great improvement with trials, and significant organization are all characteristic of performance of the American groups above the fifth grade.

A series of standard experimental manipulations (offering incentives, using lists based on functional rather than semantic classes, showing the objects to be remembered, extending the number of trials) all failed to make much difference in Kpelle performance.

However, when these same to-be-recalled items were incorporated into folk stories, when explicit grouping procedures were introduced, or when seemingly bizarre cuing procedures were used, Kpelle performance manifested organization, showed vast improvements in terms of amount recalled, and gave a very different picture of underlying capacity. Cole et al. (1971) concluded that a set of rather specific skills associated with remembering disconnected material out of context underlies the differences observed in the standard versions of the free-recall experiment with which they began. Moreover, they were able to begin the job of pinpointing these skills, their relevance to traditional activities, and the teaching techniques that could be expected to bring existing memory skills to bear in the "alien" tasks of the school.

CONCLUSION

The arguments set forth in this study can now be brought together and generalized in terms of their bearing on psychological research that is "comparative" in nature—comparing ages, cultures, subcultures, species, or even groups receiving different experimental treatments.

The central thesis derives from a reexamination of the distinction between competence and performance. As a rule, one looks for performance at its best and infers the degree of underlying competence from the observed performance. With respect to linguistic competence, for example, a single given instance of a particular grammatical form could suffice for inferring that the speaker had the competence to generate such instances as needed. By the use of such a methodology, Labov demonstrated that culturally deprived black children, *tested appropriately* for optimum performance, have the same grammatical competence as middle-class whites, though it may be expressed in different settings. Note that negative evidence is mute with respect to the status of underlying capacity—it may require a different situation for its manifestation.

The psychological status of the concept of competence (or capacity) is brought deeply into question when one examines conclusions based on standard experiments. Competence so defined is both situation blind and culture blind. If performance is treated (as it often is by linguists) only as a shallow expression of deeper competence, then one inevitably loses sight of the ecological problem of performance. For one of the most important things about any "underlying competence" is the nature of the situations in which it expresses itself. Herein lies the crux of the problem. One must inquire, first, whether a competence is expressed in a particular situation and, second, what the significance of that situation is for the person's ability to cope with life in his own milieu. As we have had occasion to comment elsewhere, when we systematically study the situational determinants of performance, we are led to conclude that cultural differences reside more in differences in the situations to which different cultural groups apply their skills than to differences in the skills possessed by the groups in question (Cole et al., 1971, Ch. 7).

The problem is to identify the range of capacities readily manifested in different groups and then to inquire whether the range is adequate to the individual's needs in various cultural settings. From this point of view, cultural *deprivation* represents a special case of cultural *difference* that arises when an individual is faced with demands to perform in a manner inconsistent with his past (cultural) experience. In the present social context of the United States, the great power of the middle class has rendered differences into deficits because middle-class behavior is the yardstick of success.

Our analysis holds at least two clear implications of relevance to the classroom teacher

charged with the task of educating children from "disadvantaged" subcultural groups.

First, recognition of the educational difficulties in terms of a *difference* rather than a special kind of intellectual disease should change the students' status in the eyes of the teacher. If Pygmalion really can work in the classroom (Rosenthal & Jacobson, 1968), the effect of this change in attitude may of itself produce changes in performance. Such difference in teacher attitude seems to be one prime candidate for an explanation of the fine performance obtained by Kohl (1967) and others with usually recalcitrant students.

Second, the teacher should stop laboring under the impression that he must create new intellectual structures and start concentrating on how to get the child to *transfer* skills he already possesses to the task at hand. It is in this context that "relevant" study materials become important, although "relevant" should mean something more than a way to motivate students. Rather, relevant materials are those to which the child already applies skills the teacher seeks to have applied to his own content. It requires more than a casual acquaintance with one's students to know what those materials are.

The Soviet psychologist, Lev Vygotskii (1962), took as the motto of his well-known monograph on language and thought an epigraph from Francis Bacon: Neither hand nor mind alone, left to themselves, amounts to much; instruments and aids are the means to perfection.[2] Psychologists concerned with comparative research, and comparisons of social and ethnic group differences in particular, must take seriously the study of the way different groups organize the relation between their hands and minds; without assuming the superiority of one system over another, they must take seriously the dictum that man is a cultural animal. When cultures are in competition for resources, as they are

2. Nec manus nisi intellectus sibi permissus multam valent; instrumentibus et auxilibus res perficitur.

today, the psychologist's task is to analyze the source of cultural difference so that those of the minority, the less powerful group, may quickly acquire the intellectual instruments necessary for success of the dominant culture, should they so choose.

REFERENCES

Bee, H. L., Van Egeren, L. F., Streissguth, A. P., Nyman, B. A., & Leckie, M. S. Social class differences in maternal teaching strategies and speech patterns. *Developmental Psychology*, 1969, 1, 726–734.

Bereiter, C., & Englemann, S. *Teaching disadvantaged children in the preschool.* Englewood Cliffs, N. J.: Prentice-Hall, 1966.

Bernstein, B. Social class and linguistic development: A theory of social learning. In A. H. Halsey, J. Floyd, & C. A. Anderson (Eds.), *Education, economy and society.* Glencoe, Ill.: Free Press, 1961.

Bernstein, B. A sociolinguistic approach to socialization: With some references to educability. In F. Williams (Ed.), *Language and poverty.* Chicago: Markham, 1970.

Blank, M., & Solomon, F. A tutorial language program to develop abstract thinking in socially disadvantaged preschool children. *Child Development*, 1969, 40, 47–61.

Bloom, B. S. *Stability and change in human characteristics.* New York: Wiley, 1964.

Bruner, J. S. *Poverty and childhood.* Merrill-Palmer Institute Monographs, 1970.

Brunswik, E. *Representative design in the planning of psychological research.* Berkeley: University of California Press, 1958.

Caldwell, B. M., et al. Infant day care and attachment. *American Journal of Orthopsychiatry*, 1970, 40, 397–412.

Campbell, D. The mutual methodological relevance of anthropology and psychology. In F. L. K Hsu (Ed.), *Psychological anthropology.* Homewood, Ill.: Dorsey Press, 1961.

Cazden, C. The neglected situation. In F. Williams (Ed.), *Language and poverty.* Chicago: Markham Press, 1970.

Chomsky, N. *Cartesian linguistics.* New York: Harper & Row, 1966.

Cole, M., Gay, J., Glick, J., & Sharp, D. W. *The cultural context of learning and thinking.* New York: Basic Books, 1971.

Deutsch, M. *The disadvantaged child.* New York: Basic Books, 1967.

Eifermann, R. *School children's games.* Washington, D. C.: Department of Health, Education, and Welfare, 1968.

Flavell, J. H., & Wohlwill, J. F. Formal and functional aspects of cognitive development. In D. Elkind & J. H. Flavell (Eds.), *Studies in cognitive development.* New York: Oxford University Press, 1969.

Garfinkle, H. *Studies in ethnomethodology.* Englewood Cliffs, N. J.: Prentice-Hall, 1967.

Gay, J., & Cole, M. *The new mathematics and an old culture.* New York: Holt, Rinehart & Winston, 1967.

Gladwin, T. *East is a big bird.* Cambridge: Belnap Press, 1970.

Goffman, E. The neglected situation. In J. Gumperz & D. Hymes (Eds.), The ethnology of communication. *American Anthropologist*, 1964, 66(6, Pt. 2), 133.

Greenberg, J. *Universals of language.* Cambridge: M.I.T. Press, 1963.

Hertzig, M. E., Birch, H. G., Thomas, A., & Mendez, O. A. Class and ethnic differences in the responsiveness of preschool children to cognitive demands. *Monographs of the Society for Research in Child Development*, 1968, 33(1, Serial No. 117).

Hess, R. D., & Shipman, V. Early experience and socialization of cognitive modes in children. *Child Development*, 1965, 36, 869–886.

Hymes, D. *On communicative competence.* (Report of a Conference on Research Planning on Language Development among Disadvantaged Children) New York: Yeshiva University Press, 1966.

Jensen, A. How much can we boost IQ and scholastic achievement? *Harvard Educational Review*, 1969, 39, 1–123.

John, V. P., & Goldstein, L. S. The social context of language acquisition. *Merrill-Palmer Quarterly*, 1964, 10, 265–275.

Kagan, J. Inadequate evidence and illogical conclusions. *Harvard Educational Review*, 1969, 39, 274–277.

Kagan, J., & Kogan, N. Individuality and cognitive performance. In P. Mussen (Ed.),

Manual of child psychology. New York: Wiley, 1970.

Klaus, R., & Gray, S. The early training project for disadvantaged children: A report after five years. *Monographs of the Society for Research in Child Development,* 1968, 33(4).

Kohl, H. *36 children.* New York: New American Library, 1967.

Kroeber, A. L. *Anthropology.* New York: Harcourt, Brace, 1948.

Labov, W. The logical non-standard English. In F. Williams (Ed), *Language and poverty.* Chicago: Markham Press, 1970.

Lévi-Strauss, C. *Structural anthropology.* New York: Basic Books, 1963.

Mehler, J., & Bever, T. The study of competence in cognitive psychology. *International Journal of Psychology,* 1968, 3, 273–280.

Mischel, W. Theory and research on the antecedents of self-imposed delay of reward. In, *Progress in experimental personality research.* Vol. 3. New York: Academic Press, 1966.

Price-Williams, D. R. A. A study concerning concepts of conservation of quantities among primitive children. *Acta Psycho-*

logia, 1961, 18, 297–305.

Rosenthal, R., & Jacobson, L. *Pygmalion in the classroom.* New York: Holt, Rinehart & Winston, 1968.

Schegloff, E. A. Sequencing in conversational openings. *American Anthropologist,* 1968, 70, 1075–1095.

Schoggen, M. An ecological study of three-year-olds at home. Nashville, Tenn.: George Peabody College for Teachers, November 7, 1969.

Smilansky, S. The effect of certain learning conditions on the progress of disadvantaged children of kindergarten age. *Journal of School Psychology,* 1968, 4(3), 68–81.

Stewart, W. A. Toward a history of American Negro dialect. In F. Williams (Ed.), *Language and poverty.* Chicago: Markham Press, 1970.

Tyler, S. *Cognitive anthropology.* New York: Holt, Rinehart & Winston, 1970.

Vygotskii, L. S. *Thought and speech.* Cambridge: M.I.T. Press, 1962.

Zigler, E., & Butterfield, E. Motivational aspects of changes in IQ test performance of culturally deprived nursery school children. *Child Development,* 1968, 39, 1–14.

The Black Family:

Myth and Reality

WARREN D. TENHOUTEN

The view that black families in America are matriarchal was developed by Frazier (1948, 1957), who describes four kinds of black families. The first type, from which the stereotype derives, is the *maternal family*. This family form was most often found in the rural South and existed during slavery. The second type is akin to the traditional American white family, with the father having undisputed authority in the family and a high level of involvement in family life. A third type originated in free black communities of mixed black, white, and American Indian origin; this structure was patriarchal. The last type delineated was composed of people who also were of a mixed ancestry, but who defined themselves as a separate, isolated race; this structure, too, was strictly patriarchal.

In the great migration of blacks from the South to the urban North during the early decades of this century, the maternal family was viewed by Frazier as unable to cope with an urban environment, becoming dependent on charity, and having its children run amuck—with sons joining delinquent gangs and daughters bearing illegitimate children. Families of the patriarchal

types, on the other hand, were better able to adjust to urbanism and formed the black middle class. Frazier, in sum, argues that there are two cultural traditions in black society: (1) the "folk culture" of the rural blacks; and (2) the genteel tradition of mulattoes and other black groups who assimilated the values and family patterns of the Southern aristocracy. Neither cultural pattern is seen as surviving among poor urban blacks, and disintegration of the folk culture is assumed to have brought about chaos, normlessness, immorality, and family pathology.[1]

The explanations offered for the development of matriarchal black families are *historical* and *socioeconomic*. The historical argument describes the black female as traditionally the most permanent and dependable member of black society (Powdermaker, p. 14; Kardiner and Ovesey, p. 348; and Glazer, pp. ix–xii). Burgess and Locke write:

Under slavery the mother remained the important figure in the family. The affectional relations of mother and child developed deep and permanent attachment.

1. An extensive critique of Frazier's research is presented in Valentine, pp. 20–28.

Excerpted from W. TenHouten. The black family: Myth and reality. *Psychiatry*, 1970, *33*, 145–173. Copyright by The William Alanson White Psychiatric Foundation, Inc. Reprinted by special permission of The William Alanson White Psychiatric Foundation, Inc.

Frequently, also, the father was a member of the family group, but often the relationship was casual and easily broken. . . . Then, too, Negro husbands were sold more often. These and other factors contributed to the development of a matricentric form of the family during slavery. [p. 62]

It is not the intention of this paper to examine the proposition that the black family in American society was at one time matriarchal. However, the assumptions and empirical evidence used in support of the foregoing historical account of matriarchy merit critical reevaluation. Frazier's use of census data, social work case histories, and public records is at best marginal in meeting the standards of evidence in present-day social science.

In modern urban society the subdominance of the black husband to the wife is attributed to employment behavior. The female in the black home has a better chance to find work than does her husband, who is at an extreme disadvantage in economic competition. Since the husband is defined as having low economic "value" in society relative to his wife, the black woman has greater control of economic resources (money, economic security, and occupational status), and brings more resources *into* the family unit. As a result of (1) the wife's contribution to the family, and (2) the husband's lack of contribution—so the argument goes—the wife wields *power* in the family and plays the dominant role. Rainwater (p. 192), in elaborating this argument, writes that in such a circumstance, the wife (and the husband) may "turn to others," and the husband is more apt to drink and become involved with his peers at the family's expense. The result of this behavior is seen as desertion and divorce.

The link between control of the economic function and power in the family is also assumed by Parsons and Bales. But the empirical evidence supporting this relationship is, as Aldous points out (p. 470), "scanty." Research by Blood and Hamblin, for instance, shows that the occupational

status of the *husband* is not very predictive of family power, relative to other social factors. There is a limited amount of empirical evidence that employment by the *wife* decreases the relative power of her husband (Blood and Wolfe, p. 34; Aldous). Middleton and Putney report (p. 605) that wives increase in dominance of *minor* decisions if they do *not* work.

The stereotype of the matriarchal black family has been given recent attention by a Department of Labor publication, *The Negro Family: The Case for National Action*, whose major author is Moynihan and which is widely known as the Moynihan Report. His description of the black family draws on both "causal" arguments—the supposed historical tradition of matriarchy, and the economic dependence of black males. Moynihan hypothesizes that:

At the heart of the deterioration of the fabric of Negro society is the deterioration of the Negro family.

The white family has achieved a high degree of stability and is maintaining that stability.

By contrast, the family structure of lower class Negroes is high unstable, and in many centers is approaching complete breakdown. [p. 5]

He goes on:

. . . the Negro community has been forced into a matriarchal structure which, because it is so out of line with the rest of American society, seriously retards the progress of the group as a whole, and imposes a crushing burden on the Negro male. [p. 29]

And on:

It was by destroying the Negro family under slavery that white America broke the will of the Negro people. Although that will has reasserted itself in our time, it is a resurgence that is doomed to frustration unless the viability of the Negro family is restored.[2] [p. 30]

2. It is in all probability an overstatement to say that the black family was "destroyed" by enslave-

Moynihan's position thus reiterates Frazier's conceptualization of the maternal family in the black community. But it also implies that the black family's adverse position has become self-sustaining, by its own internal dynamics of *family role deviancy*. Parker and Kleiner state (1969, pp. 500*ff*) that Moynihan's writings carry such an implication, and cite the following statement:

The cumulative result of unemployment and low income, and probably also of excessive dependence upon the income of women, has produced an unmistakable crisis in the Negro family, and raises the serious question of whether this crisis is beginning to create conditions which tend to reinforce the cycle that produced it in the first instance. [Moynihan, 1966, p. 147]

The Moynihan Report contains even more explicit statements on this topic:

... the circumstances of the Negro American community in recent years probably have been getting worse, not better. ... The fundamental problem, in which this is most clearly the case, is that of family structure. ... So long as this situation persists, the cycle of poverty and disadvantage will continue to repeat itself. ... [T]he present tangle of pathology is capable of perpetuating itself without assistance from the white world. [pp. 1, 47]

Parker and Kleiner conclude (1969, p. 507) that there are indeed problems in the black family, but that these problems appear to be created and maintained not by a deviant subculture, but by the social and psychological consequences of unemployment and discrimination. As a result of being unable to attain socioeconomic success because of social and economic discrimination, blacks may be apt to feel that they are not successful in family role performances.

ment. Frazier himself notes (1932, p. 1) that blacks lived in the United States for 43 years prior to the legalization of slavery, and his research suggests that there may be African cultural survivals in black family power structures.

Thus Moynihan contends that emasculation and family disorganization are basic weaknesses in the black community. To "help" the black community, it may not be sufficient to directly assault institutional and informal racism in *white* society, as it also seems necessary to directly intervene in the family in *black* society. Because family roles are deviant from the white norms, black families need to be rehabilitated to overcome the family role deviancy which perpetuates the "tangle of pathology" in the black community. This is the political consequence implied by the Moynihan Thesis.[3] It in part explains the apprehension and adverse reaction by the black community in response to the proposed "national action."

Certainly an empirical generalization used as a rationale for Government intervention in the black family merits most careful scrutiny. It is the purpose of this paper to provide such an evaluation. ...

THE MOYNIHAN THESIS:
AN EVALUATION

The Moynihan Thesis can be evaluated both as an *analytic concept* and as an *empirical generalization*. First, there exists some lack of conceptual clarity about the meaning of matriarchy. A family can be defined as matriarchal if the wife is dominant and the husband subdominant. To say the sex roles are *reversed* in black families means that the husband plays a role that a white wife would play, and the wife plays a role that a white husband would play. That is, the roles of the husband and wife are reversed vis-à-vis the "normal" pattern in white society. But it is not always clear *which* roles are reversed. Role reversal could occur for domination of the *conjugal* role, or the *parental* role. Conjugal role reversal would mean that the wife is dominant and the husband subdominant in their relations with each other. Parental role reversal would mean that the wife plays

3. For a sympathetic view of Moynihan's use of data, see Rainwater and Yancey; for an unsympathetic view, Valentine.

a dominant role in parent-child relations (control and socialization). It may be that conjugal roles are reversed in black families, but that parental roles are not; or, the obverse could be the case.

As Parker and Kleiner point out (1969), Moynihan implicitly used family role deviancy as an *intervening variable* between socioeconomic discrimination and the "pathology" of the black community. They argue that the relationship between socioeconomic discrimination and community pathology is *direct*, and that family role deviancy is not involved in the explanation of the continuing poverty of the black community.

The idea that pathology in poor and black communities is sustained through the socialization process in the family derives from a traditional mode of social science theorizing about the lower strata of society. According to this conception, poor youth learn from their parents a value system that devalues motivation to succeed. This lack of motivation—so it is argued—explains why the poor are unsuccessful and are not upwardly mobile. In short, the poor perpetuate their own poverty from generation to generation. This lack of desire for success, according to Hyman, "creates a *self-imposed* barrier to an improved position" (p. 427). This view has also been advanced by Aldous,[4] Lewis (1962, 1966), Matza, and Walter Miller. Lewis writes that lower classes have developed a "culture of poverty," in which the poor have "a high incidence of maternal deprivation, of orality, of weak ego structure, confusion of sexual identity, a lack of impulse control, [and] a strong present-time orientation with little ability to defer gratification and to plan for the future. . ." (1966, p. xlviii).

4. Aldous states that employment may be necessary to black husbands' "adequate performance" of their role but is not sufficient, because of "Lack of motivation, previous rebuffs, inability to conform to work requirements, and personal indulgence, . . . [and] abdication from family responsibility." This "makes their probability of being good family men . . . low . . . and their families are probably better off without them" (pp. 176*ff*).

Although Lewis's view of the "culture of poverty" differs from Moynihan's in that he views "male supremacy" as a part of this culture, Lewis does locate pathology in sex role identification and child socialization.

This conception of the poor has been criticized by Underhill (pp. 76–77) on the grounds that: (1) The aspirations of poor youth are higher than their attainments; (2) experimental research shows that aspirations are reduced by the denial of opportunity to succeed (he cites Lewin et al.); and (3) the positive *correlation* between aspirations and social class is well known, but social research has yet to demonstrate that high aspirations *cause* success, and suggests instead that both aspirations to success and success itself may be caused by inequality of opportunity. Ireland, Moles, and O'Shey, in a comparative study of Mexican-Americans, blacks, and Anglos (non-Mexican-American whites), find little overall support for the "culture of poverty" as a characteristic of poor people. They find minimal evidence for this among Mexican-Americans, and find blacks to be closer to Anglos than to Mexican-Americans. Liebow, in a participant-observation study of lower-class black males in Washington, D. C., found no evidence showing that these men were deviant from white middle-class norms, and found no evidence that family role deviancy is perpetuated intergenerationally. He finds the relationship between socioeconomic discrimination and family instability to be *direct*. Parker and Kleiner's data also show no such family role deviancy among blacks. Thus there exists substantial negative evidence for the view of family role deviancy and a culture of poverty in the black family.

Presumably the *pathology* attributed to low success motivation, as described by Hyman and Lewis, derives from the fact that this motivation *deviates* from the nonpoor's high motivation to succeed. Similarly, female dominance in black families is seen as pathological *because* it differs from the male dominance of the white and middle-class black family. Such an inference that *statistical* deviancy (deviation from the modal type) is pathological is stated explicitly by Moynihan in his statement that matriarchal structure retards the progress of blacks "because it is so out of line with the rest of American society" (1965, p. 29). The *causal* connection between the plight of black communities and the assumed matriarchy is not given. Certainly it cannot be assumed.

There are other factors related to the hypothesis of matriarchy which must be considered in any empirical evaluation. Differences between blacks and whites may reflect differences in socioeconomic level (roughly, "lower class" as contrasted with "middle class") as much as or more than race. Thus, social class represents an important specification of the thesis of matriarchy in the black family. As mentioned, Frazier claims that lower-class black families are matriarchal and middle-class black families patriarchal. Moynihan's view of the black family is consistent with this. He is explicit in stating that the deterioration of the black family is most intense in lower-class black families. He contends that the family structure of lower-class black families is highly unstable, and in many urban centers is approaching complete breakdown. He feels at the same time that the middle-class black family "is steadily growing stronger and more successful," and "puts a higher premium on family stability and the conserving of family resources than does the white middle-class family" (1965, pp. 5–6). It is not entirely clear if this statement means that middle-class black families are more patriarchal than are middle-class white families. Since blacks are disproportionately represented in the lower strata of society, it follows from the specified Thesis that, for an overall black-white comparison, black families are more unstable and more matriarchal than are white families. Thus the specification of the Thesis is consistent with its general formulation, that matriarchy is more predominant in black families than in white families. . . .

As a final analytic comment, female dominance in *any* role cannot be *assumed* to be dysfunctional for the particular group to which it refers. Since groups differ in their relations to important systems in society, especially the economy, it may be that different family role patterns are appropriate to different social contexts.

The Moynihan Thesis can also be evaluated as an empirical generalization. A general review of studies pertaining to the black family is beyond the scope of this paper. In the balance of this section, major empirical indicators of family "instability" and "pathology" used in the Report are critically examined. The variables to be considered are illegitimacy rates, percentages of female-headed families, and unemployment rates. Moynihan also employs statistics on participation to the Aid to Dependent Children program, failure to pass armed forces entrance examinations,[5] delinquency,[6] and crime to describe the "tangle of pathology" in the black community.

Illegitimacy Rates

Illegitimacy rates can be defined in a number of ways. In the Moynihan Report, illegiti-

5. Moynihan states, "The ultimate mark of inadequate preparation for life is the failure rate on the Armed Forces Mental Test" (1965, p. 40). He also writes: "There is another special quality about military service for Negro men: it is an utterly masculine world. Given the strains of the disorganization and matrifocal family life in which so many Negro youth come of age, the Armed Forces are a dramatic and desperately needed change: a world away from women, a world run by strong men of unquestioned authority, where discipline, if hard, is nonetheless orderly and predictable, and where rewards, if limited, are granted on the basis of performance" (p. 42).

6. References to certain of these studies are given in Parker and Kleiner (1969). The reader is also referred to Gould's study of a sample of 104 white and 220 black males from a junior high school in central Seattle. He finds that the usual race difference in official delinquency records (with blacks more delinquent than whites) does not hold for self-reported delinquency. This suggests that the "pathology" of black delinquency may result from black youth being more apt to be caught and convicted. In addition, for two kinds of delinquency related to family pathology, the percentages of blacks reporting delinquency are *lower* than the corresponding percentages for whites. The percentages "defying parents" are blacks 20 and whites 44; the percentages "running away," blacks 9 and whites 15 (p. 330).

macy rates are defined as *1000 times the ratio of illegitimate births to all live births.* Moynihan uses these rates as indicative of family pathology. This interpretation can be questioned on a number of grounds: the statistical properties of the data, including the definition of illegitimacy; the validity of the Government figures; the substantive explanation of illegitimate births; the relevance of data on illegitimacy for the measurement of family pathology; and the lack of control of the variable family socioeconomic status.

The illegitimacy rates in 1940 were, by Moynihan's definition, 20 for whites and 168 for nonwhites. (Since over 90 percent of nonwhites are blacks, the nonwhite rates are used to estimate the black rates.) By 1963, the rates for whites had increased to 31, and the rates for nonwhites to 236. Thus there has been an increase in both groups. As Moynihan observes, the total increase for whites is 11, as compared to 68 for nonwhites. But these increases can be given a second interpretation, which takes into account the differences in the 1940 base figures. As a proportion of this base, the rate has increased 55 percent among whites, as compared to 40 percent among blacks. The nonwhite figure rises more rapidly in absolute terms in part because its initial level is higher.

Thus, the claim that the black family is *increasingly* disorganized in comparison to white families is used as the empirical indicator of family disorganization. But, if the ratio of the later rate to the earlier rate is used as the indicator of disorganization, the data show that white families may be increasingly disorganized in comparison to black families. Herzog states, however, that given the uneven quality of these data—with many states submitting estimates and others no data at all—such slight differences in rates should not be regarded as significant (p. 27).

In addition, there are two difficulties with the definition of illegitimacy used in the Moynihan Report, both of which create biases toward higher rates for nonwhites.

First, black women have absolutely higher birth rates, whether married or not. Second, the proportion of women who are unmarried and of child-bearing age (15 through 44) is higher for blacks than for whites. If the illegitimacy rate is defined (Ventura, p. 446) as *1000 times the number of illegitimate births per unmarried woman 15–44 years of age,* illegitimacy is related to the population of women at risk, and nonwhite-white comparisons are more meaningful. By this measure the 1940 rates were 36 for nonwhites and 3.6 for whites, a nonwhite-white ratio of 10 to 1. This rate increased until 1950, at which time it was 12 to 1. But since 1950 the ratio of nonwhite to white illegitimacy rates has declined, so that by 1960 the rates were nonwhites 92 and whites 12, a ratio of less than 8 to 1 (Ventura, p. 447). Ventura also reports that "since 1960 the illegitimacy rate for nonwhite women has declined 6 percent while the rate for whites has risen 30 percent. . . ." (p. 447). *If these rates could be defined as valid empirical indicators of family pathology, one would conclude that the* white *family is becoming more pathological and the* black *family less pathological.*

With regard to the second criticism of illegitimacy rates as an indicator of family pathology, Moynihan concurs with Herzog that the data on illegitimacy have limited dependability. He writes:

There are almost certainly a considerable number of Negro children who, although technically illegitimate, are in fact the offspring of stable unions. On the other hand, it may be assumed that many births that are in fact illegitimate are recorded otherwise. Probably the two effects cancel each other. [p. 8]

There is some basis for believing that illegitimate black births are more apt to be recorded as such than are similar births for whites. Ventura points out that ". . . it is probable . . . that variations in reporting accuracy exist among different segments of the population. For example, it is likely that women in higher socioeconomic groups have more opportunity to under-report the incidence of illegitimate births" (p. 446). Since blacks are less apt to have high socioeconomic status than are whites, this socioeconomic effect also leads to more probable reporting of black illegitimate births as opposed to white illegitimate births. In sum, the data that *are* available are of questionable validity; and the data that *are not* available (as of 1966) represent 16 states and 30 percent of the population. The data do not constitute a random sample of the entire nation.

Third, the substantive explanation of nonwhite illegitimacy is apparently not, as is sometimes suggested, related to the availability of Aid to Dependent Children. Two factors that may be important to an explanation of the nonwhite-white difference in illegitimacy are *poverty* and *access to birth control.*

As Herzog points out (p. 28), comparisons between poor and nonpoor census tracts show a strong relationship between higher illegitimacy rates and poorer tracts. There is variation within races according to income. Pakter et al., for example, find the illegitimacy rates of blacks to be 38 in Central Harlem (poor black) but only 9 in Pelham Bay (nonpoor black). Poverty contributes to illegitimacy in at least two ways. First, poor persons are apt to be on welfare, and hence reluctant to risk eligibility by admitting that a man is living in the home. Second, poor persons and black persons are less able to afford, less likely to define as necessary, legal divorce or legal separation.

In considering other possible explanations of the illegitimacy rates, one finds that there are no reliable data indicating that unmarried black women have more interesting sex lives than do unmarried white women: there is no evidence for a "morality gap" in the black community. Since extra-marital sex is frequent in both groups, any difference in illegitimacy may depend on the greater access to birth control by white women (and men). Whites are more apt to know what

birth control *is*, are better able to afford and use it,[7] and have greater access to abortion as a means of birth control. It is this writer's opinion that much of the race difference in illegitimacy results from this factor, and that the decline in nonwhite illegitimacy will be greater as birth control becomes more available in the black community.

Fourth, the higher rate of illegitimacy reported in the black community may reflect the greater extent to which illegitimate black babies are incorporated into the family unit, rather than being expelled and concealed from the family and community. Black people in the United States are apparently far more accepting of illegitimate children and are more apt to care for them than whites. Perhaps it is a *pathology of white values* that lowers the frequency of illegitimate births accepted as members of the family. At any rate, there is an ethnocentric bias in regarding black acceptance of illegitimate babies as pathological *because* this is not done in the white family and is deviant from white "normality."

The word "legitimate," after all, means only that a certificate of legitimation of a birth is registered with some municipal officer for a fixed fee. This, per se, says nothing about a commitment to take responsibility for, and care for, and express loyalty to a child. In the black community, there are norms that the *entire family* will take responsibility for a child. In the white community, this is somewhat less apt to be the case if a child is illegitimate.

Fifth, Ventura indicates that socioeconomic level is itself an important factor contributing to nonwhite-white differences in illegitimacy. She writes: "It is likely that if it were possible to control for social class, much of the difference between the two groups would disappear" (p. 448). That is, blacks are more apt to be in a lower class

7. Ventura (p. 448) uses research by Whelpton, Campbell, and Patterson to conclude that it is likely that white couples involved in premarital sex relations are more apt to use contraceptives than are black couples.

than whites, and lower-class people are more apt to have illegitimate children, and these factors, per se, may constitute an explanation for the higher illegitimacy rates in the black group. The data on illegitimacy rates collected before 1968 contain no information on the parents' socioeconomic status. Thus, until the later data are analyzed, there is no way to know that black-white differentials in illegitimacy rates are not a spurious result of social class differences.

For all these reasons, data on illegitimacy are inappropriate for testing the Moynihan Thesis of pathology among *lower-class* blacks.

Female-Headed Families

The percentage of women with husbands absent has been stable among whites from 1950 to 1960 but has increased somewhat for blacks. Controlling for women of child-bearing age, in the decade from 1950 to 1960, the percentages of female-headed homes for nonwhites and whites, respectively, are 33 and 8 for urban areas, 15 and 6 for rural nonfarm areas, and 10 and 3 for rural farm areas. Overall, the 1960 rates are 21 percent for nonwhite and 9 for white families (Moynihan, 1965, p. 11). Thus in both urban and rural areas, female-headed families are more prevalent among blacks than among whites.

The percentage of female-headed families among blacks (as distinct from nonwhites) gradually rose from 19 in 1940 to 24 in 1959. The overall rise from 1949 to 1965 for blacks is about one-third of one percent per year (Herzog, pp. 25–26). But from 1959 through 1965, there has been no rise, and the 1965 percentage is 24 (as compared to 9 for whites). Thus the Census data show that the level of female-headed families is not rising for blacks. If the percentage of female-headed families could be defined as a valid indicator of family pathology, one would not conclude that the black family is becoming more pathological. As with illegitimacy rates (by Ventura's definition), this

empirical outcome does not contribute directional support for the Moynihan Thesis of increasing deterioration in the black family.

The most common family structure among blacks is one in which there are both a husband and a wife present in the home. In urban areas, where the black family is alleged to be rapidly deteriorating, the percentage of such families is 65. Of the remaining 35 percent, only 18 are headed by the wife (Bernard). The increase in female-headed homes for blacks may in part be a statistical artifact of urban migration, rather than family disorganization. For, as Moynihan points out, (1) blacks are more urban than whites, and (2) black families in cities are more apt to be headed by a woman than are black families in the country.

Since the Moynihan Thesis states that matriarchy is characteristic of lower-class urban black families, data comparing urban blacks and whites are necessary. If the percentage of female-headed families is a valid indicator of family pathology and matriarchy, the percentage for the lower-class black group should be higher than that for other groups. The 1960 Census data show the following: for families with children that have annual incomes under $3,000, the percentages are blacks 47 and whites 38; for families with incomes of $3,000 or more, blacks 8 and whites 4. Thus blacks at both levels are more apt to have female-headed families, but the black-white differences within income groups are only 9 and 4 percent (Rainwater). Further, percentage of female-headed families is far more closely related to income level than to race: among blacks, the low-income families are 39 percent more apt to have female-headed families; among whites, 34 percent. The effects of income level are about five times as strong as the effects of race. Female-headed families are five times more characteristic of poor families than of black families.

One reason why black women (both poor and nonpoor) are more apt to head families is a differential access to adoption. Most white women that have illegitimate babies are able to have them adopted. But since the demand for black babies is so low, black women have comparatively limited opportunities to have their illegitimate babies adopted, and thus are apt to keep them (Geismar and Gerhart, pp. 428*ff*).

The data on female-headed homes in black and poor communities undoubtedly exaggerate the extent to which the fathers are not present. Substitute father laws and welfare requirements often make financial aid contingent on there being no father in the home. This of course creates a strong economic incentive to conceal the presence of the husband, and also contributes to husbands' motivation to leave the family unit. It has been estimated that the decennial U.S. Census undercounts urban blacks by as much as 20 percent.

The Moynihan Thesis implies that black men are emasculated and subdominant in their homes. There is, however, no empirical evidence showing that black men who leave their wives do so *because* they were unable to play a dominant role in the family. To say a man is subdominant because he is *absent* reduces the meaning of dominance to that of triviality. Further, as regards the approximately 60 percent of black homes with a husband present, there is no convincing evidence that these husbands are, in comparison to white husbands, emasculated and subdominant. Evidence in support of this view would require comparative analysis of *complete* families in the black and white race groups. . . . Thus, it is most important to make a conceptual distinction between female-headed families and matriarchal families. In female-headed families there is no husband. In matriarchal families, there is a husband present, who plays subdominant conjugal and/or parental roles. For this reason, the data on female-headed families may not be valid for the measurement of family pathology.

As a final point, there is little if any justification for defining black families, or any families, as pathological on the ground that

there is no husband present (Browning, Toby). Family units in which the husband is present may be unhappy and disorganized, and family units in which the husband is absent may be happy and well organized. Duncan and Duncan have analyzed data from the Current Population Survey conducted by the U.S. Bureau of the Census in 1962. The data show that for neither black men nor white men does an intergenerational transmission of family instability (absence of a parent) appear to operate. They conclude:

There is, then, no sound basis for postulating a cycle of broken family relations, such as the failure of the parents to share a home with one another and their offspring predispose their sons to live without a spouse. [pp. 275–276]

This study, then, does not provide positive support for Moynihan's position that family role deviance perpetuates family pathology from generation to generation. The Duncan and Duncan data do show, however, that an intact family background facilitates the occupational success of sons.

Unemployment Rates

Moynihan writes that ". . . unemployment among Negroes outside the South has persisted at a catastrophic level since the first statistics were gathered in 1930" (p. 20). The high level of unemployment among blacks is certainly a sad commentary on American society and the performance of the American economy. But black unemployment has *not* increased. The data presented for the years 1930, 1940, 1950, and 1960 indicate that 1960 is the year of least unemployment for blacks. Unemployment among blacks also has declined slightly from 1960 to 1964. Unemployment among both whites and blacks has decreased, and further, the decrease has been more rapid among blacks than among whites.

It is argued that unemployment causes instability in the home (a study of white families by Bakke is cited by Moynihan). It is further argued that unemployment has more deleterious effects on the black home than on the white home. But the two conclusions imply that the decrease in black unemployment levels should *increase* family stability, just as decreased white unemployment should stabilize white families. Since unemployment has decreased faster for blacks than for whites, black homes should be increasingly stable vis-à-vis white homes. To support his Thesis, Moynihan relies on data showing that between 1960 and 1964 the number of new ADC cases rose. But the other data used in the Report as measures of family instability did not show such a rise. Marital separation, for example, continued to parallel employment. Valentine points out (p. 32) that Moynihan ignores other evidence in the Report, such as the *decline* of family income relative to white income. Valentine concludes that *there is in the Report more evidence to support the interpretation that family structure measures are caused by economic factors than to support the opposite interpretation* (p. 33). It may be too strong a statement to say that these data contradict Moynihan's argument, but any support they give to the Thesis is, at best, equivocal.

A *methodological* weakness in the use of such census data for inferences about individuals and families is that it assumes that variables correlated for groups are correlated for persons or families *within* groups. Robinson shows that this dependence on ecological correlations makes such inferences unsound. For instance, in a given time period, the unemployment rate and the percent of female-headed families may both rise in the black community. But there is no way to know, from *this*, that the husbands who left their wives are the same husbands who had become unemployed (Aldous, p. 470). Further, much of the family research consistent with Frazier's and Moynihan's conclusions was carried out in the 1930s, a time when many factors were at work which could cause both unemployment and family instability.

Further, the instability of employment of blacks as opposed to whites reflects social class as well as race. Lower-class persons work at jobs that are unstable in comparison to the jobs of the middle class. Thus part of the instability of employment behavior for blacks derives from the fact that they are more apt to be lower-class than whites. When social class is controlled, much of the race difference in employment behavior is removed (Hamel).

In summary, the evidence for deterioration of the black family (1) is derived from socio-demographic data rather than from data on family dynamics, and (2) does not support the conclusion drawn from it. As Geismar and Gerhart write, "The act of inferring functioning patterns from such structural and official, recorded behavioral characteristics, is not so much the articulation of a theoretical position as it is a form of research which grasps at available straws" (p. 480). . . .

REFERENCES

Aldous, Joan. "Wives' Employment Status and Lower-Class Men as Husband-Fathers: Support for the Moynihan Thesis," *J. Marriage and Family* (1969) 31, 469–476.

Almond, G., and Verba, S. *The Civic Culture*; Princeton Univ. Press, 1963.

Bakke, Edward Wight. *Citizens Without Work*; Yale Univ. Press, 1940.

Bernard, Jessie, *Marriage and Family Among Negroes*; Prentice-Hall, 1966.

Blood, Robert O., Jr., and Hamblin, Robert L. "The Effect of the Wife's Employment on the Family Power Structure," *Social Forces* (1955) 26, 347–352.

Blood, Robert O., Jr., and Wolfe, Donald M. *Husbands and Wives*; Free Press, 1960.

Browning, Charles J. "Differential Impact of Family Disorganization on Male Adolescents," *Social Problems* (1960) 8, 37–44.

Burgess, Ernest W., and Locke, Harvey J. *The Family*; American Book Co., 1945.

Duncan, Beverly, and Duncan, Otis Dudley. "Family Stability and Occupational Success," *Social Problems* (1969) 16, 273–285.

Frazier, E. Franklin. *The Free Negro Family*; Fisk Univ. Press, 1932.

Frazier, E. Franklin. *The Negro Family in the United States*; Dryden, 1948.

Frazier, E. Franklin, *Black Bourgeoisie*; Free Press, 1957.

Geismar, Ludwig L., and Gerhart, Ursula C. "Social Class, Ethnicity and Family Functioning: Exploring Some Issues Raised by the Moynihan Report," *J. Marriage and Family* (1968) 30, 480–487.

Glazer, Nathan, "Introduction," in Stanley M. Elkin, *Slavery*; Grosset & Dunlap, 1963.

Gould, Leroy C. "Who Defines Delinquency: A Comparison of Self-Reported and Officially-Reported Indices of Delinquency for Three Racial Groups," *Social Problems* (1969) 16, 325–335.

Hamel, Harvey R. *Job Tenure of Workers, January 1966*; U.S. Dept. of Labor, Special Labor Force Report No. 77, 1967.

Herbst, P. G. "Family Living: Patterns of Interaction," in O. A. Oeser and S. B. Hammond (Eds.), *Social Structure and Personality in a City*; Routledge and Kegan Paul, 1954.

Herzog, Elizabeth. *About the Poor*; U.S. Dept. of HEW, Children's Bureau Publ. 451, 1968.

Hoffman, L. W. "Effects of the Employment of Mothers in Parental Power Relations and the Division of Household Tasks," *Marriage and Family Living* (1960) 22, 17–35.

Hyman, Herbert H. "The Value Systems of Different Classes," in Reinhard Bendix and Seymour Martin Lipset (Eds.), *Class, Status and Power*; Free Press, 1966.

Hyman, Herbert H., and Reed, John Shelton. "Black Matriarchy' Reconsidered: Evidence from Secondary Analysis of Sample Surveys," *Public Opinion Quart.* (1969) 33, 346–354.

Ireland, Lola M., Moles, Oliver C., and O'Shey, Robert M. "Ethnicity, Poverty, and Selected Attitudes: A Test of the 'Culture of Poverty' Hypothesis," *Social Forces* (1969) 47, 405–413.

Kardiner, Abram, and Ovesey, Lionel. *The Mark of Oppression*; Meridian Books, 1962.

Kitsuse, John I., and Cicourel, A. V. "A Note on the Uses of Official Statistics," *Social Problems* (1963) 11, 131–139.

Lewin, Kurt, et al. "Level of Aspiration," in J. McV. Hunt (Ed.), *Personality and the Behavior Disorders*; Ronald, 1944.

Liebow, Elliot,. *Tally's Corner*; Little, Brown, 1967.

Lewis, Oscar. *The Children of Sanchez*; Science Editions, 1962.

Lewis, Oscar. *La Vida*; Random House, 1966.

Matza, David. "The Disreputable Poor," in Reinard Bendix and Seymour Martin Lipset (Eds.), *Class, Status, and Power*; Free Press, 1966.

Middleton, Russell, and Putney, Snell. "Dominance in Decisions in the Family: Race and Class Differences," *Amer. J. Sociology* (1960) 65, 605–609.

Miller, Daniel R., and Swanson, Guy E. *The Changing American Parent*; Wiley, 1958.

Miller, Walter B. "Lower-Class Culture as a Generating Milieu of Gang Delinquency," *J. Social Issues* (1958) 14, 5–19.

Moynihan, Daniel Patrick. *The Negro Family: The Case for National Action* (The Moynihan Report); U.S. Dept. of Labor, Office of Policy Planning and Research, 1965.

Moynihan, Daniel Patrick. "Employment, Income, and the Ordeal of the Negro Family," in Talcott Parsons and Kenneth B. Clark (Eds.), *The Negro American*; Houghton Mifflin, 1966.

Pakter, Jean, et al. "Out of Wedlock Births in New York City: I–Sociological Aspects," *Amer. J. Public Health* (1961) 51, 846–865.

Parker, Seymour, and Kleiner, Robert J. *Mental Illness in the Urban Negro Community*; Free Press, 1966.

Parker, Seymour, and Kleiner, Robert J. "Social and Psychological Dimensions of Family Role Performance of the Negro Male," *J. Marriage and Family* (1969) 31, 500–506.

Parsons, Talcott, and Bales, Robert F. *Family, Socialization and Interaction Process;* Free Press, 1955.

Powdermaker, Hortense. *After Freedom*; Viking Press, 1939.

Rainwater, Lee. "Crucible of Identity: The Negro Lower-Class Family," *Daedalus* (1966) 95, 172–216.

Rainwater, Lee, and Yancey, William L. *The Moynihan Report and the Politics of Controversy*; MIT Press, 1967.

Robinson, W. S. "Ecological Correlations and the Behavior of Individuals," *Amer. Sociol. Review* (1950) 15, 351–357.

Straus, Murray A. "Conjugal Power Structure and Adolescent Personality," *Marriage and Family Living* (1962) 24, 17–25.

TenHouten, Warren D. "Scale Gradient Analysis: A Statistical Method for the Construction and Evaluation of Guttman Scales," *Sociometry* (1969) 32, 80–99.

Toby, Jackson. "The Differential Impact of Family Disorganization," *Amer. Sociol. Review* (1957) 22, 505–512.

Udry, J. Richard. "Marital Instability by Race, Sex, Education, and Occupation Using 1960 Census Data," *Amer. J. Sociology* (1966) 72, 203–209.

Underhill, Ralph, *Youth in Poor Neighborhoods*; Natl. Opinion Research Center, Report 121-A, 1967.

Valentine, Charles, A. *Culture and Poverty*; Univ. of Chicago Press, 1968.

Ventura, Stephanie J. "Recent Trends in Differentials in Illegitimacy," *J. Marriage and Family* (1969) 31, 446–450.

Whelpton, Pascal K., Campbell, Arthur A., and Patterson, John E. *Fertility and Family Planning in the United States*; Princeton Univ. Press, 1966.

1.3
Pygmalion Black and White

PAMELA C. RUBOVITS and MARTIN L. MAEHR

It is not surprising that research on experimenter expectancies (Rosenthal, 1966; Rosenthal & Fode, 1963; Rosenthal & Lawson, 1964) has been quickly applied to the classroom, with some studies finding that students perform in line with their teachers' expectations for them (Meichenbaum, Bowers, & Ross, 1969; Rosenthal & Jacobson, 1968). These findings, controversial though they may be (Claiborne, 1969; Elashoff & Snow, 1970; Rosenthal, 1969; Snow, 1969; Thorndike, 1968, 1969), provide a perspective on a problem of major concern: the teaching of black students by white teachers. Black students have been found to believe that their white teachers have low estimates of their ability and worth (Brown, 1968; Davidson & Lang, 1960). It has also been well documented that white teachers expect less of lower-class children than they do of middle-class children (Becker, 1952; Deutsch, 1963; Warner, Havighurst, & Loeb, 1944; Wilson, 1963). In line with Rosenthal and Jacobson's proposal (1968) that teacher expectations affect teacher behavior in such a way that it is highly likely that student performance is in turn affected, it would seem probable that

differential teacher expectation for black students and white students is related to differential school achievement. Few, if any, studies have, however, directly observed and compared teacher-expectancy effects on black students and white students. The present study was designed to do just that, and it yielded surprising results—results that can be interpreted as a paradigmatic instance of "white racism."

The present study is a replication and extension of a previous study (Rubovits & Maehr, 1971) that involved the systematic observation of teacher behavior following the experimental manipulation of expectations. The teachers, college undergraduates with limited classroom experience, each met with four students who had been randomly identified for the teacher as being "gifted" or "nongifted." The teachers did not differentiate in the amount of attention given to allegedly gifted and nongifted students; however, the pattern of attention did differ: Gifted students were called on and praised more than nongifted students. Thus, in this first study, teacher expectations were found to be related to teacher behavior in such a way that gifted students appeared to be en-

From P. Rubovits & M. Maehr. Pygmalion black and white. *Journal of Personality and Social Psychology*, 1973, *25*, 210–218. Copyright 1973 by the American Psychological Association. Reprinted by permission.

couraged and average students discouraged by their teachers.

The present study replicated the above procedure with one new dimension. Whereas the previous study looked at interaction of white teachers with white students, this study considered the interaction of white teachers with white students and black students; one of the students labeled gifted and one of the students labeled nongifted were black. This provided an opportunity to investigate whether or not white teachers interact differently with white students and black students, both bright and average, in ways that would differentially affect their school performance. In addition, the study attempted to identify what kind of teacher would most likely be affected by race and label. Each teacher's level of dogmatism was, therefore, assessed under the assumption that high- and low-dogmatism teachers would react differently to the stereotyping effects of race and label.

METHOD

Subjects

Two different groups of subjects participated in the study. The group referred to as teachers was composed of 66 white female undergraduates enrolled in a teacher training course. All teachers had expressed interest in teaching, but not all were enrolled in an education curriculum, and none had yet had teaching experience. All teachers were volunteers; however, they were given course credit for participating in this project. The teachers knew nothing of the experimental manipulations; they simply thought they were taking advantage of a microteaching experience provided for them.

The group referred to as students was comprised of 264 seventh and eighth graders attending three junior high schools in a small midwestern city. These students were randomly selected within ability groups and given no instruction as to how they were to behave.

Measurement Procedures

In order to index the quality of teacher-student interaction, an instrument especially developed for this series of studies on teacher expectancy was employed. Although a more detailed description including reliability data may be found elsewhere (Rubovits, 1970; Rubovits & Maehr, 1971), the major features of this instrument should be noted. Briefly, the instrument is an observational schedule that requires a trained observer to record the incidence of six different teacher behaviors: (a) teacher *attention* to students' statements, subdivided into attention to requested statements and attention to spontaneous student statements; (b) teacher *encouragement* of students' statements; (c) teacher *elaboration* of students' statements; (d) teacher *ignoring* of students' statements; (e) teacher *praise* of students' statements; and (f) teacher *criticism* of students' statements.

The Rokeach Dogmatism Scale (Rokeach, 1960) was used to measure the teachers' authoritarianism. In addition, a questionnaire was given to each teacher in order to check the credibility of the experimental manipulations and to obtain some information on the teachers' perception of the students and the interpretations they gave to each student's behavior.

Experimental Procedure

One week before teaching, each teacher was given a lesson plan which outlined the topic to be taught and specified major points to be covered. As in the previous study, a lesson plan on the topic of television was employed. This topic and plan prompted considerable involvement on the part of both teacher and student. All students were found to be quite interested in discussing television and actively participated. The teachers had little or no difficulty in starting and sustaining a discussion on the topic and generally seemed at ease, improvising a great deal, adding and omitting points from the lesson plan, and using many original samples.

Attached to each teacher's lesson plan was a brief general description of the students she would be meeting. The teachers were told that an attempt would be made to have them teach as heterogeneous a group of students as possible. The teachers were also reminded that this was to be a learning experience for them, so they should be particularly alert to the differences between their students in terms of verbal ability, interest, quality of comments, etc.

The teachers were given no more information until just right before their teaching sessions, when each teacher was given a seating chart. This chart had on it each student's first name and also, under each name, an IQ score and a label indicating whether that student had been selected from the school's gifted program or from the regular track. The IQ score and a label had been *randomly* assigned to each student and did not necessarily bear any relation to the student's actual ability or track assignment.

For each teacher, a different group of four students was randomly selected from the same-ability-grouped class unit. Besides selecting from the same-ability units, one other restriction was placed on the selection of students; each session required two black students and two white students. One black student and one white student were randomly assigned a high IQ (between 130 and 135) and the label gifted. The other black student and the other white student were given lower IQs (between 98 and 102) and the label nongifted.

Each teacher was given the seating chart before the students arrived and was told to familiarize herself with the names and to examine closely the IQ scores and labels under each name. When the students arrived, the teacher was instructed to ask each student to sit in the seat designated on the chart. The teacher was further instructed before beginning the lesson to look at each student and read again, to herself, the IQ

score and label of each child. The necessity for doing this was emphasized to the teacher and justified by explaining that being aware of each student's ability level could help a teacher to deal with that student during the session.

The teacher then introduced herself and explained that she had come from the University of Illinois to try out some new teaching materials. In the meantime, an observer seated herself two rows behind the students. The observer began categorizing the teacher's behavior as soon as the teacher had introduced herself and continued tallying behavior for 40 minutes. It must be emphasized that the observer did not know what label had been assigned to each student.

After the teaching session, the observer and the teacher discussed what had transpired, with the observer attempting to start the teacher thinking about each student's performance in relation to his reported intelligence. The teacher then filled out a questionnaire and two personality inventories. After all of the teachers had participated, the experimenters went to the two classes from which teachers had been recruited and explained the study in detail, discussing with them the results and implications of the study.

RESULTS

Interaction Analysis

Frequency counts were collected on each teacher for each of eight categories. Each teacher met with four different kinds of students: gifted black, nongifted black, gifted white, and nongifted white. For each category, therefore, every teacher received four scores, with each score indicating her interaction with one kind of student. These scores were treated as repeated measures on the same individual.

A multivariate analysis of variance was used to analyze the data from seven of the categories (see Tatsuoka, 1971). Category 1, it will be remembered, measures the total number of times the teacher attended to the statements of the student. Attention to two specific kinds of statements were included in Category 1—attention to spontaneous responses to the teacher's questions (Category 1a) and attention to statements specifically requested by the teacher (Category 1b). Although the frequency of counts for Category 1 was not simply a combination of those for the subcategories 1a and 1b, Category 1 is clearly related to Categories 1a and 1b. For this reason, data on Category 1 were not included in the multivariate analysis of variance but were analyzed in a separate univariate analysis of variance.

In both of these analyses, there was one between-subjects variable—dogmatism (level of teacher dogmatism based on a high-low median split). This is referred to as the *teacher* variable. The two within-teachers variables are based on student differences and, for purposes of discussion, are referred to as *student* variables: race (black-white) and label (gifted-nongifted).

Student Variables: Race of Student

Each teacher met with two white students and two black students. Table 1 presents the mean number of teacher responses to black students and white students. Table 2 presents the F values from the analysis of variance and multivariate analysis of variance for the effects of race on the teacher-student interaction.

The analysis of variance for Category 1 (total attention) shows a significant difference in *quantity* of attention, with white students receiving far more attention from teachers than black students. This interpretation should be qualified in light of a Race X Label interaction and subsequent comparison of gifted and nongifted black and white means (see Tables 1 and 2 and Figure 1). Such a consideration would suggest that the significant main effect in this case is almost entirely attributable to the great amount of attention given the gifted whites. The multi-

Table 1. Mean Teacher Interactions with Gifted and Nongifted Black Students and White Students

Category	Black	White	Combined
1—Total attention			
Gifted	29.59	36.08	32.83
Nongifted	30.32	32.33	31.32
Combined	29.95	34.20	
1a—Attention to unsolicited statements			
Gifted	26.39	26.79	26.59
Nongifted	26.30	26.03	26.17
Combined	26.35	26.41	
1b—Attention to requested statements			
Gifted	3.88	10.64	7.70
Nongifted	4.77	5.67	5.22
Combined	4.32	8.15	
2—Encouragement			
Gifted	5.47	6.18	5.82
Nongifted	5.32	6.32	5.82
Combined	5.39	6.25	
3—Elaboration			
Gifted	2.09	2.08	2.08
Nongifted	2.44	2.15	2.30
Combined	2.26	2.11	
4—Ignoring			
Gifted	6.92	5.09	6.01
Nongifted	6.86	4.56	5.71
Combined	6.89	4.82	
5—Praise			
Gifted	.58	2.02	1.30
Nongifted	1.56	1.29	1.42
Combined	1.07	1.65	
6—Criticism			
Gifted	1.86	.77	1.32
Nongifted	.86	.68	.77
Combined	1.36	.73	

variate analysis of variance analyzed *qualitative* differences in teacher attention, and it also shows a significant overall effect for race. From the discriminant coefficients (Table 3) it can be seen that treatment of black students and white students differed most on the dimensions of ignoring, praise, attention to requested statements, and criticism. Across all teachers and also across labels, a pattern can be seen in the way teachers treated black students and white students. The directions of this pattern can be

Table 2. *F* Values Associated with Analysis of Variance and Multivariate Analysis of Variance

Source	ANOVA (Category 1)	MANOVA	Univariate *F*s for variables (categories) in MANOVA						
			1*a*	1*b*	2	3	4	5	6
Dogmatism (A)	.56	5.25**	.00	2.48	.00	2.88	31.30**	.49	6.72*
Race (B)	9.51**	7.48**	.00	12.51**	3.85	.25	19.05**	11.68**	9.73**
Label (C)	2.12	3.28**	.15	9.21**	.00	.36	.71	.72	13.76**
A × B	1.17	3.74**	.16	.19	18.39**	.36	6.30*	.87	1.08
A × C	3.59	1.17	1.64	.24	.13	.47	4.59*	.02	.38
B × C	4.85*	5.60**	.08	4.02*	.10	.16	.49	26.95**	10.48**
A × B × C	.10	.32	.52	.12	.01	.10	.19	.19	.42

*$p < .05$.
**$p < .01$.

seen from the means in Table 1. Fewer statements were requested of blacks than of whites. More statements of blacks than of whites were ignored. Possibly most interesting of all, black students were praised less and criticized more.

Three dependent variables contributed little to the difference in treatment of black and white students. For one of these (Category 1*a*), it had been expected that little effect would be found. This category measures the amount of student initiated interaction. Little effect for this category would allow for the inference that there was no

difference in the spontaneity of the students. Since this was the case, further confirmed by a nonsignificant univariate *F* for this category, it can be assumed that black students and white students were not treated differently by teachers because of differences in their verbosity.

Student Variables: Label of Student

Two students taught by each teacher, one black and one white, had been randomly given the label "gifted," and two, one black and one white, the label "nongifted." Table 1 presents the mean number of teacher re-

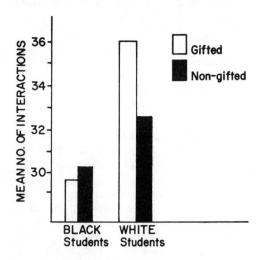

Fig. 1. Teacher Interaction with Gifted and Nongifted Black and White Students (Category 1: Total Attention).

Table 3. Discriminant Coefficients for Significant Effects in Multivariate Analysis of Variance

Category	Significant effects				
	Dogmatism (A)	Race (B)	Label (C)	A × B	B × C
1*a*	.07	.02	.22	−.20	.34
1*b*	−.23	−.40	.67	−.28	−.50
2	.12	−.16	−.16	.94	−.34
3	−.23	.14	−.04	−.04	.02
4	−.83	.63	.09	−.39	−.30
5	−.11	−.56	−.17	−.12	−.91
6	.40	.36	.72	.20	.26

Note. A convenient explanation of discriminant coefficients can be found in Tatsuoka (1971, p. 162 ff.).

sponses in each category to gifted and non-gifted students; Table 2 presents the F values for the analysis of variance and the multivariate analysis of variance.

The univariate analysis for Category 1 data shows no significant difference in total amount of attention to gifted and nongifted students. No differences had been expected for this category, as it was hypothesized that the *amount* of interaction between the teacher and the student would be fairly similar regardless of the student's label and that the crucial variable would be the *quality* of the interaction.

A significant multivariate effect was found for label, thus indicating qualitative differences in teacher interaction with gifted and nongifted students. From the discriminant coefficients in Table 3, it can be seen that two variables accounted for almost all of the difference in treatment of gifted and nongifted students. These two variables are Categories 1b (attention to requested statements) and 6 (criticism). From the means in Table 1, it can be seen that the significance occurs because more statements were requested of gifted than of nongifted students and also that gifted students were criticized more than nongifted students.

Once again, Category 1a contributed little to the total difference and also yielded a nonsignificant univariate F. This allows for the inference that gifted students were not called upon more often simply because they volunteered less.

Student Variables: Interaction of Race × Label

A prime consideration of this study was any difference in the effect of label depending on the race of the student. The univariate analysis for Category 1 revealed a significant interaction of Race × Label. Gifted white students received more attention than non-gifted white students with a reverse tendency occurring in the case of black students.

A significant multivariate F was found for the interaction of Race × Label (see Table

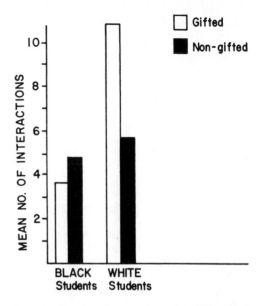

Fig. 2. Teacher Interaction with Gifted and Nongifted Black and White Students (Category 1b: Attention to Requested Statements).

2). The discriminant analysis showed this difference to be mostly attributable to Category 5 (praise) with Category 1b (attention to requested statements) also contributing addition, categories 1a (attention to unsolicited statements), 2 (encouragement), 4 (ignoring), and 6 (criticism) all contributed to the differences in treatment of differently labeled students of different races. Note from Tables 2 and 3 that Category 6 (criticism) contributed little to the overall interaction effect, although a highly significant univariate F was associated with it. This situation would suggest that the difference seemingly attributable to criticism in the univariate analysis is accounted for by the other variables with which it is correlated.

The direction of these interactions can be ascertained from Table 1. In the case of Categories 1, 1b, and 5, the interactions are also portrayed in Figures 1, 2, and 3. Considering these interactions collectively, a pattern begins to emerge in which the expectation of giftedness is associated with a generally positive response of teachers—*if*

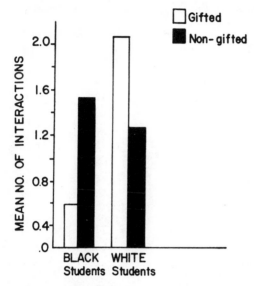

Fig. 3. Teacher Interaction with Gifted and Nongifted Black and White Students (Category 5: Praise).

the student is white. For black students, if anything, a reverse tendency is evident in which the expectation of giftedness is associated with *less* positive treatment.

Teacher Variables: Level of Dogmatism

It had been hypothesized that level of dogmatism might affect susceptibility to racial and labeling effects (see Table 4). Regardless of interaction with either student variable, level of dogmatism itself was found to affect overall teacher behavior. The analysis of variance on Category 1 (total attention) showed no quantitative differences in the attention given students by teachers high and low in dogmatism (see Table 2). The multivariate analysis of variance did, however, reveal a significant effect for dogmatism (see Table 2). This difference was due mostly to the effect of Category 3 (ignoring), with teachers higher in dogmatism ignoring many more statements than teachers lower in dogmatism. Some of the overall difference can also be attributed to Category 6 (criticism), with teachers higher in dogmatism criticizing

more statements than teachers lower in dogmatism.

Interaction of Teacher and Student Variables: Dogmatism × Race

Of particular interest in this study was whether or not teachers with different levels of dogmatism would respond differently to black students and white students. No significant interaction was found for Category

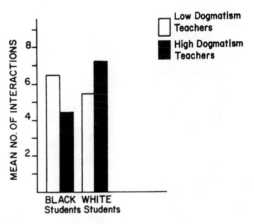

Fig. 4. Interaction Patterns of High and Low Dogmatic Teachers (Category 2: Encourage).

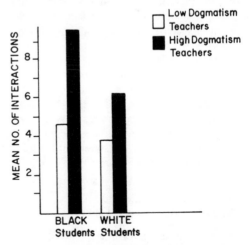

Fig. 5. Interaction Patterns of High and Low Dogmatic Teachers (Category 4: Ignore).

Table 4. Mean Interaction with Gifted and Nongifted Black and White Students X Teachers High and Low in Dogmatism

Category	Black	White	Combined	Gifted	Nongifted
1—Total attention					
High dogmatism	29.94	35.68	32.81	34.54	31.08
Low dogmatism	29.97	32.73	31.35	31.12	31.58
1a—Attention to unsolicited statements					
High dogmatism	26.06	26.67	26.36	27.27	25.45
Low dogmatism	26.64	26.15	26.39	25.91	26.88
1b—Attention to requested statements					
High dogmatism	5.47	8.82	7.14	8.85	5.44
Low dogmatism	3.18	7.48	5.33	6.56	4.11
2—Encouragement					
High dogmatism	4.44	7.17	5.80	5.88	5.73
High dogmatism	6.35	5.33	5.84	5.77	5.91
3—Elaboration					
High dogmatism	2.50	2.53	2.52	2.53	2.50
Low dogmatism	2.03	1.70	1.86	1.64	2.09
4—Ignoring					
High dogmatism	9.39	6.14	7.76	8.29	7.24
Low dogmatism	4.39	3.52	3.95	3.73	4.18
5—Praise					
High dogmatism	1.06	1.48	1.27	1.20	1.35
Low dogmatism	1.08	1.82	1.45	1.39	1.50
6—Criticism					
High dogmatism	1.86	1.02	1.44	1.76	1.12
Low dogmatism	.86	.44	.65	.88	.42

1 (total attention), but a significant multivariate F was found (see Table 2). Most of this interaction can be attributed to Category 3 (encouraging). Much less of the difference is contributed by the scores from Category 4 (ignoring). The univariate interactions for these two categories are shown in Figures 4 and 5. From Figure 4 it can be seen that dogmatism is associated with the encouraging of white rather than black students. Complementing the result is the finding that dogmatism was also associated with a tendency to ignore the statements of black students (see Figure 5).

Interaction of Teacher and Student Variables: Dogmatism X Label

A nonsignificant univariate F for Category 1 and also a nonsignificant multivariate F were found (see Table 2). One significant univariate F was found for the variables in the multivariate analysis of variance. However, since the multivariate F was not significant, this one significant univariate F may be attributed to chance.

Interaction of Teacher Variable and Student Variables: Dogmatism X Race X Label

No significant triple interactions were found for any category in any of the analyses, univariate or multivariate (see Table 2).

Credibility of Experimental Situation

A postexperiment questionnaire and an interview were given in order to check whether or not teachers accepted the experimental situation. No teacher expressed any suspicion of the experimental hypotheses. The teachers also showed great agreement with the assigned labels. One hundred and thirty-two students had been labeled gifted and 132 nongifted. Only in the case of 14 of the gifted students and 13 of the nongifted students did teachers express any reservations about accepting these labels as true indicants of the students' ability levels. These reports of the teachers, as well as clinical observations during the postexperimental interviews, suggest that the teachers not only accepted the situation as presented to them, but they also viewed each student in terms of the label assigned him.

DISCUSSION

As in a previous study (Rubovits & Maehr, 1971), teachers were found to treat students labeled gifted different from students described as average. There was no difference in the *amount* of attention given to the supposedly different-ability groups, but there were differences in the *quality* of attention. Gifted students were called on more, thus replicating a previous finding (Rubovits & Maehr, 1971). Gifted students were also criticized more, but this difference may have been caused by the inclusion of black students in the gifted group as they were the recipients of almost all the criticism.

Considering the differences due to label for whites only, it can be seen that the gifted white student was given more attention than his nongifted counterpart, called on more, praised more, and also criticized a bit more. It is interesting, incidentally, that in the informal interviews with teachers the gifted white student was also chosen most frequently as the most liked student, the brightest student, and the certain leader of the class.

Of special interest, of course, are the comparisons of teacher interaction with black students and white students. In this regard, the present study provides what appears to be a disturbing instance of white racism. Black students were given less attention, ignored more, praised less and criticized more. More startling perhaps are the Race X Label interactions that suggest that it is the gifted black who is given the least attention, is the least praised, and the most criticized, even when comparing him to his nongifted black counterpart.

It is important to stress that these results are not easily attributable to an experimental artifact of some kind. There is no reason to suppose that the expectancy communication varied for race. Moreover, it cannot be argued that teachers were responding to any actual intellectual differences between black students and white students or to any incongruity between label and actual potential. Recall that students were specifically selected so as to be of equivalent intellectual ability regardless of race.

An obvious question, of course, is whether the expectancy resided in the observer or in the teacher. It is impossible to rule out observer expectancy effects completely. While the observer could not know which students were labeled gifted or average, it is obvious that she would know black from white. However, it is difficult to see how such knowledge might have determined the pattern of results that were obtained. First, the observational instrument is reasonably objective in nature, allowing for minimal judgment on the part of the observer (Rubovits, 1970). Second, the present authors in fact had no clear and obvious basis for postulating the results that did indeed occur. For example, it would have been equally logical to argue before the fact that young, idealistic teachers, most of whom expressed liberal beliefs, would make a special attempt to ingratiate themselves to blacks. Finally, the fact that high-dogmatic teachers were more inclined toward a prejudicial pattern than low-dogmatic teachers further suggests that the reported interactions were not just a figment of the observer's expectancy. If the observer were, in fact, the responsible agent, it would be difficult to see how, not knowing the dogmatism scores, she could have effected a generally predictable pattern for high and low dogmatists as well as the overall pattern. A bias leading toward differential observation of teacher-student interaction in the case of blacks and whites would presumably operate across all teachers regardless of dogmatism, thereby making it virtually impossible to obtain any meaningful Dogmatism X Race interaction. In brief, the most logical explanation of the results is that the teachers were indeed exhibiting the negative pattern toward blacks that the reported interactions indicate.

It is important to emphasize that this prejudicial pattern was not exhibited by all teachers. Teachers higher in dogmatism seemed to differentiate more in their treatment of blacks and whites. Moreover, one may wonder about the degree to which the patterns observed are unique to young, inexperienced teachers. After all, these teachers not only had little teaching experience but, as the questionnaire data would indicate, little experience of any kind with blacks. One might at least hope that the appropriate experience could be of benefit.

All in all, then, this study clearly suggests how teacher expectations may affect teacher behavior. Although the results must be interpreted within the limits of the study, with cautious generalization, the data do suggest answers to the question of why teachers are often able to do little to equalize the performance levels of blacks and whites.

REFERENCES

Becker, H. S. Social class variations in the teacher-pupil relationship. *Journal of Educational Sociology*, 1952, 25, 451–465.

Brown, B. The assessment of self-concept among four-year-old Negro and white children. (Cited by H. Proshansky & P. Newton: The nature and meaning of Negro self-identity) In M. Deutsch, I. Katz, & A. R. Jensen (Eds.), *Social class, race and psychological development*. New York: Holt, Rinehart & Winston, 1968.

Claiborne, W. L. Expectancy effects in the classroom: A failure to replicate. *Journal of Educational Psychology*, 1969, 60, 377–383.

Davidson, H. H., & Lang, G. Children's perception of teachers' feelings toward them. *Journal of Experimental Education*, 1960, 29, 107–118.

Deutsch, M. The disadvantaged child and the learning process. In A. H. Passow (Ed.), *Education in depressed areas.* New York: Bureau of Publications, Teachers College, Columbia University, 1963.

Elashoff, J. D., & Snow, R. E. *A case study in statistical inference: Reconsideration of the Rosenthal-Jacobson data on teacher expectancy.* (Tech. Rep. No. 15) Stanford, Calif.: Stanford Center for Research and Development in Teaching, Stanford University, 1970.

Meichenbaum, D. H., Bowers, K. S., & Ross, R. R. A behavioral analysis of teacher expectancy effect. *Journal of Personality and Social Psychology*, 1969, 13, 306–316.

Rokeach, M. *The open and closed mind.* New York: Basic Books, 1960.

Rosenthal, R. *Experimenter effects in behavioral research.* New York: Appleton-Century-Crofts, 1966.

Rosenthal, R. Empirical vs. decreed validation of clocks and tests. *American Educational Research Journal*, 1969, 6, 689–691.

Rosenthal, R., & Fode, K. L. The effect of experimenter bias on the performance of albino rats. *Behavioral Science*, 1963, 8, 183–189.

Rosenthal, R., & Jacobson, L. *Pygmalion in the classroom: Teacher expectation and pupils' intellectual development.* New York: Holt, Rinehart & Winston, 1968.

Rosenthal, R., & Lawson, R. A longitudinal study of the effects of experimenter bias on the operant learning of laboratory rats. *Journal of Psychiatric Research*, 1964, 2, 61–72.

Rubovits, P. C. Teacher interaction with students labeled gifted and nongifted in a micro-teaching situation. Unpublished master's thesis, University of Illinois, 1970.

Rubovits, P. C., & Maehr, M. L. Pygmalion analyzed: Toward an explanation of the Rosenthal-Jacobson findings. *Journal of Personality and Social Psychology*, 1971, 19, 197–203.

Snow, R. E. Unfinished Pygmalion. *Contemporary Psychology*, 1969, 14, 197–199.

Tatsuoka, M. *Multivariate analysis.* New York: Wiley, 1971.

Thorndike, R. L. Review of *Pygmalion in the classroom. American Educational Research Journal*, 1968, 5, 708–711.

Thorndike, R. L. But do you have to know how to tell time? *American Educational Research Journal*, 1969, 6, 692.

Warner, W. L., Havighurst, R. J., & Loeb, M. B. *Who shall be educated?* New York: Harper & Row, 1944.

Wilson, A. B. Social stratification and academic achievement. In A. H. Passow (Ed.), *Education in depressed areas.* New York: Teachers College. Columbia University, 1963.

1.4
Police Encounters with Juveniles

IRVING PILIAVIN and SCOTT BRIAR

As the first of a series of decisions made in the channeling of youthful offenders through the agencies concerned with juvenile justice and corrections, the disposition decisions made by police officers have potentially profound consequences for apprehended juveniles. Thus arrest, the most severe of the dispositions available to police, may not only lead to confinement of the suspected offender but also bring him loss of social status, restriction of educational and employment opportunities, and future harassment by law-enforcement personnel.[1] According to some criminologists, the stigmatization resulting from police apprehension, arrest, and detention actually reinforces deviant behavior.[2] Other authorities

have suggested, in fact, that this stigmatization serves as the catalytic agent initiating delinquent careers.[3] Despite their presumed significance, however, little empirical analysis has been reported regarding the factors influencing, or consequences resulting from, police actions with juvenile offenders. Furthermore, while some studies of police encounters with adult offenders have been reported, the extent to which the findings of these investigations pertain to law-enforcement practices with youthful offenders is not known.[4]

The above considerations have led the writers to undertake a longitudinal study of

1. Richard D. Schwartz and Jerome H. Skolnick, "Two Studies of Legal Stigma," *Social Problems*, X (April, 1962), 133–42; Sol Rubin, *Crime and Juvenile Delinquency* (New York: Oceana Publications, 1958); B. F. McSally, "Finding Jobs for Released Offenders," *Federal Probation*, XXIV (June, 1960), 12–17; Harold D. Lasswell and Richard C. Donnelly, "The Continuing Debate over Responsibility: An Introduction to Isolating the Condemnation Sanction," *Yale Law Journal*, LXVIII (April, 1959), 869–99.
2. Richard A. Cloward and Lloyd E. Ohlin, *Delinquency and Opportunity* (Glencoe, Ill.: Free Press, 1960), pp. 124–30.

3. Frank Tannenbaum, *Crime and the Community* (New York: Columbia University Press, 1936), pp. 17–20; Howard S. Becker, *Outsiders: Studies in the Sociology of Deviance* (New York: Free Press of Glencoe, 1963), chaps. i and ii.
4. For a detailed accounting of police discretionary practices, see Joseph Goldstein, "Police Discretion Not To Invoke the Criminal Process: Low Visibility Decisions in the Administration of Justice," *Yale Law Journal*, LXIX (1960), 543–94; Wayne R. LaFave, "The Police and Non-enforcement of the Law—Part I," *Wisconsin Law Review*, January, 1962, pp. 104–37; S. H. Kadish, "Legal Norms and Discretion in the Police and Sentencing Processes," *Harvard Law Review*, LXXV (March, 1962), 904–31.

From I. Piliavin & Briar, S. Police encounters with juveniles. *American Journal of Sociology*, 1964, 70, 206–214. Copyright 1964 by The University of Chicago. Reprinted by permission.

the conditions influencing, and consequences flowing from, police actions with juveniles. In the present paper findings will be presented indicating the influence of certain factors on police actions. Research data consist primarily of notes and records based on nine months' observation of all juvenile officers in one police department.[5] The officers were observed in the course of their regular tours of duty.[6] While these data do not lend themselves to quantitative assessments of reliability and validity, the candor shown by the officers in their interviews with the investigators and their use of officially frowned-upon practices while under observation provide some assurance that the materials presented below accurately reflect the typical operations and attitudes of the law-enforcement personnel studied.

The setting for the research, a metropolitan police department serving an industrial city with approximately 450,000 inhabitants, was noted within the community it served and among law-enforcement officials elsewhere for the honesty and superior quality of its personnel. Incidents involving criminal activity or brutality by members of the department had been extremely rare during the ten years preceding this study; personnel standards were comparatively high; and an extensive training program was provided to both new and experienced personnel. Juvenile Bureau members, the primary subjects of this investigation, differed somewhat from other members of the department in that they were responsible for delinquency prevention as well as law enforcement, that is, juvenile officers were expected to be knowledgeable about conditions leading to crime and delinquency and to be able to work with community agencies serving known or potential juvenile offenders. Accordingly, in the assignment of personnel to the Juvenile Bureau, consideration was given not only to an officer's devotion to and reliability in law enforcement but also to his commitment to delinquency prevention. Assignment to the Bureau was of advantage to policemen seeking promotions. Consequently, many officers requested transfer to this unit, and its personnel comprised a highly select group of officers.

In the field, juvenile officers operated essentially as patrol officers. They cruised assigned beats and, although concerned primarily with juvenile offenders, frequently had occasion to apprehend and arrest adults. Confrontations between the officers and juveniles occurred in one of the following three ways, in order of increasing frequency: (1) encounters resulting from officers' spotting officially "wanted" youths; (2) encounters taking place at or near the scene of offenses reported to police headquarters; and (3) encounters occurring as the result of officers' directly observing youths either committing offenses or in "suspicious circumstances." However, the probability that a confrontation would take place between officer and juvenile, or that a particular disposition of an identified offender would be made, was only in part determined by the knowledge that an offense had occurred or that a particular juvenile had committed an offense. The bases for and utilization of non-offenses related criteria by police in accosting and disposing of juveniles are the focuses of the following discussion.

SANCTIONS FOR DISCRETION

In each encounter with juveniles, with the minor exception of officially "wanted" youths,[7] a central task confronting the

5. Approximately thirty officers were assigned to the Juvenile Bureau in the department studied. While we had an opportunity to observe all officers in the Bureau during the study, our observations were concentrated on those who had been working in the Bureau for one or two years at least. Although two of the officers in the Juvenile Bureau were Negro, we observed these officers on only a few occasions.

6. Although observations were not confined to specific days or work shifts, more observations were made during evenings and weekends because police activity was greatest during these periods.

7. "Wanted" juveniles usually were placed under arrest or in protective custody, a practice which in effect relieved officers of the responsibility for deciding what to do with these youths.

officer was to decide what official action to take against the boys involved. In making these disposition decisions, officers could select any one of five discrete alternatives:

1. outright release
2. release and submission of a "field interrogation report" briefly describing the circumstances initiating the police-juvenile confrontation
3. "official reprimand" and release to parents or guardian
4. citation to juvenile court
5. arrest and confinement in juvenile hall.

Dispositions 3, 4, and 5 differed from the others in two basic respects. First, with rare exceptions, when an officer chose to reprimand, cite, or arrest a boy, he took the youth to the police station. Second, the reprimanded, cited, or arrested boy acquired an official police "record," that is, his name was officially recorded in Bureau files as a juvenile violator.

Analysis of the distribution of police disposition decisions about juveniles revealed that in virtually every category of offense the full range of official disposition alternatives available to officers was employed. This wide range of discretion resulted primarily from two conditions. First, it reflected the reluctance of officers to expose certain youths to the stigmatization presumed to be associated with official police action. Few juvenile officers believed that correctional agencies serving the community could effectively help delinquents. For some officers this attitude reflected a lack of confidence in rehabilitation techniques; for others, a belief that high case loads and lack of professional training among correctional workers vitiated their efforts at treatment. All officers were agreed, however, that juvenile justice and correctional processes were essentially concerned with apprehension and punishment rather than treatment. Furthermore, all officers believed that some aspects of these processes (e.g., judicial definition of youths as delinquents and removal of delinquents from the community), as well as some of the possible consequences of these processes

(e.g., intimate institutional contact with "hard-core" delinquents, as well as parental, school, and conventional peer disapproval or rejection), could reinforce what previously might have been only a tentative proclivity toward delinquent values and behavior. Consequently, when officers found reason to doubt that a youth being confronted was highly committed toward deviance, they were inclined to treat him with leniency.

Second, and more important, the practice of discretion was sanctioned by police-department policy. Training manuals and departmental bulletins stressed that the disposition of each juvenile offender was not to be based solely on the type of infraction he committed. Thus, while it was departmental policy to "arrest and confine all juveniles who have committed a felony or misdemeanor involving theft, sex offense, battery, possession of dangerous weapons, prowling, peeping, intoxication, incorrigibility, and disturbance of the peace," it was acknowledged that "such considerations as age, attitude and prior criminal record might indicate that a different disposition would be more appropriate."[8] The official justification for discretion in processing juvenile offenders, based on the preventive aims of the Juvenile Bureau, was that each juvenile violator should be dealt with solely on the basis of what was best for him.[9] Unofficially, administrative legitimation of discretion was further justified on the grounds that strict enforcement practices would overcrowd court calendars and detention facilities, as well as dramatically increase juvenile crime rates—consequences to be avoided because they would expose the police department to community criticism.[10]

In practice, the official policy justifying use of discretion served as a demand that

8. Quoted from a training manual issued by the police department studied in this research.
9. Presumably this also implied that police action with juveniles was to be determined partly by the offenders' need for correctional services.
10. This was reported by beat officers as well as supervisory and administrative personnel of the juvenile bureau.

discretion be exercised. As such, it posed three problems for juvenile officers. First, it represented a departure from the traditional police practice with which the juvenile officers themselves were identified, in the sense that they were expected to justify their juvenile disposition decisions not simply by evidence proving a youth had committed a crime—grounds on which police were officially expected to base their dispositions of non-juvenile offenders[11] —but in the *character* of the youth. Second, in disposing of juvenile offenders, officers were expected, in effect, to make judicial rather than ministerial decisions.[12] Third, the shift from the offense to the offender as the basis for determining the appropriate disposition substantially increased the uncertainty and ambiguity for officers in the situation of apprehension because no explicit rules existed for determining which disposition different types of youths should receive. Despite these problems, officers were constrained to base disposition decisions on the character of the apprehended youth, not only because they wanted to be fair, but because persistent failure to do so could result in judicial criticism, departmental censure, and, they believed, loss of authority with juveniles.[13]

DISPOSITION CRITERIA

Assessing the character of apprehended offenders posed relatively few difficulties for officers in the case of youths who had committed serious crimes such as robbery, homicide, aggravated assault, grand theft, auto theft, rape, and arson. Officials generally regarded these juveniles as confirmed delinquents simply by virtue of their involvement in offenses of this magnitude.[14] However, the infraction committed did not always suffice to determine the appropriate disposition for some serious offenders;[15] and, in the case of minor offenders, who comprised over 90 per cent of the youths against whom police took action, the violation per se generally played an insignificant role in the choice of disposition. While a number of minor offenders were seen as serious delinquents deserving arrest, many others were perceived either as "good" boys whose offenses were atypical of their customary behavior, as pawns of undesirable associates or, in any case, as boys for whom arrest was regarded as an unwarranted and possibly harmful punishment. Thus, for nearly all minor violators and for some serious delinquents, the assessment of character—the distinction between serious delinquents, "good" boys, misguided youths, and so on—and the dispositions which followed from these assessments were based on youths' personal characteristics and not their offenses.

Despite this dependence of disposition decisions on the personal characteristics of these youths, however, police officers actually had access only to very limited information about boys at the time they had to decide what to do with them. In the field, officers typically had no data concerning the past offense records, school performance, family situation, or personal adjustment of apprehended youths.[16] Furthermore, files at

---

11. In actual practice, of course, disposition decisions regarding adult offenders also were influenced by many factors extraneous to the offense per se.

12. For example, in dealing with adult violators, officers had no disposition alternative comparable to the reprimand-and-release category, a disposition which contained elements of punishment but did not involve mediation by the court.

13. The concern of officers over possible loss of authority stemmed from their belief that court failure to support arrests by appropriate action would cause policemen to "lose face" in the eyes of juveniles.

14. It is also likely that the possibility of negative publicity resulting from the failure to arrest such violators—particularly if they became involved in further serious crime—brought about strong administrative pressure for their arrest.

15. For example, in the year preceding this research, over 30 per cent of the juveniles involved in burglaries and 12 per cent of the juveniles committing auto theft received dispositions other than arrest.

16. On occasion, officers apprehended youths whom they personally knew to be prior offenders.

police headquarters provided data only about each boy's prior offense record. Thus both the decision made in the field—whether or not to bring the boy in—and the decision made at the station—which disposition to invoke—were based largely on cues which emerged from the interaction between the officer and the youth, cues from which the officer inferred the youth's character. These cues included the youth's group affiliations, age, race, grooming, dress, and demeanor. Older juveniles, members of known delinquent gangs, Negroes, youths with well-oiled hair, black jackets, and soiled denims or jeans (the presumed uniform of "tough" boys), and boys who in their interactions with officers did not manifest what were considered to be appropriate signs of respect tended to receive the more severe dispositions.

Other than prior record, the most important of the above clues was a youth's *demeanor*. In the opinion of juvenile patrolmen themselves the demeanor of apprehended juveniles was a major determinant of their decisions for 50–60 per cent of the juvenile cases they processed.[17] A less subjective indication of the association between a youth's demeanor and police disposition is provided by Table 1, which presents the police dispositions for sixty-six youths whose encounters with police were observed in the course of this study.[18] For purposes

Table 1. Severity of Police Disposition by Youth's Demeanor

Severity of Police Disposition	Youth's Demeanor		
	Co-operative	Unco-operative	Total
Arrest (most severe)	2	14	16
Citation or official reprimand	4	5	9
Informal reprimand .	15	1	16
Admonish and release (least severe)	24	1	25
Total	45	21	66

of this analysis, each youth's demeanor in the encounter was classified as either co-operative or unco-operative.[19] The results clearly reveal a marked association between youth demeanor and the severity of police dispositions.

The cues used by police to assess demeanor were fairly simple. Juveniles who were contrite about their infractions, respectful to officers, and fearful of the sanctions that might be employed against them tended to be viewed by patrolmen as basically law-abiding or at least "salvageable." For these youths it was usually assumed that informal or formal reprimand would suffice to guarantee their future conformity. In contrast, youthful offenders who were fractious, obdurate, or who appeared nonchalant in their encounters with patrolmen were likely to be viewed as "would-be tough guys" or "punks" who fully deserved the most severe

This did not occur frequently, however, for several reasons. First, approximately 75 per cent of apprehended youths had no prior official records; second, officers periodically exchanged patrol areas, thus limiting their exposure to, and knowledge about, these areas; and third, patrolmen seldom spent more than three or four years in the juvenile division.

17. While reliable subgroup estimates were impossible to obtain through observation because of the relatively small number of incidents observed, the importance of demeanor in disposition decisions appeared to be much less significant with known prior offenders.

18. Systematic data were collected on police encounters with seventy-six juveniles. In ten of these encounters the police concluded that their suspicions were groundless, and consequently the juveniles involved were exonerated; these ten cases were eliminated from this analysis of demeanor.

(The total number of encounters observed was considerably more than seventy-six, but systematic data-collection procedures were not instituted until several months after observations began.)

19. The data used for the classification of demeanor were the written records of observations made by the authors. The classifications were made by an independent judge not associated with this study. In classifying a youth's demeanor as co-operative or unco-operative, particular attention was paid to: (1) the youth's responses to police officers' questions and requests; (2) the respect and deference—or lack of these qualities—shown by the youth toward police officers; and (3) police officers' assessments of the youth's demeanor.

sanction: arrest. The following excerpts from observation notes illustrate the importance attached to demeanor by police in making disposition decisions.

1. The interrogation of "A" (an 18-year-old upper-lower-class white male accused of statutory rape) was assigned to a police sergeant with long experience on the force. As I sat in his office while we waited for the youth to arrive for questioning, the sergeant expressed his uncertainty as to what he should do with this young man. On the one hand, he could not ignore the fact that an offense had been committed; he had been informed, in fact, that the youth was prepared to confess to the offense. Nor could he overlook the continued pressure from the girl's father (an important political figure) for the police to take severe action against the youth. On the other hand, the sergeant had formed a low opinion of the girl's moral character, and he considered it unfair to charge "A" with statutory rape when the girl was a willing partner to the offense and might even have been the instigator of it. However, his sense of injustice concerning "A" was tempered by his image of the youth as a "punk," based, he explained, on information he had received that the youth belonged to a certain gang, the members of which were well known to, and disliked by, the police. Nevertheless, as we prepared to leave his office to interview "A," the sergeant was still in doubt as to what he should do with him.

As we walked down the corridor to the interrogation room, the sergeant was stopped by a reporter from the local newsppaer. In an excited tone of voice, the reporter explained that his editor was pressing him to get further information about this case. The newspaper had printed some of the facts about the girl's disappearance, and as a consequence the girl's father was threatening suit against the paper for defamation of the girl's character. It would strengthen the newspaper's position, the reporter explained, if the police had information indicating that the girl's associates, particularly the youth

the sergeant was about to interrogate, were persons of disreputable character. This stimulus seemed to resolve the sergeant's uncertainty. He told the reporter, "unofficially," that the youth was known to be an undesirable person, citing as evidence his membership in the delinquent gang. Furthermore, the sergeant added that he had evidence that this youth had been intimate with the girl over a period of many months. When the reporter asked if the police were planning to do anything to the youth, the sergeant answered that he intended to charge the youth with statutory rape.

In the interrogation, however, three points quickly emerged which profoundly affected the sergeant's judgment of the youth. First, the youth was polite and co-operative; he consistently addressed the officer as "sir," answered all questions quietly, and signed a statement implicating himself in numerous counts of statutory rape. Second, the youth's intentions toward the girl appeared to have been honorable; for example, he said that he wanted to marry her eventually. Third, the youth was not in fact a member of the gang in question. The sergeant's attitude became increasingly sympathetic, and after we left the interrogation room he announced his intention to "get 'A' off the hook," meaning that he wanted to have the charges against "A" reduced or, if possible, dropped.

2. Officers "X" and "Y" brought into the police station a seventeen-year-old white boy who, along with two older companions, had been found in a home having sex relations with a fifteen-year-old girl. The boy responded to police officers' queries slowly and with obvious disregard. It was apparent that his lack of deference toward the officers and his failure to evidence concern about his situation were irritating his questioners. Finally, one of the officers turned to me and, obviously angry, commented that in his view the boy was simply a "stud" interested only in sex, eating, and sleeping. The policemen conjectured that the boy "probably already had knocked up half a dozen girls."

The boy ignored these remarks, except for an occasional impassive stare at the patrolmen. Turning to the boy, the officer remarked, "What the hell am I going to do with you?" And again the boy simply returned the officer's gaze. The latter then said, "Well, I guess we'll just have to put you away for a while." An arrest report was then made out and the boy was taken to Juvenile Hall.

Although anger and disgust frequently characterized officers' attitudes toward recalcitrant and impassive juvenile offenders, their manner while processing these youths was typically routine, restrained, and without rancor. While the officers' restraint may have been due in part to their desire to avoid accusation and censure, it also seemed to reflect their inurement to a frequent experience. By and large, only their occasional "needling" or insulting of a boy gave any hint of the underlying resentment and dislike they felt toward many of these youths.[20]

PREJUDICE IN APPREHENSION AND DISPOSITION DECISIONS

Compared to other youths, Negroes and boys whose appearance matched the delinquent stereotype were more frequently stopped and interrogated by patrolmen—often even in the absence of evidence that an offense had been committed[21] —and usually were given more severe dispositions for the same violations. Our data suggest, however, that these selective apprehension and disposition practices resulted not only from the intrusion of long-held prejudices of individual police officers but also from certain job-related experiences of law-enforcement personnel. First, the tendency for police to give more severe dispositions to Negroes and to youths whose appearance corresponded to that which police associated with delinquents partly reflected the fact, observed in this study, that these youths also were much more likely than were other types of boys to exhibit the sort of recalcitrant demeanor which police construed as a sign of the confirmed delinquent. Further, officers assumed, partly on the basis of departmental statistics, that Negroes and juveniles who "look tough" (e.g., who wear chinos, leather jackets, boots, etc.) commit crimes more frequently than do other types of youths.[22] In this sense, the police justified their selective treatment of these youths along epidemiological lines: that is, they were concentrating their attention on those youths whom they believed were most likely to commit delinquent acts. In the words of one highly placed official in the department

If you know that the bulk of your delinquent problem comes from kids who, say, are from 12 to 14 years of age, when you're out on patrol you are much more likely to be sensitive to the activities of juveniles in

20. Officers' animosity toward recalcitrant or aloof offenders appeared to stem from two sources: moral indignation that these juveniles were self-righteous and indifferent about their transgressions, and resentment that these youths failed to accord police the respect they believed they deserved. Since the patrolmen perceived themselves as honestly and impartially performing a vital community function warranting respect and deference from the community at large, they attributed the lack of respect shown them by these juveniles to the latters' immorality.

21. The clearest evidence for this assertion is provided by the overrepresentation of Negroes among "innocent" juveniles accosted by the police. As noted, of the seventy-six juveniles on whom systematic data were collected, ten were exonerated and released without suspicion. Seven, or two-thirds of these ten "innocent" juveniles were Negro, in

contrast to the allegedly "guilty" youths, less than one-third of whom were Negro. The following incident illustrates the operation of this bias: One officer, observing a youth walking along the street, commented that the youth "looks suspicious" and promptly stopped and questioned him. Asked later to explain what aroused his suspicion, the officer explained, "He was a Negro wearing dark glasses at midnight."

22. While police statistics did not permit an analysis of crime rates by appearance, they strongly supported officers' contentions concerning the delinquency rate among Negroes. Of all male juveniles processed by the police department in 1961, for example, 40.2 per cent were Negro and 33.9 per cent were white. These two groups comprised at that time, respectively, about 22.7 per cent and 73.6 per cent of the population in the community studied.

this age bracket than older or younger groups. This would be good law enforcement practice. The logic in our case is the same except that our delinquency problem is largely found in the Negro community and it is these youths toward whom we are sensitized.

As regards prejudice per se, eighteen of twenty-seven officers interviewed openly admitted a dislike for Negroes. However, they attributed their dislike to experiences they had, as policemen, with youths from this minority group. The officers reported that Negro boys were much more likely than non-Negroes to "give us a hard time," be unco-operative, and show no remorse for their transgressions. Recurrent exposure to such attitudes among Negro youth, the officers claimed, generated their antipathy toward Negroes. The following excerpt is typical of the views expressed by these officers:

They (Negroes) have no regard for the law or for the police. They just don't seem to give a damn. Few of them are interested in school or getting ahead. The girls start having illegitimate kids before they are 16 years old and the boys are always "out for kicks." Furthermore, many of these kids try to run you down. They say the damnedest things to you and they seem to have absolutely no respect for you as an adult. I admit I am prejudiced now, but frankly I don't think I was when I began police work.

IMPLICATIONS

It is apparent from the findings presented above that the police officers studied in this research were permitted and even encouraged to exercise immense latitude in disposing of the juveniles they encountered. That is, it was within the officers' discretionary authority, except in extreme limiting cases, to decide which juveniles were to come to the attention of the courts and correctional agencies and thereby be identified officially as delinquents. In exercising this discretion policemen were strongly

guided by the demeanor of those who were apprehended, a practice which ultimately led, as seen above, to certain youths, (particularly Negroes[23] and boys dressed in the style of "toughs") being treated more severely than other juveniles for comparable offenses.

But the relevance of demeanor was not limited only to police disposition practices. Thus, for example, in conjunction with police crime statistics the criterion of demeanor led police to concentrate their surveillance activities in areas frequented or inhabited by Negroes. Furthermore, these youths were accosted more often than others by officers on patrol simply because their skin color identified them as potential troublemakers. These discriminatory practices—and it is important to note that they are discriminatory, even if based on accurate statistical information—may well have self-fulfilling consequences. Thus it is not unlikely that frequent encounters with police, particularly those involving youths innocent of wrongdoing, will increase the hostility of these juveniles toward law-enforcement personnel. It is also not unlikely that the frequency of such encounters will in time reduce their significance in the eyes of apprehended juveniles, thereby leading these youths to regard them as "routine." Such responses to police encounters, however, are those which law-enforcement personnel perceive as indicators of the serious delinquent. They thus serve to vindicate and reinforce officers' prejudices, leading to closer surveillance of Negro districts, more frequent encounters with Negro youths, and so on in a vicious circle. Moreover, the consequences of this chain of events are reflected in police statistics showing a disproportionately high percentage of Negroes among juvenile offenders, thereby providing "objective" justification for concentrating police attention on Negro youths.

23. An unco-operative demeanor was presented by more than one-third of the Negro youths but by only one-sixth of the white youths encountered by the police in the course of our observations.

To a substantial extent, as we have implied earlier, the discretion practiced by juvenile officers is simply an extension of the juvenile-court philosophy, which holds that in making legal decisions regarding juveniles, more weight should be given to the juvenile's character and life-situation than to his actual offending behavior. The juvenile officer's disposition decisions—and the information he uses as a basis for them—are more akin to the discriminations made by probation officers and other correctional workers than they are to decisions of police officers dealing with non-juvenile offenders. The problem is that such clincal-type decisions are not restrained by mechanisms comparable to the principles of due process and the rules of procedure governing police decisions regarding adult offenders. Consequently, prejudicial practices by police officers can escape notice more easily in their dealings with juveniles than with adults.

The observations made in this study serve to underscore the fact that the official delinquent, as distinguished from the juvenile who simply commits a delinquent act, is the product of a social judgment, in this case a judgment made by the police. He is a delinquent because someone in authority has defined him as one, often on the basis of the public face he has presented to officials rather than of the kind of offense he has committed.

1.5

Interracial Public Housing in a Border City:

Another Look at the Contact Hypothesis

W. SCOTT FORD

THE CONTACT HYPOTHESIS

In the past two decades, a number of studies have indicated that individuals who have experienced equal-status interracial contacts are more likely to hold tolerant racial attitudes and to object less to racial desegregation than persons who have had little or no equal-status interracial contact. The research reported here reexamines this "contact hypothesis" by exploring the behavior and attitudes of a selected group of border state residents. The hypothesis that equal-status contact is positively related to racial tolerance is retested by examining interracial neighboring and a series of other equal-status situations as they are related to the racial attitudes of a sample of black and white public housing residents.

As a theoretical perspective, the "contact hypothesis" or "interaction hypothesis" is the outgrowth of several decades of social research in the area of ethnic and racial prejudice. It has been discussed at length by Williams (1964, pp. 143–222) as well as a number of other writers. A succinct summary of evidence is presented in Pettigrew (1969, pp. 54–57). This perspective of inter-group relations closely approximates that which Allport (1962) called the "situational" approach; equal-status contact is viewed as a situational determinant of prejudice, that is, racial attitudes are products of social relations. The rationale for treating behavioral factors as independent variables is found throughout the literature on race relations. For example, while cautioning that the assumption of one-way influence is an oversimplification, Raab and Lipset (1959, p. 22) conclude that the evidence indicates that attitudes shape themselves to behavior.

Among the most frequently cited studies which support the contact hypothesis are those studies of race and residence, and, particularly, studies of desegregated public housing. In fact, most conclusions concerning residential racial desegregation among lower-income persons are based upon several public-housing studies published a number of years ago (Deutsch and Collins 1951; Wilner, Walkley, and Cook 1955).

Racial prejudice and opinions concerning racial desegregation can be largely attributed to normative systems which differ from one sociocultural context to another and which alter their prescriptions with the passage of time. This suggests that at least two kinds of research regarding the interracial behavior and attitudes of public-housing residents should be profitable: (1) replication of early studies conducted in northern cities, now that we have experienced a decade of intensive civil rights activities and racial unrest, and (2) studies conducted in other regions where racial desegregation of public housing has recently begun. Although it was not designed as a replication of any of the earlier public-housing studies, the present study is an attempt to partially fulfill the latter research need.

In addition to examining the contact hypothesis in a different setting, an attempt was made to overcome some of the shortcomings of previous research. Residential desegregation and interracial contact have been viewed nearly exclusively from the perspective of the white occupant. Whereas there is evidence to suggest that the similarities in the correlates of antiblack and antiwhite prejudice exceed the differences (Noel and Pinkney 1964), few studies have examined black or other minority-group perspectives with regard to intergroup relations. This is certainly true of the analyses of residential desegregation. One of the few exceptions is the research of Works (1961) which dealt with black public-housing occupants ... Even in the otherwise comprehensive study of Deutsch and Collins (1951), only one-fifth of the respondents were black, and very little analysis is given for them. An equal amount of attention is given to black and white responses in the research presented here: half the respondents are black and half are white.

More than 20 years ago, Williams (1947, p. 70) urged sociologists to study individuals' reactions to intergroup contacts which they were actually experiencing. Few researchers have followed this advice. This study was designed with that prescription in mind; one of its primary foci is the attitudes of black and white residents toward living together as neighbors. The respondents were adults living in a housing community that was undergoing an extensive desegregation process.

A limitation of some intergroup relations research is the lack of comparability of black and white respondents with respect to such variables as socioeconomic status and family structure. These racial differentials make it difficult to interpret the meaning of attitudinal variations. White respondents, for example, are asked to record their attitudinal position toward blacks of equal social position—a category of people with whom they may be totally unfamiliar. The black and white residents studied here are generally comparable on "objective" measures of socioeconomic status. The processing procedures used for public-housing applicants assures a considerable degree of homogeneity among residents.

The literature on interracial contact is considerable and space limitations preclude an extensive review of their findings. The primary reason equal-status interracial contacts have been emphasized is that these contacts reduce stereotyped images. For example, Arnold Rose argued (1956, p. 173) that when racial prejudice is understood as an emotionally charged attitude directed toward a stereotyped object, a weakening of the stereotype results in a corresponding reduction of prejudice. When equal-status contacts are employed as explanations for a reduction of prejudice, they are viewed as interrupting the "vicious circle" in race relations (Myrdal 1944, pp. 75–78; Davis 1957, p. 446).

Equal-status contacts are not, however, autonomous occurrences unaffected by other social circumstances. Their effects are circumscribed by various social forces which may limit the hypothesized relationship between contact and attitude. Obviously, for example, where interracial status fears have gone as far as to promote open hostility, there are understandably few circumstances in which equal-status contact can occur. Nonetheless, even among the initially intolerant who have strongly resisted intergroup associations, equal-status contacts have reduced prejudices (Williams 1964, pp. 200–201).

There have been two types of studies which have explored the effects of desegregated occupancy patterns and interracial neighboring: (1) studies of public-housing residents, and (2) studies of middle-class home owners. The former are more directly related to the research reported here.[1] The most widely cited public-housing study is that of Deutsch and Collins (1951) wherein the authors first demonstrated the effects of residential desegregation in public housing. Two desegregated low-rent projects in New York City were compared with two biracial (internally segregated) projects in Newark, New Jersey. The authors found that the overall outlook of the residents in the desegregated project was more favorable on a number of counts: they displayed more friendly contacts between races, a greater willingness to engage in interracial associations, more favorability in their interracial attitudes, more tolerance toward living within a desegregated environment in general, and a closer sense of community within the projects (Deutsch and Collins 1951, pp. 122–23).

Residential proximity facilitates neighboring among families having homogeneous socioeconomic characteristics, even when residential mobility is high, as it often is in housing projects (for example, see Festinger, Schachter, and Back 1950; Caplow and Forman 1950). Physical proximity within a housing environment is best viewed as a catalyst; it requires a reaction of a majority of residents. Black and white residents may not respond favorably to desegregated living, but only when desegregation exists do they

have the opportunity. Just as residing in desegregated neighborhoods increases an awareness of members of the other race and of their symbolic equality, it also increases the probability that some of these residents will engage in interracial neighboring. Wilner, Walkley, and Cook (1955) found that where equal-status contacts did occur among members of initially estranged groups, especially where there was a lack of established opposition to such associations, intergroup attitudes improved.

Whether or not individuals are willing to engage in informal relationships with members of another race is partly a function of their own past experiences. Previous equal-status contact has been shown to be an important factor in explaining favorable racial attitudes and behavior in a variety of contexts. A number of studies—of white residents in a southern suburb, white residents in a northern city, students in a large southern university, public-housing residents, and white residents in neighborhoods adjoining the scene of a race riot—show that acceptance of and favorable attitudes toward blacks are directly related to previous extended interracial association (Greenfield 1961; Hunt 1960; Kelley, Ferson, and Holtzman 1958; Deutsch and Collins 1951; Morris and Jeffries 1968).

Attitudes and perceptions are shaped by a social-symbolic environment *and* by the length of time persons remain therein. The public-housing studies do not report the effect that duration of residence had upon residents' racial outlooks. This may be due to the normally high turnover of residents. However, it seems reasonable to argue that, the longer one resides in a desegregated housing project, the greater will be the opportunity for this environment to affect one's racial perspectives. Studies conducted in other neighborhoods show that duration of residence had an effect upon attitudinal and perceptual adjustment and the degree to which individuals, black and white alike, came to identify with their surroundings (Festinger, Schachter, and Back 1950, pp.

1. The findings of a number of studies which examined the reactions of middle-class homeowners to residential desegregation complement those conducted within public-housing projects (see Meer and Freedman 1966; Williams 1964; Hunt 1960; Rose, Atelsek, and McDonald 1953). Generally, the researchers found that when blacks and whites of equal socioeconomic status became neighbors, the number of meaningful interracial contacts increased and this, in turn, led to improved interpersonal relations.

90–99; Williams 1964, p. 202; Rose, Atelsek, and McDonald 1953; Brophy 1946).

Two other considerations are related to the attitudes of residents, especially to their perceived status threat and can qualify the contact hypothesis. One consideration is whether or not residents arrive in a neighborhood prior to or after the process of desegregation has begun. Hunt found that whites who moved into a suburb after black families had begun to enter showed "twice the proportion" of acceptance of integrated housing and far less resentment toward blacks than those white residents who lived there prior to the entrance of black families (Hunt 1960, p. 204). A second consideration involves the ratio of minority group residents to neighborhood residents. Fishman (1961) reports that in a middle-class New Jersey suburb, status fears and pressures from the "outside white world" caused many of the original white families to leave the community after increasing numbers of black families entered. Incoming blacks, in contrast, reported status gains.[2]

Consideration of research findings and theoretical perspectives in the area of intergroup contact led to the formulation of the following general hypothesis: tolerant racial attitudes by members of each race toward the other are positively associated with: (1) the amount of current equal-status interracial contact (neighboring); (2) the degree of previous equal-status contacts with members of other race; (3) the length of residence within a desegregated housing environment; and (4) the lack of perceived status threat from living in a desegregated residential surrounding.

2. In contrast to middle-class blacks who enter suburban communities, none of the black families entering public housing are buying their way out of segregated areas and into prestigious ones. However, public-housing units were often better dwellings than were otherwise available to blacks. On the other hand, low-income whites are likely to react similarly to white suburbanites upon perceiving a threat to their limited status brought about by a "Negro invasion."

METHOD

Lexington, Kentucky, is the central city of a growing SMSA which has a 1970 urbanized area population of 159,538. Thirteen percent of the population is black, and 90% of the black residents live inside the city limits (U.S., Bureau of the Census 1971). At the time of the study, there were no racially desegregated neighborhoods in the city outside the public-housing communities. There was no evidence to show that the comparative socioeconomic status of the races or the degree of residential segregation was significantly different from that found in other American cities (Taeuber and Taeuber 1965, pp. 31, 33–34). Municipal housing was comprised of 1,319 apartments located in seven projects. Prior to 1965, the resident assignment policy maintained racially segregated projects. In each of the years 1937, 1941, and 1954 two "sister" projects were completed—one for whites and the other for blacks. A seventh project, finished in 1966, had no "racial tradition."

As a consequence of the Civil Rights Act of 1964, the established segregation pattern was changed. However, the process of desegregation had not progressed uniformly. The three "black projects" remained completely segregated, while in the three "white projects," 234 of the 558 families had been "displaced" by blacks. This impression of an "invasion" and the trend toward resegregation are considered below.

Despite the rapid influx of blacks into formerly all-white projects, the proportionate distribution of the races within individual projects reflected a variety of occupancy patterns. From the occupants' perspective, the population was readily divisible into six categories (table 1): segregated blacks (Washington Park); segregated whites (Green Tree East); desegregated blacks and whites (both residents of John Harrison); a minority of blacks (Green Tree West); and a minority of whites (Washington Park Addition).[3] Table 1 shows the projects selected for study and the sample size for each respondent cate-

Table 1. Housing Projects, Sample Sizes, Sampling Ratios, and Completion Rates

Project	Racial Composition	Sample Size	Sampling Ratio*	Competion Rate†
Washington Park .	Segregated black	33	.17	.75
Green Tree East ..	Segregated white	33	.51	.75
John Harrison ...	Desegregated black	35	.19	.80
John Harrison ...	Desegregated white	34	.23	.77
Green Tree West .	Minority black	17	‡	.89
Washington Park Addition	Minority white	16	‡	.76

*The ratio of the number of residents interviewed to the total number of residents in the population subgroup.
†The ratio of the number of completed interviews to the number of housewives assigned to an interviewer.
‡No samples were drawn for these two groups; see explanation in the text.

gory. Since the John Harrison project, the city's largest, was the only one in which the racial ratio approached .50 (.56 black and .44 white), both the desegregated black and white samples were drawn from it. The Green Tree project was analytically divided into two sections, referred to here as Green Tree East and Green Tree West.[4]

The population from which samples were

drawn consisted of all housewives[5] who resided in public-housing units at the time of a preliminary survey specially designed for the study.[6] A random sample of 44 apartments was drawn from resident categories designated as segregated black, segregated white, desegregated black, and desegregated white. (The decision to draw samples this size was determined by a projected completion rate based on a pretest and available funds.) A sampling frame for each of these

3. The project names are pseudonyms. "Minority-group" residents are those who represent a numerical minority in a project comprised of members of the other race. Of the four projects from which samples were drawn, two (Washington Park and Washington Park Addition) are located in a predominantly black section of the city, whereas the other two (Green Tree and John Harrison) are located within a census tract that contains nearly equal numbers of blacks and whites, virtually all of whom live in segregated blocks. Aside from the differences in racial composition, these two areas are both within the city limits, are older sections of the city, and have comparatively high population densities.
4. At the time of the survey, there were no longer any municipal projects that did not have black residents. Green Tree had a few black families. None were located in any particular buildings, although they all resided in a particular section of the project. An imaginary line was drawn dividing the project into two sections. As a result of interviewing housewives who resided in the segregated white section (Green Tree East), it became apparent that this analytical division was perceived by many of the residents as real. Their definition of what constituted "their" project tended to exclude the western half of the project.

5. I recognize the neglect of the black male in social science research and agree fully with those who argue that it is necessary to examine his role in order to achieve a fuller understanding of the black subculture. For example, see Liebow (1967, pp. 5–8). However, the decision to survey housewives was largely determined by limited resources and by the fact that many project units were without husbands and/or children, but less than 1% were without housewives.
6. The race of each family in the projects and the location of the vacant apartments were designated by a team of "area workers" from the local Community Action Program three months before interviewing began. The public-housing administration files were not made available to me. The women interviewed included a small number who moved in after the preliminary survey. However, there were few instances of occupants who had been displaced by members of the other race. The term "housewife" is used to refer to the woman who principally takes care of the domestic affairs of the home. This includes women with or without children, married or single, living with or without male partners.

categories was constructed from site plan projections. The apartment and building designations were indicated on these projections, and a code was developed to indicate the race of each resident family and vacant apartments.

The two remaining resident categories, a minority of black and a minority of white, represented a small number of occupants in their respective projects. Site projections were used to locate these residents living in projects predominantly occupied by members of other race. All the housewives in these two categories whom the interviewers were able to contact were interviewed. In the analysis, these minority groups are often included in "desegregated" groups.

The interview schedule took, on the average, between 45 minutes and one hour to administer. Two young black women interviewed the black housewives, and I interviewed the white respondents.[7] The 168 respondents were interviewed during a two-month period in late spring and early summer of 1967. Despite an early concern that the nature of the interviews might cause detrimental rumors to spread, this did not occur. Two weeks after the interviewing began, a systematic comparison of field notes taken by the interviewers indicated that, although a number of tenants were aware that interviewers were in the projects, very few respondents knew the content of the interviews.

The amount and kind of neighboring in which housewives engaged was measured by responses to a series of questions similar to those used by Deutsch and Collins (1951,

pp. 162–64). Interviewers probed tactfully for interracial contacts and for the particular circumstances under which they occurred. Each woman living in a desegregated project received a score showing the extent of her interracial neighboring... A simple weighting method was employed to differentiate the degree of social intimacy implied in various kinds of neighborly behavior and the frequencies with which that behavior occurred. A housewife was assigned a score ranging from 0 (no interracial neighboring) to 23 (many interracial neighboring contacts). Housewives who initiated interracial neighborly visits received a somewhat higher score than if they merely received a caller of the other race. The more regularly such contacts occurred, the higher the score a respondent was assigned.[8]

The measure of previous interracial equal-status contacts was derived from a section of the schedule designed to provide an inventory of past experiences wherein the respondent related to members of the other race in a manner implying social equality. Respondents were specifically asked to recall whether or not they had contacts with members of the other race in other neighborhoods, on jobs, while in school, as playmates during childhood, and as adult friends.[9] From an analysis of the responses, a simple classifica-

7. Both women had experience interviewing in field situations. Two extensive interviewer training sessions were held prior to a pretest. During the two-month period before the fieldwork began, I spent several weeks talking with housing administration personnel, resident managers, maintenance staff, project adolescents, and selected residents. As shown in table 1, the completion rate within all respondent categories was at least 75% of the apartments selected. Before an apartment was excluded from an interviewer's list, at least three attempts were made to find the occupant at home, the initial call and two call-backs, each at different times of the day.

8. Tabular analysis was based on a further reduction of respondents into one of three categories based on the total number of points assigned: 1–3 points, "few contacts"; 4–9 points, "several contacts"; 10 or more points, "many contacts."

9. For the analysis using previous equal-status contacts, the following classification of housewives was used: 0–2 points (husband present), "little or none"; 0–1 points (no husband), "little or none"; 3–5 points (husband present), "some"; 2–4 points (no husband), "some"; 6 or more points (husband present) "considerable"; 5 or more points (no husband), "considerable." The rationale for this differential scoring procedure was based upon the fact that during the interviews it became clear that the respondents' conceptions of the other race were not independent of those views held by their husbands. In addition, the literature shows that outgroup prejudice is reduced not only by intergroup contact between status peers, but also by contact with others who have themselves experienced such contact.

tory index was constructed to differentiate housewives according to the extent of their previous interracial equal-status contacts.

Determining what constituted a "long" duration within a desegregated project was governed by two factors: the resident turnover rate and the fact that little desegregation had occurred until two years prior to the fieldwork. Discussions with the housing director, staff, and residents, together with an examination of the data, suggested that an established or "long-time" resident could be considered one who had lived in the same project for more than a year. In the data analysis, the following duration categories are used: one year or more, seven months to a year, and six months or less.

A set of four social-distance scales was used to measure the racial prejudices of black and white respondents.[10] The six items in each scale have the advantage of being applicable to both black and white respondents (by alternating the object of prejudice from "average white adult" to "average Negro adult"). Such substitution of one race for the other is made possible by the fact that items for these scales were selected on the basis of judgments of *items* rather than attitudinal responses to items; the selection and judgment was that employed in the Thurstone technique (Westie 1953, p.75). Unlike the Thurstone technique, each item, regardless of the distance it is judged to reflect, is assigned equal weight (Westie 1953). A five-alternative response pattern was used for each of the scales. A score of 24 on a scale indicates a maximum of prejudice and a score of 0 indicates a minimum. A composite racial prejudice score can be readily computed (having a range from 0–96, from least to most prejudice) or each scale can be analyzed according to the dimension of prejudice it measures.[11] The items . . . were presented to the respondent in a random order.[12]

FINDINGS

This section presents data testing the research hypothesis without extensive comment. More thorough interpretation is reserved for the concluding section. Interracial neighboring was defined as informal conservation, visits, and mutual assistance between black and white housewives. Table 2 shows the relationship between such neighboring and racial prejudice for the respondents who resided in desegregated projects.[13] The data generally support the hypothesis that housewives who engage in interracial neighboring tend to be less prejudiced than women who do little or no interracial neighboring. However, the strength of the association is quite different in the two groups. There is a strong association ($\gamma = .75$)[14] between the presence of interracial neighboring and a lesser degree of racial prejudice for white housewives. In contrast, although the association between interracial neighboring and prejudice is in

10. The scale items were developed by Westie (1953). Although the items were identical, their administration varied, as is described. These scales have subsequently been used in different research settings, with respondents varying from college students to black residents in a midwestern city. Retests on samples to which the scales were administered showed them to be consistently reliable.

11. The scalogram analysis procedure (Edwards 1957, pp. 178–84) was applied to the items in each of the four scales. Few nonscale types occurred. The coefficients of reproduciability for residential, positional, physical, and interpersonal scales were .98, .96, .98, and .94, respectively. For analysis using individuals' total racial prejudice as the dependent variable, the respondents were trichotomized.

12. Early in the pretest, it became apparent that many housewives found it difficult to choose among alternate response categories when presented a card on which they were printed. Consequently, interviewers were instructed to use their judgment in assigning a respondent to one of the five alternatives. In cases where it was not immediately apparent, probes were used to determine the intensity of respondent's attitude.

13. The 66 respondents living in segregated projects are excluded from this analysis. Early field observation and pretesting indicated that neighboring between races outside the projects was nil.

14. The coefficient of rank association (γ) varies between −1.0 and +1.0, and has its own test of significance which is used throughout the analysis (Freeman 1965, pp. 170–74).

Table 2. Interracial Neighboring Contacts and Degree of Racial Prejudice, by Race

| | Neighboring Contacts | | | | | | | |
| | White Housewives* | | | | Black Housewives† | | | |
Racial Prejudice	Many	Several	Few/ None	Total	Many	Several	Few/ None	Total
Low	7	4	3	14	2	4	18	24
Moderate ..	1	8	9	18	4	0	12	16
High	0	2	16	18	1	1	10	12
Total‡ ..	8	14	28	50	7	5	40	52

NOTE.—Total N = 102.
*γ = .75, $p < .01$.
†γ = .08.
‡γ (both groups combined) = .43, $p < .01$.

the hypothesized direction for blacks, it is not statistically significant ($p > .05$).

The issue of whether neighboring should be more appropriately treated as a result of initially tolerant racial attitudes is discussed in the concluding section. It is evident that knowing whether or not white housewives neighbor with black project residents improves prediction of the degree of their racial prejudice; the more a white respondent engages in interracial neighboring, the less prejudiced she is likely to be. Differences in the degree of interracial neighboring do not explain the variation in prejudice for black respondents as well as they do for whites. For example, 45% (18) of the black housewives reported minimal prejudice and did not engage in interracial neighboring. Black housewives, irrespective of their neighboring behavior, were less prejudiced than white respondents.[15]

Table 3 shows the relationship between the amount of equal-status contacts experienced prior to entering public housing and the degree of racial prejudice. The findings

15. There is a positive and statistically significant association (γ = .51, $p < .01$) between being black and holding racially tolerant attitudes. Race is not a behavioral variable. The association between race and tolerance cited above suggests that desegregated living generally poses less of a status threat to black housewives than their white counterparts.

affirm the hypothesized relationship that the greater the amount of previous equal-status contact, the less racial prejudice is manifested. The strength of the relationship is strong and statistically significant ($p < .01$) for both racial groups taken together as well as for each separately, although more variation in prejudice is accounted for by a knowledge of previous contacts among white respondents (γ = .72) than it is for black housewives (γ = .43). Even though previous contact is a better predictor of prejudice for white respondents than it is for blacks, examination of table 3 shows few deviant cases for black respondents. Only one black woman who had minimal prejudice had few previous equal-status contacts, and only four (12%) prejudiced blacks had many previous interracial contacts. I suggest that blacks report more previous interracial contacts than their white counterparts because the black respondents are somewhat younger than the whites and have been reared in an urban (rather than a rural) environment which provided them with more opportunities than whites to enter into "equal-status" associations (Ford 1969, pp. 96–97).

Table 4 presents a test of the hypothesis that housewives who live in a desegregated project for a longer period of time will be less prejudiced than new comers to the project. The association between duration of

Table 3. Previous Interracial Equal-Status Contacts and Degree of Racial Prejudice, by Race

| | Previous Contacts | | | | | | | |
| | White Housewives* | | | | Black Housewives† | | | |
Racial Prejudice	Many	Few/ Several	None	Total	Many	Few/ Several	None	Total
Low	6	12	0	18	22	17	1	40
Moderate ..	5	21	1	27	7	16	6	29
High	3	18	17	38	4	9	1	14
Totals‡ .	14	51	18	83	33	42	8	83

NOTE.—Total N = 166 (there was no composite prejudice score for two housewives).
*γ = .72, p < .01.
†γ = .43, p < .01.
‡γ (both groups combined) = .59, p < .01.

residence and racial prejudice for white housewives is in the direction hypothesized, but it is not statistically significant (p > .05, < .10). Therefore, the evidence for white respondents must be considered inconclusive. The absence of a clear-cut relationship between attitudes and duration of residence is partially a product of the lack of variation in length of residence. The data suggest that black housewives who lived in this particular desegregated project for a longer period of time were more likely to hold intolerant racial attitudes (γ = −.37). There would appear to be nothing about

long duration of residence in desegregated housing that was conducive to tolerant racial attitudes for black respondents. We will return to the "negative" effects of duration in a subsequent discussion.

In order to provide a more comprehensive measure of the contact hypothesis within the research context, an effort was made to measure the relationship between the combined effect of the following four variables and racial prejudice: interracial neighboring, interracial contacts implying social equality made prior to moving to public housing, living in a desegregated project, and living in

Table 4. Duration of Residence in Desegregated Project and Degree of Racial Prejudice, by Race

| | Duration of Residence | | | | | | | |
| | White Housewives* | | | | Black Housewives† | | | |
Racial Prejudice	More than 1 Year	7 Months to 1 Year	6 Months or Less	Total	More than 1 Year	7 Months to 1 Year	6 Months or Less	Total
Low	5	0	0	5	6	5	5	16
Moderate .	13	2	1	16	6	5	1	12
High	11	1	1	13	4	3	0	7
Total‡ .	29	3	2	34	16	13	6	35

NOTE.—Total N = 69.
*γ = .22, N.S. (p > .05).
†γ = −.37.
‡γ (both groups combined) = −.33.

Table 5. Number of Housewives in Each of 12 Categories of Degrees of Equal-Status Contact, Subclassified by Race and by Prejudice ($N = 166$)

RACIAL PREJUDICE	TYPE RESPONDENT ACCORDING TO EXPOSURE*												
	I	II	III	IV	V	VI	VII	VIII	IX	X	XI	XII	Total
White housewives:†													
Low	5	8	0	1	0	0	1	3	0	0	0	0	18
Moderate	7	4	2	0	1	1	3	5	3	0	1	0	27
High	1	2	0	4	2	0	4	4	8	1	2	10	38
Total	13	14	2	5	3	1	8	12	11	1	3	10	83
Black housewives:‡													
Low	5	7	0	1	3	8	6	9	0	0	0	1	40
Moderate	5	5	0	0	1	3	1	7	1	1	0	5	29
High	2	1	0	0	4	3	0	2	0	2	0	0	14
Total§	12	13	0	1	8	14	7	18	1	3	0	6	83

Types I–XII represent a descending order of interracial experience, where Type I represents housewives with most equal-status experiences and Type XII those with the least.
†$\gamma = .62, p < .01$.
‡$\gamma = .03$, N.S.
§γ both groups combined $= .38, p < .01$.

a desegregated project for a "long" period of time. During coding procedures and prior to analysis, each respondent was classified according to whether or not she had been exposed to each of these four life experiences. A respondent could have had all these experiences, none, or any possible combination—12 in all.

... Each respondent was placed in one of 12 categories. Respondents in Category I engaged in interracial neighboring, experienced previous equal-status interracial contact, were residing in a desegregated project, and had lived there for more than a year. They represent tenants who had maximum exposure to members of the other race, as measured by these particular variables. Each successive category (II–XII) represents a decreasing degree of interracial contact. It was hypothesized that women in Category I would have more tolerant attitudes than those in Categories II, III, IV, and so forth. In Cateogry XII we should find those housewives with the least tolerant attitudes.

Each of the four variables used in this composite profile was dichotomized; every respondent was classified as either having the attribute in question or not. She either neighbored with members of the other race or did not, had some previous contacts or did not, and so forth. . . .

The data in Table 5 show the degree to which residents' combined interracial experience account for variation in their prejudices. The numbers entered in the body of the table indicate the number of respondents. Expectations concerning the relationship between contact experience and prejudice are substantiated for both racial groups taken together and especially for white housewives. However, when blacks are analyzed separately, the hypothesis is unsupported. Findings for white respondents, in contrast, show a strong and statistically significant association ($\gamma = .62$, $p < .01$). Examination of table 5 shows few inversions for the white group, whereas inversions for the black group are frequent. There is a strong ordinal association among whites between the degree of exposure to equal-status experiences with blacks and less racial antipathy. On the other hand, a knowledge of black respondents' interracial profile is ineffective in predicting their degree of prejudice.

DISCUSSION AND CONCLUSIONS

Before we explore the findings, it is appropriate to discuss the possibility that a process of differential selection operated to distribute residents in the projects according to their initial racial attitudes. In any study which uses an ex post facto design and views attitude change as a result of interracial contact, the question arises as to what degree initially tolerant attitudes were responsible for one group of respondents entering a racially desegregated environment. In an appendix to their study, Deutsch and Collins (1951 pp. 150–55) claim they found little evidence to suggest that differential selection among white residents existed, that is, tenants in integrated projects were no less prejudiced initially than those in segregated projects. Their position relied on three interrelated arguments: (1) lower-income families were so in need of adequate housing that they could not afford to be selective on the basis of racial attitudes; (2) the assumption was made that the highly intolerant would be no more inclined to more into a segregated project in a black neighborhood than to move into a desegregated project; and (3) racially tolerant responses were higher in desegregated projects regardless of whether or not tenants expected to live with blacks when they applied for public housing.

I feel that differential resident selection no more adequately explains the findings presented here than it did the Deutsch and Collins research. In the Lexington projects, virtually no white applicant was unaware of the pervasively desegregated environment.[16] Residents voiced similar reservations about moving into public housing whether they entered segregated or desegregated projects. Racial desegregation or impending desegrega-

tion was not the most offensive aspect of public housing to either group of respondents. Equal proportions (20%–25%) of incoming residents were highly disturbed about the desegregation issue. Families moved into public housing because of need and a lack of suitable alternatives. Many of the whites in the desegregated project entered while it was still a "white" project. Newcomers in the desegregated project reported no more interracial neighboring than those who were there prior to or during the initial influx of black families. Reference to table 4 suggests this, and it is further confirmed by an examination of recorded interviews with residents.

The majority of white respondents grew up in rural central and eastern Kentucky surroundings, and they had comparatively few extended contacts or associations with blacks. None had lived in truly desegregated neighborhoods prior to entering public housing. Whereas they shared commonplace Negro stereotypes, they were not reared in Deep South states and exposed to their biracial cultural etiquette. This was true of white residents who entered both segregated and desegregated projects.

Again, unlike the Deutsch and Collins study (1951) and those in its tradition, it is not residential environment that is viewed as the determinant of racial attitudes. It is both neighboring and other previous interracial contacts. Whereas those who have had previous equal-status contacts are somewhat more likely to engage in interracial neighboring, housewives who had previous contacts are not disproportionately found in the desegregated housing project.

The principal hypothesis of the study reported here was that there exists a positive relationship between equal-status interracial contact and racial tolerance. The results support the contact hypothesis for white respondents, but, unlike the reported findings of earlier studies, the hypothesis was only partially and inconclusively confirmed for blacks. There are essentially two instances where the findings were contrary

16. The discussion in this and the following two paragraphs is based upon data taken from a larger study of race relations in Lexington's public-housing projects (Ford 1969).

to expectations. First, interpersonal equal-status contacts did not appear to be significantly related to reduced prejudice for blacks. Second, a longer duration in a desegregated project was either not significantly related to racial tolerance (whites) or it tended to be related to a higher degree of racial antipathy (blacks).

With regard to the first of these unexpected results, the inconclusive findings for blacks may be a partial function of the comparative lack of variability in neighboring. Most blacks reported few neighboring contacts with whites, considerably fewer than whites reported with blacks. Examination of interviews showed no evidence that whites were neighboring with a small number of interracially oriented blacks! Whereas there were a number of pairs of black-white neighbors who were quite close, there were no black women who were socially intimate with more than one white housewife. There was some evidence to show that white women were most often the initiators of interpersonal relationships, which by virtue of the measure of interracial neighboring used increased their scores. However, the findings also warrant a reexamination of what these "equal-status" contacts mean to blacks.

Although the work of Deutsch and Collins (1951) and Works (1961) suggests that blacks who neighbored with white residents held tolerant attitudes, it is unlikely that such interracial contacts are perceived similarly by blacks and whites. Some white housewives in this study refused to relate to black women as status equals, and others failed to perceive the implied social equality of such contacts. On the other hand, a number of instances arose whereby interracial neighboring led white women to call into question their stereotyped perceptions of blacks. This type of "discovery" was reported by white women who also indicated that they held initially negative feelings toward black neighbors and racial desegregation.

Black housewives entered into the same "equal-status" relationships with white neighbors with a considerably different set of life experiences. They were cognizant of the subtle nuances of dominant-subordinant relationships and had been previously subjected to rebuff and unpleasantries by whites. As Johnson (1966) suggests, because of such life experiences, blacks learn to be suspect of *any* relationships with whites—even those which do not openly suggest differential status. In the public-housing environment studies, black women were quick to perceive condescending attitudes on the part of their white counterparts, even if not recognized by the whites to whom they were relating. Such caution and suspicion could be expected in the public-housing projects described, where there was considerable tenant dissatisfaction.

The majority of black women accepted racially desegregated living, not as the result of actual contact with tolerant whites or the desire for such contact, but rather because they felt the available integrated housing offered more advantages and a healthier physical environment for their children than they otherwise could afford. This difference in the interpretation of "equal-status" contact may also explain why the net effect of a black woman's engaging in such relationships is not a reduction of prejudice comparable to that found for white respondents.

We turn now to the second result that was counter to the hypothesis—the fact that duration within the desegregated project was not positively related to racial tolerance. Originally, we argued that the opportunity to engage in interracial contacts would increase with the length of residence. Upon closer examination, it was clear that duration did not function in this fashion. Duration of residence became associated with other factors. What occurred in many instances appeared to be the following: the most prevalent sources of tenant discontent among black and white residents alike were a felt lack of privacy, a lack of discipline among young children, a high rate of delinquency among teen-agers, undue surveillance by the housing administration, and a lack of adequate project maintenance and repair. Because so many incoming project dwellers came from homes with serious inadequacies, the project apartments with their convenient facilities and relatively inexpensive rents were very welcome—especially after the typical long wait to move into the unit. The improvement in the living quarters remained a source of gratification for several months for most new comers. But after living in the projects for a time, the above sources of discontent became increasing salient. As Moore (1969), Rainwater (1970), and others found in other housing projects, at this stage many residents become resigned to the fact that their lot has not improved substantially, if indeed it has not become worse in some respects. Coser (1965) found the same reaction among welfare recipients.

In conjunction with the dissatisfactions of project living that were shared by both races, it is important to remember that the housing projects studied were undergoing a period of rapid transition; the desegregated project had two years previously been solely occupied by white families. This desegregation process had decided effects upon both black and white residents. White housewives, here designated as long-time occupants, had witnessed a rapid influx of blacks into "their" project, whereas the long-time black residents were the first of their race to enter this formerly segregated project. Among many of the white respondents who had resided in the desegregated project longest, there was marked resentment concerning the recent "Negro invasion," especially when they witnessed no similar desegregation in "Negro projects." White tenants had little financial resources, and satisfactory residential alternatives were nil. A number of those project women viewed racial desegregation in the project as an additional and unavoidable indignity. It has been shown that resistance of whites to desegregation is increased when the incoming nonwhite group is large and threatens to become the dominant group (Laurenti 1960, p. 57). Given their inability

to resist desegregation, some white women allowed their feelings of frustration to reinforce their existent fears and prejudices.

Black women who had been among the first to "desegregate" the project and who had lived there the longest often expressed similar resentment but for different reasons. In the course of the interviews, it became clear that these women objected to the lack of social recognition and the contentious attitudes some of their white neighbors held toward them and the members of their families. They also suffered from being comparatively isolated from other black women among whom they felt more comfortable and with whom they could more readily establish neighborly relations. Under the circumstances of "involuntary" biracial propinquity, black housewives and their families were cast in the role of the "intruders" which resulted in a different but no less stressful challenge than the one faced by white residents.[17]

Among their concluding remarks, Deutsch and Collins (1951, p. 126) suggested that the favorable results they found within desegregated projects would be unlikely in projects where low tenant morale and tension characterized human relationships. Unlike previous studies of interracial public housing, the present study examined interracial contacts under circumstances which were far from those likely to enhance friendly relations. It appeared for many housewives of both races, that the longer they remained in public housing, the more their general outlook became resentful.

What is surprising, under conditions wherein the lid was barely kept on open racial antagonism, is that there was an underlying realization on the part of a number of women of both races, and especially whites, that neither group was totally alien to the other. Comments made by these respondents indicated that they were aware

17. Molotch (1969) presents a related discussion of how the challenges and frustrations blacks and whites face differ from one another given such biracial neighborhood proximity.

of certain factors that transcended racial differences. In his discussion of a slum neighborhood as a territory within which different groups manage their coexistence, Suttles (1968, p. 7) says, "People who routinely occupy the same place must either develop a moral order that includes all present or fall into conflict." No well-established moral order existed across race lines in the desegregated project, and, under the circumstances, it would be somewhat surprising if one arose while the "Negro invasion" continued. Nonetheless, there was a sentiment found among many housewives that black and white women alike were sharing a similar life style within the projects.

In conclusion, the findings do not negate the contact hypothesis. They support the applicability of the contact hypothesis to the racial attitudes of lower-income whites, reaffirm the necessity for careful description of the specific conditions under which such contacts are related to interracial perspectives, and suggest that studies of black reactions to interracial contact are necessary to improve our current understanding of race relations.

REFERENCES

Allport, Gordon W. 1962. "Prejudice: A Problem in Psychological and Social Causation." In *Toward a General Theory of Action*, edited by Talcott Parsons and Edward Shils. New York: Harper & Row.

Brophy, I. N. 1946. "The Luxury of Anti-Negro Prejudice." *Public Opinion Quarterly* 9 (Fall): 456–66.

Caplow, Theodore, and Robert Forman. 1950. "Neighborhood Interaction in a Homogeneous Community." *American Sociological Review* 15 (June): 357–66.

Coser, Lewis A. 1965. "The Sociology of Poverty." *Social Problems* 13 (Fall): 140–48.

Davis, Allison. 1957. "Acculturation in Schools." In *American Minorities*, edited by Milton L. Barron. New York: Knopf.

Deutsch, Morton, and Mary E. Collins. 1951. *Interracial Housing*. Minneapolis: University of Minnesota Press.

Edwards, Allen L. 1957. *Techniques of Attitude Scale Construction*. New York: Appleton-Century-Crofts.

Festinger, Leon, S. Schachter, and Kurt Black. 1950. *Social Pressures in Informal Groups*. New York: Harper.

Fishman, Joshua A. 1961. "Some Social and Psychological Determinants of Intergroup Relations in Changing Neighborhoods." *Social Forces* 40 (September): 42–51.

Ford, W. Scott. 1969. "Racial Attitudes, Behavior and Perceptions of Public Housing Residents in a Border State City." Ph.D. dissertation, University of Kentucky.

Freeman, Linton C. 1965. *Elementary Applied Statistics*. New York: Wiley.

Greenfield, Robert W. 1961. "Factors Associated with Attitudes toward Desegregation in a Florida Residential Suburb." *Social Forces* 40 (September) 31–42.

Hunt, Chester L. 1960. "Private Integrated Housing in a Medium Size Northern City." *Social Problems* 7 (Winter): 195–209.

Johnson, Robert B. 1966. "Negro Reactions to Minority Group Status." In *Racial and Ethnic Relations*, edited by Bernard E. Segal. New York: Crowell.

Kelly, James G., Jean Ferson, and Wayne Holtzman. 1958. "The Measurement of Attitudes toward the Negro in the South." *Journal of Social Psychology* 48 (August): 305–17.

Laurenti, Luigi. 1960. *Property Values and Race*. Berkeley: University of California Press.

Liebow, Elliot. 1967. *Talley's Corner*. Boston: Little, Brown.

Meer, Bernard, and Edward Freedman. 1966. "The Impact of Negro Neighbors on White Home Owners." *Social Forces* 45 (September): 11–19.

Molotch, Harvey. 1969. "Racial Integration in a Transitional Community." *American Sociological Review* 34 (December): 878–93.

Moore, William, Jr. 1969. *The Vertical Ghetto*. New York: Random House.

Morris, Richard T., and Vincent Jeffries. 1968. "Violence Next Door." *Social Forces* 46 (March): 353–58.

Myrdal, Gunnar. 1944. *An American Dilemma*. New York: Harper.

Noel, Donald L., and Alphonso Pinkney. 1964. "Correlates of Prejudice: Some Racial Differences and Similarities." *American Journal of Sociology* 69 (May): 609–22.

Pettigrew, Thomas F. 1969. "Racially Separate or Together?" *Journal of Social Issues* 25 (January): 43–69.

Raab, Earl, and Seymour M. Lipset. 1959. *Prejudice and Society*. New York: Anti-Defamation League.

Rainwater, Lee. 1970. *Behind Ghetto Walls*. Chicago: Aldine.

Rose, Arnold M. 1956. "Intergroup Relations vs. Prejudice." *Social Problems* (October): 173–76.

Rose, Arnold M., Frank J. Atelsek, and Laurence R. McDonald. 1953. "Neighborhood Reactions to Isolated Negro Residents." *American Sociological Review* 18 (October): 497–507.

Suttles, Gerald D. 1968. *The Social Order of the Slum*. Chicago: University of Chicago Press.

Taeuber, Karl E., and Alma F. Taeuber. 1965. *Negroes in Cities*. Chicago: Aldine.

U.S., Bureau of the Census. *U.S. Census of the Population 1970 General Population: Final Report*. Washington, D.C.: Government Printing Office, 1971.

Westie, Frank R. 1952. "Negro-White Status Differentials and Social Distance." *American Sociological Review* 17 (October): 550–58.

———. 1953. "A Technique for the Measurement of Race Attitudes." *American Sociological Review* 18 (February): 73–78.

Williams, Robin M., Jr. 1947. *The Reduction of Intergroup Tensions*. Social Science Research Council Bulletin no. 57, New York.

———. 1964. *Strangers Next Door*. Englewood Cliffs, N.J.: Prentice-Hall.

Wilner, Daniel M., Rosabelle P. Walkley, and Stuart W. Cook. 1955. *Human Relations in Interracial Housing—a Study of the Contact Hypothesis*. Minneapolis: University of Minnesota Press.

Works, Ernest. 1961. "The Prejudice-Interaction Hypothesis from the Point of View of the Negro Minority Group." *American Journal of Sociology* 67 (July): 47–52.

2

POVERTY

Introduction

Two major approaches have dominated psychological inquiry into the causes of poverty: the individual approach and the situational approach.* The individual approach hypothesizes that the poor are poor because of cognitive and/or affective inadequacies; for example, it has been argued that the poor, compared to the nonpoor, are less intelligent, are unable to delay gratifying their impulses, and have little desire to achieve. In an attempt to explain these personal inadequacies, investigators have suggested that the poor are genetically inferior (Burt, 1959, 1961; Jensen, 1969a, 1969b), culturally deprived (Deutsch, 1967), and/or inadequately socialized (Lewis, 1966). The situational approach hypothesizes that the poor are poor because they only have access to a severely restricted range of opportunities; for example, the poor receive grossly inadequate health care (Birch & Gussow, 1970), are victims of the prejudice of educational institutions (Stein, 1971), and "must accept the job opportunities that have been rejected by others—unstable, low-paying work which is generally unprotected by the institutional safeguards of better paying jobs" (Ferman, Kornbluh, & Haber, 1965, pp. 186–87).

Before looking at these positions in greater detail, it might be instructive to examine why American people believe the poor are poor—since proposals to reduce poverty are unlikely to be implemented without considerable public support. Toward that end, Feagin (1972) asked a random sample of 1,017 people from all parts of the country "to evaluate the importance of a list of reasons some people give to explain why there are poor people in this country" (p. 103). These reasons fell into three categories: individualistic explanations, which held that poor people's lack of thift, lack of effort, and/or loose morals were re-

---

* Obviously, we recognize that a chronic scarcity of money is the major cause of poverty. The questions we seek to answer concern the behavioral and/or situational events that lead to and perpetuate that scarcity.

79

sponsible for their poverty; structural explanations, which assigned the blame to a paucity of jobs, low wages, poor schools, prejudice and discrimination against blacks, and/or exploitation by the rich; and fatalistic explanations, which attributed poverty to a lack of ability, illness, and/or fate. While most of the people interviewed felt that more than one explanation was needed to explain poverty, individualistic factors—or the presumed character defects of the poor— were considered far more important than structural or fatalistic factors. Feagin also tried to find out how people feel about welfare and welfare recipients. Respondents were asked whether they agreed or disagreed with seven statements; for example, "There are too many people receiving welfare money who should be working," "Many women getting welfare money are having illegitimate babies to increase the money they get," and "A lot of people are moving to this state from other states just to get welfare money here" (p. 107). On six of the seven items, a plurality expressed antiwelfare attitudes, even though "all the antiwelfare positions are questionable and many are demonstrably false" (p. 107). Given these beliefs, we need to ask two questions: what do the results of psychological research tell us about the presumed causes of poverty, and what implications do these findings have for creating change?

SOME HYPOTHESES ABOUT THE CAUSES OF POVERTY

Hypothesis 1: The poor are genetically inferior. In other words, the poor are poor because they are inherently less able than the nonpoor (Burt, 1959, 1961; Jensen, 1969a, 1969b). The results of intelligence tests, which show consistently that poor people have lower scores on the average than middle-class people, have been used to support this position. However, the understandable failure of these studies to control environmental variables that may have had confounding effects makes it impossible to determine the degree to which genetic endowment contributed to this difference. For example, there are considerable differences in the prenatal and postnatal environments of the poor and nonpoor. Women who are pregnant and poor tend to have less nourishing diets, poorer health, and markedly inferior prenatal care than pregnant women who are not poor. Their children, compared to the children of the nonpoor, are far more likely to eat irregularly, to have frequent, persistent, and severe illnesses, and to receive almost totally inadequate health care (Birch & Gussow, 1970). The importance of nutrition during pregnancy is suggested by a study in which experimental groups of pregnant, lower-class women in three neighborhoods received vitamin supplements while control groups were given placebos (Harrell, Woodyard, & Gates, 1956). When the investigators compared the intelligence test scores of the offspring, they found that children whose mothers received vitamin supplements had higher scores in two of the three neighborhoods. The research findings also suggest that the language and content of intelligence tests and the nature of the testing process have contributed to the difference in the intelligence test scores of lower- and middle-class children (Allen, 1970a; Cole & Bruner, 1971, reading 1.1; Zigler, Abelson, & Seitz, 1973).

While these findings do not rule out genetic factors as determinants of poverty, they do imply that a sizable portion of the difference in the intelligence test scores of lower- and middle-class children is due to environmental variables. The effects of carefully designed instruction on the intelligence test scores of economically disadvantaged children (e.g., Abelson, Zigler, & DeBlasi, 1974, reading 4.1; Karnes, Teska, & Hodgins, 1970; Rollins, McCandless, Thompson, & Brassell, 1974, reading 4.2) provide additional support for the proposed importance of environmental factors. Unfortunately, these studies did not determine whether improved performance was due to higher scores on tasks requiring associative ability or tasks requiring conceptual ability. As a result, they do not shed light on an important hypothesis; that is, Jensen (1969b) has argued that lower-class children are able to perform tasks requiring associative ability as well as middle-class children. He has also argued that lower-class children are inherently less able than middle-class children to apply relevant abilities and previous learning to the solution of conceptual problems. If Jensen is right, then training will not reduce the difference in conceptual task performance between lower- and middle-class children. In an attempt to test this hypothesis, Scrofani, Suziedelis, and Shore (1973, reading 2.1) compared middle-class children with above-average intelligence test scores and high scores on two measures of cognitive development, lower-class children with below-average intelligence test scores and high scores on the two measures of cognitive development, and lower-class children with below-average intelligence test scores and low cognitive development test scores. Each group contained equal numbers of whites, blacks, males, and females. Half the children in each group received two 30-minute training sessions in concept formation. The remaining children received training that was unrelated to concept formation. When the training sessions were over, every child was given a conceptual problem-solving task. The results indicate that training in concept formation eliminated the difference in conceptual task performance between middle-class children and lower-class children with high scores on the two measures of cognitive development. The results also indicate that training in concept formation did not improve the task performance of lower-class children who had low scores on the measures of cognitive development. While these findings are not conclusive, the ability of a sizable proportion of lower-class children to perform as well as middle-class children after only one hour of training in concept formation suggests that a genetically linked incapacity to apply relevant abilities and previous learning to new conceptual tasks cannot account for the poverty of many poor people.

Hypothesis 2: The poor are culturally deprived. In other words, the lower-class environment fails to provide the developing child with the kinds of learning experiences that facilitate cognitive development: that is, the processes of thinking and understanding (Deutsch, 1967). As a result, poor children enter school with verbal and intellectual deficits that seriously hamper their ability to learn, and emerge without acquiring the skills that a technological economy requires.

A sizable number of research findings have been marshaled in support of this argument. For example, Bernstein (1964) analyzed the speech patterns of lower- and middle-class children, and concluded that lower-class children fail to acquire the linguistic tools needed to function at an abstract, conceptual level. Hess and Shipman (1965), in a problem-solving situation involving middle- and lower-class mothers and their children, found that middle-class mothers offered more verbal explanations, and middle-class children performed more effectively, than their lower-class counterparts. Klaus and Gray (1968) attributed the relative inability of poor children to perceive figure-ground relations to the more confusing noise backgrounds in their homes, and Eifermann (1968) observed that the games poor children play require less strategy than the games of children who are not poor.

There is, then, a considerable body of data that appears to support the cultural deprivation hypothesis. However, a careful examination of the research raises serious questions about the validity of the findings and interpretations. For one, different subcultural groups may interpret the experimental setting, task, and/or instructions differently, and may be differentially motivated to perform effectively (Labov, 1970). Two, the ways in which investigators interpret lower-class phenomena may be misleading; for example, the sounds in the lower-class home that Deutsch (1964) interpreted as noise may be meaningful input for the people who live there. Three, since much of the data are correlational, cause and effect relationships can only be suggested (Schultz & Aurbach, 1971, reading 2.2).

This brief review of the research, and the more extensive reviews by Cole and Bruner (1971) and Schultz and Aurbach (1971), indicate that there is no substantive empirical basis for attributing the performance of poor children in school settings to cultural deprivation, though the data do not rule out cultural deprivation as a possible explanation. Accordingly, cultural deprivation remains one of a number of feasible interpretations. For example, the experience of lower-class children may be less useful in school settings than the experience of middle-class children (Getzels, 1969). In other words, since public schools are predominantly middle-class institutions, the skills that middle-class children acquire are more likely to meet the expectations of teachers than the skills that lower-class children acquire. Two, the low expectations held by teachers about the ability of poor children may affect teacher behavior in ways that discourage these children (Rist, 1970; Ryan, 1971). Three, standard English differs from black English vernacular and colloquial Spanish in ways that place many lower-

class black, Puerto Rican, and Chicano children at a considerable disadvantage in
the classroom (Baratz, 1969; Cazden, 1970). Four, curriculum materials usually
deal with subject matter that is uninteresting and/or unfamiliar to lower-class
children (Levine, 1973). Five, poor children are much more likely to eat irregularly and to receive almost totally inadequate health care (Birch & Gussow,
1970). One plausible outcome is that their school work suffers.

While these findings suggest that a number of situational factors may account
for the difference between lower- and middle-class children in scholastic performance, they are far from conclusive. Before any conclusions can be legitimately
drawn, the relationship between these factors and scholastic performance
needs to be demonstrated clearly, and more sensitive tests of the cultural
deprivation hypothesis need to be carried out.

Hypothesis 3: The poor are inadequately socialized. In other words, the poor
are members of a subculture whose norms and values deviate from the norms
and values of the nonpoor. For example, the poor, compared to the nonpoor,
have a short time perspective, little ability to delay gratifying their impulses,
little desire to achieve, and believe that their lives are controlled largely by forces
outside themselves (Lewis, 1966). As a result, lower-class children perform
poorly in school and lower-class adults perform poorly at work.

The validity of this argument and the attendant research findings were examined critically by Allen (1970b), who concluded that the "quality of much of
the research . . . is seriously deficient even when examined with charity. Failure
to provide controls for obvious confounding effects . . . , small and nonrepresen-
tative samples, and measuring instruments of dubious validity within the middle-class group—not to mention validity across classes—are all too common . . . It
would seem very risky indeed, on the basis of present meager results, to generalize research findings across the entire heterogeneous poverty group" (pp.
258, 259).

Among the more insidious implications of the inadequate socialization hypothesis are the notions that poor people do not value work, and would drop out
of the labor force if given a guaranteed annual income. Each of these notions has
recently been subjected to empirical test. In an attempt to assess the commitment to work among the poor, Goodwin (1972, 1973, reading 2.3) interviewed a
sample of approximately 4,000 people. The sample included black mothers and
their adolescent sons who were long-term recipients of welfare, black mothers
and their adolescent sons who were short-term recipients of welfare, welfare
recipients enrolled in a national job training program, and black families and
white families living in middle-class neighborhoods that were undergoing racial
change. The results indicate that:

> poor people—males and females, blacks and whites, youths and adults—identify
> their self-esteem with work as strongly as do the nonpoor. They express as much
> willingness to take job training if unable to earn a living and to work even if they

were to have an adequate income. They have, moreover, as high life aspirations
as do the nonpoor and want the same things, among them a good education and
a nice place to live. [1972, p. 112]

The results of the New Jersey graduated work incentive experiment (Kershaw
& Skidmore, 1974, reading 2.4) suggest that poor families also act in ways that
reflect a belief in the work ethic. In an attempt to determine the impact of a
guaranteed annual income on the work behavior of poor families, 1,357 poor
families containing an adult male who was able to work were randomly assigned
to two conditions: those who received a guaranteed annual income and those
who did not. Families in the experimental group were further assigned to eight
treatments defined by the amount guaranteed and the rate at which benefits
were reduced as the family's earned income increased. Data gathered during the
central two years of the experiment indicated that the employment rates, hours
worked per week, and earnings per week of the married male heads of households in the experimental and control groups did not differ. In effect, a
guaranteed annual income did not encourage male heads of households to drop
out of the labor force.

While these findings are encouraging, their generalizability appears to be
limited by the recipients' awareness of the length of the guarantee. In other
words, the subjects knew that they would be guaranteed a minimum income for
only three years. If a guaranteed annual income with no time limit were legis-
lated, it is possible that many poor people would be much less motivated to
work than the people who participated in the New Jersey study. On the other
hand, if many poor people felt that a small guaranteed income was a sufficient
income, and if they did not want to work, then many recipients in the New
Jersey study would not have held jobs for at least the first two years of the
guarantee. The data indicate that this did not happen.

SOME IMPLICATIONS FOR REDUCING POVERTY

The results of the preceding studies provide no support for the hypotheses
generated by the individual approach. Rather, they suggest that situational
factors are far more important determinants of becoming and remaining poor.
They also suggest, along with the results of studies presented in other
parts of this book, that a variety of strategies and tactics can be used to
reduce poverty. For example, the prenatal and postnatal environments of
poor children could be enhanced dramatically by nutritious diets and adequate
health care (Birch & Gussow, 1970). The scholastic performance, and consequent ability of many lower-class children to eventually compete for most
decent jobs, could be improved by implementing cognitively- and child-oriented
preschool and elementary school programs (Abelson, Zigler, & DeBlasi, 1974,

reading 4.1; Spicker, 1971), the systematic use of praise and token reinforcers (Clark & Walberg, 1968; Hamblin & Hamblin, 1972; Rollins, McCandless, Thompson, & Brassell, 1974, reading 4.2), and computer-assisted instruction (Fletcher & Atkinson, 1972; Suppes & Morningstar, 1970). Perhaps the most repercussive strategies are a guaranteed annual income and guaranteed jobs— repercussive because they would give the poor access to a far greater range of job, housing, education, and health care opportunities than they have now. The findings of the New Jersey graduated work incentive experiment (Kershaw & Skidmore, 1974, reading 2.4) suggest that a guaranteed annual income would have the intended effects. However, the results of several other studies (e.g., Goodwin, 1973, reading 2.3; Gurin, 1970) suggest that any program of job opportunities should be accompanied by job training that enables the poor to acquire new expectancies. In other words, the data imply that the harsh experiences of the poor generate negative expectations about their ability to succeed. Since expectations are important determinants of behavior, any attempt to broaden dramatically the job opportunities available to the poor would be more likely to work if it included skill training in which expectations are relearned. Toward that end, Gurin (1970) proposed that "the success experiences that the trainees have in the course of their training should be tied to their actual performance. This means programming the tasks in such a way that easy steps come first and trainees learn both skills and expectancies as they proceed through the tasks . . . To the extent that the reinforcement experiences in the training program follow a reality-based pattern of successes and failures, there is a greater possibility for learning expectancies that can handle the realities to be faced after the end of the program" (pp. 289, 291).

While the character of the training program may be an important consideration, Goodman, Salipante, and Paransky (1973, reading 2.5) indicate that training is only one of a number of role-, organizational-, and societal-level variables that can affect the work behavior of the hard-core unemployed. For example, the findings imply that considerable support from supervisors, work that is not boring, satisfactory pay, and realistic expectations held by the company may be useful strategies in retaining people who have been chronically unemployed.

REFERENCES

Abelson, W., Zigler, E., & DeBlasi, C. Effects of a four-year follow through program on economically disadvantaged children. *Journal of Educational Psychology*, 1974, 66, 756–771.

Allen, V. Theoretical issues in poverty research. *Journal of Social Issues*, 1970, 26 (2), 149–167. (a)

Allen, V. Personality correlates of poverty. In V. Allen (Ed.), *Psychological factors in poverty*. Chicago: Markham, 1970, pp. 242–266. (b)

Baratz, J. A bi-dialectal task for determining language proficiency in economically disadvantaged Negro children. *Child Development*, 1969, 40, 889–901.

Bernstein, B. Elaborated and restricted codes: Their social origins and some consequences. In J. Gumphrey & D. Hymes (Eds.), The ethnography of communication. *American Anthropologist Special Publication,* 1964, 66(6), Part 2, 55–69.

Birch, H., & Gussow, J. *Disadvantaged children: Health, nutrition, and school failure.* New York: Harcourt Brace Jovanovich, Inc., 1970.

Burt, C. Class differences in general intelligence: III. *British Journal of Statistical Psychology,* 1959, 12, 15–33.

Burt, C. Intelligence and social mobility. *British Journal of Statistical Psychology,* 1961, 14, 3–24.

Cazden, C. The situation: A neglected source of social class differences in language use. *Journal of Social Classes,* 1970, 26, 35–59.

Clark, C., & Walberg, H. The influence of massive rewards on reading achievement in potential urban school dropouts. *American Educational Research Journal,* 1968, 5, 305–310.

Cole, M., & Bruner, J. Cultural differences and inferences about psychological processes. *American Psychologist,* 1971, 26, 867–876.

Deutsch, C. Auditory discrimination and learning: Social factors. *Merrill-Palmer Quarterly of Behavior and Development,* 1964, 10, 277–296.

Deutsch, M. *The disadvantaged child.* New York: Basic Books, 1967.

Eifermann, R. *School children's games.* Washington, D.C.: Department of Health, Education, and Welfare, 1968.

Feagin, J. God helps those who help themselves. *Psychology Today,* 1972, 6(6), 101–104, 107, 108, 110, 129.

Ferman, L., Kornbluh, J., & Haber, A. (Eds.). *Poverty in America.* Ann Arbor: University of Michigan Press, 1965.

Fletcher, J., & Atkinson, R. Evaluation of the Stanford CAI program in initial reading. *Journal of Educational Psychology,* 1972, 63, 597–602.

Getzels, J. A social psychology of education. In G. Lindzey & E. Aronson (Eds.), *The handbook of social psychology,* second edition. Reading, Mass.: Addison-Wesley, 1969, vol. 5, pp. 459–537.

Goodman, P., Salipante, P., & Paransky, H. Hiring, training, and retaining the hard-core unemployed: A selected review. *Journal of Applied Psychology,* 1973, 58, 23–33.

Goodwin, L. *Do the poor want to work?* Washington, D.C.: Brookings Institution, 1972.

Goodwin, L. Middle-class misperceptions of the high life aspirations and strong work ethic held by the welfare poor. *American Journal of Orthopsychiatry,* 1973, 43, 554–564.

Gurin, G. An expectancy approach to job training programs. In V. Allen (Ed.), *Psychological factors in poverty.* Chicago: Markham, 1970, pp. 277–299.

Hamblin, J., & Hamblin, R. On teaching disadvantaged preschoolers to read: A successful experiment. *American Educational Research Journal,* 1972, 9, 209–216.

Harrell, R., Woodyard, E., & Gates, A. Influence of vitamin supplementation of diets of pregnant and lactating women on intelligence of their offspring. *Metabolism,* 1956, 5, 555–562.

Hess, R., & Shipman, V. Early experience and the socialization of cognitive modes in children. *Child Development,* 1965, 36, 869–886.

Jensen, A. How much can we boost IQ and scholastic achievement? *Harvard Educational Review,* 1969, 39, 1–123. (a)

Jensen, A. Reducing the heredity-environment uncertainty: A reply. *Harvard Educational Review,* 1969, 39, 449–483. (b)

Karnes, M., Teska, J., & Hodgins, A. The effects of four programs of classroom intervention on the intellectual and language development of 4-year-old disadvantaged children. *American Journal of Orthopsychiatry,* 1970, 40, 58–76.

Kershaw, D., & Skidmore, F. *The New Jersey graduated work incentive experiment.* Princeton, N. J.: Mathematica, 1974.

Klaus, R., & Gray, S. The early training project for disadvantaged children: A report after five years. *Monographs of the Society for Research in Child Development,* 1968, 33(4).

Labov, W. The logical nonstandard English. In F. Williams (Ed.), *Language and poverty.* Chicago: Markham, 1970.

Levine, D. The crisis in urban education. In M. Urofsky (Ed.), *Perspectives on urban*

America. Garden City, N.Y.: Anchor Press, 1973.

Lewis, O. The culture of poverty. *Scientific American,* 1966, 215, 19–25.

Rist, R. Student social class and teacher expectations: The self-fulfilling prophecy in ghetto education. *Harvard Educational Review,* 1970, 40, 411–451.

Rollins, H., McCandless, B., Thompson, M., & Brassell, W. Project success experiment: An extended application of contingency management in inner-city schools. *Journal of Educational Psychology,* 1974, 66, 167–178.

Ryan, W. *Blaming the victim.* New York: Random House, 1971.

Schultz, C., & Aurbach, H. The usefulness of cumulative deprivation as an explanation of educational deficiencies. *Merrill-Palmer Quarterly of Behavior and Development,* 1971, 17, 27–39.

Scrofani, P., Suziedelis, A., & Shore, M. Conceptual ability in black and white children of different social classes: An experimental test of Jensen's hypothesis. *American Journal of Orthopsychiatry,* 1973, 43, 541–553.

Spicker, H. Intellectual development through early childhood education. *Exceptional Children,* 1971, 37, 629–640.

Stein, A. Strategies of failure. *Harvard Educational Review,* 1971, 41, 158–204.

Suppes, P., & Morningstar, M. Technological innovations: Computer-assisted instruction and compensatory education. In F. Korten, S. Cook, & J. Lacey (Eds.), *Psychology and the problems of society.* Washington, D.C.: American Psychological Association, 1970.

Zigler, E., Abelson, W., & Seitz, V. Motivational factors in the performance of economically disadvantaged children on the Peabody Picture Vocabulary Test. *Child Development,* 1973, 44, 294–303.

Conceptual Ability in Black and White Children of Different Social Classes:

An Experimental Test of Jensen's Hypothesis

PHILIP J. SCROFANI, ANTANAS SUZIEDELIS, and MILTON F. SHORE

Jensen and his co-workers have noted that, as a group, children of low socioeconomic status (SES), repeatedly score approximately 20 to 30 points below middle-SES children on conventional IQ tests. They then attempted to investigate the nature of the cognitive differences across SES levels more thoroughly by developing laboratory learning tasks that were believed to be more culture fair (less tied to culture in content) than are conventional IQ tests. They consistently found no significant SES differences on what were later labeled Level I (LI) tasks. These involved simple associative learning; for example, serial rote learning, digit span, and free recall of uncategorized lists. However, his lower-class groups still performed significantly lower than did middle-class groups on what he labeled Level II (LII) tasks. These tasks involved conceptual problem-solving abilities that were frequently measured by culture fair IQ tests (*e.g.,* Raven Progressive Matrices) and various laboratory learning techniques of a conceptual kind. These so-called culture fair tasks, which were conceptually oriented, reflected the same significant SES differences that had been previously found with conventional IQ tests. Since the culture fairness of the task did not appear to be a major factor related to SES differences on LII tasks, Jensen [6, 7] eventually concluded that specific, genetic antecedents underlay LII task performance. These genetic factors, he believed, were differentially distributed in the general population as a function of social class. He proposed that 70% to 90% of the systematic variance on LII tasks (including IQ tests) was based on inherent factors.

Jensen [6] later theorized that conceptual ability followed a bimodal distribution (with marginally overlapping tails) in which the middle-class population represented the upper mode. Each SES distribution represented a distinct population of LII ability whose quantitative differences were seen as taking on a functional significance of a qualitative nature with regard to educability. Jensen [9] also hypothesized that LI ability was at least as heritable as LII ability, depending upon the culture fairness of the measures employed. However, LI ability was seen as being distributed about the same in all populations of social class. Although Jen-

From P. Scrofani, A. Suziedelis, & M. Shore. Conceptual ability in black and white children of different social classes: An experimental test of Jensen's hypothesis. *American Journal of Orthopsychiatry*, 1973, *43*, 541–553. Copyright © 1973, the American Orthopsychiatric Association, Inc. Reprinted by permission.

sen [6, 7, 9] believed that most cognitive tasks tapped both abilities, he reported that some tasks (especially certain laboratory tasks) are purer measures of one or the other ability. Accordingly, he believes that the purer measures could be used to validate his genetic hypothesis regarding social class and the two forms of ability.

Jensen [6, 8] has, on several occasions, cited the results reported by Glasman [4] as a major piece of supporting evidence for his two-factor theory. Glasman found that groups of lower and middle-SES, fifth-grade children differed significantly on a culture fair, LII free recall task (recall of pictures that could be conceptually categorized), in the same way as they had on a conventional IQ test. Jensen's own research [5] indicated that these children did not differ on an LI (non-conceptual) version of the task. He interpreted spontaneous conceptual classification on Glasman's task as a prime manifestation of LII ability, pointing out that middle-SES children enhanced their LII free recall on that basis, while lower-SES children did not.

Cronbach [2] presented a different interpretation of Glasman's findings and other findings based on Jensen's laboratory learning tasks. He suggested that SES differences on LII tasks such as Glasman's [4] might involve something less than inherent differences in conceptual ability. He proposed that lower-class children could equal or overtake middle-class children if they were trained in the usefulness of conceptual analysis. To bolster his argument, he cited a developmental study by Moely, Olson, Halwes, and Flavell [12], in which age differences on a task almost identical to Glasman's [4] were overcome by brief training. He implied that the same might be the case for SES differences. Cronbach [1] stated that:

Capability is not at issue when a child does not call upon an ability he possesses. (p. 343)

In a reply to Cronbach, Jensen [7, 9] refined his position. He stated that the essence of intelligence (LII ability) is the capacity to call upon relevant subabilities and previous learning when confronted with a new problem. It is the ability to transfer learning from one problem to another. This was the process that was under consideration and that had to be tested. He proposed that children in the different socioeconomic groups differed markedly in their inherent capacity to acquire mediational techniques involved in conceptual operations, and also differed in their ability to transfer these skills across situations and tasks. Accordingly, he predicted that SES differences would become accentuated by training if all children involved were trained. This prediction was, of course, a logical deduction from his genetic hypothesis.

The predictions of Cronbach and Jensen were tested in the current study. A new approach to assess conceptual ability was also introduced. Glasman's [4] LII free recall task involved conceptual classification, one of the hallmarks of LII ability. Other researchers [10, 11] had investigated this form of cognitive activity from the theoretical viewpoints of Piaget and Bruner. They employed non-verbal tasks that assessed a child's capacity for multiple classification and multiple seriation from a developmental perspective. These tasks were used in this study to identify lower-SES subjects (Ss) who generally do poorly on what Jensen referred to as LII tasks, but nevertheless may exhibit well developed conceptual abilities. It was assumed, on the basis of Cronbach's [2] arguments, that many lower SES children had adequate conceptual capabilities, which they would reveal on more verbally oriented conceptual tasks (e.g., Glasman's LII free recall task) after conceptual training. LI ability was also explored by including an LI free recall task.

The aforementioned issues led to the formulation of several empirical questions:

First: Will pretraining in simple concept

formation improve the performance of lower-SES children on more complex conceptual tasks (such as those of Glasman), as Cronbach has proposed? This is not likely when viewed from Jensen's theoretical framework. He proposed that the ability to transfer previous learning (the LII process) is a function of genetically determined factors.

Second: Will training in simple concept formation reduce or eliminate SES differences in LII performance? If Cronbach's belief is correct, a reduction of SES differences should follow from the training experience. Conversely, if Jensen's hypothesis was correct, then training would only stabilize or accentuate SES differences since these differences would be based on genetic factors.

Third: Is there a relationship between performance on the multiple classification and multiple seriation matrices (Piaget tasks) in lower-SES children and changes in LII performance as a function of training? In other words, do developmental indicators predict the effect of training? If so, are developmental indicators then a more productive way of assessing conceptual and intellectual potential among lower-SES children then Jensen-type tasks? Indeed, would Jensen's tasks alone be misleading?

Finally, is LI performance (free recall) related to SES training in concept formation, and multiple classification and seriation ability?

METHOD

Selection of Subjects

The study had three phases. The first two phases were the selection of a sample for the third phase, during which the empirical questions stated above were tested. In Phase One, 382 fourth-grade children from six public elementary schools of Prince George's County, Maryland, were passed through a series of selection techniques. Eighty-seven middle-SES Ss and 123 lower-SES Ss were selected on the basis of the Two Factor

Index of Social Position [13]. The groups differed substantially (30 IQ points) on an initial measure of LII ability similar to that which had been employed by Glasman [4]. The LII IQ measure used was a modified version of the Peabody Picture Vocabulary Test (PPVT) which correlated substantially with the conventional version of the Peabody Picture Vocabulary Test (r = .9537, p < .001). The SES groups, on the other hand, did not differ significantly on Digit Span, which Jensen [8] has cited as one of the best measures of LI ability. Therefore, the groups clearly represented the modes of the two SES populations as described by Jensen [6, 9]. If Jensen's theory was valid, these two groups would have represented two genotypically distinct samples of LII ability.

In Phase Two, the two groups were then administered the Piaget type multiple classification and multiple seriation matrix tasks. The materials and procedures employed were those described in a study by Lagattuta [10].* Over 96% of the middle-SES children achieved maximum or near maximum performance on these tasks and were called category A (A) Ss. Forty-eight percent of the low-SES children achieved an equivalent level of performance and were called category B (B) Ss. The remaining low-SES children (52%) were unable to complete the matrix tasks correctly and were labeled category C (C) Ss.

For the major part of the study, 36 Ss whose scores fell close to the mean of each category (A, B, and C) were selected, for a total of 108 Ss. The B and C Ss were equivalent on the initial LII ability measure and approximately 28 IQ points below the A Ss using the modified Peabody Picture Vocabulary Test scores (category A, mean IQ 118.75; category B, mean IQ 91.00; cate-

---

* The multiple classification task is a series of geometric forms of different colors which can be classified along the two dimensions of form and color at the same time. The multiple seriation matrix requires classification by both increasing height and geometric shape.

gory C, mean IQ 91.25). These means were within three IQ points of Glasman's [4] middle and low-SES sample means. None of the samples differed significantly on the initial LI measure, nor did they differ in age. All groups were equated on sex and race (approximately half male, half female, half black, and half white). The Ss from each category were then subdivided into two subsamples of eighteen Ss each, matched on all the measures and subject variables mentioned above (age, sex, and race). One of the subsamples from each category (A, B, and C) was randomly assigned to be trained in conceptualization, while the remaining sample did not receive conceptual training.

Final Sample and Design

The experiment in Phase Three of the study was a 3 X 2 design having 18 Ss per cell, for a total of 108 Ss. The factors were category and training. There were three categories of subjects (A, B, and C), and two conditions (trained and not trained).

Procedure

Children in the experimental condition received two training sessions in concept formation, which lasted 30 minutes each. These sessions were given by the experimenter (E), one at a time over two consecutive days. The children were trained in small groups ranging from four to six in number. The groups were heterogeneous, having at least one child from each category and no more than two children from the same category in any one group. Training during the first session involved four brief sorting exercises and four brief display exercises. The sorting exercises required children to separate a stack of picture cards into four piles according to the conceptual categories they represented (*e.g.,* food, tools, toys, and utensils). During the display exercises, E exhibited one or more pictures simultaneously, and the children took turns in suggesting a conceptual category to which the picture(s) might belong.

The second training session consisted of two sorting exercises and four display exercises, which included a few new pictures not covered in the first session. The children worked with thirteen different concepts, including two of the four concepts (animals and clothing) represented in the LII free recall task to be given later. These two concepts were not used more frequently than any of the remaining eleven concepts. *None* of the pictures used in the exercises appeared in either the LI or LII free recall tasks administered later in the study.

The children in the control condition also met with E for two sessions of identical duration to those of the trained children, which were held on the same days as the training sessions. They met in small groups of similar composition to the trained groups. The tasks they performed were unrelated to concept formation. They were a variety of recognition exercises in which the Ss had to identify pictures that were previously displayed by E. Consequently, the control Ss experienced equal contact with E and received an equal amount of experience working with picture cards. As with the trained group, none of the pictures used appeared in the later free recall tasks.

On the day following the completion of the training and control sessions, the Ss received one of the two free recall tasks (LI task or LII task). They received the second task on the next day. These tasks were individually administered to each S. The order of administration was counter-balanced; *i.e.,* half of the eighteen Ss within each cell of the design received the LI free recall task first, while the other half had the LII free recall task first.

Phase Three Measures

The LII free recall task was composed of twenty-four pictures representing four conceptual categories: animals, clothing, vehicles, and furniture. Each category consisted of six pictures (*e.g.,* animals: bear, horse, lion, etc.). The task was identical to the one used by Glasman [4], except in one respect; she employed five pictures for each conceptual category. In the current LII task a sixth picture (selected by *E*) was added to each conceptual category.

The LII free recall task was administered to each *S* individually according to the instructions and procedure described in detail by Glasman [4]. Briefly, there were five trials. During each trial, an *S* was shown all 24 pictures in random order (except that no two pictures representing the same concept were presented in sequence). Each picture was shown for three seconds, while *E* named the picture (*e.g.*, "horse"). The *S* then had a two-minute free recall period. Responses were tape-recorded.

The identical LII (conceptual) scoring techniques employed by Glasman [4] were used in the current study. The first scoring index was the LII Recall score. This was an *S*'s total recall per trial, averaged over the five trials. The second index was the LII Cluster score. An *S*'s cluster score was calculated for each trial according to the method developed by Bousfield and Bousfield [1], and then averaged over the five trials to yield a single score. The third index was the Large Cluster score. The number of triplets (three consecutive words from the same concept) occurring in each recall trial were counted and then averaged over the five trials. Glasman [4] calculated each index (LII Recall, LII Cluster, and Large Cluster) in two ways. In one method, perseverations (repetition of same word during a single free recall period) were excluded, while in a second method they were included in the calculations. Therefore, each *S* had two scores, under each index. [In the results sections, indices in which perseverations were included will be suffixed by (p)—*e.g.*, LII Cluster (p.).] Each *S* in Phase Three of the study, therefore, had six LII scores.

The LI (non-conceptual) free recall task was composed of 24 pictured objects not representing conceptual categories. The procedure and instructions were identical to those of the LII free recall task. The only scoring index for this task was the LI Recall score, calculated in the same manner described for the LII Recall score.

RESULTS

LII Free Recall

A 3 × 2 analysis of variance was performed on each of the six indices of LII (conceptual) performance. The differences in scores among the three categories (A, B, and C) on LII tasks were statistically significant for all six indices (p = <.001). These highly significant main effects for the three categories were expected, since they represented social class differences that tend consistently to emerge when variables like trainability (treatment conditions) are ignored. The statistically significant main effects were primarily based upon the simple differences between middle-class children (A *S*s) and lower-class children (B and C *S*s) that have consistently emerged in previous research on LII tasks. Glasman [4] found equally impressive SES differences yielding huge Fs reaching at least to the .001 probability level when she compared middle and lower-class fifth grade children on the same six indices of LII performance.

More importantly, however, all the 3 × 2 analyses of variance performed on each of the six LII indices yielded statistically significant category X training interaction effects. The interaction Fs on each LII scoring

Table 1. Interaction Fs and Probability Levels from Analyses of Variance on the Six LII (Conceptual) Scoring Indices

LII Index	Interaction F	df	Probability Value
LII Recall	5.02	2:102	<.01
LII Recall (p)	4.46	2:102	<.025
LII Cluster	5.12	2:102	<.01
LII Cluster (p)	7.45	2:102	<.001
Large Cluster	5.23	2:102	<.01
Large Cluster (p)	6.06	2:102	<.01

index are reported in Table 1, with their probability levels. These interactions showed that category differences could not be considered in isolation. It is necessary to consider the influence of both variables (category and training) on conceptual (LII) learning. In other words, the interaction effects make clear that the nature of conceptual performance between, for example, category A (middle-class Ss) and category B (lower-class Ss) depends upon whether or not the children of these respective categories have been trained. The interactions were then broken down to determine the meaning of these results and to answer the empirical questions posed.

The interaction effects can be seen clearly in Figure 1 and Figure 2, which show the mean scores for LII Recall and LII Cluster (p). The LII Recall means and standard deviations for the untrained Ss of categories A, B, and C were: $\overline{X}$ = 15.62 (S.D. = 1.30), $\overline{X}$ = 13.74 (S.D. = 1.23), and $\overline{X}$ = 12.62 (S.D. = 1.29), respectively. For the trained Ss they were: $\overline{X}$ = 17.49 (S.D. = 1.33), $\overline{X}$ = 16.68 (S.D. = 1.51), and $\overline{X}$ = 13.73 (S.D. = 1.47), respectively. The LII cluster (p) means and standard deviations for untrained Ss of categories A, B, and C were: $\overline{X}$ = 3.51

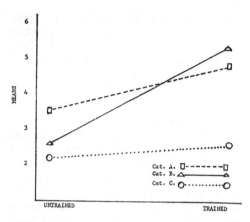

Fig. 2. Mean Number of LII Cluster (p) Units by Category for the Trained and Untrained Groups

(S.D. = 1.11), $\overline{X}$ = 2.61 (S.D. = 1.13), and $\overline{X}$ = 2.16 (S.D. = 1.08), respectively. For the trained Ss they were: $\overline{X}$ = 4.77 (S.D. = 1.28), $\overline{X}$ = 5.26 (S.D. = 1.35), and $\overline{X}$ = 2.65 (S.D. = 1.23), respectively. The means and mean profiles of the remaining four indices of LII performance followed the same patterns exhibited in Figures 1 and 2. The configuration of means for all six indices of LII performance indicated that training had the greatest effect on those lower-class children in category B, while having less of an effect on the middle-class, category A children, and the least effect on lower-class children in category C. (No child reached ever obtained the top score in any trial.) Further statistical tests were employed to break down the interactions and determine their specific significance.

Tests on the effects of training on each category were performed according to the method described by Winer [14, p. 237]. Analyses of variance for the effects of categories (A, B, and C) at each level of treatment (trained vs. untrained) were also performed by the same method. To test the differences and pattern of differences between all possible pairs of category means at either level of treatment, the Newman-Keuls procedure was used [14, p. 239]. In general,

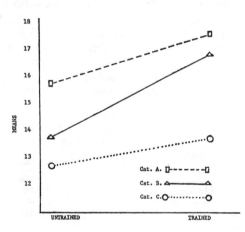

Fig. 1. Mean Number of LII Recall Words by Category for the Trained and Untrained Groups

A *S*s always scored significantly higher than did B and C *S*s when none of the *S*s were trained in concept formation. Untrained B and C *S*s did not differ significantly. Conversely, at the experimental level of treatment, where all *S*s were trained, A and B *S*s were always significantly higher than were C *S*s, but did not differ significantly from each other. Therefore, training was consistently and significantly related to improvement for B *S*s but not for C *S*s. Moreover, B *S*s were more affected by training when compared to A *S*s.

Stated another way, the results indicated that lower-class children who excelled on the matrix tasks (B *S*s) also excelled on the conceptual measures employed by Jensen, when they were trained. Without training (control condition), these *S*s showed results that would appear to support Jensen's thesis. However, when training was introduced, the lower-class B children equalled the performance of a similarly trained group of middle-class children (A *S*s) on all six scoring indices of LII ability. This finding contradicts Jensen's major thesis. The findings affirm all of Cronbach's assumptions and support his criticisms of Jensen.

LI Free Recall

A 3 X 2 analysis of variance was performed on the LI (non-conceptual) free recall scores of *S*s in Phase Three of the study. The main effects for categories or training were not statistically significant. However, the category X training condition interaction effect was significant beyond the .05 probability level. Post tests were performed to analyze the nature of the interaction. Individual cell comparisons [14] indicated that the B trained *S*s scored higher than did B untrained *S*s ($\overline{X}$'s = 13.14 and 12.20 respectively), a difference that was significant at the .05 level. The remaining four cell means differed to a much lesser extent.

Since the statistically significant interaction for LI recall followed a pattern that approximated the direction of the significant interactions found on the six LII indices, an additional question emerged. If LI and LII performance in free recall shared a portion of systematic covariance, then could the statistically significant interactions emerging for the LII indices be just as readily explainable on the basis of the systematic differences in LI ability? If the covariance between LI and LII performance was indeed substantial, then the evidence obtained from the LII indices supporting the first three empirical questions would be confounded by this relationship and difficult to interpret. It might then be suggested that the improvements on the LII free recall task that were shown by trained B *S*s were based on rote memory functions (LI learning), and not on conceptual ability (LII learning).

To investigate these possibilities, a series of 3 X 2 analyses of covariance were performed following the original 3 X 2 analysis of variance design employed in the investigation of data on the various LII indices. In each analysis of covariance, LI Recall was always the covariate and one of the LII performance indices was the criterion variable. The results of each 3 X 2 analysis of covariance were almost identical to the results of the original 3 X 2 analysis of variance involving a particular LII index. The probability levels of the main effects and interaction effects were always the same, regardless of whether a particular LII index was investigated in an analysis of covariance design, or in an analysis of variance design. The finding that many lower-class children seemed capable of functioning at the same conceptual level on these tasks was merely highlighted by these ancillary statistical checks. Many lower-class children (B *S*s) equalled the middle-class children in LII free recall on the basis of their conceptual capacities, not on the basis of rote memory capacities believed to be tapped by the LI free recall task.

Order, Sex, Race, and Concepts

A number of other variables were statistically analyzed as potential sources of variance that might have some bearing on the primary findings of the study. The variables of order of presentation of tasks (LI free recall vs. LII free recall), sex (female vs. male), race (black vs. white), and concepts (previously trained concepts vs. non-previously trained concepts) were examined separately and in combination. Because of the small sample size a comprehensive analysis of variance of these variables was not possible.

Over 40 separate analyses of variance were performed. There were no statistically significant main effects or interaction effects on the concepts that were pretrained as compared to those that were not pretrained.

A few statistically significant main effects and interactions emerged on the variables of order, sex, and race, but the patterns were highly inconsistent, and were so few in number that they did not exceed chance. There was no clear evidence to indicate that black children were different from white children in conceptual functioning when SES was systematically controlled.

DISCUSSION

The results of this study support the predictions of Cronbach [2], rather than those of Jensen [6, 7, 9]. Many of the trained low-SES, low-IQ children exhibited substantially higher LII scores than did their counterpart controls. This finding provides positive affirmation of the first empirical question and was in accord with Cronbach's [2] statement, quoted earlier, that one cannot judge capability if a child has not called upon the ability he may possess.

It was also found that lower-SES children were substantially lower in LII performance than were middle-SES children under the control (untrained) condition. Indeed, the LII recall scores of the middle and lower-SES control Ss were very similar to those reported by Glasman [4], and, taken in isolation, would appear to replicate the findings of Jensen. However, evidence of this nature proved to be exceedingly less convincing

when all of the data were taken into account. Many lower-SES children exhibited the same capacity for LII (conceptual) operations as did middle-SES children when both groups were exposed to training. These findings provided a positive answer to the second empirical question. Obviously, Cronbach's [2] belief that many lower-SES children could equal or overtake middle-class children on such measures if they were trained in the usefulness of conceptual analysis, deserves serious consideration. Jensen's statement, which asserts that lower-SES children as a group are inherently deficient in conceptual ability, appears to be highly questionable in the face of the current findings.

The experimental evidence on the third empirical question limited and refined the conclusions raised with regard to the first and second empirical questions. The multiple classification and multiple seriation matrices proved to be efficient predictors of the effectiveness of training on the LII performance among low-SES children. Specifically, the trained Ss who scored high on classification and seriation made significant gains over their counterpart untrained controls and were able to equal the middle-class level of conceptual functioning. Training had little effect among those who scored low on those two cognitive measures.

Questions arise regarding the nature of the differences between B and C children. One could speculate, for example, that the Piaget nonverbal matrices were merely more effective than the Jensen tasks in identifying the inherent conceptual inferiority of low-SES children compared with middle-SES children. This innate absence of conceptual subabilities would then explain why the C children did not improve with training. However, recent evidence [3] has shown that the times for the development of the abilities measured by Piaget tasks are themselves greatly influenced by environmental experiences. It should also be remembered that half of the low-SES children had the necessary abilities but did not use them until given a short training session. It would, therefore, seem more appropriate to explore those environmental factors in some low-SES children that delay the development of those abilities necessary to succeed on the Piaget tasks of seriation, rather than assume that the differences are genetic in origin.

With regard to the fourth question, the main effect of SES on nonconceptual performance did not emerge as significant. This corroborated the findings reported by Jensen [5, 6], in which middle and lower-SES children did not differ in LI free recall in spite of substantial SES differences in IQ. There was a significant category X training interaction on the LI free recall. It proved difficult, however, to explain why trained B Ss were significantly higher than their counterpart untrained controls, while the trained and untrained groups of A and C did not differ significantly. Interactions of this nature simply highlight the complexity of factors that might be influencing performance on these tasks and serve to caution against premature conclusions about the determinants of such performance. Of utmost importance is that the differences in LI performance were not related to differences in LII performance, and therefore did not confound the findings regarding the first three empirical questions.

The variables of order, sex, race, and age were studied. Glasman [4] confounded race and SES, making it impossible to distinguish SES differences in LII performance from race differences. Ideal designs are frequently difficult to set up, given the practical limitations imposed upon researchers. Fortunately, there were ample sampling resources for the current study to allow a careful balancing of these subject variables and avoid major confoundings. Statistical analyses were performed to study the relationship between these variables and LII performance. *The results did not support the presence of consistent, significant race differences in LII ability, when SES was adequately controlled.*

At a more general level, one of the most crucial issues was whether the current procedure allowed a valid test of LII ability. Did the introduction of training or any other procedural elements obviate this possibility? Jensen [7] described the essence of LII ability as the capacity to call upon or transfer subabilities and previous learning to a new situation or problem:

It is the appropriate calling up, integration, and transfer of various subskills that constitute what we mean by intellectual capacity. (p. 477)

The Ss in the experimental condition were trained in a very simple subability or skill, *i.e.,* verbal concept formation. They were then, from all indications, required to call upon this subability spontaneously within the context of a more complex task (LII free recall), where it had to be utilized in a new way and toward an unforeseen end, *i.e.,* enhancing recall. Furthermore, the procedure was carefully designed to go beyond the mere operationalization of Jensen's description of LII ability. It also was designed to minimize the possibility of children enhancing their LII scores on the basis of factors that would violate Jensen's [7] stated criterion for evaluating LII processes.

A significant number of lower-SES children were able to handle the conceptual operations in question, once exposed to them, and also to spontaneously transfer and integrate them appropriately. In a procedure set up to test LII capacities (as a process as well as a set of responses on an LII task), many lower-SES children did as well as middle-SES children. Why, then, was the simple form of training such a major factor in changing SES performance on the LII tasks? What did training introduce? Cronbach hinted at the need among lower SES children to experience the usefulness of conceptual analysis. Such an explanation seems plausible. However, a number of other possibilities might be generated, each of which represents a research dimension in itself. Some information was available to suggest that the shortcomings among the lower-class Ss on the LII free recall task might be, in part, a matter of specific skills rather than LII capacity or conceptual potential. After completing the final task of the study, each S was informally asked to sort the stimulus cards of the LII free recall task into groups of things that go together. As expected, all experimental Ss, regardless of category, did well. However, the performance of the untrained Ss was striking. Among A Ss, seventeen out of eighteen made perfect sorts into the four basic concepts and could verbalize the concepts afterwards. Only six of eighteen B Ss and eight of the eighteen C Ss did so. Of those few low-SES children who could sort correctly, only a few could come up with a precise concept or explanation to justify their card groupings. However, almost all the lower-SES children mastered the sorting task and provided explanations quite readily *when prompted*. These observations suggest that the middle-class children may have specific skills (for example, verbal labelling skills) and know-how that the lower-SES children do not have. Perhaps the attainment of this skill was all the B Ss needed in order to actualize their potential.

Performance deficiencies among lower-class children on LII laboratory tasks require careful and painstaking evaluation. Jensen and his colleagues have made significant contributions to exploring these cognitive deficiencies with their laboratory approach. Glasman's [4] LII free recall task proved to be a highly creative example of this form of achievement. The extent to which lower-class performance deficiencies on conceptual tasks of this sort reflect inherent cognitive deficiencies in conceptual ability is another matter, however. Certainly, the degree to which findings similar to Glasman's [4] provide validity for Jensen's genetic theory of cognitive processes has to be viewed with great skepticism in the light of the present findings. These results clearly point to the urgency for continued and extended efforts to explore the origins and functional aspects of cognitive deficiency in various groups and how they might be overcome.

SUMMARY

Jensen has asserted that socioeconomic status (SES) differences in IQ are based on genetic differences in conceptual or level II (LII) ability. He has stated that SES differences emerging on the "culture fair," LII free recall task supported this assumption. In contrast, Cronbach believed that many lower-class children are equal to middle-class children in conceptual ability and can be trained to manifest it on LII tasks.

Cronbach's assumptions were tested. Nonverbal matrix tasks were first used to assess conceptual development. Almost 96% of middle-SES children completed the matrices, as did 48% of the lower-SES children. On an LII (conceptual) free recall task, a trained group of lower-SES Ss who excelled on the matrices equalled a trained group of middle-SES children who passed the matrices. This occurred in spite of the large SES differences in IQ test scores. Untrained low-SES children scored significantly below untrained middle-SES children, regardless of matrix ability. Therefore, a significantly high number of lower-class children, who might otherwise be identified as LII deficient on such tasks, are able to reach middle-class level of functioning when trained. The findings support Cronbach's beliefs, and are in opposition to Jensen's theory that IQ differences are a function of genetic differences in conceptual ability.

REFERENCES

1. Bousfield, A. and Bousfield, W. 1966. Measurement of clustering and of sequential constancies in repeated free recall. Psychol. Rep. 19(3, Pt. 1), 935–942.
2. Cronbach, L. 1969. Heredity, environment and educational policy. Harvard Ed. Rev. 39, 338–347.
3. Furth, H. Piaget, IQ and the nature-

nurture controversy. Human Developm. (in press).

4. Glasman, L. 1968. A social class comparison of conceptual processes in children's free recall. Unpublished doctoral dissertation, University of California.

5. Jensen, A. 1961. Learning abilities in Mexican-American and Anglo-American children. Calif. J. Ed. Res. 12, 147–159.

6. Jensen, A. 1969. How much can we boost IQ and scholastic achievement? Harvard Ed. Rev. 39, 1–123(a).

7. Jensen, A. 1969. Reducing the heredity-environment uncertainty: a reply. Harvard Ed. Rev. 39, 449–483(b).

8. Jensen, A. 1969. Jensen's theory of intelligence: a reply. J. Ed. Psychol. 60, 427–43(c).

9. Jensen, A. 1970. Learning, ability, intelligence and educability. In Psychological Factors in Poverty, V. Allen, ed. Markham Publishing Co., Chicago.

10. Lagattuta, J. 1970. A developmental analysis of serial and classificatory ordering along one and multiple dimensions. Unpublished master's thesis, Catholic University of America.

11. Mackay, C., Fraser, J. and Ross, I. 1970. Matrices, three by three: classification and seriation. Child Developm. 41, 787–797.

12. Moely, B. et al. 1969. Production efficiency in young children's clustered recall. Developm. Psychol. 1, 26–34.

13. Myers, J., Bean, L. and Pepper, M. 1968. The Two Factor Index of Social Position: A Decade Later—Followup of Social Class and Mental Illness. John Wiley, New York.

14. Winer, B. 1962. Statistical Principles in Experimental Design. McGraw-Hill, New York.

The Usefulness of Cumulative Deprivation as an Explanation of Educational Deficiencies

CHARLES B. SCHULTZ and HERBERT A. AURBACH

Out of the proliferation of professional literature on the "cultural disadvantages" of the lower-class child at least one thing emerges—he does not come as well equipped to succeed in school as his middle-class counterpart. The evidence of educational deficiencies stands resolved for now at least. But there are other matters that are not resolved although they are sometimes treated as if they were. (a) Do the existent disabilities represent deficiencies in those skills and knowledges required by school or are they a genuine arrest of intellectual development? (b) If it is a matter of cognitive deficiency, does the lower-class environment merely correlate with this intellectual retardation or cause it? (c) If there is an arrest of intellectual development, is it permanent?

The discussion that follows is an attempt to make the hypothesis of cumulative deprivation more explicit by examining its theoretical and empirical bases. In questioning the cumulative deprivation hypothesis, our argument does not reject environmental influences. Rather, it doubts the permanence of educational retardation and the validity of the specific relationships that have been made between the lower-class family and important cognitive processes. We further suggest that the mediational processes central to the educational difficulties of lower-class youngsters have been developed but are not utilized by them on school and test-like tasks.

THE CUMULATIVE DEPRIVATION HYPOTHESIS: RATIONALE AND EVIDENCE

The hypothesis of cumulative deprivation asserts that the deficiencies are intellectual, that they are products of the lower-class environment, and that they tend to be permanent and irreversible. The latter point is sometimes made by implication, as in the following quotations:

The effects of lower class environment on a child's development may become even more serious during his fourth and fifth years. Furthermore, the longer these conditions continue, the more likely the effects are to be lasting (Hunt, 1964a, p. 89).

We would expect variations in environment

From C. Schultz, & H. Aurbach. The usefulness of cumulative deprivation as an explanation of educational deficiencies. *Merrill-Palmer Quarterly of Behavior and Development,* 1971, *17,* 27–39. Reprinted by permission.

to have relatively little effect on the I.Q. after age 8, but we would expect the variations to have marked effect on the I.Q. before that age, with the greatest effect likely to take place between the ages of about 1 to 5 (Bloom, 1964, p. 68).

The child who has an existing deficit in growth incurred from past deprivation is less able to profit from new and more advanced levels of environmental stimulation. *Thus, irrespective of the adequacy of all other factors—both internal and external—his deficit tends to increase cumulatively and lead to permanent retardation* (Ausubel, 1965, p. 11, our italics).

One theoretical base for the hypothesis of cumulative deprivation rests on the notions of critical periods and sensory deprivation. Since certain behaviors that cannot be acquired later are acquired at a particular stage of development (critical periods), the effects of deprivation of sensory stimulation on intellectual development are potent if not permanent at these critical times. Experiments have demonstrated convincingly that chickens won't peck, tadpoles won't swim, dogs will be stupid and shy, and chimpanzees won't see effectively when deprived of sensory stimulation at a critical period (Hunt, 1964b). The reduced intellectual capacity that results from sensory deprivation during critical periods is said to be intractable or irreversible (Bruner, 1966). Cynthia Deutsch (1964), in arguing for pre-school education, suggests that the principle of stimulus deprivation during critical or optimal times can be extended to human behavior. Thus, when deprived of stimulation at certain times, humans will not be able to recoup their intellectual losses.

A second concept used to gird the hypothesis of cumulative deprivation is the inhibitory effect of prior experience on new learning, that is, of negative transfer (Jensen, 1966a). Thus, the social environment may provide experiences that restrict the rate and direction of cognitive growth. As a consequence, the early retardation of certain

kinds of learning due to the lack of environmental opportunity has profound and cumulative effects on subsequent learning.

Ausubel's (1965) position is similar. He argues that existing deficiencies become the prior conditions which tend to keep growth rates constant. With age, the individual becomes hardened in certain intellectual channels; his degree of "intellectual plasticity" is restricted. Because of restricted rate and direction of learning, Ausubel contends, "some of this failure in developmental actualization is irreversible and cannot be compensated for later irrespective of the amount of hyperstimulation that is applied" (1965, p. 69).

Bernstein's (1967) sociological analysis of language into elaborate and restricted codes could also be considered an instance of the transfer paradigm. Here the prior condition is the reinforced use of the restricted code. Furthermore, this language code itself is a function of a particular social situation. The effect of the exclusive reliance of the lower class on this code inhibits cognitive processes that involve abstraction. The implication appears quite compelling: severe if not permanent cognitive impairment is sustained by lower-class users of the restricted code.

Bloom's (1964) examination of longitudinal studies provides further support for the hypothesis of cumulative deprivation. A number of human characteristics yield negatively accelerated growth curves; that is, they are characterized by an early and rapid development that tapers off as the individual matures. The mid-point of these curves appears to be reached about age five. It is at this time, when human growth is most rapid, that environmental influences have their greatest effect. Presumably the detrimental effects of a deprived environment early in an individual's intellectual development cannot be overcome by improved environmental conditions experienced later.

The argument of critical periods rests largely on the deprivation of sensory stimulation. The thesis of negative transfer is based on inadequate cognitive development often attributed to the home. Bloom's data describes the overall course of growth as affected by motivational and environmental influences. All three point to a lasting intellectual impairment caused by an inadequate environment. They furnish a theoretical undergirding for the hypothesis of cumulative deprivation.

Evidence supporting the hypothesis of cumulative deprivation comes from the Institute for Developmental Studies directed by Martin Deutsch and from related studies examining Bernstein's exploration of the sociology of language. Deutsch (1960), for example, related specific aspects of the social environment of Negro and white children to intellectual achievement. Using a cluster analysis procedure, Deutsch found that the "syndrome" comprised of Negro, broken home, and negative self-image had a strong, inverse relationship with a cluster of academic performance measures including reading, arithmetic, and S.A.T. scores. On the basis of these data, he observed: "The combined effect of [these] variables is probably a *major contributor* to the difference found between the performance levels of lower-class white and Negro pupils" (Deutsch, 1960, p. 17, our italics).

An important issue may be raised at this juncture. Do environmental factors, such as those identified by Deutsch, restrict only the capacity to perform the type of tasks required by the school or do they inhibit the general capacity to learn? Cynthia Deutsch (1964) found that students with reading difficulties were also deficient in auditory discrimination skills and that the poorer the reader the greater the correlation. Lower-class students with reading problems are also deficient in a basic intellectual function—the ability to differentiate and recognize auditory stimuli.

Deutsch suggests that these results can be explained by the high ratio of meaningless noise to meaningful signal in the lower-class home during a critical stage in the child's development. Unfortunately, we are not told exactly how noisy the slum environment is;

so, we cannot compute its "noise/signal ratio"; nor are we given the optimal level for learning auditory discrimination. But the implication is that because his home is too noisy, the lower-class child receives little signal and therefore little practice in any kind of auditory discrimination. In fact, he learns inattention. This results in a general impairment in his ability to discriminate auditory cues, a fundamental intellectual setback. With these studies, the Deutsches have developed two telling points: (a) specific aspects of the social environment presumably cause retardation, and (b) this retardation is of a basic sort—one that impairs the process of discrimination.

Impairment of other cognitive processes has been related to the social environment. For example, Vera John (1963) explored labeling, relating, and categorizing—tasks that involve abstraction in one form or another. She found that at the first grade level, lower-class Negroes did not perform significantly different from middle-class Negroes on tasks requiring enumeration, integration, classification, and concept sorting. By the fifth grade they were behind significantly in tasks requiring more precise and abstract language such as concept sorting. John contends that the deficiency in "the acquisition of more abstract and integrative language seems to be hampered by the living conditions in the homes of the lower-class children" (1963, p. 821).

The failure of the lower-class child to use language as a "conceptual tool" is related to Bernstein's (1962) language codes hypotheses. Because of their exclusive use of a less explicit, restricted code, lower-class children engage in less verbal planning (complex encoding-decoding processes emphasizing language). Bernstein further hypothesizes that the time a speaker spends in hesitation is an index of his verbal planning. In a study that related hesitation phenomena to social class (1962), he found that when controlled for intelligence, working-class Ss spent less time pausing during and between phrases.

Hess and Shipman (1965), experimenting with the effect of categorical statements on learning, explicitly related Bernstein's restricted and elaborate codes to family types. Middle-class mothers offered more verbal explanations which presumably accounted for the fact that middle-class youngsters learned better and were able to verbalize principles they did learn.

In summary, the work of Bernstein, John, and Hess and Shipman demonstrates that the intellectual fate of the lower-class child has been tied to his poorly developed language. The relevance of this to the hypothesis of cumulative deprivation is clear: lower-class youngsters learn an intellectually limited language which restricts their very thought process and, because of the pervasiveness of language, retards their further intellectual development. This evidence relates to the studies of scholastic achievement and auditory discrimination explored by the Deutsches. Together, these studies provide an empirical base for the hypothesis of cumulative deprivation.

SOME NAGGING DOUBTS

The logic of the hypothesis of cumulative deprivation and the conclusiveness of the findings are quite convincing to many; but, even so, doubts arise. If members of an American subculture are intellectually inferior for social rather than biological reasons, how would "backward" peoples who haven't developed a written language stack up against us? Would their restricted codes, the dearth of variety in their puzzles and games, their lack of blocks of various sizes and colors, and their generally "drab" life consign them to the status of inferior peoples? This clearly is *not* the intent of the advocates of this viewpoint, but it is an unfortunate implication. It is all too familiar but it flies in the face of history. Russians have advanced from a "backward" status to a literate and intellectually developed nation in two generations. Africans with the marks of tribal rites on their bodies compile excel-

lent records in American and British universities—a fantastic accomplishment. Many black Americans, and white Americans too, have achieved intellectual stature in a single generation despite slum origins and "deprived" sociocultural backgrounds.

We will examine further doubts regarding the rationale and the evidence of the hypothesis of cumulative deprivation by focusing on three assertions implied by that hypothesis: (a) retardation is intellectual rather than educational; (b) it is a function of lower-class environment; and (c) it is permanent.

1. *Retardation is intellectual rather than educational.* Those who hold that lower-class retardation is an arrest of intellectual development must account for the factor of value bias in the conduct of their research.* The hassle over a culture-free and culture-fair intelligence test suggests that this will not be done easily.

Failures to consider alternative interpretations of experimental findings may reflect such value biases. One example is M. Deutsch's (1960) explanation of the poor results of Negroes in the digit span backwards test. Attention span clearly is in part a function of the interest in what is being attended to and the importance attached to that task. Deutsch reported lower-class Negro children's comments about the digit span test like, "so what?" or "who cares?" or "what does it matter?" and yet he did not examine the possibility that cultural influences could account for the poor showing of black children on these tests.

In explaining her findings that lower-class black children do not discriminate auditory stimuli as well as middle-class children, C. Deutsch (1964) characterized the sounds in lower-class homes as noise. The difference

---

*A similar argument has recently been presented by Joan and Stephen Baratz (1970) in respect to early childhood intervention programs such as Headstart. They suggest that the failure of social scientists to recognize and utilize existing cultural forms of the lower-class Negro community leads to perceiving Negro children as inferior and pathological. They further argue that this represents a form of institutional racism.

between noise and signal is only a matter of attaching arbitrary, culturally established meanings to the stimuli. What is noise to Deutsch may be signal to a lower-class Negro child. And it may not. In order to substantiate her explanation, the actual noise/signal ratio of the lower-class Negro child must be established in terms of the child's perspective.

Moreover, Deutsch's findings are not necessarily evidence of poor auditory discrimination. Subjects who use a dialect that tends to slur endings of words and, perhaps, who may recognize words as much by their context and inflection as by their sound would be expected to do poorly on the Wepman test. They did. It was the final phoneme that distinguished whites from Negroes. In addition, the words themselves may be more familiar to one group than another.

The imaginative effort of Hess and Shipman (1965) to substantiate Bernstein's theory using a learning task rather than merely correlating test data is also open to question. The superior results of the middle-class Negro children may be a function of factors other than verbalization with their mothers. Both experimental tasks, sorting blocks and the etch-o-sketch problem, utilized common toys which is one version or another may be found in more affluent homes. Thus, the results may be more a function of practice than verbalization. Also, the atmosphere of a university may provide a more stressful testing situation for lower-class mothers than for their middle-class counter-parts.

Hess and Shipman assume that the best parental instruction is that which verbally provides the essential information the child needs to solve a problem, and that it is best measured by successful completion of the task. Assuming verbal explanation as the best means of instruction is certainly open to question. It may be that the four-year-old, lower-class child learns independence and problem coping at the expense of completing the task. Reissman (1962) distin-

guished between the slow-gifted learner characteristic of the lower-class and the poor learner. He argued that society emphasizes speed to the advantage of quick, bright students and to the disadvantage of the slow-gifted. Independence and problem coping may be important dependent variables not considered by Hess and Shipman.

2. *Retardation is a function of lower-class environment.* In the Hess-Shipman study the adult role is central to establishing lower-class environment as the cause of deprivation. It is for others too. Hunt states that "continuing development appears to demand a relationship with adults who enable the infant to pursue his locomotor and manipulative intentions and who answer his endless questions of 'What's that?' " (Hunt, 1964a, p. 89). Martin Deutsch (1963) also emphasized the adult role in the child's intellectual development. John and Goldstein (1964) posited that the acquisition of labels requires verbal interaction with corrective feedback of a special sort—the kind that adults provide.

Yet the relative unavailability of adults to lower-class children could be questioned as could the instrumentality of their function in lower-class language and cognitive development. It could be argued that since the black household is often an extended family, the black child has "multi-mothers," a variety of familiar surrogate mothers who would have the effect of widening the child's range of curious interests in human behaviors and so facilitate the development of cognitive skills especially during infancy.

The larger size of many lower-class families, the reduced sibling rivalry among their children, and the authority given to older brothers and sisters in caring for the young, all suggest that much learning could result from interaction among older siblings—not adults. Also, Lewis (1968) found that when the child is relatively young the urban Negro mother surrenders parental control to authority outside the home, presumably the peer group society of the street. Black youngsters, and probably white lower-class children too, may learn much from people other than the adults in their families and it is probably well learned because of its relevance to their lives.

Another problem lies with the data used to undergird the alleged causal relationship between educational achievement and social environment. Measurement of the environment must be made before relationships are established, *but we simply do not now have adequate and precise devices to measure the social environment* (Bloom, 1964). Even so, sweeping conclusions are sometimes reached on the basis of limited data. There seems no direct support for Strom's (1964) assertion that: "Where no father is present during the evening, there is usually no organized meal, no organized opportunity for language exchange, no real interaction. A common result is a cumulative deficit in the language component of a child's development" (pp. 191–192). Deutsch (1963) also relates cognitive deficiencies to the lower class without the kind of rigorous environmental measure Bloom proposes.

Visually, the urban slum and its overcrowded apartments offer the child a minimal range of stimuli. There are usually few if any pictures on the wall, and objects in the household, be they toys, furniture, or utensils, tend to be sparse, repetitious, and lacking in form and color variations. The sparsity of objects and the lack of diversity of home artifacts which are available and meaningful to the child, in addition to the unavailability of individualized training, gives the child few opportunities to manipulate and organize the visual properties of his environment and thus perceptually to organize and discriminate the nuances of that environment (p. 170).

A number of questions could be asked of this passage. Do the objects seem repetitious and lacking in form to the middle-class observer or to the lower-class child? Who delimits the range of stimuli, the observer or the observed? What is the optimal range of stimuli? Even granting the similarity among stimuli, would this produce greater acuity of visual discrimination or breed inattention? One might also wonder how representative these observations are. These questions do not deny the influence of environment on an organism; they caution that the specific relationship between environmental variables and selected intellectual capacities has not been established, partly due to the present inability to measure the environment.

The establishment of a causal relationship between educational retardation and lower class suffers from important weaknesses. Most notable are exclusive reliance on adult-child relations, difficulties in measuring the lower-class environment, and the descriptive rather than experimental nature of the studies. Regarding this latter point, much of the data tying cognitive deficiencies to the lower-class environment is based on correlations which at best can only suggest cause. Rosenhan (1967) is one of the few authors to note that extreme caution is required in suggesting a causal relationship.

3. *Retardation is permanent.* The application of critical periods and sensory deprivation to lower-class students implies permanence because certain stimuli are purported to be effective only during that critical stage. This thesis has been doubted by others; these objections will be little more than recorded here.

Ausubel (1964) argued against the application of critical periods to human learning. The critical periods hypothesis has been validated only in infant, infrahuman species. Furthermore, it has not been demonstrated that optimal readiness exists at any particular age period for specific kinds of intellectual development. In fact, it is Ausubel's claim that adults are superior to children in ability to learn when they are equally unsophisticated.

Bereiter and Englemann (1966) are caustic in their rejection of sensory deprivation as applicable to the human condition. The major neurological effects of sensory deprivation occur only in early infancy when nerve cells are not fully developed. Furthermore, the amount of deprivation is drastic, far beyond any that can occur in normal life. Finally the subjects in sensory deprivation experiments are not able to seek increased stimulation, unlike free organisms which tend to maintain optimal levels of stimulation.

It is our contention that experiments dealing with imprinting during the "critical period" offer a poor analogy to the lower-class home. It is submitted that immobilizing tadpoles with chloretone or keeping baby chicks in total darkness is not comparable with the vital family life of the lower-class infant even if a comparison among species can be made.

Whether retardation is permanent depends on what is retarded. Perhaps deficiencies in social studies achievement, punctuation skills, or even reading skills could be more easily overcome than an intellectual arrest, that is, the inability to perform such cognitive operations as discrimination, mediation, and concept formation. Further, the identification of the most instrumental deficiency, one that when corrected will best facilitate improvement in other areas, is important in assessing the permanency of deprivation. The difficulty of this task is attested to by the array of over one hundred variables listed and studied by Deutsch (1965).

Jensen (1968a) constructed a continuum with associative learning at one end (Level I) and concept formation and problem solving, two processes involving mediation, at the other (Level II). Controlling for IQ, Jensen found that lower-class, low IQ children were superior to those of the middle class in Level I learnings and that there was little difference between the middle and lower class with high IQ's on these skills. Differences became apparent at Level II, indicating that, if an impairment exists, it is with mediational processes. He contended these skills are necessary for the attainment of educational potential because of their broad transferability to other tasks (Jensen, 1966b). The issue of permanence is placed in sharper perspective by identifying mediational skills

of lower-class youngsters as the cognitive process that may be both impaired and instrumental for other learning.

The difficulties lower-class children have with Level II tasks may not be due to their inability to engage in mediation or even acquire appropriate mediators. Rather, lower-class youngsters may not produce mediators for school and test-like tasks, even though they have acquired and can use such mediators for other purposes. Evidence supporting the production deficiency hypothesis (Flavell, Beach, & Chinsky, 1966) is analogous to the mediational difficulties of the lower-class child. That hypothesis holds that younger children have acquired the ability to mediate and the mediators necessary for a particular task, but do not produce mediators at the appropriate and necessary points in the task as do older children. This is exactly the categorizing difficulties Jensen (1969) reports for lower-class children. However, with instructions and training, mediation does occur and is used to aid younger children's cognitive operations such as memory (Moely, Olson, Halwes, & Flavell, 1969). Perhaps, what Flavell and his colleagues found for younger children may also be true for lower-class and black youngsters, i.e., they also may be subject to the facilitative effects of similar instructions and training.

It could also be argued that poor results of lower-class youngsters on tasks requiring mediation may not reflect a low level of learning (they have acquire; mediators and can mediate) but a low level of performance (they do not mediate with certain tasks). As learning (they have acquired mediators and more "self-initiated activity" is necessary, suggesting that greater motivation is required. If so, the lower motivation of the lower-class child (Katz, 1967) would yield a depressed growth curve that would show relatively rapid improvement with reinforcement. Moreover, most of the acquisition of mediators and skill in their use may be incidental. "Most mediational processes take place subvocally below our level of awareness" (Jensen, 1966b). It seems reasonable to hypothesize that lower-class youngsters have incidentally acquired mediational skills which they do not produce and use on school and test-like tasks. If this is the case, it seems incorrect to speak of their difficulties as permanent.

ALTERNATIVE DIRECTIONS

The hypothesis of cumulative deprivation needs to be made more explicit, and its power to explain subjected to systematic experimentation. One tack would be replication of earlier studies with experimental paradigms. These efforts should manipulate variables of the learning-teaching situation rather than correlate test results with social class antecedents. When conducting such replications the effects of value bias should be eliminated.

A more fruitful tack to test the hypothesis of cumulative deprivation would be the direct examination of verbal mediation. Characterizing the problem as one of verbal mediation has several advantages. First, it allows for theoretical reevaluation. When Bernstein described covert verbal planning employed by users of the elaborate codes as "inner verbal sequences below the threshold of incipient articulation" in problem solving (1967, p. 243), it sounded like Jensen's (1966b) description of verbal mediation as being sub-vocal and below the level of awareness. It may be that the difference in verbal planning for the restricted and elaborate codes is one of facility with verbal mediation. If this were the case, some fundamental aspects of Bernstein's theory would need further exploration. His theory might be embellished by a sharper focus on cognitive differences between users of the two codes. On the other hand, it might minimize the role of the social context of language if verbal mediation processes are found to be easily learned or even to be already acquired by members of the lower class. If "verbal planning" and verbal mediation are similar, if not identical, processes, and if lower-class

speakers do mediate on topics relevant to them, it would seem that Bernstein's scheme should explain this.

Hess and Shipman's (1965) characterization of cultural deprivation as deprivation of meaning also relates to mediation. Since verbal mediators serve as vehicles for meaning, the ability to mediate is an index of the existence of deprivation. Verbal mediation also figures in the explanation of John and Goldstein (1964) for the failure of lower-class youngsers to acquire words with "low stability," such as action words. The acquisition of these labels, they suggest, requires greater corrective feedback by means of adult interaction. Through this process the child "fits" the label to varying forms of action that he has seen or experienced. The more the forms vary, the lower the stability of the word. In this sense, the label or word could be considered a mediator and the John-Goldstein assertion seems to be that lower-class children have not acquired the ability to establish mediative connections among many acts that they actually experience.

Furthermore, the verbal mediation approach helps clarify the direction for instructional applications. If lower-class students cannot mediate, a cognitive orientation is suggested with instructional sequences designed to teach this skill. If they can mediate—that is, they have learned but do not perform this skill with school subjects—an affective orientation is suggested with a motivational emphasis.

Finally, and most relevant to this discussion, the consideration of verbal mediation makes a body of psychological and sociological theory and experimental procedures available to facilitate the examination of the hypothesis of cumulative deprivation. Jensen (1968b) employed just such an approach in which the reversal-nonreversal shift was used to compare lower-class Mexican-American and Anglo-American children. The findings indicated that among the Mexican-Americans there was less evidence of mediation even though both groups preferred the reversal condition, which suggests that both employed mediation.

There is another variable that could be operating to account for the results Jensen reported and may facilitate the production of mediators, namely, motivation. Perhaps the non-mediators were unmotivated. Their performance may have been depressed by the lower expectations that teachers or experimenters held for them. That such lower expectations are communicated to both *S*s and students and that this affects their performance has been suggested by Rosenthal (1968). Moreover, the effects of approval and disapproval are most extreme on the more alienated lower-class and Negro younsters (Rosenhan, 1966).

The motivational variable is central to the test of the hypothesis of cumulative deprivation. By manipulating motivation in experimental tasks requiring mediation, the extent of cognitive deficiency can be clarified and the adequacy or inadequacy of the hypothesis of cumulative deprivation to explain educational retardation can be further revealed.

In the face of the present, unsettled research, it is difficult to justify school programs that assume that the educational deficit is intellectual, that it is caused by the lower-class environment, and that the phenomenon is permanent. These assumptions underlie characterizations such as "deprived" and "disadvantaged." The logic of the self-fulfilling prophecy suggests that the use of these labels in programs designed to uplift lower-class youth ironically would have a debilitating effect. In addition, the case for permanency has been oversold in the concentration on pre-school and head-start programs. The feeling seems to be that learning disabilities must be corrected before school or in the early grades if they are to be corrected at all. Overriding commitments to the pre-school program at the expense of comparable attention to the upper grades has produced unbalanced programs. Such commitments reflect premature acceptance of the hypothesis of cumulative deprivation.

Rather, efforts should be devoted to the full range of elementary and secondary levels. An important component of these efforts would be a candid, self-examination of teacher attitudes toward impoverished and black youth.

REFERENCES

Ausubel, D. P. How reversible are the cognitive and motivational effects of cultural deprivation? *Urb. Educ.*, 1964, 1, 16–38.

Ausubel, D. P. The effects of cultural deprivation on learning patterns. *Audiovisual Instruction*, 1965, 10, 10–12.

Baratz, J. C. & Baratz, S. S. Early childhood intervention: the social science base of institutional racism. *Harvard Educ. Rev.*, 1970, 40, 29–50.

Bereiter, C. & Englemann, S. *Teaching the disadvantaged child in the preschool.* Englewood Cliffs, N.J.: Prentice-Hall, 1966.

Bernstein, B. Linguistic codes, hesitation phenomena, and intelligence. *Lang. & Speech*, 1962, 5, Part I, 31–46.

Bernstein, B. Social structure, language, and learning. In A. H. Passow, M. Goldberg, & A. J. Tannenbaum (Eds.), *Education of the disadvantaged.* New York: Holt, Rinehart, & Winston, 1967.

Bloom, B. S. *Stability and change in human characteristics.* New York: Wiley, 1964.

Bruner, J. The cognitive consequences of early sensory deprivation. In J. L. Frost & G. R. Hawkes (Eds.), *The disadvantaged child.* New York: Houghton Mifflin, 1966.

Deutsch, C. P. Auditory discrimination and learning: social factors. *Merrill-Palmer Quart.*, 1964, 10, 277–296.

Deutsch, M. Minority group status as related to social and personality factors in scholastic achievement. *Soc. Applied Anthro. Monogr.*, 1960.

Deutsch, M. The disadvantaged child and the learning process: some social psychological, and developmental considerations. In A. H. Passow (Ed.), *Education in depressed areas.* New York: Teachers College Press, 1963.

Deutsch, M. The role of social class in language development and cognition. *Amer. J. Orthopsychiat.*, 1965, 35, 78–88.

Flavell, J. H., Beech, D. H., & Chinsky, J. M. Spontaneous verbal rehearsal in a memory task as a function of age. *Child Developm.,* 1966, 37, 283–299.

Hess, R. & Shipman, V. Early blocks to children's learnings. *Children,* 1965, 12, 189–194.

Hunt, J. McV. The psychological basis for lectually. *Children,* 1964a, 11, 83–91.

Hunt, J. McV. The psychological basis fr using pre-school enrichment as an antidote for cultural deprivation. *Merrill-Palmer Quart.,* 1964b, 10, 209–248.

Jensen, A. R. Cumulative deficit in compensatory education. *J. school Psychol.,* 1966a, 4, 37–47.

Jensen, A. R. Verbal mediation and educational potential. *Psychol. in Schools,* 1966b, 3, 99–109.

Jensen, A. R. Intelligence, learning ability, and socio-economic status. Paper read at the annual meeting of the American Educational Research Association, Chicago, Feb. 8–10, 1968a.

Jensen, A. R. Social class and verbal learning. In M. Deutsch, I. Katz, & A. R. Jensen (Eds.), *Social class, race, and psychological development.* New York: Holt, Rinehart, & Winston, 1968b.

Jensen, A. R. How much can we boost I.Q. and scholastic achievement? *Harvard Educ. Rev.,* 1969, 39, 1–123.

John, V. P. The intellectual development of slum children: some preliminary findings.

Amer. J. Orthopsychiat., 1963, 33, 813–822.

John, V. P. & Goldstein, L. S. The social context of language acquisition. *Merrill-Palmer Quart.,* 1964, 10, 265–275.

Katz, I. Some motivational determinants of racial differences in intellectual development. *Internat. J. Psychol.,* 1967, 2, 1–12.

Lewis, H. Child rearing among low income families. In L. A. Ferman, J. L. Kornbluth, & A. Haber (Eds.), *Poverty in America.* Ann Arbor: Univer. of Michigan Press, 1968, pp. 433–443.

Moely, B. F., Olson, F. A., Halwes, T. G., & Flavell, J. H. Production deficiency in young children's clustered recall. *Develop. Psychol.,* 1969, 1, 26–34.

Reissman, F. *The culturally deprived child.* New York: Harper & Row, 1962, ch. 7.

Rosenhan, D. L. The effects of social class and race on responsiveness to approval and disapproval. *J. Pers. & Soc. Psychol.,* 1966, 4, 253–259.

Rosenhan, D. L. Cultural deprivation and learning: an examination of method and theory. In H. L. Miller (Ed.), *Education for the disadvantaged.* New York: Free Press, 1967.

Rosenthal, R. & Jacobson, L. *Pygmalion in the classroom.* New York: Holt, Rinehart, & Winston, 1968.

Strom, R. D. The school dropout and the family. *Sch. & Soc.,* 1964, 92, 191–192.

Middle-Class Misperceptions of the High Life Aspirations and Strong Work Ethic Held by the Welfare Poor

LEONARD GOODWIN

Important persons in our country believe that the welfare poor do not want to work. Academicians such as Banfield [1] claim that the poor have a deviant psychology that militates against work. Political leaders such as Russell Long, chairman of the powerful Senate Finance Committee, suggest that welfare recipients are looking for a handout rather than wanting to earn their way [5]. And even the President of the Unted States [9] takes the poor to task for not having the work ethic. Such views are consistent with those of middle-class persons in general. A nationwide survey [3] conducted for the National Advisory Committee on Civil Disorders showed that whites attribute the low status of Negroes to their lack of motivation. A recent national survey by Feagin [4] indicates that a large proportion of Americans believe that many welfare recipients could be out working.

The deprecating view of the middle class toward the poor has been confirmed but its validity challenged in this author's previous writings [6, 7, 8]. He found that welfare recipients—black and white, male and female, teenager and adult—maintain as strong

a work ethic and as high life aspirations as do middle-class employed persons. The present paper presents additional data that illuminate the psychological adaptation of poor people to failure in the work world and the kind of misinterpretations that stand in the way of middle-class people comprehending the situation of the poor. More specifically, there will be a three-way comparison of responses to sets of items measuring life and work orientations. Responses of welfare recipients will be compared with those of middle-class persons, and both sets will be compared with additional responses that two of the middle-class groups make when they put themselves in the place of welfare recipients. On the basis of this analysis it is possible to suggest what kind of help the poor do and do not need from the middle class.

THE RESPONDENTS

Mothers of the three family groups described below were interviewed in their homes in the Baltimore area (1968–70), providing a range of respondents from long-time welfare re-

From L. Goodwin. Middle-class misperceptions of the high life aspirations and strong work ethic held by the welfare poor. *American Journal of Orthopsychiatry*, 1973, *43*, 554–564. Copyright © 1973, the American Orthopsychiatric Association, Inc. Reprinted by permission.

cipients to affluent suburbanites. (Data on other family members are not presented here, but can be found in earlier reports [6, 9].)

1. Two hundred sixty-seven (267) long-term welfare mothers who had teenage sons, lived in the inner city, and had been on welfare the longest period of time in Baltimore. Names of the mothers were drawn from the Baltimore Department of Welfare's list of Aid to Families with Dependent Children recipients, beginning with those who had been on welfare the longest period of time and who had teenage sons. The average number of years on welfare was sixteen. Only blacks were chosen from this group because over 95% of long-term welfare recipients in Baltimore were black. This group was interviewed by persons of differing race, class, and sex in order to test for possible bias in responses, as explained later.

2. One hundred seventy-five (175) white mothers who lived within the limits of Baltimore, but outside the inner city. They were members of families that contained a father and a teenage son or daughter. The families were chosen on an area probability basis from census tracts into which black families had been moving, representing lower-middle to middle-middle income white families. (Data on the black families also interviewed from these census tracts have been presented elsewhere [6].)

3. Two hundred ten (210) white mothers who lived in the affluent suburbs of Baltimore, and were members of families containing a husband and teenage child. Families were selected on an area probability basis from census tracts that showed an average income in 1960 of about $10,000. The mothers were asked for their own work orientations and then for the orientations they would project for a woman on welfare who had entered a work-training program.[1]

4. Nine hundred fifty-seven (957) black welfare mothers enrolled in the Work Incentive Program (WIN) were interviewed in group sessions at six sites across the country.[2] These mothers were attempting to obtain training and jobs through the federally supported program, and hence from an important comparison group to the long-term welfare mothers. The WIN mothers also approximate the description given to suburban Baltimore women for their projection of the work orientations of the poor.

5. One hundred thirty-three (133) staff members of the WIN program, coming from the same sites as trainees were asked to complete the same sets of questions as trainees, but by putting themselves in the place of the average (female) trainee in their particular program. A key aspect of this paper is to

1. The statement read by the interviewer to the middle-class interviewee with respect to projecting the rating of a welfare mother was as follows: "I now would like you to put yourself in the position of another person and answer some questions the way you think this person would do so. In particular, think of a mother who is living on welfare in the inner city. She is about 30 years old, has three or four children and no husband is present in the house. This woman, however, has recently enrolled in one of the work-training programs designed to train her for a job. Now, I would like you to answer some of the earlier questions about life and work the way you think this welfare mother would do so."

2. Responses only from black WIN trainees are reported because projections made by the Baltimore suburban mothers and the WIN staff (group 5) are generally based upon that group. That is, most of the WIN mothers in this study—and all of them from Baltimore—are black. This occurs because the study focused on northern metropolitan centers rather than looking at a random sample of WIN trainees across the entire country. The number and location of black female trainees are as follows: 567 from Baltimore and District of Columbia in the East; 229 from Detroit and Milwaukee in the Midwest; 161 from Seattle and the San Francisco Bay Area in the West. Similarity of responses to the scales by these geographic subgroups indicated that they could be combined into a single group [6]. (There were a total of 228 white WIN mothers coming primarily from the West.) Trainees completed the questionnaire shortly after entering WIN. This was done in group sessions in which staff members read the questionnaire, item by item, to the trainees, each of whom had a copy in front of her. After completing the questionnaire, the trainee placed it in a stamped envelope addressed to the project director. Less than one percent of trainees refused to complete the questionnaire or returned unusable ones, although only about 80% of those expected on a given day actually appeared.

Table 1. Characteristics of Respondents[a]

Characteristics	Long-Term Welfare Mothers	WIN Mothers	Outer-City Mothers	Suburban Mothers	WIN Staff[b]
Age	43	29	45	44	35
Years of schooling	8	10	12	13	15
Number of children	3.9	2.8	3.0	2.5	X
Currently employed (percent)	14	X	56	45	100
Dollars per hour	1.80	X	2.60	3.30	X
Total family job income (dollars per year)	2,800	X	11,200	16,000	X
Years on welfare	16	3	X	X	X
Number	267	957	175	210	133

[a]All figures are averages except number of cases.
[b]Sixty percent of this WIN staff is female.

compare the projections of the staff with those of the suburban mothers and, in turn, with the actual responses of WIN trainees. When data were first gathered from staff (1969), only the projected ratings were requested. Afterward, it seemed desirable to have the ratings given by staff for themselves. Visits were made again to WIN sites a year later (1970) and staff asked to complete the questionnaire for themselves. Only 48% of the 147 second-time respondents had completed the original set of questions projecting the views of trainees. This indicates a high turnover among staff. But demographic characteristics of both sets of staff respondents were similar, and no significant correlations appeared between ratings given the second set of responses about one's own orientations and whether or not one had completed the first set of questions.

Certain demographic characteristics of the several groups are presented in Table 1. Differences between the welfare and nonwelfare groups are clear. The latter are much better educated and have the capability of earning much more money. The high educational level of the WIN staff indicates that most of them are middle class. With respect to the two welfare groups, one would expect differences in orientation between them because

of differences in age, education, and years on welfare. But greater differences should separate the welfare from the nonwelfare mothers.

ASPIRATIONS AND AVOIDANCES

Each respondent gave ratings to items that had been clustered into reliable scales that measured several different orientations toward life and work.[3] Among the items were a series dealing with life aspirations and avoidances. These were rated on a four-step ladder that was labeled "Worst Way of Life" at the bottom and "Best Way of LIfe" at the top. The items included, for example, "Having a job that is well paid," along with its converse, "Having a job that pays very little." In the process of clustering items into scales, most of these pairs of items split so that the positive statement emerged on the scale called Life Aspirations and the negative

3. A series of factor analyses of several thousand responses marked the initial step in clustering the items into scales. The clustering was done separately for poor and nonpoor groups in order to be sure that poor people were not interpreting the same items in a fundamentally different way from nonpoor people. No differences were observed. Reliabilities of all scales are above .60. Creation and properties of the scales are discussed at length in an earlier report [6].

statement on the one called Life Avoidances. The score of a person on each scale is the average of his scores on the individual items comprising it.

Table 2 presents mean values of the several groups on these and other scales. For Life Aspirations, the mean values of the different groups answering for themselves are approximately the same. The same holds for Life Avoidances. Hence the experience of failure does not seem to have dimmed the overall level of aspirations of welfare mothers or to have made them different from middle-class persons with respect to avoiding negative events.

Certain differences between welfare and nonwelfare mothers do emerge, however, when the rank orders of life aspirations and avoidances are examined. Admittedly, it is risky to rank order ratings on individual items because of low item reliabilities; however, attention will be given only to large differences in rank ordering and to overall correlations between rank orders of groups. Table 3 presents the rank order of all groups for both aspirations and avoidances.

Both sets of welfare mothers rank the goal of a well paid job above half the other goals, whereas outer-city and suburban mothers, who are more affluent, rank it near the bottom. Welfare mothers give high rank to "Having a nice place to live," while low rank is given his item by the nonwelfare mothers who already live in a nice environment. A similar trend is seen with respect to having a good education. Welfare mothers, with little education, rank it very high whereas the other mothers—especially the suburban mothers who have the highest education of all—rank the goal much lower. Respondents appear to be influenced in their rankings by their own social-economic circumstances. The results argue for the poor wanting to have what the more affluent already possess.

Table 2. Mean Values for Orientations[a]

Orientation	Long-Term Welfare Mothers	WIN Mothers	WIN Staff[b]	Outer-City Mothers	Suburban Mothers
1. Life aspirations	3.66[c]	3.75	3.58 (3.32)[d]	3.71	3.62 (3.32)[d]
2. Life avoidances	1.38	1.48	1.41 (1.54)	1.39	1.44 (1.53)
3. Work ethic	3.21[c,e]	3.45	3.10 (2.87)[d]	3.34	3.22 (2.69)[d]
4. Lack of confidence in ability to succeed	3.13	2.77	2.29 (2.81)	2.61	2.36 (3.12)[d]
5. Acceptability of welfare	2.92	2.28	1.86 (2.27)	1.51	1.60 (2.78)[d]
Number	267	957	147 (133)	175	210 (210)

[a]All items making up each orientation were rated on four-step ladders. The higher the rating the more strongly the orientation is held. Differences between means of .33 or more points are both large and statistically significant beyond the .01 level of probability.
[b]Projected ratings for WIN mothers given by this group appear in parentheses below the rating given for itself.
[c]Adjusted for bias from interviewer's race. Interviewers with different characteristics were used to test whether respondents were biasing their answers. Lower ratings were given to black as against white interviewers. The former were taken as more valid and used in computing mean values.
[d]Difference between projected mean value and that of the WIN mothers is at least .33 points.
[e]Adjusted for bias from interviewer's class. The ratings given to lower class interviewers (high school dropouts) used for the mean value.

Table 3. Rank Order of Life Aspirations and Life Avoidances

Life Aspirations	Life Avoidances	Numbered Rank Order[a]				
		Long-Term Welfare Mothers	WIN Mothers	Projected by WIN Staff	Outer-City Mothers	Suburban Mothers
1. Having good health.	Being in poor health.	1–3	4–4	3–3½	1–4	1–2
2. Having a good education.	Having very little education.	2–10	1–5	7–10	4–9	9–9
3. Having a husband who supports you and your family.	Having a husband who does not support you and your family.	3–2	10–1	4–5	3–2	X–X[b]
4. Having a nice place to live and plenty of food.	Being poor.	4–6	3–3	1–1	10–12	8–11
5. Getting along well with your family.	Having difficulties with your family.	5–9	9–14	8–7	5–6	2–5
6. Having a job that is well paid.	Having a job that pays very little.	6–11	6–6½	2–2	12–13	10–12
7. Being honest.	Being dishonest.	7–1	2–6½	13–6	2–1	3–1
8. Making this a better world to live in.	Not helping to make this a better world.	8–7	7–8	12–14	7–7	6–7
9. Having a job that you like.	Having a job that you do not like.	9–12	5–11	6–12	9–11	4–8
10. Having important goals in life.	Having no important goals in life.	10–4	8–2	10–11	6–3	5–3
11. Helping other people.	Not caring about other people.	11–8	12–10	14–13	8–8	7–6
12. Getting along with your neighbors.	Living in a place where you don't get along with your neighbors.	12–13	13–12	11–9	13–10	11–10
13. Having a regular job.	(None)[c]	13–X	11–X	9–X	11–X	12–X
14. Having plenty of money to get what you want.	Not having enough money to buy the things you want.	14–14	14–13	5–3½	14–14	13–13
15. (None)[c]	Your friends do not respect you.	X–5	X–9	X–8	X–5	X–4

[a] In each column of figures the numbered rank of each life aspiration is followed by the rank of the corresponding life avoidance, separated by a dash. Rank 1 for aspirations indicates the goal is most desired; rank 1 for avoidances indicates the goal that is least desired.

[b] This item was inadvertently omitted from the questionnaire for suburban mothers.

[c] The counterpart item to the aspiration (or avoidance) item did not cluster on the Life Aspiration or Life Avoidance scales during the statistical analysis, and hence has been omitted.

Similarities among rankings provide an important insight into the work orientation of mothers. All mothers assign low priority to having a regular job. Higher priority is given to having the support of a husband. The goal of good family relations, moreover, is placed higher than a regular job. Hence the chronically poor as well as the affluent mothers appear to see themselves as something other in the family than just a breadwinner. Efforts at moving welfare women into the work force may lose sight of the important fact that many mothers feel their role in the home is important.

The relatively low rank given by WIN women to having the support of a husband may be explained by their relatively recent negative experience of having to go on welfare—based perhaps on the desertion of a male provider. It is necesary in this context to note that WIN mothers rank the having of a husband who does not support you as the situation to be most strongly avoided— ranked 1 on the Life Avoidance scale.

The relation between aspiration and avoidance rankings is of special interest. Looking down these pairs of rankings for welfare and nonwelfare mothers (Table 3), one gets the impression of more consistency of response among the latter. Take for example the pair of items: "Getting along well with your family," and "Having difficulties with your family." The difference in the ranks given these two items is greater for the welfare groups. They seem to be saying that it is desirable to have good family relations, but if there are difficulties it is not a disaster. The nonwelfare mothers seem to be saying that not only is it desirable to have good family relations, but family difficulties are something of a disaster.

The overall consistency between aspiration and avoidance rankings in a group can be tested by examining the product-moment correlations between rankings. Table 4 shows that the rank order correlations for the middle-class mothers are substantially higher than those for the welfare mothers— about .86 versus about .48. There is, then, a

general tendency among the poor to regard certain aspirations as important to fulfill, but to regard lack of fulfillment as not having serious impact on their lives.[4] Rodman [10] noted a similar occurrence several years ago. He found that lower-class persons held the higher-class values about the importance of legal marriages, but simultaneously believed that violation of those values—living together and having children outside of formal marriage—was also acceptable.

The interpretation offered here is that persons who aspire to a given goal but also express little regret about not obtaining it, or are willing to accept contrary goals as well, are protecting themselves from feelings of failure. That is, one way of coping with inability to fulfill important goals is to play down their significance and perhaps show apathy about their fulfillment. The psychology of this kind of situation is discussed in the literature on adaptation to failure and fear of failure [2].

Testing of this interpretation would require further empirical study. It would be necessary, for example, to determine whether those trainees with large discrepancies in rank ordering show signs of apathy about fulfilling goals. It is not unlikely that WIN trainees give certain cues that are interpreted by middle-class staff as indications of not wanting to work. The staff, as seen in Table 2, project a mean value for Life Aspirations that is substantially below that expressed by the trainees themselves. The nature of staff misperceptions is made clearer by examining the projected rank ordering of aspirations and avoidances in Table 3.

Staff, reasonably enough, believe that WIN

4. One might argue that the low rank order correlations for the poor groups may be merely the result of their tending to rate the aspiration and avoidance items at random on the 4-step ladder. Such a possibility is ruled out by the fact that the items cluster into the same scales for the poor and the nonpoor and the reliability of the scales for the poor is even greater than for the nonpoor. See reference [6].

Table 4. Rank Order (Product-Moment) Correlations Involving Life Aspirations and Avoidances Items[a]

Orientation	Long-Term Welfare Mothers	WIN Mothers	Outer-City Mothers	Suburban Mothers	WIN Staff Projections
Life Aspirations versus Life Avoidances	.52	.45	.86	.87	.78
WIN Staff Projected Life Aspirations versus Life Aspirations of WIN Mothers	X	.26	X	X	X
WIN Staff Projected Life Avoidances versus Life Avoidances of WIN Mothers	X	.23	X	X	X

[a]These correlations are based on the rankings given to items that appear both as life aspirations *and* life avoidances—a total of 13 pairs for all groups except suburban mothers, where the number is 12.

mothers put greater stress upon money. They project a Life Aspiration rank 1 for "Having a nice place to live and plenty of food," and a Life Avoidance rank 1 for the converse item, "Being poor." This is not far from the actual rankings, which are both 3. What staff fail to realize is that WIN women's concerns go beyond money. These women give top rank to the positive goal of "Having a good education." Staff project a rank of only 7. "Making this a better world to live in," is projected by staff to have a rank of 12, whereas the WIN mothers give it a rank similar to other mothers—7. The greatest discrepancy between staff and trainee rankings comes with the item, "Not having enough money to buy the things you want." Staff believe that trainees strongly reject such a supposition, and project a ranking of 3½. Trainees, like all the other mothers, give this item a very low rank—13.

The low overall correspondence between staff projects and WIN trainee rankings is seen in the low rank order correlations in Table 4—around .24. The relatively high correlation between staff projected aspirations and avoidances—.76—points to the middle-class belief in the symmetry of aspirations and avoidances and so to a further misperception of the poor.

WORK ETHIC AND OTHER ORIENTATIONS

Another series of fifteen items was designed to measure identification of self with work. Among the items, rated on a 4-step ladder labelled "Agree" at the top and "Disagree" at the bottom, were: "Getting recognition for my own work is important to me;" "I feel good when I have a job;" "Success in an occupation is mainly a matter of how much effort you put into it." These items define what is generally meant by the Work Ethic, the extent to which one's respect is bound up with work.

Table 2 reveals that the WIN and long-term welfare mothers hold as strong a work ethic as do the nonwelfare mothers. WIN staff and suburban mothers project decidedly lower means for WIN mothers than actually observed. The middle-class groups deny that welfare recipients have strong work ethic. What underlies that view is illuminated by considering the relation between work ethic scores and those of two other orientations.

Table 5. Selected Correlations Among Orientations

Variables Correlated	Long-Term Welfare Mothers	WIN Mothers	Outer-City Mothers	Suburban Mothers	WIN Staff[a]
Work Ethic versus Lack of Confidence	.26[b]	.22[b]	.08	.15 (−.36)[b]	.05 (−.27)[b]
Work Ethic versus Acceptability of Welfare	.07	.03	.01	−.06 (−.39)[b]	−.30[b] (−.32)[b]

[a]Correlations in parentheses are between variables whose values have been projected for WIN mothers. The other correlations are for the respondents themselves.
[b]Significantly different from zero beyond the .01 level of probability.

The first of these other orientations consists of eight items that measure lack of confidence in ability to succeed in the work world.[5]

It is also reasonable to expect that those who score high in lack of confidence, with its emphasis on luck and other people providing success, would score low in work ethic, with its emphasis on achievement of success through one's own efforts. Negative or zero correlations should appear between the two orientations. Table 5 presents these correlations for the several groups. Essentially zero correlations are observed for middle-class groups answering for themselves. However, significant *positive* correlations are observed for the two welfare groups.

Among the poor, those with higher work ethic exhibit greater lack of confidence. How is this result to be explained? All welfare women experience economic failure, and must subsist on inadequate incomes provided by the government. There is an additional failure, however, for those who score high on the work ethic. For them, inability to succeed in the work world lowers their feeling of self-worth because they are unable to participate in an important activity. Women with low work ethic scores, on the other hand, do not find their self-worth challenged by failure in the work world. This means that just those poor women with the strongest work ethic have the greatest lack of confidence in their abilities, and this interplay accounts for the positive correlation between the two orientations. It is being suggested, in short, that poor people cope with high work ethic by losing confidence in themselves.

A crucial point is that middle-class persons—both WIN staff and suburban mothers—miss this interpretation altogether. The correlations projected by them between work ethic and lack of confidence are significant and *negative*. Work ethic is seen to carry with it for the poor a feeling of strong confidence in self. And, conversely, middle-

5. The items were rated on a 4-step ladder labelled "Agree" at the top and "Disagree" at the bottom. Some mention money: "The most important part of work is earning good money." Others mention sources of success: "Success in an occupation is mainly a matter of luck." Why should extreme emphasis on money and a belief in external forces controlling success cluster on the same scale? The interpretation made is that persons who are extremely concerned about money, who view it as the most vital occupational goal, tend to have little of it or to be uncertain about their ability to maintain an adequate income. (This is not to say that affluent people in secure jobs have no concern about money, but that after achieving a certain level of economic security, persons become more interested in other, non-monetary goals). Persons who strongly believe that such things as luck control success also are expressing an uncertainty about, or lack of confidence in, their own efforts. Hence, a high score on this orientation indicates low confidence in one's ability to achieve success in the work world.

class persons mistakenly tend to see a great lack of confidence among poor people as an indication of their low work ethic.

A similar misperception is observed with respect to the orientation measuring the acceptability of welfare. Five items comprise the scale, including the following which are rated on a 4-step ladder that is labelled "Best Way of Getting Enough to Live On" at the top and "Worst Way of Getting Enough to Live On" at the bottom: "Being on welfare;" "Having the government send you enough money every week." The correlations between ratings on this scale and the Work Ethic scale are essentially zero for both sets of welfare mothers (see Table 5). The WIN staff and suburban mothers, however, project strong negative correlations. They seem to be saying that persons who are accepting of welfare have low work ethic. Such a view is unsupported by data from the poor themselves.

It is clear from Table 2 that welfare recipients are much more accepting of welfare than are middle-class respondents. This seems in keeping with their precarious economic position. And it has been shown in another report [6] that acceptance of welfare increases as WIN trainees fail to get jobs—experience another failure in the work world. Hence high scores tend to be the direct result of negative environmental encounters. Middle-class persons appear to take a perverse view of the situation. To them, the greater the acceptance of welfare and lack of confidence of poor people, the greater the evidence that these people lack work ethic.

SUMMARY AND CONCLUSIONS

Persons who have failed in the work world, such as welfare recipients, reasonably might be expected to lower their aspirations and work ethic. For them to bring their aims into line with reality would seem appropriate. It is here that middle-class persons tend to go wrong, failing to recognize the importance to the poor of maintaining major cul-

tural images. Rather than deny important life aspirations, welfare recipients play down the negative effects of not fulfilling such aspirations. Rather than deny the work ethic, welfare recipients tend to lose confidence in their efforts to succeed. These adaptations may result in poor people appearing to be apathetic, lacking interest in trying to succeed in the work world. Such apathy as exists may stand in the way of further effort. The point is that it results from the experience of failure rather than from low work ethic, as middle-class persons mistakenly believe.

Middle-class persons who hope to help the poor, such as counselors or trainers, are unlikely to do so if they misperceive the orientations of the poor. Most welfare recipients do not need to have their level of aspirations or work ethic raised. They desperately need experiences of success in the work world. It would be worthwhile to help overcome the lack of confidence or dependency of welfare recipients in order to help them complete training that would *assure* them access to decently paid jobs. Such "helping" efforts become destructive when there are no jobs, or no better jobs, at the end of the line.

While research on the orientations of the poor should continue, it is necessary to study the perceptions of those who would help the poor. Especially important is study of how perceptions change—for example, what kinds of events alter the orientations staff hold about trainees—and the relation between accuracy of perception and effectiveness of program action.

REFERENCES

1. Banfield, E. 1970. The Unheavenly City. Little, Brown, Boston. (pp. 45 ff, 211 ff)
2. Birney, R., Burdick, H. and Teevan, R. 1969. Fear of Failure. Van Nostrand-Reinhold Co., New York (p. 200 ff)
3. Campbell, A. and Schuman, H. 1968. Racial Attitudes in Fifteen American Cities: Supplemental Studies for the

National Advisory Commission on Civil Disorders. U.S. Government Printing Office, Washington, D.C. (pp. 29–38)

4. Feagin, J. 1972. American welfare stereotypes. Soc. Sci. Quart. (March): 921–933.

5. Goodwin, L. 1973. Bridging the gap between social research and public policy: welfare, a case in point. J. Appl. Behav. Sci. 9(Feb.):85–114.

6. Goodwin, L. 1972. Do the Poor Want to Work? Brookings Institution, Washington, D.C.

7. Goodwin, L. 1972. How suburban families view the work orientations of the welfare poor: problems in social stratification and social policy. Soc. Problems 19(Winter):337–348.

8. Goodwin, L. 1971. On making social research relevant to public policy and national problem solving. Amer. Psychol. 26(May):431–442.

9. Nixon, R. 1971. Remarks of the President at the Republican Governors' Conference. Office of the White House Press Secretary, Washington, D.C. (April 19)

10. Rodman, H. 1966. Illegitimacy in the Carribean social structure: a reconsideration. Amer. Sociol. Rev. 31 (Oct.):673–683.

The New Jersey Graduated
Work Incentive Experiment[1]

DAVID N. KERSHAW and FELICITY SKIDMORE

On June 30, 1967, the Office of Economic Opportunity approved a grant to the Institute for Research on Poverty of the University of Wisconsin, to undertake a controlled experiment in negative income taxation in conjunction with Mathematica, Inc., a research firm in Princeton, New Jersey. The central question the experiment hoped to address was the cost of a nation-wide guaranteed annual income as determined by the extent to which families would reduce their work effort in response to negative income tax payments. It was also expected that the experiment would provide policy makers with estimates of the administrative costs of such a program.

The first 14 months of the grant were spent in planning, the next four years in the actual operating phase of the experiment, and the final 16 months in the analysis of the data collected and the production of the final report. The experiment cost a total of 8 million dollars, of which about one-third (2.7 million dollars) went for cash payments to the participating families.

The basic criterion for eligibility to participate in the experiment was twofold. First, the family had to contain an able-bodied male aged between 18 and 58, who was neither going to school full time, nor institutionalized, nor in the armed forces. Second, the family's normal or expected income could not be more than 150 percent of the official poverty line. Originally enrolled in the experiment were 1,216 such families— 725 in the experimental groups and 491 in the control group. They were enrolled sequentially in four sites, as follows:

August, 1968—Trenton, New Jersey

January, 1969—Paterson-Passaic, New Jersey

1. This paper draws heavily from two sources: David N. Kershaw and Jerilyn Fair (Eds.), *Operations, Surveys and Administration*, The Final Report of the New Jersey Work Incentives Experiment, Volume IV, Institute for Research on Poverty Monograph Series, Academic Press, 1976; and Felicity Skidmore, "Operational Design of the Experiment," in Joseph A. Pechman and P. Michael Timpane (Eds.), *Work Incentives and Income Guarantees: The New Jersey Negative Income Tax Experiment.* Copyright © 1975 by The Brookings Institution, Washington, D.C. Section 3, on the results, uses statistical material from Harold Watts and Albert Rees (Eds.), *Central Labor Supply Response*, Volume I, Final Report of the New Jersey Graduated Work Incentive Experiment; and *Summary Report: New Jersey Graduated Work Incentive Experiment*, U.S. Department of Health, Education, and Welfare, December, 1973.

Excerpted from *The New Jersey Graduated Work Incentive Experiment* by David N. Kershaw and Felicity Skidmore, Mathematica, Inc., Princeton, New Jersey, 1974. Reprinted by permission.

June, 1969—Jersey City, New Jersey

September, 1969—Scranton, Pennsylvania

In October, 1969, 141 additional families in Trenton and Paterson-Passaic were added to the control group.

The operating phase of the experiment lasted three years in each site. Each family in the experimental groups filled out an Income Report Form every four weeks which formed the basis for calculating their payments. The payments were thus recalculated every four weeks, and the family received the indicated amount in two bi-weekly checks. These transfer payments were ruled by the Internal Revenue Service to be non-taxable.

A negative income tax plan is defined by a guarantee level (the level of payment the family receives if its other income is zero), and a tax or reduction rate (the rate at which the payment is reduced for each dollar of other income). Eight such negative income tax plans were finally chosen for the experiment (combinations of three tax rates and four guarantee levels), as follows:

Plan	Guarantee (Percent of Poverty Line)	Tax Rate (Percent)
I	50	30
II	50	50
III	75	30
IV	75	50
V	75	70
VI	100	50
VII	100	70
VIII	125	50
Control Group	0	0

In addition to the negative income tax transfer payments, every family receiving payments was paid a bi-weekly amount of $10 (included in their regular check) in return for sending in the Income Report Form. The controls were paid $8 a month for sending in a small card giving their current address. Every three months, an hour-long interview was administered to controls and experimentals alike, for which they were paid $5. All these other payments were considered as taxable income, unlike the negative income tax payments themselves.

Every effort was made to use the mails for sending these forms and payments back and forth, because the experiment was explicitly designed to minimize, in contrast to welfare, discretionary personal contact with the families. It was found essential, however, to have a field office at every site to deal with the filing problems that did arise.

From the beginning, the personnel administering the interviews were completely separate from those dealing with the report and payments forms. Two different names were in fact used for the two groups in an effort to underline their independence in the eyes of the families. The Payments Group was called the Council for Grants to Families (a registered trade name), and the Interviewing Branch was entitled Urban Opinion Surveys (a name now applied to an entire division of Mathematica).

The 12 regular quarterly interviews provided the main data source for the experiment. They were approximately one hour long and included two sections: a 20-minute section repeated every time on the labor force status and participation of all family members 16 years of age and older, and a 40-minute section that varied by quarter and covered at differing frequencies other kinds of economic behavior items such as expenditure and debt accumulation, plus information on health and social behavior. In addition to the quarterly interviews there were four special one-shot interviews: (1) a short screening interview, simply designed to assess eligibility for inclusion in the experiment; (2) a "pre-enrollment" interview, to collect extensive baseline data on all the families selected, before they were actually enrolled; and (3) a follow-up interview administered three months after the last transfer payment, designed to explore labor force behavior after payments had ended and to determine the families' understanding of the experiment and their reactions to the interviews and the transfer payments (for experimentals only). . . .

RESULTS FROM THE NEW JERSEY EXPERIMENT

. . . The Technical Papers in the Final Report of the experiment provide extensive, rigorous, and sophisticated statistical analyses of the labor-supply results that we shall not attempt to summarize here. Instead we shall include tables showing treatment-control differentials as estimated by regression analysis for the Summary Report on the experiment released by HEW, along with parts of the commentary on the tables also contained in that report. These regressions include as control variables age, education, number of adults, number and ages of children, sites, and pre-experiment family earnings and labor supply.

Husbands' Labor Supply

Table 1 shows treatment-control differentials of married male heads of households for four measures of labor-supply response—labor force participation, employment, hours, and earnings—for the middle eight quarters of the experiment. The striking features of these results are that all the differentials are small in both absolute and relative terms—none exceed 10 percent of the control mean and most are less than five percent—and all are statistically insignificant (i.e., one cannot rule out the possibility that these differentials occurred purely by chance). There are no findings here to indicate a significant reduction in labor supply resulting from the experimental payments. Moreover, many of the differentials (including all of those for blacks) are positive, indicating greater labor supply among husbands

Table 1. Husband Totals: Regression Estimates of Differentials in Labor Force Participation, Employment, Hours, and Earnings for Quarters 3 to 10[1]

	Labor Force Participation Rate[2]	Employment Rate	Hours Worked per Week	Earnings per Week
White				
Control group mean	94.3	87.8	34.8	100.4
Absolute differential	−.3	−2.3	−1.9	.1
Treatment group mean	94.0	85.5	32.9	100.5
Percent differential	−.3	−2.6	−5.6	.1
Black				
Control group mean	95.6	85.6	31.9	93.4
Absolute differential	0	.8	.7	8.7
Treatment group mean	95.6	86.4	32.6	102.1
Percent differential	0	.9	2.3	9.3
Spanish-speaking				
Control group mean	95.2	89.5	34.3	92.2
Absolute differential	1.6	−2.4	−.2	5.9
Treatment group mean	96.8	87.1	34.1	98.1
Percent differential	1.6	−2.7	−.7	6.4

[1] The data for this table consist of 693 husband-wife families who reported for at least 8 of the 13 quarters when interviews were obtained. Percent differentials are computed using the mean of the control group as base.
[2] This includes those employed and unemployed. Someone is unemployed if he is actively seeking employment, waiting recall from layoff or waiting to report to a new wage or salary job.
Note: For a complete explanation of the data and methods used for these calculations, please refer to the *HEW Summary Report* (December, 1973).

in the treatment group than in the control group. It is also worth noting that the means for both groups indicate that the vast majority (approximately 95 percent) of the husbands were labor force participants, working, when employed, close to full time (37 to 40 hours per week).

The further statistical refinements on the data for husbands pursued in the Technical Papers still found no significant treatment effect for whites and blacks. They did, however, uncover a small but statistically significant decrease in labor force participation on the part of Spanish-speaking husbands. Significant treatment effects were again found for Spanish-speaking husbands for hours worked per week. If one evaluates the estimated response function[2] for an average Spanish-speaking husband on a plan with a basic benefit equal to the poverty line and a 50 percent implicit tax rate, the treatment effect on weekly hours worked is a reduction of 3.2 hours (mean hours worked by Spanish-speaking control husbands were 34.3). A similar calculation for white husbands yields a statistically significant reduction of 2.4 hours per week. For black husbands there was once again no significant treatment effect.

Much of the reduction in hours among Spanish-speaking husbands can be accounted for by declines in their employment rate (that is, the fraction of all Spanish-speaking husbands in the experimental population who were employed). This implies that Spanish-speaking husbands were unem-

ployed more when in the treatment group, a result which is given independent confirmation when data on unemployment are analyzed directly. For white husbands, whose hours were reduced as noted above, the employment effect was small (and positive) so that all the experimental effect would appear to be in hours worked per week for those at work. As yet we do not know if this result arises from less overtime work, a reduction in multiple job holding, or some other source.

Viewing the results by experimental plan, it was found that the reduced labor supply for Spanish-speaking husbands varied, as we would expect, with the implicit tax rate— higher implicit tax rates produced substantially stronger disincentives. For whites the reverse was true—the largest disincentives were estimated for plans with the lowest implicit tax rates. In neither case was there a strong or consistent ordering by basic benefit level; indeed, the most generous plan (125-50) showed the smallest treatment effects. Overall, then, the experiment produced no consistently significant effects by implicit tax rate or basic benefit. These results do not, of course, allow prediction of the labor supply effects of implicit tax rates or basic benefits outside the range employed in the experiment—that is, implicit tax rates below 30 percent or above 70 percent, or basic benefits less than 50 percent, or greater than 125 percent of the poverty line.[3]

By far the most surprising result of the analysis for husbands is the complete failure to find any significant effect for blacks, despite the fact that black husband-wife families received slightly larger average payments than the other two ethnic groups. Indeed, the estimated supply response for blacks is not only insignificant, but preponderantly positive. The data indicate that earnings of the black control group increased more

2. The "response functions" on which the results presented in this section are based are regression equations relating the labor supply response variables to a set of control variables and the basic benefit levels and implicit tax rates of the experimental plans. These regressions were estimated using data from all continuous husband-wife families, in all plans and the control group. By inserting specific values of the control and treatment variables in these equations, one can predict the labor supply response of a particular type of family on a particular plan. References to responses under a specific plan are based on this type of calculation. In general, these predictions will be more precise than those based only on data from families in a particular plan.

3. Even results for the 70 percent tax rate must be interpreted skeptically, because (as mentioned above) of the very small numbers of families in the 70 percent tax rate cells who were below their breakeven point and not receiving welfare.

Table 2. Wife Totals: Regression Estimates of Differentials in Labor Force Participation, Employment, Hours, and Earnings for Quarters 3 to 10[1]

	Labor Force Participation Rate[2]	Employment Rate	Hours Worked per Week	Earnings per Week
White				
Control group mean	20.1	17.1	4.5	9.3
Absolute differential	−6.7*	−5.9*	−1.4	−3.1
Treatment group mean	13.4	11.2	3.1	6.2
Percent differential	−33.2	−34.7	−30.6	−33.2
Black				
Control group mean	21.1	16.8	5.0	10.6
Absolute differential	−.8	−.3	−.1	.8
Treatment group mean	20.3	16.5	4.9	11.4
Percent differential	−3.6	−1.5	−2.2	7.8
Spanish-speaking				
Control group mean	11.8	10.7	3.4	7.4
Absolute differential	−3.8	−5.2	−1.9	−4.1
Treatment group mean	8.0	5.5	1.5	3.3
Percent differential	−31.8	−48.3	−55.4	−54.7

[1],[2] See notes to Table 1.
*Significant at the .95 level (two-tailed test).

slowly over the course of the experiment than those of the other control and treatment groups. Thus, when treatment-control comparisons are made for blacks the differential in favor of the treatment group is noticeably large. This kind of finding for blacks is not limited to husbands; it recurs in the analysis of other components of the household. We have no plausible explanation for this outcome.

The Labor-Supply Response of Wives

Table 2 shows the regression results for wives—predominantly negative labor supply differentials. These were small in absolute magnitude, but, because of the low levels of market supply of wives, these differentials represent relatively large percentage differentials—at least for white and Spanish-speaking wives.[4] Even so, only two of the differ-

entials shown in the Table—those for labor force participation and employment rates of white wives—are statistically significant. This lack of significance reflects the small absolute size of the differentials and the small sample sizes of working wives in each of the three ethnic groups; for example, in any given survey week there were only about 15 working wives among the Spanish-speaking families in the entire sample. It is important to note that the labor supply of wives in the experiment as reflected by both of these measures, particularly labor force participation, are well below their average values for the population as a whole. For example, the pre-enrollment labor force participation rates of 16.0 percent and 13.4 percent for treatment and control wives, respectively, are less than one-half their values for all married women in the population. This re-

4. The means presented in the tables are averages over *all* individuals within a given group, including non-workers. Corresponding means for workers only can be readily calculated from the numbers

presented. For example, while all white wives worked an average of 26.3 (4.5/.171) hours per percent of the control group who were employed worked an average of 26.3 (4.5/.171) hours per week.

sults from the way in which the sample was selected. Only families with income less than one and one-half times the poverty line were admitted to the sample. Therefore, families with multiple earners had a low probability of selection. In addition, because the poverty line is adjusted upward as family size increases, the higher-income families in the experiment were likely to have larger families and younger children. Both these factors lead to an underrepresentation of working wives. Because pre-enrollment labor supply was quite small the absolute differentials seem large indeed in percentage terms.

In distinguishing among experimental plans, as was done in the Technical Papers, responses were generally consistent with expectations. For all wives the estimated negative response is consistently larger the more generous the plan, and the differences in response by plan are usually significant. A similar comparison by implicit tax rates found larger effects the higher the implicit tax rate, but these differences were usually small and never significant.

The estimated effects on labor supply of wives are subject to two rather different interpretations. The average estimated reduction in labor-force participation for all wives referred to above is 3 percentage points; for white wives it is 8 percentage points. These do not represent large absolute changes taken alone. But, because the mean participation rate for all control wives is only 17 percent, the estimated percentage reduction in labor supply for all wives in the treatment group (compared to controls) is 20 percent, and, for white wives, it is a sizeable 50 percent.

It should be noted that these estimated effects may be larger than those to be expected in an otherwise similar but permanent income maintenance program. For the control families, no more than 19 percent of wives were in the labor force in any one quarter, but 41 percent were in the labor force in at least one of the 13 quarters (counting pre-enrollment). In other words, this is a group that enters and leaves the labor force frequently. The experimental treatment creates a strong incentive to concentrate periods out of the labor force during the life of the experiment. A permanent program might therefore be expected to have a somewhat smaller impact.

The Family

Table 3 shows similar mean labor-supply differentials for the family as a whole—preponderantly negative but again relatively small.[5] In no case do the differentials exceed 14 percent of the control mean, and most are less than 10 percent. All the differentials for white families except for the earnings measure are statistically significant, while none of those for black or Spanish-speaking families are significant.

Earnings is particularly important as a labor supply measure for the family in that it provides a natural way to value or weight the hours worked by different family members; the weight is the wage rate of each member. Unfortunately, there is a possible bias in the experiment's measurement of the earnings variable not present in the other measures. Treatment families filled out an income report form every four weeks, while control families did not. The treatment families may therefore have learned more quickly than control families that what was to be furnished was gross rather than net earnings (that is, earnings before taxes and other deductions, *not* take-home pay). If this were the case, earnings in the treatment group (since gross exceeds net) would appear greater, relative to control earnings, than they actually are. This differential learning process could have caused a spurious differential in earnings in favor of the treatment group, especially during the early part of the experiment. Therefore, the results for hours worked and labor-force participation may be more reliable than for earnings.

5. Family means and differentials include the labor supply of all workers in the family, not just husband and wife.

Table 3. Family Totals: Regression Estimates of Differentials in Labor Force Participation, Employment, Hours, and Earnings for Quarters 3 to 10[1]

	Number in Labor Force per Family[2]	Number Employed per Family	Hours Worked per Week	Earnings per Week	Percent of Adults in the Labor Force, per Family	Percent of Adults Employed, per Family
White						
Control group mean	1.49	1.30	46.2	124.0	57.6	51.1
Absolute differential	−.15*	−.18*	−6.2*	−10.1	−5.3*	−6.1*
Treatment group mean	1.34	1.12	40.0	113.9	52.3	45.0
Percent differential	−9.8	−13.9	−13.4	−8.1	−9.1	−12.0
Black						
Control group mean	1.38	1.17	41.7	114.0	54.3	46.9
Absolute differential	−.07	−.07	−2.2	4.1	−1.6	−1.6
Treatment group mean	1.31	1.10	39.5	118.1	52.7	45.3
Percent differential	−5.4	−6.1	−5.2	3.6	−2.9	−3.3
Spanish-speaking						
Control group mean	1.15	1.04	39.0	102.4	48.9	44.7
Absolute differential	.08	−.02	−.4	5.0	2.4	−1.0
Treatment group mean	1.23	1.02	38.6	107.4	51.3	43.7
Percent differential	6.7	−1.5	−.9	4.9	5.0	−2.2

[1,2] See notes to Table 1.
*Significant at the .99 level (two-tailed test).

In the more sophisticated analysis in the Technical Papers, hours worked and earnings both showed a significant reduction for white families, ranging from 8 to 16 percent for hours and 8 to 12 percent for earnings. For blacks, the earnings effects were significantly positive, rising by 9 to 13 percent. Effects on hours worked by black families are small and show no consistent pattern; in one analysis a decline of 3 percent was found, while in another an increase of 1 percent appeared.

For Spanish-speaking families estimates of significant hours reductions in the neighborhood of 2 percent to 6 percent were found, while earnings were estimated to fall anywhere from 2 percent to 28 percent. These estimates are based on evaluation of the estimated response functions for families in plans with a 50 percent implicit tax rate.

In parts of the analysis the statistically predicted variance of family income was included as a control variable. This variable represents the fluctuation in income over time—for example, from $200 per month in February to $600 per month in July for a construction laborer. Such a variable was included for two reasons. First, families with variable income may have weaker attachments to the labor force, and therefore the experimental payments may have a stronger effect on their behavior. Second, variation in income gives the family experience with the effect of the implicit tax rate on the level of payments. This variance of income measure had a highly significant effect on the labor supply of whites. The more variable was income, the more labor supply declined. Other ethnic groups did not evidence such behavior.

The results for white families are thus consistent with those from the separate analyses of husbands and wives in that significant negative effects on labor supply are found. For blacks, the results again show predominantly positive responses, though not consistently so for hours worked. For Spanish-speaking families, the labor supply effects are negative, though generally smaller and less significant than for whites.

SUMMARY OF FINDINGS

There was no widespread withdrawal from work on the part of the experimental group. This is clear from the fact that average benefit payments to the experimental families increased over the period of the experiment by less than the cost-of-living correction built into the benefit calculation. In the first year of the experiment, the average four-weekly payment was $92. In the third year this had increased by only 3.8 percent, to $96.

The most important group for any national income maintenance policy with respect to the potential cost of such a program is that constituted by the non-aged able-bodied males with family responsibilities. These are the people with the most solid attachment to the labor force. These are the people with the most labor to withdraw. These are the people about whom there is the most widespread fear that, given an income alternative, they will decide not to work. As it turned out, the effect for this group was almost undetectable. Over the central two years of the experiment (the period least contaminated by start-up and end effects), the employment rate for male family heads in the experimental group was only 1.5 percent less than that for the controls. For the number of hours worked per week the difference amounted to just over 2 percent. For earnings per week the experimentals actually were higher by 6.5 percent. This finding is at least partly spurious, due to a probable accelerated learning effect whereby experimentals learned to report gross rather than net earnings faster than controls. It also appears partly due to the fact that the younger and better-educated experimentals were able to use the insurance provided by the payments to look for (and find) better, more stable, jobs.

The second group in terms of policy interest is the wives. The average family size in the sample was six, so these wives must be considered on the average to be mothers of four children. These wives had lower labor force participation than the national average, about 15 percent working at any survey point. For this group the differential between experimentals and controls was substantial, with experimental wives working 23 percent fewer hours per week than controls, their employment rate being 24 percent less, and their average earnings per week 20.3 percent less. This should not be regarded necessarily as an adverse outcome, given the fact that wives in six-person families work very hard inside the home, and that this work could well be more beneficial (cost-effective) from a national point of view than low-wage market labor. It should be noted, in addition, that although this relative reduction is large, it in fact starts from an average figure of only 4.4 hours a week. So from the point of view of family labor supply and national costs, it is not a large absolute change.

This brings us to total family labor supply—a composite of market work by the husband, the wife, and other adult family members. Predictably, these estimates lie between those for husbands and wives. Over the central two years, the number employed per family was 9.5 percent less for experimental families than controls. The hours worked per week per family were 8.7 percent less for experimentals than controls. The average earnings per week were almost the same. This disincentive was almost entirely made up of relative work withdrawal by secondary earners—wives who decided to work more inside the home, teenagers who may have been enabled by the payments to stay in school longer, and older workers who were able to take it a bit easier. As such, the disincentive effect may well be considered to be socially useful.

The analysis has shown a persistent difference in response according to ethnic groups—white, Black, and Spanish-speaking. Such disincentive as was found for husbands was restricted mainly to whites. The substantial disincentive for wives was also largely due to white wives. For both males and females the Spanish-speaking showed more disincentive than the Blacks, who showed none. No satisfactory explanation has yet been found for this difference. It is apparent that Black controls had an unusually bad labor-market experience in the last year of the experiment, both compared with Black experimentals and with the controls from the other two ethnic groups. Further research is underway to try and pin down the causes for this ethnic difference.

Response in areas other than labor force participation were generally slight. In the area of expenditures, the experimentals showed a tendency to move from public to private rental housing, and to buy relatively more homes. They also bought somewhat more furniture and other durables, and consequently incurred more debt.

In the area of psychological and sociological responses, the effects were negligible. Cash assistance at the levels involved in this study does not appear to have a systematic effect on the recipients' health, self-esteem, social integration, or perceived quality of life, among many other variables. Nor does it appear to adversely affect family composition, marital stability, or fertility rates.

What we can say with certainty is that these benefits represented a net increase in family income, allowing these families greater command over material goods and services, and enhancing their economic well-being. The anti-poverty effectiveness of the payments was not seriously vitiated by offsetting reductions in earnings due to reduced work effort.

Hiring, Training, and Retaining the Hard-Core Unemployed:

A Selected Review

PAUL S. GOODMAN, PAUL SALIPANTE, and HAROLD PARANSKY

Many organizations are involved in programs to hire, train, and retain the so-called hard-core unemployed (HCU),* and recent years have seen an increasing amount of research on this problem. The purpose of this paper is (*a*) to provide a conceptual framework which serves to organize these research studies and (*b*) to evaluate what has been learned and what directions for future research are needed.

One hundred and ninety-two articles on training or employing the HCU (private sector only) were examined; 28% (54) of these related to firms' experiences in HCU programs. From this group 44% (24) were selected on the basis of an empirical criterion, that is, they presented some systematic analysis between independent variables (e.g., type of training, individual differences) and criterion variables (e.g., turnover).

*It is difficult to precisely define the term "HCU" as used in these studies because of lack of information. However, a general characterization would be: the HCU is a member of a minority group, not a regular member of the work force, has less than a high school education, is often under 22 and of a poverty level specified by the Department of Labor.

CONCEPTUAL FRAMEWORK

The HCU worker operates in a complex social system. The focal organization providing the training and job, community organizations, government agencies, informal peer groups, and the HCU worker's family are all components of this social system that bear on the HCU worker's behavior. Within each organization there are role relationships and other structural properties (e.g., type of job available, promotion opportunities, pay level) that directly affect the HCU worker's behavior. Recognition of these multiple factors seems necessary in order to understand the HCU worker. Too often, researchers have defined a very limited social system composed primarily of the HCU worker, trainer, and supervisor (cf. Goodman, 1969a).

A social system implies not only multiple variables, but the interdependence of these variables. Change in one variable has a complex effect on the other dimensions. A major theme in most HCU studies is that change should be focused primarily on the HCU worker—that is, how to change him to fit (i.e., be retained by) the organization. A

From P. Goodman, P. Salipante, & H. Paransky. Hiring, training, and retaining the hard-core unemployed: A selected review. *Journal of Applied Psychology* 1973, *58*, 23–33. Copyright 1973 by the American Psychological Association. Reprinted by permission.

social system model focuses on a broader perspective—what changes at the individual, organizational, or societal level are necessary to provide employment opportunities for the HCU worker.

An expectancy-performance model may also be used in viewing the HCU literature. Basically, this model holds that behavior is a product of the expectancies about behavior-reward contingencies and the attractiveness of these rewards. High retention rates would occur, then, when workers believe that remaining on the job leads to desired rewards, whereas leaving the job does not. Recent studies (cf. Heneman & Schwab, 1972) on the relationship between expectancies and rewards seem to indicate that these concepts are useful predictors of work behavior and that, therefore, they should be applicable to HCU worker behavior.

The basic thesis of this framework is that the HCU worker operates in a complex social system. The multiple factors in this social system affect his expectancies about behavior-reward contingencies and the relative attractiveness of these rewards. These expectancies and rewards, in turn, combine to determine the propensity of the HCU worker to remain on the job and to produce.

This review is organized around different dimensions of the social system that are arranged in terms of levels of social analysis. First, data relevant to individual factors are examined and then other levels of analysis, such as role and structural characteristics of the organization, are examined. The expectancy-performance component is then employed to explain the findings on the relationships between the individual or structural factors and the behavior of the HCU worker.

INDIVIDUAL CHARACTERISTICS

Age

In a study of 347 HCUs in a large manufacturing company's program for hiring and retaining the disadvantaged, Quinn, Fine, and Levitin (1970) report that termination after

job placement was greater for HCUs under 21 (50%) than for those over 21 (37%); age was not related to turnover during the prejob training. In a study of a similar HCU program, Hinrichs (1970) reports a greater turnover for trainees under 21 during training, after training, and 2 years after the training program. Greenberg (1968), Gurin (1968), Rosen (1969), Shlensky (1970), Lipsky, Drotning, and Fottler (1971), Davis, Doyle, Joseph, Niles, and Perry (1973), and Kirchner and Lucas (1972) report a similar relationship between age and dropouts during a training program. In terms of our model, younger HCU workers probably experience greater feelings of distrust toward the focal organization (Clark, 1968). Accordingly, they would perceive lower expectancies about the likelihood of receiving rewards and would be more likely to leave. Older workers probably have higher expectancies and a greater desire for the rewards (i.e., regular salary) that are contingent on attendance. Only Allerhand, Friedlander, Malone, Medow, and Rosenberg (1969) report no relationship between age and any of the criterion variables. There is not enough information on the comparability of this study with other studies we reviewed to determine why the results of Allerhand et al. differ from the other findings on age.

Sex

The evidence indicates that female job retention is significantly higher than the retention of males (Davis et al., 1973; Greenberg, 1968; Gurin, 1968; Shlensky, 1970). Females are also more likely to have a job at the completion of training (Lipsky et al., 1971). Only Allerhand et al. (1969) does not support these relationships.

Marital Status, Family Responsibilities and the Family Environment

Unmarried HCU workers exhibit higher turnover rates than married HCU workers (Hinrichs, 1970; Lipsky et al., 1971; Quinn et al., 1970). The degree of family responsibilities also seems to affect the HCU's behavior. Quinn et al. (1970) and Gurin (1968) report that male HCUs who are the main breadwinners are less likely to drop out. If HCU workers own or rent their own home or apartment, they are more likely to remain on their job (Hinrichs, 1970) and to earn higher wages (Gurin, 1968). (Gurin's study supported this relationship for males but not for females.) The impact of number of dependents—another measure of family responsibility—is more ambiguous. Gurin (1968), Rosen (1969), and Shlensky (1970) did not find number of dependents to be a significant predictor of HCU behavior. One study (Hinrichs, 1970) reports that number of dependents was positively related to retention, but since that study did not control other individual characteristic variables (e.g., age), its conclusions must be tentatively accepted.

The findings supporting relationship between family responsibilities (e.g., marital status, owning a home) and retention reflect the greater need for job-related rewards (e.g., money); that is, greater responsibilities demand greater resources which can be attained by job attendance. Following the expectancy model, the greater the attraction of rewards related to holding a job, the higher the retention rates.

Birthplace

The birthplace or the geographical area where the trainee spent his formative years seems related to turnover of HCU workers. Higher retention rates were reported for those born in the rural South (Quinn et al., 1970; Purcell & Cavanagh, 1969) and the West Indies or Latin America (Shlensky, 1970) as opposed to those from the urban North. This relationship seems to parallel findings on rural-urban differences (cf. Hulin & Blood, 1968) which suggest that the value premises of rural-born individuals might be more congruent with organizational requirements.

Education

Evidence on the relationship between education and the criterion variables is mixed. Greenberg (1968) and Shlensky (1970) report significant positive relationships between education and job retention; in the latter study, the finding holds only for the black HCU. Gurin (1968), Quinn et al. (1970), Lipsky et al. (1971), and Davis et al. (1973) report no relationships for education. Unfortunately, there is little information in these studies on the distribution of education or the relationships between educational attainment and job requirements to permit a reconciliation of these findings.

Previous Job History

Present job behavior should reflect, to some extent, the patterns of past job behavior and earnings. Quinn et al. (1970) report that terminations were greater (54%) for those with more than two jobs in the last 2 years as compared with those (25%) who held less than two jobs in the same time period. Many of the other studies (cf. Greenberg, 1968; Hinrichs, 1970) report similar relationships. It seems that the inability to stay on past jobs leads to lower expectancies that rewards will follow from job attendance and to lower expectancies by the individual that he is capable of remaining on jobs. Following our model, these lower expectancies should lead to lower job retention.

Personality and Description of Self

Researchers interested in explaining HCU trainee behavior have examined the role of personality. Some studies have used traditional measures of personality characteristics, while others have employed single-item scales to tap specific attitudes and values. In general, the results are not encouraging. Quinn et al. (1970) introduced some 21 indexes in their study; only two exhibited significant differences in the criterion variables, of which one was in the direction opposite from the prediction. Frank (1969) used a more extensive battery of tests and also obtained few significant results. Gurin's (1968) analysis of five scales dealing with orientation toward work, personal efficacy, and attitudes about the Protestant Ethic also did not reveal any strong consistent relationships to the criterion.

Research by Allerhand et al. (1969), Hinrichs (1970), and Teahan (1969) indicates that there may be some relationship between personality factors and the criterion variables for HCU trainees. Hinrichs (1970) reports that trainees who rated their own ability as high were more likely to be considered highest in performance during a training program. Allerhand et al. (1969) report that individuals who indicated a strong need to be perceived as smart by their boss and who perceived themselves as having a high level of energy and activity were less likely to drop out of a prejob orientation program. Teahan's (1969) study focused on the time span concept. He indicates that terminators from an HCU training program possessed shorter time spans and were less optimistic about their future than were those who remained in training. Data from each of these studies seem to indicate that a favorable self-image and orientation toward producing positive results are related to successful outcomes in an HCU program.

It is interesting to note two differences between the sets of studies presented above. The first set examined more generalized personality traits, while the second set examined attitudes and beliefs about more specific objects. The first set also relied on more traditional personality batteries, while the second set used single items that are designed for the specific research. Since there seemed to be some relationship between personality type variables and the criterion variables in the second set of studies, it may be that the methodology of this set is more appropriate to an HCU population. That is, given a population with low education and potentially negative attitudes toward test taking, it may be preferable to use a smaller set of specific items instead of the traditional personality batteries. However, before one can weigh the relative importance of personality differences, future research must examine the implications of these different strategies. (See Friedlander, 1970, and Goodman, 1970, for a discussion of methodological issues relevant to research in HCU populations.) Also, there is need for a theoretical perspective to aid in identifying relevant personality variables.

ROLE CHARACTERISTICS

Within the organization the trainee interacts with supervisors, peers, counselors, trainers, and other organizational participants. The characteristics of these role relationships have a bearing on the likelihood that the HCU workers will remain in the company. For example, the supervisor can affect the amount of rewards the HCU worker receives. Or he can affect the expectation that certain behaviors are rewarded. The modification of rewards, or of expectations that certain behaviors and rewards are connected, should affect the HCU worker's behavior.

Supervisor Role

A number of studies indicate that the supportiveness of the supervisor affects HCU behavior. Beatty (1971) reports that consideration (measured by the Leadership Behavior Description Questionnaire) was positively correlated with performance ($r = .38$). A further analysis, however, indicated that for those trainees in the extremes of the distribution of performance scores, the relationship with consideration was negative. Another important finding is that only first-level supervisory behavior, and not second-level supervisory behavior, was related to HCU trainees' performances. Friedlander and Greenberg (1971) report a similar positive relationship between supervisory supportiveness and performance. Another interesting finding in their analysis is that significant discrepancies existed between the

HCU worker and the supervisor in their perception of the supportiveness of the organization; that is, HCU trainees defined the work climate as much less supportive. Friedlander and Greenberg suggest that this differential perception of work climate increases the chances that some reliable (low-absenteeism) HCU workers will find this work situation intolerable and leave, while others will exhibit withdrawal behaviors such as tardiness or absenteeism. Quinn et al. (1970), using different measures of supervisory style, found that being treated fairly reduced the HCU worker's propensity to terminate. Also, HCU workers with more than one supervisor experienced greater turnover (57%) than those with one supervisor (31%). Davis et al. (1973) find no consistent positive relationships between supervisory behavior and the criterion variables. However, their measures of supervisory behavior (e.g., time spent with the worker) are not very specific in terms of how the supervisor deals with the HCU trainee.

In general, the studies seem to indicate supervisory style does affect HCU worker behavior. Supportiveness from the supervisor probably allays some of the HCU worker's fears about the new work situation and provides feelings of positive reinforcement about the work setting. Having a single supervisor increases the predictability of the job and probably clarifies the expectations about rewards and expected performance. Following our model, these conditions seem to lead to higher retention and performance.

Counselor and Trainer Roles

Unfortunately there are few studies meeting our criteria which deal with the effect of the counselor-trainee role on HCU trainee behavior. Quinn et al. (1970) report findings similar to their analyses of the first-line supervisor—the fairness of treatment by the counselor during training is positively related to job retention.

Gurin (1968) provides a provocative analysis of the sources of attractiveness of counselors and trainers for the HCU trainees. Counselors (versus vocational and basic education teachers) were defined as the most attractive staff members by the HCU trainees. Black counselors, however, were perceived as more attractive than white counselors for male trainees, while race differences did not differentiate the attractiveness of the occupants of the training roles. This difference in preference for black versus white counselors may be attributed to the fact that black counselors expressed values and beliefs more congruent with those of the trainees. However, an analysis of trainees' perceptions indicated that they felt black counselors stressed middle-class values more than white counselors did. This finding would seem to indicate that HCU trainees were more willing to accept middle-class socialization attempts from a black than a white counselor. Gurin confirms this point by indicating that there was a positive association (+.27) between stressing middle-class values and the attractiveness of the counselor for black male counselors but no association (−.04) for white male counselors. These findings and others reported by Gurin are important because they indicate that certain combinations of race and sex with specific roles have a more powerful effect on the socialization of the HCU worker. In terms of the model, it suggests that these combination effects will have a greater impact in changing expectancies and the attractiveness of rewards and, thus, on retention and job performance.

Peers in the Work Organization

Friedlander and Greenberg (1971) report that HCU workers' perceptions of the supportiveness of their peers and others in the organization to new workers was related to supervisory ratings of performance. In general, the more supportive the trainee viewed his peers and others in the organization, the more likely he was to be evaluated by his supervisor as competent, congenial, friendly, and conscientious, but not necessarily as more reliable. Case studies by Campbell (1969) and Kirchner and Lucas (1971), as well as an experiment by Baron and Bass (1969), also point to the importance of peer-group relationships.

Morgan, Blonsky, and Rosen (1970) examined the reactions at different levels of the existing work force in the firm to a program for the HCU. They found a shift from positive to neutral feelings at the end of the 12-week program. Differences in attitudes toward the HCU and the program varied in terms of the role distance between the trainee and the respondent. For example, individuals at the vice presidential level showed an increase in positive attitudes. For foremen and the rank-and-file group, there was a tendency for positive attitudes to decrease and for negative attitudes to increase ($p < .01$ for change in overall attitudes). The modification in perceived positive and negative consequences at different levels probably reflects greater realization of problems in dealing with HCU workers. The closer one is to the day-to-day problems, the more likely it is that one's perceptions and attitudes should reflect these problems. There are no data in this study to indicate the consequences of this attitude change on the criterion variables. On one hand, the changes might merely reflect reality testing—actual experiences and expectations are more congruent. On the other hand, especially at the foreman and rank-and-file level, it might lead to less positive relationships with the HCU worker.

Roles Outside the Work Organization

Some researchers have looked at the social context of the HCU's family and peer group. Gurin (1968), for example, found that male HCU trainees in the lowest earning quartile more often came from families (reference is to the household of the trainees' mothers) where a greater percentage of adult males were unemployed. Friends of these HCU trainees also were more likely to be unem-

ployed. Other findings (cf. Quinn et al., 1970) on the characteristics of the HCU worker's family, however, have not supported the relationships between indexes of family disorganization and the criterion variables. Therefore, although there is some indication that external role relationships affect HCU behavior, the process by which they affect expectancies, perceived attractiveness of rewards, retention, and performance is not clearly defined.

ORGANIZATION PROGRAM CHARACTERISTICS

Organizations involved in hiring and retaining the hard core have adopted a variety of training and counseling programs, as well as other supportive services.

Training

The selection of no training versus some, vestibule versus on-the-job training, and attitudinal versus skill training (general or specific) represent some of the choices in designing the training program portion of a program for the HCU. The Quinn et al. (1970) study permits analysis of a group that was trained and a matched control group of direct hires who received no training. The training program in question was prejob and primarily company oriented in nature. An analysis of individuals on the job who had been trained versus those not trained indicated that there were no significant differences in the perceived levels of competence in job-related skills. Trained individuals were more likely to value work, to exhibit positive attitudes toward time schedules, and to show increased feeelings of personal efficacy concerning achievement. Since data for this analysis were collected after the trainee was on the job, it is difficult to separate the effects of training from the effects of successfully completing training on these responses. In either case, the trained individual's sense of personal efficacy about accomplishment did increase.

Training, of course, may have dysfunctional consequences by raising expectations beyond the realities of the work situation. Quinn et al. (1970) indicate that trained individuals preferred more autonomy than they experienced on an entry-level job and they perceived the quality of supervision as lower than did direct hires. That is, training leads to greater expectations than the job situation can fulfill. Hinrichs' (1970) study of 300 trainees in a 17-week vestibule training program also indicates some possible dysfunctional consequences of training. Not only did training not change attitudes in the intended direction, but in some cases it seems to have facilitated a change toward feelings of powerlessness. Unfortunately there are no other data presented on the effects of training that could put this result in a broader perspective.

In Allerhand et al.'s (1969) and Frank's (1969) analyses of the effects of training on certain attitudinal and motivational dimensions, there do not seem to be any significant changes as a result of the training experiences. Similarly, Goodale (1971) found that changes in work values of HCU trainees over 8 weeks of training were not significantly different from those of non-equivalent controls (insurance agents and college students).

The impact of training on job retention or performance seems negligible (Friedlander & Greenberg, 1971; Quinn et al., 1970). A study by Rosen (1969) indicates that company orientation training led to lower termination among HCU workers than did quasi-therapeutic training. However, the retention rate of the company-trained HCU workers did not differ substantially from that of regular new hires. Farr (1969) reports that among HCUs placed under sensitivity-trained supervisors, trained HCUs had lower retention (20%) than did untrained HCUs (55%).

There are many case studies concerned with the effects of turnover and performance training. Some (cf. Gudyer, 1970; Habbe, 1968; Janger, 1969) indicate training affects the HCU's behavior (e.g., turnover);

other studies (cf. Saltzman, 1969) do not.

In general, reviewing all the studies and their respective methodologies, it seems unlikely that training itself affects job retention or performance. This conclusion is quite congruent with our model of HCU behavior. Job retention is related to the expectancy that job attendance will lead to desired rewards. Although the training might initially affect these expectations, it is the actual work experiences which determine the HCU behavior; that is, the types and amount of rewards available and the frequency of and criteria for their allocation determine the expectancies and the perceived attractiveness of rewards. These factors are quite independent of the training experience.

Counseling

There are no experimental data on the relative effects of different counseling strategies. The earlier discussion of the counselor role sheds some light on how the demographic characteristics of the counselor may influence his effectiveness. Several studies (cf. Allerhand et al., 1969; Hearns, 1968; Purcell & Webster, 1969; Rutledge & Gass, 1968) indicate that counseling may contribute to lower HCU termination rates. However, it is difficult to evaluate the impact of counseling on retention, since these studies do not separate its effect from other structural dimensions.

Although there is no evidence supporting any significant effects of a particular program characteristic (e.g., training), several studies (Davis et al., 1973; Janger, 1972; Sedgwicks & Bodell, 1972) indicate that the combined effects of many program dimensions (e.g., counseling, training, providing transportation) increase job retention. The problem with this conclusion is that we do not know whether other uncontrolled variables might explain this relationship, nor do we know the nature of the interaction effects. Also, Davis et al. (1973) provide a contrasting finding for those considering formal, elaborate programs—the more visible the program, the higher the absenteeism and turnover.

ORGANIZATION STRUCTURAL CHARACTERISTICS

Job Structure

The nature of the job on which the trainee is placed affects his work attitudes and propensity to remain on the job. Quinn et al. (1970) identified four job characteristics which seem related to negative job attitudes and turnover. The inability to change one's job assignment now or in the future was related to higher termination rates for the HCU worker. Assignment to multiple work stations, or not having an idea what their work routine would be like, was also positively related to turnover. Trainees who did not understand some aspects of their job, or how it fit into the larger picture, were more likely to terminate than those who had a better understanding. When job activities were perceived as boring, turnover was more likely (63%) than when HCU workers did not find their job boring (18%); similarly, involuntary terminations were negatively related to skill level (Davis et al., 1973). In addition, a number of case studies (Bonney, 1971; Campbell, 1969; Goodman, 1969b) indicate that job status and job mobility are positively related to retention rates.

Pay

Another organizational characteristic which bears on HCU workers' behavior is the pay system. Although none of the studies we reviewed examined the effects of different pay systems, a number of studies did examine the effect of pay levels. In Shlensky's (1970) analysis, pay was a major predictor among groups (e.g., blacks, young people, and males) that were more likely to terminate and thus served to reduce the propensity to terminate in these groups. Pay did not seem to relate to turnover for whites and older workers. Other studies (cf. Allerhand,

1969; Davis et al., 1973; Purcell & Cavanagh, 1969) also indicate a positive relationship between pay and job retention and between pay and completion of training (cf. Lipsky et al., 1971).

Organizational Commitment and Change

In a few multifirm studies that were reviewed, there is some indication that higher commitment (Allerhand et al., 1969; Hearns, 1968; Janger, 1972), company willingness to change policies and procedures (Allerhand et al., 1969; Goodman, 1969b; Hearns, 1968; Janger, 1972), and more realistic company expectations of the HCU (Allerhand et al., 1969) are associated with higher retention rates.

Employment Stability, Size, Industry

Companies with lower turnover rates in entry-level jobs seemed to have higher retention rates with HCU workers than did other firms (Allerhand et al., 1969). Medium-sized companies (100–500 employees) seemed to retain more HCU workers than did larger or smaller firms (Allerhand et al., 1969). Using multivariate analysis, Lipsky et al. (1971) found that white-collar versus blue-collar jobs and jobs in manufacturing versus non-manufacturing industries were two significant predictors of training program completions.

DISCUSSION

The evidence indicates that many factors—individual, role, and structural—affect the behavior of the HCU worker. Age, sex, family responsibilities, and place of birth are associated with termination and subsequent earnings of HCU workers. These variables probably relate to the expectancies that job attendance will lead to certain rewards and to the relative attractiveness of these rewards. The product of expectancies and rewards leads to job retention.

The relationships between these individual

differences and the criterion variables are by no means simple. First, the individual-level variables may be interrelated. For example, Shlensky (1970) finds age related to turnover among males, but not among females; further, he finds sex related to turnover among HCU aged 16–20, but not among those over 20. It appears, then, that age, sex, and other individual differences do not have simple effects on the criteria; rather, there is evidence of some fairly strong interactions.

A second problem is the relative independence of the individual-level variables and the organizational-level variables. For example, it may be that HCU workers with certain characteristics (e.g., being older) might be placed in more desirable and higher paying jobs. If such were the case, it would be difficult to assess whether a relationship among the HCU between age and turnover were due to age differences or to the more desirable nature of the jobs in which older workers were placed. The evidence concerning this issue is that the relationships between individual variables and the criteria are reduced, but not eliminated, when organizational variables are entered into a regression analysis (cf. Greenberg, 1968; Shlensky, 1970).

Although the relationships are complex, both between individual and organizational variables and among the individual level variables, a number of observations can be drawn from these studies. First, there are clearly no simple selection rules. Also, selecting out HCU workers based on the individual-difference information would be inappropriate given the purpose of HCU programs. Second, the design of a program should reflect the differences among the HCU work force. If a firm must select HCU workers with heterogeneous characteristics, it would seem important to design the program to reflect differences in their expectations and preferences for rewards. That is, a young unmarried male would receive different program inputs than a married female with two children.

The HCU trainee operates in a large social system with many interconnected role relationships. The degree of conflict between the HCU trainee and his counselor, trainer, supervisor, and peers clearly can affect his behavior. In one study there was some indication of an interaction effect between the counselor-trainer role and the similarity of the background characteristics of the role occupant and the HCU trainee. This finding would seem to have implications for selection of individuals as counselors-trainers in an HCU program. In the area of supervision, the perceived supportiveness of one's supervisor is related to job retention. However, there may be large perceptual discrepancies between supervisors and HCU workers on the degree of supportiveness existing in the organization (cf. Friedlander & Greenberg, 1971). Bridging the gap between the supervisor's and HCU worker's perception of the work climate and increasing the level of supportiveness in the organization may be one strategy to increase performance and job retention. At the same time, it is important to remember that other roles (e.g., peers) bear on HCU worker behavior; attention to only one role is not a useful strategy.

Much of the literature on the HCU worker focuses on the effectiveness of the different training strategies to reorient this individual to the world of work. Unfortunately, in the studies reviewed, there is no clear indication that training significantly affects the turnover or performance of the HCU worker. These results seem consistent with our model; that is, it is unlikely that training would have a major impact on job expectancies and the availability and attractiveness of rewards. Our conclusion is not that training of HCU workers should be discontinued. On the other hand, large investments in intensive training programs may not be warranted. Future studies that examine the effects of different training combinations such as short prejob orientation combined with on-the-job training versus extended vestibule training will provide more definitive answers to this question.

Dimensions of the organization such as the

type of job and pay system affect the HCU worker's behavior. The HCU workers were more likely to terminate from jobs that they did not understand or that afforded little opportunity for movement, etc. The implication of these findings is that the trainee's behavior must be understood within the technological system in which he operates and that job redesign may represent a useful strategy in affecting the HCU worker's behavior. The level of pay also affects the HCU worker's behavior. The data seem to indicate that firms with relatively lower wage rates for entry-level jobs should avoid HCU programs. Higher paying firms, on the other hand, are in a position to hire HCU workers who would otherwise be most likely to leave; that is, there is some evidence that higher pay reduces the propensity to terminate for those most likely to leave.

Our analysis of structural characteristics has been primarily at the intraorganizational level. Little attention has been paid to the larger institutional forces which bear on the expectations and values of the HCU worker. For example, limited housing opportunities affect the HCU worker's cost of going to work. Often employers are some distance from ghetto areas. Similarly, limitations in educational systems and in health and child care systems bear on the HCU worker's propensity to come to work. Changes in these larger institutional forces must be considered when analyzing HCU behavior and HCU programs.

The overall theme of this review is that multiple variables affect the HCU worker as he operates in a complex social system. Changes in the behavior of the HCU worker are related to changes in the role-, organizational, and societal-level variables. In many studies on the HCU worker, there has been an unfortunate assumption that the worker must be changed to fit the organization. Our concept of the complex social system suggests changes must occur at all the main levels of analysis—that is, individual, role, organizational, and societal.

Two other issues, until now implicit in this review, need to be specified. First, designing a program to hire and to retain the HCU worker is an exercise in decision making. It requires a judgment about the allocation of resources to a variety of options (e.g., type of training, counseling, pay). Basically the manager is interested in the effect of this allocation on the retention (or performance) of HCU workers in relationship to the costs of this decision. What is surprising is that given the large investment of resources by many firms in programs for the HCU worker is an exercise in decision making. It lect and develop data systems that would provide guidance in the design or reevaluation of such a program. There are studies cited in this review that may serve as models for developing data systems to aid in decision making about HCU programs. Quinn et al. (1970) demonstrate how an experimental design may be successfully used in evaluating an organization's HCU program. Although their study is more elaborate than a firm would undertake, their general design could be utilized to evaluate the contribution of different factors (e.g., training) to the retention of the HCU worker. A different data collection strategy, which includes a number of firms in a cross-sectional design, is suggested by the Shlensky (1970) study. This type of study is valuable since it permits the assessment of variables such as pay level, type of job, and size of the firm, which are more amenable to multifirm investigations. The critical issue, however, is that designing programs for the HCU worker requires data which indicate the relative importance of the multiple variables identified in this review.

The second issue concerns the role of the industrial psychologist and research on the HCU worker. Research in this area provides a number of opportunities. One can test theories about work attitudes, motivation, and performance. Empirical results from other studies can be cross-validated in this population. Psychologists interested in organizational change and action research have a "ready-made" laboratory. The research opportunity is also unique, since the data bear on an immediate social issue in our country. What is interesting in reviewing the studies in this area is that relatively few psychologists have become actively involved in research in what would seem to be a fertile area. The question is, Given an area with good theoretical research opportunities, one in which managers need data that could be gathered by psychologists, and one which concerns a relevant social problem, why is there not greater utilization of the skills of industrial psychologists?

REFERENCES

Allerhand, M. E., Friedlander, F., Malone, J. E., Medow, H., & Rosenberg, M. *A study of the impact and effectiveness of the comprehensive manpower project of Cleveland (AIM-JOBS).* (Office of Policy, Evaluation and Research, U.S. Department of Labor, Contract No. 41-7-002-37) Cleveland, Ohio: Case Western Reserve University, Cleveland College, AIM Research Project, December 1969.

Baron, R. M., & Bass, A. R. *The role of social reinforcement parameters in improving trainee task performance and self-image.* (Final Report, U.S. Department of Labor, Office of Manpower Administration, Contract No. 81-24-66-04) Detroit, Mich.: Wayne State University, September 1969.

Beatty, R. W. First and second level supervision and the job performance of the hard-core unemployed. Paper presented at the meeting of the American Psychological Association, Washington, D.C., September 1971.

Bonney, N. L. Unwelcome strangers: A study of manpower training programs in the steel industry. Unpublished doctoral dissertation, University of Chicago, 1971.

Campbell, R. Employing the disadvantaged: Inland Steel's experience. *Issues in Industrial Society,* 1969, 1, 30–42.

Clark, K. No gimmicks please whitey. *Training in Business and Industry,* 1968, 5, 27–30.

Davis, O., Doyle, P., Joseph, M., Niles, J., & Perry, W. An empirical study of the NAB-JOBS Program. *Public Policy,* 1973, in press.

Farr, J. L. Industrial training programs for hard-core unemployed. Paper presented at the Seventeenth Annual Workshop in Industrial Psychology (Division 14, American Psychological Association), Washington, D.C., August 1969.

Frank, H. H. On the job training for minorities: An internal study. Unpublished doctoral dissertation, University of California, Los Angeles, 1969.

Friedlander, F. Emerging blackness in a white research world. *Human Organization,* 1970, 29, 239–250.

Friedlander, F., & Greenberg, S. Effect of job attitudes, training, and organization climate on performance of the hard-core unemployed. *Journal of Applied Psychology,* 1971, 55, 287–295.

Goodale, J. G. Background characteristics, orientation, work experience, and work values of employees hired from human resources development applicants by companies affiliated with the National Alliance of Businessmen. Unpublished doctoral dissertation, Bowling Green State University, 1971.

Goodman, P. S. Hiring and training the hard-core unemployed: A problem in system definition. *Human Organization,* 1969, 28, 259–269. (a)

Goodman, P. S. Hiring, training and retaining the hard core. *Industrial Relations,* 1969, 9, 54–66. (b)

Goodman, P. S. Methodological issues in conducting research on the disadvantaged. In W. Button (Ed.), *Proceedings of Conference on Rehabilitation, Sheltered Workshops, and the Disadvantaged.* Binghamton, N.Y.: Vail-Ballou Press, 1970.

Greenberg, D. H. *Employers and manpower training programs: Data collection and analysis.* (U.S. Office of Economic Opportunity Memorandum RM-5740-OEO) Santa Monica, Calif.: Rand Corporation, October 1968.

Gudyer, R. H. A corporate experience: American Airlines. In W. D. Drennan (Ed.), *The fourth strike: Hiring and training the disadvantaged.* New York: American Management Association, 1970.

Gurin, G. *Inner city youth in a job training project.* Ann Arbor: University of Michigan, Institute for Social Research, 1968.

Habbe, S. Hiring the hard-core unemployed: Pontiac's operation opportunity. *The Conference Board Record,* 1968, 5, 18–21.

Hearns, J. P. New approaches to meet post-hiring difficulties of disadvantaged workers. In, *Proceedings of the Twenty-First Annual Winter Meeting, Industrial Relations Research Association.* Madison, Wisc.: Industrial Relations Research Association, 1968.

Heneman, H. G., III, & Schwab, D. P. Evaluation of research on expectancy theory predictions of employee performance. *Psychological Bulletin*, 1972, 78, 1–9.

Hinrichs, J. R. *Implementation of manpower training: The private firm experience.* Unpublished paper, IBM Corporation, White Plains, N.Y., 1970.

Hulin, C., & Blood, M. Job enlargement, individual differences and worker responses. *Psychological Bulletin*, 1968, 69, 41–56.

Janger, A. New start for the harder hard core. *The Conference Board Record*, 1969, 6, 10–20.

Janger, A. *Employing the disadvantaged: A company perspective.* New York: The Conference Board, 1972.

Kirchner, W., & Lucas, J. Some research on motivating the hard-core. *Training in Business and Industry*, 1972, 8, 30–31.

Kirchner, W., & Lucas, J. The hard-core in training—who makes it? *Training and Development Journal*, 1972, 26, 34–38.

Lipsky, D., Droitning, J., & Fottler, M. *The Quarterly Review of Economics and Business*, 1971, 11, 42–60.

Morgan, B. S., Blonsky, M. R., & Rosen, H. Employee attitudes toward a hard-core hiring program. *Journal of Applied Psychology*, 1970, 54, 473–478.

Purcell, T. V., & Cavanagh, G. F. Alternative routes to employing the disadvantaged within the enterprise. In, *Proceedings of the Twenty-Second Annual Winter Meeting, Industrial Relations Research Association.* Madison, Wisc.: Industrial Relations Research Association, 1969.

Purcell, T. V., & Webster, R. Window on the hard-core world. *Harvard Business Review*, 1969, 47, 118–129.

Quinn, R., Fine, B., & Levitin, T. *Turnover and training: A social-psychological study of disadvantaged workers.* Unpublished paper, Survey Research Center, University of Michigan, 1970.

Rosen, H. *A group orientation approach for facilitating the work adjustment of the hard-core unemployed.* (Final Report, U.S. Department of Labor) Washington, D.C.: U.S. Government Printing Office, 1969.

Rutledge, A. L., & Gass, G. Z. *Nineteen Negro men: Personality and manpower retraining.* San Francisco, Calif.: Jossey-Bass, 1968.

Saltzman, A. W. Manpower planning in private industry. In A. Weber, F. H. Cassell, W. L. Ginsberg (Eds.), *Public-private manpower policies.* (IRRA publication No. 35) Madison, Wisc.: Industrial Relations Research Association, 1969.

Sedgwicks, R., & Bodell, D. The hard-core employee—key to high retention. *Personnel Journal*, 1972, 50, 948–953.

Shlensky, B. Determinants of turnover in NAB-JOBS programs to employ the disadvantaged. Unpublished doctoral dissertation, Massachusetts Institute of Technology, 1970.

Teahan, J. E. Future time perspective and job success. In, *Supplement to H. Rosen, A group orientation approach for facilitating the work adjustment of the hard-core unemployed.* (Final Report, U.S. Department of Labor) Washington, D.C.: U.S. Government Printing Office, 1969.

3

HOUSING

Introduction

About 2.3 million families, or 7.6 million people, live in substandard urban housing the United States: that is, housing that is either dilapidated or lacking at least one plumbing facility (U.S. Bureau of the Census, 1967).[1] Millions of other families live in housing that is not dilapidated by Census standards, but that does violate the somewhat higher standards of many local housing codes (Frieden, 1968). How do these people feel about their homes and neighborhoods? What characteristics make their neighborhoods desirable or undesirable places to live? What impact have government strategies designed to provide adequate housing for large numbers of low-income families had on the attitudes and behavior of the participating families? Let us review some of the studies that have addressed each of these questions.[2]

ATTITUDES TOWARD LOW-INCOME PRIVATE HOUSING

A number of studies have tried to find out how people who live in low-income private housing feel about their homes and neighborhoods. Although the failure of most of these studies to use control groups limits the conclusions that can be drawn, the results suggest that residents' attitudes in some low-income neighborhoods are primarily favorable (Gilbert & Eaton, 1970; Hartman, 1963a, reading 3.1; Yancey, 1971, reading 3.2), while residents' attitudes in other low-income neighborhoods are largely negative or neutral (Cagle & Deutscher, 1970; Levine, Fiddmont, Stephenson, & Wilkerson, 1972; Wolf & Lebeaux, 1967). The results also suggest that the extent to which social networks evolve

1. The *Estimate of substandard housing (vol. 6), 1970 census of housing* had not been issued prior to 1975. As a result, we have referred to data collected in 1966.

2. The effects of densely populated urban housing are examined in the introduction to the readings on effects of the urban environment.

and the degree to which residents feel their neighborhoods are safe are often important determinants of these attitudes.

In a study of 473 female residents of Boston's West End, a white working-class neighborhood that was about the be cleared and redeveloped, Hartman (1963a, reading 3.1) found that 76% of the women interviewed expressed a great deal of satisfaction with the neighborhood. Hartman also found that the number of neighbors with whom the women interacted was an influential determinant of their attitudes toward their apartments. For example, among residents of physically poor housing, 85% who interacted with many neighbors, compared to 53% who interacted with few neighbors or none, liked their apartments. Interviews with 785 residents of an integrated Akron, Ohio neighborhood yielded fairly similar findings (Barresi & Lindquist, 1970). Thirty-two percent of the residents who said they did not visit their neighbors, 39% of the residents who visited some of their neighbors, and 45% of the residents who visited most of their neighbors expressed positive attitudes toward the neighborhood. While Barresi and Lindquist's findings suggest that interaction with neighbors was one determinant of attitudes toward the neighborhood, they also imply that it may not have been a particularly influential one. In a study of 62 families in a predominantly black neighborhood slated for urban renewal, Cagle and Deutscher (1970) reported considerably weaker, albeit suggestive, findings. They found that many of the respondents reportedly disliked their apartments and over half said they were looking for new housing or thinking about moving before finding out that they had to move. They also found that 61% of the respondents disliked the neighborhood's residents and 16% were neutral. Unfortunately, Cagle and Deutscher did not tell us whether the people who disliked their apartments and/or who were looking for new housing were also the people who disliked the neighborhood's residents.

Studies by Wolf and Lebeaux (1967) and Kasl and Harburg (1972) shed light on the relationship between perceiving one's neighborhood as unsafe and attitudes toward that neighborhood. Wolf and Lebeaux (1967) interviewed 216 occupants of a largely black, low-income neighborhood in Detroit. The findings indicate that only 25% expressed predominantly positive feelings about the neighborhood, and almost two-thirds were planning to move, thinking about moving, or would have liked to move if they could. Wolf and Lebeaux suggested that these attitudes were due primarily to two factors. One, many residents felt that the neighborhood was dangerous; that is, one-third of the sample said that the area wasn't safe, and an additional third talked about the reassuring presence of constant police surveillance. Two, the neighborhood contained a considerable number of broken homes, temporary unions between men and women, and residents on public assistance. Kasl and Harburg (1972) sought to determine the impact of socioeconomic level and social disorganization on perceptions of the neighborhood and the desire to move. Toward that end, they used archival measures of education, income, unemployment, marital and residential instability, density, proportion of home ownership, and juvenile and adult crime to select four census tracts in Detroit: a white low stress tract, a white high stress tract, a black low stress tract, and a black high stress tract. Although Kasl and Harburg attempted to locate equivalent tracts, the black tract was higher on the indices of disorganization than the white tract within each category of stress. Within each tract, interviews with approximately 250 residents were carried out. The data indicate that people tend to perceive accurately the conditions under which they live; that is, residents in high stress areas evaluated their homes and neighborhoods much less favorably than residents in low stress areas, and blacks had less favorable perceptions than whites within each category of stress. The data also indicate that perception of the neighborhood as unsafe was an important correlate of disliking the neighborhood in the high stress areas, and that disliking the neighborhood was more closely related to the desire to move than was dissatisfaction with one's house. Unfortunately, Kasl and Harburg presented standardized scores, but not summaries of raw scores. As a result, they provide information about differences between groups, but not about how favorably or unfavorably the residents of each census tract evaluated their homes and neighborhoods. For example, we don't know whether residents in high stress areas were extremely dissatisfied with their homes and neighborhoods, mildly dissatisfied, or mildly satisfied.

A recent study of the residents of a white lower-class neighborhood in St. Louis (Wolfe, Lex, & Yancey, 1968) documents the impact of social networks on residents' perception of the neighborhood as safe and on their consequent satisfaction with the neighborhood. The results indicate that "persons who were not integrated into such networks were more likely to express concern over allowing their children out of the house, felt that they were vulnerable to strangers entering the neighborhood, felt unsafe on the street at night, and felt that children in the neighborhood were out of control" (Yancey, 1971, p. 6).

SOME STRATEGIES FOR HOUSING THE POOR

In an attempt to provide adequate housing for large numbers of low-income families, the federal government has implemented some strategies and tried to evaluate others. For example, the government has constructed public housing, provided rent supplements, leased private housing, and studied the feasibility of direct housing allowances. Unfortunately, several million people in cities still live in substandard dwellings. Obviously, a great deal more housing suitable for low-income families needs to be created. Toward that end, studies of the psychological impact of public housing, rent supplements, leased housing, and direct housing allowances are examined in an attempt to identify some of the factors that make housing programs desirable from the vantage point of these families.

Public Housing

Studies of the residents of low-income private housing shed light on some of the individual and situational variables that influence the attitudes of potential occupants of public housing toward that housing. For example, 76% of the people interviewed in the West End (Hartman, 1963b) said they would not like to live in a public housing project. Families that did express interest were usually families with little choice: that is, large families, fatherless families, and the aged. Among those who felt that public housing had undesirable characteristics, one-third made statements referring to the people that live in housing projects and to the absence of a sense of community, and 25% objected to the institutional features of public housing. Elsewhere, both complete and fatherless families whose neighborhood was about to be cleared and redeveloped expressed fairly favorable attitudes toward public housing (Cagle & Deutscher, 1970). For example, 54% of the sample cited better apartment facilities and 40% mentioned low rents. On the other hand, 25% of the fatherless families and 41% of the complete families also thought there was no privacy in public housing, and 22% of the sample felt there were too many rules. Unfortunately, comparable questions about private housing were not asked.

In an attempt to determine the impact of public housing on the occupants' attitudes and behavior, Wilner, Walkley, Pinkerton, and Tayback (1962) compared several hundred families who moved into public housing from a slum with several hundred matched families who remained in the slum. The housing project was designed to provide adequate room space, many opportunities for daily contact among neighbors, and use of project facilities by neighbors under noncompetitive circumstances. The results indicate that the housing project had a favorable impact. For example, 60% of the women in the project, compared to 33% of the women who continued to live in the slum, said they liked their apartments a lot; 59% in the project, versus 35% in the slum, helped and were helped by neighbors; 66%, compared to 30%, felt their neighborhood was a good place to live; and 59%, compared to 23%, thought it was a good place to raise children. A study of former West End residents conducted two years after the West End was vacated (Hartman, 1963b) revealed that 89% of the people who relocated to public housing liked their apartments. However, 42% of these people, compared to 16% of the West End residents who moved into private housing, missed a sense of community and said they were lonely and isolated. While much of the difference in feelings of community may have been due to

differences in the neighborhoods and their residents, the relatively large proportion of elderly West End dwellers who moved into public housing projects may
have also accounted for a sizable portion of the variance. In a study of the
tenants of a 300 unit, two-story row house public housing project in Richmond,
California, Cooper (1965) found that 43% of the sample commented favorably
about the project while 30% commented unfavorably. Among the features
people liked were an enclosed front porch and front and back yards. Among the
disliked features were poor construction, poor maintenance, lack of privacy, and
lack of playgrounds.

Studies by Yancey (1971, reading 3.2) and Newman (1972, 1973, reading 3.3)
suggest that the way buildings and grounds are designed has a marked impact on
how safe residents feel and on how they behave. Based on interviews with 154
residents of Pruitt-Igoe, a public housing project containing 43 eleven-story
buildings and located in St. Louis, Yancey (1971, reading 3.2) argued that the
design of the buildings severely impeded development of the networks of relationships that maintain informal social control:

> Absent from the architectural design of Pruitt-Igoe is what has sometimes been
> referred to as wasted space. We choose to call it "defensible space." In lower- and
> working-class slums, the littered and often trash-filled alleys, streets, and backyards
> provide the ecological basis around which informal networks of friends and relatives
> may develop. Without such semi-public space and facilities, the development of such
> networks is retarded; the resulting atomization of the community can be seen in the
> frequent and escalating conflict between neighbors, fears of and vulnerability to the
> human dangers in the environment, and, finally, withdrawal to the last line of de-
> fense—into the single-family dwelling unit. The sense of security and control that is
> found in other working- and lower-class neighborhoods is not present. [p. 17]

The results of a study of two public housing projects in New York City
(Newman, 1972, 1973, reading 3.3) underline the importance of defensible
space. The Brownsville and Van Dyke projects were similar in a number of ways.
They each housed approximately 6,000 people, contained 288 persons per acre,
and averaged about 4.6 rooms per apartment. The racial composition, average
family size, proportion of minors, average family income, percent on welfare,
and percent of broken homes were nearly identical. They were also located
across the street from one another. As a result, they were served by the same
Housing Authority police and New York City police. Despite these similarities,
the two projects differed markedly in layout and design. For example, Van Dyke
was comprised primarily of fourteen-story rectangular-shaped buildings, while
Brownsville consisted of three- to six-story cross-shaped buildings. The one
functional entrance to each Van Dyke building was about 60 feet from the
street, invisible to street surveillance, and served approximately 125 families.
Each Brownsville building contained several entrances. Each entrance was used by

nine to thirteen families and was usually located only a few feet from the street. In Van Dyke, enclosed, soundproof fire stairwells became areas in which crimes were frequently committed. In Brownsville, open stairwells were surrounded by apartment doors.

The behavior of tenants and the incidence of crime suggest that these differences in layout and design had a considerable impact on the quality of life in each project. While crime and vandalism were major problems in both housing projects, more than twice as many robberies, and 60% more felonies and misdemeanors, were reported in the Van Dyke housing. In Brownsville, children were allowed to play in corridors and on stairwells. In Van Dyke, they were not. Similarly, young children in Brownsville were allowed to roam over more outdoor space than were young children in Van Dyke. Brownsville tenants, compared to Van Dyke tenants, were also more active in keeping their buildings clean, and were less likely to move out of their apartments.

Based on this study and on studies of 165 other public housing projects in New York City, Newman (1972) proposed that defensible space is produced by three interacting features of design. One, the space outside the individual apartment units should be designed in ways that cause tenants and outsiders to perceive that the public spaces comprising the project are part of the tenants' personal territory. For example, locate the apartment buildings in ways that define and break up the grounds they occupy; limit the project to 1,000 units or less; and use low walls, hedges, stoops, changes in the texture of the walking surface, and entry portals to create symbolic barriers between the public street and the semipublic grounds of the project. Wtihin each building, separate the elevators so that each one serves about four to eight apartments per floor, and cluster small numbers of apartments around corridors and open stairwells. Two, the grounds of the project and the building interiors should be designed in ways that provide residents and formal authorities with natural opportunities to observe all public and semiprivate spaces and paths. For example, divide housing projects into small, recognizable enclaves; locate building entrances close to the street and facing the street; illuminate paths and entrances; make lobbies and elevator entrances visible to passersby; build windows into firestair walls; and have kitchen windows face building entrances, play areas, and parking lots. Three, projects should be designed in ways that minimize residents' and outsiders' perception of the project as unique, isolated, and stigmatized. For example, build two to three, rather than ten to twenty high-rise buildings; avoid materials that create an institutional atmosphere, such as glazed tiles and mercury-vapor type exterior lighting; and provide automobiles with access to streets within the project.

Rent Supplements and Leased Housing

In an attempt to respond more effectively to the problem of housing the poor, the federal government created the rent supplement and leased housing programs in 1965.[3] The rent supplement program sought to encourage private groups to construct and manage housing for low-income families by providing these groups with rent subsidy payments. The leased housing program was designed to lease privately owned housing units and sublease those units to families qualified for public housing. Shortly before these programs were created, the Boston Housing Authority funded an experimental rent subsidy program that contained many of the features of the rent supplement and leased housing programs. In an attempt to determine the effectiveness of the Boston program from the vantage point of the participants, Tilly and Feagin (1970, reading 3.4) compared the responses of 35 low-income black families who moved into a newly constructed middle-in-come development and 24 low-income black families who moved into a public housing project. Both the development and project were located in the Roxbury ghetto area. The 35 families in the middle-class development paid the rents they would normally pay in public housing. The Boston Housing Authority paid the rest. The findings indicated that 83% of the rent subsidy wives, compared to 29% of the public housing wives, said they liked their new residence "very much" (Feagin, Tilly, & Williams, 1972). The findings also indicate that most of the rent subsidy wives liked their new homes better than the homes they moved from; for example, almost everyone was more satisfied with the size and external appearance of the building, the amount of apartment space, the quietness of the street, and the neighborhood as a place to raise children. Although a majority of the public housing wives were also more satisfied with their buildings and apart-ments, sizable minorities were less satisfied with the proximity of public trans-portation, the class of people living nearby, and the quietness of the street. The social ties of the women in both groups were affected similarly by the move; that is, most of the wives cut some social ties when they moved and made new friends several weeks afterward. Within the middle-income development, there was no indication that rent subsidy families were treated as a stigmatized group by their middle-class neighbors, or that unusual problems developed between the two groups.

Rent supplements and leased housing appear to have several advantages. One, they can provide a considerable number of poor families with housing that meets desired standards. Two, "they are flexible; in all but a very tight market they can

---

3. Rent supplements and leased housing do not include the subsidized purchase by poor families of newly constructed or rehabilitated homes.

be used to rapidly increase the number of units available for relocated families"
(Tilly & Feagin, 1970, p. 328). Three, "they give redevelopment and housing
authorities the means to assure that relocated families receive dwellings in good
condition" (Tilly & Feagin, 1970, p. 328). Unfortunately, rent supplements and
leased housing may also have disadvantages. One, they may have an adverse
impact on the quality of housing in a city. For example, Tilly and Feagin suggested that the owners of substandard dwellings may respond to rising vacancy
rates by abandoning or destroying the buildings. However, Tilly and Feagin also
noted that these owners might improve, convert, or reduce rents on their properties. Two, landlords who participate in rent subsidy programs may collude
with inspectors in order to maintain low standards while setting high rents. While
some policing may be needed, Tilly and Feagin argued that "the local housing
authority operating a rent subsidy program under its own control has several
advantages over the city's code enforcement officer. It is offering something
precious to a landlord: a guarantee of continuous rent payments. It can negotiate the rent directly . . . for many units at a time, rather than relying on piecemeal landlord-tenant agreements . . . [and] can supervise maintenance, or it can
contract with a third party for maintenance" (p. 329).

While further research on the impact of rent supplements and leased housing is
clearly needed, the results of the Boston experiment suggest that they are
desirable strategies from the vantage point of the participating families.

Direct Housing Allowances

The shortcomings of public housing—long waiting lists, little or no opportunity
to choose where to live, and the creation of pockets of high density housing in
ghetto areas—led Model Cities agencies in Kansas City, Missouri and Wilmington,
Delaware to conduct preliminary examinations during 1971–72 of the feasibility
of a direct housing allowance (Peabody, 1974, reading 3.5). Approximately 200
low-income families living primarily in substandard units or in public housing
were selected to participate in the Kansas City program. Eighty-five percent of
the families chosen were black, 79% were headed by a female, and 75% were
receiving welfare. Each family was given the opportunity to rent housing anywhere in the Kansas City metropolitan area as long as that housing met city code
standards. In other words, each family was given a monthly housing allowance
when they found acceptable housing. The amount of the allowance was the
standard cost of housing appropriate to the family's size and composition less
25% of the family's income (adjusted for family size). If families rented housing
for less than the standard cost, they could keep the difference as long as the
allowance was less than or equal to the rent. In other words, they could reduce
their own expenses.

The results indicate that most black families moved to black working-class neighborhoods while most white families moved to white working-class neighborhoods; that 90% of the participants liked choosing their own homes and preferred a direct allowance to public housing; and that the allowances averaged about $95.00 a month, or only about 40% of the cost of subsidizing a new public housing unit each year. Although the Wilmington study produced fairly similar findings, the use of only two cities and about 250 families makes generalization imprudent. As a result, the Department of Housing and Urban Development is currently funding major studies of the direct housing allowance in eleven metropolitan areas.

While direct housing allowances seem to have a number of desirable features, Gans (1974) argued that they also have several drawbacks. One, a housing allowance will not work in cities whose vacancy rate is less than 5%. In other words, unless there is an adequate supply of moderately priced vacant housing, many poor people will not be able to take advantage of the allowance. Although the vacancy rate in many metropolitan areas is at least 5%, it is less than 5% in a considerable number of others; for example, New York and Rochester (Peabody, 1974). Two, a direct housing allowance will not benefit poor families who already reside in standard housing. Three, the units that allowance recipients select will have to be inspected to make sure that they meet city code standards. Unfortunately, this may generate considerable corruption, since it costs less to bribe an inspector than to renovate a buliding. Four, the residents of working-class neighborhoods are likely to react hostilely to a large influx of poor families, and many may move voluntarily or be frightened into moving by block-busting realtors. In an attempt to minimize or eliminate these drawbacks, Gans proposed that allowances be given to poor, near poor, and barely-moderate-income people without requiring them to move; that rent control be a part of direct housing allowance legislation; and that the construction of housing for the nonpoor accompany an allowance program, except in cities with abundant vacancies.

CONCLUSIONS

Studies of low-income private and public housing suggest that residents' attitudes are primarily favorable in some neighborhoods and largely negative or neutral in others. The findings also suggest that the degree to which social networks evolve and the extent to which residents feel their homes and neighborhoods are safe are important determinants of these attitudes. Given these findings, several studies of the effects of public housing have useful implications—for both present and future private and public housing. These studies suggest that the way housing is designed has a considerable impact on the extent to which social networks evolve and on the rate at which crimes are committed.

Newman's studies of the public housing projects in New York City are especially instructive. These studies indicate that three interacting features of design produce housing that facilitates the development of social networks and reduces considerably the incidence of crime.

The findings also imply that many of the people who live in low-income private dwellings would be satisfied with their neighborhoods and homes if neighborhood crime were substantially reduced and the dilapidated conditions in their homes were corrected. Accordingly, the assignment of considerably more police to low-income areas and the creation of a home-repair allowance may also be useful strategies.

Additional implications for providing low-income families with satisfactory housing come from the studies of rent subsidies and direct housing allowances. Although further research is clearly needed before conclusions about their effectiveness can be drawn, the studies that have been done suggest that these are desirable strategies from the viewpoint of the participating families.

While public housing, rent supplements, leased housing, and direct housing allowances may provide decent housing for substantial numbers of poor people, the impact of any housing policy is clearly limited. As Gans (1974) noted: "Ultimately, a house is only a physical shell for people's lives; it cannot affect the deprivation forced by unemployment or underemployment; or lessen the anxiety of an unstable or underpaid job; or reduce the stigma and dependency of being on welfare; or keep out pathology. A housing policy is not and cannot be an antipoverty policy" (p. 58).

REFERENCES

Barresi, C., & Lindquist, J. The urban community: Attitudes toward neighborhood and urban renewal. *Urban Affairs Quarterly*, 1970, 5, 278–290.

Cagle, L., & Deutscher, I. Housing aspirations and housing achievement: The relocation of poor families. *Social Problems*, 1970, 18, 243–256.

Cooper, C. *Some social implications of house and site plan design at Easter Hill Village*. Berkeley: University of California Institute of Urban and Regional Development, 1965.

Feagin, J., Tilly, C., & Williams, C. *Subsidizing the poor: A Boston housing experiment*. Lexington, Mass.: D. C. Heath, 1972.

Frieden, B. Housing and national urban goals: Old policies and new realities. In J. Q. Wilson (Ed.), *The metropolitan enigma*. Cambridge: Harvard University Press, 1968.

Gans, H. A poor man's home in his poorhouse. In *The New York Times Magazine, The New York Times*, March 31, 1974.

Gilbert, N., & Eaton, J. Who speaks for the poor? *Journal of the American Institute of Planners*, 1970, 36, 411–416.

Hartman, C. Social values and housing orientations. *Journal of Social Issues*, 1963, 19 (2), 113–131. (a)

Hartman, C. Limitations of public housing: Relocation choices of a working-class community. *Journal of the American Institute of Planners*, 1963, 29, 283–296. (b)

Kasl, S., & Harburg, E. Perceptions of the neighborhood and the desire to move out. *Journal of the American Institute of Planners*, 1972, 38, 318–324.

Levine, D., Fiddmont, N., Stephenson, R., &

Wilkerson, C. Are the black poor satisfied with conditions in their neighborhood? *Journal of the American Institute of Planners*, 1972, 38, 168–171.

Newman, O. *Defensible space.* New York: Macmillan, 1972.

Newman, O. Defensible space: Crime prevention through urban design. *Ekistics,* 1973, 36, 325–332.

Peabody, Jr., M. Housing allowances. *The New Republic*, 1974, 170 (10), 20–23.

Tilly, C., & Feagin, J. Boston's experiment with rent subsidies. *Journal of the American Institute of Planners*, 1970, 36, 323–329.

U.S. Bureau of the Census. Social and economic conditions of Negroes in the United States. In *Current population reports,* series P-23, no. 24, 1967.

Wilner, D., Walkley, R., Pinkerton, T., & Tayback, M. *The housing environment and family life.* Baltimore: The Johns Hopkins University Press, 1962.

Wolf, E., & Lebeaux, C. On the destruction of poor neighborhoods by urban renewal. *Social Problems*, 1967, 15, 3–8.

Wolfe, A., Lex, B., & Yancey, W. *The Soulard area: Adaptations by urban white families to poverty.* St. Louis: Social Science Institute of Washington University, 1968.

Yancey, W. Architecture, interaction, and social control: The case of a large-scale public housing project. *Environment and Behavior*, 1971, 3, 3–21.

Social Values and Housing Orientations

CHESTER W. HARTMAN

INTRODUCTION

Traditionally, description and analysis of the problems of slums, as well as the various governmental programs aimed at their amelioration, have been dominated by concern for the physical aspects of the environment: facilities, housing condition, hygiene, quantity of living space. In more recent considerations of the ways in which planning and social policy can most effectively improve the lot of the slum-dweller, increasing attention is being paid to the range of social and cultural values and how they modify attitudes toward and use of the "objective" physical world. Research in this area has focused largely on the process of dislocation and relocation from urban redevelopment areas, prompted by the personal and social problems many displaced families have experienced in leaving old neighborhoods and in adjusting to new ones. However, the broader questions of the nature and determinants of residential attitudes and choices and how they vary among different groups have not yet been subjected to careful inquiry.

This problem is particularly pertinent with respect to working-class populations, since their lives are most subject to conscious and drastic intervention through the urban renewal and public housing programs. We know little about the basic issues involved in the formation of residential patterns and choices generally, and our knowledge about residential orientations in the working class is particularly meager. This gap in our knowledge is usually filled with assumptions and impressions about standards and goals based largely on experience with middle-class and professional people. Working-class residential attitudes and goals may, however, be founded on entirely different needs and desires. What appears irrational or neglectful in working-class residential patterns may, upon deeper inquiry, prove to be quite reasonable and meaningful. *In order to reassess physical standards in terms of personal values and living patterns and come to a view of the physical environment as a setting for social action, we must understand the meaning and functional importance that so-called slum areas have for their inhabitants.*

In the course of studying the effects on mental health of forced relocation from

From C. Hartman. Social values and housing orientations. *Journal of Social Issues*, 1963, *19*(2), 113–131. Reprinted by permission.

Boston's West End,[1] we have tried to clarify the prevalent values and patterns of a stable and vital urban working-class neighborhood. Through questionnaires, surveys and observation of almost 500 households, a fairly clear picture emerges of life in this community. These findings serve to suggest some alternative considerations for reviewing our conceptions of slums and slum housing.

HOUSING ATTITUDES

If the ostensible purpose of slum clearance and urban renewal is to improve the lot of the slum-dweller, a crucial consideration is the attitudes of slum residents toward their own housing situations. Planning cannot of course be wholly guided by what is, at first sight, preferred by the community; certainly one of the tasks of the planner is to communicate alternative possibilities and their implications in order to guide community decisions. Nonetheless, empirical evidence of preferences serves as a valuable indicator of residential values and the role that housing plays among various groups. These can, in turn, provide the basis for meaningful social change oriented toward human needs.

The people of West End in general were very strongly attached to their neighborhood.[2] An overwhelming proportion of the

1. The West End, a 48-acre neighborhood located in the center of Boston, was demolished in 1958–1959 as part of the city's urban renewal program. At the time of land-taking about 2700 households—7500 persons—were living in the area. The population was predominantly working-class, with a scattering of students and professional people, the latter for the most part associated with the adjacent Massachusetts General Hospital. The inhabitants were primarily first- and second-generation American, and the predominant ethnic groups were Italian (42%), Jewish (11%), and Polish (10%). Most of the data in this paper are taken from a 2–3 hour interview conducted with a sample of 473 female household members. This represented roughly one out of every five families living in the West End. A second, post-relocation, interview was conducted with the same persons after a lapse of several years, to determine the effects of relocation, but no data from these interviews are included in the present report.
2. Fried, Marc, "Grieving for a lost home," in Duhl, Leonard J. (ed.), *The Urban Condition*, New

sample (78%) also reported that they liked the apartments in which they were living, while very few (13%) expressed unqualified dislike. In the light of more generalized conceptions of so-called slum areas, this is indeed a remarkable finding. It must inevitably lead us to question whether the usual descriptive criteria of substandard living conditions are adequate indicators of either objective physical standards or subjective value preferences.

This high rate of satisfaction takes on added significance in view of the fact that West Enders were not severely limited in their choice of residence, as may be the case with many slum residents. The West End population was almost exclusively white; thus they did not suffer from the racial restrictions on housing choice which operate for Negroes. Moreover, on the basis of income, most West Enders could have lived in more fashionable housing and neighborhoods, had they so chosen; 20% of the sample had family incomes in excess of $100 per week, and 43% in excess of $75 per week.[3] Since West End rents were extremely low—average monthly housing costs, including heat but not utilities, were $42—most persons were spending a very low proportion of their incomes for housing. Sixty-three per cent of the sample devoted less than 1/6 of their total income to housing, and 20% less than 1/10. However, financial reasons were rarely mentioned by West Enders as motives for living there, and the rate of housing satisfaction is no higher among persons paying lower proportions of their incomes for housing. While there were many persons for whom the low rent levels, both in absolute terms and proportionate to income, must

York: Basic Books, 1963; Fried, Marc, and Gleicher, Peggy, "Some sources of residential satisfaction in an urban slum," *J. Amer. Inst. Planners*, 1961, *27*, 305–315; and Gans, Herbert, "The human implications of current redevelopment and relocation planning," *J. Amer. Inst. Planners*, 1959, *25*, 15–25.
3. Post-relocation housing surveys brought out dramatically this potential for better housing; some West Enders relocated in suburban homes in the $20–25,000 class.

have been important sources of satisfaction with the West End, the desire to economize on housing cannot stand as a general explanation of the fact that nearly 4/5 of the population in an area of ostensibly substandard housing liked their apartments. The most obvious question to ask initially is whether the description of the West End as a slum is an accurate one.

HOUSING CONDITION

Examination of the physical status of housing in the West End shows that there were certainly a great many substandard dwellings, but that there was also a fairly large stock of decent housing. The general quality of housing was considerably higher than that implied in our usual notions of slums. According to a pre-relocation survey of housing conditions (see Table 1), only 36% of all buildings and 25% of all apartments were in poor or very bad (dilapidated) condition, while 23% of all buildings and 41% of all apartments were in good or excellent (sound) condition.[4]

4. While not part of the main argument of this paper, it should be noted that the true proportion of good and bad housing in an urban renewal area has important implications for both social policy and personal reactions. Planners must consider carefully the number of non-dilapidated units to be eliminated in a clearance project—and their particular characteristics in terms of rental levels, housing type, availability and desirability to various ethnic groups, and location—to determine what sorts of imbalances are thereby created in the housing stock.

In aggregate statistical terms, evaluation of the results of urban renewal projects with respect to relocation of displaced residents may be quite deceptive if it fails to take into account over-all pre-relocation housing conditions. If post-relocation surveys find that, say, 60% of an area's population has been relocated in standard housing, this may be no gain at all, and perhaps a loss, since an equal or greater proportion may have been living in standard housing before relocation. As planning and urban renewal powers expand in the direction of allowing increased amounts of non-slum acreage to be included in a clearance project to permit large-scale planning, this consideration increases in importance.

Furthermore, persons displaced from sound housing in the course of an urban renewal plan probably feel a great sense of personal injustice, which may

One of the most striking features of housing conditions in the West End is the frequency with which apartment quality was superior to building condition. In the majority of cases (61%), of course, condition of dwelling unit and condition of building were at approximately the same level. In only a small group (7%) was building condition better than dwelling unit condition. But for almost one-third of the sample (32%) dwelling unit condition represented an improvement over building condition. This alerts us to the fact that, in some sense, good physical living conditions were highly valued in the West End. Despite structural limitations, a great many West End apartments showed evidence of considerable care and attention; their inhabitants improved and maintained them, undaunted by the physical shabbiness of the immediate and general environment.[5]

Our interviewers were constantly surprised by the quality of West End apartments, quite unexpected in view of external appearances. The pride that many West Enders took in their apartments can be gleaned from interviewers' comments such as the following:

Well furnished, elaborately decorated, kitchen with all modern utilities and conveniences.

Extremely well appointed—very modern. Since almost on Charles River, could be very expensive apartment, even with West End the way it is.

Respondent's apartment . . . is extremely well kept, very nicely furnished. The floors are fine hardwood and walls are hand-painted murals or such, done by her husband.

intensify negative consequences of relocation, such as feelings of bitterness and grief as well as adjustment difficulties.

5. Data on apartment furnishings and appearance also indicate that West Enders exhibited considerable concern for their apartments: 80% of the sample had furnishings rated as "good condition—old or new," and in 80% of the cases apartment appearance was rated as "neat and clean."

Table 1. Condition of Building and Dwelling Unit,*
West End Sample

| | Building Condition | | | |
Dwelling Unit Condition	Excellent/ Good (n)	Fair (n)	Poor/ Very Bad (n)	Total
Excellent/Good	60	54	10	124 (41%)
Fair	11	61	33	105 (34%)
Poor/Very Bad	1	11	66	78 (25%)
Total	72 (23%)	126 (41%)	109 (36%)	307** (100%)

*The evaluative criteria used by our interviewers approximate those used by Census enumerators. Our ratings "poor/very bad," "fair," and "excellent/good" are the respective equivalents of "dilapidated," "deteriorating," and "sound." The 1950 Housing Census block statistics indicated that slightly over 20% of all units in the project area were dilapidated or lacked private bath. Our data show that 25% of the units are "poor/very bad" (4% lacked private bath, but virtually all of these are also in poor or very bad condition), which is roughly the increase to be expected over seven years due to natural deterioration of the housing stock and the accelerated deterioration that followed the original announcement of redevelopment plans in 1952.
**The first (pre-relocation) interview was conducted during late 1958 and early 1959. The sample was drawn from Relocation Office listings of all persons living in the area as of approximately mid-Winter 1957–1958. Many persons moved out of the area between the time of the listing and the interview (in an accelerated fashion after residents began to receive eviction notices in the Spring of 1958). Therefore, interviewers' ratings on the condition of the respondents' housing were available for only 307 of the 473 cases (those whose initial interviews were held in the West End apartments). This sample represents about 1/3 of all West End buildings and about 1/8 of all occupied dwelling units.

This apartment is furnished in excellent furniture of outstandingly good taste—a beautiful place in any league.[6]

The difference in quality of interior and exterior residential spaces is a vital factor to be considered in evaluating slum areas. It evidences the importance of good dwelling

6. Naturally, examples of the other extreme were also to be found. One of the more distressed comments by an interviewer: "This is the worst apartment I have been in—it smells of urine and dog feces—there is very little furniture and that in hopeless repair and the place has not been cleaned in perhaps months."

units for a large proportion of slum inhabitants and the motivation to achieve this, within the limitations of the physical environment. Residential attachment and the significance of housing attributes can be expressed in a variety of ways, and it would be a mistake to conclude from the external attributes of a dwelling or neighborhood alone the prevalent values and orientations toward housing.

The considerable proportion of decent housing cannot, however, wholly explain the high rate of satisfaction with apartments. It is true that housing satisfaction showed a strong positive relationship to objective condition. On the basis of an over-all housing rating, 89% of the occupants of "good housing" liked their apartments, while 65% of the occupants of "poor housing" expressed equivalent satisfaction.[7] The remarkable fact, however, is that so high a proportion of persons with poor housing—nearly 2/3— stated that they liked their apartments. The apparent paradox of satisfaction with poor housing conditions when there was ample opportunity for awareness of and change to better housing can be adequately understood only if we take account of the social values which guide and define residential attitudes and behavior.

SOCIAL VALUES AND HOUSING ATTITUDES

One of the most important social values we must consider is that "people do not live *only* in houses, and this is most strikingly true for working-class people."[8] The apartment proper can play quite different parts in the residential patterns of different people. For some, it is *home* and every movement away from this central area is temporary and

carried out for a specific purpose. But, in the working class, external areas are far more extensively and casually used and, by comparison, the surrounding neighborhood is a far more important component of the residential "life space." If the apartment is considered as a connected part of an entire residential context, it may be that feelings about the residential situation as a whole are likely to "rub off" and affect many discrete residential and housing experiences which, considered by themselves, might not be intrinsically satisfying.

A number of factors strongly suggest that feelings about the area as a whole markedly influenced attitudes toward the apartment. Certainly there was an extremely high rate of global satisfaction with the West End as a residential neighborhood. The great majority of people living in the area (76%) expressed quite unreserved positive feelings about the West End; and only a small proportion (10%) expressed unqualified negative feelings about the area. Several recent studies have also pointed to the deep attachment that many slum-dwellers develop for their homes and neighborhoods.[9] A review of some typical responses reveals the depth of feelings experienced by West Enders in considering their local neighborhood. The following examples are selected from responses to the question, "How do you feel about living in the West End?"

It's home to me, because it's the place I've lived in all my life. It's nearest to my heart— just home to me—a wonderful thing.

I love it. I was born and brought up here. I like the conveniences, the people, I feel safe ... I'm going to miss it terribly.

---

7. Unless specific mention is made of building or dwelling unit condition, "good," "fair," and "poor" housing refer to a Housing Index derived from ratings on five separate items: household density, building condition, dwelling unit condition, furnishings and household appearance. The unweighted summation of these ratings gave a scale with a possible scoring range of 5–14 (as was noted in the footnote to Table 1, only 2/3 of the sample could be rated). "Poor housing" was that which received a score of 5–9, "fair housing" 10–12, and "good housing" 13–14. "poor housing" is of course not a very precise term, but descriptively it would range from "3 persons living in 5 rooms, building and dwelling unit dilapidated, furnishings old but in good condition, appearance very disorderly" (9 points on the Housing Index) to "6 persons living in 4 rooms, building and dwelling unit dilapidated, makeshift furnishings, appearance very disorderly (5 points on the Housing Index).

8. Fried, Marc, "Personal and Social Deprivations and Family Roles: The Working Class Situation." (Unpublished manuscript. Paper delivered before the National Conference on Social Welfare, New York, May, 1962).

9. Fried, Marc, in Duhl, Leonard J. (ed.), *The Urban Condition, loc. cit.*; Fried, Marc, and Gleicher, Peggy, *op. cit.*; Marris, Peter, *Family and Social Change in an African City*, London: Routledge and Kegan Paul, 1961; Mogey, J. M., *Family and Neighbourhood*, London: Oxford University Press, 1956; and Young, Michael, and Willmott, Peter, *Family and Kinship in East London*, Glencoe: The Free Press, 1957.

Good. Lovely. I'll never find any better than the West End. I love the West End.

Wonderful. We had such lovely times as kids. Wonderful memories.

I loved it very much. It was home to me. I was very happy. Everyone was so nice. All my relatives lived here.

I enjoyed it. I liked it very much. People were wonderful. Everyone was nice. Stores are very convenient and it was like a big family.

I feel so badly. I've got the blues about leaving here. Have lived here so long. It's really my only place.

You're asking an old-timer who loves it here. Do you think I can get used to any other place? I don't think so.

I love the West End—this is my country.

I love the West End. I love America, the people. I pray to God that they'll let me stay here.

I loved it. I don't know no other place. I loved it.

As these responses suggest, the West End was a place to which people were deeply committed and in which they were rooted by an abundance of interpersonal ties and attachments to meaningful places. There were strong feelings of belonging, of being "at home." Most of these responses have a diffuse, generalized quality which communicates a sense of total embeddedness, the feeling that the area was the setting for their entire lives. Under these circumstances, the evaluation of discrete places or experiences is likely to be dominated by the more general sense of satisfaction and meaningfulness of the total environment, of its dominant values, and of the life styles characteristic of the people living in the area. Housing will be perceived in a quite different way in this case, compared with the more usual situation in which the dwelling unit itself is of predominant importance.

In the West End, the apartment was merely one aspect of residential life. Its functions and significance were, to a large extent, defined by the broader personal and social setting and the attitudes of people toward their housing situation. If we examine attitudes toward the dwelling unit, we find that: (a) feelings expressed about the apartment were quite pallid and unemotional compared with comments about the West End; and (b) the responses frequently by-passed the actual question with allusions to factors extrinsic to the apartment itself, such as neighbors, relatives, view, contact with the street, general accessibility. This becomes quite apparent when we consider a series of responses from the same persons whose comments about the neighborhood are reported above, in answer to the question, "What do you like about your apartment?"

Within my means, clean and nice-looking—I like the cleanliness and heat and hot water.

A good-sized kitchen. It's airy. I can look out on the street. Friendly neighbors.

It's just because I stay here a long time. It's just that I haven't found anything wrong. It's all okay.

The neighborhood.

Steam heat. First floor.

Convenient to everything. Large rooms, heat supplied. Large bathroom.

The rooms are laid out nice and I have a hall.

Convenient. Nothing wrong. Found refrigerator here. Warm, cozy rooms.

Nothing special. I'm just used to it here.

Nice rooms, friendly location.

Well, once it's cleaned up, it's cozy. It's got enough room for what I have.

It's clean. One flight up. It's nice, that's all.

These responses convey both the limited affective tone in the orientation to the apartment and the sense of the apartment as part of a larger world with many other dimensions. It is also notable that there was a considerable amount of intra-West End mobility—moves from one apartment to another within the neighborhood. Of the 295 residents who lived in the West End at least 15 years and thus indicated their deep commitment to the area, 50% had changed apartments within the last 10 years, and 17% had moved more than once. Thus, for many residents the basic sense of residential satisfaction and continuity was not necessarily tied to a specific dwelling but was inherent in the larger residential context. Dwellings were often replaceable; the area seems, for a very great many, to have been utterly irreplaceable.

HOUSING CONDITION, HOUSING ATTITUDES AND SOCIAL VALUES

If it is true that West Enders viewed their apartments in a context provided by more general residential satisfactions and meaning, we should expect that attitudes toward the apartment will be considerably influenced by attitudes toward broader aspects of residential experience. In particular we must examine the interaction of attitudes toward the West End and objective housing quality as determinants of attitudes toward the apartment. It is quite clear from the data presented in Table 2 that if one had strong positive feelings about the West End, one also had positive feelings about the apartment. Under these conditions objective housing quality was almost irrelevant as a determinant of housing attitudes. Among those who liked the West End very much, almost everyone with good housing (98%) liked his apartment, and only a slightly smaller proportion of those with poor housing (86%) liked their apartments. As feelings about the area itself became less positive, however, rates of satisfaction with apartments of comparable quality decreased. And only then did objective quality of housing appear to affect attitudes toward the apartment. Thus, among those with good housing, 98% of those who liked the West End very much liked their apartments, but only 59% of those who did not have positive

Table 2. Relation of Attitude Toward West End, Attitude Toward Apartment, and Objective Housing Quality

Housing Quality	Attitude Toward West End		
	Like Very Much	Like	Other (mixed/indiff., dislike, dislike very much)
Good Housing			
Like Apartment	98%	91%	59%
	(n = 44)	(n = 34)	(n = 17)
Mixed/Indiff., Dislike	2%	9%	41%
Fair Housing			
Like Apartment	92%	83%	65%
	(n = 60)	(n = 46)	(n = 31)
Mixed/Indiff., Dislike	8%	17%	35%
Poor Housing			
Like Apartment	86%	67%	38%
	(n = 22)	(n = 33)	(n = 21)
Mixed/Indiff., Dislike	14%	33%	62%

feelings about the West End liked their apartments. There is only a 12% difference in the proportion of persons who liked good and who liked poor housing among those who were very positive about the West End, but the gap increases to 24% among those with only moderately positive feelings about the neighborhood and remains at approximately the same level with more negative feelings about the area.

We may note that, among those who expressed no positive feelings about the West End and who lived in poor housing, 38% still liked their apartments. At first sight, this is a puzzling group, although it represents only a very small number of persons (8 cases). Why should so high a proportion of those people who did not have good housing and who were not satisfied with the surrounding environment like their apartments? A closer analysis of these cases and a review of the original responses is quite revealing. Only one person of the eight expressed actual dislike for the neighborhood; the other seven were either ambivalent or indifferent. Moreover, among most of these there was the explicit or implicit reference to a recent impairment in their attitudes, due to the actual deterioration of the West End during the redevelopment period, starting in 1952 (five of the seven had been living in the West End at least 20 years). The one person who specifically stated disliking the West End, when asked what she liked about her apartment, began by saying, "The street outside. . . ." In short, a closer consideration of this "deviant" group lends further support to the notion that attitudes toward housing are closely related to feelings about the general residential environment.

That this relationship between objective physical quality and the larger sense of residential meaning and satisfaction is highly general and based on quite concrete local experience is further documented by considering the relationship between attitudes toward the apartment and several "social" variables, holding objective housing quality constant. Two of the more striking examples

Table 3. Relation of Contact with Neighbors, Attitude Toward Apartment, and Housing Quality

Housing Quality	Contact with Neighbors	
	Contact with Many	Contact with Few or None
Good Housing		
Like Apartment	95%	84%
	(n = 38)	(n = 56)
Mixed/Indiff., Dislike	5%	16%
Fair Housing		
Like Apartment	93%	75%
	(n = 57)	(n = 79)
Mixed/Indiff., Dislike	7%	25%
Poor Housing		
Like Apartment	85%	53%
	(n = 26)	(n = 47)
Mixed/Indiff., Dislike	15%	47%

of this general pattern are presented in Tables 3 and 4, where the influence of contact with neighbors and size of extended family living in the West End on attitudes toward the apartment can be observed. People who had frequent contact with neighbors or a large extended family living in the same neighborhood were highly likely to be satisfied with their apartments, almost irrespective of objective apartment quality. These data again demonstrate that, in varying degrees, *the experience of social and personal satisfaction in the local area markedly limits the effect of objective housing quality on attitudes toward the apartment. Only in the absence of these meaningful experiences does the objective physical quality of the dwelling become an important determinant of housing satisfaction.*

Residential satisfactions, thus, are not experienced discretely, but may be related to an entire living pattern and a larger set of social and personal values. For many people, particularly the working class,[10] the social

10. As noted earlier, the West End contained several large ethnic concentrations. No significant dif-

Table 4. Relation of Size of Extended Family in the West End, Attitude Toward Apartment, and Housing Quality

Housing Quality	Extended Family in West End	
	4 or More Related Households Living in West End	0–3 Related Households Living in West End
Good Housing		
Like Apartment	96%	85%
	(n = 28)	(n = 65)
Mixed/Indiff., Dislike	4%	15%
Fair Housing		
Like Apartment	81%	83%
	(n = 36)	(n = 101)
Mixed/Indiff., Dislike	19%	17%
Poor Housing		
Like Apartment	93%	56%
	(n = 15)	(n = 59)
Mixed/Indiff., Dislike	7%	44%

and personal satisfactions that derive from the total living situation may be of primary importance. It is inevitable then that conflict will frequently arise between the desire to retain these critical features of life style, personal meaning and continuity and desires for physical housing quality, whether these are based on the intrinsic significance of a good apartment or on status aspirations related to housing. When this conflict occurs, some compromise is necessary in order to retain the maximum benefit within the limits of the physical reality. It cannot be denied that the West End was characterized by many shoddy-looking buildings, lack of light and air and green space, considerable dirt, and street patterns inadequate for many aspects of urban life. But the primary satisfactions connected with West End living were able to flourish within this physical setting. Implicit was a compromise: to

ferences have been found between these groups regarding the findings reported in this paper; nor have they yet appeared as critical variables for most of the results of our study.

accept the external space as it was and to restrain desires for physical quality, applying efforts to achieve this within the more easily controlled area of the apartment. Thus, apart from any ideal desires regarding the physical habitat, over-all physical quality of the living space necessarily assumed a secondary place in the hierarchy of residential values.

Relegating physical quality to a secondary position, however, does not mean that it was unimportant or that efforts at individual improvement were wholly satisfactory. In fact, most West Enders felt that their dwellings fell short of the standards they desired. When asked what they disliked about the apartment, only 29% expressed complete satisfaction. The majority stated one or more reservations, and the most frequent complaints referred to lack of space (18%), deterioration (13%), inconvenience (14%), and general physical atmosphere (14%). But these reservations and complaints hardly signify any serious disaffection and certainly were insufficient to motivate many moves out of the neighborhood or even seriously to interfere with expressed feelings of satisfaction with the apartment or with the area. As indicated, only in the absence of other social and personal satisfactions does the objective quality of the apartment become a primary determinant of housing satisfaction. These data, of course, refer to a sample from a population which was predominantly working class. From the point of view of physical planning, it would be of considerable importance to know if some of these interrelationships also hold for other population groups. In general, middle-class housing does not even provide an opportunity for the operation of those communal factors which made the West End so meaningful an area for most of its residents. Thus, even if these same dynamic relations would hold in theory, practically speaking most middle-class urban dwellers have little choice but to base their evaluations of their residential situations primarily on the quality of their housing and on other physical attributes of their habitat.

It is, at the very least, a reasonable hypothesis that if urban planning were to create large-scale physical spaces for all socio-economic groups with a greater potentiality for becoming meaningful personal and social settings, the traditional primacy of the dwelling unit might diminish considerably.

RESIDENTIAL DENSITY

Like housing quality, quantity of individual residential space—in its relative form, housing density—can properly be evaluated only within a context of living patterns and values. There has been little attempt to build flexibility into density standards, taking account of the ways in which traditions and values of different class and ethnic groups relate to desired amounts of space; of the effects of inter-personal contact and affective style on the thresholds at which crowding is perceived as overcrowding; or of the mutual relationships between usable interior apartment space and usable exterior residential space.[11] A pattern of more intimate and frequent interpersonal contact requires a very different spatial setting from a pattern in which privacy and independence are highly valued.

The West End was a high density area, and overcrowding, both internal and external, was one of the putative evils that led to the neighborhood's condemnation. The streets were noisy, narrow and crowded, and there was virtually no internal open space, although the Charles River and its parks formed the western boundary of the area and the Boston Common was within walking distance. According to the Boston Housing Authority's *Declaration of Findings:* "Almost all [of the 798 residential structures in the West End] cover 90% of the lot on which they are situated, and almost all of these structures have no setback from the

street." Compared with several other Boston neighborhoods generally considered to be crowded, and with the city as a whole, housing densities were also relatively high. Sixteen per cent of West End households were living at density ratios higher than 1.00, compared with 9% of all Boston households; and 27% were living at ratios of 0.50 or less, compared with 48% of all Boston households.[12] There were, however, only 10 families in the sample (2%) living at density ratios higher than 1.50, the Census criterion for extreme over-crowding. And, despite the generally high apartment densities, 13% of the sample were living in apartments in which the number of rooms exceeded the number of occupants by at least three.

When the residential situation is characterized by considerable choice and minimal restriction, as was generally true in the West End, density patterns are likely to be a product of certain critical features of living patterns. Thus, density cannot be regarded as a discrete variable and evaluated without reference to the larger residential context provided by other physical and social variables. In the West End it is clear that residential stability and the ways in which living space was organized with reference to a

11. An excellent exposition of the difference between these two spaces and their significance for planning is to be found in Jane Jacobs' recent book *The Death and Life of Great American Cities*, New York: Random House, 1962, pp. 205–208.

12. "Density ratio" is simply the ratio of total number of regular household members to the number of rooms in the dwelling unit (including the kitchen, but not the bathroom). Although person/room ratio is the generally accepted index of household density, and possibly the only feasible way of collecting data on relative spatial quantity for large numbers of households, it is an index which has many shortcomings (the lack of an adequate measuring tool is of itself a hindrance to deeper knowledge about the entire question of amount of living space). Number of rooms alone says nothing about the size of rooms (height as well as floor area), nor about shape and layout of rooms (e.g., the difference between an apartment in which rooms have to be traversed in order to enter other rooms and an apartment in which rooms are entered separately off a central corridor). Number of people alone says nothing about the particular household composition (age, sex, kinship), occupational and leisure patterns (who is around, when, doing what) and sleeping arrangements. The very quality of space—its basic condition and the way it is furnished and maintained—tends, moreover, to modify perception of and judgments about spatial quantity.

range of important physical spaces and social relationships were key determinants of the observable density patterns.

DENSITY AND MOBILITY

Our usual conceptions about optimum amounts of dwelling space in the urban environment necessarily imply a fairly high rate of residential mobility. Particularly in lower income housing, the relative restriction of dwelling space to minimal current needs means that any change in family composition is likely to lead to altered space requirements. Thus, changes in family size during different phases of the life cycle, given such minimal spatial areas for the family and the inelasticity of these housing spaces, lead to altered spatial requirements which can only be met by moving to a larger (or smaller) unit. Where powerful tendencies toward residential stability exist, this adjustment of physical space to altered family size may not take place or may occur only within narrow limits. Therefore, if the value of the residential area and of continuity in residence is to be maintained despite changed spatial needs or spatial desires, the amount and distribution of household space must assume a lower place in the hierarchy of residential values.

The West End population was highly stable. Seventy-one per cent of the sample had been living in the area nine years or more; and fully 56% had been living there at least 19 years. Quite a large proportion (24%) of this sample of adults (minimum age for inclusion in the sample was 20) had been born in the West End. A large proportion had been living in the same apartment for quite extensive periods: 59% had been living in their present apartments for at least five years, and 44% had been in the same apartment nine years or more. During this time, moreover, many of these same families experienced major shifts in family composition due to life cycle changes. Thus many West End families were living at densities higher (or, in some cases, lower) than those which

ceteris paribus they would have preferred and for the most part were able to afford. [13] However, rather than disrupt personal ties, attachment to places, and a general sense of continuity in the area, the minor discomforts which resulted from changes in spatial needs and desires were adjusted to and absorbed as alternative costs.

To examine this hypothesis more closely, a smaller sample was drawn from those persons who had lived in the same apartment for at least ten years. [14] This permitted a check as to whether these extremely stable respondents were also at a stable phase of the life cycle, or whether they had remained in the same apartment despite changes in family status. Among the 41 cases examined, the great majority experienced changes in family composition without any corresponding changes in dwelling unit. Thus, 19 (46%) experienced addition of one to five children without any shift in dwelling; in 12 other instances (29%), although the number of family members remained stable, the children went through significant age changes and hence through altered space needs without change in dwelling; and several others experienced departure of a spouse or children from the household and/or addition of non-nuclear family members without a shift in residence. It is clear from these data that many families remained in the same dwelling despite changes in household size and age composition that might ordinarily have led to a change in dwelling unit, were it not for powerful "pulls" in the direction of stability.

Thus, in those urban communities or urban areas in which widespread commitment to the specific local area exist—and profound attachments to particular local regions may be characteristic for the working

13. As noted above, 18% of the sample cited insufficient space as their dominant complaint about the apartment, and many more mentioned it as a secondary complaint.
14. One hundred sixty-two households, or 35% of the entire sample, fell into this category. Of these, every fourth case was selected for detailed analysis.

class—we can expect to find a wide range of housing densities. And to the extent that living patterns and the hierarchy of cultural values do not encourage "normal" space adjustments according to changing physical and social constellations in the household, higher densities, as well as some extremely low densities, can be expected and must be regarded as a chosen alternative cost.

INTERNAL AND EXTERNAL RESIDENTIAL DENSITY

In discussing the determinants of housing attitudes it was apparent that the residential patterns in the West End and in similar high-density working-class neighborhoods could be understood only in the context of the central importance of widespread associational networks of local kin and friends and an abundance of nearby places which were part of the daily life-pattern. This would imply that the individual apartment and individual household tend to function less clearly as discrete units than is characteristic for the middle class. In the West End, and in most urban working class communities which have been reported in the literature, there was considerable interaction with the surrounding physical and social environment, an interaction which formed an integral part of the lives of the people. This has important implications for the entire notion of residential densities, for it meant that the West Ender had available far more living space than his own apartment. Among a population for whom sitting on stoops, congregating on street corners, hanging out of windows, talking with shopkeepers, and strolling in the local area formed a critical part of the *modus vivendi,* the concept of personal living space must certainly be expanded to include outdoor as well as indoor space. Likewise a high level in intimate and casual social interaction with immediately surrounding neighbors means that other dwelling units may be used as extensions of or escapes from one's own apartment.[15] In

15. In one case from our sample, for instance, a child regularly slept in the upstairs apartment of

other words, if the prevalent life-style is such that the street scene, hallways,[16] and the apartments of others are the locus for a considerable part of the day's activities, measures and standards of residential density must be revised to include a realistic assessment of available living space as well as consideration of the preferred pattern and intensity of interpersonal contact.[17]

A further consideration in evaluating the effects of housing conditions generally and of density specifically relates to concepts of privacy. A good deal of our thinking about optimum amount and type of living space is based on an explicit or implicit regard for the virtues of privacy and the ways in which privacy permits and encourages orientation toward individual responsibility and achievement. However, this orientation, generally associated with the middle class in our society, is not universal and there still remain large segments of the population for whom kinship ties, interpersonal relations, spatial identity, and a sense of belonging in an area are critical orientations. For groups like this, "apartment" connotes something quite different from its meaning for the middle class. For the middle class, housing is an apart-

her grandmother to relieve the crowding in her own family's apartment, although her meals and other household activities took place in the family apartment. More detailed study might show, moreover, that visiting patterns resulted in an unplanned readjustment of living space: persons living in high density apartments may do a lot of informal visiting with neighbors and choose low density households as the outlet for their socializing.
16. Hallways, too, were considered part of one's personal living space: children played there, neighbors gossiped there, and large household gatherings overflowed into the corridors.
17. One might, of course, argue that these patterns of extended spatial use are, in fact, evidence of dissatisfaction with the dwelling unit; that people extrude themselves into the street because the home has so little to offer or is the focus for conflict and unpleasantness. There is, however, no basis for viewing the situation in this light. Not only do we have the fact of an extremely high rate of expressed satisfaction with the apartment and the frequency with which apartments were well furnished and maintained, but the integration and interweaving of interior and exterior spaces would also contradict the idea that the extensive use of outdoor space was merely an avoidance of intolerable indoor space.

ment contained within walls: the quantity and quality of internal space, apart from its adjacent setting; and the home life refers to the interpersonal contacts that take place within the confines of the apartment. By contrast, working-class housing is not so clearly oriented around an "*apart*ment" (the word itself is quite revealing), defined or conceived of in this discrete way; it represents a constant interplay between "inside" and "outside," both in a physical and social sense. It is not that distinctions between the interior and exterior are non-existent, but they are less rigid, less important. Apartment walls, windows and doors are relatively "permeable," in terms of sights, smells, sounds and persons from the outside entering the apartment, as well as the "inside" moving out—the high degree of informal socializing, the intensive use of the street.

Density must be regarded in terms of over-all spatial use and organization. Fried and Gleicher have used the term "territorial" to describe the organization of space in the West End, and, more generally, in many working-class neighborhoods.[18] That is, the space immediately surrounding one's dwelling is regarded and used as a stable, meaningful locus for interpersonal contact, leisure time activities, shopping and services. It is a particular, non-interchangeable, contiguous territory to which an individual belongs and within which he feels "at home." Since this territory is readily and immediately available, it is in fact one's personal living space, even though it is not exclusive or private, and therefore must in some way be included in the evaluation of density. In contrast, organization of space among the middle class is far more selective and exclusive, defined in terms of a far-flung network of chosen relevant points, connected by a series of functional paths.

If we limit our conception of housing orientations solely to the activities and space of the apartment, we tend both to obscure connections to a larger physical environment and to confine our observations to physical

18. Fried, Marc, and Gleicher, Peggy, *op. cit.*

criteria without regard for their place in a larger residential context which includes a diversity of social factors. Physical attributes are important, but their specific meaning and functional relevance are determined by social and personal values and life-styles.

CONCLUSION

This paper has attempted to show that for certain people the accepted standards of housing quality and quantity may be of secondary importance in determining residential satisfaction or dissatisfaction. More generally, it suggests the significance of social values and the ways in which they can modify attitudes toward and use of the physical world. Traditionally, physical factors alone have been stressed in the evaluation of housing conditions and in planning for improved residential areas. Physical factors are important, but they have no invariant or "objective" status and can only be understood in the light of their meaning for people's lives—which in turn is determined by social and cultural values. The tendency to regard the physical environment as having independent meaning and significance is in part related to middle-class values of individuality. But in part, too, it may reflect a failure of existing neighborhoods and communities to provide the kinds of settings wherein meaningful communal life can take place.[19]

The extreme "apartness" and inward quality of so much of today's housing, the exclusive personal involvement in one's own home, may in fact be a function of limited alternative choice. It is quite possible that a

19. British experience with housing estates has led some observers to a similar conclusion. Vere Hole writes: "So far, however, the ideological emphasis in rehousing has been on the dwelling rather than the estate where it is located. In spite of protestations to the contrary, estates are still being planned as dormitories rather than as communities, and the tenants moving onto them have had neither the expectations, the incentives nor the opportunities that would be necessary if genuine communities are to be created." Hole, Vere, "Social effects of planned rehousing," *Town Planning Review*, July 1959, 30:2, 161–173.

great many features of working-class residential life could have far wider appeal and applicability. In studying working-class residential orientations, the importance of the larger residential experience within a meaningful physical area is revealed. While the nature of this relationship may be quite different for the middle class, greater attention to a meaningfully designed neighborhood might have widespread significance and offer an opportunity for different conceptions of residential life. Certainly within the working class, the interaction of inner and outer space and the effect of social values on housing behavior is a critical consideration. Only with a deeper understanding of working-class orientations and life-styles and of the familiar or unfamiliar alternatives which can be meaningful in working-class perspectives may we hope to design housing which is more gratifying than the slums we wish to eradicate.

3.2

Architecture, Interaction, and Social Control:

The Case of a Large-Scale Public Housing Project

WILLIAM L. YANCEY

In this paper we will argue that the architectural design of the Pruitt-Igoe Housing Project, located in St. Louis, Missouri, has had an atomizing effect on the informal social networks frequently found in lower- and working-class neighborhoods. Without the provision of semi-public space and facilities around which informal networks might develop, families living in Pruitt-Igoe have retreated into the internal structures of their apartments and do not have the social support, protection, and informal social control found in other lower- and working-class neighborhoods.

It is clear that social and economic factors, particularly the level and stability of incomes and occupations, are major determinants of the life styles of the poor. Yet there is also evidence which indicates that the physical environment in which families live, in particular the design and condition of dwelling units, has an effect on the manner in which they live (Schorr, 1963; Wilner et al., 1962).

Among the effects of architectural design which have been identified by previous research is that of the physical proximity of dwelling units on the development of informal relationships between families. Gans (1963) has pointed out that the effects of proximity on informal relationships is somewhat contingent on differences in life styles exhibited by various groups. Gans' research indicates that it cannot be assumed that a particular architectural design will have the same effect on all social groups. The presence or absence of a particular design should have a variant effect on the total social life of a particular group, depending on the interdependence of the architecturally related behavior to other dimensions of the group's life. More specifically, we should find that the architectural relationships between dwellings and the effects of such spatial relationships on the social relationships that develop between families will have varying degrees of significance, depending on the importance of informal neighboring relationships in a particular social group.

In this paper, we will argue that informal networks among neighbors are an important means by which the urban lower and working classes cope with poverty and deprivation and that these networks are at least in

From W. Yancey. Architecture, Interaction, and Social Control: The case of a large-scale public housing project. *Environment and Behavior*, 1971, *3*, 3–21. Reprinted by permission of the Publisher, Sage Publications, Inc.

169

part dependent on the semi-public space and facilities that are present in many working- and lower-class neighborhoods. Finally, we will review results of an ethnographic study of the Pruitt-Igoe Housing Project which indicate the nature of the consequences stemming, in part, from the absence of such space and facilities and the networks that might otherwise have developed.

SOCIAL CLASS AND INFORMAL NETWORKS

There is some ambiguity in the sociological literature concerning the importance of informal networks among different social classes. On the one hand, there are authors who argue that the frequency of neighboring and sociability is particularly prevalent in upper- and middle-class suburbs (Whyte, 1956; Bell and Boat, 1957; Fava, 1957). On the other hand, studies of the urban working and lower classes have shown rather strong interpersonal networks of neighbors and strong attachment to neighborhoods (Bott, 1957; Young and Wilmott, 1957; Gans, 1962; Fried and Gleicher, 1961; Fried, 1963; Suttles, 1968).

Careful reviews of these studies indicate that there is a difference in the character of social relationships with neighbors found in the middle class as compared to the working and lower classes. While neighboring is found to be frequent in both areas, "the intensity of social interaction tends to decrease as one moves from working class areas to upper income bracket residential suburbs" (Herberle, 1960: 279).

Illustrative of this debate are the results of a survey directed by John McCarthy and me in Nashville and Philadelphia. The survey was taken in which were principally lower- and working-class neighborhoods in the two cities, with a smaller proportion of what might be considered lower-middle-class respondents. A total of 1,178 interviews were completed, 712 in Nashville, and 466 in Philadelphia. Approximately equal numbers of these were with black households

(576) and white households (602). Samples were systematic, rather than random, and were not designed so as to be representative of either city.

Using a scale developed by Wallin (1953), we found no relationship between casual neighboring relationships and social status.[1] In contrast to these results were those obtained when we asked our respondents to tell us how far away their closest friends lived. In this case, lower-status respondents were more likely to have friends living nearby than were those of higher status.[2]

These results conform to statements by Alan Blum (1964) and Rudolf Herberle (1960), suggesting that once the distinction is made between casual acquaintances and relatively high levels of interdependence, lower-class respondents are more closely tied to their neighbors. Among the lower class, friends are more likely to be neighbors. While, among the middle class, one might be friendly with his neighbors, friendships are more likely to be based on common in-

---

1. When status was measured by education, we found a positive, although weak, relationship. When status was measured by income, we obtained the opposite results.

Neighboring and Social Status. Percentage of each status group scoring "high" on neighboring items:

Education Completed			Weekly Income		
0–7 yrs	25.2	(306)	00–$59	41.2	(240)
8–11 yrs	33.8	(409)	60–129	29.9	(421)
12 yrs	33.8	(225)	$130+	28.6	(318)
College	30.7	(192)			

2. *Friends' Distance and Social Status.* Percentage with first friend living on same block:

Education Completed			Weekly Income		
0–7 yrs	43.7	(300)	00–$59	40.7	(231)
8–11 yrs	31.6	(415)	60–129	29.3	(413)
12 yrs	26.8	(220)	$130+	19.9	(311)
College	14.5	(186)			
Probability	.0074		.0027		

Similar results were obtained with each of three friends.

terests, rather than upon physical proximity[3] (see Gans, 1961).

There is also considerable literature suggestive of the functions of informal networks for the lower and working class. Marc Fried's (1963) research on the depressing effects of urban renewal and relocation, particularly for families who had strong personal ties to the Boston West End, is illustrative. Gerald Suttles' recent research in Chicago's Adams area documents the manner in which the development of neighborhood networks based on physical proximity, age, sex, and ethnicity provided social and moral norms, as well as a means of integration into the larger groups. He writes

Within each small, localized peer group, continuing face-to-face relations can eventually provide a personalistic order. Once these groups are established, a single personal relation between them can extend the range of such an order. With the acceptance of age grading and territorial usufruct, it becomes possible for slum neighborhoods to work out a moral order that includes most of their residents [Suttles, 1968: 8].

A recent study of an all-white slum neighborhood in St. Louis found similar informal networks. Of particular interest here, and complementing the work of Suttles (1968), is the finding that the level of personal integration into networks was strongly related to the perception of human dangers in the environment. Persons who were not integrated into such networks were more likely to express concern over allowing their children out of the house, felt that they were vulnerable to strangers entering the neighborhood, felt unsafe on the street at night, and felt that children in the neighborhood were out of control (Wolfe et al., 1968).

There are also some indications that the presence of ecologically local networks is more important to lower- and working-class urban dwellers than to their middle-class counterparts. Herbert Gans has noted that the move to suburban areas by middle-class families results in part in having more privacy from neighbors than they had in inner-city apartments. Gans' research suggests that, for the middle class, the move to suburban areas results in few changes in life style that were not intended. He writes: "They are effects, not of suburban life, but of the larger cultural milieu in which people form their aspirations" (Gans, 1963: 192).

The limited consequences of moving to suburbs by middle-class families stand in sharp contrast to those reported by Marris (1962) and Young and Wilmott (1957). These studies of the relocation of lower- and working-class communities indicate that the move to suburbia resulted in significant and unintended changes in their life styles. No longer available in the suburban housing estates were the amenities of the slum—the close proximity to work, the pub, and to friends and relatives. They changed their way of life and began focusing energies more sharply on their homes and jointly pursued family lives, and much less on separate activities by husband and wife participating in sex-segregated peer groups.

In addition to the ethnographic evidence on the relative importance of ecologically local informal networks, there is considerable research indicating that, much to the dismay of urban renewers, lower- and working-class populations are as satisfied with their neighborhoods as are members of the middle class (Foote et al., 1960; Fried, 1963). Our recent survey in Nashville and Philadelphia indicated that there was no relationship between social status and neighborhood satisfaction. Over sixty percent of our respondents were satisfied with their neighborhoods, no matter what their social and economic status.

The works of Fried (1963), Gans (1962), and Foote et al. (1960) also indicate that among the lower and working classes, neighborhood satisfaction is rather closely tied to

---

3. We also found that higher-status persons are more likely to have friends whose occupations are similar to their own, in level of prestige, than are members of the lower and working classes.

the presence of informal networks of friends and relatives. Results from our survey support this proposition. Without social class controls, we found no relationship between the proximity of friends and neighborhood satisfaction. When we controlled on the social class, we found that neighborhood satisfaction was related to the proximity of friends in the lower socioeconomic group, while there was no relationship in the higher-status respondents.[4]

These survey data suggest that, not only are the existence and integration into ecologically local informal social networks significant for the lower and working classes, but our results go slightly beyond the earlier studies in that they are suggestive of the relative importance of such networks for different social and economic levels. While social and economic factors are the principal variables that determine the life styles of the poor, they have developed ways of coping with and adapting to poverty, thus making the condition less oppressive. We have argued that among these adaptations is the

4. *Neighborhood Satisfaction and Proximity of First Friend by Social Status:* Percentage satisfied with neighborhood:

		Distance in Blocks		
		0–4	5–25	26+
Total Sample		72.9(541)	69.4(264)	70.0(240)

Education completed

0–8 yrs	LO	74.8(262)	76.0 (71)	71.0 (60)
9–12 yrs	MD	70.0(203)	61.9(126)	63.2 (87)
College	HI	77.3 (66)	67.3 (61)	78.2 (78)

As these data reveal, without social and economic controls there is little or no relationship between friends' distance and neighborhood satisfaction. Yet when we control on the level of education, we find that there is a relationship in the lower class, but not in the middle class.

Similar results were obtained with the second- and third-friend responses and when social status was measured by income and occupation. The levels of significance, beyond the .05 level, are not always achieved, but in every case the pattern of a stronger relationship between the proximity of friends and satisfaction with neighborhood is found in the lower-status groups.

development of ecologically local informal neighborhood relationships. When these are disrupted, or a community is designed which makes their development almost impossible, we should expect to see their importance made manifest by other differences that emerge in the life styles of a particular group. The Pruitt-Igoe Housing Project community is illustrative of one such group.

THE CASE OF PRUITT-IGOE

The Pruitt-Igoe Housing Project consists of 43 11-story buildings near downtown St. Louis, Missouri. The project was opened in 1954, had 2,762 apartments (many of which are currently vacant), and has as tenants a high proportion of female-headed households, on one form or another of public assistance. Though originally containing a large population of white families, the project has been all-Negro for the past several years. The project community is plagued by petty crimes, vandalism, much destruction to the physical plant, and has a rather widespread reputation as being an extreme example of the pathologies associated with lower-class life (Demerath, 1962; Rainwater, 1966a, 1966b).

Pruitt-Igoe represents, in its architectural design, an extreme example of a national housing policy whose single goal is the provision of housing for individual families, with little knowledge about or concern for the development of a community and neighborhood. Unlike normal slums, with their cluttered streets and alleys, Pruitt-Igoe provides no semi-private space and facilities around which neighboring relationships might develop. There is a minimum of what is often considered "wasted space"—space within buildings that is outside of individual family dwelling units. An early review of the project's design (Architectural Forum, 1951) praised the designers for their individualistic design and the absence of such wasted space between dwelling units.

Walking into the project, one is struck by the mosaic of glass that covers what were

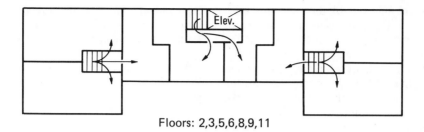

Floors: 2,3,5,6,8,9,11

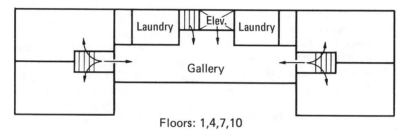

Floors: 1,4,7,10

Pruitt Igoe Typical Floor Plan

grassy areas and playgrounds. The barren dirt, or mud when it rains, is constantly tracked into the apartments. Windows, particularly those on the lower floors, are broken out. The cost of replacing glass in vacant apartments led the Housing Authority to cover many with plywood. Streets and parking lots are littered with trash, bottles, and tin cans. Derelict cars provide an attractive source of entertainment for children. Fences around "tot lots" are torn; swings, sliding boards, and merry-go-rounds are noticeably unpainted, rusted, and broken.

Within the buildings themselves, the neglect is more apparent. Entering the buildings via one of the three stairwells, one is struck with the stale air and the stench of urine, trash, and garbage on the floors. One is also struck by the unfinished construction—the unpainted cinderblocks and cement. These unfinished walls in the stairwells are decorated with colorful graffiti.

The alternative route into the building is the single elevator. The elevator is used as a

public restroom, as well as a means of transportation up into the buildings. Even though it is mopped every morning, the smell of urine is noticeable throughout the day. Many individual building elevators are without handrails and in need of painting; all have the reputation of breaking down between floors.

On the fourth, seventh, and tenth floors, there is an open gallery, or hall, the only level public space within the building, one side of which is lined with broken windows and steel gratings. Next to the incinerator, open garbage is often found on the floor. The laundry rooms, located off the gallery, are sometimes used as lavatories. We observed residents and officials urinating in them.

The physical danger and deterioration of Pruitt-Igoe is but a reflection of the more pressing human dangers. Residents of Pruitt-Igoe continually expressed concern with being assaulted, beaten, or raped. We were frequently warned of such dangers and told that we should never enter buildings alone and should stay out of the elevators, especially after dark. We were told stories of people being cut by bottles thrown from the buildings and warned never to stand immediately outside of a building. In addition to the physical violence, there was also the danger to one's self—the verbal hostility, the shaming and exploitation from children, neighbors, and outsiders (see Rainwater, 1966a).

One of the first things pointed out by the residents of Pruitt-Igoe was the distinction between "private" space within apartments and the "public" space and facilities. In our early interviews with families, we asked what they liked about living in the housing project. Almost without exception, what they liked was limited to the physical space and amenities within the family unit. Characteristic of these interviews is the following exchange:

Interviewer: How do you like living here in Pruitt-Igoe?

Respondent: I like living here better than I like living on O'Fallon Street [in a private housing slum] where we had a first floor, but did not have heat provided in the winter and windows were broken out. We did have an inside toilet, but no modern plumbing— we had no water. I like living here because it's convenient.

Interviewer: What do you mean by "convenient?"

Respondent: The apartment itself—it's easier to take care of and to clean. Although the paint on these walls holds dirt badly, the Housing Authority does furnish the paint. We don't have a choice of what kind of paint, but I painted the walls. It's real convenient here, especially in the wintertime. It's always so nice and warm here, and I only have one rent to pay. I don't have to pay for gas and electricity and all that. I just pay once. I like that. I like this apartment, it's good for the kids. Here we have separate rooms.

Interviewer: Each child has a separate room?

Respondent: No, but this way the children have a bedroom and the parents have a bedroom. It gives them and us more freedom.

When the interviewer changed the focus of the interview by asking, "How do you feel about this building?" the character of the interview changed.

Respondent: Well, I don't like being upstairs like this. The problem is that I can't see the kids. They're just too far away. If one of them gets hurt, needs to go to the bathroom, or anything, it's just too far away. And you can't get outside. We don't have any porches. And there are too many different kids around here. Some of them have parents, some do not. There are just a variety of families. Some have husbands, some not. If it weren't for the project police, the teen-agers would take over. I've got some children that are teen-agers, but I still think they are the most dangerous group.

This pattern of responses repeats itself throughout our research. The results of a survey taken in the housing project indicate that 78% of the residents were satisfied with their apartments, while only 49% were satisfied with living in the project. This pattern of satisfaction and dissatisfaction with one's dwelling unit as compared to one's neighborhood is exactly the opposite of that found in most studies of housing and neighborhood satisfaction. In contrast with Pruitt-Igoe, slum dwellers generally are dissatisfied with their specific dwellings, while satisfied with their neighborhoods.[5] In Pruitt-Igoe, the familiar aspects of slum living, such as fires and burning, freezing and cold, poor plumbing, dangerous electrical wiring, thin walls, and overcrowding of children and parents into single rooms are somewhat abated. *Yet the amenities of lower-class neighborhoods are apparently lost.*

5. A survey taken in the private slum neighborhood directly adjacent to Pruitt-Igoe found the more usual pattern of satisfaction with housing and

Complementing the pattern of satisfaction with apartment and neighborhood, and again in sharp contrast to the research reviewed above, informal social networks did not form in the corridors and stairwells of Pruitt-Igoe. Residents of the projects had a similar number of friends as in other lower-class populations, yet these friendships bore little or no relationship to the physical proximity of families to each other.

In Pruitt-Igoe, relationships with neighbors ranged from occasional friendship and helping patterns to (more frequently found) open hostility or isolation. As one woman explained when we asked about troubles in the project:

I think people bring trouble on themselves, but like the kids—see, the kids get fighting and the parents they get into it too. Now us, we mind our own business. I say little to the people across the hall. We don't have any friends in the building. Most of our friends are from work. Some of them we have known for a long time.

Still another replied, when asked about her neighbors:

They are selfish. I've got no friends here. There's none of this door-to-door coffee business of being friends here or anything like that. Down here, if you are sick you just go to the hospital. There are no friends to

neighborhood. The results of this and a survey taken in Pruitt-Igoe are presented below.

	Percentage Satisfied	
	Pruitt-Igoe	adjacent slum
with apartment	78	55
with project living	49	
with neighborhood	53	74
	(n = 154)	(n = 69)

In more recent years, vandalism and lack of maintenance have resulted in the deterioration of the plumbing and heating of the building. Thus these data, if gathered more recently, would probably not be found to be as striking as they were when this study was done in 1965.

help you. I don't think my neighbors would help me and I wouldn't ask them to anyway. I don't have trouble with my neighbors because I never visit them. The rule of the game down here is *go for yourself.*

THE CONSEQUENCES OF ATOMIZATION

Gerald Suttles notes that in the Adams area in Chicago, conflict between residents in the area results in the reinforcement of the small informal group. He writes (1968:228):

Individuals in the Adams area achieve a positive association with co-residents of the same age, sex and ethnicity primarily because conflict with other persons forces them together into small face-to-face groupings. Otherwise, people might remain almost wholly isolated, associate indiscriminately, and be dependent on such dyadic relations as they could form.

Of particular interest here is his discussion of the sequence through which such groups develop. New residents of the area restrict their children's movement to the areas immediately around or close by their homes. As a result, small and continuous face-to-face associations develop around the immediate proximity of the home. They provide means of controlling children and provide "assurances that relieve their apprehension." Conflict with persons outside these small groups forces the residents to "throw their lot in with a definite group of people" (Suttles, 1968:228).

In a similar manner, mothers in Pruitt-Igoe attempt to keep their children in close proximity to their apartments. Yet in contrast to the slum, the architectural design of the project is such that as soon as a child leaves an apartment he is out of his mother's sight and direct control. There are no areas within buildings, except the galleries (which cannot be seen from the apartments and which are shared by some twenty families) in which children can play. As one mother explained:

I find that I can't keep up with the children when they leave the house to play. When they go out they play with just anybody; there are some people in the project who raise their children and some who don't. I want to have control over who they play with and when so many people live in one place you just can't choose your kid's playmates. If we were in a house I could keep them in a yard and see who they play with.

Mothers fear the early introduction and socialization of their children into sex and other troubles. They also see the adults in the housing project as being irresponsible, deviant, and beyond control. Said one:

They tell their children one thing and go out and do the very opposite. They see kids in a fight and rather than break it up, will get into it themselves.

Yet attempts to control children who are members of unknown families frequently resulted in conflict between adults. Thus one woman reported:

I used to watch the kids in this building. In the beginning I tried to discipline them. I'd tell them every time I found them doing something mischievous what was wrong and what was right. But kids don't like that; their parents don't like it. They don't want somebody else to discipline their children. They put the blame on you. Watching children is dangerous.

Another explained that after she had "made one of the neighbor's boys do right," his mother came and said she was going to bring a gun.

The conflict is further escalated when one of the two adults calls the police. As one woman explained, after she was told the police had been called because her son had gotten into a fight:

Well, I'm not going to get shook because the police are coming. They always come to this house and tell me how bad my children are. It's too bad the parents had to call the police and could never take the time to come up and talk to me first.

Apparently without the informal networks, informal social control that might otherwise be based on the small social group is not strong enough to resolve such conflicts. Thus, as a means of resolving what might otherwise have been a relatively small complaint, a more powerful authority—the policeman—is called upon. This, in turn, further exacerbates the atomization that exists.

Our interviews and observations with families in the housing project contain many references to the police. A sample survey of the Pruitt-Igoe Housing Project showed that over 90% of the residents of the project indicated that there should be more policemen patrolling the area. As one lady explained:

In other projects they have enough policemen, but not here. You put lights in and they take them out, or the police never turn them on. They have policemen but they don't do any good. They are not here long enough. They used to have auxiliary policemen down here. But as soon as they took them away there was all kinds of raping and stealing all over the project. It has turned into a jungle.

Other features of the architecture, apart from the lack of semi-public space and facilities, have contributed to the fears that characterize the community. The design of the stairwells is such that they represent almost completely uncontrolled space. They are public in the sense that anyone can enter them without being challenged, yet they are private in that no one is likely to be held accountable for his behavior in the stairwell. This lack of accountability is particularly prevalent in the center stairwell, where a small anteroom separates the individual apartments from the stairwell. This room creates a buffer zone between the totally private apartment and the stairwell. Pruitt-Igoens fear this stairwell more than the others, and it is said to be used by teen-agers as a relatively private place in which they can engage in sexual intercourse. As one teen-ager explained, "All you have to do is knock

out the light on the landings above and below you. Then when someone comes, if they
are not afraid of the dark, they tumble
around and you can hear them in time to get
out."

The isolation, the lack of accountability
for entry into the stairwells, and the fears
that are centered around them are somewhat
interdependent with the lack of informal
networks. Given the number of families who
have rights to this space, it should not be
surprising that strangers can enter it without
being challenged. While interviewing in
lower- and working-class neighborhoods, one
often encounters persons on the street who
question you as to where you are going.
After an introduction, such persons often
give interviewers instructions as to where a
family can be found, when they will return
home, or how to get through an alley to an
apartment. Later, when such an interviewer
returns and introduces himself, he often gets
a response such as, "Oh yes, you were here
earlier." During our three years of intensive
research in Pruitt-Igoe, such an experience
never occurred. The presence of outsiders
was noticed by the residents, but they were
never challenged.

Absent from the architectural design of
Pruitt-Igoe is what has sometimes been referred to as wasted space. We choose to call
it "defensible space." In lower- and working-
class slums, the littered and often trash-filled
alleys, streets, and backyards provide the
ecological basis around which informal networks of friends and relatives may develop.
Without such semi-public space and facilities, the development of such networks is
retarded; the resulting atomization of the
community can be seen in the frequent and
escalating conflict between neighbors, fears
of and vulnerability to the human dangers in
the environment, and, finally, withdrawal to
the last line of defense—into the single-
family dwelling unit. The sense of security
and control that is found in other working-
and lower-class neighborhoods is not
present.

There are at least two alternative hypotheses which might be used to explain the
atomized nature of the Pruitt-Igoe community. The first of these stems from the
research and literature on social stratification, which rather clearly show that the level
of interpersonal trust is lower in the lower
class than in any other segment of the population. Thus it is argued that Pruitt-Igoe,
being representative of the lowest class, is
therefore a community of people none of
whom trust one another. A comparison of
Pruitt-Igoe's residents' responses to questionnaire items measuring the level of trust indicates that, while they are less trustful than
are persons of higher status, they are not
different from other lower-class populations
(see Rainwater and Schwarts, 1965).

Perhaps a more credible hypothesis, one
which might be termed the "police state"
theory, stems from the public nature of life
in public housing. Over fifty percent of the
residents are on some form of welfare assistance. Welfare workers and housing authority officials maintain a rather close
scrutiny of their clients who might otherwise
break one of the many rules governing residence in the project. Under such a "police
state," residents of the project may fear that
becoming friendly with neighbors will result
in their being turned into the authorities. We
observed neighbors calling the police about
one another, as discussed above, and some
families complained that neighbors had reported them to the housing authority or
welfare office for an infraction of one of
their rules.

Without a comparative study of Pruitt-Igoe
with another housing project with a similar
population, similar reputation, and similar
administration by caretakers, it is difficult to
adequately judge the effects of architecture
per se. David Wilner's study of public housing in Baltimore shows, in contrast with
Pruitt-Igoe, that with an architectural design
which facilitated interpersonal interaction
by the provision of common space and facilities, an increased amount of neighboring,
visiting, and mutual aid was found among
persons moving from a slum into a public

housing project (Wilner et al., 1962: 161).

We obviously believe that architecture does have an effect on the manner in which the poor cope with poverty. And we further suggest that designers of housing for the poor, rather than viewing the space between dwelling units as something to be avoided or reduced as far as possible, should provide semi-public space and facilities around which smaller identifiable units of residence can organize their sense of "turf." Designers should minimize space that belongs to no one and maximize the informal control over the space required to get from one dwelling to another. In a word, if housing must be designed for the ghetto—if we must reconcile ourselves to not being able to change the social forces which produce the world of danger that lower-class families experience— the architect can make some small contribution by facilitating the constructive adaptations that have emerged as a means of defense against the world of the lower class.

REFERENCES

Architectural Forum (1951) "Slum surgery in St. Louis." (April): 128—136.

Bell, W. and M. Boat (1957) "Urban neighborhoods and informal social relations." Amer. J. of Sociology 62 (January): 391—398.

Blum, A. F. (1964) "Social structure, social class, and participation in primary relationships," in A. B. Shostak and W. Gomberg (eds.) Blue Collar World. Englewood Cliffs, N.J.: Prentice-Hall.

Bott, E. (1957) Family and Social Networks. London: Tavistock.

Demerath, N. J. (1962) "St. Louis public housing study sets off community development to meet social needs." J. of Housing 19: 472—478.

Fava, S. F. (1957) "Contrasts in neighboring New York City and a suburban county," in R. L. Warren (ed.) Perspective on the American Community. Chicago: Rand McNally.

Festinger, L., S. Schacter, and K. Back (1950) Social Pressures in Informal Groups. New York: Harper & Row.

Foote, N. N., J. Abu-Lughod, M. M. Foley, and L. Winnick (1960) Housing Choices and Housing Constraints. New York: McGraw-Hill.

Fried, M. (1963) "Grieving for a lost home," pp. 151—171 in L. J. Duhl (ed.) The Urban Condition. New York: Basic Books.

——— and P. Gleicher (1961) "Some sources of residential satisfaction in an urban slum." J. of Amer. Institute of Planners, No. 4: 305—315.

Fried, M. and J. Levin (1968) "Some social functions of the urban slum," pp. 60—83 in B. Friedman and R. Morris (eds.) Urban Planning and Social Policy. New York: Basic Books.

Gans, H. (1963) "Effect of the move from city to suburb," pp. 184—198 in L. J. Duhl (ed.) The Urban Condition. New York: Basic Books.

——— (1962) The Urban Villagers. New York: Free Press.

——— (1961) "Planning and social life: friendship and neighbor relations in suburban communities." J. of Amer. Institute of Planners 27, 2: 135—139.

Herberle, R. (1960) "The normative element in neighborhood relations." Pacific Soc. Rev. 3, 1: 3—11.

Marris, P. (1962) Family and Social Change in an African City. Evanston, Ill.: Northwestern Univ. Press.

Rainwater, L. (1966a) "Crucible of identity: the Negro lower-class family." Daedalus 95, 1: 172—216.

——— (1966b) "Fear and the house-as-haven in the lower class." J. of Amer. Institute of Planners 32 (January): 23—31.

——— and M. J. Schwarts (1965) "Identity, world view, social relations, and family behavior in magazines." Social Research, Inc.

Schorr, A. L. (1963) Slums and Social Insecurity. Washington, D.C.: Government Printing Office.

Suttles, G. D. (1968) The Social Order of the Slum. Chicago: Univ. of Chicago Press.

Wallin, P. (1953) "A Guttman scale for measuring women's neighboring." Amer. J. of Sociology 59 (November): 243—246.

Whyte, W. H. (1956) The Organization Man. Garden City, N.Y.: Doubleday.

Wilner, D. M., R. P. Walkley, T. C. Pinkerton, and M. Tayback (1962) The Housing

Environment and Family Life. Baltimore, Md.: Johns Hopkins Univ. Press.

Wolfe, A., B. Lex, and W. Yancey (1968) The Soulard Area: Adaptations by Urban White Families to Poverty. St. Louis: Social Science Institute of Washington University.

Young, M. and P. Wilmott (1957) Family and Kinship in East London. Glencoe: Free Press.

Defensible Space:

Crime Prevention through Urban Design

OSCAR NEWMAN

Defensible space is a model for residential environments which inhibits crime by creating the physical expression of a social fabric that defends itself. All the different elements which combine to make a defensible space have a common goal—an environment in which latent territoriality and sense of community in the inhabitants can be translated into responsibility for ensuring a safe, productive, and well-maintained living space. The potential criminal perceives such a space as controlled by its residents, leaving him an intruder easily recognized and dealt with. On the one hand this is target hardening—the traditional aim of security design as provided by locksmiths. But it must also be seen in another light. In middle-class neighborhoods, the responsibility for maintaining security has largely been relegated to the police. Upper-income neighborhoods—particularly those including high-rise apartment buildings—have supplemented police with doormen, a luxury not possible in other neighborhoods. There is serious self-deception in this posture. When people begin to protect themselves as individuals and not as a community, the battle against crime is effectively lost. The indifferent crowd witnessing a violent crime is by now an American cliché. The move of middle- and upper-class population into protective high-rises and other structures of isolation—as well guarded and as carefully differentiated from the surrounding human landscape as a military post—is just as clearly a retreat into indifference. The form of buildings and their arrangement can either discourage or encourage people to take an active part in policing while they go about their daily business. "Policing" is not intended to evoke a paranoid vision but refers to the oldest concept in the Western political tradition: the responsibility of each citizen to ensure the functioning of the *polis*.

"Defensible space" is a surrogate term for the range of mechanisms—real and symbolic barriers, strongly defined areas of influence, and improved opportunities for surveillance—that combine to bring an environment under the control of its residents. A defensible space is a living residential environment which can be employed by inhabitants for the enhancement of their lives, while providing security for their families, neighbors,

Abridged from O. Newman. Defensible space: Crime prevention through urban design. *Ekistics*, 1973, 36(216), 325–332. Reprinted by permission of Macmillan Publishing Co., Inc. Copyright © 1972 by Oscar Newman.

and friends. The public areas of a multi-family residential environment devoid of defensible space can make the act of going from street to apartment equivalent to running the gauntlet. The fear and uncertainty generated by living in such an environment can slowly eat away and eventually destroy the security and sanctity of the apartment unit itself. On the other hand, by grouping dwelling units to reinforce associations of mutual benefit; by delineating paths of movement; by defining areas of activity for particular users through their juxtaposition with internal living areas; and by providing for natural opportunities for visual surveillance, architects can create a clear understanding of the function of a space, and who its users are and ought to be. This, in turn, can lead residents of all income levels to adopt extremely potent territorial attitudes and policing measures, which act as strong deterrents to potential criminals.

THE PROBLEM

There are five or six physical characteristics that reinforce criminal behavior, and these occur both in developments built for low- and middle-income occupancy. The projects are usually very large, accommodating over a thousand families, and consist of high-rise apartment towers over seven stories in height. The sites are usually an assembly of what was previously four to six separate city blocks, amalgamated into one giant super block, closed to city traffic. The buildings are positioned on the site in a rather free compositional fashion. The grounds are designed as one continuous space, moving freely among the buildings and open to the surrounding streets. In the detailed site design, there is seldom any attempt at differentiating the grounds so as to make portions relate to a particular building or cluster of buildings.

The buildings themselves are commonly slab or cruciform towers, housing from 150 to 500 families. They are generally designed with a single lobby which faces onto the interior grounds of the development. The lobby itself contains a mailbox area and a waiting space for a bank of two to four elevators. A typical floor consists of a long central corridor with apartments lining both sides, which is designated in the building profession as a "double-loaded corridor." The elevator bank is located at the center of this corridor.

To furnish sufficient exits in fire emergencies, two, and occasionally four sets of emergency stairwells are provided, running the height of the building. Sometimes two sets of stairs are grouped together behind the elevators in what is called a scissors-stair configuration; at other times the emergency stairs are located at the ends of the corridors. (Location requirements are determined by local building codes.) Every set of stairs requires its own exit at the ground level. One or two exits may be allowed to be located within the lobby. A high-rise tower, depending on its size, will have from one to four exits in addition to the main entry.

What has just been described will no doubt be seen as a common enough phenomenon, well within the experience of most urbanites. The only difference between a low-income and a high-income development is the presence of fences and guards in the upper-income project, or a doorman provided for each of its buildings. These slight but expensive additions, however, are what make the one a workable habitat and the other not. The same urban high-rise residential developments for low- and middle-income families, devoid of the doormen, guards, and resident superintendents, become pasturelands for criminals.

It is the apartment tower itself, however, that is the real and final villain of the piece. It is inconceivable that one genius alone could have been responsible for its creation. High-rise, elevator-serviced, double-loaded corridor apartment buildings for the use of low- and middle-income families have proven disastrous. Their provision in many cases is the result of a set of circumstances now common to most inner city developments: land

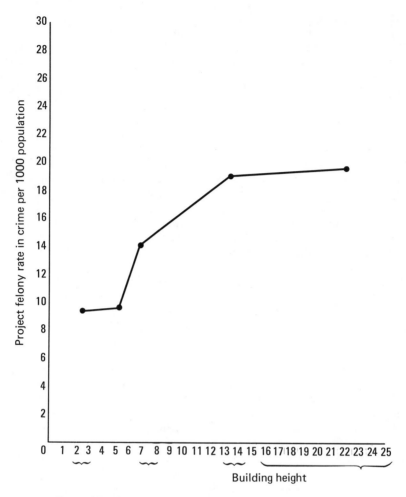

Fig. 1. Project Felony Rate by Building Height

costs driven up by land speculation; zoning increased by city planning departments so as to provide more housing; pressed housing officials; harried Federal mortgage financiers; and indifferent architects. No one person would have dared so much.

The high-rise apartment tower is primarily a by-product of the need to build higher densities to justify inflated land costs. Where, at under sixty units to the acre, a variety of building prototypes are still available for use by a housing designer, once seventy-five units per acre is reached, the high-rise slab becomes about the only option

open. Crime rate has been found to increase almost proportionately with building height, as illustrated by Fig. 1.

Project size has also been found to affect crime rate. If the two variables of building heights and project size are coupled, the probability of crime increases to the extent that it is possible to guarantee a higher crime rate in virtually all projects of excessive height and size. In New York City, 95 percent of the Housing Authority's projects greater than six stories in height and larger than a thousand units in size have higher crime rates per thousand population than those which are both smaller and lower.

In a high-rise, double-loaded corridor apartment tower, the only defensible space is the interior of the apartment itself; everything else is a "no-man's-land," neither public nor private. The lobby, stairs, elevators, and corridors are open and accessible to everyone. But unlike the well-peopled and continually surveyed public streets, these interior areas are sparsely used and impossible to survey; they become a nether world of fear and crime.

The investigation of the relationship between building height and crime was begun with the basic hypothesis that a positive correlation exists between the two; that as building height increases, so. does crime. Recognizing the fact that height alone was not the reason for such a connection, we took into account the various other factors that usually attend high buildings: a larger number of apartment units and people using a single lobby, entry, and elevators, with resulting anonymity; more interior public space hidden from view and so on.

From the computer tapes of the New York City Housing Authority Police, the 1969 crime records for 100 projects were examined. These projects were selected to meet the following criteria: (1) buildings throughout an individual project had to be of uniform building type, and (2) the project had to be seen as a separate entity from the surrounding community. Projects were divided into two groups, those with buildings six stories or less, and those with buildings seven stories or greater. In addition, these projects were divided by size, those under 1000 units and those greater than 1000 units. Population can be substituted for units to indicate project size. An examination of data revealed a linear correlation between the two, allowing such interchangeability. The crime rate for a project was found by taking the total number of felonies, misdemeanors, and offenses occurring in 1969 and dividing it by the project population. An analysis of variance was performed on the subsequent data, and the results are shown in Table 1.

Table 1. Project Size and Building Height versus Crime

		Building height	
		Equal to or less than 6 stories	Greater than 6 stories
Project size	Equal to or less than 1000 units	N = 8 M = 47 SD = 25	N = 47 M = 51 SD = 23
	Greater than 1000 units	N = 11 M = 45 SD = 26	N = 34 M = 67 SD = 24

Note: N = number of cases; M = mean number of crimes per thousand; SD = standard deviation.

The apparent effect of building height on crime is quite evident. In both project size categories, the mean or average rate jumps significantly when one compares low buildings with high buildings. But what is most interesting is the fact that in buildings of six stories or less, the project size or total number of units does not really make much difference. In fact, projects of 1000 units, but under six stories in height, have a lower crime rate than smaller-sized projects of similar height. In terms of our hypothesis, larger projects encourage crime by fostering feelings of anonymity, isolation, irresponsibility, lack of identity with surroundings, etc. Our evidence indicates that low buildings seem to offset what one may assume to be a factor conducive to high crime rates. In the higher buildings, a significant increase in average crime rate is seen when one compares the smaller-size project category with the larger. The fact that projects greater than 1000 units, with buildings of seven or more stories, have the highest rate, indicates that it is not large size alone. but large size in combination with higher buildings that contributes to a more criminally active situation. It seems that one can still maintain high density (size) and not encounter higher crime rates, as long as building height remains low.

A TALE OF TWO PROJECTS

Brownsville and Van Dyke are strikingly different in physical design, while housing comparatively identical populations in size and social characteristics. The high-rise towers at Van Dyke are almost totally devoid of defensible space qualities, while the buildings at Brownsville are comparatively well-endowed with such qualities. It should be mentioned, even before beginning the comparison, that Brownsville, the better of the two projects, is still far away from answering all defensible space design directives.

Review of the objective data on the physical characteristics of the two projects reveals many striking parallels. The projects are almost identical in size, each housing approximately 6,000 persons, and are designed at exactly the same density: 288 persons per acre. Major differences arise in the composition of buildings and the percentage of ground-level space they occupy. Brownsville buildings cover 23 percent of the available land, whereas Van Dyke buildings cover only 16.6 percent of the total land area—including nine three-story buildings which occupy a large percentage of space but house only 24 percent of the total project population. In addition, the two projects differ in design (see Fig. 2) in that Brownsville is comprised of low, walk-up and elevator buildings, three to six stories, while the latter is comprised of a mix of three-story buildings and fourteen-story high rise slabs (87 percent of the apartment units at Van Dyke are located in the high-rise slabs). The two projects are located across the street

Brownsville
Houses

Van Dyke Houses

Fig. 2. Site Plan of Brownsville and Van Dyke Houses

from one another and share the same Housing Authority police and New York City police services.

Differences in physical design of the Brownsville and Van Dyke projects are apparent even to the casual observer. Van Dyke Houses has the appearance of a large, monolithic project. The most dominant buildings are the thirteen fourteen-story slabs. In less evidence are the nine three-story structures. Each of the buildings at Van Dyke sits independently on the site, with large open spaces separating it from its neighbors. At the center of the project is a single, large open area, used for a Parks Department playground and for automobile parking. By means of its design, this large open area has been distinctly separated from and is unrelated to the surrounding buildings.

None of the buildings at Van Dyke may be entered directly from the public street. Entrance requires that tenants leave the public street and walk onto project paths that wind into internal project areas, blind to street surveillance. The only areas of the project grounds which relate somewhat to buildings are the small seating areas in the channel of space between the double row of buildings. The functional entrance to the high-rise buildings is a small door shared by 112 to 136 families. This door is located directly off the project paths, with no gradation or distinction indicated by the design of the grounds in front of the building lobby.

Two low-speed elevators carry families to their living floors in each of the high-rise buildings. Elevators are placed directly opposite the building entrances, as mandated by the Housing Authority, to improve surveillance from the outside. Full benefit is not derived from this arrangement, however, since entrances face the interior of the project rather than the street.

The housing floors of the high-rise buildings are each occupied by eight families. The elevator stops in the middle of the corridor, and the apartment units are reached by walking left or right down a dead-end cor-

ridor with apartments positioned on both sides (a double-loaded corridor).

In contrast, Brownsville Houses presents the appearance of being a smaller project, due to the disposition of units in smaller and more diverse clusters of buildings. It might be said that the buildings and the way in which they were placed on the site has been used to divide the project into smaller, more manageable zones. The ground areas have been humanized through their relationship with the individual residential buildings. Activities that take place in small project spaces adjoining buildings have become the business of the neighboring residents, who assume a leading role in monitoring them.

All residents and police who have been interviewed at Brownsville perceive the project as smaller and more stable than Van Dyke. All intruders, including police and interviewers, feel more cautious about invading the privacy of residents at Brownsville. By contrast, their attitude toward the invasion of the interior corridors at Van Dyke is callous and indifferent.

This emphasis on space division carries over into the design of the building interiors of Brownsville Houses. Individual buildings are three- and six-story structures with six families sharing a floor. The floor is further divided, by an unlocked swinging door, into two vestibules shared by three families each. In the six-story buildings there is an elevator which stops at odd floors, requiring residents of upper stories to walk up or down one flight, using an open stairwell around which apartment doors are clustered. Vertical communication among families is assured by this relationship of elevators to apartments, and also by the presence of open stairwells connecting the floors.

At the ground level, the building lobby leads up a short flight of stairs to several apartments that maintain surveillance over activity in this small entryway. On all floors, tenants have been found to maintain auditory surveillance over activity taking place in the halls by the device of keeping their doors slightly ajar. These features of the building have allowed occupants to extend their territorial prerogatives into building corridors, hallways, and stairs. Those mothers of young children at Brownsville who allow their children the freedom to play on landings and up and down the stairwells monitor their play from within the apartment. A mere interruption in the din of children at play was found to bring mothers to their doors as surely as a loud scream.

By contrast, most young children at Van Dyke are not allowed to play in the corridors outside their apartments. The halls of Van Dyke and other high-rise buildings are designed solely for their corridor function and are inhospitable to the fantasy-play of children. In addition, too many families utilize a typical high-rise hall for a mother to comfortably leave her child there unsupervised. For the same reason, mothers are reluctant to leave their doors ajar for surveillance—too many people, including strangers and guests of neighbors, wander through the Van Dyke halls unchecked and unquestioned. Finally, to give children real freedom in the use of the building would require their using the elevator or fire stairs to gain access to other floors. But both these areas are frightening and would take the children out of the surveillance zone of the mother and other tenants.

The elevator cab is sealed by a heavy metal door that cannot be opened manually. The fire stairwells are designed to seal floors in the event of a fire. A by-product of their fireproofing is that noises within the stairwells cannot be heard in the corridors outside. Criminals often force their victims into these areas because the soundproofing feature and low frequency of use make the detection of a crime in progress almost impossible.

The sense of propriety which is apparent in the way tenants of Brownsville Houses use their halls to monitor and maintain surveillance over children and strangers appears to have carried over to the grounds adjacent to building entrances. Because of the unique construction of the buildings, there are areas

on the ground level just outside the front door of the building where parents can allow their children to play, while maintaining contact with them through their kitchen windows. Interviews have revealed that the range of spaces into which young children are permitted to roam is greater in Brownsville than in Van Dyke.

Finally, where entries to Van Dyke highrise buildings serve 130 families, Brownsville buildings are entered through different doors, each serving a small number of families (nine to thirteen). The ground area adjacent to these entries has been developed for use by adults, and for play by young children. Parents feel confident about allowing their children to play in these clearly circumscribed zones. Frequently, these entry areas are located just off the public street, and serve to set off the building from the street itself by acting as an intervening buffer area. The placement of entrances just off the street avoids the dangers created at Van Dyke: forcing tenants to walk along blind interior project paths to get to their buildings.

Inspection of Tables 2 and 3 reveals that the tenants of Brownsville and Van Dyke are rated similarly on overall indexes of socioeconomic status, family stability, and ethnic, racial, and family composition. It is also clear that these rough similarities are consistent from year to year. Comparison of demographic data over the period 1962 to 1969 reveals few exceptions to this overall pattern of identity between the projects.

It was a widely held belief that many so-called "problem families," displaced by the Model Cities renewal programs, were among recent move-ins to Van Dyke. Many people drew an immediate correlation between the higher crime rate at Van Dyke and this change in population. Information was therefore obtained on a representative sample of families who have moved into the two projects over the past three years. Sample data on one of every five move-ins reveal no striking differences in the social characteristics of residents in both projects.

Table 2. Tenant Statistics

Characteristic	Van Dyke	Brownsville
Total population	6,420	5,390
Average family size	4.0	4.0
Number of minors	3,618(57.5%)	3,047(57.8%)
Percent families black	79.1%	85.0%
Percent families white	5.6%	2.6%
Percent families Puerto Rican	15.3%	12.4%
Average gross income	$4,997	$5,056
Percent on welfare	28.8%	29.7%
Percent broken families	29.5%	31.7%
Average number of years in project	8.5	9.0
Percent of families with two wage earners	12.2%	11.0%
Number of children in grades 1–6	839	904

Source: New York City Housing Authority Records, 1968.

The total number of move-ins in the past three years in any case constituted fewer than 5 percent of the project population in both Van Dyke and Brownsville. To blame problems of the Van Dyke project on a small number of "bad seeds" is clearly gratuitous.

Crime and vandalism are major problems at both Van Dyke and Brownsville Houses. The problem has become serious over the past ten years, with the decline of the old Brooklyn community and the failure to create renewal opportunities. The area surrounding both projects is severely blighted; store owners conduct business in plexiglass booths to protect themselves from addicts.

The local library requires two armed guards on duty at all times. The local hospital claims it records fifteen teenage deaths per month due to overdoses of drugs.

Table 4 presents data on major categories of crime expressed in terms of rate per thousand population. Data are also presented on specific crimes, including robbery, possession of drugs, and loitering. A comparison of 1969 crime incident rates (see Table 4) and maintenance rates (see Table 5) for the two projects was quite revealing. In summary, Van Dyke Homes was found to have 66 percent more total crime incidents, with over two and one-half times as many rob-

Table 3. A Comparison of Physical Design and Population Density

Physical measure	Van Dyke	Brownsville
Total size	22.35 acres	19.16 acres
Number of buildings	23	27
Building height	13-14 story 9-3 story	6-story with some 3-story wings
Coverage	16.6	23.0
Floor area ratio	1.49	1.39
Average number of rooms per apartment	4.62	4.69
Density	288 persons/acre	287 persons/acre
Year completed	1955 (one building added in 1964)	1947

Source: New York City Housing Authority Project Physical Design Statistics.

Table 4. Comparison of Crime Incidents

Crime incidents	Van Dyke	Brownsville
Total incidents	1,189	790
Total felonies, misdemeanors, and offenses	432	264
Number of robberies	92	24
Number of malicious mischief	52	28

Source: New York City Housing Authority Police Records, 1968.

beries (264 percent), and 60 percent more felonies, misdemeanors, and offenses than Brownsville.

Another measure of security can be understood from examination of the rate of decline of facilities. Even though Brownsville Houses is an older project, beginning to suffer from natural decay, Van Dyke annually required a total of 72 percent more maintenance work. It is interesting to note that the average outlay of time and funds for upkeep of Van Dyke is significantly higher than that of Brownsville. Not only is there less need of repair at Brownsville, but tenants themselves play a greater role in seeing to the cleanliness of buildings either through insistence on the upkeep of janitorial services or by individual effort.

One of the most striking differences between the two projects concerns elevator breakdowns. The far greater number of breakdowns at Van Dyke is primarily a func-

tion of more intensive use. However, more breakdowns are due to vandalism at Van Dyke than at Brownsville. This form of vandalism is especially diagnostic, showing that adolescents who tamper with Van Dyke elevators do not have a sense of identity with the people they inconvenience.

As a measure of tenant satisfaction, Brownsville Houses, with smaller room sizes in similarly designated apartment units, has a lower rate of move-outs than Van Dyke Houses. To avoid historical accident and subsequently limited conclusion, results were tabulated annually over an eight-year period, including sampling of move-ins to the two projects.

There are some elementary differences in the physical construct of the projects which may contribute to the disparity of image held by officials. Police officers revealed that they found Van Dyke Houses far more difficult to patrol. To monitor activity in the

Table 5. Comparison of Maintenance

Maintenance	Van Dyke (constructed 1955)	Brownsville (constructed 1947)
Number of maintenance jobs of any sort (work tickets) 4/70	3,301	2,376
Number of maintenance jobs, excluding glass repair	2,643	1,651
Number of nonglass jobs per unit	1.47	1.16
Number of full-time maintenance staff	9	7
Number of elevator breakdowns per month	280	110

Source: New York City Housing Authority Project Manager's bookkeeping records.

enclosed fire stairs requires that a patrolman take the elevator to the upper floor and then walk down to the ground level, alternating at each floor between the two independent fire-stair columns.

Police express pessimism about their value at Van Dyke Houses. About Brownsville they are much more optimistic and, in subtle ways, respond to complaints with more vigor and concern. All these factors produce a significant positive effect in Brownsville. At Van Dyke the negative factors of anonymity, police pessimism, pessimism about police, and and tenant feelings of ambiguity about strangers (caused by large numbers of families sharing one entrance) conspire progressively to erode any residual faith in the effectiveness of community or official response to crime.

In summary, it seems unmistakable that physical design plays a very significant role in crime rate. It should also be kept in mind that the defensible space qualities inherent in the Brownsville design are there, for the most part, by accident. From a critical, defensible space viewpoint, Brownsville is far from perfect. The comparison of the crime and vandalism rates in the two projects was made using gross crime data on both projects. Twenty-three percent of the apartments at Van Dyke consist of three-story walk-up buildings serving a small number of families. It is likely that comparative data on crime rates in the low buildings versus the towers at Van Dyke would reveal significant differences. This would make the comparison of crime rates between Van Dyke and Brownsville even more startling.

FOUR CHARACTERISTICS OF DEFENSIBLE SPACE

There is always a danger in categorical subdivision in that it may suggest that any one of the mechanisms can operate independently. Whereas some are independent, others are rendered almost meaningless if used alone. As an example, the definition and assignment of territorial areas to groups of inhabitants has been found to operate most effectively where occupants have also been given visual control of the defined area. Equally, improving visual surveillance opportunities may be a pointless task if the resident is viewing activity taking place in an area he does not identify with. Therefore, in the discussion of each defensible space mechanism, continuous cross-reference will be made to other categories where the two act in tandem or symbiotically.

The four major cateogires created for the discussion of defensible space are:

1. The capacity of the physical environment to create perceived zones of territorial influence: mechanisms for the subdivision and articulation of areas of the residential environment intended to reinforce inhabitants in their ability to assume territorial attitudes and prerogatives.

2. The capacity of physical design to provide surveillance opportunities for residents and their agents: mechanisms for improving the capacity of residents casually and continually to survey the nonprivate areas of their living environment, indoor and out.

3. The capacity of design to influence the perception of a project's uniqueness, isolation, and stigma: mechanisms which neutralize the symbolic stigma of the form of housing projects, reducing the image of isolation, and the apparent vulnerability of inhabitants.

4. The influence of geographical juxtaposition with "safe zones" on the security of adjacent areas: mechanisms of juxtaposition—the effect of location of a residential environment within a particular urban setting or adjacent to a "safe" or "unsafe" activity area.

Boston's Experiment with Rent Subsidies

CHARLES TILLY and JOE FEAGIN

Until recently low-income families displaced by urban renewal or other public actions have generally faced a choice between unsubsidized housing in the private market and subsidized housing under public ownership. Those who opted for the private market either moved into substandard dwellings elsewhere in the city or paid significantly more for their new housing than for the old, or both. Those who went to public housing normally found themselves in large, segregated, institutional developments populated entirely by families who had also gone through a lengthy process of administrative screening. The experience of the movers in the private market has intensified the feeling that urban renewal essentially displaces slums instead of eliminating them and victimizes the helpless in the process. The experience of those who have moved to public housing has fostered the accusation that urban renewal segregates the poor and stores them out of sight.

Within the last four years, several new housing programs designed for low-income families have been authorized by Congress, each involving income redistribution in the form of federal housing subsidies. However, some "low-income" programs, such as the 221 (d) (3) Below Market Interest Rate program and the new Rental Housing Program, are not real alternatives to public housing, because the limited federal subsidies involved mean that housing generally cannot be rented for sums that many families in the public housing income range can be expected to pay.[1]

Currently, the two major low-income programs that seem to provide workable alternatives to public housing and the substandard private market are the Rent Supplement program and the LHA Leasing program.[2] The Rent Supplement program created by the 1965 Housing Act, is administered directly through federal agencies, bypassing local housing authorities; the program relies on private groups to build and manage low-rent

1. This is not to say that some low-income families will not benefit from these programs, especially those in the upper range of the public housing level. The as yet untested Section 235 Homeownership Program (1968 Housing Act) will probably serve families in this same income range. See, President's Committee on Urban Housing, *A Decent Home* (Washington, D.C.: U.S. Government Printing Office, 1968), pp. 60–79.
2. Even these programs do not reach the poorest of American families.

C. Tilly, & J. Feagin. Boston's experiment with rent subsidies. *Journal of the American Institute of Planners*, 1970, **36**, 323–329. Reprinted by permission.

housing developments. Contracts for rent subsidy payments are made directly between the FHA and private owners. Hedged in by a growing number of restrictions on eligibility requirements, construction costs, and maximum rentals, this program has so far provided only a small percentage of the number of housing units originally authorized.

Unlike the Rent Supplement program, the Section 23 Leasing program is administered th ough local housing authorities. This ap roach provides for leasing by the LHA of ex.sting housing units from private owners, followed by the subleasing of these units to tenants who would otherwise qualify for public housing. Also in its early stages, this leasing program has great potential for meeting the housing needs of low-income families.

Before these low-income housing programs came into existence, an experimental rent subsidy program in Boston anticipated many of their features and characteristics.[3] What is more, it worked. This article reports on the costs, effectiveness, and policy implications of the Boston program.

THE BOSTON PROGRAM

Until 1964, the Boston Housing Authority had put most of its energy into large public housing developments. Then it began an experiment with rent subsidies, financed by the federal Department of Housing and Urban Development with funds allocated by Congress in the early 1960's for experimental housing programs. For the three-year period from 1964–1967, forty large, low-income families displaced by public action (thirty-five of them black, five mixed or white) paid the rents they would normally have paid in public housing, but lived in apartments or row houses in one of three

3. Actually, the technical name of the Boston program was "rent supplements"; to avoid confusion with the somewhat different government program now bearing that name we have referred throughout to the Boston experiment with the term "rent subsidies."

newly constructed 221 (d) (3), middle income developments. The three projects were sponsored by non-profit organizations with a definite interest in Boston's black community and were located in the ghetto or on its fringe. Two of them were, in fact, side by side in the midst of a cleared site within a major ghetto urban renewal project.

Thus, the Boston rent subsidy program dealt with a common situation in what may become a typical way. Although its designers did not realize how typical it would become when they were planning in 1963, certain critical features of their resulting program were prophetic: (1) provision of housing for families displaced by public action; (2) restriction to families with incomes low enough for admission to public housing; (3) payment of rent subsidies to development owners on behalf of selected tenants; and (4) substantial local housing authority control over tenant selection, rent, and administrative procedures. Subsequently, both the Rent Supplement program and the LHA Leasing program incorporated some of these features. Both were designed for poor families with incomes in the public housing range; both have facilitated housing poor families displaced by public action. (The Rent Supplement program formally focuses on such families.) Both programs involve federal rent subsidies. Under the Rent Supplement program, subsidies are (typically) paid directly to the development owners; while under the LHA Leasing program, they are indirectly paid through the local housing authority. In regard to the fourth characteristic, local housing authority control, the Boston experimental program was similar to later LHA Leasing programs though it differed substantially from current Rent Supplement programs. This is an important point to emphasize, since such LHA control generally means local public control over tenant qualifications, administrative procedures and housing standards.

The experimental rent subsidy program differed from currently existing Rent Supplement and LHA Leasing Programs in several other respects. The Boston program, unlike the Rent Supplement program, was not as severely hemmed in by federal restrictions on construction costs, maximum market rentals, and housing amenities—limitations that have not only virtually eliminated the possibility of building qualifying housing that will attract the income mix of the Boston experimental program but also made the "Rent Supplement program generally unworkable for new construction in major central cities outside the South and Southwest."[4] The Boston program reflected greater flexibility in this regard, a flexibility to which the Rent Supplement program will probably have to return, if it is to serve a large number of low-income families.

The Boston experiment differed from many current LHA Leasing programs in (a) its involvement with new construction (the Kaiser Report recommends an expansion of the leasing program to include new construction) and (b) its contractual arrangements (the private owners, or their managers, played an important role in selecting tenants and in the administration of the Boston project).[5]

The BHA program was also prophetic in that two circumstances associated with its implementation seem characteristic of many local projects built under subsequent low-income housing programs including: (1) a very high proportion of Negro families as participants; and (2) housing built on a renewal site, frequently in or near a ghetto area.

The three ghetto developments involved in the BHA program, newly constructed 221 (d) (3) "middle-income" housing, varied in design (Charlame Park Homes and Marksdale Gardens were mainly row houses while Academy Homes consisted of two- and three-story apartments.), but all three were attractive and convenient. Largely because of their

locations, they attracted mostly black tenants—close to 90 percent.

The forty families were scattered throughout the three developments, occupying about one unit in eleven. Aside from a few administrative accidents, the only segregation was due to the families' need for larger apartments, which were clustered to some extent; but there were no areas that could reasonably be labeled "rent subsidy areas." So far as we could determine, no areas ever were labeled that way by local residents. Nor were the recipients of rent subsidies ever singled out by their neighbors as a separate class of people.

The normal rents in Charlame, Marksdale, and Academy ran from $85 to $150 per month. For the forty families, the Housing Authority paid the difference between those rents and the amounts they would normally pay in public housing. The rent subsidy averaged about $51 per month per family.

The experimental rent subsidy program lasted three years. Because of the construction schedule, the last families moved in when it had little more than a year to run. At the end of the three-year period, thirty-five families of the original forty still remained in the program. Three had, in effect, been evicted for bad housekeeping; two more had, so far as we can tell, dropped out voluntarily. When the program officially ended, the BHA simply shifted the remaining families to a new leasing arrangement so that none of them had to move from the dwellings they were currently occupying. By September 1968, three of the thirty-five families had sufficient income to pay the full rent themselves; altogether, then, 88 percent of the families who started the program in 1964 and 1965 were still in their dwellings three or four years later.

The Evaluation

Our systematic observation of the Boston subsidy experiment ran from June 1964 (two months before the first families moved into their new dwellings) to June 1966 (eight months after the last families moved

---

4. For a critical review of the current Rent Supplement program, see, *A Decent Home*, p. 65.
5. *Ibid.*, p. 79. Technically, private owners can play an important role in the tenant selection process under the Section 23 program, although so far that function has usually been in the hands of the LHA.

in). During that time we stayed in close contact with the people running the program, examined records of the Boston Housing Authority and several other agencies dealing with housing low-income families, collected general information about the Boston housing market, and interviewed a number of officials and local leaders concerned with housing and other problems of Boston's ghetto. Our largest effort, however, went into a series of interviews with the forty families in the rent subsidy program and with other families chosen for comparison.

The comparison samples included three important housing groups: families who moved into public housing: families who found dwellings in the private market; and a group of higher income families who moved into the same three developments as the rent subsidy families. Interviews were conducted both before and after the housing moves. Because of the ghetto location of the projects in which rent subsidy families were to live, most of the families we interviewed were black.[6]

In general, our investigation showed that the experimental rent subsidy program met its objective of providing sound, attractive housing to low-income families without major difficulties and at moderate cost. The selection process, it is true, was excessively cumbersome, partly as a result of being grafted onto the Boston Housing Authority's regular procedures for placing families in public housing. But once families had joined the program there was little that could go wrong. The chief mishap was the eviction of three families, allegedly for "bad housekeeping," by the local management. Such cases seem to point to the desirability of putting even more control over the conditions of tenure and renting in the hands of the public housing authority. In general, the subsidy

families kept their dwellings in good condition; they paid their rents regularly and from every point of view fulfilled their obligations as tenants. In short, the administration of the program did not present any exceptional problems, and it required much less apparatus than the running of public housing developments does.

What about the administrative and subsidy costs of the experimental subsidy program particularly as compared with other housing alternatives? We have no usable information on the cost of providing standard housing for low-income families through income redistribution or direct intervention in Boston's private housing market. However, we do have some comparative data on the apparent costs of three programs being operated by the BHA: (1) large project public housing; (2) leased housing; and (3) experimental rent subsidy housing. We stress *apparent* here, because the data have two important flaws: (1) they deal with current costs for units already on hand, rather than the cost of adding new units; (2) they do not genuinely reflect the differences in administrative costs among the programs. Figures indicating costs per unit per month are shown in Table 1.

The low subsidy of the non-elderly public housing units comes largely from the fact that many were built some years ago, when construction costs were substantially lower than today. As Table 1 shows, the public housing subsidy rises regularly with the recency of construction; the apparent costs of recently constructed public housing for the elderly *greatly* surpass those of leased housing and the experimental rent subsidy housing. Based on these data on elderly units, one would also expect subsidy costs for newly constructed non-elderly public housing to be much higher than they were fifteen or more years ago.[7]

6. Most of the statistical analysis in the larger report, on which this summary is based, deals with the 129 families in the several housing groups that were best matched with regard to income, size, and composition, and with whom we had comparable interviews both before and after the move. One hundred and twenty of these families were Negro.

7. We have no reason to expect any substantial difference in subsidy between the rent subsidy and leasing programs for 221 (d) (3), although Table 1 shows an apparent difference of almost $3 per month. We have good reason, on the other hand, to expect the administration of leasing scattered private units to cost more than the administration of

Table 1. Apparent Costs of BHA-Low-Income Housing Programs[a]

| | Costs ($) per unit per month | | |
Program	Current administrative costs	Current federal subsidy	Total
Public housing			
Non-elderly units built 1940–54	7.40	24.87	32.27
Elderly units built 1960–63	7.40	62.12	69.52
Elderly units built 1966	7.40	75.52	82.92
Other BHA programs			
First nine private units leased (first three months)	7.37	50.56	57.93
Estimated cost of first thousand 221 (d) (3) units leased	7.37	54.00	61.37
Experimental rent subsidies in 221 (d) (3) units	7.37	51.01	58.38

[a]Calculated from figures provided us by Frank Donahue, Director of Finance and Accounts, Boston Housing Authority.

The average rent subsidy of $51 per month, plus estimated administrative expenses, brought the cost of the experimental program to about $58 per unit per month. Rent subsidies of the type involved in the BHA experimental and leasing programs appear to be a somewhat less expensive method of adding dwellings to stock available to a local housing authority than construction of new publicly owned developments. Yet these figures on the Boston experimental program do not include an additional hidden rent subsidy, a result of construction of the housing projects being financed under the 221 (d) (3) BMIR mortgage program. Inclusion of this additional subsidy, difficult to calculate, might increase the total subsidy per unit to the $70–$80 range, closer to that for recent public housing.[8] Moreover, whatever cost advantages rent subsidies have over public housing programs are only for the short run of five to ten years. In the long run, obviously, capital costs per unit of publicly owned housing

decline, even if maintenance costs rise, while rent subsidies tend to rise with average rents; the financial advantage of one over the other will depend on borrowing costs, durability of publicly owned housing, and rate of increase in rents in the local area.

In addition, public construction of housing does guarantee the addition of new housing, accessible to low-income families, to the housing stock. Rent subsidies like those in the BHA experimental program do not. The Boston experiment essentially opened up to low-income families forty units that would have been built anyway, would have had the same locations, and would have been occupied by middle income families. Yet a rent subsidy program on a much larger scale than this experiment and directed toward new dwellings, could certainly encourage construction that would otherwise not occur.[9]

But what of the effect of the moves on the low-income families themselves? All rent subsidy and comparison families participating

leasing units in 221 (d) (3); however, the data in Table 1 seem to indicate the opposite conclusion.
8. There are, of course, hidden subsidies involved in public housing, such as local tax concessions.

9. The new Section 236 Rental Housing program makes an attempt to do this, but it provides for only limited subsidies and probably cannot reach the same income levels as public housing.

in the Boston experiment came from the ghetto or its fringe. Most remained within the ghetto or on its fringe after the move. This was particularly true of the rent subsidy families; all remained in or near the center of the Roxbury area ghetto. Respondents in the comparison housing samples, those moving into private, public, and 221 (d) (3) housing (without subsidy), tended to report somewhat greater contact with whites after the move yet so did the rent subsidy families. Actually, none of the housing alternatives we examined produced a significant amount of residential integration.

The moves did, however, produce important changes in the quality of the housing people occupied and in their feelings about the housing. Almost everyone in every housing category, private or public, moved into somewhat better housing than he had before—better in terms of structural soundness, space, comfort, and the family's satisfaction with it. The general enthusiasm of the rent subsidy families is illustrated by the

data in Table 2, which presents the post-move comparisons of present and previous residences made by the rent subsidy wives and the public housing wives in our sample. Both groups are composed of black respondents; a few white and mixed-race families have been omitted from the two samples to increase comparability. It should be noted that at the time of their selection (in 1964–1965), public housing was the only major alternative, outside the private housing market, available to these low-income families.

Examining the two columns for the rent subsidy wives, it is clear that on every item the proportion liking their 221 (d) (3) apartments better than the last places they had lived far exceeds the proportion not liking them as much. This is particularly true of the items bearing on space, design, safety, quietness, and childrearing features of the new 221 (d) (3) environment. In each of these cases the "like it better-don't like as much" differential and the absolute percentage exceed the comparable figures for the

Table 2. Comparison of Present and Previous Residence, After the Move[a]

	Rent subsidy wives (N = 35)		Public housing wives (N = 24)	
Compared to the last place you lived, do you like "x" better, worse, or the same (selected dimensions)	*Percent replying "like it better"*	*Percent replying "don't like it as much"*	*Percent replying "like it better"*	*Percent replying "don't like it as much"*
The size of this place	91	3	75	4
The outside of the building	94	3	75	13
The amount of rent you pay	66	26	96	4
Amount of space you have to invite friends over	91	6	67	8
As a place to bring up children	83	3	58	17
Nearness to public transportation	60	20	42	25
Schools	40	26	33	17
Class of people who live near	46	3	21	25
The quietness of the street	86	9	29	46

[a]"About the same" and "can't say" responses have been omitted from the tabulations in this table, but can be calculated by subtraction. The data are for the Negro families in the two samples.

public housing sample, although the public housing figures also indicate overall satisfaction with the new environment. In only one case is the "like it better" percentage for the public housing sample greater than that for the subsidy group. This is in regard to the issue of rent paid. Some of the subsidy families also had minor complaints about the design of their new dwellings, but their general attitude toward rent subsidies was quite enthusiastic. One articulate respondent commented: "It helps a lot to know that you can live happy and decent like one who can really afford it."

Moreover, we found that most people in each of our housing samples cut some informal social ties when they moved and slowly made new friends afterward. Those who moved into the private market (and thus had the greatest control over their new locations and relied most often on friends and relatives in the search for housing) appear to have cut the fewest ties; those who moved into public housing appear to have cut the most. In the new neighborhood, our data suggest that the subsidy families joined in local affairs faster and more actively than those moving into other types of housing. The net effect of the move appears to have included a heavier involvement in neighborhood activities.

Contrary to some published criticisms of the rent subsidy approach, we could detect no signs that higher income neighbors of the subsidy families singled them out as a special group, or that any special frictions developed from grouping together households with different income levels. Of course, the income differences were not as great as might be expected; moreover, middle income families, the overwhelming majority of families in the developments, had seen enough of the housing problems of poor Negroes to react favorably to the general principle of government rent subsidies.

Implications for Public Policy

Rent subsidies of the type involved in the Boston experiment, along with those in the closely comparable LHA Leasing programs, have many advantages as an instrument of housing policy. Some of these advantages are shared with federally financed programs that bypass local housing authorities, particularly the Rent Supplement program, but many are not. So far we have concentrated on whether rent subsidies under the auspices of a local housing authority work, without too much bother and expense, as a means of providing sound housing for poor families. In our view, they certainly do. We should also consider their implications for other persistent problems of housing policy: relocation, desegregation, economic integration, code enforcement, and special-need households.

The subsidy families in the Boston experiment, and many of those in other housing markets with whom we compared them, were being relocated as a consequence of urban renewal in and around the ghetto. Our findings indicate that the families who relocated through the private market had the smallest personal adjustment to make, because they continued a routine they already knew well from previous moves. Low-income families moving into public housing and 221 (d) (3) developments had greater adjustments to make; in almost every respect the families moving into 221 (d) (3) dwellings were far happier with those adjustments.

Several features of rent subsidies (from this point on, we will take this phrase to include both the experimental Boston program and LHA Leasing arrangements) make them handy tools for relocation of poor families. They are flexible: in all but a very tight market they can be used to rapidly increase the number of units available for relocated families. They give redevelopment and housing authorities the means to assure that relocated families receive dwellings in good condition. Furthermore, location of dwellings is not a great problem. In principle, it makes little difference whether they are scattered or clustered, central or suburban. The main limit in all these respects is the state of the city housing market.

Whether or not rent subsidy programs produce racial desegregation in housing depends entirely on location of the subsidized units. The Boston program did not produce any substantial amount of desegregation. Programs working with the existing stock of housing, even if run by people committed to equal opportunity, are likely to feel the subtle pressures that produce current forms of residential segregation—if only because the equal opportunity policy itself will affect which units are offered to the public authority for leasing or subsidy. A greatly expanded program of rent subsidies, especially if it concentrated on new 221 (d) (3) middle income dwellings or their equivalent, would have a strong impact on the pattern of racial segregation *only if* the developments were distributed around the city. The more scattered the units, the greater the desegregation, as long as a substantial proportion of the families involved belonged to racial minorities. A policy of clustering, on the other hand, would tend to perpetuate, or possibly even consolidate, the ghetto.

The Boston experiment did produce a small measure of *economic* integration, since families of somewhat different income levels lived together without notable difficulty. We have no reason to believe that it could not happen on a larger scale. This feature of rent subsidies deserves further scrutiny, because the Boston arrangements were especially favorable: a relatively narrow income gap; a very low proportion of poor families; no notable racial difference between the two groups. We suspect that significantly changing any one of these conditions would reduce contact between families receiving rent supplements and their neighbors. We also suspect that it would take a *huge* change in these conditions to produce systematic hostility between the two groups. The best way to find out is to carefully examine cases in other cities in which the proportions have been different, the income differentials larger, the racial cleavage more definite.

It is also hard to judge the effect of an expanded program of rent subsidies on the *quality* of a city's housing. For the particular dwellings involved, local housing authority control over rent payments and tenure would help maintain landlord concurrence with building and health codes. Such a program ought to reduce the demand of very poor families for substandard dwellings, but whether landlords would respond to rising vacancy rates by improving, converting, abandoning, razing, or reducing rents on their properties is hard to say. No doubt a combination of all of these would occur, and the net effect would be a modest improvement in housing quality.

This brings up a danger many people have seen in rent subsidies. What if they gave unscrupulous landlords an opportunity to collude with inspectors in setting high rents and low standards? The association of rent subsidies with housing built by nonprofit or limited-dividend corporations, as in the Boston experiment, does not pose much of a threat. But what about slum properties operated for maximum profit? There is a risk here, and it will take some policing. Nevertheless, the local housing authority operating a rent subsidy program under its own control has several advantages over the city's code enforcement officer. It is offering something precious to a slum landlord: a guarantee of continuous rent payments. It can negotiate the rent directly, with plenty of experience behind it, for many units at a time, rather than relying on piecemeal landlord-tenant agreements. The LHA can supervise maintenance, or it can contract with a third party for maintenance.

Households with special needs may not be so well served by rent subsidies. Old people are perhaps the best example. Housing built specifically for the elderly often has such features as ramps, few and easy stairways, low cabinets, and specially equipped bathrooms. Although there are excellent reasons for avoiding construction of large enclaves of buildings for old people, there are also many advantages—social, practical, financial—to producing such dwellings in small clusters. Rent subsidies do not easily lend themselves to this purpose. They work best providing for households who need the sorts of dwellings that *normally* come onto the market but that, without subsidy, would be beyond the households' means.

CONCLUSION

In fitting rent subsidies, under the auspices of local housing authorities, into the spectrum of available means to assure that every poor family has sound housing and maximum freedom of choice, the framers of public policy face two major decisions. The first decision is between public ownership and management, on the one hand, and rent subsidies (including leasing), on the other. The second is between the use of housing already available and the creation of new dwellings. Public ownership gains in attractiveness when the demand for publicly subsidized housing is relatively constant; rent subsidies seem more viable when that demand varies.[10] Available housing is most likely to

meet public needs when vacancy rates and turnover are high, discriminatory barriers few, and average quality of housing good; new construction makes greater sense in cases of tight markets, extensive discrimination, and low housing quality. Therefore, rent subsidies in existing housing are likely to work best where demand for publicly subsidized housing is quite variable, the housing stock good, discrimination weak, and the market relatively loose. A program like the one tried in Boston—combining rent subsidies with earmarking newly constructed units—is likely to reach its maximum effectiveness where the housing market is tight and discriminatory, the housing stock inferior, and the demand either somewhat less variable or far greater than can be met with current public resources.

10. Although public ownership gains in attractiveness in situations of more or less constant demand, this does not mean that rent subsidy programs in private housing are necessarily unattractive in many such situations.

Housing Allowances

MALCOLM E. PEABODY, JR.

When in St. Louis in March of 1972, the plunger was pushed to blow the first building of the Pruitt-Igoe public housing project into a pile of rubble, it symbolized the end of the federal policy of building housing for the poor begun 36 years ago. Built in 1956 to house 2700 families, Pruitt-Igoe won architectural awards but shortly deteriorated into an unlivable slum—good only for a demolition experiment. The actual end came in January of 1973 when the White House declared a moratorium on the subsidized programs, charging that they were "wasteful, inequitable and scandal prone," and called for a major study of federal housing policies to develop a new approach.

As the dust settled on Pruitt-Igoe, across the state in Kansas City, Missouri Louise Garrett, a welfare mother with four children, was being interviewed about her reactions as one of the first participants in a demonstration of a new approach to housing the poor. It was called "the housing allowance," and it consisted of giving cash assistance to needy families and allowing them to choose their own housing on the private market, rather than subsidizing housing authorities and private developers to build new low-rent housing.

When chosen for the experiment Garrett was living in a dilapidated one-bedroom apartment in a Kansas City slum. Within 60 days she had rented a simple but attractive three-bedroom, single-family house in a pleasant working-class area, with good schools and recreation for her children. She was delighted. "The house and the neighborhood has exceeded my highest expectations of what I ever thought I could afford," she said. Officials in charge of the demonstration were also pleased because in addition to housing the participants so happily, the allowance program had done so at one-half the annual cost of subsidizing new public housing units, done it in a fraction of the time, and with no resistance from Garrett's new neighbors.

With the results of a federal study in hand, the President last September declared that direct cash assistance was "the most promising way to achieve decent housing for all our families at an acceptable cost." He then filed

Malcolm E. Peabody, until recently the Deputy Assistant Secretary of Equal Opportunity at HUD, pioneered the development of the housing allowance program.

legislation to expand the national experiment in housing allowances, which had been set up to test the findings of the Kansas City approach. Congress, stung by the President's impounding of housing funds and now weighing the possibility of impeachment, is unlikely to respond positively to his proposals. And yet the Congress, too, has lost stomach for subsidizing new housing for the poor, which it had enthusiastically endorsed when it passed the 1968 Housing Act.

Dubbed the "Magna Carta of Housing" by its sponsor, Lyndon Johnson, the '68 act launched the section 235 and section 236 housing programs under which the government subsidized moderate-income ($5000–$10,000 a year, depending on family size and geographic location) home buyers purchasing housing under $35,000, and developers who built housing for moderate-income families by lowering mortgage payments to the equivalent of one percent. The act also permitted FHA to guarantee single-home mortgages in inner-city areas, expanded the public housing program and set forth for the first time a national housing goal of 26 million new units to be built within the next 10 years, six million of which were to be subsidized. In a rare act of putting its money where its mouth was, Congress appropriated the funds to meet these goals. Subsidized housing production took off, and in the four years that followed over 1.6 million units were started, more than doubling the one million that were in place in 1968.

What went wrong after such an auspicious start? In simple terms the act produced financial, political and sociological monsters. The annual costs for subsidizing individual units were outrageous. It took $2500 in direct and indirect subsidies to lower the rent of a new unit of public housing to the $70 level (the average monthly rent that public housing tenants pay). In one program annual subsidies were running in excess of $2000 per unit or substantially more than what the average family pays for housing. The President's study showed that it would cost $2.5 billion annually just to pay for the

units started during the past four years, and billions more to reach the six million unit goal. And even if this goal were reached, it would provide but one unit for every four families or individuals eligible under current statutes.

Politically the subsidized construction approach has become increasingly unpopular. Locating a public low-rent or even moderate-rent multifamily housing development raises issues of race, class and high-density development all at once. Any of these is explosive enough, but when combined they trigger community reactions of nuclear proportions. . . .

During the late '60s and late '70s resistance grew rapidly to the location of new federal housing developments—particularly multifamily projects. The fight over the Forest Hills public housing project in Queens, New York and the one over a project in Blackjack, Missouri, were typical of what was happening in many metropolitan areas.

The single-family housing program had fewer political problems at first, since it did not raise any controversy over building apartments. However, congressional mailbags soon swelled with complaints from irate homeowners who were struggling to make their own living and who felt keenly the inequity of having the government subsidize neighbors who paid less and owned better and newer equipped housing. The outcry was such that a local approval requirement was added to the '72 housing bill in the House. The bill was blocked by the Rules Committee for other reasons, but it would have effectively killed the program had it passed. Not only neighbors were objecting, so were tenants, because too often the subsidies were producing poor housing, particularly the public housing for families. Even before the '68 act we knew it was a ghastly mistake to erect monster public housing projects like Pruitt-Igoe, Columbia Heights in Boston and Taylor Homes in Chicago. These were built in the '50s when social planners believed in concentrating the poor geographically, thereby permitting more efficient delivery of social services. Experience proved instead that packing multiproblem families together was like packing oily rags, risking spontaneous combustion. Many of the riots in the '66–'69 period began in such public housing projects. Smaller projects on scattered sites were preferable, but these proved to be much costlier to build and maintain, and not much easier to locate.

The basic defect of the public housing program in my opinion was not that it concentrated the poor but that it discouraged their escape from the poverty cycle. The public housing tenant was at the bottom of a many-tiered sociological totem pole. Benefits flow down this pole from central, regional and area offices of HUD, thence to the mayor of the city who selects the housing authority board, which in turn hires the authority director who then supervises the project directors who finally control the tenants. Tenants cannot reach up that long pole to complain about the filthy hallways or the lack of security. Their only contact is with the project director who does as he pleases because he knows the tenants have no other housing choice. This reinforces the feeling of powerlessness and hopelessness that are the first emotional hurdles to clear before a family can break out of poverty.

Although the political and financial problems would have been enough to knock out the subsidized housing, the corruption and confusion produced by the explosive expansion of the programs following the '68 act hastened their demise. In 1972 grand juries in nine cities were uncovering collusion between HUD staffs and sharp real estate developers and brokers. In one HUD office, corruption was so rife that the office was closed out entirely. The headlines produced by these revelations figured importantly in the decision to impose a moratorium.

Thus the United States may well be at the end of an era of subsidized housing construction and at the beginning of a new one using direct cash assistance to house the poor. The question is will the new approach be better?

In my judgment the answer is yes. By giving cash directly it lessens the dependency of the poor; they have the power to choose. At one stroke this inverts the sociological totem pole, putting the beneficiary on top and the people who provide him housing below. If they are not sensitive to his needs, he has the freedom to go elsewhere. The housing they find may be older than public housing but it is likely to be in better neighborhoods. Moreover the beneficiaries will not be stigmatized as wards of the state since few will know they are being aided. And with all these advantages, the direct approach will cost far less per family housed, and thus will be far more equitable since more needy people can be helped with the same amount of money.

These are the conclusions that were reached as a result of two experiments with housing allowances for some 250 families, conducted in Kansas City and Wilmington during 1971 and 1972. In Kansas City the program worked this way: a survey was taken of the metropolitan area to determine the lowest rents at which standard units were generally available. Low-income families were then selected with first priority given to families living in substandard units or in public housing. Of those selected, 85 percent were black, 79 percent female, 75 percent on social welfare, 70 percent unemployed, and their average annual incomes were close to $3000. Average age was 32 years old; the families had three to four children. In short these were the families ordinarily judged the toughest to house.

Allowance amounts were determined by deducting what the family could afford in rent (25 percent of their income, adjusted to family size) from the cost necessary to rent a suitably sized, standard apartment. For example if a family needed a three-bedroom apartment (standard cost $200) and could only pay $75 with 25 percent of their income, they would be entitled to an allowance of $125. If families found standard apartments at less than the standard cost, they could keep the difference as long as the rent equaled or exceeded the allowance. This gave families an incentive to find bargains, but also allowed them to choose higher-quality housing if they were willing to pay more. Units were inspected prior to move-ins to assure that they met city code standards. Beneficiaries had to show proof of rents paid to assure that allowances were used for housing.

Armed with their prospective allowances most of the families found housing within the 60 days allowed. Many, lacking cars, had difficulty seeing available units. Others couldn't find enough listings or had trouble finding housing that could pass inspection. Their experience pointed up a need for better counseling and transportation, which features are being built into the national experiment. There was some awkwardness with landlords who refused to rent to families with children or to persons on welfare, or who practiced outright racial discrimination. A great majority, however, did not. Seventy-five percent of the landlords were even willing to decorate and make repairs to pass city inspections, and 60 percent continued to make prompt repairs afterward.

The participants were successful in finding rents below the standard. The average rental paid by participants from their own funds was $18.96. The remainder was made up by the allowances that averaged about $95.00 a month, or *about 40 percent of what it takes to subsidize a new public housing unit each year.*

Where the families moved was fascinating. Some stayed in their own low-income neighborhoods but shifted to better housing. Most moved to better neighborhoods but stayed within the same ethnic community. About eight to 10 percent of the minority families moved into white areas. It seemed that when decent housing was available in neighborhoods within their own ethnic community, minority families were less likely to move outside, particularly poor families. One of the participants, a Mexican-American, was reluctant to leave the Spanish community but failed to find decent housing within it.

He chose a home in the southwestern part of the city near his job and outside the Spanish community.

Ninety percent of those interviewed felt that the allowance program was preferable to public housing, and they were uniformly pleased with the freedom to choose their own home. They mentioned frequently the pleasure of privacy, the peace and quiet of their larger houses in less crowded neighborhoods, and the feeling of pride they got from living there. As one lady put it; "If he [the landlord] don't do what he is supposed to, he don't get paid and he knows it."

But administrators benefit as well. For example a housing allowance is more flexible in that it does not tie the federal government to a specific unit in a specific location for 40 years, as do existing programs. Moreover housing allowances avoid the political problems of where to locate subsidized developments. In Kansas City a number of housing allowance participants moved easily into a neighborhood whose residents had just sued to prevent the construction of a small 236 project. Few residents realized how the newcomers had arrived, but even if they had there was no legal way they could have stopped them. There are a dozen good legal ways, however, of stopping a building.

Housing allowances are no panacea. Though superior in almost every respect to the subsidized construction approach, they cannot be used in tight markets where vacancy rates are less than five to six percent without some parallel program to expand production. Otherwise there will be an imbalance of supply and demand and rents will be driven up without improving overall housing quality. Most of our metropolitan areas today do have vacancy rates of over six percent, however. The 1970 housing census indicated that Chicago had a rate of 6.7 percent; Cleveland, 7.8; Fort Worth, 12.2; Louisville, 7.2; Pittsburgh, 7.7; and Tampa, 9.3. Housing is still tight in many urban areas, mostly in the Northeast. In New York, for example, the vacancy rate is near two percent, one of the lowest in the nation;

Philadelphia, five percent; Washington, 5.3; and Rochester, 4.5. In these cities production must continue to be stimulated.

How to do that is a real teaser, for resistance to subsidized housing is highest in markets that are tightest, particularly to housing projects in white neighborhoods. Building in minority areas is politically easier but legally more difficult. A series of recent federal court decisions have circumscribed the government's ability to assist housing construction in minority areas where the effect of such construction is to perpetuate racial concentration—which most of them do. Finding sites that are both politically and legally allowable would now be extremely hard. So reestablishing the present programs will not get us far. The programs must either be made more palatable, or the courts or Congress must grant power to override local opposition to the location of subsidized projects. The latter seems highly unlikely. Congress is headed in the opposite direction, and though some lower courts seem ready to force communities to accept such projects, the Supreme Court does not.

Thus the emphasis will have to be on wider community acceptance. Many attempts toward this goal have been made before without success—scattering developments, lowering project size, better architecture—all have been used and have improved the housing, but they are costly and public resistance has not declined. Why? Because the resistance is due not primarily to the housing itself but to the race and class of people for whom it is built, and no matter how silky one makes the purse, the public sees only a sow's ear.

There is a way out of this dilemma, but it requires giving up the notion that subsidized construction must directly help the poor. Trying to solve the problems of low-income and poor housing together has made it impossible to solve either. They *can* be solved separately by a program that stimu-lates housing for the *general* public and relies primarily on an income approach to assist the poor. Such a program would use government subsidies and loan guarantees to build housing for *middle income* families. Subsidies would be available only to tight-market cities and would continue until vacancy rates climbed over the six percent level. Until this level was reached, housing allowances would have to be limited probably to the same number of new units produced under the construction program. For this reason it will take time in tight-market cities to solve the housing problems of the poor. But using the double-barreled approach of building for the middle class and assisting the poor to rent existing decent housing will work far faster than the current approach of building for the poor.

Thus far, subsidized middle-income construction has not been proposed by either branch of government. The House is considering block grants—sending subsidy funds to cities and leaving them to decide how best to build low-income housing. The emphasis in the Senate is on continuing the present subsidized construction programs with modifications. The administration has proposed an interim construction program—pending a final decision on how best to administer a direct cash assistance program——wherein subsidies will be available in tight market cities to builders to rent a portion of their units to the poor (no more than 20 percent). How the direct cash assistance approach will fare in this climate is hard to predict. One can only predict that the differing approaches will produce a debate that should continue for at least a year. As that debate rages, the national housing allowance experiment will continue in several states, and if the results validate the findings of the initial experiments in Kansas City and Wilmington, then they may provide the weight necessary to tip the balance and a new era of housing will open.

4

EDUCATION

Introduction

A distressingly large proportion of lower-class children either drop out of school or graduate without acquiring the skills needed to compete for most decent jobs. In an attempt to explain why so many lower-class children do poorly in school, two sets of hypotheses have been proposed. The deficit hypotheses state that lower-class children are inferior to middle-class children in ways that affect scholastic performance. For example, it has been argued that poor children are genetically inferior (Burt, 1959, 1961; Jensen, 1969), that the lower-class environment fails to provide the developing child with the kinds of learning experiences that facilitate cognitive development (Deutsch, 1967), that poor children are inadequately socialized (Banfield, 1971; Lewis, 1966), and/or that lower-class children are much more likely than middle-class children to eat poorly and to receive inadequate health care (Birch & Gussow, 1970). The difference hypotheses state that the cultural background of lower-class children is different from, though not inferior to, the cultural background of middle-class children, and that the schools fail to respond constructively to this difference. For example, it has been argued that the experience of lower-class children may be less useful in school settings than the experience of middle-class children (Getzels, 1969); that standard English differs from black English vernacular and colloquial Spanish in ways that place many lower-class black, Puerto Rican, and Chicano children at a considerable disadvantage in the classroom (Baratz, 1969; Cazden, 1970); that the low expectations held by teachers about the ability of poor children may affect teacher behavior in ways that discourage these children (Rist, 1970; Ryan, 1971); and that curriculum materials usually deal with subject matter that is uninteresting and/or unfamiliar to lower-class children (Levine, 1973). Although the research findings do not permit conclusions about the relative validity of the deficit and difference hypotheses to be drawn, they do suggest that a variety of

207

strategies designed to produce change in urban schools can have a considerable impact on the scholastic performance of lower-class children.[1]

STRATEGIES FOR CHANGE

A number of strategies designed to improve the scholastic performance of lower-class children have been subjected to empirical test. We have placed these strategies in two categories: instructional and institutional. Instructional strategies deal with the ways and means of learning; for example, compensatory education, token reinforcement, and computer-assisted instruction. Institutional strategies seek to alter the character of existing schools or to create alternative schools; for example, desegregation and community control.

We recognize that the education of lower-class children is only one of many problems that confront urban schools. Nevertheless, we have chosen to examine the impact of the preceding strategies on the scholastic performance of these children for several reasons. One, we feel that the failure of so many lower-class children to acquire an adequate education has severely damaging individual and social consequences. Two, most of the programs that have been designed to improve the performance of these children have been implemented in schools. Three, educators have much more control over strategies used in school than over strategies used outside school. For example, we know that children are exposed to school programs, and we can monitor these programs and the children's performance. However, we cannot compel mothers who are taught to facilitate the development of their children's school-related skills to practice what they have learned, nor can we compel preschool children to watch programs such as "Sesame Street." Although strategies such as parent training and educational television programs may be beneficial, we feel that the creation of effective in-school strategies is considerably more useful. Accordingly, let us examine the research findings in an attempt to determine the effects of some of these strategies.

Instructional Strategies

Numerous preschool compensatory education programs, primarily under the aegis of Project Head Start, have been created in recent years in an attempt to increase the school readiness of economically disadvantaged children. While the research findings suggest that many of these programs have not succeeded (Cicirelli, 1969), Spicker (1971) noted that they vary considerably in content and quality, and that some programs have had favorable results. In an attempt to

1. For a more detailed discussion of the deficit and difference hypotheses, see the introduction to the readings on Poverty and the Cole and Bruner article (reading 1.1).

identify the features that make compensatory education work, Spicker reviewed a number of carefully designed studies. For example, Karnes, Teska, and Hodgins (1970)[2] compared the effects of four programs: a traditional nursery school program that used informal and incidental learning opportunities to foster personal, social, motor, and general language development; a community integrated nursery school program in which two to four disadvantaged children were placed in classes containing middle- and upper-class children; a Montessori program in which children played with materials of their choice, sang, told stories, played games, and took field trips; and a highly structured experimental program that used a variety of techniques to teach mathematical concepts, science, social studies, language arts, and reading readiness. Approximately 60 black and 30 white four-year-olds from economically and educationally disadvantaged families participated in the study. Each class contained about 15 children and two or three teachers, lasted about two hours a day, and met daily for approximately eight months. The results indicate that children in the experimental program improved their IQ scores considerably, eliminated substantial linguistic deficits (or overcame differences), and made sizable gains in vocabulary comprehension. Children in the traditional nursery school program showed some improvement in each of these areas, while children in the community integrated and Montessori programs displayed little or no improvement. In a study of the impact of a cognitively structured one-year kindergarten program, Hodges, McCandless, and Spicker (1971) found that lessons designed to teach the skills needed to cope with formalized, rote-memory types of tasks enabled lower-class children to perform as well as their middle-class peers in the second grade. These studies and related studies led Spicker (1971) to conclude that:

> Curriculum models which stress cognitive or academic skill development produce the largest IQ score increases . . . Structured programs other than cognitively or academically oriented ones produce intellectual gains only when they incorporate strong oral language development components . . . Unless the primary grade curriculum can be modified, preschool programs must develop the fine motor, memory, and general language abilities of disadvantaged children. These skills, rather than abstract reasoning, critical thinking, and creative thinking, appear to be needed to succeed in the primary grades of many existing elementary schools located in inner city ghettos and rural communities. [p. 645]

While a number of studies indicate that children who participate in cognitively oriented preschool programs display greater intellectual and linguistic skills than children who do not participate (Beller, 1969; Blank & Solomon, 1968; Karnes, Teska, & Hodgins, 1970; Weikart, 1971), the data also indicate that these gains usually disappear or diminish greatly after one year of elementary school (Bron-

2. Spicker reviewed an earlier version of this paper.

fenbrenner, 1974). As a result, some have called compensatory education a failure (Eysenck, 1971; Jensen, 1969), while others have contended that one year of preschool experience is not enough to overcome the economic, social, and educational disadvantages that poor children encounter (Kohlberg, 1968; Zigler, 1973). In an attempt to test the latter hypothesis, Abelson, Zigler, and DeBlasi (1974, reading 4.1) evaluated a four-year program of compensatory education at the elementary school level. The Follow Through program was characterized by considerable contact between teachers and individual children, an emphasis on learning how to learn by mastering underlying concepts and principles, and an abiding interest in the social-emotional development of each child. Although the regular, or comparison classes were characterized initially by traditional instruction, enrichment programs were introduced in two comparison schools and an extensive program of extracurricular activities was started in a third comparison school during the second year of the study.

Thirty-five economically disadvantaged children who participated in Follow Through and 26 economically disadvantaged children enrolled in regular classes were compared at the beginning and end of kindergarten and at the end of the first and third grades. Comparisons were also made between the 35 economically disadvantaged children and 10 middle-class children enrolled in Follow Through at the end of kindergarten, first, and third grades; and between 42 economically disadvantaged children in Follow Through and 100 economically disadvantaged children attending regular classes at the end of the third grade.

The results suggest that the program had a considerable impact. The longitudinal comparison of disadvantaged children indicates that third-grade children in Follow Through were superior to third-grade children in regular classes on measures of intellectual ability, achievement in mathematics and general information, and task-related verbal behavior. While Head Start attendance had a favorable effect on test scores in kindergarten and first grade, it had no impact on test performance by the end of the third grade. The cross-sectional comparison—42 children in Follow Through and 100 children in regular classes at the end of the third grade—yielded fairly similar findings. Children in Follow Through had higher scores on measures of intellectual ability, achievement in mathematics, reading comprehension, spelling, and general information, self-image, and task-related verbal behavior. Comparison of the economically disadvantaged and nondisadvantaged children in Follow Through indicates that the superiority of the nondisadvantaged children on an assortment of measures diminished considerably from the end of the first grade to the end of the third. While the findings need to be interpreted with caution because the children were not randomly assigned to Follow Through and regular classes (Abelson *et al.*, 1974), they do suggest that "the program was highly beneficial to the children who participated in it. The longitudinal and cross-sectional evidence together

point to the conclusion that the gains accruing from compensatory education
programs are commensurate with the duration and amount of effort which are
expended on these programs" (Abelson *et al.,* 1974, p. 770).

The effects of incentives on classroom behavior have received a considerable
amount of attention (Kazdin, 1975; Lipe & Jung, 1971; O'Leary & Drabman,
1971). Part of that attention has been given to the academic performance of
economically disadvantaged children. Hamblin and Hamblin (1972) examined
the effects of token reinforcement and peer tutoring on the reading achievement
of 26 white and six black preschool children from a low-income St. Louis neighborhood. Classes were held each day for eight weeks. Half the children were
given tokens for reading and half were given tokens for coming to class. At the
end of each session, tokens could be exchanged for things to eat and small toys.
Half the children in each reinforcement condition were also tutored by teenage
Job Corps workers. Among the remaining children, fast learners were tutored by
the teenagers while slower learners were tutored by their fast learning peers. The
results indicate that peer tutoring and tokens for reading had favorable independent and additive effects on the number of words learned, symbols learned, and
books read. Benewitz and Busse (1970) also studied the impact of material reinforcers on test performance. Subjects were 101 fourth-grade black children
attending elementary schools in a large urban ghetto. During one week, the
pupils in two classes were told that they would be given a box of crayons if they
did well on a spelling test. The pupils in the other two classes were given the
same spelling test, though no reward was offered for good grades. During the
second week, conditions in the four classes were reversed. The results indicate that
the children obtained higher scores when they were offered the crayons as an incentive. Wolf, Giles, and Hall (1968) designed a remedial program for sixth-grade
children from a low-income Kansas City neighborhood whose reading level was
at least two years below the norm. Classes met in the afternoon during the
school year and in the morning during the summer. Fifteen children participated
in the program while 15 children with equivalent reading scores did not. Token
reinforcers—which could be exchanged for field trips, daily snacks, money,
novelties, clothes, inexpensive watches, and used bicycles—were awarded for
work completed and/or corrected in regular classes, homework and remedial
assignments completed in the remedial class, report card grades, good behavior,
and attendance. The results indicate that the remedial program had a considerable impact. Participating children gained, on the average, 1.5 years in achievement test scores and an entire grade in their report card averages. The average
gains of children in the control group were significantly and substantially lower.
Clark and Walberg (1968) examined the influence of a great deal of praise on
reading achievement. One hundred and ten black children in a Chicago elementary school whose scholastic performance was one to four years below average

were randomly assigned to nine remedial reading classes. Each child was given a card containing the numbers 1 to 50. Teachers were instructed to praise each child's work several times a day. Each time a child was praised, the teacher told him to check a number on his card, beginning with the number "one." At the end of each day, the children wrote down the number of times they were praised and returned their cards to the teacher. After several sessions, teachers in five randomly chosen classes were instructed to double or triple the number of times they praised each child while teachers in the remaining classes were told merely to "keep up the good work" (p. 308). Reading tests administered five weeks later indicate that children who received a great deal of praise obtained considerably higher scores than children who were praised several times a day.

In an attempt to determine the effectiveness of training teachers to use behavior modification techniques, Rollins, McCandless, Thompson, and Brassell (1974, reading 4.2) implemented and evaluated a one-year program of token reinforcement in four schools in low-income Atlanta neighborhoods. Subjects were 730 black students in the first, second, third, fourth, sixth, and eighth grades. Sixteen classes containing 22 to 25 pupils each were assigned to the experimental group and 14 classes containing 25 to 28 pupils each were placed in the control group. The teachers of the 16 experimental classes—13 were black and three were white—were trained in a three-week summer workshop before the school year began. The workshop "was designed to provide instruction in the theory and practical application of operant conditioning and to involve the teachers in planning for the classroom implementation of behavior management procedures and various curricular activities" (p. 169). Throughout the year, help was provided whenever problems with pupils arose, and individual sessions in curriculum implementation were held weekly.

During the first weeks of school, teachers in the experimental classes rewarded desirable classroom behavior and ignored disruptive behavior. Once the students were behaving appropriately, teachers principally reinforced academic behavior and evidence of academic achievement. Reinforcers included praise and tokens. During the first two weeks, reinforcers were distributed on a continuous and predictable basis, and students were able to obtain a variety of fun items and school supplies. As the children began to behave in desired ways, tokens were dispensed less frequently and less predictably. During the third and fourth months of school, all tangible rewards—except some school supplies—were replaced by access during school hours to activity rooms that contained a variety of toys, games, kits, puzzles, magazines, and records. Experimental classrooms were divided into a mastery center—where children received instruction and completed assignments—and five academically oriented interest stations designed to foster learning without direct teacher assistance. The control classes were taught by the traditional lecture method.

Systematic observation of teachers and students during the school year indicates that experimental teachers administered substantially more reinforcements and fewer punishments than control teachers, and that students in experimental classes were much less disruptive and more often attentive to academic tasks than students in the control classes. The results of several tests administered at the beginning and end of the school year reveal that experimental students made greater IQ gains than control students in the third, fourth, sixth, and eighth grades; that experimental students made greater reading grade-level gains in the first, second, third, sixth, and eighth grades; and that experimental students made greater arithmetic grade-level gains in every grade. While these findings are encouraging, the structure of the experimental classes makes it hard to say if praise and token reinforcement would have the same impact in traditionally run classrooms. In other words, experimental classes were characterized by the use of praise and token reinforcement and by the establishment of mastery centers and interest stations. While it seems likely that praise and token reinforcement contributed heavily to the difference between experimental and control students, it also seems likely that part of that difference was due to the mastery centers and interest stations. Perhaps teachers of economically disadvantaged children should consider establishing mastery centers and interest stations as well as using praise and token reinforcement.

The results of several studies suggest that computer-assisted instruction can also enhance the academic performance of economically disadvantaged children. Suppes and Morningstar (1970) developed a drill-and-practice mathematics program in which the student typed his/her name on a teletypewriter each day. The computer responded by typing a problem. If the student answered correctly, the computer typed another problem. If the student answered incorrectly, he/she was told to try again. After a third error, the correct answer was typed and a new problem was presented. In an attempt to determine the impact of this program on economically disadvantaged children, Suppes and Morningstar compared 515 first to sixth graders who received computer-assisted instruction for a year (first graders received computer-assisted instruction for a half year) and 543 first to sixth graders who did not. The results indicate that children in the experimental classes made greater gains on a test of arithmetic achievement than children in the control classes in every grade. Evaluation of a comparable mathematics program in 16 New York City elementary schools yielded similar findings (Suppes & Morningstar, 1970). In a study that tried to determine the effectiveness of a low-cost computerized reading curriculum designed to supplement classroom instruction, Fletcher and Atkinson (1972) compared 50 economically disadvantaged first-graders who received approximately 10 minutes of computer-assisted instruction a day during the second half of the year and 50 economically disadvantaged first-graders who studied reading in the classroom during these

10-minute periods. Tests administered at the end of the first grade indicate that experimental pupils had an average reading grade-level of about 2.3 while control pupils had an average of 1.8. Tests administered at the end of the second grade revealed that the difference between the two groups had been maintained even though the experimental children did not receive additional computer-assisted instruction (Atkinson, 1974). The data suggest that this particular system of instruction is also cost effective; that is, "the yearly cost is roughly $97.00 per student. If this is multiplied by three, we have a figure of $291.00, a cost that places students at grade level by the end of the third grade who would normally be over a year behind" (Atkinson, 1974, p. 177). While it would probably be more difficult to provide 10 minutes of effective individual instruction using people instead of computers, research designed to determine the relative effectiveness of human and computer-assisted instruction may have useful implications.

Many lower-class children do not speak standard English when they begin school. For example, many lower-class black children speak black English vernacular rather than standard English (Labov, 1972). In an attempt to make use of this difference, Leaverton (1972, reading 4.3) used black English vernacular to help a class of economically disadvantaged black first-graders make the transition to standard English. The materials consisted of eight stories concerning the child, his community, and his ethnic group. Each story focused on a particular verb form that the children frequently used in informal conversation. Stories were presented in black English vernacular, then in standard English, and were accompanied by oral instruction dealing with the same verb forms. After a story was read and the verbs were reviewed, each child gave a talk in standard English. The results of an assortment of tests indicate that children who were given the stories in black English vernacular and standard English obtained higher scores on 19 of 20 measures than a matched group of children in the same class who were given the stories in standard English only. A reading test administered at the start of the third grade reveals that children who were in the experimental group as first graders had substantially higher scores than the other third graders in the school. Cornett, Ainsworth, and Askins (1974) tried to determine the effectiveness of a bilingual program for economically disadvantaged Mexican American preschool children. Thirty children participated in the program while 20 children served as controls. The program contained a variety of learning activities designed to develop intellectual abilities and linguistic skills. Half-day sessions were held for nine months. Analysis of covariance using pretest scores as the control variable indicate that the gain scores of participants on a measure of English language development were considerably greater than the gain scores of children who did not participate. Zirkel (1972) evaluated bilingual and quasi-bilingual programs in schools in four Connecticut cities. In one quasi-bilingual program, a small amount of instruction in Spanish was provided by teacher aides. In the other quasi-bilingual program, children received bilingual instruction during selected periods only. Participants and controls were economically disadvantaged Puerto Rican first, second, and third graders. Using pretest scores on measures of linguistic and intellectual ability to equate statistically the three groups, Zirkel found that second and third graders in the bilingual program displayed greater academic skills in both English and Spanish than second and third graders in regular classes. He also found that first-grade children in the bilingual program and children in the quasi-bilingual programs did not differ academically from children in regular classes. The results of these studies suggest that carefully designed bi-dialectal and bilingual programs may increase the ability of many linguistically different children to use standard English.

Homogeneous ability grouping, or the assignment of students to separate ability groups and classes on the basis of intelligence, aptitude, or achievement test scores, is practiced in many elementary and secondary schools (Esposito, 1973). Unfortunately, the research findings suggest that this practice has detrimental effects on many lower-class children. Such children tend to be placed in low ability groups, where they do worse than lower-class children who are not subjected to homogeneous ability grouping. The findings also indicate that homogeneous ability grouping results in improved performance in some high ability groups only (Esposito, 1973). If schools are to provide each child with the same educational opportunities, these findings suggest that *heterogeneous* ability grouping is one of the strategies they need to implement.

While a causal relationship between teachers' expectations about the ability of lower-class children and the scholastic performance of those children has not been established, there is indirect evidence that such a relationship may exist. One, teachers expect middle-class children to do better academically than lower-class children (Becker, 1952; Deutsch, 1963; Wayson, 1965; Wilson, 1963). Two, teachers who do not expect students to do well are more likely to behave in ways that discourage those students (Beez, 1970; Brophy & Good, 1970; Rothbart, Dalfen, & Barrett, 1971; Rubovits & Maehr, 1971). Three, students perform less effectively when their teachers have naturally induced low expectations about their ability (Parlardy, 1969; Rist, 1970; Seaver, 1973); for example, expectations that result from teaching a child's older sibling, from discussions with other teachers, and/or from a child's appearance. One implication of these findings is that seminars which make prospective and actual teachers of lower-class children aware that these children can do well in school need to be established.

Institutional Strategies

The effects of desegregation on the academic performance of black students have been subjected to considerable inquiry (e.g., Coleman *et al.*, 1966;

McCullough, 1972; Wilson, 1967). Unfortunately, these studies did not rule out the effects of the students' ability, their socioeconomic level, and/or the quality of the schools they attended (St. John, 1975, reading 4.4). As a result, St. John concluded that "adequate data have not yet been gathered to determine a causal relation between school racial composition and academic achievement . . . Suggestive trends have been uncovered, however, as has one important . . . finding: desegregation has rarely lowered academic achievement for either black or white children" (p. 36). Despite the inconclusiveness of the findings, the data do suggest that the academic performance of black children in desegregated schools may be moderated by several variables. One, the younger black children are when they enter desegregated schools, the better they are likely to perform (Mahan, 1968; Purl, 1971; St. John, 1971). Two, black children are likely to perform more effectively when they receive staff support (Mahan, 1968). Three, the larger the proportion of white children in the class, the more black students' verbal achievement is likely to improve (McPartland, 1969). Using data gathered from about 5,000 black ninth-graders in several metropolitan areas, McPartland found that average verbal achievement increased as the proportion of whites in the classroom increased. He also found that this relationship was not due primarily to the assignment of high achieving blacks to predominantly white classes.

In an attempt to provide their children with high quality education, people in many lower-class communities have tried to gain control of neighborhood schools. A number of urban school systems have responded by transferring some power to the communities. While the effects of decentralization are likely to be determined by such factors as the amount of control that the school system relinquishes, the ways in which members of the community compete to exercise that control, and the relations between teachers and parents, a study of a community controlled school district in a low-income neighborhood (Guttentag, 1972, reading 4.5) suggests that decentralization can have a favorable impact on the schools and the students.[3]

Guttentag compared five elementary schools in a community controlled district in Harlem with the schools in a neighboring district in Harlem, the schools in a suburban school district, and a sample of other schools in New York City. The findings suggest that the climate of the community controlled schools was more open and more responsive to change than the climate in the sample of New York City schools. Observation of school visitors indicates that parents in the community controlled district were far more likely to visit the schools than were parents in the neighboring and suburban districts. For example, parents in the experimental district were more likely than parents in the neighboring district to bring things to their children, observe classes, and attend PTA meetings. While reading achievement declined in many of New York City's elemen-

3. Very few attempts have apparently been made to determine the impact of community control on teachers and students. We were able to find only one other study, a case study conducted in New York City (Zimet, 1973).

tary schools, reading achievement was stable in some community controlled schools and increased in others. The data also indicate that children who attended experimental schools during the community's three-year term of control had higher reading and math achievement scores than children in the same grade who attended experimental schools for less than three years.[4] Although Guttentag was unable to assign children randomly to experimental and control groups or to determine if the several comparison groups were equivalent to the experimental group before the community acquired control of the schools, the range and consistency of the differences between the experimental schools and the various comparison schools suggest that these differences were due primarily to community control.

CONCLUDING REMARKS

The research findings indicate that a number of instructional strategies may have favorable effects on the academic performance of lower-class children; however, they do not shed light on the interactive effects of strategies and students. Accordingly, studies designed to determine which strategies work best with which children need to be carried out. The findings also indicate that studies are needed to determine the conditions under which desegregation and community control enhance student performance.

Unfortunately, even if urban schools dramatically increase the educational opportunities available to economically disadvantaged children, several studies suggest that those opportunities would enable relatively few poor children to escape poverty as adults. The results of these studies imply that inadequate nutrition and health care impair the scholastic performance of many poor children (Birch & Gussow, 1970), and that discriminatory employment practices diminish the ability of education to improve the lives of many lower-class blacks (Cook, 1970; Eidson, 1968). Accordingly, high quality education is unlikely to have a sizable impact on the lives of many poor children unless strategies designed to reduce poverty and discriminatory employment practices are also implemented. This is not to say that quality education should not be provided; clearly, it should.

REFERENCES

Abelson, W. Zigler, E., & DeBlasi, C. Effects of a four-year follow through program on economically disadvantaged children. *Jour-* *nal of Educational Psychology*, 1974, 66, 756–771.

Atkinson, R. Teaching children to read using

4. While differences in student performance may have been due to increased parental involvement as well as to changes in the schools, it seems likely that any increase in parental involvement was due to community control.

a computer. *American Psychologist*, 1974, 29, 169–178.

Banfield, E. *The unheavenly city.* New York: Harper & Row, 1971.

Baratz, J. A bi-dialectal task for determining language proficiency in economically disadvantaged Negro children. *Child Development*, 1969, 40, 889–901.

Becker, H. Social class variations in the teacher-pupil relationship. *Journal of Educational Sociology*, 1952, 25, 451–465.

Beez, W. Influence of biased psychological reports on teachers' behavior and pupil performance. In M. Miles & W. Charters (Eds.), *Learning in social settings.* Boston: Allyn & Bacon, 1970.

Beller, E. The evaluation of effects of early educational intervention on intellectual and social development of lower-class, disadvantaged children. In, *Critical issues in research related to disadvantaged children.* Princeton, N. J.: Educational Testing Service, 1969.

Benewitz, M., & Busse, T. Material incentives and the learning of spelling words in a typical school situation. *Journal of Educational Psychology*, 1970, 61, 24–26.

Birch, H., & Gussow, J. *Disadvantaged children: Health, nutrition, and school failure.* New York: Harcourt Brace Jovanovich, Inc., 1970.

Blank, M., & Solomon, F. A tutorial language program to develop abstract thinking in socially disadvantaged preschool children. *Child Development*, 1968, 39, 379–389.

Bronfenbrenner, U. *A report on longitudinal evaluations of preschool programs.* Vol. 2. *Is early intervention effective?* Washington, D.C.: U.S. Department of Health, Education and Welfare, 1974.

Brophy, J., & Good, T. Teachers' communication of differential expectations for children's classroom performance: Some behavioral data. *Journal of Educational Psychology*, 1970, 61, 365–374.

Burt, C. Class differences in general intelligence: III. *British Journal of Statistical Psychology*, 1959, 12, 15–33.

Burt, C. Intelligence and social mobility. *British Journal of Statistical Psychology*, 1961, 14, 3–24.

Cazden, C. The situation: A neglected source of social class differences in language use. *Journal of Social Classes*, 1970, 26, 35–59.

Cicirelli, V. *The impact of Head Start: An evaluation of the effects of Head Start on children's cognitive and affective development.* Springfield, Va.: U. S. Department of Commerce Clearinghouse, PB 184: 328, 1969.

Clark, C., & Walberg, H. The influence of massive rewards on reading achievement in potential urban school dropouts. *American Educational Research Journal*, 1968, 5, 305–310.

Coleman, J., & Campbell, E., Hobson, C., McPartland, J., Mood, A., Weinfeld, F., & York, R. *Equality of educational opportunity.* Washington, D.C.: U.S. Government Printing Office, 1966.

Cook, T. Benign neglect: Minimum feasible understanding. *Social Problems*, 1970, 18, 145–152.

Cornett, J., Ainsworth, L., & Askins, B. Effect of an intervention program on "high risk" Spanish American children. *Journal of Educational Research*, 1974, 67, 342–343.

Deutsch, M. The disadvantaged child and the learning process. In A. Passow (Ed.), *Education in depressed areas.* New York: Bureau of Publications, Teachers College, Columbia University, 1963.

Deutsch, M. *The disadvantaged child.* New York: Basic Books, 1967.

Eidson, B. Major employers and their manpower practices. In P. Rossi, R. Berk, D. Boesel, B. Eidson, & W. Groves, *Between black and white: The faces of American institutions in the ghetto.* Supplemental studies for the National Advisory Commission on Civil Disorders. Washington, D.C.: Government Printing Office, 1968, pp. 115–123.

Esposito, D. Homogeneous and heterogeneous ability grouping: Principal findings and implications for evaluating and designing more effective educational environments. *Review of Educational Research*, 1973, 43, 163–179.

Eysenck, H. *The IQ argument.* New York: Library Press, 1971.

Fletcher, J., & Atkinson, R. Evaluation of the Stanford CAI program in initial reading. *Journal of Educational Psychology*, 1972, 63, 597–602.

Getzels, J. A social psychology of education. In G. Lindzey & E. Aronson (Eds.), *The handbook of social psychology*, second edition. Reading, Mass.: Addison-Wesley, 1969, vol. 5, pp. 459–537.

Guttentag, M. Children in Harlem's community controlled schools. *Journal of Social Issues*, 1972, 28 (4), 1–20.

Hamblin, J., & Hamblin, R. On teaching disadvantaged preschoolers to read: A successful experiment. *American Educational Research Journal*, 1972, 9, 209–216.

Hodges, W., McCandless, B., & Spicker, H. *Diagnostic teaching for preschool children*. Arlington, Va.: The Council for Exceptional Children, 1971.

Jensen, A. How much can we boost IQ and scholastic achievement? *Harvard Educational Review*, 1969, 39, 1–123.

Karnes, M., Teska, J., & Hodgins, A. The effects of four programs of classroom intervention on the intellectual and language development of 4-year-old disadvantaged children. *American Journal of Orthopsychiatry*, 1970, 40, 58–76.

Kazdin, A. *Behavior modification in applied settings*. Homewood Ill.: Irwin, 1975.

Kohlberg, L. Early education: A cognitive-development view. *Child Development*, 1968, 39, 1013–1062.

Labov, W. *Language in the inner city*. Philadelphia: University of Pennsylvania Press, 1972.

Leaverton, L. Nonstandard speech patterns. In H. Walberg & A. Kopan (Eds.), *Rethinking urban education*. San Francisco: Jossey-Bass, 1972.

Levine, D. The crisis in urban education. In M. Urofsky (Ed.), *Perspectives on urban America*. Garden City, N.Y.: Anchor Press, 1973.

Lewis, O. The culture of poverty. *Scientific American*, 1966, 215, 19–25.

Lipe, D., & Jung, S. Manipulating incentives to enhance school learning. *Review of Educational Research*, 1971, 41, 249–280.

Mahan, T. *Project Concern–1966–1968: A report on the effectiveness of suburban school placement for inner-city youth*. Hartford, Conn.: Board of Education, 1968.

McCullough, J. Academic achievement under school desegregation in a southern city. Chapel Hill: Department of City and Regional Planning, University of North Carolina, January, 1972. (mimeographed)

McPartland, J. The relative influence of school and of classroom desegregation on the academic achievement of ninth grade Negro students. *Journal of Social Issues*, 1969, 23 (3), 93–102.

O'Leary, K. D., & Drabman, R. Token reinforcement programs in the classroom: A review. *Psychological Bulletin*, 1971, 75, 379–398.

Parlardy, J. What teachers believe, what children achieve. *Elementary School Journal*, 1969, 69, 370–374.

Purl, M. *The achievement of pupils in desegregated schools*. Riverside, California: Unified School district, 1971.

Rist, R. Student social class and teacher expectations: The self-fulfilling prophecy in ghetto education. *Harvard Educational Review*, 1970, 40, 411–451.

Rollins, H., McCandless, B., Thompson, M., & Brassell, W. Project success experiment: An extended application of contingency management in inner-city schools. *Journal of Educational Psychology*, 1974, 66, 167–178.

Rothbart, M., Dalfen, S., & Barrett, R. Effects of teacher's expectancy on student-teacher interaction. *Journal of Educational Psychology*, 1971, 62, 49–54.

Rubovits, P., & Maehr, M. Pygmalion analyzed: Toward an explanation of the Rosenthal-Jacobson findings. *Journal of Personality and Social Psychology*, 1971, 19, 197–203.

Ryan, W. *Blaming the victim*. New York: Random House, 1971.

Seaver, W. B. Effects of naturally induced teacher expectancies. *Journal of Personality and Social Psychology*, 1973, 28, 333–342.

Spicker, H. Intellectual development through early childhood education. *Exceptional Children*, 1971, 37, 629–640.

St. John, N. *School integration, classroom climate and achievement*. U.S. Office of Education, Final Report, Project No. OA-026, 1971.

St. John, N. *School desegregation outcomes for children.* New York: Wiley, 1975.

Suppes, P., & Morningstar, M. Technological innovations: Computer-assisted instruction and compensatory education. In F. Korten, S. Cook, & J. Lacey (Eds.), *Psychology and the problems of society.* Washington, D.C.: American Psychological Association, 1970.

Wayson, W. Expressed motives of teachers in slum schools. *Urban Education,* 1965, 1, 222–238.

Weikart, D. Early childhood special education for intellectually subnormal and/or culturally different children. Manuscript prepared for the National Leadership Institute in Early Childhood Development in Washington, D.C. Ypsilanti, Michigan: High/Scope Educational Research Foundation, 1971.

Wilson, A. Social stratification and academic achievement. In A. Passow (Ed.), *Education in depressed areas.* New York: Bureau of Publications, Teachers College, Columbia University, 1963.

Wilson, A. Educational consequences of segregation in a California community. In U.S. Commission of Civil Rights, *Racial isolation in the public schools.* Vol. II. Washington, D.C.: U.S. Government Printing Office, 1967.

Wolf, M., Giles, D., & Hall, V. Experiments with token reinforcement in a remedial classroom. *Behaviour Research and Therapy,* 1968, 6, 51–64.

Zigler, E. Project Head Start: Success or failure? *Learning,* 1973, 1, 43–47.

Zimet, M. *Decentralization and school effectiveness: A case study of the 1969 school decentralization law in New York City.* New York: Teachers College Press, 1973.

Zirkel, P. An evaluation of the effectiveness of selected experimental bilingual education programs in Connecticut. *Dissertation Abstracts International,* 1972(Dec.), 33 (6-A), 2680.

4.1

Effects of a Four-Year Follow Through Program on Economically Disadvantaged Children

WILLA D. ABELSON, EDWARD ZIGLER, and CHERYL L. DeBLASI

Optimism concerning the effectiveness of preschool compensatory programs such as Project Head Start has waned considerably in the last few years. Findings have been generally consistent that at the end of a year of Head-Start-type experience, children are superior to comparison children without this preschool experience in both intellectual and social-emotional functioning (cf. Beller, 1969; Klaus & Gray, 1968; Weikart, 1971; Zigler & Butterfield, 1968). However, with some exceptions (Ryan, 1974), the evidence also indicates that the superiority of Head Start children vanishes or is greatly diminished by the end of one year of formal public school (Bronfenbrenner, 1974; Westinghouse Learning Corporation, 1969).

In the face of this evidence, some have concluded that compensatory education in general, or Head Start in particular, is a failure (Eysenck, 1971; Jensen, 1969). Others (Kohlberg, 1968; Zigler, 1973) have responded to these findings with the view that the expectation of long-term benefits from a one-year preschool program was an unrealistic one, since it was based on the questionable assumption that children could

somehow be inoculated against the social, economic, and educational disadvantages which they would encounter later in life. Within this view, compensatory education would be seen as having a positive impact on the lives of economically disadvantaged children provided the effort were of long enough duration. At the level of national social policy, this viewpoint resulted in the creation of the Follow Through project.

The Follow Through project sponsors four-year compensatory education programs for both Head Start graduates and non-Head-Start children. The project is an experimental effort permitting a variety of pedagogical approaches. (See Maccoby & Zellner, 1970, for a description of the many models employed.) Although Follow Through programs have been in operation for several years, available national evaluation data are limited to longitudinal findings for children who have been in the program for only one year (Stanford Research Institute, 1971). This initial evaluation revealed enough differences in favor of Follow Through children to lead some to conclude that the project is a success, although others regard the results as disappointing in view of the relatively high cost of the project and the small absolute size of the differences between Follow Through and non-Follow-Through children. Officials responsible for the Follow Through project have taken the position that "a definitive interpretation of the first-year findings must await the results of ongoing evaluation efforts."[1]

The major purpose of the present paper is to report the findings of one such evaluation effort. A Follow Through program based on a model which has been employed in a number of Follow Through centers was studied for four years. The effectiveness of the program was assessed through longitudinal data, cross-sectional data, and a special longitudinal comparison of economically disadvantaged and nondisadvantaged Follow Through children.

The longitudinal portion of the evaluation involved 35 economically disadvantaged children who attended the full four years (kindergarten through third grade) of the Follow Through program and 26 comparison children who were attending three non-Follow-Through schools during this same period. In view of the small numbers remaining in the longitudinal study at the end of the fourth year, the decision was made to also conduct a cross-sectional study comparing the performance of the entire group of 42 economically disadvantaged children graduating from the Follow Through program (7 children transferred to the program from other schools during the first and second years) with the entire group of 100 economically disadvantaged children of the same age and grade in four non-Follow-Through schools (74 children plus the 26 longitudinal comparison children).

The 35 longitudinal Follow Through children were also compared with 10 nondisadvantaged children who had attended the full

1. Wilson, R. C. Communication from the U. S. Department of Health, Education, and Welfare, Office of Education, Washington, D. C., February 13, 1969.

four-year Follow Through program. This final comparison was conducted in order to illuminate two issues: (a) the progress of nondisadvantaged children attending school classes composed primarily of economically disadvantaged children and (b) the comparative performance of economically disadvantaged and nondisadvantaged children under this special program.

METHOD

Subjects

Longitudinal. At the outset of the study, the subjects included 61 children attending Follow Through (FT) kindergartens and 48 children attending kindergartens in three non-Follow-Through (NFT) schools. All of the children resided in New Haven, Connecticut, and all were from economically disadvantaged families, defined as follows: (a) lived in low-income housing, (b) parents had no more than a high school education, and (c) parents were employed as semiskilled or unskilled workers or were unemployed. The FT group was recruited for the program by soliciting parents in several low-income areas. The NFT group was made up of all of the economically disadvantaged children in one classroom from each of three schools located in similar low-income areas.

Upon completion of the longitudinal study four years later, 35 of the original 61 FT children and 26 of the original 48 NFT children were completing third grade in these schools. Three of the original FT children and three of the original NFT children were held back in kindergarten or first grade and were dropped from the longitudinal samples. The others who were dropped withdrew from these schools during the course of the study. An examination of the children's demographic characteristics and their test scores at kindergarten entrance revealed no systematic differences between either (a) those who stayed in or dropped out of the Follow Through program or (b) those

Table 1. Characteristics of Longitudinal Groups

School program	n	M CA at school entrance (years, months)	Sex		Head Start		Race		Father absent	
			Boys	Girls	Yes	No	Black	White	Yes	No
Follow Through	35	5–1	21	14	32	3	30	5	15	20
Non-Follow-Through	26	5–2	12	14	7	19	19	7	5	21

Note. Abbreviation: CA = chronological age.

who stayed in or dropped out of the non-Follow-Through programs.[2]

The characteristics of the economically disadvantaged longitudinal groups are presented in Table 1. The groups differed in four respects: As compared to the non-Follow-Through group, the Follow Through group had (*a*) a higher proportion of boys than girls, (*b*) a higher proportion of blacks than whites, (*c*) a higher incidence of Head Start attendance, and (*d*) a higher incidence of father absence. In addition to these children, 10 nondisadvantaged children (5 girls, 5 boys; 4 black, 6 white) completed four years of the Follow Through program. These children resided in two-parent homes located in middle-income neighborhoods and the occupations of their fathers ranged from lower-middle to upper-middle class (e.g., fireman, salesman, professor).

Cross-sectional. The cross-sectional sample consisted of all third-grade children in the Follow Through program and in three non-Follow-Through programs who were economically disadvantaged (as defined by the criteria given above), who were completing their fourth year of school, and for whom English was the primary language. The FT cross-sectional group consisted of 42 children: the 35 longitudinal children plus 7 children who had transferred to the FT program during kindergarten or first grade. The NFT group of 100 children consisted of the longitudinal NFT group plus an additional

2. Comparisons involving the larger samples tested in kindergarten and first grade have been reported elsewhere (Abelson, 1974).

74 children. This group was made up of the following school samples:

1. Inner-city tutorial (*n* = 48): nine longitudinal children and their 35 classmates in a New Haven inner-city school with a tutorial program, plus 4 longitudinal children in another New Haven inner-city school with the same program;

2. Outer-urban enriched (*n* = 30): thirteen longitudinal children and their 17 economically disadvantaged classmates in a New Haven school attended by both economically disadvantaged and nondisadvantaged children; and

3. Inner-city traditional (*n* = 22): twenty-two children in an inner-city school 35 miles from New Haven.

The characteristics of the FT and NFT cross-sectional groups are presented in Table 2. As was true of the longitudinal groups, the cross-sectional groups differed in proportion of boys and girls, incidence of Head Start attendance, and incidence of father absence. Unlike the longitudinal groups, the cross-sectional groups had similar proportions of blacks and whites.

School Programs

Follow Through. The Follow Through program under study was conducted by the public schools of New Haven and Hamden, Connecticut. The program was based from its inception on the educational model which is usually identified with Bank Street College of Education (see Maccoby & Zellner, 1970), and staff from Bank Street

Table 2. Characteristics of Cross-Sectional Groups Tested at End of Third Grade

School program	n	M CA (years, months)	Sex		Head Start		Race		Father absent	
			Boys	Girls	Yes	No	Black	White	Yes	No
Follow Through	42	8–9	25	17	37	5	37	5	17	25
Non-Follow-Through	100	8–10	51	49	26	74	89	11	27	73

Note. Abbreviation: CA = chronological age.

were involved in the training of Follow Through teachers during the last two years of the study. The FT classes were composed of no more than 20 children and at least two full-time staff (head teacher and assistant teacher). Although the majority of children were economically disadvantaged, each class included some children from middle- to upper-middle-income families.

The features which most markedly distinguished the FT program from programs in the NFT schools in the study were (a) an individual rather than a group-oriented approach, (b) an explicit interest in the social-emotional development of the child, or what is often called the "whole child" approach, and (c) an emphasis on learning how to learn through the mastery of underlying principles and concepts. These features led to more frequent contacts between teachers and individual children in FT classrooms than in NFT classrooms. They also resulted in the use of a broad array of teaching methods, for the manner in which a lesson was conducted in an FT classroom depended on the needs, interests, and ongoing responses of the children in that classroom, rather than on a preset curriculum or technique. The FT program emphasized verbal communication skills. In addition, adult-child relations were oriented specifically toward fostering children's self-esteem and interpersonal trust.

Non-Follow-Through. In the longitudinal study, three NFT schools in New Haven were employed; these same schools plus a school in another Connecticut city were employed in the cross-sectional study. The four schools served neighborhoods which were comparable to those of the economi-

cally disadvantaged FT children. Three of the schools (including the one outside New Haven) were in inner-city neighborhoods with predominantly black and Spanish-speaking populations. The other school was in a non-inner-city New Haven area with a 60% black, 40% white population. Children attending this school either came from low-income families residing in a public housing project or from middle-income families in the surrounding neighborhood.

At the beginning of the study, the three schools in New Haven had quite similar, traditional public school programs. Classes were larger than in the FT program, and classroom teachers seldom had more than occasional outside assistance. Lessons were usually organized for each class group as a whole, with the exception of reading which was traditionally taught with small groups.

During the second year of the longitudinal study, class sizes were reduced and a number of experimental projects were initiated in the New Haven schools. In the two inner-city schools attended by NFT children, low-achieving children began to be tutored individually (several NFT children in the present study were tutored). In one of these schools, some children were placed in a busing program to schools in middle-class neighborhoods (five of the original NFT children were selected for this program and were therefore dropped from the study). The non-inner-city school in the socioeconomically mixed neighborhood was not involved in these projects, but the facilities of this school were greatly expanded at this time and the school staff initiated an extensive program of extracurricular activities.

The programs of these three NFT schools thus changed in some significant respects during the course of the longitudinal study. Although the pedagogical approaches used in the classrooms continued to reflect the group-oriented, didactic model which has traditionally been followed in public schools, the range of educational opportunities that were available to the children broadened considerably. It was primarily because of these changes that the fourth NFT school, located in another city, was sought out and added to the cross-sectional study. As the children in this fourth NFT school had not received any special remedial or enrichment programs, they provided a sample of comparison children with a more traditional type of inner-city school experience than the children in the other NFT schools.

Measures

Academic achievement. Academic achievement at the beginning and end of kindergarten was measured with the Screening Test of Academic Readiness (STAR; Ahr, 1966). The STAR is a group-administered instrument designed to appraise general information, conceptual maturity, and perceptual-motor development in preschool- and kindergarten-aged children. Academic achievement in Grade 1 was assessed with the Metropolitan Achievement Tests, Primary I Battery, Form A (Bixler, Durost, Hildreth, Lund, & Wrightstone, 1958–1962). This group-administered battery includes four tests: Word Knowledge, Word Discrimination, Reading Comprehension, and Arithmetic.

Since NFT children took school-administered Metropolitan Achievement Tests twice a year during the last two years of the study, they became considerably more familiar with these instruments than did the FT children. For this reason, a different instrument was employed for all children in Grade 3 to measure academic achievement—the Peabody Individual Achievement Tests (PIAT;

Dunn & Markwardt, 1970). The PIAT is an individually administered battery of Mathematics, Reading Recognition, Reading Comprehension, Spelling, and General Information tests.

Intellectual abilities. Form B of the Peabody Picture Vocabulary Test (PPVT; Dunn, 1965) was used to investigate verbal intellectual development throughout the four years of the study. The PPVT is an individually administered test which assesses verbal conceptual knowledge independent of reading ability. In addition, the individually administered Picture Arrangement Test of the Wechsler Intelligence Scale for Children (Wechsler, 1949) was administered in Grade 3 to assess the children's nonverbal, problem-solving abilities.

Problem-solving style. Several measures were administered in first grade to assess the children's effectiveness in handling unfamiliar tasks. One of these measures, the Sticker Game (Zigler & Turnure, 1964), was designed to investigate the extent to which children rely on imitation rather than on their own ideas in carrying out a task. The Sticker Game yields imitation scores based on the similarity of designs the child makes to three designs constructed by the examiner. The frequency with which the children spontaneously engaged in verbal communication with the examiner was also recorded during the Sticker Game.

Also administered in first grade were the Circles Test from the Torrance Tests of Creative Thinking (Torrance, 1966), which was used to measure creativity on a nonverbal task, and a modified form of Torrance's Just Suppose Test, which was used to measure creativity on a verbal task. These tests assess creativity by the originality, fluency, and flexibility of ideas expressed by the child. The Sticker Game and Circles Test were individually administered to each child in one session. The Just Suppose Test was individually administered in a second session.

The Picture Arrangement Test employed in Grade 3 to measure nonverbal, problem-solving ability also provided an index of the degree to which children were impulsive as opposed to reflective when tackling new problems. Impulsivity was gauged by the amount of time children spent studying the pictures before attempting to arrange them in the correct order. Since the Picture Arrangement Test problems differ in difficulty and in time allowed to complete them, a relative time measure was used, a latency score consisting of the ratio of the preliminary study time (time from the "start" signal to the first reordering of the pictures) to the overall problem-solving time. A latency score of 15% thus indicated that a child spent 15% of his problem-solving time in preliminary study of the pictures. Lower latency scores imply a more impulsive approach; high latency scores imply a more reflective approach.

Attitude toward school. Children's attitudes toward school were assessed in Grade 3 with the Attitude Toward School Questionnaire (ASQ; Klein & Strickland, 1970). The children were presented 54 situations involving classmates, teachers, lessons, and other aspects of school life. By circling one of three faces in their test booklets, the children indicated whether they would feel happy, neutral or don't know, or unhappy in each situation. The ASQ was group-administered in two sessions to each class. Responses to the 53 scored items (the first item was a practice item) were quantified on a scale of 1 equals unfavorable attitude, 2 equals neutral, and 3 equals favorable attitude. Attitude scores could thus range from 53 (totally unfavorable) to 159 (totally favorable).

The attitude data were factor analyzed to determine whether there were meaningful item clusters. Two main factors were revealed: an eight-item factor in which the items all concerned schoolwork and a seven-item factor in which all items involved situations where children were in contact with a teacher or principal. The subscores on these two factors (attitude toward academic work and attitude toward authorities) and the overall attitude scores were analyzed.

Self-image. A 32-item form of Coopersmith's Self-Esteem Inventory (Coopersmith, 1967) was administered in third grade, but the results are not reported because a considerable number of NFT children were unable to respond in a discriminating way to the Coopersmith items. After it became evident that Coopersmith results could not be used, a semiprojective, exploratory measure of children's perceptions of themselves as students in school was specially developed for this study. The instructions for this Student Self-Image measure (SSI), which was administered individually, were as follows:

Now we're going to draw a picture and you have to pretend you are somewhere else. Here is a sheet of paper and a pencil. Pretend that you are in class. It is morning and the class is working. The picture could be called "[child's name] class at work." I'll write the title up here. Okay, you draw a picture here of your class at work ... Now pretend the teacher said, "Today we are going to start on some new work. It is something we have never had before. Now listen and try to get it the first time." Would you probably get it the first time or not until later? ... Pretend you're having trouble with the new work. Pretend you don't understand it. What would you do? ... What would you do if you still didn't get it? ... Do you think you'd ever get it? ... Are there some kinds of work you do in school that you feel pretty good at? ... What do you like best about school?

Three dimensions of the child's image of himself as a student were assessed on the SSI. The child's *sense of membership* in his class group was inferred from the manner in which he presented himself in his drawing of his class. Sense of membership was rated on a scale of 0–4 (0 = the child left himself out of the picture entirely; 1 = the child drew himself alone; 2 = the child drew himself with one other person; 3 = the child drew himself as part of a group; and 4 = the child drew himself as part of a group and the self-figure was given prominence by reason of size, detail, or central position).

The child's *feelings of effectiveness* in school were assessed from the confidence and initiative which he expressed in his responses to the questions concerning a new lesson. Confidence was rated as follows: 0, if the child did not think he would learn a new lesson the first time it was presented and thought he probably would never learn it; 1, if the child was uncertain about whether or not he would learn a new lesson; and 2, if the child was confident he would learn a new lesson and would probably learn it the first time it was presented. Initiative was rated as follows: 0, if the child could suggest no plan for coping with a learning difficulty in class; 1, if the child suggested asking someone else for help; and 2, if the child suggested a plan which entailed adaptive, self-initiated activity.

The child's *involvement in academic learning* was assessed from what he said he liked best about school. Learning involvement was rated as follows: 0, if the child said he liked nothing about school except lunch or recess; 1, if the child expressed a vague, general liking for school but not for any specific activity; 3, if the child said he most liked a nonacademic activity such as music or gym; and 4, if the child said he most liked an academic activity such as math, phonics, or reading. (No Number 2 rating was used in order to give this dimension the same range as the others.)

The ratings were summed to obtain an overall SSI score. These scores could range from 0 (negative self-image) to 12 (positive self-image). In order to insure impartial ratings, all identifying information was blocked out of the drawings and answer sheets. Each protocol was then scored independently by two raters, neither of whom had previously been associated with the study. The product-moment correlation coefficient for the two raters' SSI scores was +.87, indicating a satisfactorily high degree of interrater agreement. (Interrater agreement for the four individual ratings ranged from +.84 to +.95.)

Test behavior. A behavior checklist was employed to record each child's behavior during the two sessions in which the ASQ was administered in the third grade. Task-related verbal behavior of three types was recorded: (*a*) requests for assistance (e.g., "Can you erase this for me?"); (*b*) comments about procedures or materials (e.g., "How many pages are left?"); (*c*) comments or questions about the meaning of the test items (e.g., in response to the item, "You came to school in the morning. There is a sign near the door. It says 'No School Today.' " "What day is school closed? How I feel depends on what day school is closed."). Each type of verbal behavior was recorded as either present or absent during the presentation of each of the 54 ASQ items. Maladaptive behaviors (disruptions, withdrawal, refusal to do the task) were also recorded but are not reported because they occurred very infrequently.

Procedure

The testing schedule over the four years of the longitudinal study was as follows:

Kindergarten:
  September—PPVT (1 individual session)
  October—STAR (1 group session)
  April—STAR (1 group session)
  May—PPVT (1 individual session)
Grade 1:
  March—Problem-solving style (2 individual sessions)
  May—PPVT (1 individual session)
  June—Metropolitan Achievement Tests (2 group sessions)
Grade 3:
  March—ASQ, behavior checklist (2 group sessions)
  April—PPVT, SSI (1 individual session)
  May—Picture Arrangement Test, PIAT (1 individual session)

Testing of cross-sectional subjects was confined to Grade 3 and followed the Grade 3 schedule shown above.

Intelligence and academic achievement tests were administered in accordance with the standardized instructions given in the test manuals. The testing was carried out by

12 female examiners (4 for the kindergarten testing, 3 for the Grade 1 testing, and 5 for the Grade 3 testing). Group testing took place in the classrooms with 1 of the examiners presenting the test items and 2 or 3 others serving as proctors. (Teachers assisted the proctors, except during the Grade 3 administration of the ASQ when school staff were excluded from the classrooms.) Children were taken out of their classrooms for individual testing. The individual testing followed a schedule which insured that (a) every examiner tested both FT and NFT children on each measure and (b) no child was individually tested more than once by the same examiner.

RESULTS

Analyses were performed on IQ, mental age (MA), and raw scores for the PPVT measure, but since in all cases the findings were the same for all three scores, only IQ scores are reported. For all other measures, analyses were performed on raw scores. Since the FT and NFT groups differed in their proportion of boys and girls, all analyses incorporated sex as a separate dimension.

Longitudinal Study

In order to assess the comparability of the FT and NFT groups at the outset of the longitudinal study, 2 × 2, Program (FT × NFT) × Sex unweighted means analyses of variance were conducted on the PPVT and STAR scores obtained at the beginning of kindergarten. No significant effects were found in the analysis of the PPVT scores. While no program effect was found for the STAR scores, a sex effect ($F = 8.47$, $df = 1/55$, $p < .01$) and a significant Program × Sex interaction ($F = 4.23$, $df = 1/55$, $p < .05$) were discovered. Comparisons among the four groups by the Newman-Keuls method (Winer, 1971) indicated that the sex effect was largely due to the high scores of the NFT girls.

As can be seen in Table 1, the FT and NFT groups differed in incidence of father absence and of Head Start experience.[3] The father absence variable was ignored after preliminary analyses revealed that it was not significantly related to any dependent measure at any testing.

Because of the extremely small number of non-Head-Start children in the FT program, the effects of Head Start experience were examined in 3 × 2, Education (FT–Head Start × NFT–Head Start × NFT–Non-Head-Start) × Sex unweighted means analyses of variance on each dependent measure at each testing.[4] Head Start effects were found only at the beginning of kindergarten and the end of first grade (see Table 3). Head Start experience had a significant effect on PPVT performance at the beginning of kindergarten (main effect for education, $F = 4.61$, $df = 2/52$, $p < .05$) when both FT and NFT Head Start groups scored higher than the NFT–non-Head-Start group. At the end of kindergarten, there were no differences in the PPVT performance of these three groups. The PPVT scores obtained at the end of first grade showed a combined Head Start–Follow Through effect. A main effect for education ($F = 3.47$, $df = 2/52$, $p < .05$) was found; however, comparisons among the groups revealed that only two of the three groups differed from each other: FT–Head Start children scored significantly higher than NFT–non-Head-Start children.

3. The groups also differed in proportion of blacks and whites, but there were too few white children in the sample to permit meaningful analyses for race effects.
4. Covariance adjustment was possible for the PPVT measure since it was administered at every testing. End-of-kindergarten raw scores were used as the covariable for three-group comparisons (FT–Head Start × NFT–Head Start × NFT–Non-Head-Start) and two-group comparisons (FT × NFT) of Grade 1 raw scores and Grade 3 raw scores. (Beginning kindergarten scores could not be used because the PPVT performance of many children appeared to be attenuated by motivational factors at that testing.) The findings were comparable to those reported for the unadjusted analyses of variance except that the significance levels for the Grade 1 differences were improved.

Table 3. PPVT Performance of Head Start Samples in FT and NFT Longitudinal Groups During Kindergarten and First Grade

	FT–Head Start		NFT–Head Start		NFT–non-Head-Start	
Time of testing	Boys ($n = 20$)	Girls ($n = 12$)	Boys ($n = 4$)	Girls ($n = 3$)	Boys ($n = 8$)	Girls ($n = 11$)
Beginning of kindergarten	92.60	77.58	94.50	87.33	64.38	67.09
End of kindergarten	102.55	89.58	99.50	88.67	96.25	86.36
End of first grade	104.85	94.82	104.00	88.33	90.38	86.70

Note. Abbreviations: PPVT = Peabody Picture Vocabulary Test, FT = Follow Through, and NFT = non-Follow-Through.

Table 4. Scores for FT and NFT Longitudinal Groups

	Follow Through				Non-Follow-Through			
	Boys ($n = 21$)		Girls ($n = 14$)		Boys ($n = 12$)		Girls ($n = 14$)	
Measure	M	SD	M	SD	M	SD	M	SD
End of kindergarten								
PPVT	101.19	9.90	88.36	18.67	97.33	15.37	86.86	17.31
STAR	50.05	10.70	51.79	11.99	47.18	9.06	53.14	9.44
End of Grade 1								
PPVT	103.52	10.10	94.23	11.20	94.09	10.41	87.08	12.90
MAT, Word Knowledge	19.39	7.54	20.69	9.29	19.10	7.11	16.50	9.69
MAT, Word Discrimination	19.50	9.38	21.31	9.35	19.30	9.50	18.42	7.44
MAT, Reading Comprehension	15.06	6.95	20.17	10.11	13.67	5.77	14.92	8.12
MAT, Arithmetic	39.35	12.04	39.92	15.38	42.20	11.72	40.08	10.08
Imitation	9.70	5.25	9.38	4.56	10.73	5.44	12.50	5.23
Frequency of communication	7.85	9.44	9.54	14.16	2.82	4.19	1.64	2.34
Creative thinking, nonverbal	35.15	21.78	28.08	17.58	32.46	19.18	32.14	18.79
Creative thinking, verbal	9.10	5.97	7.62	6.28	6.18	6.51	4.36	4.77
End of Grade 3								
PPVT	100.95	11.51	89.57	10.46	92.92	9.10	86.07	12.55
Picture Arrangement Test	23.67	6.95	20.64	6.26	19.46	8.10	17.29	8.92
PIAT, Mathematics	37.05	8.29	33.57	8.51	32.91	10.42	29.93	7.71
PIAT, Reading Recognition	32.14	8.52	30.64	8.48	34.09	8.83	30.64	6.17
PIAT, Reading Comprehension	30.48	7.62	31.00	9.65	31.54	7.54	30.64	4.83
PIAT, Spelling	33.48	9.30	34.93	13.22	36.46	9.21	33.14	7.56
PIAT, General Information	26.81	8.69	19.00	8.37	18.82	7.51	19.36	6.61
Problem-solving latency	31.05	7.45	27.00	5.39	32.64	6.07	25.36	8.68
ASQ, academic work	15.94	4.28	17.15	4.24	16.58	5.00	18.00	3.02
ASQ, school authorities	12.59	3.16	13.08	2.96	12.75	2.56	13.08	2.58
ASQ, overall attitude	114.71	8.64	119.08	13.09	115.25	16.09	123.17	6.47
Student Self-Image	8.00	3.12	8.00	2.63	6.50	3.00	8.75	2.80
Comments on procedures	11.33	10.02	7.62	7.18	7.25	6.94	3.57	4.38
Request for help	.86	1.42	1.92	2.02	1.00	1.48	.64	1.65
Comments on meaning	2.10	3.08	1.92	2.63	.50	.91	.29	.61

Note. Abbreviations: FT = Follow Through, NFT = non-Follow-Through, PPVT = Peabody Picture Vocabulary Test, STAR = Screening Test of Academic Readiness, MAT = Metropolitan Achievement Test, PIAT = Peabody Individual Achievement Test, and ASQ = Attitude Toward School Questionnaire.

Group comparisons indicated that FT–Head Start children also scored significantly higher than NFT–non-Head-Start children on the two verbal measures of problem-solving style administered in first grade (frequency of verbalization and creative thinking, verbal), although main effects for education were not found in the analyses of variance of these measures. No Head Start effects were found on any other kindergarten or Grade 1 measure nor were they found on any of the grade 3 measures.

The scores of the FT and NFT children at every testing for school program effects are presented in Table 4. A 2 × 2 (Program × Sex) unweighted means analysis of variance was performed on each measure at each testing.[4] (One-tailed tests of statistical significance were employed to assess program main effects in view of the expectation that the FT children would have higher scores. Two-tailed tests were employed to assess sex main effects and interaction effects.) The results of these analyses are summarized in Table 5. The three program effects found at the end of Grade 1 were combination Head-Start–Follow Through effects, as reported above. On every Grade 3 measure where a program

Table 5. Summary of Findings for FT and NFT Longitudinal Groups

Measure	Program	Sex	Program × Sex
End of kindergarten			
PPVT	ns	boys > girls*	ns
STAR	ns	ns	ns
End of Grade 1			
PPVT	FT > NFT**	boys > girls**	ns
MAT, Word Knowledge	ns	ns	ns
MAT, Word Discrimination	ns	ns	ns
MAT, Reading Comprehension	ns	ns	ns
MAT, Arithmetic	ns	ns	ns
Imitation	ns	ns	ns
Frequency of communication	FT > NFT**	ns	ns
Creative thinking, nonverbal	ns	ns	ns
Creative thinking, verbal	FT > NFT*	ns	ns
End of Grade 3			
PPVT	FT > NFT*	boys > girls**	ns
Picture Arrangement Test	FT > NFT*	ns	ns
PIAT, Mathematics	FT > NFT*	ns	ns
PIAT, Reading Recognition	ns	ns	ns
PIAT, Reading Comprehension	ns	ns	ns
PIAT, Spelling	ns	ns	ns
PIAT, General Information	FT > NFT*	boys > girls*	ns
Problem-solving latency	ns	boys > girls**	ns
ASQ, academic work	ns	ns	ns
ASQ, school authorities	ns	ns	ns
ASQ, overall attitude	ns	ns	ns
Student Self-Image	ns	ns	ns
Comments on procedures	FT > NFT*	ns	ns
Requests for help	ns	ns	ns
Comments on meaning	FT > NFT**	ns	ns

Note. Abbreviations: FT = Follow Through, NFT = non-Follow-Through, PPVT = Peabody Picture Vocabulary Test, STAR = Screening Test of Academic Readiness, MAT = Metropolitan Achievement Test, PIAT = Peabody Individual Achievement Test, and ASQ = Attitude Toward School Questionnaire.
*$p < .05$.
**$p < .01$.

Table 6. Scores for FT and NFT Cross-Sectional Groups at End of Third Grade

| | Follow Through | | | | Non-Follow-Through | | | |
| | Boys (n = 25) | | Girls (n = 17) | | Boys (n = 51) | | Girls (n = 49) | |
Measures	M	SD	M	SD	M	SD	M	SD
PPVT	101.84	11.10	90.24	9.69	91.26	12.33	86.41	11.04
Picture Arrangement Test	23.92	6.63	20.88	6.18	19.41	7.72	16.61	7.65
PIAT, Mathematics	36.48	8.36	35.29	8.62	33.27	9.56	28.29	7.98
PIAT, Reading Recognition	32.64	9.00	31.65	8.25	30.78	8.41	30.61	6.36
PIAT, Reading Comprehension	30.80	7.91	31.88	9.17	29.18	7.05	29.14	5.41
PIAT, Spelling	33.80	9.18	36.18	12.78	32.12	8.36	32.22	6.95
PIAT, General Information	27.84	9.94	20.88	9.95	20.16	7.76	17.74	5.77
Problem-solving latency	31.20	7.82	27.94	5.36	26.76	9.68	23.35	8.99
ASQ, academic work	15.96	4.10	17.63	3.95	17.11	4.21	18.29	3.41
ASQ, school authorities	12.92	3.59	13.38	3.05	12.69	3.62	12.67	3.66
ASQ, overall attitude	114.56	10.36	120.25	12.44	116.54	15.19	122.23	10.91
Student Self-Image	8.12	2.85	8.06	2.44	6.77	2.35	7.41	2.95
Comments on procedures	12.36	9.81	7.25	7.25	7.17	6.75	3.92	4.18
Requests for help	.80	1.35	2.50	3.37	1.15	1.73	.75	1.50
Comments on meaning	3.16	4.49	2.38	2.90	.22	.59	.46	1.34

Note. Abbreviations: FT = Follow Through, NFT = non-Follow-Through, PPVT = Peabody Picture Vocabulary Test, PIAT = Peabody Individual Achievement Test, and ASQ = Attitude Toward School Questionnaire.

effect was found, FT children scored higher than both NFT–Head Start and NFT–non-Head-Start children.

Cross-Sectional Study

Preliminary analyses of the Grade 3 cross-sectional data revealed that father absence and Head Start attendance did not significantly influence performance on any of the dependent measures. The scores of the FT and NFT children are presented in Table 6. A 2 × 2 (Program × Sex) unweighted means analysis of variance was conducted on each of the measures. The results of these analyses are summarized in Table 7.

Since the NFT children attended three types of school program (mixed socioeconomic grouping with enriched program, tutorial program, traditional program), a 3 × 2, School (Mixed × Tutorial × Traditional) × Sex unweighted means analysis of variance was performed on the NFT children's scores on each of the dependent measures. The results are summarized in Table 8. On 2 of the 11 measures on which a significant FT effect was found (Mathematics and problem-solving latency), a significant difference among the three NFT schools was also found. On these 2 measures, the analysis was rerun with the FT children included as a fourth school group. On the Mathematics test, a school main effect (F = 6.03, df = 3/132, p < .001) was again found. Employing the Newman-Keuls procedure, comparisons of the four schools indicated that FT children scored significantly higher than NFT children in the tutorial and traditional schools, but FT children did not score differently from NFT children in the socioeconomically mixed school. On the problem-solving latency measure, a school main effect (F = 7.50, df = 3/132, p < .001) was again found. Comparisons of the four schools indicated that FT children had significantly higher latency scores than NFT children in only one of the NFT schools, the traditional school.

Table 7. Summary of Findings for FT and NFT Cross-Sectional Groups at End of Third Grade

Measure	Program	Sex	Program × Sex	
PPVT	FT > NFT**	boys > girls***	ns	
Picture Arrangement Test	FT > NFT**	boys > girls*	ns	
PIAT, Mathematics	FT > NFT**	ns	ns	
PIAT, Reading Recognition	ns	ns	ns	
PIAT, Reading Comprehension	FT > NFT*	ns	ns	
PIAT, Spelling	FT > NFT*	ns	ns	
PIAT, General Information	FT > NFT***	boys > girls**	ns	
Problem-solving latency	FT > NFT**	boys > girls*	ns	
ASQ, academic work	ns	ns	ns	
ASQ, school authorities	ns	ns	ns	
ASQ, overall attitude	ns	girls > boys*	ns	
Student Self-Image	FT > NFT*	ns	ns	
Comments on procedures	FT > NFT**	boys > girls**	ns	
Requests for help	FT > NFT*	ns	FT girls > NFT boys >	FT boys > NFT girls**
Comments on meaning	FT > NFT***	ns	ns	

Note. Abbreviations: FT = Follow Through, NFT = non-Follow-Through, PPVT = Peabody Picture Vocabulary Test, PIAT = Peabody Individual Achievement Test, and ASQ = Attitude Toward School Questionnaire.
*p < .05.
**p < .01.
***p < .001.

Table 8. Summary of Findings for Three NFT Schools (Mixed Socioeconomic Status, Tutorial, Traditional) in Cross-Sectional Group at End of Third Grade

Measure	School	Sex	School × Sex
PPVT	ns	ns	ns
Picture Arrangement Test	ns	ns	T boys & M girls > others*
PIAT, Mathematics	M & T > Tr*	boys > girls**	ns
PIAT, Reading Recognition	ns	ns	ns
PIAT, Reading Comprehension	ns	ns	ns
PIAT, Spelling	ns	ns	ns
PIAT, General Information	ns	ns	ns
Problem-solving latency	M & T > Tr**	ns	ns
ASQ, academic work	ns	ns	ns
ASQ, school authorities	M > T > Tr**	ns	M girls > others > Tr girls**
ASQ, overall attitude	ns	girls > boys*	ns
Student Self-Image	ns	ns	ns
Comments on procedures	ns	boys > girls**	ns
Requests for help	ns	ns	ns
Comments on meaning	ns	ns	ns

Note. Abbreviations: NFT = non-Follow-Through, M = mixed socioeconomic status, T = tutorial, Tr = traditional, PPVT = Peabody Picture Vocabulary Test, PIAT = Peabody Individual Achievement Test, and ASQ = Attitude Toward School Questionnaire.
*p < .05.
**p < .01.

232

In the major cross-sectional analyses, then, FT children were compared with a group of NFT children whose performance on these two measures was influenced by the program of the particular school they were attending.

Comparisons of FT Economically Disadvantaged and FT Nondisadvantaged Children

The scores of the FT nondisadvantaged children at every testing are presented in Table 9. At the outset of the program (beginning kindergarten), these children scored higher than the FT economically disadvantaged children on both the PPVT ($F = 8.84$, $df = 1/44$, $p < .01$) and STAR ($F\,9.99$, $df = 1/42$, $p < .01$). Analyses revealed no significant changes in the nondisadvantaged children's PPVT IQs over the course of the four-year program. A 2 × 2, Income Group (Disadvantaged × Nondisadvantaged) × Sex unweighted means analysis of variance was conducted on every measure at every testing

Table 9. Scores for FT Nondisadvantaged Boys and Girls

Measure	Boys ($n = 5$)		Girls ($n = 5$)	
	M	SD	M	SD
End of kindergarten				
PPVT	120.20	9.73	101.60	21.69
STAR	62.00	8.83	65.50	3.70
End of Grade 1				
PPVT	126.00	28.28	105.50	15.16
MAT, Word Knowledge	29.00	6.24	27.00	7.52
MAT, Word Discrimination	30.33	5.03	27.60	7.89
MAT, Reading Comprehension	31.00	18.52	29.50	14.06
MAT, Arithmetic	46.33	20.11	42.60	10.67
Imitation	9.75	5.56	10.20	6.22
Frequency of communication	22.50	24.09	8.60	7.80
Creative thinking, nonverbal	52.75	15.31	20.00	13.78
Creative thinking, verbal	—[a]	—[a]	7.00	3.83
End of Grade 3				
PPVT	116.60	9.92	97.80	11.01
Picture Arrangement Test	31.00	7.87	23.00	5.83
PIAT, Mathematics	49.60	14.98	34.60	11.33
PIAT, Reading Recognition	40.80	17.24	36.20	7.36
PIAT, Reading Comprehension	37.00	12.90	32.80	7.60
PIAT, Spelling	41.40	14.66	42.80	13.54
PIAT, General Information	43.60	13.65	28.60	10.94
Problem-solving latency	25.40	5.46	25.80	8.29
ASQ, academic work	16.40	4.04	17.25	3.40
ASQ, school authorities	12.80	1.64	9.50	1.92
ASQ, overall attitude	111.40	8.26	115.00	16.31
Student Self-Image	8.20	2.59	8.80	2.95
Comments on procedures	9.60	6.15	1.75	2.36
Requests for help	.20	.45	.00	.00
Comments on meaning	4.40	3.29	.00	.00

Note. Abbreviations: FT = Follow Through, PPVT = Peabody Picture Vocabulary Test, STAR = Screening Test of Academic Readiness, MAT = Metropolitan Achievement Test, PIAT = Peabody Individual Achievement Test, and ASQ = Attitude Toward School Questionnaire.

[a]Scores were obtained for only two nondisadvantaged boys on this measure.

Table 10. Summary of Findings for Economically Disadvantaged (D) and Nondisadvantaged (ND) Children in Follow Through

Measure	Income group	Sex	Income Group × Sex
End of kindergarten			
PPVT	ND > D**	boys > girls**	ns
STAR	ND > D**	ns	ns
End of Grade 1			
PPVT	ND > D***	boys > girls***	ND boys > $\frac{\text{D boys}}{\text{ND girls}}$ > D girls*
MAT, Word Knowledge	ND > D*	ns	ns
MAT, Word Discrimination	ND > D*	ns	ns
MAT, Reading Comprehension	ND > D**	ns	ns
MAT, Arithmetic	ns	ns	ns
Imitation	ns	ns	ns
Frequency of communication	ns	ns	ns
Creative thinking, nonverbal	ns	boys > girls**	ns
Creative thinking, verbal	_a	_a	_a
End of Grade 3			
PPVT	ND > D*	boys> girls***	ns
Picture Arrangement Test	ns	boys > girls*	ns
PIAT, Mathematics	ns	boys > girls*	ns
PIAT, Reading Recognition	ND > D*	ns	ns'
PIAT, Reading Comprehension	ns	ns	ns
PIAT, Spelling	ns	ns	ns
PIAT, General Information	ND > D***	boys > girls**	ns
Problem-solving latency	ns	ns	ns
ASQ, academic work	ns	ns	ns
ASQ, school authorities	ns	ns	ns
ASQ, overall attitude	ns	ns	ns
Student Self-Image	ns	ns	ns
Comments on procedures	ns	ns	ns
Requests for help	D > ND*	ns	ns
Comments on meaning	ns	boys > girls*	ns

Note. Abbreviations: PPVT = Peabody Picture Vocabulary Test, STAR = Screening Test of Academic Readiness, MAT = Metropolitan Achievement Test, PIAT = Peabody Individual Achievement Test, and ASQ = Attitude Toward School Questionnaire.

[a]This analysis was not performed becuase scores were available for only two nondisadvantaged boys.

*p < .05.
**p < .01.
***p < .001.

which assessed the effects of the FT program. The results of these analyses are summarized in Table 10.

DISCUSSION

Effects of Head Start

Given the very small number of FT children who had not had Head Start, essentially what was examined in this study was the impact of a five-year compensatory effort—one year of Head Start and four years of Follow Through. Consistent with current views, the findings of the present study indicate that a one-year Head Start experience, if not followed by a subsequent compensatory effort, has little lasting effect on children's performance. The Head Start effects that were found were limited to the beginning of kindergarten and end of first grade, and these pose certain problems of interpretation. At. the beginning of kindergarten, the PPVT effect was due to the inordinately low scores obtained by non-Head-Start children. This effect disappeared at the end of kindergarten when the non-Head-Start children showed a 25-point IQ increase. In view of the evidence (Beller, 1969; Thomas, Hertzig, Dryman, & Fernandez, 1971; Zigler, Abelson, & Seitz, 1973; Zigler & Butterfield, 1968) that deleterious motivational factors attenuate the intelligence test performance of disadvantaged children, it seems probable from the large IQ increase of the non-Head-Start children that their low PPVT scores at school entrance were due to such factors rather than being accurate indicators of their actual cognitive abilities.

The reemergence of a significant PPVT performance difference at the end of first grade between FT–Head Start children and NFT–non-Head-Start children was partly due to the gains made by FT children and partly due to losses by NFT–non-Head-Start boys. These boys seem not to have profited as much from their schooling—at least as measured by PPVT performance—as the other children in NFT schools. The poorer

performance of these boys again may have been due to motivational factors, in that it was evident that NFT first-grade classrooms did not provide as warm and supportive an environment for the children as did NFT kindergartens.

The findings for the first-grade, verbal problem-solving style measures show the same transitional pattern as the PPVT IQ results. The FT children were generally ahead of NFT children in verbal performance abilities, but their superiority was clear-cut only in comparison to NFT children who had not had Head Start. Two years later this was no longer the case. On all Grade 3 measures where FT children were superior, they were superior to both the Head Start and non-Head-Start children in NFT schools.

Effects of Follow Through

The findings at the end of third grade showed a consistent pattern of superior performance by FT over NFT children. In the longitudinal study, the FT children were superior on such intelligence-achievement measures as the PPVT, the Picture Arrangement Test, Mathematics, and General Information. In regard to social-motivational characteristics, the FT children demonstrated greater curiosity than the NFT children by commenting more frequently about the meaning and significance of tasks presented to them. These same differences favoring FT children were discovered in the cross-sectional study. In addition, in the cross-sectional study, the FT children were superior to NFT children on the intelligence-achievement measures of Reading Comprehension and Spelling. The FT children also displayed a more reflective approach to problem solving, a greater willingness to ask adults for assistance, and a more positive image of themselves as students.[5]

5. The similarity in the test scores of the NFT cross-sectional and NFT longitudinal groups suggests that the performance of the cross-sectional

It was particularly noteworthy to find that a Bank Street approach, which emphasizes the discovery method, was associated with superior performance not only on intelligence and social-motivational measures but on academic achievement measures as well. National assessment findings (Stanford Research Institute, 1971) suggested that discovery approaches were not as effective as more structured curriculum approaches in producing gains on achievement measures. These national findings, which were based on assessments after a year of school attendance, are consistent only with the kindergarten and Grade 1 findings of the present study indicating no differences between FT and NFT children on the kindergarten Screening Test of Academic Readiness and the Grade 1 Metropolitan Achievement Tests. However, FT children were superior to NFT children on achievement measures after FT children had experienced a Bank-Street-type program for four years. There is no way of determining from the present study whether even better achievement performance would accrue with a more structured approach. It is important to note, though, that these third-grade findings do not support the view which has developed (Pines, 1967) that the "whole child" approach does not effectively improve the achievement scores of disadvantaged children.

The findings of this study must be interpreted with some caution in view of the fact that children were not randomly assigned to FT and NFT programs at the beginning of the study. Whether there were selective factors operating and in what direction such factors might have influenced the results cannot be assessed until replication studies are completed in which there has been random assignment of children.[6] (Such a study is now in progress at this FT program.) It was nevertheless encouraging that

children was not impaired by having less testing experience.
6. A penetrating discussion of these issues may be found in Campbell and Erlebacher (1970).

positive effects were visible in the FT children studied here. The findings certainly call into question the general proposition that compensatory education is a failure. In addition to demonstrating that children who received a special program for several years were superior on a wide array of measures to children who did not receive such a program, the findings also suggest that other types of remedial efforts benefit disadvantaged children. Comparison children attending a school with a mixed socioeconomic grouping and enriched program and a school with a tutorial program displayed a less impulsive approach to problem solving, greater mathematics achievement, and a more positive attitude toward school authorities than did children who were attending a school which had no special remedial or enrichment programs of any kind.

In interpreting the Follow Through program effects, it is important that the FT children not only had a prior year of Head Start experience but that during their four years in the program they were in interaction with a number of children from better-educated, higher-income families. The finding of better performance in the FT and NFT schools with mixed socioeconomic and racial groupings is consistent with the findings of the Coleman report (Coleman, 1966). This finding also supports the view recently expressed by defenders of busing (Pettigrew, Useem, Normand, & Smith, 1973) that in order for achievement to be higher in desegregated schools, other crucial conditions (such as adequate school services and remedial training) must be met, as they were in this FT program. Just how important socioeconomic mixing was to this program will be clarified when studies are completed of similar FT programs attended only by economically disadvantaged children.

Economically Disadvantaged and Nondisadvantaged Comparisons

Although there was no nondisadvantaged non-FT group with which to compare the

FT nondisadvantaged children at the end of third grade, there is no evidence that attending a program in which disadvantaged children were in the majority was detrimental to the learning growth of the nondisadvantaged children. These children's PPVT IQ scores did not change over their four years in the program. Furthermore, converting the nondisadvantaged children's scores on the third-grade achievement tests into grade equivalent levels indicated that these children were performing at or (more typically) above grade level in all academic areas.

The nondisadvantaged children attending the Follow Through program were generally superior to the economically disadvantaged children in the program on intelligence and achievement measures at all testings. This superiority was less marked in the fourth year of school than it was in the first two years. At the end of Grade 3, no significant differences were found between the economically disadvantaged and nondisadvantaged children on the Picture Arrangement, Mathematics, Reading Comprehension, or Spelling tests, or on any of the social-motivational measures. It would be erroneous to conclude from this that the FT program resulted in the disadvantaged children attaining a level of intellectual functioning equivalent to that of the nondisadvantaged children, since on every measure where a difference was found, the difference was in favor of the nondisadvantaged children. But, given the striking differences in the home lives of these children, it would surely be naive to expect that a compensatory program alone would be powerful enough to produce equivalent intellectual functioning.

In sum, the findings of this study indicate that while the Follow Through program assessed was not capable of ameliorating all of the negative effects of living in an economically disadvantaged environment, the program was highly beneficial to the children who participated in it. The longitudinal and cross-sectional evidence together point to the conclusion that the gains accruing from compensatory education programs are commensurate with the duration and amount of effort which are expended on these programs.

REFERENCES

Abelson, W. D. Head Start graduates in school: Studies in New Haven, Connecticut. In S. Ryan (Ed.), *A report on longitudinal evaluations of preschool programs*. Vol. 1. *Longitudinal evaluations*. Washington, D.C.: U.S. Department of Health, Education, and Welfare, 1974.

Ahr, A. E. *Screening test of academic readiness*. Skokie, Ill.: Priority Innovations, 1966.

Beller, E. K. The evaluation of effects of early educational intervention on intellectual and social development of lower-class, disadvantaged children. In, *Critical issues in research related to disadvantaged children*. Princeton, N.J.: Educational Testing Service, 1969.

Bixler, H. H., Durost, W. N., Hildreth, G. T., Lund, K. W., & Wrightstone, J. W. *Metropolitan Achievement Test series*. New York: Harcourt, Brace, & World, 1958–1962.

Bronfenbrenner, U. *A report on longitudinal evaluations of preschool programs*. Vol. 2. *Is early intervention effective?* Washington, D.C.: U.S. Department of Health, Education, and Welfare, 1974.

Campbell, D. T., & Erlebacher, A. How regression artifacts in quasi-experimental evaluations can mistakenly make compensatory education look harmful. In J. Hellmuth (Ed.), *Disadvantaged child*. Vol. 3. New York: Brunner/Mazel, 1970.

Coleman, J. S. *Equality of educational opportunity*. Washington, D.C.: U.S. Government Printing Office, 1966.

Coopersmith, S. *The antecedents of self-esteem*. San Francisco: W. H. Freeman, 1967.

Dunn, L. M. *Peabody Picture Vocabulary Test*. Minneapolis, Minn.: American Guidance Service, 1965.

Dunn, L. M. & Markwardt, F. C. *Peabody Individual Achievement Tests*. Circle Pines, Minn.: American Guidance Service, 1970.

Eysenck, H. J. *The IQ argument.* New York: Library Press, 1971.

Jensen, A. R. How much can we boost IQ and scholastic achievement? *Harvard Educational Review,* 1969, 39, 1 −123.

Klaus, R. A., & Gray, S. W. The early training project for disadvantaged children: A report after five years. *Monographs of the Society for Research in Child Development,* 1968, 33(4), 1−66.

Klein, S. P., & Strickland, G. *The child's attitude toward school.* Los Angeles, University of California, Center for the Study of Evaluation, 1970. (ERIC Document Reproduction Service No. Ed 048 324)

Kolhberg, L. Early education: A cognitive-development view. *Child Development,* 1968, 39, 1013−1062.

Maccoby, E., & Zellner, M. *Experiments in primary education: Aspects of Project Follow-Through.* New York: Harcourt-Brace, 1970.

Pettigrew, T. F., Useem, E. L., Normand, C., & Smith, M. S. Busing: A review of "the evidence." *Public Interest,* 1973, 30, 88−118.

Pines, M. *Revolution in learning.* New York: Harper & Row, 1967.

Ryan, S. (Ed.) *A report on longitudinal evaluations of preschool programs.* Vol. 1. *Longitudinal evaluations.* Washington, D.C.: U.S. Department of Health, Education, and Welfare, 1974.

Stanford Research Institute. *Longitudinal evaluation of selected features of the national Follow Through program.* Menlo Park, Calif.: Author, 1971, (ERIC Document Reproduction Service Nos. Ed 057 266 and Ed 057 267)

Thomas, A., Hertzig, M. E., Dryman, I., & Fernandez, P. Examiner effect in IQ testing of Puerto Rican working-class children. *American Journal of Orthopsychiatry,* 1971, 41, 809−821.

Torrance, E. P. *Torrance Tests of Creative Thinking.* Princeton, N.J.: Personnel Press, 1966.

Wechsler, D. *Wechsler Intelligence Scale for Children.* New York: Psychological Corporation, 1949.

Weikart, D. B. Early childhood special education for intellectually subnormal and/or culturally different children. Manuscript prepared for the National Leadership Institute in Early Childhood Development in Washington, D.C. Ypsilanti, Mich.: High/Scope Educational Research Foundation, 1971.

Westinghouse Learning Corporation. *The impact of Head Start experience: An evaluation of the effects of Head Start on Children's cognitive and affective development.* Vol. 1. *Text and Appendices A−E.* Ohio University Report to Office of Educational Opportunity, Clearinghouse for Federal, Scientific, and Technical Information, Washington, D.C., 1969.

Winer, B. J. *Statistical principles in experimental design.* (2nd. ed.) New York: McGraw-Hill, 1971.

Zigler, E. Project Head Start: Success or failure? *Learning,* 1973, 1, 43−47.

Zigler, E., Abelson, W. D., & Seitz, V. Motivational factors in the performance of economically disadvantaged children on the Peabody Picture Vocabulary Test. *Child Development,* 1973, 44, 294−303.

Zigler, E., & Butterfield, E. C. Motivational aspects of changes in IQ test performance of culturally deprived nursery school children. *Child Development,* 1968, 39, 1−14.

Zigler, E., & Turnure, J. Outer-directedness in the problem solving of normal and retarded children. *Journal of Abnormal and Social Psychology,* 1964, 69, 427−436.

Project Success Environment:

An Extended Application of Contingency Management in Inner-City Schools

HOWARD A. ROLLINS, BOYD R. McCANDLESS,
MARION THOMPSON, and WILLIAM R. BRASSELL

Both black and white children from low socioeconomic backgrounds are failing to gain an adequate education in the nation's central-city schools (e.g., Coleman et al., 1966; Dittman, 1967; Kvaraceus, 1965; McCandless, 1967, 1970). In fact, the educational achievements of these children have been repeatedly documented as dismal. As a group, they fall further and further behind their economically advantaged, suburban peers with each year of schooling (e.g., McCandless, 1970).

The list of variables offered as explanations for the academic plight of the inner-city child appears endless (c.f., Bronfenbrenner, 1974). However, as Becker, Engelmann, and Thomas (1971), among others, suggest, etiology may be less important than the academic environment in which these children are placed. Our schools are designed to build successively year after year upon skills acquired by the children in previous years. If at any point a child has not acquired the appropriate prerequisite skills, failure is likely. For inner-city children, such failures often occur early, since they typically enter school poorly prepared to handle both the standard public school curriculum and the middle-class format of the classroom. Further, a history of failure may promote expectations of failure which in turn make actual failure more likely. Thus, inner-city children are forever behind, confused, and as a consequence, probably lose all interest in undertaking new academic tasks. As a result, inner-city classrooms are filled with unhappy, restless children who are relatively uninvolved in academic work and often are highly disruptive.

If this analysis is correct, then one logical course of action is to replace failure with success. To guarantee inner-city children success, the school curriculum must be modified to provide opportunities for success by matching the material presented to the level at which these children function, and teachers must be trained to emphasize success while minimizing failure.

Contingency management is one vehicle available for providing inner-city students with success experiences. Based on the principles of operant conditioning, contingency management has proved to be an effective motivational system (e.g., Staats, 1964;

From H. Rollins, B. McCandless, M. Thompson, & W. Brassell. Project success environment: An extended application of contingency management in inner-city schools. *Journal of Educational Psychology*, 1974, *66*, 167–178. Copyright 1974 by the American Psychological Association. Reprinted by permission.

Staats & Staats, 1963). Both social and token reinforcements have been used in classroom settings to accelerate appropriate behaviors, such as attending behavior, and to decrease disruptive behaviors. Praise and teacher attention have provided adequate incentives for many students to perform effectively (e.g., Becker, Madsen, Arnold, & Thomas, 1967; Harris, Wolf, & Baer, 1964; Madsen, Becker, & Thomas, 1968; Zimmerman & Zimmerman, 1962). Token reinforcements—tangible objects or symbols which, when exchanged for a variety of other objects such as edibles or playthings, acquire reinforcing power themselves—have also proved effective in modifying pupil behavior (e.g.. Kupers, Becker, & O'Leary, 1968; McLaughlin & Malaby, 1971; O'Leary, Becker, Evans, & Saudargas, 1969).

Other investigators have shown that academic achievement can be accelerated through manipulating contingencies. In a series of studies, Staats (1964; Staats, Minke, Finley, Wolf, & Brooks, 1964; Staats & Staats, 1963) reported significant gains in reading achievement using token reinforcement. Staats and his colleagues (e.g., Staats & Staats, 1963), among other relevant theoretical projections, suggest "work" rooms in schools where token reinforcers are earned for learning activities and other rooms and situations where the child receives the reinforcement that backs up the tokens. This was a key strategy employed in the present study. Among others, Clark and Walberg (1968) and Wolf, Giles, and Hall (1968) have reported similar results. Teachers have also been trained to manipulate contingencies in the classroom, and the results have been encouraging (e.g., Hall, Lund, & Jackson, 1968; Hamblin, Buckholdt, Ferritor, Kozloff, & Blackwell, 1971; Thomas, Becker, & Armstrong, 1968).

The following points should be made about the present study. First, it has been clearly demonstrated, and is supported by our own observations made early in the course of conducting this study, that teachers of inner-city pupils typically employ negative and even punitive methods as their major incentive technique for behavior control and academic learning. Second, it is clear that behavior modification is not necessarily a positive technique, but can be and often is accomplished by means of aversive incentives. Third, most of those reporting in the literature, either by themselves or by way of specialists trained by them, have been interested in finding whether the behavior modification technique worked but have been less interested in training classroom teachers in its use.

In the present study, we have worked to move teachers from the employment of a preponderance of negative to a preponderance of positive incentives. Appropriate behavior is rewarded, inappropriate behavior is ignored, and almost no aversive incentives are used. Also, our emphasis has been on the pre-service and in-service training of teachers rather than on that of specialists in the use of positive behavior modification. Further, most behavior modification investigators who have reported in the literature have worked with individual students or small groups for limited periods of time, such as six weeks. In the present study, a contingency management technique was implemented in a large number of inner-city classrooms from the first to the eighth grades for an entire academic year.

Entitled "Project Success Environment," the pilot 1970–1971 study included eight experimental classes with appropriate comparison classes at the first-, second-, third-, and seventh-grade levels (c.f. Thompson, Brassell, Persons, Tucker, McCandless, & Rollins, 1973). Following this initial developmental effort and its encouraging results, the program was expanded to include twice the number of students within a wider age range during the second year of operation, 1971–1972. A reasonably rigorous experimental design was also incorporated in the second year.

As a group study, Project Success Environment was not designed as an exercise in scientific analyses of behavior. Its purpose, rather, was to answer an actuarial question of the sort suggested by Baer (1971): Can behavior modification solve the recurring social problem, which has been analyzed into two sets of behavior—those too high and those too low in rate? The central question in this study is whether teachers can be trained to use the techniques made available through behavioral analysis to provide large numbers of students from economically disadvantaged backgrounds with some modicum of individual success.

METHOD

Subjects and Setting

Three hundred and sixty-seven male and 363 female black pupils enrolled in a public middle school and three of its feeder elementary schools participated in the study. The four schools are located on the fringe of inner-city Atlanta and are characterized by substandard educational achievement and a high proportion of pupils from low-income families; for example, 54.8% of the pupils in one of the elementary schools are from families with annual incomes of $2,000 or less.

The subject population during the second year of the study (the present data) consisted of pupils in the first, second, third, fourth, sixth, and eighth grades. The total sample was divided into an experimental group and a control group of 16 and 14 classes, respectively, with from 22 to 25 pupils per experimental class and from 25 to 28 pupils per control class. The control classes at the elementary level were in a nearby elementary school, while those at the middle-school level (sixth and eighth grades) were in the same school. Of the 355 experimental subjects, 154 were exposed to the treatment over a period of two consecutive years. The rest were involved in the study for the second year alone, so that the percentage of "two-year" pupils in the experimental classes during the second year ranged from 0% in seven classes to 81% in two classes. Thirteen experimental and 10 con-

trol teachers were black, the others were white.

Although control subjects were identified during both years of the study, those for whom data are reported here were selected just before the beginning of the second academic year. With the exception of the first-grade pupils, the experimental and control subjects were matched on the basis of reading scores obtained the previous April on the Metropolitan Achievement Tests.

Procedures

Behavior modifiers. The teachers of the 16 experimental classes served on a voluntary basis as behavior modifiers within the framework of the public school setting. Eight of the teachers participated in the study from its inception, while the remaining 8 participated only during the second year. The 14 control teachers were selected at the beginning of the second year by their respective principals from the available faculty at the appropriate grade levels. Most of the experimental and control teachers were female, with previous classroom experience of from 1 to 13 years. A paraprofessional aide was available to each experimental and control teacher for approximately 90 minutes per day to assist with clerical and logistical tasks.

Teacher training. Most of the training for the experimental teachers was accomplished in a three-week workshop during the summer preceding the second academic year. (The eight experienced teachers had also participated in a similar three-week seminar in the first year.) The workshop was conducted by three psychologists and three educators and was designed to provide instruction in the theory and practical application of operant conditioning and to involve the teachers in planning for the classroom implementation of behavioral management procedures and various curricular activities.

During the mornings, the teachers participated in discussion sessions that were primarily focused on readings in behavior modification from *Teaching: A Course in Applied*

Psychology (Becker, et al., 1971) and other sources. The teachers then had the opportunity to apply behavioral management principles in classroom settings while being observed by their peers, and a videotape recording was made of them, which was to serve as the basis for further discussion in classroom management. The teachers were also exposed to systematic classroom observation by collecting data in actual classrooms using the procedures and forms that trained observers would use later in their classrooms. In addition, each teacher shared in the identification of the pupil behaviors to be modified during the following year and in the establishment of a token economy to support the behavior modification effort.

The afternoons during the workshop were devoted to curriculum planning, especially for the initial weeks of school. Emphasis was placed on formulating behavioral objectives for pupils, developing and using individualized instruction techniques, using programmed reading materials and academic diagnostic instruments, and establishing and maintaining a specific classroom arrangement.

Throughout the year, an experienced behavioral management technician was available at least twice weekly to assist each teacher with current problems in classroom management. Individual in-service sessions concerning curriculum implementation were also conducted weekly by two curriculum coordinators, one of whom concentrated on the elementary curriculum and the other on the middle-school curriculum.

Target behaviors. For the first six to eight weeks of school, the emphasis was on the positive reinforcement of desirable classroom conduct in an effort to increase the frequency of on-task behavior and to decrease the frequency of disruptive behavior. On-task behavior was defined as apparent attention to assigned academic tasks, while disruption subsumed any unsolicited behavior serving to distract pupils from academic tasks, for example, physical contact or inappropriate social conversation among pupils. Appropriate classroom behavior in the elementary classes was stipulated by the following set of conduct rules agreed upon by the elementary teachers during the summer workshop: (*a*) stay in your seat, (*b*) work hard, (*c*) pay attention, and (*d*) raise your hand to speak. The rules agreed upon by the middle-school teachers were as follows: (*a*) pay attention, (*b*) have necessary tools for work, (*c*) stay on task, and (*d*) raise your hand for recognition.

Although these behavioral guidelines were common across classes, each teacher was encouraged to interpret them according to her individual teaching style and to relate her precise interpretation of the guidelines to her pupils on the first day of school. Some teachers chose to specify that their pupils remain in their seats except when granted permission to move; others indicated to their pupils that they could circulate freely within the classroom, provided they were engaged in an academic task. In any event, the teachers were consistent within their respective classrooms in the specification and execution of behavioral contingencies. Once desired conduct was established within a class, the emphasis shifted partially to the reinforcement of academic behavior. For most classes, this shift to the reinforcement of academic behavior occurred no later than the third week of school.

Behavior management. The teachers adhered to a basic premise of "ignore and praise;" that is, they attempted to attend and reward suitable behavior while disregarding improper conduct. Behavioral management, then, was implemented overtly by means of positive reinforcement, although the possibility exists that the teachers may have also used subtle forms of punishment, such as the withdrawal of attention. In addition to praise and other forms of social reinforcement, the teachers relied heavily on a token system in which checkmarks on "reward cards" and tickets were dispensed in the elementary and middle-school classes, respectively. Since the elementary classes were self-contained, the elementary pupils were exposed to the behavioral contingencies throughout each school day. The middle-school classes, however, were taught by teams (three teachers per team in the sixth grade and four in the eighth grade), so that the pupils were exposed to the contingencies for approximately four hours daily during the mornings while they attended the basic classes (reading, mathematics, social studies and, in the eighth grade, science) taught by the experimental teachers. During the afternoons, the middle-school pupils attended nonexperimental exploratory classes, such as music, art, and home economics.

Throughout the first day of school and for several days thereafter, immediate primary reinforcement (M & Ms and hard candy) was paired with praise and token reinforcement contingent upon approximations of desired social conduct, including such behaviors as simply coming to school and sitting at a desk. Enough tokens were distributed within the first two days for every pupil to exchange them for a variety of backup reinforcers, including both inexpensive "fun" items and school supplies. During the initial two weeks of school, reinforcement was dispensed on a generally continuous and predictable basis, but as the desired behaviors were gradually shaped, the tokens were dispensed on more intermittent, less predictable schedules. In order to generate more intermittent schedules and to provide a mechanism for delay of reinforcement, the number of checkmarks required to complete a reward card for the elementary pupils increased progressively from 25 to 150. In the middle-school classes, not only were less expensive items (in terms of tokens) replaced by more expensive items, but the prices of various items were increased so that, for instance, an item which could be obtained for 5 tickets on the first day of school was worth 25 tickets by the end of the second week.

During the third and fourth months, all tangible rewards, with the exception of certain school supplies, were replaced by activity reinforcers in that the pupils traded tokens for access during school hours to the activity room supervised by the paraprofessional aides. The activity rooms at the elementary schools were stocked with such items as games, toy cars, comic books, sewing kits, dolls, Tinker Toys, and Lincoln Logs, while the middle-school activity room contained not only games, magazines, and puzzles, but also records for listening and dancing, as suggested by a student committee. The elementary pupils were also able to exchange tokens for the privilege of assisting the teacher in such capacities as playground monitor, chalkboard monitor, and "mini-teacher" or tutor.

Although there had been some concern that the pupils would find the transition from tangible to intangible rewards unpalatable, there were no apparent detrimental effects, perhaps because there was a four- to six-week overlap between the two types of reinforcement and because the pupils were told of the impending change six weeks in advance. Immediately prior to the final conversion to activity reinforcers, auctions were held in each classroom to dispose of the remaining tangible rewards. From this point through the remainder of the year, tokens could be exchanged only for activity reinforcers and a limited assortment of school supplies, such as pencils and notebooks.

Classroom arrangement. A classroom arrangement, consisting of a mastery center for instruction and five academically oriented interest stations, served to structure the instructional program and concomitantly to free the teachers for more interaction with individual pupils and small groups. Within the mastery center, the pupils were divided into three ability groups in which they received instruction and completed academic assignments. While one group received instruction and the second completed assigned tasks, the third group visited the various interest stations that were designed to foster individual and small group exploratory behavior without direct teacher intervention. The five stations included a library station with books, magazines, and newspapers; an art station with a variety of paints, crayons, and other materials; a communications station with a language master, phonograph, and tape recorder; and an exploratory station with an assortment of science materials keyed to the instructional program; and a games and puzzles' station equipped primarily with academically related materials. The materials at the stations were changed or rotated among the classrooms at least weekly by the paraprofessional aides.

Control classes. All control classes were conducted in a traditional manner with a single teacher managing each class in a lecture format. Control teachers had access to numerous academic materials but seldom used materials other than those prescribed by the school system. None of the control teachers received any formal training in the use of contingency management procedures.

Behavioral Observations

Five paraprofessional data gatherers systematically observed teacher and pupil behavior in each class for 45 minutes daily during the first three weeks of school and twice weekly during the remainder of the year. Each observer gathered data in both the experimental and the control classes during observation sessions, which varied from morning to afternoon and occurred only during periods of academic activity.

During each 45-minute observation session, the relevant behaviors were observed three times in structured 15-minute sequences in order to obtain more typical behavioral samples. Within a single 15-minute sequence, data were obtained using three different procedures to observe and record teacher reinforcement and punishment, pupil disruption, and pupil attention, in that order.

Positive reinforcement and punishment. The teacher alone was observed for 5 minutes in each sequence (for a total of 15

minutes during the entire 45-minute observational session). The data gatherer counted and classified every instance of teacher-administered positive reinforcement according to the nature of the reinforcer (tangible or nontangible) and according to the nature of the behavior being reinforced (academic or conduct). The average number of positive reinforcements administered per student in a 15-minute period constituted a criterion measure, which was obtained by dividing the total number of reinforcements administered by the number of pupils present during the observation session. A second criterion measure consisted of the total number of instances of punishment.

Teacher behaviors recorded as positive reinforcement included verbal praise, positive physical contact, the granting of privileges, and the administration of tangible rewards such as candy or tokens (which were administered only in the experimental classes). Punishment included criticism implied explicitly or implicitly through threats of consequences, voice tone, or facial expression; aversive physical contact with pupils; withdrawal of pupil privileges; and isolation of pupils.

Disruption. During the second 5-minute period in each 15-minute sequence, the data gatherer ignored the teacher while continuously scanning the entire class for instances of disruptive pupil behavior. In general, disruption encompassed any unsolicited pupil behavior serving to distract other pupils from academic tasks, such as talking or being out of one's seat without permission; generating loud noises; or disturbing other pupils either verbally, by means of physical contact, or by handling another pupil's possessions. A single pupil could not be observed for disruption more often than once every 10 seconds. The criterion measure was the average number of disruptions per pupil per 15 minutes, obtained by dividing the total number of disruptions recorded by the number of pupils present during the observation session.

Attention. Attentive behavior was observed during the final 5-minute period of the 15-minute sequence. One third of the pupils assigned an academic task were observed during each of the three 5-minute periods, with the focus being on attention; therefore, each pupil was observed for attentive behavior one time only for 20 seconds within the entire 45-minute observation session. The data gatherer recorded the number of seconds during which the pupil was off task; that is, during each 20-second interval, the behavior of one pupil was observed and the amount of time apparently devoted to other than academic tasks was recorded. Each pupil observed was classified as involved (0–5 seconds off task), medium involved (6–15 seconds off task), or uninvolved (16–20 seconds off task). The criterion measure was the percentage of time on task for the entire class, calculated by adding the number of pupils classified as involved to one half of the number classified as medium involved, then dividing the sum by the total number of pupils observed, and multiplying the quotient by 100.

Interrater reliability. Reliability coefficients were obtained periodically for the five data gatherers by comparing their observations with the simultaneous observations of one of the behavioral management technicians. Most of the resulting coefficients were above .80. The median coefficients (over 12 reliability checks) for reinforcement, punishment, disruption, and attention were .94, .78, .90, and .88, respectively.

Academic aptitude and achievement. One of the primary goals of the program was to accelerate both academic aptitude and achievement. In order to assess these objectives, the short forms of the California Test of Mental Maturity and the California Achievement Test were administered to all experimental and control subjects in mid-September and again in early May. The latter test was administered at reading level rather than grade level, since testing during the first pilot year of the study had indicated that these children frequently performed at chance when tested at grade level.

RESULTS

Behavioral Observation

The teacher training program, among other things, was designed to increase the frequency of teacher-administered reinforcements and to reduce the frequency of teacher-administered punishments. The effects of the training program on teacher reinforcements are given in Figure 1 relative to controls across the entire school year. Each data point in Figure 1 is an average of the observations within a one- or two-week period. It is evident in Figure 1 that experimental teachers administered more reinforcements per student than control teachers. In fact, the experimental teachers essentially doubled the rate of reinforcement administered by control teachers. The number of reinforcements delivered by project teachers dropped over the course of the school year, reflecting progress toward an intermittent schedule. However, even at the end of the year, project teachers reinforced their students at more than twice the rate of control teachers.

A 2 × 2 × 18 (Frequency of Reinforcement Delivery with Treatment Group × Elementary versus Middle-School Grade Level × Observation Interval) analysis of variance was performed. Consistent with the above observations, experimental teachers administered reliably more reinforcements than control teachers ($F = 36.98$, $df = 1/26$, $p < .01$). In addition, the Treatment Group × Observation Interval interaction was reliable ($F = 4.63$, $df = 17/442$, $p < .01$), reflecting the reduced separation of experimental and control teachers across the school year. There were no reliable effects of grade level.

Figure 2 is a representation of the average number of punishments per 15-minute interval delivered by project and control teachers

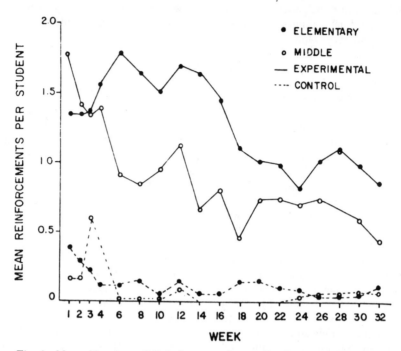

Fig. 1. Mean Number of Reinforcements per Student over Weeks as a Function of Treatment Condition and Grade Level.

by grade level. As shown in Figure 2, project teachers were much less punitive than control teachers, particularly during the first few weeks of school. For the first two weeks, project teachers at both elementary and middle schools administered fewer than one fourth as many punishments as control teachers. The rate of punishment declined over the school year for all groups. At the elementary level, project and control teachers punished at about the same level during the last two weeks, while controls at the middle-school level continued to administer more punishment throughout most of the year. In line with these observations, an analysis of variance yielded significant effects for treatment ($F = 3.35$, $df = 17/442$, $p < .01$). In addition, grade level and weeks interacted ($F = 4.20$, $df = 17/442$, $p < .01$), indicating the greater decline in punishment

rate at the elementary level than at the middle-school level.

These data demonstrate quite clearly that the project teachers' behaviors were appropriately modified by the summer and in-service training. As a result of these changes, students in project classes received a rather massive dose of contingent "success" and minimal punishment. The alterations of classroom environment produced some marked changes in pupil behavior as evidenced by the data for disruptions and task involvement presented in Figures 3 and 4. As indicated in Figure 3, students in project classes emitted fewer disruptions than children in control classes ($F = 33.99$, $df = 1/26$, $p < .01$). At both elementary and middle-school levels, disruption in project classes was approximately one half to one third that of control classes. The Trials X Treatment

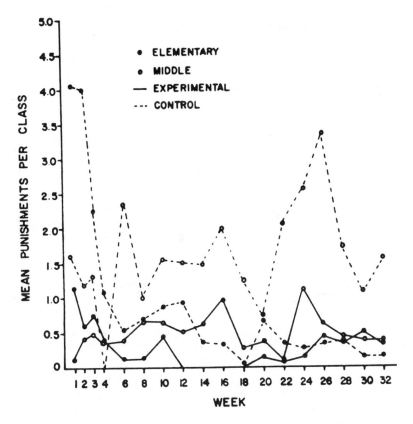

Fig. 2. Mean Number of Punishments Delivered per 15 Minutes as a Function of Treatment Condition and Grade Level.

interaction was also reliable (F = 2.30, df = 17/442, $p <$ .01). The level of disruption in project classes declined slightly over the first few weeks and then remained relatively stable for the remainder of the year. In control classes, on the other hand, there was a gradual drop at mid-year and then a rise in disruptive level. This was particularly noticeable in the middle-school control classes.

Project teachers were instructed to ignore disruptive behaviors in order to reduce their frequency and to reinforce any behaviors that evidenced work on assigned academic material. The effect of this procedure on task involvement is apparent in Figure 4.

Project students increased from about 75% task involved near the beginning of the year to more than 90% task involved by mid-October. Control students, on the other hand, remained from 65% to 75% involved throughout the school year. A 2 × 2 × 18 (Frequency of Reinforcement Delivery with Treatment Group × Elementary versus Middle-School Grade Level × Observation Interval) analysis of variance indicated a reliable effect of treatment (F = 60.89, df = 1/26, $p <$ .01) favoring project classes. In addition, the difference between project and control classes increased across observation intervals (F = 3.42, df = 17/442, $p <$ .01).

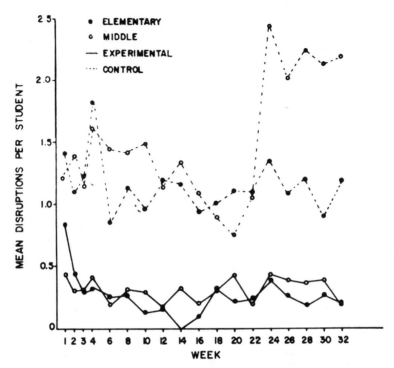

Fig. 3. Mean Number of Disruptions per 15 Minutes over Weeks for Each Treatment by Grade Level Group.

Thus, in terms of in-class observation, the behaviors of both teachers and students shifted dramatically in the predicted direction in project classes. Such behavioral changes are, in themselves, significant, since the inner-city classroom has become a pleasant, success-oriented environment and students appear willing, if not eager, learners. However, the experiences of the first year of the project suggested that simply reducing the level of disruption and increasing task involvement did not guarantee changes in academic aptitude or achievement (Thompson, et al., 1972). Consequently, in the second year, teachers were encouraged to reinforce evidence of academic achievement almost exclusively, once appropriate social behaviors were established.

Academic aptitude. The mean IQ scores for the September and May administrations of the California Test of Mental Maturity and the mean gain for project and control classes at each grade level are presented in Table 1. Students in project classes outgained students in control classes by a factor over 2 (for project, M gain = 5.98; for control, M gain = 2.51). In fact, project students at every grade level, with the exception of the first, achieved greater IQ gains than control pupils. As indicated in Table 1, the most impressive change occurred at the fourth grade. The outstanding performance of this group may be due to the fact that 81% of these children were exposed to the technique for two consecutive years. Over the two-year period, the fourth-grade project pupils have gained 20 IQ points: from 85.69 in September, 1970, to 105.56 in May, 1972.

A 2 × 6 (Treatment × Grade Level)

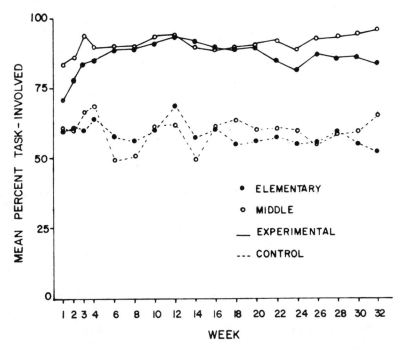

Fig. 4. Mean Percentage of Pupils on Task for Each Treatment Group at Middle and Elementary Grade Levels.

analysis of variance was performed on gains in IQ. Project pupils gained reliably more than controls ($F = 12.14$, $df = 1/602$, $p <$

Table 1. Mean Total IQ (California Test of Mental Maturity) at Pre- and Post-test and Mean Gain as a Function of Treatment and Grade Level (September to May)

Grade	Group	n	Pretest	Post-test	Gain
1	Project	35	98.60	98.49	−.11
	Control	34	86.60	96.18	9.58
2	Project	38	86.03	94.21	8.18
	Control	44	86.11	92.00	5.89
3	Project	61	88.28	95.54	7.26
	Control	35	90.54	92.94	2.40
4	Project	36	91.69	105.56	13.87
	Control	43	86.70	88.17	1.47
6	Project	57	85.70	91.40	5.70
	Control	49	85.76	86.27	.51
8	Project	76	71.63	74.67	3.04
	Control	106	73.86	74.08	.22

.01). There was some drop in the amount of gain from the first to the eighth grade ($F = 3.85$, $df = 5/602$, $p < .01$). Finally, Grade X Treatment interacted ($F = 5.90$, $df = 5/602$, $p < .01$), indicating the large reversal in gain at the first-grade level. Project students reliably outgained controls by specific comparison for third, fourth, sixth, and eighth grades.

Academic achievement. The effects of project treatment on reading achievement are presented in Table 2 for the second through the eighth grades. On the average, project pupils gained .69 years (based upon a 10-month year) and this doubled the gain of .34 years made by controls for the 8-month interval. Further, project students gained more than controls at every grade level. A 2 X 5 analysis of variance was performed on gains in reading grade equivalent. Project pupils gained reliably more than controls (F

Table 2. Mean Total Reading Grade Equivalent on California Achievement Test at Pre- and Post-test and Mean Gain as a Function of Treatment and Grade Level

Grade level	Treatment group		Reading		
		n	September	May	Gain
2nd	Project	46	1.54	2.72	1.18
	Control	40	1.46	2.11	.65
3rd	Project	61	1.87	2.48	.61
	Control	34	2.19	2.50	.31
4th	Project	46	3.28	3.90	.62
	Control	23	2.74	3.31	.57
6th	Project	57	4.55	5.05	.50
	Control	37	4.51	4.90	.39
8th	Project	77	4.67	5.29	.62
	Control	117	4.90	5.08	.18

Table 3. Mean Total Arithmetic Grade Equivalent at Pre- and Post-test and Mean Gain as a Function of Treatment and Grade Level

Grade level	Treatment group		Arithmetic		
		n	September	May	Gain
2nd	Project	46	1.45	2.01	0.56
	Control	43	1.47	1.87	0.40
3rd	Project	64	1.76	2.34	0.58
	Control	30	2.14	2.56	0.42
4th	Project	43	3.58	4.26	0.68
	Control	50	3.29	3.72	0.43
6th	Project	55	4.98	5.94	0.96
	Control	28	5.04	5.34	0.30
8th	Project	69	5.32	5.83	0.51
	Control	104	5.55	5.95	0.40

= 167.60, df = 1/528, $p < .001$). As for IQ, the amount of gain decreased with increasing grade (F = 53.64, df = 4/528, $p < .001$). Finally, Treatment $\times$ Grade interacted (F = 3.65, df = 4/528, $p < .05$). Comparisons of project and control means at each grade level yielded reliable differences favoring project students at second, third, sixth, and eighth grades ($p < .01$).

Children in first-grade classes were given the achievement tests only at the end of the year. However, since IQ scores were obtained in September and since project students scored higher on this pretest, an analysis of covariance was performed comparing year-end reading scores for first-grade students with IQ as the covariate. This analysis indicated that project first graders had better reading skills at the end of their first year than did controls (F = 7.85, df = 1/62, $p < .01$). The mean raw scores (adjusted scores are in parentheses) in reading were 60.94 (59.22) for project pupils and 46.70 (48.71) for controls. These mean raw scores translate to 1.80 and 1.55 in grade equivalent for project and control groups, respectively.

Results for arithmetic achievement for Grades 2 through 8 are presented in Table 3. Overall, project pupils gained .65 years in

mathematics (based upon a 10-month school year) as compared to a .39 gain for control pupils. As for reading, project students outgained controls at every grade level. A 2 $\times$ 5 analysis of variance yielded reliable effects for treatment (F = 135.07, df = 1/522, $p < .001$), for grade (F = 20.76, df = 4/522, $p < .001$), and for Grade $\times$ Treatment (F = 9.00, df = 4/522, $p < .01$). Specific comparisons between project and control means were reliable at each grade level. However, there was a much larger gain by project pupils in the sixth grade.

An analysis of covariance was performed on the year-end arithmetic scores of first-grade children with pretest IQ scores as the covariate. First-grade project children outperformed controls in mathematics (F = 8.99, df = 1/62, $p < .01$). The mean raw scores (adjusted scores are in parentheses) in arithmetic were 59.34 (57.39) for project students and 43.83 (46.11) for controls. In terms of grade equivalent, first-grade project pupils scored at 1.70 grade level and controls at 1.40 grade level.

DISCUSSION

The results of this study are promising. The authors believe a clear demonstration has been made that most, if not all, inner-city teachers can learn to use a positive contingency management procedure to insure behavior control, accelerated academic achievement, and probably as a function of the latter, substantial tested IQ gain. Further, it appears that teachers can maintain use of such a procedure over extended periods of time (two years for eight teachers in the present study) and that the technique works as well or better for children in the second year than in the first. In other words, there is substantial evidence that results of this contingency management procedure are enduring and not produced by some halo effect.

As Baer (1971) notes, research workers, including the present authors, have clearly shown that operant principles *can* be effectively applied in the classroom. However, previous investigators have not answered actuarial questions concerning the proportion of teachers that can be trained to use these principles or the proportion of children that can benefit from the program. The present study provides some preliminary answers to these questions. First, all 16 teachers participating in this project reduced their delivery of punishment and increased their delivery of reinforcement. At a subjective level, the authors, who visited these classes regularly, believe that all but 1 teacher learned to use these procedures effectively. Further, in all 16 classrooms, disruptive behavior dropped dramatically, and more significantly, task involvement increased. Finally, a simple count of the proportion of children showing any gain in reading from pre- to posttest indicated that 91% of the project children gained, whereas only 72% of the control children gained. Thus, contingency management appears to work well for most inner-city teachers and is effective with most inner-city children.

Informal observation also suggests many side benefits of the study, such as higher teacher morale, few if any disciplinary referrals by teachers to principals, and improved relations between school personnel and the commuity (as represented by the parents of children in the experimental classes).

The authors believe that the procedures of this study offer real hope for inner-city education and, they think, for the education of all children.*

REFERENCES

Baer, D. M. Behavior modification: You shouldn't. In E. A. Ramp & B. L. Hopkins (Eds.), *A new direction for education: Behavior analysis 1971*. Vol. 1. Lawrence: University of Kansas, Department of Human Development, 1971.

Becker, W. C., Engelmann, S., & Thomas, D. R. *Teaching: A course in applied psychology*. Chicago: Science Research Associates, 1971.

Becker, W. C., Madsen, C. H., Arnold, C. R., & Thomas, D. R. The contingent use of teacher attention and praise in reducing classroom behavior problems. *Journal of Special Education*, 1967, 1, 287–307.

Bronfenbrenner, U. *Is early intervention effective?* Washington, D.C.: U.S. Department of Health, Education, and Welfare, Office of Child Development, 1974.

Clark, C. A., & Walberg, A. J. The influences of massive rewards on reading achievement in potential urban school dropouts. *American Educational Research Journal*, 1968, 5, 305–310.

Coleman, J. S. et al. *Equality of educational opportunity*. Washington, D.C.: U.S. Government Printing Office, 1966.

Dittman, L. L. (Ed.) *Parent and child centers: A guide for the development of parent and child centers*. Washington, D.C.: Office of Economic Opportunity, 1967.

Hall, R. V., Lund, D., & Jackson, D. Effects of teacher attention on study behavior. *Journal of Applied Behavior Analysis*, 1968, 1, 1–12.

Hamblin, R., Buckholdt, D., Ferritor, D., Kozloff, M., & Blackwell, L. *The humanization process*. New York: Wiley, 1971.

*The cost per pupil of this project was $375 per academic year including costs for research and project staff. If the latter two costs are removed, this program can be implemented for about $25 per pupil.

Harris, F. R., Wolf, M. M., & Baer, D. M. Effects of adult social reinforcement on child behavior. *Young Children*, 1964, 20, 9–17.

Kupers, D. S., Becker, W. C., & O'Leary, K. D. How to make a token system fail. *Exceptional Children*, 1968, 35, 101–109.

Kvaraceus, W. Negro self-concept. New York: McGraw-Hill, 1965.

Madsen, C. H., Jr., Becker, W. C., & Thomas, D. R. Rules, praise, and ignoring: Elements of elementary classroom control. *Journal of Applied Behavior Analysis*, 1968, 1, 139–150.

McCandless, B. R. *Children: Behavior and development*. New York: Holt, Rinehart & Winston, 1967.

McCandless, B. R. *Adolescents: Behavior and development*. Hinsdale, Ill.: Dryden Press, 1970.

McLaughlin, T. F., & Malaby, J. E. Development of procedures for classroom token economics. In E. A. Ramp & B. L. Hopkins (Eds.), *A new direction for education: Behavior analysis 1971*. Vol. 1. Lawrence: University of Kansas, Department of Human Development, 1971.

O'Leary, K. D., Becker, W. C., Evans, M. B., & Saudargas, R. A. A token reinforcement program in a public school: A replication and systematic analysis. *Journal of Applied Behavior Analysis*, 1969, 2, 3–13.

Staats, A. W. A case in and a strategy for the extension of learning principles to problems of human behavior. In A. W. Staats (Ed.), *Human learning*. New York: Holt, Rinehart & Winston, 1964.

Staats, A. W., Minke, K. A., Finley, J. R., Wolf, M., & Brooks, L. O. A reinforcement system and experimental procedure for the laboratory study of reading acquisition. *Child Development*, 1964, 35, 209–231.

Staats, A. W., & Staats, C. K. *Complex human behavior*. New York: Holt, Rinehart, & Winston, 1963.

Thomas, D. R., Becker, W. C., & Armstrong, M. Production and elimination of disruptive classroom behavior by systematically varying teacher's behavior. *Journal of Applied Behavior Analysis*, 1968, 1, 35–45.

Thompson, M., Brassell, W., Persons, S., Tucker, R., McCandless, B. R., & Rollins, H. *Project Success Environment: A behavior modification program for inner-city teachers*. (Tech. Rep. APS-PSE-6 of Project Success Environment) Atlanta, Ga.: Atlanta Public Schools, 1973.

Wolf, N. K., Giles, D. K., & Hall, R. V. Experiments with token reinforcement in a remedial classroom. *Behavior Research and Therapy*, 1968, 6, 51–64.

Zimmerman, E. H., & Zimmerman, J. The alteration of behavior in a special classroom situation. *Journal of the Experimental Analysis of Behavior*, 1962, 5, 59–60.

4.3

Nonstandard Speech Patterns

LLOYD F. LEAVERTON

There is vigorous disagreement among and between educators, psychologists, and linguists concerning the acceptability of nonstandard speech patterns as legitimate forms of communication. The "standard English advocates" insist that nonstandard patterns interfere with effective thinking. The "nonstandard advocates" maintain that nonstandard speech patterns permit the user to engage in just as high-level abstract reasoning and overall problem solving as does the standardized dialect.

Bernstein's (1964) research has possibly exerted the strongest influence in support of the first position. After comparing the speech patterns of lower-class and middle-class children, he concluded that lower-class children fail to learn a linguistic code that enables them to deal with the complex and abstract situations they will encounter in formal education. The "restricted" code (as Bernstein has labeled it) tends to fixate the child at a limited conceptual level. On the other hand, the "elaborated" code learned by the middle-class child prepares him to function at the abstract conceptual level required for effective problem solving in our complex society. Bereiter and Engelmann

(1966) take a similar position. When confronting children from communities where nonstandard speech patterns are used, they conclude, the teacher must "start from zero" and proceed on the assumption that the children have no prior knowledge of English. . . .

Sledd (1969), an eminent linguistic scholar, questions the wisdom of imposing the standard dialect on children at all. He suggests that the rejection of "black English" may be a form of displaced racial prejudice: "The fact is, of course, that Northern employers and labor leaders dislike black faces but use black English as an excuse" (p. 1311).

A child's self-concept, in Sledd's opinion, can be badly damaged when he is forced to learn standard English by repetitive drill, derived by analogy from structuralist methods of teaching foreign languages: "Professor Troike can argue the success of his methods by showing that after six months of drills a little black girl could repeat *'his hat'* after her teacher, instead of translating automatically to *'he hat.'* Unfortunately, tapes do not record psychological damage, or compare the effectiveness of other ways of

Abridged from L. Leaverton. Nonstandard speech patterns. In H. Walberg & A. Kopan (Eds.), *Rethinking urban education.* San Francisco: Jossey-Bass, 1972, pp. 49–57. Reprinted by permission.

teaching, or show what might better have been learned in the same time instead of learning to repeat 'his hat' " (p. 1312).

Instead, Sledd offers the following recommendations: "Bidialectalism would never have been invented if our society were not divided into the dominant white majority and the exploited minorities. Children should be taught that. They should be taught the relations between group differences and speech differences, and the good and bad uses of speech differences by groups and by individuals. The teaching would require a more serious study of grammar, lexicography, dialectology, and linguistic history than our educational system now provides—require it at least of prospective English teachers" (p. 1315).

Kochmann (1969) has also strongly urged that we should not force standard English speech patterns on black urban children—especially the adolescent living in the black ghetto. Instead, we should focus on intensive language instruction within the framework of the nonstandard forms with which the child can identify.

During the past seven years, I and my colleagues have been testing an approach in language-arts instruction that differs in some basic aspects from the two positions just discussed (Leaverton, 1965, 1967, 1969, 1971a). We feel that the ultimate acceptance of Bernstein's position would force one to conclude that the "elaborated" code used by the columnist William Buckley results in more effective thinking than the "restricted" code frequently used by Samuel Clemens or Will Rogers. We cannot accept this conclusion. On the other hand, the position taken by those who feel that it is undesirable or unnecessary to have children learn the standardized dialect is also unrealistic. Sledd, I feel, is correct in his concern for the psychological damage that can be done by belittling the established speech patterns of the child's home and community. He is wrong, in my opinion, in concluding that standard English cannot be taught in a way that respects the established speech patterns of the child

when he enters school. Children—especially primary-grade children—usually want to please their teacher. If standard English is introduced as another way of saying something already familiar to them, the negative results described by Sledd need not occur. In fact, our research has shown that if the children's established speech forms are accepted as legitimate forms of communication while those speech forms used in the school by the teacher and observed in the books are systematically introduced, the children readily accept and enjoy learning the speech forms traditionally fostered by the school.

Our research was initiated to test a model of language-arts instruction based on the following conjectures and assumptions.

The first conjecture is based on substantial research findings concluding that the material to which the learner is introduced should be meaningful to him; that is, in the area of language-arts instruction, the child's established speech patterns must be accepted and used—especially when his speech patterns are different in some basic respects from standard English.

Second, at no time during the learning situation should the child be given the impression that his basic established speech patterns are inferior speech. He is, however, expected to learn to distinguish between his familiar speech patterns and the standard ones, which may be unfamiliar to him. To facilitate this distinction, we introduce in our research model the concepts of *everyday talk* and *school talk*. Everyday talk refers to the nonstandard pattern with respect to verb usage. School talk refers to the statement or story in which the verb form corresponds to the standardized dialect. Since the child feels most comfortable using the everyday talk patterns that are familiar to him, the initial emphasis in the approach we are testing—in beginning reading and oral-language activities—is placed on having the child make a transition from the familiar everyday talk form to the unfamiliar school talk form. Once the child has mastered the school talk form, the teacher may ask him whether a particular statement is everyday talk or school talk. If it is school talk, the child may be asked to change the statement to everyday talk, or vice versa.

In considering programs for children whose speech patterns differ from standard English, we had to ask ourselves what aspect of standard English should be emphasized in the program. Differences occur in grammatical form, pronunciation, and vocabulary. Which pronunciation system can be identified as corresponding to the standard dialect? Also, even if a standard pronunciation system can be identified and justified, will it be educationally feasible with primary children to focus on this aspect of the standard dialect? Even if it were possible and feasible to identify and teach a standard pronunciation system to primary-grade children, there is far more tolerance in our society toward regional variation's in pronunciation and vocabulary than toward differences in verb usage. In considering these questions, we concluded that in our research we would focus only on the difference between the standard and nonstandard dialects that existed in the area of verb usage. Pronunciation would be considered only if it determined the form of the verb (for instance, *work, works*).

The decision to focus on verbs *only* as the distinguishing variable between the nonstandard and the standard was also influenced by the fact that transition from the nonstandard to the standard pattern often can be made by *adding* to the nonstandard pattern. For example, the statement "My daddy strong" can be changed to the standard pattern by adding *is*. Similarly, "My daddy work" can be changed to the standard pattern by adding *s*. This aspect of the model is consistent with research studies showing that learning is enhanced if it starts at a point meaningful to the learner and does not force him to unlearn previously learned material. Therefore, in developing our research materials we tried to focus primarily on speech patterns that could be changed into standard forms by *adding* to the nonstandard form.

The reading series (Davis, Gladney, and Leaverton, 1969) consists of eight units. The focus of each unit is on a particular verb form that frequently appears in nonstandard form in the child's informal conversation. The content of the stories focuses on the child, his community, and his ethnic group. The everyday talk story is introduced first, followed by the same story with the verb form changed to correspond to the school talk form (see Table 1).

Each unit is printed as a separate paperback book. As soon as a child has completed a book, it becomes his property to take home and share with his younger brothers and sisters. Space is provided in several of the books for the children to write their own stories. If the child's story uses the nonstandard verb form under consideration, he is asked to change it into the standard form. If the child's story uses "school talk" verb forms, he may be asked to change to "everyday talk" verb forms.

Oral language instructional activities were also developed as a companion program to the reading series (Gladney and Leaverton, 1968). These activities, organized by units, focus on the same verb forms used in the reading materials. Each unit introduces a new verb form systematically to prevent errors of distribution. For example, the verb form *are* is introduced immediately following the completion of the unit dealing with *is* to avoid overcorrections such as *they is*. In introducing each unit, the teacher tells a story or asks a question structured to elicit from the children their speech patterns in the verb area being studied. The children's statements in nonstandard and standard forms are recorded on the chalkboard. For example, some of the responses given by the children in a conversation about their friends during a lesson on the use of *is* in simple sentences were: "Marie my friend." "Timuel is smart." "Robert he bad in school." The teacher then describes each sentence as everyday talk or school talk, pointing out to the children that the sentences omitting *is* are everyday talk and the sentences includ-

Table 1. Verb Forms in Experimental Reading Materials

	Reading Materials	Everyday Talk	School Talk
Unit 1	All about Me	Employs the verb got	Introduces the verb have
Unit 2	All about Me and My Family	Absence of is and are	Introduces is and are
Unit 3	In My House and in My School	Absence of third person singular	Introduces the verb ending -s
Unit 4	Yesterday	Absence of -ed ending	Introduces the -ed ending
Unit 5	Working and Playing	Use of do	Introduces does
Unit 6	At School	Use of be in place of am, is, are	Introduces am, is, and are in place of be
Unit 7	I Be (Am) Scared When . . .	Use of he be, we be, they be	Introduces standards forms he is, we are, they are
Unit 8	Afro-Americans	Serves as a review for the verb patterns introduced in the preceding books. This book has only one set of stories; in the stories the verb slot is left blank and the child is to fill in the blank with the school talk form.	

ing *is* are school talk. The teacher explains that school talk and everyday talk are simply different ways of expressing the same ideas, neither one "wrong" or "right" but used in different situations, that is, in school or out of school.

After the activities stemming from the children's own statements are concluded, prewritten sentences and stories in everyday talk and dialogue in school talk which include the verbs being studied are given to the children for practice in changing the nonstandard dialect to the standard dialect in orally spoken sentences. Finally, at the close of each unit, each child is asked to give an informal oral presentation using school talk.

At no time during the lessons is the teacher required to interrupt the child to correct his speech. If a nonstandard form occurs in a child's statement with respect to a verb form studied in a previous unit, the teacher asks the child or the class whether the statement was everyday talk or school talk. If, however, the verb form is one that has not been introduced in the oral language activities, the teacher does not call attention to the nonstandard form.

A comprehensive analysis of the research findings is reported in another paper (Leaverton, 1971b). Hence, it will not be repeated here. The major findings, briefly summarized, are as follows: (1) The group of first-grade children who received both versions of the materials (everyday talk followed by school talk) excelled in nineteen of twenty measures investigated as compared with a matched group of children in the same class who were given only the school talk version of the reading materials (Leaverton, 1971). (2) The children who received the experimental treatment in first grade were retested when they reached third grade. The results were then compared with those

Table 2. Scores of Experimental and Control Groups on Reading Subtests of Metropolitan Elementary Test

	Above 1.5	Above 2.0	Above 2.5	Above 3.0	Above 3.5
			Per Cent		
Reading					
Experimental	100	100	58	36	18
Control	97	89	50	19	04
Word Knowledge					
Experimental	100	71	47	29	17
Control	87	75	48	20	07
Word Discrimination					
Experimental	100	82	47	35	29
Control	96	93	53	28	17
Language					
Experimental	100	94	64	52	17
Control	88	80	64	34	13

N for Experimental Group = 17.
N for Control Group = 76.

of all other third-grade children in the school. Table 2 gives the results of these findings. In all of the subtests the low children in the experimental group were higher than the low children in the control group.

Several studies in progress are using the Psycholinguistic Reading materials to replicate and/or investigate our findings in further detail.

Possibly the most significant value of our model is its influence on the attitude and behavior of the teacher toward the children's oral language. The traditional approaches to reading and oral-language programs frequently have not taken into account the effect of the nonstandard dialect on the interaction between teacher and child. Possibly to a large extent, the teacher's attitude has contributed to the difficulty many of the children have had in learning to read and achieve ultimate success in the school situation. In using this model, the teacher is at no time required to criticize the speech of the children while they are beginning to read or during the oral-language activities.

What are the implications of this model for future research? The model places emphasis on the phrase as the initial unit given to the child in the beginning reading situation, as contrasted to the isolated word (emphasized in the "look-see" approach) or the individual sounds contained in the word (emphasized in the phonic approach). When the phrase is used as the primary unit, the variables of pitch and stress also are introduced as possible aids to comprehension. There is essential agreement among scholars of language that in early speech development pitch and stress take precedence over vocabulary as indicators of meaning. Parents, for example, have little difficulty in determining from the early babblings of the child not only what mood the child is communicating but also whether the utterance is a question or a command.

In view of the importance of pitch and stress in early speech development, investigations should be made of the possible effect of the phrase used as the initial emphasis in beginning reading instruction—not only with children whose speech patterns differ from standard English but also with the large group of children who speak standard English.

REFERENCES

Bereiter, C., and Engelmann, S. *Teaching Disadvantaged Children in the Preschool.* Englewood Cliffs, N.J.: Prentice-Hall, Inc., 1966.

Bernstein, B. "Elaborated and Restricted Codes: Their Social Origins and Some Consequences." In J. Gumphrey and D. Hymes (Eds.), "The Ethnography of Communication," *American Anthropologist Special Publication*, 1964, 66(6), Part 2, 55–69.

Carroll, J. B. "Language Development and Reading." International Reading Association Conference, Preconvention Institute VIII, Atlantic City, N.J., April 1971.

Davis, O., Gladney, M., and Leaverton, L. *The Psycholinguistics Reading Series: (A Bi-Dialectal Approach).* Chicago: Board of Education, 1969.

Fasold, R. W. "What Can an English Teacher Do about Nonstandard Dialect?" *English Record*, 1971, 21(4), 82–91.

Gladney, M. R., and Leaverton, L. "A Model for Teaching Standard English to Non-Standard English Speakers." *Elementary English*, Oct. 1968, 758–763.

Kochmann, T. "Rapping in the Black Ghetto." *Trans-Action*, 1969, 6(4), 26–34.

Leaverton, L. "An Experimental Language Arts Program for Potentially Gifted Culturally Disadvantaged Primary Children."

Proposal to Superintendent of Public Instruction, State of Illinois, March 1965.

Leaverton, L. "Identification and Assessment of the Language Potential of Culturally Disadvantaged Negro Children Whose Established Language Patterns Differ from Standard English Usage." Proposal to Superintendent of Public Instruction, State of Illinois, March 1967.

Leaverton, L. "In-Service Training Program to Accompany Field Testing and Dissemination of the Psycholinguistic Reading Series." Proposal to Superintendent of Public Instruction, State of Illinois, April 1969.

Leaverton, L. "Dialectal Readers—Rationale, Use and Value." International Reading Association Conference, Preconvention Institute VII, Language Development and Reading, Atlantic City, N.J., April 1971a.

Leaverton, L. "Follow-Up Three Years Later of 1,400 Children Who Learned to Read Using the Psycholinguistics Reading Series." Proposal to Superintendent of Public Instruction, June 1971b.

Shuy, R. W. "Dialectology and Usage." *Baltimore Bulletin of Education*, 1966, 43, 40.

Shuy, R. W., and Baratz, J. C. (Eds.), *Teaching Black Children to Read.* Washington, D.C.: Center for Applied Linguistics, 1969.

Sledd, J. "Bi-dialectalism: The Linguistics of White Supremacy." *English Journal*, 1969, 38, 1307–1315.

Stewart, W. A. "Current Issues in the Use of Negro Dialect in Beginning Reading Texts." *The Florida FL Reporter*, Spring/Fall 1970.

Desegregation and Academic Achievement[1]

NANCY ST. JOHN

MEASUREMENT OF ACHIEVEMENT

Do desegregated black children read or subtract better than segregated black children?

Does black growth in verbal skill accelerate over time in reacially mixed schools?

Does the achievement of white children decline if black children are bused to their schools?

Does the black-white gap in mean test scores tend to close following the desegregation of a school system?

Questions such as these, which reflect the hopes of integrationists and the fears of segregationists, have preoccupied those engaged in studying the effects of school desegregation. Academic achievement may be a multidimensional concept, but its operational definition tends to be one- or two-dimensional. Many possible outcomes of schooling—creativity, curiosity, civic responsibility, moral judgment, artistic taste, leadership skill, human sensitivity, to name a few—however important, typically go unmeasured in educational research. Therefore, though the subject of this chapter

could be the relation of school racial composition to children's total intellectual, artistic, and social development, I can report only research that treats verbal or mathematical skill as the measure of achievement.

In most studies of the outcome of desegregation the criterion is the raw or grade-equivalent score on a standardized achievement test (or composite score on a battery of such tests). In a few studies "mental ability" or "scholastic aptitude" or IQ is the criterion variable, whereas in others mental ability or IQ is used as a control when estimating achievement in reading or arithmetic. There are serious problems in the use of either type of test in desegregation research. If the tests have not been standardized and validated on a similar population (and they rarely have), they may have low predictive validity for black children or differentiate poorly among them.[2] Though the comparison is between black children and other black children, rather than between black and white children, the tests may neverthe-

1. This chapter is a revised and much expanded version of a paper that appeared in *Review of Educational Research*, Volume 40, February 1970.
2. See Fishman et al. (1964).

less show unreliable or unreal differences or fail to show differences that are reliable and real.

Beyond this there is the further question of whether IQ should be used as a control in estimating differences in achievement. As long as IQ was considered fixed at birth and immune to the effects of environment, it seemed reasonable to focus on "achievement" within the limits set by "ability" in any study of the outcomes of different types of schooling. The contemporary shift in outlook of psychologists to the view that intelligence is plastic and the product of the interaction of genetic and environmental factors means that we can expect differences in school environment to result in differences in performance on IQ tests, as well as on tests which measure the results of instruction in skills. Controlling on the results of a contemporaneous IQ test therefore may make it difficult to detect differences in achievement between experimental and control groups. The difficulty is especially great in the case of children of any minority subculture.

Studies in which IQ is controlled are not the rule in desegregation research and their findings can thus be discounted. On the other hand it is not possible to ignore all studies that depend on the evidence of standardized achievement tests. No better criteria are generally available. The consequent uncertainty as to the meaning of their findings in regard to minority group children must be kept constantly in mind.

The experimental model discussed in the previous chapter suggests a logical way of classifying research on the relation of school racial composition and academic achievement. The ideal design provides for measurement in four cells:

	Before	After
Experimental Group	(1) Segregated	(3) Desegregated
Matched Control Group	(2) Segregated	(4) Segregated

But in many designs one or more of these cells are empty. I will first review cross-sectional studies that lack prior measurement of achievement, then longitudinal studies that lack a proper control group, and finally studies with before and after data for both control and experimental groups. Such four-celled studies are quasi experiments rather than true experiments, in that the two samples are rarely randomly drawn or randomly assigned to segregated or desegregated schools, nor is there precision matching of the groups on home background or school quality. Moreover, the early measurement is in many cases determined post facto. Black children are the focus of the discussion that follows. A later section summarizes evidence on the effect of the racial composition of schools on white children.

A NATIONAL CROSS-SECTIONAL STUDY

The most important source of cross-sectional data for the comparison of segregated and nonsegregated school children is the Equality of Educational Opportunity Survey (EEOS). Since the findings by the authors of the original report[3] and of *Racial Isolation in the Public Schools*[4] have been widely disseminated and argued and since the data have been subjected to careful reanalyses by many social scientists,[5] I will not discuss the matter here. But to set these studies in their rightful place in this review of school desegregation research, I must summarize briefly those findings of the original and subsequent analyses that are most relevant to the topic of this chapter and note those methodological limitations that inevitably affect our acceptance of such findings.

The Coleman Report stated that the proportion white in a school was positively

3. Coleman et al. (1966).
4. U.S. Commission on Civil Rights (1967).
5. For example, see Bowles and Levin (1968); McPartland (1968); Hanusheh (1969); Mayeske et al. (1972); Mosteller and Moynihan (1972); Armor (1972b).

related to individual performance, but that the "effect appeared to be less than, and largely accounted for, by other characteristics of the student body than the racial composition of the school per se" (i.e., by their SES). The Commission on Civil Rights' reanalysis of the data for twelfth-grade black students in the metropolitan northeast and ninth-grade blacks in eight regions indicated that the racial composition of the classroom in the previous year did have an independent relationship to students' verbal achievement. As suggested in the previous chapter, however, if pupils are assigned to classrooms on the basis of test scores, the direction of causality may not be from classroom percentage white to achievement, as assumed by the commission. On the other hand, in support of their assumption, the commission found that the earlier the grade at which blacks first reported having white classmates, the higher their achievement.

Further analysis of the EEOS data by McPartland (1968) agrees with the commission's conclusion on the relation between classroom composition and achievement. He shows that school desegregation is associated with higher achievement for black pupils only if they are in predominantly white classrooms, but classroom desegregation is favorable irrespective of school percentage white. The classroom racial composition effect, says McPartland, is not entirely explained by selection into track or curriculum.

A reanalysis by Cohen, Pettigrew, and Riley (1972) reaffirms the Coleman finding that the racial composition of the schools has little effect on the verbal achievement of blacks when school quality and the background of individuals and their peers are controlled. But, as the commission and McPartland had earlier reported, the racial composition of the classroom does have a modest relationship to verbal achievement (not apparently purely a result of selection processes) even after controlling for the foregoing factors. "A moderate proportion of the variance attributed to school social class

is, in fact, shared with school percent Negro, and cannot be uniquely decomposed into either its racial composition or social-class components" (Cohen et al., 1972, p. 347).

Regardless of the finesse of the several analyses of the EEOS data, the following major criticisms of the quality of those data suggest that any conclusions as to the influence of school race on children must be considered tentative:

1. Without prior measures of academic performance there is no assurance that segregated and integrated children were comparable in scholastic aptitude when they entered these schools.[6]

2. The measures of home background are of doubtful validity and certainly do not measure or control on all facets of family influence.

3. School and classroom percentage white refer to one point in time and may not be accurately reported.

4. In spite of the many school characteristics measured in the survey, the quality of schooling in respects other than racial mixture is probably inadequately controlled. Failure to match teachers and their own pupils or to allocate per pupil expenditure by schools are among the sources of slippage.

Each of these could mask an actual relationship between school race and pupil achievement. If pupils are coded as "integrated" (though they had just arrived that week in a mixed school after eight years of segregation) or as "middle class" (though they are in fact from poverty-level homes), or as the recipients of "quality" schooling (though actually their class had a series of poorly trained substitutes all last year), then their low test scores coupled with "integra-

6. Jencks and Brown (1972) use an ingenious method of controling for variations in initial ability among students sampled in the EEO survey. They compare first and sixth graders in the same elementary schools. They find that both black and white achievement rose (relative to national norms) in elementary schools 51 to 75% white. The effects in secondary schools were small but suggested that blacks gain more in schools 26 to 90% white.

tion," "middle-class status," or "equal school resources" would diminish the apparent relation between integration and achievement for the group of which they were a part.

LOCAL CROSS-SECTIONAL STUDIES

The Equality of Educational Opportunity Survey was not the first cross-sectional study which, without the benefit of base-line data, compared the school achievement of segregated and desegregated black children. Chart A-1 (in the Appendix)* lists 13 other such studies, all at the local rather than national level. This listing, like similar ones to follow, includes all published and unpublished studies of the specified type that I have found reported in sufficient detail to allow classification. Though my search has been long and hard, I undoubtedly have missed some relevant research.[7]

It is probably no accident that most of these studies were initiated before the release of the Coleman Report in 1966. That important document demonstrated so clearly the need for longitudinal data that few subsequent investigators have failed to incorporate some "before" as well as "after" measurement into their research designs. It is also noteworthy that the studies (in at least nine different northern states from Connecticut to California) all had small samples and compared the achievement of "naturally" desegregated and segregated pupils. In other words, racially mixed schools were the result of demographic changes in school districts, not of deliberate action on the part of school boards, a feature also symptomatic of the era in which the data were gathered.

Differences in social and economic status

*Editor's note. With the exception of Chart 2-1, we have omitted the charts referred to by the author because of their length. These charts can be found in Nancy St. John, *School desegregation outcomes for children.* New York: Wiley, 1975.

7. The work of Weinberg (1970), O'Reilly (1970), and Pettigrew et al. (1973) were especially helpful in locating studies and are here gratefully acknowledged. All dissertations referred to have been read, usually on microfilm.

between the segregated and the desegregated were controlled in some fashion in most of these investigations, but it is doubtful that the two groups were thereby equated in family background. The only two researchers who reported unmixed findings of significantly higher achievement for the integrated (Jessup, 1967; Lockwood, 1966) had very little control on family background.

Several studies treated IQ as a control rather than as another measure of the outcome of desegregation. As noted, this presents a problem of interpretation. If the IQ test is contemporaneous with the reported achievement score, then to "remove its effect" may reduce not merely the initial difference between groups, as these researchers assume, but also the hypothesized relation between the race of classmates and achievement. The findings of no significant difference between the two groups of children tested reported by several researchers (Crowley, 1932; Long, 1968; Robertson, 1967) or the mixed findings reported by other researchers (Matzen, 1965; Samuels, 1958) may be artifacts of this procedure.

Chart A-1 summarizes four cross-sectional studies (in Chicago, Pittsburgh, Plainfield, and New Haven) that measured school race longitudinally. In each case secondary or postsecondary school achievement was the criterion and earlier desegregation experience the predictor. In these studies the previously integrated tended to outperform the previously segregated, but the controls were not stringent, nor were the differences reported to be large or statistically significant, with the exception of the Pittsburgh study.

Since the Pittsburgh study which I conducted (St. John, 1973) is a good example of the problems of interpreting the results of such research, I will describe it in some detail. Eight of the 21 secondary schools in that city were selected as representative of the schools attended by minority group students in 1966. The 1388 black ninth graders in those schools were 72% of the black ninth graders in the city and were graduates of 60 different elementary schools that varied considerably in their racial and social class composition. For each student I calculated the average percentage of white students and the average social class level of the schools he had attended in grades 1 to 8.

Pupils' elementary school percentage white (which ranged from 0 to 99%) was the independent variable in subsequent tabular and regression analyses and proved to be positively and significantly related to eighth-grade Metropolitan Achievement Test score in arithmetic. The relationship did not disappear either when sex and family SES were controlled or when boys and girls or students of high and low SES and IQ were analyzed separately. However, other achievement test scores (in reading, language, or science) were not related to school percentage white, though they were related to school SES.

The results of the Pittsburgh analysis are thus ambiguous: desegregation apparently encouraged skill in arithmetic but not in other subjects. One possible explanation for this discrepancy is that arithmetic in contrast to reading is a school-learned skill and was perhaps better taught in racially mixed schools. Another possible explanation is that segregated and desegregated students were not originally alike in their potential for learning arithmetic. Without random assignment, matching, or a pretest, it is impossible to determine the reason for the difference in results.

The other cross-sectional studies suffer from the same weakness, but since a strong relationship between integration experience and achievement was seldom found, there is little danger of a spurious conclusion. Only if the integrated were *less* advantaged than the segregated could their gains by greater and their final scores the same. Given the usual demography of cities, such a possibility is unlikely. It is in connection with the few studies in this group that find the desegregated significantly ahead that the question of inadequate controls and possible spuriousness must be seriously considered.

Longitudinal Studies

The last few years have seen an increase in studies that have the benefit of before and after measurement of achievement but lack a genuine control group. Fourteen such studies are listed in Chart A-2, in three southern and five northern states from East to West Coast, plus the District of Columbia. In most cases the studies followed total district desegregation; therefore the samples were fairly large and no contemporary control group of segregated peers was possible. The duration of the study was only one year in the case of five of these reports, from two to five years in the others. The focus of most of the studies was the elementary level. The busing of black children was a feature of the desegregation plan in most of these studies, but only in Boston were black children transported out of the city to suburban schools.

Few of these studies reported clear gains for desegregated minority group children in comparison with national norms, local whites, or their own previous growth in a segregated setting. Methodological problems detracted from the Washington, D.C., and Louisville findings. Systemwide desegregation did not mean desegregated classes for most children in these cities at the time of the studies. No tests of statistical significance were reported for Berkeley, but trends there did not favor the desegregated. No consistently significant gains were reported for White Plains, Evanston, or Riverside. In several other cities findings were mixed, with significant gains in some subjects but not others or at some grade levels but not others. The most clear-cut positive findings were those in Hoke County and Goldsboro, North Carolina, where blacks showed postdesegregation gains relative to national norms.

In none of these longitudinal studies was individual family background measured or controlled, though this may not be a serious limitation if the sample includes all children in the system. However, it is probable that the classmates of black children were of higher average SES after desegregation than before and that any relative growth that occurred might have been due to this factor as much as to school race. It is also probable that desegregation meant changes for the better in school quality for the black children involved. There is good evidence that in Washington, D.C., and Louisville, for instance, major systemwide educational improvements accompanied desegregation. However, in some cities (e.g., in Berkeley, according to a study by Frelow, 1971), there was a reduction in services in the years following desegregation.

The Riverside experiment in desegregation is the most longterm, completely documented, and widely noted study in this group, and its findings are therefore particularly discouraging. In 1965 the school board voted a phased closedown of three very imbalanced elementary schools involving the busing of 225 pupils (47% black and 53% Mexican-American) to 17 other schools in the city. In their February 1973 report, Purl and Dawson summarized the findings after seven years of desegregation:

1. The achievement of kindergarten and first-grade minority students rose steadily and significantly and in 1972 was near the median of the norming sample. Second graders showed no trend and third graders decreased slightly.

2. Receiving pupils showed trends similar to those of bused pupils. Thus the gap between bused and receiving pupils narrowed only slightly.

3. The authors suggest that the gains in the first two years were the result of instructional improvement and greater individualization of classes. In the higher grades low achieving pupils showed the least progress and the need for compensatory programs.

4. Pupils attending certain schools consistently scored high or low. Sometimes the SES of receiving pupils and sometimes the quality of the instructional program seemed to be responsible.

Thus the gains of the younger children in Riverside might not be lost in the older grades if services were maintained at predesegregation levels and if minority group children were all allocated to classrooms in which the achievement level was high. But as it stands neither the Riverside evidence nor that of any of the other longitudinal studies provides strong support for the hypothesis that desegregated schooling benefits minority group children.

QUASI-EXPERIMENTAL FOUR-CELLED STUDIES

The last group of studies to be considered are four-celled, in that the achievement of segregated and desegregated subjects is measured at two points in time. These studies are quasi experiments rather than true experiments since subjects are neither assigned randomly from a common population to segregated or desegregated schools nor matched on all relevant variables. The presumed validity of their findings, although greater than that of two-celled studies, is not beyond question. Chart A-3 lists 37 such studies.

The dates of these reports range from 1958 to 1972, clustering in the late 1960s. The locations are New York state for 10, other northeastern cities for 9, with the others well distributed across the nation. Eleven samples had less than 50 black pupils in the experimental group, while five had over 1000; the modal size was between 100 and 500 desegregated black children. The great majority (29) were at the elementary level.

In most of these experiments, as compared to those with a longitudinal design, desegregation was not systemwide and mandatory for all. For research purposes this situation is useful, in that a control group of segregated children was thus available, but it also poses a serious research hazard, in that most of the desegregated were in one way or another self-selected. The desegregated were either children whose families chose an integrated neighborhood or, in most cases, those who volunteered for open enrollment or a busing program. Careful matching of subjects in the control and experimental groups on family background as well as early achievement was therefore essential. But such matching was rare, and only 11 studies made any attempt to control on socioeconomic status.

Two ways of handling the choice of control group are especially promising. The METCO studies reported by Walberg (1969) and Armor (1972a) tested segregated siblings of the pupils bused out to suburban schools and found that bused pupils did not show significantly greater gains than their brothers or sisters. Unfortunately, due to nonresponse the sample of siblings was too small and nonrandom to constitute an adequate control group. Project Concern reported by Mahan (1968) randomly selected whole classrooms to be bused to Hartford suburbs. Though a few parents refused this opportunity, such a procedure insured a large measure of comparability between experimental and control groups. In the younger grades (K to 3) bused Hartford pupils made significantly greater gains in IQ and achievement than pupils who remained in the city. In grades 4 to 6 the differences in achievement favored the segregated.

Another interesting feature of the Hartford study is that half of the receiving suburban classrooms were assigned extra "supporting" teachers. Greater gains were reported for pupils in these classrooms than for bused pupils without such support. On the other hand, there was no evidence that such assistance benefited pupils who remained in the inner city. The chief drawback of this project as a scientific experiment is, of course, the fact that the effects of racial composition and quality of schools are completely confounded.

The Wilson Study

Among studies of the effect of "natural" or unplanned desegregation on minority group performance, the one with the most nearly adequate design is Wilson's (1967) survey, reported in an appendix to the Civil Rights Commission Report. The sample is a stratified random sample of over 4000 junior and senior high school students in one school district in the San Francisco Bay area. The design is a cross-sectional comparison of verbal test scores, according to the racial and social class composition of neighborhoods and schools, but retrospective longitudinal control is introduced by the data on school racial and social class composition at each grade level, and by the availability of first-grade individual mental maturity test scores. Wilson argues that controlling on these test scores equates children on the effects of both genetic differences and preschool home environment, so that changes can be attributed to new (school?) experiences and not to uncontrolled initial differences. I do not share Wilson's faith in the early test score.

Though the sample is large (N = 905 blacks in crucial tables), analysis of the separate effects of neighborhood and school segregation or of racial and social class segregation is hampered for blacks by the confounding of these variables and by the fact that few blacks live in integrated neighborhoods, thus seriously reducing the number of cases in some cells. Nevertheless, by means of regression analysis, Wilson showed that after controlling for variation in first-grade IQ and for parental and neighborhood SES, the social class of the primary school had a significant effect on sixth-grade reading level and the social class of the intermediate school a significant effect on eighth-grade verbal reasoning scores. School racial composition, however, had no significant effect on achievement over and above school social class (pp. 180–184).

Beyond the small size of the numbers in some of the cells, there are further limitations to this study:

1. First-grade scores would have been available only for the most stable members of the sample, and its representativeness may have been affected by attrition.

2. Children were matched only by father's occupation and primary mental maturity

scores; in other respects segregated and integrated children could have been quite different.

3. Parental and school social class assignment based on the questionnaire replies of students are potentially inaccurate.

4. No evidence is offered as to the equality of segregated and integrated schools in Richmond.

5. If the relation between school racial composition and achievement was not linear, the regression analysis could have underestimated the effect.

But in spite of these quibbles, the study is impressive in design and quite convincing that in this community, at least, racial integration per se was not significantly related to the academic performance of blacks. But, given the strong intercorrelation of school racial and social class composition ($r \pm .77$), the combined effect of the two types of segregation was plainly a strong deterrent to achievement.[8]

The Goldsboro Study

A most interesting study of planned total district desegregation in a southern community is that by Mayer et. al. (1973) and McCullough (1972) of Goldsboro, North Carolina. Desegregation was accomplished there in a manner that equalized facilities, equipment, and staff for all pupils. Black schools were kept open and remodeled. All teachers were reassigned, and the principals of black schools became the principals of white schools and vice versa. Pupils were assigned by grade level rather than residence so that busing affected blacks and whites alike.

Longitudinal comparison was made of the third- and fifth-grade scores of a cohort of pupils who experienced systemwide desegregation between their third- and fourth-grade years. Both blacks and whites gained significantly relative to national norms in verbal

8. See O'Reilly (1970) for a careful and detailed critique of this study.

and mathematical skills. The white-black gap, however, was not reduced. The authors suggest that desegregation may not have altered the status relationships between blacks and whites. Structured observations in fourth-grade classrooms revealed much less teacher-pupil intereaction of a substantive nature and much more interaction of a disciplining nature for black males than for white males.

A quasi-experimental design was then achieved by controlling on degree of desegregation experience. Pupils were classified according to the racial composition of their school in the year before systemwide desegregation and according to whether their school was desegregated in the first or second year of the experiment. In verbal achievement all groups made significant gains, with no significant differences according to desegregation experience. Apparently the fact of systemwide desegregation, not attendance at a desegregated school, boosted verbal achievement, since similar gains were experienced by those who remained at a segregated school in the fourth grade and by those who did not.

Achievement in arithmetic, on the other hand, *was* related to desegregation experience: black pupils who had longer experience in desegregated schools made significantly greater gains than the newly desegregated. The effect was not due to changes in teaching methods; a comparison of pupils experiencing open classroom teaching style with those who remained in traditional classrooms revealed that the latter made significantly greater improvement in arithmetic. Nor did social class alone account for the improvement, though the researchers did not examine possible interaction between social class and desegregation experience.

The authors claim the effect of desegregation experience on mathematical but not verbal achievement occurs because "Social structural change is more likely to work in performance areas that are narrow and depend on recently acquired skills, than in

Chart 2.1. Frequency Distribution of Four-celled Studies of Relation of Schools Racial Composition and Black Achievement, by Direction of Findings and by whether Design Included Control on SES and Tests of Significance

Direction of Findings	No SES Control, No Test of Significance	No SES Control, Yes Test of Significance	Yes SES Control, Yes Test of Significance	Total
Positive on all tests reported	Banks and DiPasquale (1969) Dressler (1967) Heller et al. (1972) Johnson (1967)	Anderson (1966) Zdep and Joyce (1969)	Griffin (1969)	7
Mixed positive and negative or no difference	None	Beker (1967) Carrigan (1969) Clinton (1969) Fortenberry (1959) Laird and Weeks (1966) Mahan (1968) Mayer et al., (1973) Rochester School Board (1970) Rock et al. (1968) Sacramento School Board (1971) Samuels (1971) Williams (1968) Wolman (1964) Wood (1969)	Frary and Goolsby (1970) Slone (1968) Walberg (1969) St. John and Lewis (1971)	18
No difference	Fox (1966, 1967, 1968)	Danahy (1971) Gardner et al. (1970) Moorefield (1967) Rentsch (1967)	Denmark and Guttentag (1969) Klein (1967) Laurent (1969) Wilson (1967)	9
Mixed no difference and negative	Shaker Heights (1972)	None	Armor (1972a) Evans (1969)	3
Negative on all tests reported	None	None	None	0
Total	7	19	11	37

performance areas that depend on more pervasive skills built up over a longer time period" (p. 42).

Chart 2-1 shows the frequency distribution of the 36 four-celled studies summarized in Chart A-3 according to the direction of their findings and whether SES was controlled and tests of significance reported. It is evident that the findings are partially or wholly positive much more frequently than they are negative. However, it is also evident that the tighter the design the more often is no difference found between segregated and desegregated minority group children. We therefore cannot ignore the possibility that positive findings would disappear completely in studies with more perfect control of all relevant variables.[9]

Space does not allow full description of each of these four-celled studies. Taken together, however, they suggest that the achievement of black children is rarely harmed thereby, but they provide no strong or clear evidence that such desegregation boosts their achievement. A countdown by grade level and achievement tests, rather than by cities, reveals that a report of no difference is more common than a report of significant gain. Even studies over several years are as often negative as positive in their findings. And where gains are established, we are left to wonder whether the effective agent was the quality of desegregated schools, the selection of the busing program by the children of mobility-oriented families, or contact with middle-class or white schoolmates.

Two findings already noted in connection with two-celled studies receive further support from four-celled studies: five of these reports note that gains of desegregated black children are more evident in earlier than in later grades; and achievement in arithmetic but not reading was found to be significantly and positively related to school race in New York, Boston, and Goldsboro.[10] Both of these tendencies deserve further testing.

WHITE STUDENTS

Research on the effect of desegregation on school achievement has usually focused on minority group students, whereas research on the effect of prejudice has focused on white students. In the majority of the studies summarized above, the achievement of white students is either ignored entirely or else treated as the norm against which the gains of black students should be measured. But the prospect of reverse busing of white students to formerly black schools has stimulated interest in the probable effects on their academic progress. Chart A-4 summarizes 24 studies of the achievement of desegregated whites.

The Coleman et al. (1966) cross-sectional finding that school percentage white bears little relation to verbal achievement that is independent of the influence of individual and school social background referred to white children as well as to minority group children. The U.S. Commission on Civil Rights Report (1967) reaches the same conclusion in regard to classroom rather than school racial composition.[11] Armor's (1972b) reanalysis of the Coleman data clearly shows that the verbal ability of white pupils in majority-black schools is as low or lower than that of black schoolmates. It is apparently not the school's racial composition but the low SES of such pupils (and perhaps that of their classmates as well) that seems to be primarily responsible for their low achievement.

Using longitudinal data, Wilson (1967) found that for white students as well as black students the racial composition of the school had a negligible effect but was confounded with social class composition, which had a significant effect. For whites in comparison with blacks, school social class was less related to achievement, and family social class was more related to achievement.

In contrast, I found that residence in racially changing neighborhoods in Boston was associated with lower test scores for white children. The greater the percentage of black classmates in earlier grades, the lower the later achievement of whites in arithmetic and reading, even with parental and school SES and a measure of early achievement

9. Pettigrew (1969) reasons that "soft research . . . strongly suggests that desegregation has sustained and marked effects on the achievement of Negro children" (p. 104) and therefore feels it is likely that "hard" research will support this evidence. I find, rather, that "soft" research tends to show little effect and am therefore less sanguine than he that hard research will reveal clear benefits unless the conditions under which desegregation normally occurs are changed.
10. Slone (1968); St. John and Lewis (1971); Mayer et. al., (1973).

11. See page 47 and Tables 8-3, 8-4, and 8-6 of *Racial Isolation in the Public Schools.*

controlled. Fifty percent black was an important boundary. White children who had attended majority-black schools scored considerably below those who had attended majority-white schools (St. John and Lewis, 1971).

The longitudinal data from desegregating school systems—Berkeley, Chapel Hill, Evanston, Goldsboro, Louisville, Riverside, Washington, D.C., White Plains—indicate in every case that racial mixture in the schools had no negative consequences for majority group pupils. In busing experiments in which selected central city children are transported to outlying communities the universal report also is no significant difference in achievement between children in classrooms that do or do not receive bused pupils (Buffalo, Denver, Hartford, Westport, Verona, West Irondequoit). It should be noted, however, that in almost all these experiments, white children remained in the majority in their schools and classrooms.

A few reports are available on the academic progress of white children bused to schools in the ghetto. In Shaker Heights white pupils in grades 4 to 6 who accepted reassignment to a majority-black school gained more than whites in the rest of the system. In Evanston self-selected white children bused to a formerly black school had scores above the norm. O'Reilly (1970) reports on two similar cases. One study in Queens, New York, found that white students transported to a majority-black school made less academic progress than white students who remained home (Wrightstone et al., 1966). In the other study of reverse busing in Rochester, New York, no significant differences between the two groups of white students were found except that fourth-grade students transferred to an inner city school made significantly higher scores on vocabulary and arithmetic achievement tests (Rock et al., 1968).

The evidence appears convincing that the achievement of white students is not adversely affected by the addition of a few black students to their classrooms. Classrooms over 50% black are quite possibly detrimental to white achievement, but this has been tested so little with longitudinal data that it remains an open question. The rare studies of reverse busing of suburban children to ghetto schools show gains more often than losses, but families who choose reverse busing may have unusual children.

CONCLUSION

In sum, adequate data have not yet been gathered to determine a causal relation between school racial composition and academic achievement. More than a decade of considerable research effort has produced no definitive positive findings. In view of the political, moral, and technical difficulties of investigation on this question, it is doubtful that all the canons of the scientific method will ever be met or a causal relationship ever established. Suggestive trends have been uncovered, however, as has one important negative finding: desegregation has rarely lowered academic achievement for either black or white children.

Light and Smith argue that "little headway can be made by pooling the words in conclusions of a set of studies. Rather progress will only come when we are able to pool, in a systematic manner, the original data from the studies" (1971, p. 343). Their argument is persuasive; but until such pooling can be accomplished we may learn something from noting the shortcomings of existing studies and the direction of their findings.

The studies reviewed in this chapter were conducted in communities that range across the country and vary greatly in population. But there is no evidence that city size or region affects the influence of desegregation on achievement. The northern, middle-sized city was until recently the most frequent location because this is where desegregation was most possible and probable in the 1960s. Since 1970, however, a number of studies of southern school systems have appeared, but their findings are as mixed as those of northern systems.

Similarly, research has focused on the elementary grades because at this level neighborhood housing patterns have produced the greatest variation in school racial mixture. Here there is some indication that younger children, especially those of kindergarten age, tend to benefit more than older children from desegregation. The length of exposure to desegregation, however, has not so far proved to be an important variable, perhaps because most experiments or studies thereof have been of very short duration. A further cause for uncertainty in this regard is that childrens' total experience with school desegregation from kindergarten on is usually not measured at all or measured imprecisely.

When significant differences in favor of the desegregated are reported, in some but not all tests, there is no consistency as to which academic skill is most affected. However, gains in mathematical rather than verbal achievement are reported frequently enough to deserve further study.

In the studies reviewed there is considerable variation in the definition of the independent variable. In most studies school racial composition rather than classroom racial composition is the focus, and reports do not specify whether grouping practices resulted in within-school desegregation. Since classroom race may be the result of grouping based on test scores, school race seems the preferable independent variable. But within-school desegregation should be measured and controlled.

The Coleman Report and a few of the other studies reviewed treat school racial composition as a continuous variable, but it is far more frequently treated as a nominal variable, with the scores of the same pupils being compared before and after "desegregation" or the scores of different pupils, either "segregated" or "integrated," being compared. A "segregated" school is variously defined as majority-black (greater than 50%) or predominantly black (greater than 80% or 90%) or totally black. Similarly "integrated" or "desegregated" refers sometimes to a majority-white school, but more often to a

predominantly white situation in which desegregation is "token." There is no clear evidence in this literature that findings depend on the definition of desegregation. Tabular analyses of the EEOS data (U.S. Commission on Civil Rights, 1967) suggest that in some regions or at some SES levels there is a curvilinear relationship between school or classroom percentage white and achievement, with lowest mean achievement for black pupils where that percentage is between 25 and 50. But this finding may be a function of incomplete control on SES and other factors. Further study is needed before we can be sure whether, as some researchers have found, both races perform better in schools at least 50% white or whether tokenism, either for whites in black schools or blacks in white schools, affects achievement adversely.

The desegregation referred to in these studies came about in at least four different ways: through "natural" demographic changes in residential neighborhoods; through school board rezoning of districts or closing of a segregated school and mandatory transfer of its pupils, with or without busing; through voluntary transfer of selected pupils to distant schools through open enrollment or busing; and through total district desegregation in which all children, white or black, are assigned to schools of similar racial mix. In this last case, black children are more frequently bused than are white children. We have seen that the method by which a community achieves desegregation largely determines what type of evaluation is technically possible. However, available evidence does not suggest that the method determines whether academic gains result, though the matter has not been studied systematically. In many cases of desegregation through redistricting, some children must walk and some must be bused to the new school. But in only one city, Evanston (Hsia, 1971), were the achievement gains of busers and walkers compared. In this case the busers gained more.

More serious than ignorance as to the most

favorable black-white ratio or the most favorable method of achieving that ratio is lack of research evidence as to the conditions under which desegregation (however defined or achieved) benefits children. Researchers have not controlled on such variables as the level of community controversy over desegregation, the friendliness of white parents and students, the flexibility or prejudice of the staff, the content of curriculum, or the method of teaching. There is some evidence, however, that individualization of instruction and the provision of support services for students in need of remedial work is an important concomitant of desegregation.

In the introduction to this chapter the point was made that the twin challenges to desegregation research are assurance as to the original equivalence of segregated and desegregated pupils and the equivalence of their schooling in all respects other than interracial exposure. We have found that "no significant difference" between segregated and desegregated black children is the finding of over half of the most carefully controlled studies and of many more than half of the tests of the relationship, if subject matter areas and grade levels rather than communities are counted. The question then before us is: Is it likely that tighter control on the equivalency of pupils and treatments would change the verdict? Wherever desegregation is found to *benefit* minority group children we must assure ourselves that this is not a spurious finding. But where *no difference* is found, it is unlikely that tighter controls would reveal a relationship. Experience suggests that it is unlikely that the absence of effect is due to the *lower* initial ability or SES of the desegregated pupils or to the *lower* objective quality of desegregated schools. The research hazard is rather that the desegregated may be children of greater initial potential than the segregated and that desegregated schools will be superior on tangible criteria. On the other hand it is entirely possible, and unfortunately highly probable, that many desegregated schools are unfriendly, irrelevant, and unsupportive to black pupils. Without control on such intangible qualities of schools it is impossible to measure the contribution to achievement of their black-white ratios.

One further point in regard to the academic consequences of desegregation deserves consideration. Does the way we pose our research question place the burden of proof unfairly on the minority group rather than the majority group? Desegregation is supposed to benefit the achievement of black children, not white children. It is pronounced a success if black achievement rises but white achievement remains stationary; in other words, it is successful if the racial gap is reduced. Given the demonstrated importance of early childhood influences and the high correlation for children generally between early and late test scores, why should we expect only one aspect of school experience—racial mix—to have a pronounced effect on achievement and, what is more, on the achievement of one racial group only? Moreover, why do we continue to measure minority group children's progress in school with tests normalized on the population at large, tests which may reflect very poorly their own group strengths, interests, and priorities?

REFERENCES

Anderson, Louis V. *The Effect of Desegregation on the Achievement and Personality Patterns of Negro Children,* unpublished doctoral dissertation, George Peabody College for Teachers, University Microfilm 66-11, 237, 1966.

Armor, David J. "The Evidence on Busing," *The Public Interest,* 28 (Summer 1972), 90–126.(a)

Armor, David J. "School and Family Effects on Black and White Achievement: A Reexamination of the USOE Data," in Frederick Mosteller and Daniel P. Moynihan (eds.), *On Equality of Educational Opportunity,* New York, Random House, 1972, 168–229.(b)

Banks, Ronald, and Di Pasquale, Mary E. "A Study of the Educational Effectiveness of Integration," Buffalo, N.Y., Buffalo Public Schools, January 1969.

Beker, Jerome. "A Study of Integration in Racially Imbalanced Urban Public Schools," Syracuse University Youth Development Center, Final Report, May 1967. (mimeographed)

Bowles, Samuel, and Levin, Henry M. "The Determinants of Scholastic Achievement: An Appraisal of Some Recent Evidence." *The Journal of Human Resources*, 3 (Winter 1968), 3–24.

Carrigan, Patricia M. "School Desegregation via Compulsory Pupil Transfer: Early Effects on Elementary School Children," Ann Arbor, Michigan, Public Schools, September 1969.

Clinton, Ronald R. *A Study of the Improvement in Achievement of Basic Skills of Children Bused from Urban To Suburban School Environments*, unpublished masters thesis, Southern Connecticut State College, 1969.

Cohen, David K., Pettigrew, Thomas F., and Riley, Robert T. "Race and the Outcomes of Schooling," in Frederick Mosteller and Daniel P. Moynihan (eds.), *On Equality of Educational Opportunity*, New York, Random House, 1972.

Coleman, James S., et al. *Equality of Educational Opportunity*. Washington, D.C., U.S. Department of Health, Education and Welfare, Office of Education, 1966.

Crowley, Mary R. "Cincinnati's Experiment in Negro Education: A Comparative Study of the Segregated and Mixed School," *Journal of Negro Education*, 1 (April 1932), 25–33.

Danahy, Ann Hechter. "A Study of the Effects of Bussing on the Achievement, Attendance, Attitudes, and Social Choices of Negro Inner-City Children," unpublished doctoral dissertation, University of Minnesota, 1971.

Denmark, Florence L. and Guttentag, Marcia. "Effect of Integrated and Non-Integrated Programs on Cognitive Change in Pre-School Children," *Perceptual and Motor Skills*, 29 (October 1969), 375–380.

Dressler, Frank J. "Study of Achievement in Reading of Pupils Transferred from Schools 15 and 37 to Peripheral Schools to Eliminate Overcrowding, to Abandon an Obsolete School, and to Achieve a more Desirable Racial Balance in City Schools," Buffalo Public Schools, Division of Curriculum Evaluation and Development, March 1967. (mimeographed)

Evans, Charles Lee. *The Immediate Effects of Classroom Integration on the Academic Progress, Self-Concept and Racial Attitudes of Negro Elementary Children*, unpublished doctoral dissertation, North Texas State University, 1969.

Fishman, Joshua A., et al. "Guidelines for Testing Minority Group Children," *Journal of Social Issues*, 20, (April 1964), 129–145.

Fortenberry, James. H. *The Achievement of Negro Pupils in Mixed and Non-Mixed Schools*, unpublished doctoral dissertation, University of Oklahoma, University Microfilm No. 59-5492, 1959.

Fox, David J. "Free Choice Open Enrollment–Elementary Schools," New York, Center for Urban Education, August 1966. (mimeographed)

Fox, David J. "Evaluation of the New York City Title I Educational Projects 1966–1967: Expansion of the Free Choice Open Enrollment Program," New York, Center for the Urban Education, September 1967. (mimeographed)

Fox, David J., et al. "Services to Children in Open Enrollment Receiving Schools: Evaluation of ESEA Title I Projects in New York City, 1967–1968," New York, Center for Urban Education, November 1968, (mimeographed)

Frary, Robert B., and Goolsby, Thomas M., Jr. "Achievement of Integrated and Segregated Negro and White First Graders in a Southern City," *Integrated Education*, 8 (July/August 1970), 48–52.

Frelow, Robert D. *A Comparative Study of Resource Allocation: Compensatory Education and School Desegregation*, Unpublished doctoral dissertation, University of California, Berkeley, 1971.

Gardner, Burleigh B., et al. "The Effect of Busing Black Ghetto Children into White Suburban Schools," July 1970 (ERIC ED 048 389).

Griffin, J. L. *The Effects of Integration on Academic Aptitude, Classroom Achievement, Self-Concept and Attitudes toward the School Environment of a Selected*

Group of Negro Students in Tulsa, Oklahoma, unpublished doctoral dissertation, University of Tulsa, 1969.

Hanusheh, Eric Alan. *The Education of Negroes and Whites*, unpublished doctoral dissertation, Massachusetts Institute of Technology, 1969.

Heller, Barbara R. et al. "Project Concern: Westport, Connecticut Center for Urban Education, New York, N.Y., June 1972.

Hsia, Jayjia. "Integration in Evanston, 1967–1971," Educational Testing Service, Princeton, N.J., August 1971. (mimeographed).

Jencks, Christopher, and Brown, Marsha. "The Effects of Desegregation on Student Achievement: Some New Evidence from the Equality of Educational Opportunity Survey," Center for Educational Policy Research, Harvard Graduate School of Education, November 1972, (mimeographed)

Jessup, Dorothy K. "School Integration and Minority Group Achievement," in Robert A. Dentler, Bernard Mackler, and Mary Ellen Warschauer (eds.), *The Urban R's: Race Relations as the Problem in Urban Education*, New York, Praeger, 1967.

Johnson, Norman J., Wyer, Robert, and Gilbert, Neil. "Quality Education and Integration: An Exploratory Study," *Phylon*, 28 (Fall 1967), 221–229.

Klein, Robert Stanley. *A Comparative Study of the Academic Achievement of Negro Tenth Grade High School Students Attending Segregated and Recently Integrated Schools in a Metropolitan Area in the South*, unpublished doctoral dissertation, University of South Carolina, 1967.

Laird, Mary Alice, and Weeks, Grace. "The Effect of Bussing on Achievement in Reading and Arithmetic in Three Philadelphia Schools," The School District of Philadelphia, Division of Research, December 1966. (mimeographed)

Laurent, James A. *Effects of Race and Racial Balance of School on Academic Performance*, unpublished doctoral dissertation, University of Oregon, 1969.

Light, Richard J., and Smith, Paul V. "Accumulating Evidence: Procedures for Resolving Contradictions among Different Research Studies," *Harvard Educational Review*, 41 (November 1971), 429–471.

Lockwood, Jane Durand. *An Examination of Scholastic Achievement, Attitudes and Home Background Factors of 6th Grade Negro Students in Balanced and Unbalanced Schools*, unpublished doctoral dissertation, University of Michigan, 1966.

Long, David. *Educational Performance in Integrated and Segregated Elementary Schools*, unpublished doctoral dissertation, Yeshiva University, 1968.

Mahan, T. W. "Project Concern–1966–68: A Report on the Effectiveness of Suburban School Placement for Inner-City Youth," Hartford, Connecticut, Board of Education, August 1968.

Matzen, Stanley Paul. *The Relationship between Racial Composition and Scholastic Achievement in Elementary School Classrooms*, unpublished doctoral dissertation, Stanford University, 1965.

Mayer, Robert R., et al. *The Impact of School Desegregation in a Southern City*, Boston, Heath, 1974.

Mayeske, G., et al. *A Study of Our Nation's Schools*. Washington, D.C., U.S. Department of Health, Education and Welfare, 1972.

McCullough, James S. "Academic Achievement under School Desegregation in a Southern City," University of North Carolina, Chapel Hill Department of City and Regional Planning, January 1972. (mimeographed)

McPartland, James. *The Segregated Student in Desegregated Schools: Sources of Influence on Negro Secondary Students*, Center for the Study of Social Organization of Schools, Baltimore, Md. The Johns Hopkins University, Report No. 21, 1968.

Moorefield, Thomas. *The Bussing of Minority Group Children in a Big City School System*, unpublished doctoral dissertation, University of Chicago, 1967.

Mosteller, Frederick, and Moynihan, Daniel P. *On Equality of Educational Opportunity*, New York, Random House, 1972.

O'Reilly, Robert P., ed. *Racial and Social Class Isolation in the Schools*. New York, Praeger, 1970.

Pettigrew, Thomas F. "The Negro and Education: Problems and Proposals," in Irwin Katz and Patricia Gurin (eds.), *Race and the Social Sciences*, New York, Basic Books, 1969.

Pettigrew, Thomas F., et al. "Busing: A Review of the Evidence", *Public Interest* (Winter 1973), 88–118.

Purl, Mabel C., and Dawson, Judith A. "The Achievement of Students in Primary Grades after Seven Years of Desegregation," Riverside, Calif., Riverside Unified School District, February 1973. (mimeographed)

Rentsch, George Jacob. *Open-Enrollment: An Appraisal*, unpublished doctoral dissertation, State University of New York, Buffalo, 1967.

Robertson, William Joseph. *The Effects of Junior High School Segregation Experience on the Achievement Behavior and Academic Motivation of Integrated 10th Grade Students*, unpublished doctoral dissertation, University of Michigan, 1967.

Rochester City School District. *Final Report: A Three-Year Longitudinal Study to Assess a Fifteen-Point Plan to Reduce Racial Isolation and Provide Quality Integrated Education for Elementary Level Pupils*, September 1970.

Rock, William C., et al. "A Report on a Cooperative Program Between a City School District and a Suburban School District," Rochester, N.Y., June 28, 1968.

Sacramento City Unified School District, *Focus on Reading and Math, 1970–71: An Evaluation Report on a Program of Compensatory Education*, E.S.E.A., Title 1, July 1971.

St. John, Nancy Hoyt. "School Racial Context and the Aspirations of Ninth Graders," unpublished paper, 1973.

St. John, Nancy Hoyt, and Lewis, Ralph G. "The Influence of School Racial Context on Academic Achievement," *Social Problems* 19 (Summer 1971), 68–78.

Samuels, Ivan G. *Desegregated Education and Differences in Academic Achievement*, unpublished doctoral dissertation, Indiana University, 1958.

Samuels, Joseph Maurice. *A Comparison of Projects Representative of Compensatory: Busing; and Non-Compensatory Programs for Inner-City Students*, unpublished doctoral dissertation, University of Connecticut, 1971.

Shaker Heights School Board. *An Interim Evaluation of the Shaker Schools Plan,*

1970–71, Shaker Heights, O., February 1972. (mimeographed)

Slone, Irene Wholl. *The Effects of One School Pairing on Pupil Achievement, Anxieties and Attitudes*, unpublished doctoral dissertation, New York University, 1968.

U.S. Commission on Civil Rights. *Racial Isolation in the Public Schools*, Washington, D.C., U.S. Government Printing Office, 1967(a).

U.S. Commission on Civil Rights. *Southern School Desegregation, 1966–67*, Washington, D.C., U.S. Government Printing Office, July 1967, (b).

Walberg, Herbert J. "An Evaluation of an Urban-Suburban School Bussing Program: Student Achievement and Perception of Class Learning Environments," Draft of Report to METCO, Cambridge, Mass., July 1, 1969.

Weinberg, Meyer. *Desegregation Research: An Appraisal*, 2nd ed. Bloomington, Ind., Phi Delta Kappa, 1970.

Williams, Daniel E. *Self-Concept and Verbal Mental Ability in Negro Pre-School Children*, unpublished doctoral dissertation, St. John's University, 1968.

Wilson, Alan. "Educational Consequences of Segregation in a California Community," in U.S. Commission on Civil Rights, *Racial Isolation in the Public Schools*, Vol. II, Washington, D.C., 1967, 165–206.

Wolman, T. G. "Learning Effects of Integration in New Rochelle," *Integrated Education*, 2 (December 1964–January 1965), 30–31.

Wood, Bruce Hartley. *The Effect of Bussing vs. Non-Bussing on the Intellectual Functioning of Inner City, Disadvantaged Elementary School Children*, unpublished doctoral dissertation, University of Massachusetts, 1968.

Wrightstone, J. Wayne, McClelland, S. D., and Forleno, G., *Evaluation of the Community Zoning Program*, New York City: Bureau of Educational Research, Board of Education, 1966.

Zdep, Stanley M., and Joyce, Diane. *The Newark-Verona Plan for Sharing Educational Opportunity*, Educational Testing Service, Princeton, N.J., September 1, 1969. (mimeographed)

4.5
Children in Harlem's Community Controlled Schools

MARCIA GUTTENTAG

COMMUNITY CONTROL OF SCHOOLS IN NEW YORK CITY

... Education is a route to social mobility. Parents in the inner city want their children to succeed in school. They distrust the central school administration, usually made up of people different from them in social class and ethnic background. They want a say in the schools. Yet, they are confronted by school professionals who make all the decisions. Community control of schools in New York City is an example of an experiment in which parents and local community people did, for a brief time, acquire power over the conduct of their public schools.

It was accompanied by conflict of many kinds, the most pronounced between the professional-educational bureaucracy and the community boards and parents of three poor areas in New York City. From the viewpoint of newspapers and public, community control was only a political struggle. Was there more to it than the disordered surface of events?

The IS-201 board asked some basic questions about the effects of community control on schools and children. Were community controlled schools different from other schools? How were children affected by experiences in these schools? Did the schools create a sense of community, in contrast to the anomie of other New York city schools?

Parents said the purpose of community control was to change the schools and, in doing so, to benefit the children. Their long-term aim was improvement of the quality of education.

Effects on children are of interest from several points of view. In New York City the size of minority populations is so great that integrated schools are unlikely under any plan. One must ask whether there are alternative forms of school organization which have beneficial effects on children. Is community control one of these?

One objective of the study was to understand how the schools functioned at several different levels. To do so required measurement of general school characteristics and specific features of subsystems, such as parent involvement, teacher-pupil interactions, and children's expectancies and achievements.

Background

In the late 1960s, three groups of schools in New York City were designated "com-

Abridged from M. Guttentag. Children in Harlem's community controlled schools. *Journal of Social Issues*, 1972, *28* (4), 1–20. Reprinted by permission.

Table 1. Ethnic Composition of Schools and School
Boards

Percentage Nonwhite	6 Urban School Districts	Demonstration Districts
Pupil Population	57	56
School Board Members	23	61

Note. Data for these comparisons are from Gittell et al.
(1971).

munity controlled": Ocean Hill-Brownsville, Intermediate School 201, and Two Bridges. In contrast to the typical New York City school district with 30,000 children, each of these districts had between four and eight thousand children. Local elections for school board membership were held for the first time since 1900. Each district elected a local community school board. Throughout the country, demonstration school districts have community boards which are more representative of the ethnic populations in their schools than are typical urban school boards (see Table 1).

The IS-201 board was representative of the community. Its 21 elected members included parents, teachers, community representatives, and one school administrator. Membership on the board roughly reflected the educational and social class make-up of the community.

The elected local board gained some direct control over fiscal, personnel, and curricular matters. A grant from the Ford Foundation gave each district a small measure of independence from the New York City Board of Education. The IS-201 district additionally received funds from Rockefeller, Carnegie, New York, Field, and Episcopal foundations along with support from the Michael Schwerner Fund, Warner Fund, Columbia University Urban Center, U.S. Office of Education, and State and City educational authorities.

In the IS-201 district in Harlem, community organizations and parent groups had become heatedly involved in the local schools when a new junior high school was built several years before. Over parent protests, the school was placed where it could not become an integrated school. After this occurred, community groups demanded autonomy for their schools, and the IS-201 schools became one of the three experimental community controlled districts.

Seven studies were conducted in these schools for the IS-201 governing board. Among the studies were: organizational climate in the schools; parent use of school buildings; administrator's use of time; health and other innovative programs in the schools; teacher-pupil interaction in classrooms, and pre-school and grammar school children's expectancies. A neighboring school district in Harlem with pupils of similar SES and ethnic background was used for comparison.

Organizational Climate in the Schools[1]

The organizational climate study used Stern's (1963) Organizational Climate Index,

Table 2. Ethnic Backgrounds of Lay Board
Members, Pupils, and Community in IS-201
District (Percentages)

Source	Black	Puerto Rican	Other
Pupils	83	16	1
Board Members	73	20	7
Community	92	7	1

1. This study was conducted by C. Steinhoff and
M. Roberts.

a measure of the environmental press as experienced by individuals in an organization. Stern's (1963) Activities Index, an individual self-descriptive measure, also was used. The two instruments share a common taxonomy and supplement one another as reciprocal measures of the individual's characteristics and his perception of his environment. Only three of the five elementary schools in IS-201 yielded enough returns to be represented.

Compared with a sample of New York City elementary schools for which normative data were available, two of the IS-201 schools in the district provided a significantly stronger expressive climate and one which was stronger in development press. The third school was average compared with the reference population. Sub-scales showed IS-201 schools provided a climate characterized by intellectual activity, social action, individual responsibility, and open-mindedness. Faculty members in these schools described themselves as having personal needs of intellectual aspiration and competitiveness. They perceived the climate of the schools to be supportive of their personal needs.

The self descriptions of IS-201 teachers compared with other New York City teachers also are of interest. IS-201 teachers saw themselves as significantly higher in acceptance of criticism and in purposefulness. They believed they were more organized and self-reliant.

These findings are surprising because the comparison sample was biased in the direction of middle-class schools. Nevertheless, it was the IS-201 schools, with a lower-class population, which showed the stronger expressive climate and placed greater stress on intellectual matters, on achievement standards, and on personal dignity. In Stern's terms, the IS-201 schools had a press for achievement, change, tolerance, objectivity, and sensuality. This translates into a juicier, more vivid environment, one with more sights and sounds, one less repressively controlled.

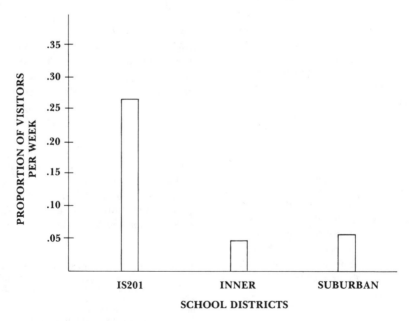

Fig. 1. School Visitors per Week Relative to Enrollment (Based on Rothenberg's Study).

Parent Involvement in IS-201 Schools[2]

In their fight to obtain community control, one of the strongest arguments marshalled by community groups was that inner-city schools tend to be closed to parents. Community groups wanted an open atmosphere where parents would be able to communicate directly with school staff through the district level. It was hoped that this would create greater involvement in school affairs on the part of parents. It would also permit community residents to rely on their own observations about what happened in the schools. School board members then could be held directly accountable.

This study investigated the use of school buildings by visitors. Observations were made on randomly selected days in community controlled and comparison districts. The survey included the name of each person who entered the school, his purpose, the identity of persons seen, the length of stay, and whether the person had a child attending the school.

Observations also were made for after-school-hours use as well as in the evening, when types of activity and numbers of people involved were recorded. To supplement the survey data, the calendars of administrators were examined for the names of groups and individuals they had seen.

Two comparison school districts were used: the neighboring school district in Harlem and a suburban school district with the same number of schools.

The number of visitors for randomly selected days was totalled and divided by school enrollment to make possible a comparison of proportions. In the IS-201 district there was one visitor for every four pupils; in the two comparison districts, one visitor for every 20 pupils. The relative number of visitors to the community controlled schools was overwhelmingly greater than either comparison district.

2. The parent involvement study was done by Marilyn Rothenberg.

Table 3. Percentage of Visitors by Purpose and School Category

| Purpose | School Category | | |
	IS-201	Urban Controls	Suburban Controls
Parent/Child	49	7	52
Parent/Re: Child	10	36	9
Organizational/Parent	10	7	20
Health	2	0	2
Professional	16	14	9
Other	13	36	8

Note. Data are from parent involvement study conducted by M. Rothenberg.

Table 3 shows the percentages of visitors classified by stated purpose. The first three categories are of greatest interest.

The category, *Parent/Child*, includes visits by parents primarily to deliver a child, to take a child from school, or to bring something to him. It provides an indication of the ease with which parents entered the schools in IS-201. About half of all visitors were parents who entered the building when walking their children to or from school. This contrasts with 7 percent for the urban control schools. This activity was encouraged at IS-201. Parents often brought their children to the classroom and remained for a while. At pickup time parents arrived early and spent time observing or helping. People in this category averaged a stay of more than ten minutes.

Parent/Re: Child includes only those parent visits to discuss a child, usually his misbehavior, with a teacher or principal. These were not casual visits; they were requested by school personnel. In IS-201, few parents came to discuss the behavior of their child.*

*Editors' note. This statement is misleading. The author notes that one person per four pupils visited IS-201 schools and one person per 20 pupils visited schools in the neighboring district. The author also notes that 10% of the visits to IS-201 schools and 36% of the visits to neighboring schools were made by parents to discuss their children's behavior. Accordingly, only one person per 40 pupils visited

Organizational/Parent includes parents' visits for group activities, such as observing a class unit, PTA meeting, or parent education. Some visitors in this category said they were there to help in the reading course, or with multi-media. Still others said they were there "to look in on the children" or "to visit a class."

In the (urban) comparison schools, the most frequent category was that of parents entering the school to discuss a child's misbehavior. In the suburban school district the breakdown of visitors by purpose was not unlike that of IS-201.

Were parents who came to the IS-201 schools representative of the low SES families in the neighborhood or were they just the better educated ones? Parents were asked to write a brief phrase about why they had come to the school. Linguistic analysis of these showed that they were representative.

School administrators in IS-201 and the comparison district had diverse attitudes toward this study. In IS-201, they were concerned only that the study might hinder parents' access to the buildings or deflect them even briefly from their purpose in coming to the schools. In contrast, an administrator of the comparison schools agreed to the survey with the comment that she didn't know how profitable the study would be because when parents come to the school "they are liable to be too angry" to sign the survey—implying that they came only when summoned.

Community Use of Schools

All schools in the IS-201 complex had active afternoon, evening, and weekend centers open to the community, all with a large range of activities. Activities were diverse and encouraged participation by people of

IS-201 schools and only one person per 55.5 pupils visited neighboring schools to discuss a child's behavior. In other words, relatively few parents in either school district came to school to discuss their children's behavior.

all ages and interests. The school buildings were vital community centers. The study of administrator's calendars showed a great many community organizational contacts and much time spent with parents and students.

In contrast to the comparison district, school staff devoted a considerable time to telling the community what was going on in the schools. Flyers were sent to homes on a variety of topics. Adults in the community felt free to enter the schools and took advantage of this opportunity. Many assumed responsibility for part of an educational program. The amount of face-to-face contact between parents and staff was much greater than in the comparison schools. Parents and teachers worked together with fewer status differences.

One can infer that parents perceived the schools to be less anonymous and alienating than schools in the comparison district. Parents of low SES, with limited education, usually are hesitant to enter the schools and rarely participate in school activities. IS-201 differed sharply from this pattern.

Innovative Programs

Big city school systems suffer from a lack of flexibility and a limited number of innovative programs, though cities are most in need of them. Proponents of community control believed that it would permit innovative educational programs which would be related to local needs. In the absence of a centralized bureaucracy, many more such programs were expected.

This proved to be the case (see Gittell, 1971). We studied several in the IS-201 district. I will briefly mention two and discuss the health program more fully.

Programs initiated in each demonstration district ranged from brief to long-term. For example, IS-201 had a "teach-out," to demonstrate the school curriculum to the community. On a spring day, classes were held outside on the school mall and in the street. A great many people observed these lessons.

A variety of programs in reading and math were initiated in schools in the district. One school, which used the Gattegno reading method, showed a dramatic increase in reading achievement.

Of the number of these programs we assessed, the health program can serve as an illustration.[3] In a suburban area where general health is good and children see private physicians frequently, a health program in the schools would arouse little comment. In Harlem, however, health services in the schools are inadequate or nonexistent. Despite unusually high rates of tuberculosis, sickle cell anemia, and vision and hearing problems, few children ever receive examinations. The IS-201 district initiated a system of diagnostic examinations and established relationships with nearby hospitals, medical schools, and colleges. For the present study, a one-fifth sample of the school population was selected. Of the children sampled, 87% had received visual screening tests and 97% auditory tests at the time of the study. Serious visual or hearing problems were found in 10%. Diagnostic examinations revealed that there were physical problems at a rate of 54 per 100 children. At the time of our study 41% of these problems had been treated. Most children had received immunizations for the first time. Free eyeglasses were provided.

Findings were similar on all the innovative programs studied. There were many more of them, and those we studied were highly effective.

Teacher-Pupil Classroom Interaction

Were the classrooms of IS-201 different? We conducted a study of teacher-pupil interactions in the community controlled school and the comparison district.[4] Interaction

3. This study was carried out by Liebman.
4. The study of teacher-pupil classroom interaction was conducted by Wiser and Fanin.

analysis, using the Flanders-Dunbar technique (Flanders, 1960), was the observation system used in the classrooms in each school. This technique codes both teacher and pupil talk and the contingency relationships between them. Black and white, male and female teachers were sampled.

In IS-201, student-initiated talk was more often directly followed either by teacher praise or teacher acceptance of the student's ideas, a highly significant finding. Furthermore, although teacher's race was significantly related to verbal behavior in the comparison schools, this was not true of the community controlled schools.

These findings suggest that a social climate had been created in the community controlled schools which was more powerful than the individual characteristics of teachers, for in the comparison district race predicted interaction patterns. Children in the community controlled classrooms were exposed to a distinctive academic and social experience, one which was more strongly positive than that in comparison schools.

Each of the previously mentioned studies of the IS-201 district schools indicated that these schools were markedly different from those of the neighboring district. Teachers and administrators perceived them to have a stronger, freer intellectual atmosphere and a more growth-inducing climate. Parents were actively involved in school programs and had free access to the schools. The schools themselves had more varied and successful innovative programs. Teacher's responses to pupils were more positive.

Clark and Clark Replication

Given the school characteristics reported above, what were the effects on children?

A flurry of studies in recent years have replicated the Clark and Clark doll preference and identification studies (1947). Nearly all have found that black preschool children, at least those who live in cities, now prefer black dolls and accurately identify them. In fact one recent study (Fox &

Barnes, 1972) has shown that Chinese children are much more likely to choose white dolls and to make derogatory statements about same-race dolls than are black children.

Therefore it is not surprising that when we replicated the Clark and Clark study with preschool children, no differences in racial identification were found between the IS-201 preschool children and those in the comparison district. But on racial preference, the IS-201 preschool girls showed a stronger preference for their own race dolls than did the controls. The same was true for boys, though it was not as pronounced as it was for girls.

All children in Harlem are exposed to a strong emphasis on black pride; most have black dolls. One would not expect to find differences between preschool children in the IS-201 and comparison district. That such differences were found suggests that the special social climate of these schools had penetrated even to the preschool level, where girls, as usual, showed the greatest responsiveness to social inputs.

Achievement

We turn now to changes in the achievements and expectancies of older children in the grammar and junior high schools of IS-201. Achievement often is treated as the only important output of schools. Although higher achievement certainly was one of the aims of the community board, it was by no means the only one. As well as improved achievement, the board also wanted schools that were open to parents, and a change in classroom and school atmosphere.

Achievement results must be pieced together from two sources, neither of which provides adequate information. The first is the standard achievement testing given throughout New York City. It does not provide valid data. All the community controlled districts were hostile toward the standardized achievement tests sent from the City Bureau of Educational Research. Many teachers did not administer them. Others gave them carelessly or idiosyncratically.

A second source is a study of achievement in IS-201 conducted by the Psychological Corporation in the spring of 1971. In this study, teachers gave special achievement measures to preschool, kindergarten, and first grade children. New York City group tests were used for higher grades. To provide a comparison population, children who had been in the complex for three successive years were compared with those who had been in the complex for only two years. This analysis aimed to reveal the effect of different amounts of educational experience in the IS-201 schools.

Generally, the gap between national norms and the norms of New York City schools increases by grade. In 1968–69 one-fourth of all children in elementary schools were two or more years behind in reading, an increase from the previous year's figure of one-fifth of all children. In the IS-201 schools, however, first and second graders reached national norms in both reading and arithmetic. In one school of the complex the mean in reading surpassed the national norm by two months. While New York City's reading achievement norms declined in 1968–69, reading achievement levels at IS-201 did not decline. Moreover, some individuals schools in IS-201 showed considerable advances. A school which had a special reading program showed a rise in reading level for the entire school. Second and third grade children were reading at nearly a full year above the national norm. Between 1969 and 1971, the means for successive pupil groups at the same grade levels in the IS-201 district increased from second to sixth grade level.

To evaluate the effect of community control on achievement, the most useful information is the comparison of the achievement scores of children in the district for three years with those in the district for a shorter period. The three-year children had means significantly higher than the average child in their grade.

To summarize, despite the scattered and

fragmented nature of the achievement data, achievement in the community controlled schools apparently improved over the three-year period of their existence. One school in the district was significantly above national norms for reading. Children who had been in the district for three years showed significantly higher reading and math scores than did other children. Moreover, IS-201 did not share in the general decline in New York City achievement scores. The picture was best for young children in kindergarten and first grade; for children from second to sixth grade it was somewhat better than the comparison schools. Seventh and eighth-grade children did not show similar gains.

Expectancies

"Expectancies" are what children think will happen to them—in school, with adults, in the political arena, and in the future. The cluster of expectancies called "locus of control" accounts for much of the variance in the academic achievement of poor and minority children. Locus of the control refers to the child's belief that chance, luck, and other external factors as opposed to his own actions, intentions, and other internal factors determine what happens to him.

The research literature indicates that changes in expectancies are associated with changes in academic achievement. The Coleman report (1966) suggested that expectancies are more internal for children who attend integrated schools. Other studies show that expectancies can become more internal after children experience control over what happens to them. Undoubtedly there are many situations which can affect expectancies.

Expectancies of poor and minority children are more complex and differentiated than those of middle-class children. They also are more responsive to environmental changes.

Do community controlled schools affect children's expectancies? Community control provided parents with greater power and participation in the schools. Children in the IS-201 schools had the opportunity to see their parents in autonomous roles. It seemed reasonable that children's own beliefs about their likelihood of success in the schools should be altered by these experiences. If this were so, then long term changes in academic achievement were possible even if no immediate effects were apparent.

When this study began, no expectancy questionnaires had been standardized on a large population of poor, urban, and minority children. Therefore several instrumentation studies were done with large samples of such grade school, poor, urban, and minority children, in which all relevant children's expectancy scales were used. In each of these studies, it was found that expectancy scores made an appreciable contribution to achievement variance.

Children in the community controlled and comparison districts received expectancy questionnaires in 1970 and 1971. These questionnaires contained items distilled from previous studies and a number of others written together with the IS-201 board.

No differences were found between the districts for total expectancy scores, but there were many significant subscale and item differences. For example, on a subscale of expectancies of personal effectiveness, means for the IS-201 children were all significantly higher.

Were children more aware of the active and influential roles of parents and teachers? If they were, then IS-201 children should have made more external choices on items relating to school and parents and should not have differed from the controls on non-school-related questions. Table 4 shows some illustrative data on this question. Each tally for the two districts represents a significant Chi-square for treatment effects for a single item.

Every one of 13 significant Chi-squares for school-related items is in the external direction for IS-201 pupils and in the internal direction for controls. On non-school-related

Table 4. Differences in Locus of Control Between IS-201 and Comparison Schools

	School-Related Items	
	External response	Internal response
IS-201	13	0
Comparison Schools	0	13
	Non-School-Related Items	
	External response	Internal response
IS-201	12	11
Comparison Schools	11	12

Note. Frequencies represent the number of items having significant Chi-squares in the labeled direction.

items, there is no systematic difference for internality–externality. Clearly, IS-201 pupils responded vigorously to the changed school environment, especially to the influence of parents and teachers on school performance.

One can get a better idea of the meaning of this finding from the content of some items. On one, IS-201 pupils attribute a child's learning something quickly in school to the teacher's clear explanation. On another, they attribute difficulty in working arithmetic problems to the teacher's having given problems that were too hard.

There are some straightforward implications to be drawn from the expectancy findings and some questions left open by them. The clarity of results leaves no doubt that the changed school environment was directly perceived and responded to by children in IS-201 schools. School related items sharply differentiated IS-201 from comparison children. Whenever IS-201 children made causal attributions which required a choice between teachers or parents and themselves, they overwhelmingly placed the locus of cause in adults. Teachers and parents were a more salient feature of the school environment to these children.

In previous studies, chidlren's external expectancies about success in school generally are associated with low achievement; internal expectancies are related to higher academic achievement, at least for middle-class children. If poor children's expectancies mirror reality, they must believe that external circumstances make a difference in whether they succeed in school. The data just reported show a new combination: a shift toward more external expectancies about who has power in the schools (parents and teachers) combined with higher academic achievement. In IS-201 schools, the children's perception of teachers' and parents' responsibility for the schools was correlated with higher academic achievement. Externality of school expectancies for lower-class children has different meanings in different contexts. When the child believes the school is alien, that adults are remote or hostile, and that what he does will not influence what happens to him, his external expectancies are linked to lower academic achievement. When, however, he perceives the school to be accepting of him, and his parents support the school and have some power in it, his realistic appreciation of this changed school environment is reflected in external expectancies and higher achievement.

IS-201 children thus attribute the success or failure of their school performance to parents, teachers, and the school rather than to their own characteristics. This is especially revealed in answers to expectancy questions on blame for failure. IS-201 children, much more often than controls, place blame for a specific failure on parents, teachers, or the school; the IS-201 children were not self-blaming. Similarly, they more often gave credit to teachers for their own good performance than did comparison children.

CONCLUSION

No one of the studies just reported can stand by itself. Taken together they show that a major social change with far-reaching effects had taken place in the community-controlled schools. This change created a radically different school structure. Despite many problems, the IS-201 schools were doing what the community school board wanted them to do. They were more innovative; the school climate was more intellectual and stimulating; teacher pupil interaction, more positive. Parents made their presence known in the schools; they were frequently in the schools for a variety of constructive purposes. Children showed somewhat higher academic achievement. The school children were acutely aware of the power and salience of parents and teachers in their schools. An outsider had the impression of one cohesive group from school board members to pupils, all committed to and enthusiastic about the IS-201 schools.

IS-201 no longer exists. It was swallowed up into a larger school district following a change in New York State law. This law created a weakened form of school decentralization throughout New York City. The law permitted elected boards, but these were stripped of the fiscal, personnel, and curricular power which the experimental community controlled districts had assumed. District size was considerably larger.

The state legislature passed the weak decentralization law as a way of ridding New York City of the troublesome experimental districts, and, at the same time, placating critics of centralization. In the process of incorporation into the larger district, all of IS-201's special programs were dismantled. Ironically, the district into which IS-201 was absorbed had served as the comparison school district in the studies just reported.

In New York City, as in other parts of the country, decisions about community control are settled solely in the political sphere. The decision to abolish the experimental districts was made in the absence of data on the effects of this experiment on schools and children. It was made in complete awareness of the intense conflict which had erupted between organizational professionals and inner-city residents. It was clear to the law-

makers that community control experiments attempted to shift the power of educational policy decisions to new groups.

The political future of community control is an uncertain one. There are at least two possible future outcomes, and undoubtedly more. One likely outcome is that within the next ten years teachers, school administrators, and central school board members will be much more representative of the population of children in the schools. This trend is accelerating in most urban centers. When ethnic minorities see board members, teachers, and administrators from their own groups, the demands for community control of schools in cities may decline. From this point of view, demands for community control represent a transitional phase in the ethnic make-up of public organizations in cities.

The second—and I think a more likely—outcome is that even when ethnic homogeneity exists, experiments in community control will continue. Pressure for community control today is found in ethnically homogeneous school systems. This continued pressure is to be expected, since differences in social class between the poor and professionals in charge of the schools are likely to remain. The problem of the gap between centralized decision-making and the attitudes and desires of the consumers of education will continue, as will the issue of the sheer size of educational and other public organizations in cities.

Therefore it is worth asking why the experiment in community control just reported was successful. There were, I think, two reasons. The first was the small size of the community controlled district. In Harlem most informal social organization is linked to the block in which a person lives. People do not drive, they walk or take the subway to their destinations. Thus in Harlem a small school district in which the schools are within walking distance maximizes the likelihood of face-to-face contact between parents and school personnel, as was apparent in IS-201.

Undoubtedly the optimal size of a public organization varies according to a number of technological, physical, and social characteristics of the population it serves. The purpose of the agency, whom it serves, where it is located, and the social organization of the community are a few of the many factors which should be balanced in the identification of optimal size. At present this is not done; most ecological considerations are ignored. Decisions about size are currently made on political and intra-organizational grounds, not on the basis of optimal psychological size. More data are needed on the critical variables and weights which should enter into size decisions; thus a variety of natural experiments must be studied. ·

The second reason for the success of IS-201 was the powerful and shared ideological commitment of people in the district. It originated with the history of the district when community organizations banded together to fight a common enemy—the central school board—in the dispute over the placement of the "integrated" school. The community's commitment was maximized during the life of the district by the successful policy of active parent participation and involvement in the schools. Such shared ideological commitments had pervasive effects throughout the school organization.

Yet one cannot discover such an ideology without looking for it. Let me illustrate. The ghost of reductionism lingers on in research with children. Research continues to be conducted as though children were isolated from the larger social system, as though they were immune to the ideology and rules which govern the whole social context. Generally only the immediate environment of the classroom is studied. Explanations of children's attitudes and behaviors extend only to the face-to-face level of interactions. Yet it is the social and ideological system within which these interactions are imbedded which provides the truest and most general explanation for the observed interactions.

Ideology counts even with children. They

do respond to a major change in the distribution of power in a school district. If in the study of IS-201 only teacher-pupil interactions had been studied, or only achievement scores reported, little would be known about community control of schools in Harlem. Such single results ignore the "why" of it all.

Philosophers of human action, the symbolic interactionists, Goffman, Garfinkel, and many others, stress how important both the social context and the implicit rules which govern behavior are in understanding the meaning and thus the explanation of individual behavior. These ideas apply with equal force to the understanding of social systems of every size. The growth of a vigorous ideology in IS-201 was also undoubtedly helped by the small size of the district.

The study of just one natural experiment in community control has been reported. This experiment happened to have been successful. Undoubtedly, many unsanctioned social experiments are failures. Nevertheless, these fleeting, unsanctioned experiments in participation must be studied. They can provide some partial answers to the problems of urban organizations—size, complexity, centralization, and accountability. Decisions about organizational changes in the future should be made on the basis of more than elitist or egalitarian biases. In the absence of data, elitist views win.

REFERENCES

Clark, K., & Clark, M. P. Racial identification and preference in Negro children. In T. M. Newcomb & E. L. Hartley (Eds.), *Readings in social psychology*. New York: Holt, 1947.

Coleman, J. S., et al. *Equality of educational opportunity*. Washington, D.C.: U.S. Government Printing Office, 1966.

Flanders, N. A. *Teacher influence, pupil attitudes, and achievement*. Minneapolis: University of Minnesota, 1960. (Mimeo)

Fox, D. J., & Barnes, V. B. Racial preference and identification of black, American Chinese, and white children. Unpublished manuscript, CUNY, 1972.

Gittell, M., et al. *Demonstration for social change: An experiment in local control.* New York: Institute for Community Studies, Queens College, CUNY, 1971.

Stern, G. G. Measuring noncognitive variables in research on teaching. In N. L. Gage (Ed.), *Handbook of research on teaching.* Chicago: Rand McNally, 1963.

5

DRUG USE

Introduction

The use and presumed effects of drugs have aroused a great deal of concern in American cities, suburbs, and towns. In an attempt to determine the extent to which this concern is warranted, we will examine briefly the research findings on the extent of drug use and some effects of drugs on the individual and on society. For those drugs that warrant serious concern, we will also try to determine why some people become intensive or compulsive users and how effective different strategies designed to reduce the individual and social costs of drug use appear to be.

EXTENT AND EFFECTS OF DRUG USE

Research findings suggest that a substantial proportion of adults use alcohol. A national probability sample survey (Cahalan, Cisin, & Crossley, 1969) indicates that 28% of the people sampled (21 years and over) reported drinking at least once a month and usually having one or two drinks at each sitting, 13% said they normally drink several times a month and usually have three or four drinks each time, and 12% said they drink at least once a week and have at least five drinks on each occasion. The data also indicate that most of the heavy drinkers were men aged 21 to 59; that is, approximately 25% of these men reportedly drink at least once a week and have at least five drinks at each sitting. Similar findings were reported by the National Commission on Marihuana and Drug Abuse (1973). The results of a national survey indicate that 53% of the sample (18 years and over) reported having an alcoholic beverage during the week preceding the survey, and that approximately 25% said they consumed at least seven drinks during this period. The data also indicate that 56% have used one or more propietary or ethical tranquilizers, sedatives, or stimulants.

289

Illicit or illegal drugs were reportedly used considerably less often by the respondents in the National Commission on Marihuana and Drug Abuse survey. However, it seems likely that the percentages do not reflect the actual use of these drugs because of the Commission's understandable failure to include "street" users in its survey and because a number of people who used illegal drugs may have chosen not to say so. Sixteen percent of the sample (18 years and over) said they tried marihuana, and 8% said they were currently using it. Among those aged 18 to 25, about 47% said they had used marihuana at least once. Approximately 5% of the sample said they tried LSD or a similar hallucinogen at least once, 3% said they tried cocaine, and 1.3% reportedly tried heroine.

The National Commission on Marihuana and Drug Abuse (1973) also looked at a sizable number of surveys of student drug use and concluded that the large majority of high school and college students has never used, and does not intend to use, drugs other than tobacco, alcohol, and marihuana. Among students who try psychoactive drugs, many discontinue use after satisfying their curiosity in a few experimental trials. Among those who continue to use psychoactive drugs, relatively few go from occasional social and recreational use to more frequent and intensive use.

The research findings on the impact of drugs on the individual and on society indicate that "the most serious concern in contemporary America should attach to the use of alcohol and heroin. Moderate social concern should attach to the use of amphetamines, barbiturates, hallucinogens, methaqualone and cocaine . . . The use of marihuana and the so-called minor tranquilizers appears to require relatively minimum social concern at the present time" (National Commission on Marihuana and Drug Abuse, 1973, p. 36). Let us look at some of the findings that led to this conclusion.

Alcohol, when used intensively or compulsively, has an assortment of deleterious effects on the individual and on society. For example, the findings indicate that there is a relationship between alcoholism and cirrhosis of the liver, heart disease, and suicide (Wallgren & Barry, 1970); studies of the blood/alcohol concentration of fatally injured drivers suggest that chronic drinking is an important determinant of fatal automobile accidents (e.g., Arthur D. Little, Inc., 1966); there is a sizable relationship between alcohol use and violent crime (Molof, 1967; Shupe, 1964; Voss & Hepburn, 1968); and the treatment of alcoholics costs the federal and state governments several hundred million dollars a year (National Commission on Marihuana and Drug Abuse, 1973). However, alcohol also has recognized and accepted functions; for example, it induces feelings of warmth and relaxation, it is used in religious ceremonies, and it provides a sizable number of jobs and considerable revenue from taxes. The existence of both positive and negative uses and effects has made it difficult to devise ways of dealing effectively with the problems caused by alcohol use.

Studies of heroin addiction suggest that the property crimes committed by addicts to purchase heroin cost the victims approximately two billion dollars a year (Holahan, 1972). The data also indicate that heroin addicts, in an attempt to obtain the money they need to purchase heroin, tend to commit more serious crimes and to be arrested more often after becoming dependent on heroin (Blum, 1967; Friedman & Friedman, 1973; Jacoby, Weiner, & Wolfgang, 1973); that most heroin addicts continue to be arrested after their release from prisons, hospitals, or treatment programs (Cuskey, Ipsen, & Premkumar, 1973; Friedman & Friedman, 1973; Tinklenberg, 1973; Winick, 1967); and that the costs of arresting, trying, incarcerating, and treating the heroin-dependent offender are considerable (National Commission on Marihuana and Drug Abuse, 1973).

Studies of marihuana use in this country suggest that its use is generally experimental or intermittent and is confined largely to the less potent forms of the drug. Under these conditions, there is little or no psychological dependence and no evidence of physical dependence or organ injury. However, when the most potent preparations of marihuana are used intensively for a long period of time, the data suggest that there are adverse physical and psychological effects (National Commission on Marihuana and Drug Abuse, 1972). Surveys of drug use also suggest that the use of marihuana does not lead to the use of other drugs. The results of these surveys indicate that while almost all people who use barbiturates, amphetamines, hallucinogens, and/or the opiates have also used marihuana, tobacco, and alcohol, most marihuana users do not become multi-drug users or users of more dangerous drugs (National Commission on Marihuana and Drug Abuse, 1973). Data on the impact of marihuana on crime contain no evidence that marihuana use, by itself, causes people to commit crimes (National Commission on Marihuana and Drug Abuse, 1972). Accordingly, it seems plausible to argue that serious public concern about marihuana use, as well as harsh legal penalties for possession of marihuana, are unwarranted. Rather, the individual and social costs of drug use indicate that public concern should be accorded primarily to problem drinking and heroin addiction. In an attempt to give useful direction to that concern, we will examine research that has tried to find out why some people become problem drinkers or heroin addicts and studies of different strategies designed to reduce the individual and social costs of problem drinking and heroin addiction.

PROBLEM DRINKING

Cultural forces are an important determinant of alcohol use; however, there is considerable variation in problem drinking *within* different cultural and subcultural groups. In an attempt to account for this variation, a number of psychological theories have been constructed. Some of these theories—such as constitutional theories and psychoanalytic theories—argue that individual characteristics are responsible for problem drinking. Other theories—such as problem behavior theory—propose that problem drinking results from the interaction of individual and sociocultural variables. While both approaches are instructive, the research findings suggest that the interactive approach is considerably more useful. Accordingly, we will take a cursory look at constitutional and psychoanalytic theories and a more detailed look at problem behavior theory.

Constitutional Theories

Constitutional theories argue that biochemical factors are the major determinant of problem drinking. Several types of studies have been designed to test this hypothesis: comparisons of identical and fraternal male twins (e.g., Kaij, 1960; Partanen, Bruun, & Markkanen, 1966), studies of the half-siblings of alcoholics (e.g., Schuckit, 1972), studies of different strains of rats and mice (e.g., Erikkson, 1970; Thomas, 1969), and studies of the relationship between endocrine or metabolic dysfunction and alcoholism (e.g., Kissin & Hankoff, 1959; R. Williams, 1959). While the results of these studies suggest that constitutional factors may be one determinant of problem drinking, the data can be interpreted in a number of other ways. For example, we don't know if an endocrine dysfunction caused the individual to drink heavily or if heavy drinking led to an endocrine dysfunction. Similarly, the results of half-sibling research may mean that hereditary factors increase the probability of becoming addicted to alcohol, or that problem drinking is a symptom of a genetically influenced psychological disorder. Accordingly, more definitive research is needed before conclusions about the influence of constitutional factors can be drawn.

Psychoanalytic Theories

Psychoanalytic theory has characteristically regarded alcoholism as a symptom of oral passivity and regression. For example, Fenichel (1945) argued that problem drinkers use the effects of alcohol "to satisfy the archaic oral longing which is a sexual longing, a need for security, and a need for the maintenance of self-esteem" (p. 376). While a small number of correlational studies (e.g., Bertrand & Masling, 1969; Wolowitz & Barker, 1968) provide some support for the oral passivity hypothesis, the results of a longitudinal study indicate that boys who displayed oral tendencies—such as thumbsucking in childhood and playing with their mouths—were not more likely to become alcoholics than boys who did not display oral tendencies (McCord, McCord, & Gudeman, 1960). Unfortunately, the characteristic difficulty of operationalizing psychoanalytic concepts and establishing causal links makes it hazardous to draw conclusions from the findings.

Problem Behavior Theory

Problem behavior theory proposes that problem drinking is part of a class of functionally related problem behaviors (Jessor & Jessor, 1973, reading 5.1). Such behaviors are "purposive or goal-oriented, the outcome of social learning processes which endow [them] with personal, functional significance" (Jessor & Jessor, 1973, p. 4). In an attempt to explain problem drinking, Jessor and his co-workers (Jessor, Carman, & Grossman, 1968; Jessor, Collins, & Jessor, 1972; Jessor, Graves, Hanson, & Jessor, 1968; Jessor, Young, Young, & Tesi, 1970) constructed a theoretical network of personality, perceived environmental, and behavioral variables. Personality is regarded as a system comprised of three sets of variables: motivational instigators, beliefs, and personal controls. The perceived environment includes compatibility with parents and peers, influence of parents and peers, social support for drug use, and peer and parental support for drinking. The behavioral variables consist of problem drinking behaviors, other problem behaviors, and nonproblem behaviors (see Figure 1 in Jessor & Jessor, 1973, reading 5.1).

In a preliminary attempt to determine the validity of the theory, Jessor and Jessor administered a 50-page questionnaire to 949 junior- and senior-high school students. During each of the next two years, Jessor and Jessor readministered the questionnaire to the members of the sample who had not yet graduated. At the end of the third year, 605 students remained in the sample. These students were classified into four groups: abstainers, minimal drinkers, no-problem drinkers, and problem drinkers.

Jessor and Jessor analyzed the data in two ways. One, they compared the third-year responses of no-problem drinkers and problem drinkers in an attempt to identify the correlates of problem drinking. Two, in an attempt to identify some of the causes of problem drinking, they compared the responses made during the second year by two groups of students who were no-problem drinkers in year two: the first group remained no-problem drinkers in year three while the second group *became* problem drinkers in year three. Jessor and Jessor also compared the residual gain scores between the second and third years that were made by these groups in an attempt to determine the amount and direction of change on the personality, environmental, and behavioral variables from the second year to the third.

The results of the analyses designed to identify the correlates of problem drinking indicate that problem drinkers and no-problem drinkers differed on some of the variables in each of the major portions of the theory.[1] Among the personality variables, problem drinkers had lower expectations for their own achievement, valued achievement less, placed a comparatively greater value on indepen-

---

1. Since studies of alcohol use (e.g., Cahalan, Cisin, & Crossley, 1969) indicate that problem drinkers are predominantly male, we will present results for the males only.

dence than on achievement, and were more tolerant of deviance. Among the perceived environment variables, problem drinkers said they received more peer support for drinking and more social support for drug use than did no-problem drinkers. Among the behavioral variables, problem drinkers reportedly engaged in more deviant behavior, used marihuana more often, had more sexual encounters, and had lower grade-point averages.

The results of the longitudinal analyses—the comparison of no-problem drinkers in year two who remained no-problem drinkers in year three with no-problem drinkers in year two who became problem drinkers in year three—provided additional support for the usefulness of the theory. As a result, Jessor and Jessor concluded that "problem drinking in youth . . . seems to emerge from a combination of influences: greater motivational instigation to problem behavior, less personal controls, and a social context of peer involvement and peer support for drinking" (p. 22).

The results of several investigations provide support for this conclusion. In a study of alcohol use among 1,300 adolescents living in a small, semi-industrial city, Wechsler and Thum (1973) found that heavy drinkers, compared to light drinkers and nondrinkers, were more likely to have several friends who drank, to feel that almost all their peers drank, and to engage in problem behaviors such as shoplifting, property damage, and illicit drug use. Heavy drinkers were also less likely to feel very close to their families. In a national survey of 1,561 men, Cahalan and Room (1972) found that problem drinking was associated with impulsivity, tolerance of irresponsible behavior, drinking by relatives and friends, and positive attitudes toward drinking. In a small sample longitudinal study of personality characteristics and alcohol use, Jones (1968) indicated that men who became problem drinkers, compared to men who drank moderately or who abstained, were hostile, impulsive, and rebellious as adolescents. Using Thematic Apperception Test scores, McClelland (1973) argued that men who drink heavily have an excessive concern with personal power and little sense of restraint. In a study of male college students, A. Williams (1970) found that problem drinkers were relatively independent, anxious, aggressive, impulsive, unconcerned about others, and had low opinions of themselves. Taken together, the results of these studies argue persuasively that peer support for drinking and little personal control are influential determinants of problem drinking.

Strategies to Reduce Problem Drinking

In an attempt to reduce the individual and social costs of problem drinking, a variety of treatments have been used; for example, psychoanalysis, group therapy, Alcoholics Anonymous, therapeutic communities, psychodrama, classical and operant conditioning, and drug therapy. In a review of research that tried to evaluate the impact of psychotherapy on alcoholics, Chafetz, Blane, and Hill

(1970) found that "the bulk of the studies are gross retrospective surveys, usually with large groups of patients, . . . with reliance on unreliable and unvalidated superficial measures and with inadequate follow-up procedures" (pp. 185–86). Accordingly, Chafetz *et al.* argued that the data do not permit conclusions about the effects of psychotherapy to be drawn.

Alcoholics Anonymous is comprised solely of alcoholics who try to help one another stop drinking. Toward that end, members discuss their feelings and experiences as alcoholics, and rely upon each other for consultation and support. While studies of 1,058 members in New York City (Bailey & Leach, 1965) and 11,355 members throughout the United States and Canada (Norris, 1970) have been conducted, each study contains a number of understandable methodological weaknesses. For example, there were no control groups, and a large segment of the New York sample reportedly received clinical treatment, chemotherapy, psychotherapy, and/or counseling in addition to the support of Alcoholics Anonymous (Leach, 1973). Despite these shortcomings, the findings suggest that Alcoholics Anonymous works for a substantial number of people. Forty-one percent of the North American sample reported that they had not taken a drink since attending their first meeting, 23% said they stopped drinking within a year or less after joining Alcoholics Anonymous, and 18% stopped drinking within two to five years after becoming members. Similar findings were reported in the New York City survey. The results also indicate that many members remain abstinent. Approximately 25% of the North American sample and 25% of the New York sample were reportedly abstinent for at least five years, about 35% in each group were abstinent for one to five years, and 38% had not taken a drink in less than one year.

While the number of well-designed studies that have used operant conditioning to change the drinking behavior of alcoholics is small, the consistency of the findings suggests that operant conditioning may be able to reduce considerably the extent of alcoholism. In a study designed to provide individualized behavior therapy for alcoholics, Sobell and Sobell (1973) interviewed 70 male alcoholic patients to find out which treatment goal—nondrinking or controlled drinking— was more appropriate for each patient. When each patient's treatment goal was determined, the patient was randomly assigned to a control group that was given conventional hospital treatment or to an experimental group that received 17 behavioral treatment sessions and conventional hospital treatment. The behavior treatment sessions were administered in a simulated bar and cocktail lounge and a simulated home environment. Subjects in the nondrinker experimental group received a one second electric shock when they ordered a drink. When the drink was served, subjects were shocked from the moment they touched the glass to the moment they released it. Subjects in the controlled drinker experimental group were given a one second shock for a variety of inappropriate drinking behaviors; for example, ordering a straight drink and ordering two drinks within

20 minutes. After they had three drinks in a session, controlled drinker subjects were placed on the same schedule of shocks as nondrinker subjects. Subjects in both groups were shocked on a variable ratio schedule; that is, a shock was randomly assigned to one of every two inappropriate drinking behaviors. Most subjects left the hospital shortly after treatment was completed. During the next six months, Sobell and Sobell maintained contact with each subject and with one or more persons who were close to the subject.

The results indicate that the drinking behavior of experimental subjects was considerably more restrained than the drinking behavior of control subjects six months after the subjects left the hospital.[2] For example, 78% of the controlled drinker experimental subjects, 75% of the nondrinker experimental subjects, 30% of the controlled drinker control subjects, and 17% of the nondrinker control subjects reportedly practiced controlled drinking or abstinence during a majority of the six-month interval. The results also indicate that the vocational status of 58% of the experimental subjects and 14% of the controls had improved; that 73% of the experimental subjects and 14% of the controls used therapeutic supports such as community counseling services; and that persons close to the subjects felt that 85% of the experimental subjects and 24% of the controls handled interpersonal relationships and coped with stressful situations more effectively than they had in the year preceding hospitalization.

The ability of electrical aversion conditioning to increase to a considerable degree controlled drinking or abstinence among alcoholics has also been documented by Vogler, Lunde, Johnson, and Martin (1970), Lovibond and Caddy (1970), and Baer (1973). Vogler et al. (1970) found that hospitalized alcoholics who received electrical aversion conditioning before and after leaving the hospital were much slower to relapse—get drunk again—than alcoholics in an assortment of control groups. Lovibond and Caddy (1970) trained 28 alcoholics to assess their blood/alcohol concentration. When the concentration rose above 0.065%, the subjects, who were instructed to continue drinking, were shocked electrically as they drank. Comparison with a control group whose members were given shocks that were not contingent on their actions indicated that experimental subjects consumed considerably less alcohol shortly after the sessions began. Follow-up data indicated that 21 of the 28 experimental subjects were reportedly practicing controlled drinking. Baer (1973) found that 20 alcoholic patients who received electrical aversion conditioning reportedly drank considerably less after three months of treatment than they had before beginning treatment. The data also indicate that the experimental group drank less and had fewer alcohol-related symptoms than the control group.

In a study that sought to rearrange the vocational, family, and social reinforcers of the alcoholic so that these reinforcers would be withheld if he began to

2. Six-month follow-ups had been completed on 48 of the 70 subjects.

drink, Hunt and Azrin (1973, reading 5.2) randomly assigned the members of eight matched pairs of hospitalized male alcoholics to a group that received community-reinforcement counseling or to a group that did not. Both groups received standard hospital counseling and instruction. Community-reinforcement counseling included vocational counseling, marital and family counseling, and social counseling. Vocational counseling was designed to help the subject find a satisfactory job. For example, the subject was told to prepare a resumé, call the major plants and factories in the area, and interview for available jobs. Active assistance was provided by the counselor. When the subject found a job he was satisfied with, he was released from the hospital. Marital and family counseling sought to create conditions that would reinforce the subject for being a functioning marital partner, that would reinforce the subject's wife for maintaining the marital relationship, and that would make drinking incompatible with an improved relationship. If the subject was unmarried and lived with his parents, reciprocal benefits between the subject and his parents were arranged. Benefits were withheld if the subject failed to remain sober. If the subject did not have a wife or a family, Hunt and Azrin attempted to provide the subject with a form of foster family. Social counseling tried to restore and improve the subject's social relationships and to make these relationships contingent upon sobriety rather than drinking. Toward that end, a self-supporting social club for the subjects and their friends was established.

The results indicate that the community-reinforcement group spent much less time drinking, unemployed, away from home, and institutionalized than the control group during the six months following discharge from the hospital. Comparison of the experimental and control groups during each month also indicate that the reported differences were stable over the six-month period.

While the results of these studies suggest that operant conditioning techniques may be able to alter considerably the drinking behavior of many alcoholics, a recent study of alcoholics admitted to an aversion conditioning hospital, an outpatient clinic, a halfway house, or a police work center suggests that no one approach can effectively treat all alcoholic subpopulations (Pattison, Coe, & Doerr, 1973). As Pattison et al. noted: "In the planning and implementation of comprehensive community alcoholism programs there is a need for multiple treatment approaches . . . serving particular population needs" (p. 200).[3]

HEROIN ADDICTION

Many studies have tried to identify the factors that cause people to become addicted to heroin. Unfortunately, the process of becoming a heroin addict is an

---

3. One approach that clearly failed was Prohibition: the attempt to outlaw the sale and distribution of alcoholic beverages.

extremely difficult process to study rigorously. As a result, most of the research has been retrospective, has used clinical or criminal samples, and has not included control groups. Accordingly, the findings need to be interpreted with much caution.

Several sociocultural variables currently appear to be related to the use of heroin. Known heroin users usually live in low-income urban areas (Chein, 1959; Preble & Casey, 1969), are often members of ethnic minorities (Narcotics Register Statistical Report, 1969; Vaillant, 1966a), and frequently start using heroin in response to peer group enticement (Brown, Gauvey, Meyers, & Stark, 1971; Cameron, 1963; Chein, Gerard, Lee, & Rosenfeld, 1964; Gamso & Mason, 1958; Vaillant, 1966b). For example, Chein et al. (1964) found that about 75% of the adolescent heroin users in their sample were introduced to heroin by a group of friends. In a study of 73 adolescent addicts, Brown et al. (1971) found that 66% were reportedly persuaded by friends to use heroin for the first time. A sizable proportion of adult addicts also appear to have been influenced by their peers. Studies of 167 addicts in a Chicago jail (Abrams, Gagnon, & Levin, 1968) and 133 addicts in District of Columbia treatment centers (Brown et al., 1971) indicate that curiosity and the influence of friends were reportedly the major reasons for initially using heroin. Studies of juvenile and adult addicts also indicate that most known heroin users engaged in a variety of delinquent or criminal acts before being identified as drug users, and that heroin use was apparently a further expression of a delinquent life style (Cuskey et al., 1973; Friedman & Friedman, 1973; Jacoby et al., 1973; Tinklenberg, 1973; Winick, 1967).

In an attempt to account for the variance in heroin use that sociocultural variables are unable to explain, numerous studies of the relationship between personality characteristics and heroin use have been carried out. Unfortunately, the findings are very hard to interpret. As Braucht, Brakarsh, Follingstad, and Berry (1973, reading 5.3) noted:

> . . . addicts have been found to be immature, insecure, irresponsible, and egocentric. However, the way in which all these traits fit together within any given narcotic addict is unclear. This can be seen as the result of a lack of a sound theoretical structure as the point of origin for these studies. Furthermore, although there is some agreement that the narcotic addict suffers from a personality disorder, there is hardly any agreement as to the specific dynamics of this disorder. Indeed, one should be aware that the population of adolescent drug addicts is very loosely defined and includes more than one personality type. [p. 98]

There are several possible strategies for reducing the individual and social costs of heroin addiction: drug education, reducing the supply of heroin, passing and enforcing more stringent laws, legalizing heroin, treatment, and altering the situational forces that make members of low-income minorities relatively vulnerable to heroin addiction.

A study of heroin use in the District of Columbia (DuPont & Greene, 1973) suggests that reducing the supply of heroin can have favorable effects—*if* treatment is available. Based on the findings, DuPont and Greene argued that the availability of treatment and a reduction in the supply of heroin due to vigorous law enforcement were instrumental in curbing the escalating use of the drug. "When heroin is scarce and treatment is available, addicts have both a disincentive to heroin abuse and an alternative to an increasingly desperate criminal lifestyle" (p. 722). Whether the supply of heroin is also reduced by harsh penalties is debatable; for example, we know of no evidence indicating that the stringent drug laws enacted by the New York State legislature in 1973 have reduced the availability of heroin or the number of addicts.

In an attempt to reduce adolescent use of heroin and other drugs, numerous drug education programs have been developed. Unfortunately, the few programs that have been evaluated rigorously have not reduced the drug use of participating adolescents. As a result, there is little consensus on which goals are realistic or desirable, and a paucity of information on how to communicate effectively with students about drug use (Wald & Abrams, 1972).

There are two major kinds of treatment: abstinence and methadone maintenance. Abstinence programs, which include detoxification, civil commitment, and therapeutic communities, are designed to help the addict to stop using heroin without providing a substitute drug for heroin. While the data are fragmentary, they suggest that detoxification "is primarily a service for the drug user who needs a respite and a short-term way of protecting society against crime rather than a long-term treatment for addiction" (DeLong, 1972, p. 183), that civil commitment does not produce long-term abstinence (Vaillant, 1973), and that therapeutic communities have very low rates of success (Coghlan & Zimmerman, 1972; Deitch, 1973). For example, Coghlan and Zimmerman found that only 5% of the addicts who entered Daytop Village completed the program and remained abstinent, and Deitch found that Synanon retained only 10% of its entrants after a year.

Methadone, which is taken orally and whose effects last 24 hours, is a synthetic opiate that purportedly blocks the euphoric effects of heroin and prevents the user from feeling withdrawal symptoms. Given these properties, several hundred programs of methadone maintenance have been established. Each program gives the addict a dose of methadone every day. Many programs also offer ancillary services such as individual or group therapy, vocational rehabilitation, employment counseling, and medical and dental care (DeLong, 1972).

In an attempt to determine the efficacy of methadone maintenance, a sizable number of evaluative studies have been carried out. While these studies contain a number of methodological flaws,[4] the findings suggest that methadone main-

4. Detailed critiques are presented by Coghlan and Zimmerman (1972), DeLong (1972), and Maddux and Bowden (1972).

tenance has had a favorable impact on the behavior of a substantial proportion of participants. For example, studies of three groups of 500 patients in a methadone maintenance treatment program in New York City (Gearing, 1970) indicated that 16% left the program or were dropped during the first year, 23% left or were terminated after 21 months, 34% had departed after 33 months, and 42% were gone after 48 months. While these rates of attrition are sizable, they were due primarily to the dismissal of addicts who violated the fairly strict standards of behavior that the program required its participants to meet. Among the addicts who remained in the program, employment rose and arrests declined dramatically. Twenty-six percent were employed when they began treatment, 66% were employed after 12 months, and 78% were working after 48 months. In the three years preceding admission to the program, the group of participants had 120 arrests and 48 incarcerations for every 100 man-years. During the four years on methadone maintenance, the group had 4.5 arrests and 1.0 incarcerations for every 100 man-years. The data also indicate that none of the participants returned to regular heroin use while on methadone maintenance. Although the program's selection procedures—addicts who were considered most likely to respond to treatment were selected—make it difficult to estimate the representativeness of the findings, a 12-month study of the impact of methadone maintenance on 814 addicts who were selected simply if they had failed to respond to at least one other type of treatment reported similar findings (Dale & Dale, 1973, reading 5.4). Additional support is provided by a study of 600 unscreened addicts in a District of Columbia program (Brown, DuPont, Bass, Brewster, Glendinning, Kozel, & Meyers, 1973). The results indicate that addicts who were placed on high-dose methadone maintenance (mean dosage was 89 mg) were far more likely to remain in treatment than addicts who entered abstinence, methadone detoxification, or low-dose methadone maintenance programs. Among those who remained on high-dose methadone maintenance, 56% were employed or in school, only 11% had been arrested, and only 7% used heroin regularly and continuously six months after beginning treatment. While further research on the effects of dosage level, ancillary services, and eventual withdrawal from methadone needs to be carried out,[5] these findings suggest that methadone maintenance "has definitive value in decreasing antisocial behavior and contributing to the initial steps toward social rehabilitation" (Dale & Dale, 1973, p. 305).

Perhaps the most controversial treatment is heroin maintenance: that is, the creation of clinics which provide addicts with heroin. England, which treats heroin addiction as a medical rather than as a criminal problem, has established a

---

5. Research has been done on the short-term effects of dosage level (e.g., Jaffe, 1970; H. Williams, 1970) and on the effects of therapy as part of a methadone-maintenance program (e.g., Cheek, Tomarchio, Standen, & Albahary, 1973; Willet, 1973).

number of heroin prescribing clinics. Although the data are fragmentary, they suggest that these clinics have reduced dramatically the antisocial behavior of participating heroin addicts (May, 1972).

Would heroin maintenance work in the United States? DeLong (1972) suggests that it might attract addicts who do not volunteer for methadone maintenance and addicts who do not succeed on methadone maintenance. If many of these addicts did participate, the crimes they commit in an attempt to obtain money to purchase heroin should decline dramatically, since the cost of maintaining a habit would be eliminated. The incidence of infection, overdose, and imprisonment would also be reduced sharply. On the other hand, DeLong noted that there are several possible drawbacks. For one, many addicts may buy more heroin on the street in order to continue to experience its euphoric effects, then ask the clinics to maintain the new, higher dosage. Two, the high doses that could tend to be the norm in a heroin maintenance program would tranquilize addicts and make rehabilitation impossible. Three, many prospective and actual participants in methadone maintenance programs may be attracted to heroin maintenance. Unfortunately, addicts on heroin maintenance are likely to be much more difficult to rehabilitate than addicts on methadone maintenance. Four, heroin maintenance may encourage people to experiment with heroin. Despite these possible shortcomings, the individual and social costs engendered by laws prohibiting the sale and use of heroin and the apparent effectiveness of the English clinics make careful experimentation with heroin maintenance desirable (DeLong, 1972; May, 1972).

REFERENCES

Abrams, A., Gagnon, J., & Levin, J. Psychosocial aspects of addiction. *American Journal of Public Health*, 1968, 58, 2142–2155.

Arthur D. Little, Inc. *Summary report: The state of the art of traffic safety.* New York: Praeger, 1966.

Baer, P. Aversion and avoidance conditioning as a treatment for alcoholism: Short term effects. In M. Chafetz (Ed.), *Research on alcoholism: Clinical problems and special populations.* Proceedings of the First Annual Alcoholism Conferences of the National Institute on Alcohol Abuse and Alcoholism. Washington, D.C.: U.S. Government Printing Office, 1973.

Bailey, M., & Leach, B. *Alcoholics Anonymous, pathway to recovery: A study of 1,058 members of the A.A. fellowship in New York City.* New York: The National Council on Alcoholism, 1965.

Bertrand, S., & Masling, J. Oral imagery and alcoholism. *Journal of Abnormal Psychology*, 1969, 74, 50–53.

Blum, R. Drugs, behavior and crime. *Annals of the American Academy of Political and Social Sciences*, 1967, 374, 135–146.

Braucht, G., Brakarsh, D., Follingstad, D., & Berry, K. Deviant drug use in adolescence: A review of psychosocial correlates. *Psychological Bulletin*, 1973, 79, 92–106.

Brown, B., DuPont, R., Bass, U., Brewster, G., Glendinning, S., Kozel, N., & Meyers, M. Impact of a large-scale narcotics treatment program: A six month experience. *International Journal of the Addictions*, 1973, 8, 49–57.

Brown, B., Gauvey, S., Meyers, M., & Stark,

S. In their own words: Addicts' reasons for initiating and withdrawing from heroin. *International Journal of the Addictions*, 1971, 6, 635–645.

Cahalan, D., Cisin, I., & Crossley, H. *American drinking practices*. New Brunswick: Rutgers Center of Alcohol Studies, 1969.

Cahalan, D., & Room, R. Problem drinking among American men aged 21–59. *American Journal of Public Health*, 1972, 62, 1473–1482.

Cameron, D. Addiction: Current issues. *American Journal of Psychiatry*, 1963, 120, 313–319.

Chafetz, M., Blane, H., & Hill, M. (Eds.). *Frontiers of alcoholism*. New York: Science House, 1970.

Cheek, F., Tomarchio, T., Standen, J., & Albahary, R. Methadone plus–A behavior modification training program in self-control for addicts on methadone maintenance. *International Journal of the Addictions*, 1973, 8, 969–996.

Chein, I. The status of sociological and social psychological knowledge concerning narcotics. In *Narcotic drug addiction problems*. Washington, D.C.: U.S. Department of Health, Education and Welfare, 1959.

Chein, I., Gerard, D., Lee, R., & Rosenfeld, E. *The road to H*. New York: Basic Books, 1964.

Coghlan, A., & Zimmerman, R. Self-help (Daytop) and methadone maintenance: Are they both failing? *Drug Forum*, 1972, 1, 215–225.

Cuskey, W., Ipsen, J., & Premkumar, T. *An inquiry into the nature of changes in behavior among drug users in treatment*. Paper prepared for the National Commission on Marihuana and Drug Abuse, 1973.

Dale, R., & Dale, F. The use of methadone in a representative group of heroin addicts. *International Journal of the Addictions*, 1973, 8, 293–308.

Deitch, D. *Treatment of drug abuse in the therapeutic community: Historical influences, current considerations and future outlook*. Paper prepared for the National Commission on Marihuana and Drug Abuse, 1973.

DeLong, J. Treatment and rehabilitation. In P. Wald *et al.* (Eds.), *Dealing with drug abuse*. New York: Praeger, 1972.

DuPont, R., & Greene, M. The dynamics of a heroin addiction epidemic. *Science*, 1973, 181 (4101), 716–722.

Erikkson, K. The estimation of heritability for the self-selection of alcohol in the albino rat. *Quarterly Journal of Studies on Alcohol*, 1970, 31, 728–729.

Fenichel, O. *The psychoanalytic theory of neuroses*. New York: Norton, 1945.

Friedman, C., & Friedman, A. *Drug abuse and delinquency*. Paper prepared for the National Commission on Marihuana and Drug Abuse, 1973.

Gamso, R., & Mason, P. A hospital for adolescent drug addicts. *Psychiatric Quarterly Supplement*, 1958, 32, 99–109.

Gearing, F. Evaluation of methadone maintenance treatment program. *International Journal of the Addictions*, 1970, 5, 517–543.

Holahan, J. The economics of heroin. In P. Wald *et al.* (Eds.), *Dealing with drug abuse*, New York: Praeger, 1972.

Hunt, G., & Azrin, N. A community-reinforcement approach to alcoholism. *Behaviour Research and Therapy*, 1973, 11, 91–104.

Jacoby, J., Weiner, N., & Wolfgang, M. *Drug use and criminality in a birth cohort*. Paper prepared for the National Commission on Marihuana and Drug Abuse, 1973.

Jaffe, J. Further experience with methadone in the treatment of narcotics users. *International Journal of the Addictions*, 1970, 5, 375–389.

Jessor, R., Carman, R., & Grossman, P. Expectations of need satisfaction and drinking patterns of college students. *Quarterly Journal of Studies on Alcohol*, 1968, 29, 101–116.

Jessor, R., Collins, M., & Jessor, S. On becoming a drinker: Social-psychological aspects of an adolescent transition. In F. Seixas (Ed.), *Nature and nurture in alcoholism*. New York: Annals of the New York Academy of Sciences, 1972.

Jessor, R., Graves, T., Hanson, R., & Jessor, S. *Society, personality and deviant behavior: A study of a tri-ethnic community*. New York: Holt, Rinehart, & Winston, 1968.

Jessor, R., & Jessor, S. Problem drinking in youth: Personality, social, and behavioral antecedents and correlates. In M. Chafetz (Ed.), *Psychological and social factors in drinking and treatment and treatment evaluation*. Proceedings of the Second Annual Alcoholism Conference of the National Institute on Alcohol Abuse and Alcoholism. Washington, D.C.: U.S. Government Printing Office, 1973.

Jessor, R., Young, H., Young, E., & Tesi, G. Perceived opportunity, alienation, and drinking behavior among Italian and American youth. *Journal of Personality and Social Psychology*, 1970, 15, 215–222.

Jones, M. Personality correlates and antecedents of drinking patterns in adult males. *Journal of Consulting and Clinical Psychology*, 1968, 32, 2–12.

Kaij, L. *Alcoholism in twins: Studies on the etiology and sequels of abuse of alcohol*. Stockholm: Almquist and Wiksell, 1960.

Kissin, B., & Hankoff, L. The acute effects of ethyl alcohol and chlorpromazine on certain physiological functions in alcoholics. *Quarterly Journal of Studies on Alcohol*, 1959, 20, 480–492.

Leach, B. Does Alcoholics Anonymous really work? In P. Bourne & R. Fox (Eds.), *Alcoholism: Progress in research and treatment*. New York: Academic Press, 1973.

Lovibond, S., & Caddy, G. Discriminated aversive control in the moderation of alcoholics' drinking behavior. *Behavior Therapy*, 1970, 1, 437–444.

Maddux, J., & Bowden, C. Critique of success with methadone maintenance. *American Journal of Psychiatry*, 1972, 129, 440–446.

May, E. Narcotics addiction and control in Great Britain. In P. Wald *et al.* (Eds.), *Dealing with drug abuse*. New York: Praeger, 1972.

McClelland, D. Drinking as a response to power needs in men. In M. Chafetz (Ed.), *Psychological and social factors in drinking and treatment and treatment evaluation*. Proceedings of the Second Annual Alcoholism Conference of the National Institute on Alcohol Abuse and Alcoholism. Washington, D.C.: U.S. Government Printing Office, 1973.

McCord, W., McCord, J., & Gudeman, J. *Origins of alcoholism*. Stanford: Stanford University Press, 1960.

Molof, M. *Differences between assaultive and non-assaultive juvenile offenders in the California Youth Authority*. Research report no. 51, state of California, Department of the Youth Authority, 1967.

Narcotics Register Statistical Report–1969. Department of Health, Research, and Professional Training, 125 Worth Street, New York, N.Y.

National Commission on Marihuana and Drug Abuse. *Marihuana: A signal of misunderstanding*. Washington, D.C.: U.S. Government Printing Office, 1972.

National Commission on Marihuana and Drug Abuse. *Drug use in America: Problem in perspective*. Washington, D.C.: U.S. Government Printing Office, 1973.

Norris, J. Alcoholics Anonymous. In E. Whitney (Ed.), *World dialogue on alcohol and drug dependence*. Boston: Beacon Press, 1970.

Partanen, J., Bruun, K., & Markkanen, T. *Inheritance of drinking behavior*. Helsinki: The Finnish Foundation for Alcohol Studies, 1966.

Pattison, E., Coe, R., & Doerr, H. Population variation among alcoholism treatment facilities. *International Journal of the Addictions*, 1973, 8, 199–229.

Preble, E., & Casey, J., Jr. Taking care of business—the heroin user's life on the street. *International Journal of the Addictions*, 1969, 4, 1–24.

Schuckit, M. Family history and half-sibling research in alcoholism. *Annals of the New York Academy of Sciences*, 1972, 197, 121–125.

Shupe, L. Alcohol and crime. *Journal of Criminal Law, Criminology and Police Science*, 1964, 4, 661–664.

Sobell, M., & Sobell, L. Individualized behavior therapy for alcoholics. *Behavior Therapy*, 1973, 4, 49–72.

Thomas, K. Selection and avoidance of alcohol solutions by two strains of inbred mice and derived generations. *Quarterly Journal of Studies on Alcohol*, 1969, 30, 849–861.

Tinklenberg, J. *Drugs and crime*. Paper prepared for the National Commission on Marihuana and Drug Abuse, 1973.

Vaillant, G. Parent-child cultural disparity and drug addiction. *The Journal of Ner-*

vous and Mental Disease, 1966, 142, 534–539. (a)

Vaillant, G. A twelve-year follow-up of New York narcotic addicts: Some social and psychiatric characteristics. *Archives of General Psychiatry*, 1966, 15, 599–609. (b)

Vaillant, G. A 20-year follow-up of New York narcotic addicts. *Archives of General Psychiatry*, 1973, 29, 237–241.

Vogler, R., Lunde, S., Johnson, G., & Martin, P. Electrical aversion conditioning with chronic alcoholics. *Journal of Consulting and Clinical Psychology*, 1970, 34, 302–307.

Voss, H., & Hepburn, J. Patterns in criminal homicide in Chicago. *Journal of Criminal Law, Criminology and Police Science*, 1968, 59, 499–508.

Wald, P., & Abrams, A. Drug education. In P. Wald *et al.* (Eds.), *Dealing with drug abuse*. New York: Praeger, 1972.

Wallgren, H., & Barry, H. *Actions of alcohol*, Vol. II. Amsterdam: Elsevier Publishing Company, 1970.

Wechsler, H., & Thum, D. Alcohol and drug use among teenagers: A questionnaire study. In M. Chafetz (Ed.), *Psychological and social factors in drinking and treat-*

ment and treatment evaluation. Proceedings of the Second Annual Alcoholism Conference of the National Institute on Alcohol Abuse and Alcoholism. Washington, D.C.: U.S. Government Printing Office, 1973.

Willet, E. Group therapy in a methadone treatment program: An evaluation of changes in interpersonal behavior. *International Journal of the Addictions*, 1973, 8, 33–39.

Williams, A. College problem drinkers: A personality profile. In G. Maddox (Ed.), *The domesticated drug: Drinking among collegians*. New Haven, Conn.: College and University Press, 1970.

Williams, H. Low and high methadone maintenance in the out-patient treatment of the hard core heroin addict. *International Journal of the Addictions*, 1970, 5, 439–447.

Williams, R. *Alcoholism: The nutritional approach*. Austin: The University of Texas Press, 1959.

Winick, C. Drug addiction and crime. *Current History*, 1967, 52, 349–353.

Wolowitz, H., & Barker, M. Alcoholism and oral passivity. *Quarterly Journal of Studies on Alcohol*, 1968, 29, 592–597.

5.1

Problem Drinking in Youth:

Personality, Social, and Behavioral Antecedents and Correlates

RICHARD JESSOR and SHIRLEY L. JESSOR

The concept of problem drinking, when applied to adolescent youth, is obviously different from the meaning it carries for adults later on in life. Nevertheless, research on youth may be especially important for the understanding of problem drinking in general. Youth is the time when initial experiences with alcohol occur, and initial experiences may have more than their share of influence on later patterns of alcohol use. Further, the onset and early stages of a behavior pattern—in this case problem drinking—can often be peculiarly revealing of its nature; thus, the role played by alcohol in the life of an individual may well be seen in sharper relief at the time when beginning to drink heavily than later on when heavy drinking is established.

This paper is derived from a larger research project that is concerned with a variety of areas of problem or problem-prone behavior in high school and college youth. The design of the larger project is longitudinal in nature and involves obtaining information from each subject annually, over a 4-year period. Data collected by a lengthy questionnaire can be used to examine the development of personality and behavior over time, as well as their interrelations at any given point in time. The present paper reports on that aspect of the larger project that concerns drinking and problems associated with drinking among high school students. Its aims are twofold: first, to show that problem drinking is systematically related, at a given point in time, to a variety of theoretically derived personality, social, and behavioral variables; and second, to examine whether these same variables may also be *predictive of the development of problem drinking* over time, an objective made feasible by the longitudinal nature of the research design. These aims together lead us to the specification of a network of variables that can begin to account for both cross-sectional and temporal variation in problem drinking among adolescents.

Our general orientation toward problem behavior, including problem drinking, is social-psychological and is based upon a social learning theory of personality (Rotter 1954; Rotter et al. 1972). Problem behavior,

From R. Jessor, & S. Jessor. Problem drinking in youth: Personality, social, and behavioral antecedents and correlates. In M. Chafetz (Ed.), *Psychological and social factors in drinking and treatment and treatment evaluation.* Proceedings of the Second Annual Alcoholism Conference of the National Institute of Alcohol Abuse and Alcoholism. Washington, D.C.: U.S. Government Printing Office, 1973, pp. 3–23.

as with any other class of behavior, is considered purposive or goal-oriented, the outcome of social learning processes which endow it with personal, functional significance. From this perspective, it is possible to specify a variety of potential functions of youthful problem drinking: as an instrumental effort to achieve goals otherwise unavailable; as a learned way of coping with personal frustrations and anticipated failures; as an expression of opposition to or rejection of conventional society and its norms; as a negotiation for status transformation on a developmental ladder; or as a manifestation of solidarity with peers or of membership in a subculture. Given the variety and complexity of these possible alternatives, it is unlikely that any single personality or situational variable will be able to provide a sufficient explanation of problem drinking. What seems to be required is a multivariate network of both person- and situation-attributes logically connected with the class of behavior at issue.

Such a network, or portions of it, have been described in previous publications (Jessor et al. 1968a; Jessor et al. 1968b; Jessor et al. 1970; Jessor et al. 1972), but especially in the report of the Tri-Ethnic Project (Jessor et al. 1968b). For present purposes, our focus will be on only a portion of the network, a subset of the variables presently being assessed in the longitudinal study of high school youth mentioned earlier.

There are three major classes of variables which we have been concerned with in trying to account for problem behavior in general and for problem drinking in particular—variables referring to personality, to the social environment, and to behavior. Personality is treated as a system composed of three structures—a motivational instigation structure, a belief structure, and a personal control structure. Each personality structure, in turn, consists of specific variables or attributes linked directly or indirectly to the occurrence of problem behavior. The social environment is treated primarily as perceived, but also demographically. Behavior is treated as action, with associated meanings or functions and consequences. The schema presented in fig. 1 represents the way in which the classes of variables to be dealt with in this paper are conceptualized in relation to variation in problem drinking.

It can be seen from the schema that youthful problem drinking is indeed embedded in a multivariate, social-psychological network. The relationships hypothesized are actually more complex than represented, but the major concerns of this paper can be dealt with adequately in terms of this schema. Two comments, however, should be made. First, some of the variables more directly implicate drinking or problem drinking than do others. For example, the variable, Peer Support for Drinking, more directly implies an association with drinking behavior than does the variable, Expectation for Achievement. Variables more directly implicative of a specific behavior are characterized as "proximal;" variables more remote from a behavior are referred to as "distal." The distal variables are, in some sense, more interesting, since their linkage to behavior depends on theory rather than on their obvious association with the behavior. Thus, we will be especially interested in significant relationships of distal variables in the schema to problem drinking. Second, no causal direction is represented in the schema; in fact, all the arrows are shown as bidirectional. This indicates not an absence of ideas about causal priority, but an awareness of the difficulty of getting beyond mere covariation in most research. Despite this difficulty, longitudinal data presented later in this paper may suggest causal precedence among some of the variables in the schema.

Some of the expected relationships can be stated in general terms. First with respect to Behavior, there should be a positive relation between problem drinking and other problem behaviors, such as drug use or general deviant behavior, since they all occupy a similar conceptual location in the schema. Also, a negative relation should be found

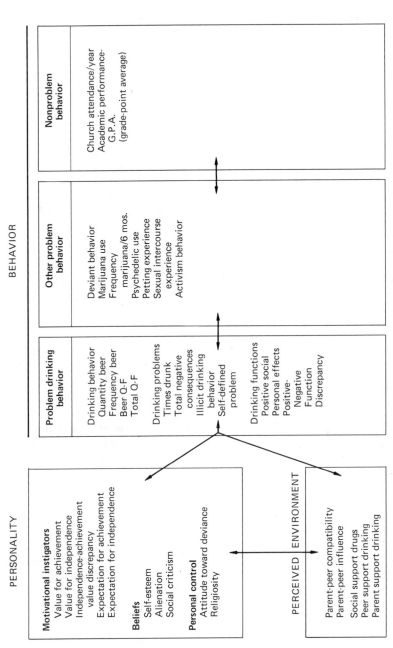

Fig. 1. Schema: Conceptual Network for Study of Problem Drinking in Youth.

between problem drinking and nonproblem (conforming) behavior such as church attendance or academic performance represented by grade point average. With respect to Personality, both values and expectations are considered to motivate behavior choice. Value for conventional goals such as academic achievement should be negatively related to problem drinking, whereas value for independence should show a positive relation to problem drinking. More important to actual behavioral directionality should be the discrepancy between these two values—the more that independence is valued *relative* to the value placed on achievement, the more likely is problem behavior, including problem drinking. Low expectations for attaining conventional goals such as academic achievement should be conducive to alternative behavior, including problem drinking. High expectations for independence should be conducive to problem drinking, provided that expectation for achievement is not also high. The belief variable, Alienation, should be positively related to problem drinking, but the other two belief variables, Self-esteem and Social Criticism, have conceptually-equivocal relationships to problem drinking. The general hypothesis about the two personal control variables is clear; the higher the personal controls, the lower the expected degree of problem drinking. Concerning the Perceived Environment, that structure has two subclasses of variables. The first two variables, Parent-Peer Compatibility and Parent-Peer Influence, are more distal from problem drinking and refer to aspects of the adolescent's reference orientation to parents versus friends: compatibility involves the degree of consensus or agreement between parents and friends in their general expectations for the adolescent; and influence refers to whether parents' or friends' opinions are considered more important by the adolescent. The more the orientation is to peers rather than to parents, and the less the compatibility between parents and peers, the more likely is problem drinking. The latter three variables shown in the Perceived

Environment structure are more proximal and involve assessments of the magnitude of perceived support for drinking and for the behavior of drug use: the greater the perceived support for drinking and drug use, the greater the likelihood of problem drinking.

When dealing with several classes of variables, as shown in the schema, a variety of important questions arise about their interrelationships. While all of these need eventually to be explored, the focus of this paper will remain on their relation to problem drinking: first, whether they can be shown to be correlates of problem drinking, and, second, if so, whether they can be shown to be predictive of the development of problem drinking over time.

METHOD

The details of sampling and of the nature of measurement development and data collection have been presented elsewhere (Jessor et al. 1972) and will be mentioned here only briefly. From an original, randomly selected sample of 2,220 junior-senior high school youths in a single school district, an initial Year I cohort of 949 students agreed to participate in the research for a 4-year period unless graduating before then. Of those who had not graduated in the interim, 81 percent were retained in Year II, and of the latter, 82 percent were subsequently retained in Year III (N = 605). The Year III subjects are distributed in grades 9 through 12 in school (the 7th graders in the initial cohort having reached 9th grade by Year III). Data were collected by a 50-page questionnaire made up largely of psychometrically developed scales assessing the variables mentioned earlier as well as other concepts not dealt with in this paper. Homogeneity ratios and Cronbach alphas indicate that the scale properties are adequate in nearly all cases. Subjects sign their names to the questionnaire in order to enable longitudinal followup, but they are identified by code number only to fulfill our guarantee of complete confidentiality. The names are locked in a safe deposit box in a bank vault off campus. Interest in the research is uniformly high, especially among the subjects who have continued through the third year of the study.

Establishment of the Problem Drinker Groups

The method of examining the relations in the schema (fig. 1) was to establish three contrasting groups of drinkers along a dimension of drinking problems, and to test the relevance of a specific variable to variation in problem drinking by employing one-way analyses of variance and t-tests between the groups. All tests were done separately for males and females.

The concept of problem drinking as used in this research refers to the joint consideration of two indicators associated with alcohol intake: frequency of drunkenness in the previous year, and number of life-areas (friends, school, dates, police, driving, family) in which negative consequences such as censure or trouble associated with drinking have occurred in the past year. Beyond a certain frequency of drunkenness which the adolescent or his significant others may consider acceptable or tolerable, frequent drunkenness, itself, may reasonably be considered to represent problem behavior or problem-prone behavior for the adolescent or for those with whom he interacts. The report of negative consequences associated with drinking directly implicates problems experienced by the adolescent in relation to important areas of life.

The groups for the analyses were established as follows. Of the 605 subjects in Year III, 388 were classified as drinkers (rather than abstainers) based on questionnaire responses indicating more than two or three drinks (not just sips or tastes) of beer, wine, or liquor. Since any socially meaningful definition of problem drinking implies at least a level of alcohol intake capable of resulting in problems, an intake cutting point was established such that those whose average quantity of intake of any beverage was one drink or less per sitting, were considered Minimal Drinkers (Group A) for whom the concept of problem drinking is a priori considered inapplicable. Of the 221 female drinkers, 51 were minimal; of the 167 male drinkers, 34 were minimal. The frequency of drunkenness and negative consequences scores of the remaining drinkers were employed jointly to assign them either to a No-Problem-Drinker Group (Group B) or to a Problem-Drinker Group (Group C). Problem drinkers were those who reported five or more times drunk in the past year (three or more for 9th graders), or two or more areas of negative consequences, or both. While these particular cutting points are arbitrary, they are based both on the empirical distributions of the two criterion measures and on their meaningfulness for high school youth. For the females, these criteria resulted in 104 No-Problem Drinkers and 66 Problem Drinkers; for the males the comparable figures are 65 and 68. The percentage of drinkers with problems among the males is 41, and among the females is 30, according to the criteria used.

The present definition of problem drinking is relative to the high school age group rather than to some absolute standard, but it results in a meaningful approach to variation in drinking patterns as can be seen in table 1.

Data are presented, separately for females and males, on a variety of measures of drinking or drinking-related variables for the three groups: Minimal Drinkers, No-Problem Drinkers, and Problem Drinkers. Several aspects of the data are worth noting. First, in every case and for both sexes, the data are ordered as expected from Group A to Group C. Further, for every measure the one-way analysis of variance across the three groups within each sex yields a significant F-ratio. For our present concern with significant separation between the No-Problem and the Problem Drinkers, the key comparisons are the t-tests between Groups B and C. It can be seen from the table that the mean scores of these two groups are different at a high

Table 1. Year III Mean Scores on Drinking Measures for Minimal Drinkers (Group A), No-Problem Drinkers (Group B), and Problem Drinkers (Group C)

Measure	Females			Males		
	Group A (N = 51)	Group B (N = 104)	Group C[a] (N = 66)	Group A (N = 34)	Group B (N = 65)	Group C[a] (N = 68)
Drinking behavior						
Quantity beer	1.6	4.5	6.2 §	1.7	4.5	7.3 §
Frequency beer	1.3	2.8	5.1 ‡	0.9	2.8	5.5 ‡
Beer Q-F	0.01	0.11	0.35 §	0.01	0.13	0.48 §
Total Q-F	0.05	0.24	0.70 §	0.03	0.24	0.78 §
Drinking problems						
Times drunk	0.4	1.1	14.3 §	0.4	1.0	17.9 §
Total negative consequences .	0.1	0.4	2.0 §	0.1	0.4	2.0 §
Illicit drinking behavior	4.1	5.6	6.6 §	4.5	5.3	6.1 ‡
Self-defined problem	1.0	1.0	1.2 ‡	1.0	1.0	1.2 §
Drinking functions						
Positive social	7.9	10.4	11.6 ‡	8.9	9.9	11.3 ‡
Personal effects	5.4	6.8	9.4 §	5.9	6.3	7.8 §
Positive-negative function discrepancy	22.9	28.5	35.5 §	27.4	31.1	35.5 ‡

[a]The symbols, shown for Group C means, refer to the significance level of a two-tailed t-test between Groups B and C as follows: ‡$p < .01$; §$p < .001$.

level of statistical significance in every case. By looking first at the two criterion measures used for establishing Groups B and C, it can be seen that the mean frequency of drunkenness of Group C is more than ten times that of Group B for both sexes; mean negative consequences in Group C is about five times that of Group B for both sexes. These resultant absolute differences on the two problem-drinking criterion measures provide strong evidence that contrasting problem and nonproblem groups have been successfully achieved. The contrast can be elaborated further by reference to the other measures in the table. Intake of alcohol is substantially greater in Group C whether considering quantity or frequency of drinking. Group C's drinking takes place significantly more often illicitly (outside of the home or without parents present). Also, significantly more of Group C than B self-define their drinking as a problem; these are a minority in Group C (13 of the males and 18 of the females) but there are none in Group B.

Of further interest in table 1 are the data on drinking functions. Group C, both males and females drink more for positive social reasons (e.g., "just to have a good time") and for personal effects reasons (e.g., "helps me forget I'm not the kind of person I'd like to be") than Group B. They also endorse more positive functions *relative to* negative functions for drinking than does Group B. These differences in drinking function, perhaps more than the other drinking measures, help to bridge the gap in the schema between problem-drinking behavior and the other, more distal personality variables and perceived environment variables invoked to explain it. Insofar as problem drinking involves more reasons and different reasons for drinking than does nonproblem drinking, variables in the person and the situation related to those reasons become implicated in the explanation of problem drinking.

Since the data in table 1 demonstrate the differentiation of problem-drinking from nonproblem-drinking groups, for both males and females, we can now turn to the presentation of the main findings on personality, social, and behavioral correlates and antecedents of problem drinking in high school youth.

RESULTS

The results will be presented in two major parts. The first part consists of the cross-sectional findings for the three drinker groups on the Year III data. The second part exploits the longitudinal nature of the research and examines whether earlier data,

collected prior to Year III, are predictive of the development of problem drinking by Year III. The two parts, taken together, may provide a more thorough evaluation of the variables in the network than either part considered by itself.

Part I—Cross-Sectional Analysis of the Year III Drinker Groups

The Year III data are presented, separately for males and females, in table 2. Most of

Table 2. Year III Mean Scores on Personality, Social, and Behavioral Measures for Minimal Drinkers (Group A), No-Problem Drinkers (Group B), and Problem Drinkers (Group C)

Measure	Females			Males		
	Group A (N = 51)	Group B (N = 104)	Group C[a] (N = 66)	Group A (N = 34)	Group B (N = 65)	Group C[a] (N = 68)
Personality						
Motivat. instigators						
Value-achievement	66.9	58.6	52.8*	67.9	64.5	55.1‡
Value-independence	74.6	74.3	74.8	69.5	75.5	75.9
Independence-achievement discrepancy	97.7	105.7	112.0*	91.6	101.0	110.8‡
Expectations for achievement	58.3	54.0	46.4†	58.8	58.1	49.3‡
Expectations for independence	69.2	71.0	69.9	63.8	67.7	71.7*
Beliefs						
Self-esteem	30.4	30.2	29.6	29.1	29.8	30.0
Alienation	36.2	35.3	37.3†	36.4	36.9	36.1
Social criticism	30.8	31.5	31.1	29.7	30.6	31.2
Personal control						
Attitude toward deviance	182.0	162.0	143.7‡	162.7	156.0	134.5§
Religiosity	12.3	12.4	12.4	13.8	11.2	10.8
Perceived Social Environment						
Parent-peer compatibility	8.5	7.8	6.8†	8.3	7.7	7.7
Parent-peer influence	3.7	3.9	4.3	3.1	3.6	3.7
Social support drugs	11.8	14.0	18.0§	10.2	12.2	16.9§
Peer support drinking	11.4	13.1	14.5§	11.8	12.7	13.6†
Parent support drinking	6.1	5.7	5.5	5.4	5.7	5.5
Behavior						
Deviant behavior	34.0	37.8	44.3§	37.1	39.0	47.0§
Marijuana use	0.9	1.8	3.9§	0.3	1.7	4.5§
Frequency marijuana/6 mos.	2.3	4.8	16.4§	0.4	2.9	26.2§
Psychedelic use	0.1	0.3	0.6‡	0.0	0.1	0.9§
Petting experience	0.9	1.5	1.8‡	0.9	1.4	1.7†
Sexual intercourse experience	0.2	0.5	0.8†	0.1	0.3	0.8§
Activism behavior	0.3	0.2	0.4	0.3	0.3	0.5*
Grade point average	3.1	2.9	2.5‡	3.0	2.9	2.6†
Church attendance/year	23.3	22.4	20.6	39.8	17.0	15.1

[a]The symbols, shown for Group C means, refer to the significance level of a two-tailed t-test between Groups B and C as follows: *$p < .10$; †$p < .05$; ‡$p < .01$; §$p < .001$.

the variables show mean scores with the theoretically expected contrast between Groups A and C, with the No-Problem Drinkers occupying an intermediate position between the Minimal Drinkers and the Problem Drinkers. One-way analyses of variance across the three groups for each measure and for both sexes yield F-ratios which are significant in 34 of the 48 comparisons. The data are very similar for both males and females, as were the drinking data presented earlier in table 1.

Our main concern is with the comparison of Groups B and C, the No-Problem Drinker and the Problem Drinker groups respectively; differences between these groups in mean scores were assessed by t-test. It can be seen in table 2 that 15 of the 24 t-test comparisons are significant ($p < .10$) for females, and the same number for males also. While the preponderance of significant differences occurs among the Behavior measures, some measures in the Personality category and in the Perceived Environment category also reach statistical significance. This outcome supports the validity of the multivariate network as applied to problem drinking.

Relative to the Personality measures, the strongest findings are in the motivational instigation structure and the personal control structure. Both value for achievement and expectation for achievement are lower among Problem Drinkers; and Problem Drinkers place greater value on independence, relative to the value they place on achievement, than do No-Problem Drinkers. In the personal control structure, the religiosity measure is nondiscriminating, but the measure of attitudinal tolerance of deviance is highly significant with Problem Drinkers evidencing considerably greater tolerance. The Problem Drinkers thus appear less involved with conventional achievement goals and place higher relative value on independence, both factors being associated with alternative or problem behavior; and their greater tolerance of deviance indicates weaker control against transgression. Both

instigations and controls, then, suggest problem-proneness.

With the exception of the alienation measure for the females (and even on that one Group A was intermediate between Groups B and C), none of the belief variables—self-esteem, alienation, or social criticism—is capable of discriminating between No-Problem and Problem Drinkers.

The first two measures in the Perceived Environment indicate significantly less parent-peer compatibility and a tendency for greater peer influence for the female Problem Drinkers. The measures of peer support for drinking and social support for drugs indicate higher support for the Problem Drinkers, male and female. In contrast to these findings, there is no difference between the groups in parent support for drinking. Given the instigation and personal control findings noted earlier, and adding now the greater peer involvement and greater peer support for drinking, the problem drinking of Group C seems to be a logical outcome.

With respect to the Behavior measures, the data are highly consistent and significant in showing an association of other problem or problem-prone behavior with problem drinking for both males and females. These findings are important in suggesting that problem drinking, rather than being a unique behavior dependent upon the use of alcohol, is probably more accurately described as an instance of a class of functionally related problem behaviors. Problem Drinkers engage more in deviant behavior (aggression, stealing, lying), are more involved with marijuana, have used it more often in the previous 6 months, and have greater sexual activity. Considering the two conventional behavioral indicators, the Problem Drinkers have lower grade-point averages as expected, but they do not differ significantly from No-Problem Drinkers in church attendance. Data for a measure of activist behavior, not shown in table 2, are equivocal and suggest that it may not co-vary with these other instances of problem behavior.

In summary, the data in table 2 demonstrate that Problem Drinkers differ from No-Problem Drinkers in at least some respects in each of the three main areas of our social-psychological network—Personality, Perceived Environment, and Behavior. These differences logically relate to problem drinking; they provide a plausible account of its occurrence, and their magnitude and frequency encourage greater conviction about the utility of the network itself.

Part II—Longitudinal Analysis of the Development of Problem Drinking

The preceding data provide strong support for the association of a number of personality, social, and behavioral variables in the theoretical network with variation in problem drinking. But such co-variation always remains open to a variety of alternative interpretations, involving other variables not dealt with or controlled for, or involving ambiguity in the direction of influence or of causal priority. It would be plausible, for example, to argue that problem drinking leads to or results in lower Expectation for Achievement rather than, as our theoretical predilection would have it, the other way around. In order to obtain a somewhat firmer grasp on the inference of causal priority and, at the same time, to strengthen the evidence in support of the network of variables employed, we undertook a longitudinal analysis of the development of problem drinking over time. The objective was to examine whether any of the cross-sectional

correlates of problem drinking in Year III existed *prior to* the appearance of problem drinking and, in a sense, signaled the prospective onset or occurrence of the behavior.

This analysis proceeded as shown in table 3. For the subjects dealt with in Part I, their Year II drinking data were also examined in order to classify them into either a No-Problem or a Problem-Drinker group according to the same criteria used for Year III. Since our interest now is in the shift from no-problem to problem drinking, the Minimal Drinker group is combined with the No-Problem group. The procedure results in a two-by-two classification matrix representing for each subject his Year II and his Year III problem-drinker status, as shown.

Since not all of the Year III subjects had Year II data, the female total is 193 and the male total is 144 for this analysis. A group of subjects has now been identified as No-Problem Drinkers in Year II (145 females and 97 males) some of whom remain No-Problem Drinkers by Year III (118 females and 74 males) and some of whom have become Problem Drinkers by Year III (27 females and 23 males). Our critical concern is with whether *at Year II*, any differences were already evident which indicate the prospective likelihood of the shift from No-Problem to Problem-Drinker status. Such evidence, since it would have antedated the shift in behavior, would indicate stronger causal inference than is possible from cross-sectional differences alone.

Our focus in this section of the results, then, is on the Year II differences that are

Table 3. Number of Cases Classified as No-Problem and Problem Drinkers in Year II and Year III

	Year III status			
	Females (N = 193)		Males (N = 144)	
Year II status	No-problem	Problem	No-problem	Problem
No-problem ..	118	27	74	23
Problem	24	24	13	34

Table 4. Year II Mean Scores on Selected Personality, Social, and Behavioral Measures. Comparison Between No-Problem Drinkers in Year II who Remain No-Problem Drinkers by Year III (N-P$_{II}$ − N-P$_{III}$), and No-Problem Drinkers in Year II who Shift to Problem-Drinker Status by Year III (N-P$_{II}$ − P$_{III}$)

Measures	Females		Males	
	N-P$_{II}$ − N-P$_{III}$ (*N* = 118)	N-P$_{II}$ − P$_{III}$[a] (*N* = 27)	N-P$_{II}$ − N-P$_{III}$ (*N* = 74)	N-P$_{II}$ − P$_{III}$[a] (*N* = 23)
Personality				
Motivation instigators				
Value-achievement	64.4	60.9	66.7	63.6
Independence-achievement				
discrepancy	101.1	103.3	96.8	103.2
Expectations for achievement	55.1	41.6‡	56.4	46.5†
Personal control				
Attitude toward deviance	169.6	159.3	166.6	151.8
Perceived Social Environment				
Parent-peer compatibility	12.0	9.8‡	11.6	12.0
Social support drugs	11.2	13.4*	9.3	12.3†
Total support drinking	21.2	22.6*	20.4	20.0.
Behavior				
Drinking-related				
Total Q-F	0.04	0.05	0.03	0.04
Times drunk	0.48	1.07†	0.26	2.00‡
Total negative consequences ..	0.26	0.48	0.15	0.96†
Positive social functions	8.8	10.0†	8.9	9.8
Personal effects functions	6.5	8.4†	6.6	7.2
Other behavior				
Deviant behavior	37.3	40.6†	37.7	42.9‡
Marijuana use	0.63	1.15	0.51	1.35*
Frequency marijuana/6 mos. .	1.6	4.3	0.51	6.48
Psychedelic use	0.05	0.15	0.00	0.17
Petting experience	1.0	1.2	0.68	0.96
Sexual intercourse experience	0.23	0.56	0.15	0.33
Grade point average	2.8	2.4†	2.7	2.6
Church attendance/year	30.2	28.3	25.2	17.2

[a]The symbols for the means in this column refer to the significance of a two-tailed *t*-test between the two group means within each sex as follows: *$p < .10$; †$p < .05$; ‡$p < .01$; §$p < .001$.

found between those who remained No-Problem Drinkers (N-P$_{II}$−N-P$_{III}$) and those who changed from No-Problem to Problem Drinkers (N-P$_{II}$−P$_{III}$) by Year III. The other direction of change shown in the matrix, from Problem to No-Problem status, is also of considerable interest, but it will not be dealt with here. Data relevant to this comparison are presented, separately for females and males, in table 4. The variables selected for presentation are limited to those which showed strong relations with problem drink-

ing in the Year III cross-sectional analyses, those for which there is clear theoretical rationale, or those which have been discriminating in other areas of behavior such as in the shift from nondrug use to drug use or in the shift from virginity to nonvirginity.

Despite the year interval involved and the possibilities for a variety of intervening experiences and events to occur, the data in table 4 do provide evidence that several of the variables are capable of differentiating between those who will remain No-Problem

Drinkers and those who will shift to Problem-Drinker status by a year later. Of the 40 possible comparisons, 38 showed the expected direction, and 16 of these reach statistical significance (3 at the $p < .10$ level). At least one comparison is significant in each part of the network of personality, social, and behavioral variables. Looking first at the drinking-related behavioral variables (those likely to be most closely linked to subsequent drinking patterns), it can be seen that although the absolute frequency of drunkenness and negative consequences is quite low (far below the differences which result later on at Year III), there is already a greater frequency among those who will become problem drinkers by Year III. There is also a difference in functions for drinking (significant only for females, however). Of interest is the fact that, despite these differences in consequences and meanings of alcohol use, there is no Year II difference in alcohol intake (Total Q-F) for either males or females. Considering the other behaviors, deviant behavior is significantly higher for those who will become problem drinkers, among both males and females, and grade-point average is lower, but for females only. None of the other behavior differences is statistically reliable even though all are in the direction expected. It is of special theoretical interest to examine the more distal variables. Among the motivational attributes, expectation for achievement is significantly lower in those males and females who will become problem drinkers; they also manifest greater attitudinal tolerance of deviance and this finding reaches significance for the males.

These findings are only for a selected set of the measures; those other measures which did not yield cross-sectional Year III differences generally do not show differences in the present longitudinal analysis. However, these results provide further support for the social-psychological approach to problem drinking. The data in table 4 indicate that variation on measures taken at Year II is associated with problem-drinker status at Year III; the data thereby add an increment to the relevance of the variables and to the inferential claim of causal priority.

A further approach was taken to show the relevance of this set of variables to the process of shifting from nonproblem to problem-drinker status. This approach entails assessing *the amount and direction of change* on the personality, social, and behavioral variables from Year II to Year III. The appropriate procedure for assessing change on measures taken at two points in time is one which controls for or partials out differences in initial scores (such as those shown in table 4) rather than employing raw score gains between the two times, since raw score gains tend to be correlated with initial score levels on a measure. The method used was to employ residual gain scores, scores which represent the discrepancy between a subject's *actual* Year III score and the score that would be predicted for him from the regression of Year III scores on Year II scores. Separate regression lines for the males and for the females were used in computing residual gain scores for each of the subjects in table 4. The mean residual gain scores for the two female and the two male groups are shown in table 5. The plus or minus signs indicate the direction of gain for a given group *relative to* the direction of overall gain for the combined groups (males or females) from which the regression line was derived.

The residual gain scores add considerable support to the relevance of the variables in table 5 to the development of problem drinking. Both the male and the female groups that shift from nonproblem to problem drinking between Year II and Year III show greater magnitude of change in the theoretically-expected direction on a variety of the measures (28 out of the 40 residual gain score comparisons reach significance) than the group that retains No-Problem status by Year III. Several of the measures which did not show initial Year II differences in table 4 now do yield significant differences in magnitude of change; this is true for the behavior measures, especially those that are drinking-related, but also for

Table 5. Mean Residual Gain Scores Between Year II and Year III on Selected Personality, Social, and Behavior Measures. Comparison Between No–Problem Drinkers in Year II who Remain No-Problem Drinkers by Year III (N-P$_{II}$ – N-P$_{III}$), and No-Problem Drinkers in Year II who Shift to Problem-Drinker Status by Year III (N-P$_{II}$ – P$_{III}$)

	Females		Males	
Measures	N-P$_{II}$ – N-P$_{III}$ (N = 118)	N-P$_{II}$ – P$_{III}$[a] (N = 27)	N-P$_{II}$ – N-P$_{III}$ (N = 74)	N-P$_{II}$ – P$_{III}$[a] (N = 23)
Personality				
Motivation instigators				
Value-achievement	2.0	–9.0‡	2.8	–9.0‡
Independence-achievement				
discrepancy	–1.9	8.2‡	–2.9	9.3‡
Expectations for achievement	0.41	–1.78	1.6	–5.1†
Personal control				
Attitude toward deviance	2.4	–7.0	2.4	–7.6
Perceived Social Environment				
Parent-peer compatibility	0.14	–0.61	–0.05	0.16
Social support drugs	–0.45	1.96†	–0.27	0.90
Total support drinking	–0.23	1.00‡	–0.22	0.72†
Behavior				
Drinking related				
Total Q-F	–0.11	0.41 §	–0.13	0.37†
Times drunk	–1.96	7.35 §	–2.02	5.80†
Total negative consequences ..	–0.47	1.78§	–0.50	1.46‡
Positive social functions	–0.33	1.38‡	–0.31	1.02†
Personal effects functions	–0.27	1.15‡	–0.21	0.74*
Other behavior				
Deviant behavior	–0.71	3.08‡	–0.53	1.69
Marijuana use	–0.36	1.57‡	–0.40	1.27†
Frequency marijuana/6 mos. .	–1.45	6.17†	–1.07	3.45*
Psychedelic use	–0.05	0.23†	–0.08	0.25†
Petting experience	–0.07	0.33†	–0.05	0.17
Sexual intercourse experience	0.02	–0.12	–0.06	0.17
Grade point average	0.05	–0.26†	0.05	–0.16†
Church attendance/year	1.28	–1.55	–0.26	0.81

[a]The symbols for the means in this column refer to the significance of a two-tailed t-test between the two group means within each sex as follows: $*p < .10$; $†p < .05$; $‡p < .01$; $§p < .001$.

the distal personality measures—for example, value for achievement and the independence-achievement discrepancy. The group that shifts to problem drinking has a mean *decrease* in value for achievement (as theoretically expected) over the time period (−9.0 for both females and males) *relative to* its comparison group (2.0 for females and 2.8 for males), and this relative decrease is significant in magnitude for both sexes.

To sum up this part of the results, we have shown that certain of the variables in our

network discriminate *in advance* between those No-Problem Drinkers who will remain in this status and those who will shift to Problem-Drinker status by a year later. We have shown, further, that *change* on measures of these variables over the year interval is also associated significantly with change in drinking-problem status. These results, taken together with the cross-sectional findings presented earlier, encourage a high degree of conviction about the explanatory possibilities of the network involved.

One other line of longitudinal evidence may be added briefly. Earlier work (Jessor et al. 1972) had shown the utility of several of the variables discussed above for predicting the shift from abstainer to drinker status over a 1-year time interval. Current analyses have replicated the earlier demonstration over a longer time interval. The topic of the present paper led to the following question: Considering only the subjects who were classified as Abstainers in Year I ($N = 234$), can any of our measures discriminate *at year I* those who will remain Abstainers by Year III, those who will become No-Problem Drinkers by Year III, and those who will become Problem Drinkers by Year III? Two variables yielded significant findings: Expectation for Achievement (respective Year I means were 60.9, 59.0, and 48.8), and Deviant Behavior (32.0, 34.6 and 36.5, respectively). While these are obviously only a chance number of findings, their consistency with the previously presented data makes them a source of further support for the network.

CONCLUSIONS

The aim of this paper has been to apply a more general social psychology of problem behavior to the specific area of problem drinking among high school youth. The results give us confidence that the theoretical framework can be useful and has promise of revealing important social-psychological information about adolescent involvement with alcohol.

The limitations of the research should not be minimized, however, and several need to be mentioned. Because these analyses have only recently been completed, we have not yet been able to carry out controls for obvious social background or demographic variables such as socioeconomic status or religious-group membership which conceivably could be contributing to the patterning of the results. In view of the restricted socioeconomic variation in our community, and our previous experience with instituting such controls in other analyses, we do not expect the findings to change; nevertheless, the possibility exists and needs to be ruled out. Second, we have not given adequate attention to those measures which, while expected to discriminate, failed to do so. Our search for evidence supporting the utility of a complex, multivariate network has led us to emphasize the positive findings and, in the long run, the balance will need to be evened with additional attention to negative outcomes—for example, the general failure of the belief variables to discriminate problem drinking. Third, although the logic of our approach requires multivariate analyses, only single-variable analyses were presented. The full assessment of the utility of the network will depend on a multiple regression or discriminant analysis. Until that is done, it is not possible to describe the amount of variance in adolescent problem drinking that the theoretical scheme as a whole is capable of accounting for.

Our conviction about the findings, despite these limitations, stems from several sources. First, the results show noteworthy consistency and convergence. Second, some of the findings replicate previous analyses of problem drinking carried out at an earlier stage of the research (Abramowitz 1971). Most important, however, is the fact that the results from the analysis of problem drinking are consistent with similar analyses that we have made in other problem-behavior areas. The same general network has been applied to variation among these high school youth in general deviance, in drug use, in activism, and in sexual behavior, and also to behavior change in some of these areas. The pattern of results is compellingly similar for most of these areas and, for drug use especially, is even stronger and holds across more of the variables in the network than was shown for problem drinking.

The content of the specific variables associated with problem drinking ought not to be overlooked in the emphasis on support for the network as a whole. Of immediate interest is the demonstrated association of problem drinking with other problem or problem-prone behaviors. It seems clear that problem drinking is not a unique behavioral phenomenon. It seems clear also that other behaviors such as marijuana use do not substitute for but, instead, co-vary with problem drinking. The associations among the various behaviors suggest their syndrome character, and it is at least for this reason that a more abstract concept such as problem behavior seems useful, since it can subtend the behavioral diversity included in such a syndrome.

Also noteworthy is the importance to problem drinking of the distal personality variables. Problem Drinkers tend to value achievement less and to expect to attain achievement goals less than No-Problem Drinkers. They tend also to place greater value on independence relative to achievement. Problem drinking may reflect, then, both a means of coping with expected academic failure and an asssertion of independence. Greater attitudinal tolerance of deviance indicates that Problem Drinkers can be characterized as having relatively weaker personal controls against transgression. Problem drinking in youth thus seems to emerge from a combination of influences: greater motivational instigation to problem behavior, less personal controls, and a social context of peer involvement and peer support for drinking.

The concern for social-psychological theory, the reliance on a multivariate network, and the recourse to longitudinal design have all been part of the research effort reported here. Our commitment to such an approach has been strengthened by the nature of the present findings.

REFERENCES

Abramowitz, Christine V. "Personality and Social Factors Associated with Drinking Context and Problem Drinking among Adolescents." Project Research Report No. 18, August 1971, pp. 1–92. (Mimeo.)

Jessor, R.; Carman, R. S.; and Grossman, P. H. Expectations of need satisfaction and drinking patterns of college students. *Quart J Stud Alc*, 29:101–116, 1968a.

Jessor, R.; Graves, T. D.; Hanson, R. C.; and Jessor, S. L. *Society, Personality and Deviant Behavior: A Study of a Tri-Ethnic Community.* New York: Holt, Rinehart & Winston, 1968b.

Jessor, R.; Collins, M. I.; and Jessor, S. L. On becoming a drinker: Social-psychological aspects of an adolescent transition. *In*: Seixas, F. A., ed. *Nature and Nurture in Alcoholism.* New York: Annals of the New York Academy of Sciences, 1972, pp. 199–213.

Jessor, R.; Young, H. B.; Young, E. B.; and Tesi, G. Perceived opportunity, alienation, and drinking behavior among Italian and American youth. *J of Personality Soc Psychol*, 15:215–222, 1970.

Rotter, J. B. *Social Learning and Clinical Psychology.* Englewood Cliffs, N.J.: Prentice-Hall, 1954.

Rotter, J. B.; Chance, J. E.; and Phares, E. J. *Applications of a Social Learning Theory of Personality.* New York: Holt, Rinehart & Winston, 1972.

5.2

A Community-Reinforcement Approach
to Alcoholism

GEORGE M. HUNT and N. H. AZRIN

Alcoholism is perhaps the number one public health problem in the United States: alcoholics number approximately 10 million (Wilkinson, 1970); half of all fatal accidents involve a drunken driver (Wilkinson, 1970); cirrhosis of the liver, heart disease and suicide have been linked to alcoholism (Wallgren and Barry, 1970). Yet, as two recent reviews have concluded (Hill and Blane, 1967; Wallgren and Barry, 1970) alcoholism continues to be a major problem for which even a partial solution is being sought. A variety of approaches for treating alcoholism have been developed including the psychodynamic and psychoanalytic model (Freytag, 1967), transactional analysis (Steiner, 1969), the medical and physiological approach (see review by Jellinek, 1960; Wallgren and Barry, 1970), the anxiety model (Vogel-Sprott, 1967) and the peer-friendship model of Alcoholics Anonymous (Alcoholics Anonymous, 1960). A fairly recent emphasis has been the learning theory approach which uses the Pavlovian reinforcement model (see review by Rachman and Teasdale, 1969).

Another learning theory approach is the operant reinforcement approach (Skinner, 1938). The operant approach stresses the interaction between behavior and the environment whereas classical conditioning stresses the associations between different environmental events. With the exception of a case study by Sulzer (1965), an operant approach to alcoholism treatment has not been evaluated.

One method of developing an operant method of deterring alcoholism is to examine the natural deterrents of alcoholism and conceptualize them in operant terms. The principles of operant conditioning might then be used to alter these natural deterrents to maximize their effectiveness. It appears that individuals are deterred from drinking because of the interference that drinking produces with other sources of satisfaction. In the alcoholic state, one may incur social censure from friends as well as from one's family. Discharge from one's employment is likely. Pleasant social interactions and individual recreational activities cannot be performed as satisfactorily, if at all, when one is alcoholic. Conceptually, this state of affairs may be characterized in learning terms as postponement or omission of positive reinforcers as a result of alcohol intake. This statement suggests that deterrents will be

From G. Hunt, & N. Azrin. A community-reinforcement approach to alcoholism. *Behaviour Research and Therapy*, 1973, *11*, 91–104. Reprinted by permission of Pergamon Press, Ltd.

maximized if the postponed reinforcers are of maximum quality, frequency, varied in nature and regularly occurring. The general process seems to be that of time-out from positive reinforcement (Leitenberg, 1965; Ferster, 1958; Holz and Azrin, 1963) which has been studied extensively and has been applied to a variety of clinical situations including classroom disorders (Wahler, 1969), tantrums (Wolf, Risley and Mees, 1964) and self-injurious behavior (Bucher and Lovaas, 1967). An additional major factor is the distribution of these reinforcers in time. Time-out from positive reinforcement cannot be a new event if the natural distribution of reinforcers is such that extended interruptions normally occur. Consequently, for maximum effectiveness of this time-out dimension, the normal reinforcers should be grouped closely together in time, as well as being of qualitatively great value.

This type of operant reinforcement approach to alcoholism incorporates essential features of the recent emphasis in mental health programs known as the community mental health approach, (Bindman and Spiegel, 1969; Caplan, 1964; 1970; Klein, 1968). This approach may be characterized by a realization that mental disorders result from forces operating in and by the community on the individual and suggests that treatment be conducted by rearranging these community influences on the patient in the community rather than in a hospital. Examples of community based treatments include the home care program for schizophrenics (Pasaminick, Scarpitti and Denitz, 1967), the home based reinforcement program for school aged children (Tharp and Wetzel, 1969), the community located business owned and operated by former mental patients (Fairweather, Sanders, Maynard and Cresslor, 1969) and an open facility for skid-row alcoholics (Meyerson and Mayer, 1967). Since the operant based model described above deals with the rearrangement of the alcoholics' vocational, social, recreational and familial satisfactions, most of which are found in the community, this approach is in

accord with the general community treatment approach and may be designated therefore, as a Community-Reinforcement approach to alcoholism.

The present study developed a method of treating alcoholics and evaluated the effectiveness of this Community-Reinforcement procedure with hospitalized alcoholics, a group which is known to have an extremely poor prognosis. A matched control group was included since recent reviews (Hill and Blane, 1967; and Wallgren and Barry, 1970) have concluded that virtually no treatment procedure can be stated to have been effective because of the lack of a suitable control group against which to evaluate that procedure.

METHOD

Subjects

The population consisted of those patients admitted to a State Hospital for treatment of alcoholism who suffered withdrawal symptoms and were diagnosed alcoholic. This institution was responsible for the hospital treatment of all alcoholics and mental patients in a sparsely populated rural Midwestern region. Sixteen males were selected from this population. Patients were excluded who had serious medical ailments which precluded employment.

Design for Evaluation

Eight available alcoholics were selected arbitrarily and then matched individually with eight others on the basis of employment history, family stability, previous drinking history, age and education (see Table 1). The rationale for the matching according to these characteristics is based on studies by Gerard and Saenger (1966) and Schmidt, Smart and Moss (1968). A coin flip determined which member of each pair received the Community-Reinforcement counseling. The other pair member did not receive the Community-Reinforcement counseling procedures. Both

Table 1. Patient Characteristics

	Control (Mean)	Reinforcement (Mean)
Age	36.75	39.87
Education	11	10.2
Number of hospitalizations	2.5	2.6
Marital status	5 M–3 S	5 M–3S
Recent job	5 yes–3 no	5 yes–3 no

groups received the same housing, didactic program and other services of the hospital.

The Community-Reinforcement Program

The Community-Reinforcement program was designed to rearrange the vocational, family and social reinforcers of the alcoholic such that time-out from these reinforcers would occur if he began to drink. On the first day, a brief description of the nature of the procedures, and the reasons for them were presented to the alcoholic. For example, he was told by the counselor that extensive research and experience have shown that the alcoholic's chances of staying sober are improved if he has a satisfying steady job. Therefore, one part of this counseling program involved helping him achieve a satisfactory job. The family and social adjustment procedures were introduced to the alcoholic in a similar manner. Also, on the first day, the alcoholic was asked if he had any pressing problems. If he had a legal problem, he would be referred to a lawyer. If his major problem was financial, then the job-finding procedures would begin immediately. The clients' reluctance to attempt these large scale changes was overcome by assuring him that such changes were possible and that the counselor would be accompanying him at every step of the way.

The specific manner and sequence in which these procedures were carried out varied somewhat from patient to patient depending on the specifics of his situation. For example, if he stated that he was happy with his job, and it seemed that he did not drink at work, the family counseling procedures were begun. Typically there was continued overlap in the procedures.

Vocational Counseling

Those patients without jobs were instructed to (1) prepare a resumé, (2) read the pamphlet "How to get the job" (Dreese, 1960), (3) call all friends and relatives on the phone to inform them of the need for employment and ask them for job leads, (4) call the major factories and plants in the area, (5) place a 'Situations-Wanted' advertisement in the local papers, (6) rehearse the job interview and (7) place applications and interview for the jobs which are available. While the alcoholic was following the above procedures, the counselor was physically present and actively assisted the client. He stood by while phone calls were made, role-played interviews with the client and arranged for typing of the resumé. Also, he escorted the alcoholic to the job interviews and immediately following the interview discussed the results. These procedures are based on recent studies concerning the relevant considerations in successful job-finding (Jones and Azrin, 1972; Sheppard and Belitsky, 1966). As soon as the patient acquired a job, which he said would be satisfactory to him, he was released from the hospital. The counselor typically accompanied the client to the job on the first day. The counselor arranged for transportation to work by friends when necessary. In some cases employer-employee situations were role-played.

Marital and Family Counseling

The marital counseling attempted to (1) provide reinforcement for the alcoholic to be a functioning marital partner, (2) provide reinforcement for the spouse for maintaining the marital relation and (3) to make the drinking of alcohol incompatible with this improved marital relation. The first sessions usually took place in the hospital, the remainder in the home after discharge. The alcoholic and his wife were given the Marriage Adjustment Inventory (Manson and Lerner, 1962) which identified twelve specific problem areas in the marriage, including money management, family relations, sex problems, children, social life, attention, neurotic tendencies, immaturity, grooming, ideological difficulties, general incompatibility and dominance. The husband and wife met jointly with the counselor who assisted them in listing specific activities which each spouse agreed to perform to make the other spouse happy in the identified problem area, thereby providing reciprocal benefits to each other. This list typically included preparing meals, listening to the partner with undivided attention, picking up the children from school, redistributing the finances, engaging in sexual activities of a particular type or at a minimal frequency, visiting relatives together and spending a night out together. To facilitate communication about sexual interaction, a marriage manual with specific instructions on sex (Ellis, 1966) was given to the partners. Absolute sobriety was a stipulation by all of the wives as one of the agreements. The rationale for this general approach to marital counseling has been described by Stuart (1969).

For unmarried patients living with their families, a similar procedure was used of providing reciprocal benefits between the patient and his parents, to be maintained only when the patient was sober. For patients with neither a marital or parental family attempts were made to arrange a 'synthetic' or foster family. The synthetic family consisted of those persons who might have some natural reason for maintaining regular interactions with the patient: relatives, or an employer or a minister. These synthetic families were encouraged to invite the ex-patient over for dinner on a regular basis, and to expect him to help with chores or offer his services in some other way. Again, sobriety was made a condition for maintaining these 'family' benefits.

Several major problems arose in attempting to carry out the marital and family counseling procedures. A list of the major problems and the attempted strategy for solution is presented as follows: (1) Both the client and his wife often refused to engage in marital counseling on the grounds that the marital situation was so distressful that neither of them had a desire to return to it. The strategy for overcoming this objective was to strongly assure both the client and his spouse that no attempt would be made to return to the marital situation until the spouse had given convincing assurance that the distressful problems would be eliminated. (2) Great difficulty was often experienced by the patient and his wife in designating activities that would make their marriage a pleasant one, often because of their lack of verbal articulation and often because of general reticence and skepticism. The strategy used in overcoming these problems was for the counselor to suggest satisfactions that other married persons enjoyed, to phrase possible satisfactions in specifiable terms, to have the clients imagine what an ideal marriage would consist of, and to ask what satisfactions they might have received in the past or had expected to receive when first married. (3) They often expressed doubt that they could discontinue providing the agreed upon satisfactions when the client began drinking. The strategy for solving this problem was to advise the wife to discontinue physical and social contact with the client as much as possible during that time; in the extreme case she was advised to move out of the house into a motel or with a relative until the client in a sober state requested her return. (4) The client sometimes refused to initiate any unaccustomed activity that had been requested by the spouse such as different type of sexual behavior, the visiting of a particular relative or attending a social club together. The strategy for solving this was the principle of Reinforcer Sampling (Ayllon and Azrin, 1968) in which the clients were asked to "just try it for one week and then we will decide after that whether to continue it". (5) Even after agreements had been made and the couple was following them, a frequent difficulty was that new problems arose that were not covered by the agreements or some of the old agreements were found to be distasteful. The solution was to teach the couple how to draw up these reciprocated agreements on their own.

About five marital and family counseling sessions were conducted in drawing up the complete set of agreements between the spouses or between the patient and his parental or synthetic family.

Social Counseling

Most social interaction of the alcoholic had been reduced to a small circle of friends who also had a severe drinking problem. Consequently, drinking became a behavioral prerequisite for maintaining those social relationships. A social counseling procedure was developed which attempted to restore and improve the client's social relationships and to make continuation of these improved relationships dependent upon sobriety rather than upon drinking. The clients were counseled to schedule social interactions with friends, relatives and community groups with whom alcoholic drinking was not tolerated. At the same time they were discouraged from interacting with those friends known to have a drinking problem. In many instances the client's circle of friends had become circumscribed because of his drinking problem. Hence, a more structured method of creating these incompatible social reinforcers was devised. A former tavern was converted into a self-supporting social club for the clients. This organization provided a band, jukebox, card games, dances, invited female companions, picnics, fish fries, bingo games, movies and other types of social activities. The wives of the clients were strongly invited to attend and often did. Each client was given paid membership to the club for a period of one month, after which he paid his own membership dues. Each member was encouraged to invite personal friends to the club as guests. The club's principal meeting was on Saturday night. For those members without transportation, the other club members made a deliberate effort to provide transportation. Alcoholic beverages were strictly forbidden at the club and any member who arrived at the club with any indication of drinking was turned away. In this manner the clients experienced a greatly improved social life which was incompatible with alcoholic drinking.

Reinforcer-Access Counseling

An improved adjustment in the aforementioned three areas of the family, the job and the social life was often hindered by the absence of facilities that are commonly available to the non-alcoholic. For example, one might find it difficult to obtain employment without a telephone or newspaper. Successful social adjustment was also often hindered by this inability to call and speak with friends, by the absence of transportation facilities (no public transportation was available in this rural area) and by the absence of timely topics of conversation (some of the clients did not read newspapers, listen to the radio or watch television). The attractiveness of the home or family situation was also diminished by the absence of these facilities. In order to make the home a more attractive place, to facilitate communication with potential employers, and to increase access to friends and social occasions, the counselor encouraged and arranged for the clients to obtain a radio and/or television set in their home, to subscribe to the area newspaper, to subscribe to magazines, to obtain an automobile or driving license and to have a telephone installed in their home. If necessary, the counselor arranged for payment of the initial costs in order to prime the activity. So, for example, the required installation charge by the telephone company was paid by the counselor but not the monthly payments thereafter; likewise the first month's payment on the newspaper but not the succeeding months. The rationale for priming these activities was to increase the ease with which the alcoholic could engage in the areas of vocational, marital, and social activities, these three areas of activities already being incompatible with drinking. A second reason why these 'access' activities would be expected to be incompatible with drinking is that most of these activities required continued payments and thereby provided an additional incentive for the client to maintain his remunerative employment. Also it might be expected that these activities would reduce the need for obtaining reinforcement from drinking by providing alternative sources of reinforcement.

Existing Hospital Program

Both the reinforcement and control groups received the counseling and instruction that was standard at the institution. This consisted of approximately 25 one-hour didactic sessions which presented by means of lectures and audio-visual aids: (1) a description of the basic workings of Alcoholics Anonymous, (2) information regarding the statistics on drinking and the problems of alcoholics, (3) examples of alcoholics' behavior, (4) examples of physiological pathologies resulting from alcoholism, (5) examples of sex problems caused by alcohol and the means of overcoming the problems and (6) other related topics.

Community Maintenance

For the first month after discharge, the alcoholic was visited by the counselor once or twice a week. During these visits he was reminded of the reinforcers which existed for family, job, and social life participation. Also, any problems which might have arisen in following the procedures were discussed and several alternative solutions were offered. The visits also functioned as a means of following up the progress of the ex-patient in terms of his sobriety, employment, and social life. After the first month, these visits continued on the average of twice a month, then decreased thereafter to

once a month. If the alcoholic attended the social club, contact was made on a more frequent, although more informal basis.

Recording and Reliability

On every visit, the counselor obtained information about the days unemployed, days drinking occurred and days spent away from home. In most cases, a member of the family was present for the purpose of helping the ex-patients to remember the exact situation. In addition, an assistant who was in no way connected with the counseling, and was unaware that the patients were treated differently, called on the ex-patients after the 6 months period and explained that he was collecting information for the purpose of better understanding alcoholism. The information he collected correlated with that of the counselor at greater than 0.95 using the Pearson r (Edwards, 1969).

RESULTS

Figure 1 shows that the mean per cent of time spent drinking, unemployed, away from home, and institutionalized was more than twice as high for the control group as for the Community-Reinforcement group. The mean per cent of time spent (1) drinking was 14 per cent for the reinforcement group and 79 per cent for the control group; (2) unemployed was 5 per cent for the reinforcement group and 62 per cent for the control; (3) away from family or synthetic family was 16 per cent for the reinforcement group and 36 per cent for the control group; (4) institutionalized was 2 per cent for the reinforcement and 27 per cent for the control group. The t test of differences for paired comparisons (Edwards, 1969) yielded significant differences ($p < 0.005$) for all measures. The dependent measures were calculated by dividing the number of days the patient was drinking, unemployed, away from home, and institutionalized by the total number of days since discharge. For the drinking measure, time spent in an institu-

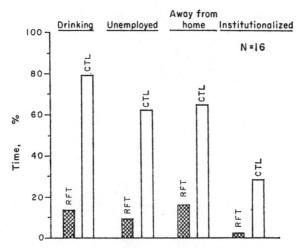

Fig. 1. A Comparison of the Key Dependent Measures for the Reinforcement and Control Groups since Discharge: Mean Percentages of Time Spent Drinking, Unemployed, Away from Home and Institutionalized.

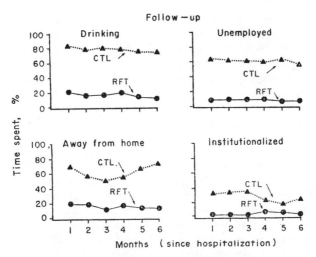

Fig. 2. The Stable Difference Between Groups over the 6 Months After Discharge of the Key Dependent Measures: Mean Percentages of Time Spent Drinking, Unemployed, away from Home and Institutionalized.

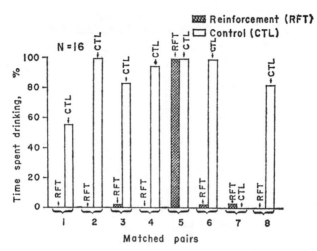

Fig. 3. Sobriety: A Comparison of the Matched Pairs—One Receiving the Community-Reinforcement Procedures, the Other the Control-in Terms of Mean Percentage of Time Spent Sober since Discharge.

tion was not included. If a person had a job but did not work because of temporary weather conditions, illness, being on vacation or weekends or holidays, he was still considered to be employed full-time.

Figure 2 shows that the mean per cent of time spent for all measures computed monthly remained stable over the 6 month period. In no month was there a major fluctuation in any of the measures. For every month and for every measure, the t test of differences yielded significant differences between the control group and the Community-Reinforcement group ($p <$ 0.005). Analysis of the earnings of the patients revealed that the reinforcement group, having a mean income of $355 per month per patient, made more money than did the control group which had a mean income of $190 per month. Analysis of the patients' social activities showed that the Community-Reinforcement patients spent a mean of 13 weekends per patient in a structured social activity out of the home whereas the mean of the control patients was four such weekend activities.

Figure 3 shows the per cent time spent drinking for each of the matched pairs. For 6 of the 8 pairs, the counseled group differed radically from the control group. However, both members of pair 7 remained sober and neither member of pair five remained sober. The counseled member of pair 5 was the only patient for whom counseling produced only minimal changes. He was retarded (IQ = 70), remained single, lived with his alcoholic father, had a low status job, did not attend the social club, and even though a synthetic family was arranged, they lived eight miles away and lack of transportation seemed to prohibit active involvement with them. This patient had the least resources of all patients in this study prior to counseling, and seemed to change the least. Also, he was accidentally discharged from the hospital without the counselor's consent and before the initial hospital-based portion of the counseling was completed. The control member of pair 7 was the highest functioning member in the control group. He returned from the hospital to his well-established family and job situation. Not only did he express satisfaction with his well-paid job as manager of a dairy business, but he also seemed happy with his family and regularly participated in Alcoholics Anonymous.

The job-finding procedures led to satisfactory employment for 4 of the 8 counseled alcoholics. Two were located by systematically checking with the major places of employment. The other 2 were located through advertisement. One job proved unsatisfactory because it was too far from the alcoholic's home and after 2 weeks the job hunt procedures were resumed until a closer job was obtained. For one patient, the 'Situations Wanted' procedure located a variety of what seemed to be acceptable job leads. However, this alcoholic turned down every job offer since he was satisfied with his former job as a trade union construction worker. The remaining 4 counseled patients returned to former jobs. All jobs were located within 10 days after the procedures were started.

All 5 of the married couples in the Community-Reinforcement group initially suggested the possibility of divorce. Two had already separated by the time the husband was admitted to the hospital. Within a short time after counseling had begun, the couples decided to remain married for a while longer. It seemed that counseling was particularly valuable in pointing out the reinforcers which existed for remaining married. All 5 couples in the Community-Reinforcement group eventually remained together while two of the four control couples permanently separated or divorced.

The counseled group participated actively in the social club. Three of the 8 held offices in the club and attended over 80 per cent of the Saturday night meetings; 4 attended about 25 per cent; only 1 failed to attend. The club had been equally available to the control group alcoholics but without the special encouragement and structuring. Yet, only 2 members of the control group ever attended, and neither came more than 3 times.

DISCUSSION

Although the present procedure was tested in a hospital, the procedure does not require hospitalization except as a means of helping the patient through his withdrawal symptoms and physical debility, if any. The present results show that the patients who received the Community-Reinforcement procedures remained more sober than their matched controls. This improvement did not diminish over the 6 month period. The Community-Reinforcement patients also spent greater percentages of time gainfully employed, with their families, and out of institutions. Their average earnings were twice as great as the control group and they spent more time during weekends in acceptable social activities. These positive results for treating alcoholism are unusual in that no controlled study with state hospital patients has reported such general success (Chafetz, Hill and Blane, 1971; Hill and Blane, 1967; Mayer and Meyerson, 1971; Pittman and Tate, 1969).

To evaluate meaningfully the large benefits produced by the present procedure, it is necessary to compare the effects of the present procedure with the effects obtained by previous methods of treating alcoholism. In making such comparisons, a major problem is assuring that comparable populations were used since the rate of spontaneous recovery from alcoholism after hospitalization is often extremely high even among otherwise untreated patients. Improvement rates as high as 100 per cent have been reported for particular subgroups of alcoholics after simple hospitalization, such as the control group whose members refused treatment in one study (Voegtlin, Lemere, Broz and O'Hallaren, 1941), whereas improvement or cure rates have been as low as 20 per cent for other sub-groups, even with treatment (Pittman and Tate, 1969). A reported effectiveness of 90 per cent with a given treatment procedure may, therefore, reflect no improvement by that procedure, since that percentage may have been even less than the spontaneous rate of improvement. Conversely, a reported rate of improvement of only 20 per cent by a given treatment method may represent a substantial effect if the spontaneous rate would have been only 10 per cent. Thus, judgement of the effectiveness of a given treatment procedure requires a comparison with a comparable group of controls. Yet, as recent reviews of alcoholism treatment programs and related studies (Hill and Blane, 1967; Chafetz, Hill and Blane, 1971; Wallgren and Barry, 1970) have concluded, only a handful of studies have been conducted containing a comparable control group. Among this handful are the studies by Madill, Campbell, Laverty, Sanderson and Vandewater (1966); Pittman and Tate (1969) and Wallerstein (1957). Although their measure of sobriety and related social behaviors are presented in terms different from the present study, a general comparison indicates that the present Community-Reinforcement procedure was at least as effective.

Examination of the post-hospital conduct of the control group reveals what the spontaneous rate of improvement would have been without the special Community-Reinforcement procedure. The results show that in the absence of this treatment the patients spent most of their time drinking, worked very rarely, had few acceptable social activities and did not form stable family relationships. Correlational studies have demonstrated that patients exhibiting this type of life style have extremely poor prognosis under virtually all treatment procedures (Gerard and Saenger, 1966).

A question to be raised is whether the present results can be accounted for in terms of the time-out explanation. Did the procedure raise the actual reinforcement density and thereby make the time-out produced by drinking especially aversive? Two lines of evidence support an affirmative answer. First the density of reinforcement of the Community-Reinforcement group was definitely higher than that of the control group

as seen by the increased amount of time at work, increased time spent with families, increased salaries and increased social life. Second, the Community-Reinforcement patients often reported spontaneously that they were now more satisfied with their life. Actually, time-out did not occur in many cases since drinking never occurred. However, the patients all stated that time-out would occur if they did take a drink and this knowledge of the consequence seemed to be the deterrent.

The present study was concerned with specific variables such as time-out and immediacy of reinforcement. In a larger sense, the present results can be considered to offer support for a general Community-Reinforcement model for describing (1) the etiology of alcoholism, (2) the basis of effectiveness of current treatment methods, (3) the direction in which future treatment methods may have the grestest likelihood of success and (4) the epidemiological facts about alcoholism.

Consider first a reinforcement conceptualization of the etiology of alcoholism. Alcohol can be considered as a reinforcer. One source of reinforcement for drinking alcohol is probably the pleasant and relaxing subjective state which it produces. Purely taste factors seem to constitute another basis for the reinforcing value as seen in preferences for one specific type of alcoholic beverage. A third basis for the reinforcement value is the social reinforcement that is given by one's family, friends and peers directly for drinking as at a cocktail party or for drinking as part of a desired group activity, such as at a poker game. Or the social reaction may be that of social tolerance (non-punishment) of otherwise disapproved activities. A fourth source of reinforcement arises after prolonged drinking, namely, the individual becomes addicted to the alcohol and requires ever-increasing amounts to maintain the same subjective sensations and to avoid withdrawal symptoms. At this state the individual is usually characterized as being an alcoholic. In the absence of any inhibitory influences, these four combined sources of subjective, physical, social and addictive reinforcement could be expected to maintain drinking indefinitely, depending on the accumulated strength of these factors for a given individual.

Opposed to these factors that facilitate drinking are various influences that serve to inhibit drinking and which can be conceptualized as negative reinforcers. The major types of negative reinforcers correspond roughly to the major types of positive reinforcers. Under excessive alcohol consumption many of the subjective sensations become unpleasurable such as nausea, dizziness, incoordination and sexual impotence. Unpleasant social reactions rather than approval may result from one's friends, family, legal authorities and employers who then reject the alcoholic. The deterrent value of these negative reinforcers on a given individual will depend on whether they are operative on him (does he have a family or job), on the magnitude of the negative reinforcer (how much is lost when losing a given job or family) and the immediacy with which the negative reinforcer follows the act of drinking (how much does the employer tolerate drinking).

Current treatment methods may be conceptualized as emphasizing one or more of the above reinforcement influences. Shock-aversion therapy emphasizes the physical negative reinforcers and the importance of immediacy by arranging for very painful electric shocks to be delivered in an immediate association with the act or thought of drinking. Antabuse therapy emphasizes the importance of frequency of negative reinforcement by insuring that a painful, nauseous reaction will result shortly after each act of drinking. The Alcoholics Anonymous program emphasizes the social types of negative reinforcement by providing a social peer group which reacts negatively to drinking but arranges social positive reinforcement for non-drinking. Treatment approaches which include vocational and general counseling can be considered to be emphasizing

the negative reinforcement influences in that by providing regular gainful employment to the alcoholic, he will be assured of a time-out from positive reinforcement resulting from drinking. The detoxification procedure that has become standard in hospitals emphasizes the elimination of the withdrawal symptom as a source of reinforcement in that once the alcoholic individual has been forcibly kept sober for a period of time he no longer has the same want to keep drinking in order to avoid the withdrawal symptoms. Efforts to discover a central nervous system center for alcoholism can be considered to be an emphasis on discovering the neurological basis for the pleasurable subjective sensations caused by drinking (St-Laurent and Olds, 1967).

This Community-Reinforcement model of alcoholism also appears capable of conceptualizing some of the major findings concerning the epidemiology of alcoholism. As noted below, the major association of alcoholism is with cultural factors (Bales, 1946; DeLint and Schmidt, 1971) which can be taken to mean that particular sub-cultures, such as the French and Italian, reinforce drinking whereas other sub-cultures, such as the Scandinavians, Jews and Moslems, give negative reinforcers for drinking. The lower rate of alcoholism among married individuals and those with stable families (Gerard and Saenger, 1966) is taken to show that negative reinforcers will be encountered to a greater extent by the time-out from positive family reinforcers. The finding that alcohol consumption decreases when the cost of alcohol is increased (DeLint and Schmidt, 1971) follows directly from the inhibitory properties of monetary cost as a negative reinforcer. Similarly, the lower rate of alcoholism among the regularly employed (Gerard and Saenger, 1966; Trice, 1962) is taken to be the result of the negative reinforcer of job dismissal that results only when one is regularly employed. The relatively high rate of alcoholism among the self-employed (Gerard and Saenger, 1966; Trice, 1962) can be explained on the basis of this negative reinforcer not being as immediate as when one is employed by others. The general observation of a higher rate of alcoholism during the 'off-seasons' for various employment categories shows that in the absence of regular vocational reinforcement, a time-out from reinforcement will not occur for drinking. The varying susceptibility to alcohol by different individuals (Jellinek, 1960) is taken to indicate varying degrees of positive reinforcement and varying degrees of unpleasant medical reaction, i.e. negative reinforcement such as is normally encountered with all drugs (Wallgren and Barry, 1970). The common observation that some persons have a high level of social, economic and family satisfactions and yet become alcoholic can be analyzed by examining whether their drinking is immediately followed by loss of these satisfactions or whether a long delay occurs such as by the alcoholic's circumventing detection.

The relationship between the present model and the theory of tension reduction is especially relevant because of the general acceptance of that tension reduction theory as an explanation of alcoholic drinking. The tension reduction theory considers that alcohol is consumed primarily because it reduces anxiety or tension: the proposed model also assumes that alcohol is a reinforcer but not necessarily because of its ability to reduce tension. The Community-Reinforcement model assumes that alcohol is pleasant to drink (a reinforcer), that this reinforcement value will be great at moments of pleasure as well as stress, and that alcohol consumption will be governed by social, economic and other such reactions to the drinking. Only with respect to the stress of the withdrawal symptoms do the two theoretical statements necessarily coincide. Evidence in favor of the Community-Reinforcement theory over the tension reduction theory can be seen from two major sources: (1) As a very recent review has concluded, laboratory studies show that the evidence for the tension-reduction theory "is negative, equivocal and often contradictory" (Coppell and Herman,

1972). (2) As noted previously, epidemiological studies such as by DeLint and Schmidt (1971) show alcoholic consumption to be associated primarily with social and cultural factors and not with factors that might be considered as stressful such as low income level (Schmidt *et al.*, 1968) and neurotic or anxious personality (Lisansky, 1967).

The promise of different alcohol treatment approaches may be estimated on the basis of the known correlates of alcoholism. In general, the search for genetic, personality and economic correlates of alcoholism have shown little association (Wallgren and Barry, 1970; Schmidt, *et al.* 1968). The major factors associated with alcoholism have been the social-cultural and familial factors (Gerard and Saenger, 1966; Schmidt, *et al.*, 1968; Wallgren and Barry, 1970). These findings may be taken to indicate that the greatest progress in future treatment research will come from treatments that alter these social-cultural influences and that community-based treatment procedures therefore hold great promise.

REFERENCES

Alcoholics Anonymous (1960) *The Story of how Many Thousands of Men and Women Have Recovered from Alcoholism.* Alcoholics Anonymous Publishing, New York.

Ayllon T. and Azrin N. H. (1968) Reinforcer sampling: A technique for increasing the behavior of mental patients. *J. Appl. Behav. Anal.* 1, 13–20.

Bales R. F. (1946) Cultural differences in rates of alcoholism. *Q. J. Stud. Alcohol.* 6, 480–499.

Bindman A. J. and Spiegel A. D. (Eds.) (1969) *Perspectives in Community Mental Health.* Aldine Publishing Co., Chicago.

Bucher B. and Lovaas O. I. (1968) Use of aversive stimulation in behavior modification, In *Miami Symposium on the Prediction of Behavior 1967: Aversive Stimulation* (Ed. M. R. Jones). University of Miami Press, Coral Gables, Florida.

Caplan G. (1964) *Principles of Preventive Psychiatry.* Basic Books, New York.

Caplan G. (1970) *The Theory and Practice*

of Mental Health Consultation. Basic Books, New York.

Chafetz M. E., Blane H. T. and Hill M. J. (Eds.) (1970) Frontiers of Alcoholism. Science House, New York.

Coppell H. and Herman C. P. (1972) Alcohol and tension reduction. Q. J. Stud. Alcohol 33, 33—64.

DeLint J. and Schmidt W. (1971) Consumption averages and alcoholism prevalence: A brief review of epidemiological investigations. Br. J. Addict. 66, 97—107.

Dreese M. (1960) How to Get the Job. (Rev. Edn). Science Research Associates, Chicago.

Edwards A. L. (1969) Statistical Analysis. Holt, Rinehart & Winston Inc., New York.

Ellis A. (1966) The Art and Science of Love. Bantam Books, New York.

Fairweather G. W., Sanders D. H., Maynard H. and Cressler D. L. (1969) Community Life for the Mentally Ill. Aldine Publishing Co., Chicago.

Ferster C. B. (1958) Control of behavior in chimpanzees and pigeons by time-out from positive reinforcement. Psychol. Monogr. 72, No. 8 (Whole No. 461).

Freytag Fredericka (1967). Psychodynamisms with special reference to the alcoholic, In Alcoholism: Behavioral Research, Therapeutic Approaches (Ed. Ruth Fox). Springer Publishing Co., New York.

Gerard D. L. and Saenger G. (1966) Outpatient Treatment of Alcoholism. University of Toronto Press, Toronto, Monograph No. 4.

Hill M. J. and Blane H. T. (1967) Evaluation of psychotherapy with alcoholics: A critical review. Q. J. Stud. Alcohol 28, 76—204.

Holz W. C. and Azrin N. H. (1963) A comparison of several procedures for eliminating behavior. J. Exp. Anal. Behav. 6, 399—406.

Jellinek E. M. (1960) The Disease Concept of Alcoholism. College and University Press, New Haven.

Jones R. J. and Azrin N. H. (1972) An experimental application of social reinforcement approach to the problem of job finding J. Appl. Behav. Anal. To be published.

Klein D. C. (1968) Community Dynamics and Mental Health. Wiley, New York.

Leitenberg H. (1965) Is time-out from positive reinforcement an aversive event? Psychol. Bull. 64, 428—441.

Lisansky E. S. (1967) Clinical research in alcoholism and the use of psychological tests: A reevaluation, In Alcoholism: Behavioral Research, Therapeutic Approaches (Ed. Ruth Fox). Springer Publishing Co., New York.

Madill M., Campbell D., Laverty S. G., Sanderson R. E. and Vandewater S. L. (1966) Aversion treatment of alcoholics by Succinylcholine-induced apneic paralysis. Q. J. Stud. Alcohol 27. 483—510.

Manson M. P. and Lerner A. (1962) The Marriage Adjustment Inventory. Western Psychological Services, Los Angeles.

Mayer J. and Meyerson D. J. (1971) Outpatient treatment of alcoholics. Q. J. Stud. Alcohol 32, 620—627.

Meyerson D. S. and Mayer J. (1967) The origins, treatments and destiny of skid row alcoholic men, In Alcoholism: Behavioral Research, Therapeutic Approaches (Ed. Ruth Fox). Springer Publishing Co., New York.

Pasaminick B., Scarpitti F. R. and Denitz S. (1967) Schizophrenics in the Community. Appleton-Century-Crofts, New York.

Pittman D. J. and Tate R. L. (1969) A comparison of two treatment programs for alcoholics. Q. J. Stud. Alcohol 30, 888—899.

Rachman S. and Teasdale J. (1969) Aversion Therapy and Behavior Disorders: An Analysis. University of Miami Press, Coral Gables, Florida.

Schmidt W. G., Smart R. G. and Moss M. K. (1968) Social Class and the Treatment of Alcoholism. University of Toronto Press, Toronto, Monograph No. 7.

Sheppard H. L. and Belitsky H. H. (1966) The Job Hunt. The Johns Hopkins Press, Baltimore.

Skinner B. F. (1938) The Behavior of Organisms. Appleton-Century-Crofts, New York.

Steiner C. M. (1969) The alcoholic game. Q.s, J. Stud. Alcohol 30, 920—938.

St. Laurent J. and Olds J. (1967) Alcohol and brain centers of positive reinforcement, In Alcoholism: Behavioral Research, Therapeutic Approaches (Ed. Ruth Fox). Springer Publshing Co., New York.

Stuart R. B. (1969) Token reinforcement in marital treatment, In *Advances in Behavior Therapy* (Ed. R. Rubin and C. Franks). Academic Press, New York.

Sulzer E. S. (1965) Behavior modification in adult psychiatric patients, In *Case Studies in Behavior Modification* (Ed. L. Ullmann and L. Krasner). Holt, Rinehart and Winston, Inc., New York.

Tharp R. G. and Wetzel R. J. (1969) *Behavior Modification in the Natural Environment*. Academic Press, New York.

Trice H. M. (1962) The job behaviors of problem drinkers, In *Society, Culture and Drinking Patterns* (Ed. D. Pittman and C. Snyder). John Wiley, New York.

Voegtlin W. L., Lemere F., Broz W. R. and O'Hallaren P. (1941) Conditioned reflex therapy of chronic alcoholism—IV. A preliminary report on the value of reinforcement. *Q. J. Stud. Alcohol.* 2, 505–511.

Vogel-Sprott, M. (1967) Alcoholism as learned behavior: Some hypotheses and research, In *Alcoholism: Behavioral Research, Therapeutic Approaches* (Ed. Ruth Fox). Springer Publishing Co., New York.

Wahler R. G. (1969) Setting generality: Some specific and general effects of child behavior therapy. *J. Appl. Behav. Anal.* 2, 239–246.

Wallerstein R. S. (Ed.) (1957) *Hospital Treatment of Alcoholism: A Comparative Experimental Study*. Basic Books, New York.

Wallgren H. and Barry H. (1970) *Actions of Alcohol*, Vol. II. Elsevier Publishing Co., Amsterdam.

Wilkinson R. (1970) *The Prevention of Drinking Problems*. Oxford University Press, New York.

Wolf M., Risley R. and Mees H. (1964) Application of operant conditioning procedures to the behavior problems of an autistic child. *Behav. Res. & Therapy* 1, 305–312.

Deviant Drug Use in Adolescence:

A Review of Psychosocial Correlates

G. NICHOLAS BRAUCHT, DANIEL BRAKARSH,
DIANE FOLLINGSTAD, and K. L. BERRY

Deviant adolescent drug use has come to occupy center stage among the long list of contemporary problems concerning America's youth. Given the current drive for intervention into this widespread and seemingly increasing deviant use of drugs (including alcohol) by today's youth, the need for psychosocial explanation of adolescent drug use is of pressing practical concern. Comprehensive, cogent identification of the sociocultural and personality determinants of various forms of youthful drug use is fundamental to the development and administration of primary prevention and treatment efforts in this area. Accordingly, it is the authors' intention to review critically the literature concerning the sociocultural and personality correlates of deviant adolescent drug use in an attempt to assess the level of psychosocial description and explanation which is presently available. . . .

SOCIOCULTURAL CORRELATES OF ADOLESCENT NARCOTIC USE

Much research has focused on the familial environment of the adolescent addict. Family fragmentation, in the form of either the actual physical loss (Vaillant, 1966b) or the separation of parents (Rosenberg, 1968) has often been noted in the family backgrounds of adolescent addicts. These findings are further supported by those of both Rosenberg (1969) who pointed out that less than half of his subject group of youthful addicts had reached the age of 15 with both their parents living continuously at home, and by Lewis and Osberg (1958) who noted that the family of the addict generally lacks cohesiveness.

Although many researchers agree that the parents of addicts are extreme personality types (Modlin & Montes, 1964), there is a marked lack of agreement as to the nature of the extreme personality type. Three major parental personality patterns have emerged in the literature. The first is the overprotecting parent, found in the research of Ausubel (1961), Bender (1963), and Laskowitz (1961). The second pattern is that of the underdominating parent (Ausubel, 1961; Bender, 1963). This personality pattern is supported by Rosenberg's study (1968) which discovered a relationship between inadequate parental control and adolescent addiction and the research of Robins (1966), which found that subjects who were diagnosed as psychopaths having problems with alcohol and drugs were early in the sibling birth order and frequently came from families whose parents were uninterested in them and exercised little discipline. While Rosenberg (1969) has isolated the trait of underdominance as typical of the mother of the adolescent addict, Lewis and Osberg (1958) hypothesize that the father, if not absent, is the weak individual in the family.

The third parental personality pattern thought to be related to adolescent addiction is overdomination (Ausubel, 1961; Bender, 1963). Zimmering (1952) and Lewis and Osberg (1958) feel that the pattern consists specifically of an overdominating mother, while Mason (1958) posits that these overpowering mothers simulate aggression and sexual drives in their children, then deny and punish these drives. Rosenberg (1969) found that the father of the adolescent addict represented the overdominating influence in the family, frequently the symbol of punishment and rejection.

Another theme in the research on sociocultural correlates of adolescent addiction is parental rejection during the formative years. While Rosenberg (1969) points to frequent paternal rejection, Hirsh's (1961) theory suggests that sons who are infantilized by rejecting narcissistic mothers are prone to addiction. Gold (1957) also suggests the salience of a rejecting environment within families, producing insecurity feelings. Rosenberg (1968, 1969) concludes that the early life of the addict is marked by either a general deprivation of parental models or the presence of inadequate models, as indicated by a high degree of parental alcohol abuse or mental or physical illness. Nyswander (1956) disagrees to some extent with the deviant family model by stating that addicts have no more or less problems with their parents than the average emotionally disturbed patient. Although there is a lack of consensus as to specifics in the studies noted

above, this body of research (primarily retrospective studies) seems to point to the hypothesis that the adolescent addict, in his early years, suffers from mentally disturbed parents, from rejecting parents, or from the absence of one or both parents.

The ethnic composition of adolescent narcotic addicts has been studied by Chein (1959), Bender (1963), and Vaillant (1966a), who agree that most addicts are members of a minority community. There seem to exist two implications of this finding. First, being a member of an ethnic minority leads to the possibility of racial discrimination; both Murray (1967) and Zimmering (1952) found racial discrimination to be a relevant factor in narcotics addiction. Second, Vaillant's (1966a) sample of adolescent addicts were not only from a minority community but were first generation, native born Americans. This finding points to the possibility that one of the sociocultural factors relevant to narcotics addiction is a cultural clash between parent and child.

Chein (1959), Bender (1963), and Vaillant (1966b) found that narcotic addicts are generally found in urban and metropolitan areas. These addicts usually grow up in poor residential areas (Murray, 1967) and come from families in low-income groups (Bender, 1963; Chein, 1959; Vaillant, 1966b).

The hypothesis that there is some parent-child conflict regarding status achievement is supported by the studies of Rosenberg (1968, 1969), Vaillant (1966b), and Laskowitz (1961) who found an inadequate vocational adjustment history in the backgrounds of their addict sample. The studies of Ausubel (1961, Scher (1966), Gamso and Mason (1958), Cameron (1963), and Modlin and Montes (1964) also indicate that it is in these urban, poor residential areas that there is a relatively high availability of narcotics, and it is this availability which also helps to determine who becomes a drug addict.

A number of studies (Cameron, 1963; Gamso & Mason, 1958; Modlin & Montes, 1964; Scher, 1966; Vaillant, 1966b) have shown that adolescent narcotics addiction is usually connected with peer-group enticement to deviance. Furthermore, Little and Pearson (1966) attribute perpetuation of drug addiction to the interdependence of an addict and others whom the addict persuades to experiment with narcotics.

In summary, research indicates that the adolescent narcotic user is frequently a member of an ethnic minority, often from an impoverished urban environment, often from a broken home. There is further consensus regarding the importance of peer group enticement and availability of narcotics. While there seems to be agreement on the general point that adolescent users are usually subject to deficient parental models, there is marked disagreement as to the nature of this deficiency; one or both of the parents are characterized as being either overprotecting, overdominating, underdominating, or rejecting. This lack of consensus can be attributed to the heavy reliance on retrospective studies of the narcotic users' parents.

PERSONALITY FACTORS RELATED TO NARCOTIC USE

Intelligence has been a variable considered by several researchers. Zimmering (1952) found that most addicts to be of dull normal intelligence, but Rosenberg (1968), Vaillant (1966b), and Knight and Prout (1951) disagree. They found their subjects to range from average to superior intelligence. Immaturity is considered a personality characteristic of youthful addicts by Rettig and Pasamanick (1964), Ausubel (1961), and Bender (1963). Both Bender (1963) and Zimmering (1952), even though their observations were conducted a decade apart, agree that addicts show low frustration tolerance, that they tend to repress their troubles, and that they tend to withdraw into fantasies. Knight and Prout (1951) described their clinic population of addicts as being introverted, shy, insecure (also Gilbert & Lombardi, 1967), having a flat affect,

shallow interests and immature goals, and lacking healthy resources and adequate structure. Gilbert and Lombardi (1967), using Minnesota Multiphasic Personality Inventory data, concluded that addicts generally are depressed (also Leeds, 1965), tense, feel inadequate (also Laskowitz, 1961), are irresponsible (also Laskowitz, 1961), are impatient and irritable, lack persistence, are hypersensitive and apprehensive, and have poor morale. Both Gilbert and Lombardi (1967) and Laskowitz (1961) noted the egocentrism of addicts in their disregard for social mores and in their view of themselves as members of an elite group. Restlessness and quick dissatisfaction, private logic following, limited problem solving, and overvaluation of the masculine role are described by Laskowitz (1961). Savitt (1963) describes the addict as a person unable to experience love and gratification through the usual channels. An interesting study by Cooper (1959) suggests that the personality descriptions of drug addicts in literature are not at all like the self-perceptions of these individuals.

Most researchers agree that most narcotic addicts have some mental problems or a weak or disturbed personality (Ausubel, 1961; Chein, Gerard, Lee, & Rosenfeld, 1964; Gerard & Kornetsky, 1954; Holmberg & Jansson, 1968; Laskowitz, 1961; Savitt, 1963; Vogel, Isbell, & Chapman, 1948; Wakefield, 1963). The consensus ends here. Many authors suggest their own theories and findings as to the mental status of addicts: Cameron (1963) describes addicts as inadequate personalities; Sorio (1967) discusses a pathological desire for drugs; Rosenberg (1968) characterizes his subjects as having high levels of anxiety and neuroticism; and Laskowitz (1961) also stresses the neurotic tendencies of addicts, considering them to have low ego strength or poorly developed superegos. Vaillant (1966b) and Bender (1963) call the syndrome a personality disorder, Gilbert and Lombardi (1967) and Cameron (1963) call addiction a basic character disorder, while Murray (1967) and

Laskowitz (1961) use the term social deviant, and Hill (1957) employs the term conduct disorder. Psychopathic traits are considered to be present in many addicts by Gilbert and Lombardi (1967), Hill (1957), Monroe, Miller, and Lyle (1964) and Laskowitz (1961). Hill, Haertzen, and Glaser (1960) used Minnesota Multiphasic Personality Inventory data to conclude "Personality characteristics of narcotic addicts are either associated with psychopathy or are predominately psychopathic in nature although they may include many of the classical psychoneurotic and psychotic features [p. 97]." Rosenberg (1969) reported less disturbance on psychological tests by addicts than alcoholics, although Gilbert and Lombardi (1967) found addicts to have deeper and more widespread pathology than nonaddicts. Holmberg and Jansson (1968) consider schizoid curiosity to be a factor in narcotic use, Hill (1957) suggests that some addicts are schizoid psychopaths, and Bender (1963) reports evidences of schizoid blocking of the perceptual field in addict samples. Clark (1962) reports that psychiatric illnesses precede or accompany 40% of drug addiction cases and that 20% of the cases appear to be sociopathic. Nyswander (1956) has found that the reported incidence of mental illness among addicts is no different from the rate in the general population, and she suggests that this is the result of addicts' failure to seek or avail themselves of help, and because their psychopathology is often subclinical.

In summary, addicts have been found to be immature, insecure, irresponsible, and egocentric. However, the way in which all these traits fit together within any given narcotic addict is unclear. This can be seen as the result of a lack of a sound theoretical structure as the point of origin for these studies. Furthermore, although there is some agreement that the narcotic addict suffers from a personality disorder, there is hardly any agreement as to the specific dynamics of this disorder. Indeed, one should be aware that the population of adolescent drug addicts is very loosely defined and includes more than one personality type. Psychological predispositions to recruitment into this population may be different for different sociocultural strata, different patterns of drug use (e.g., chronic or episodic) and differential involvement of various psychological functions of drug use. On this last point, see Chein et al. (1964) and Chein (1969).

Almost all of the personality research and much of the sociocultural research focuses on the psychopathological nature of adolescent narcotic use. Although such an approach is reasonable if the goal is the treatment of the young addict, it is not readily apparent that the psychopathology orientation is appropriate to the primary prevention of narcotic use. In addition, the use of uncontrolled convict and clinic populations in this body of research casts considerable doubt on the validity, reliability, and representativeness of the research findings. Furthermore, the personality results reported are primarily the product of small sample observational research, or in many cases, conjecture. . . .

REFERENCES

Ausubel, D. P. Causes and types of narcotic addiction: A psychosocial view. *Psychiatric Quarterly*, 1961, 35, 523–531.
Barron, F. Motivational patterns in LSD usage. In R. C. DeBold & R. C. Leaf (Eds.), *LSD, man, and society*. Middletown, Conn.: Wesleyan University Press, 1967.
Bender, L. Drug addiction in adolescence. *Comprehensive Psychiatry*, 1963, 4, 131–134.
Blum, R. *Utopiates*. New York: Atherton Press, 1966.
Blumenfield, M., & Glickman, L. Ten months experience with LSD users admitted to a county psychiatric receiving hospital. *New York State Journal of Medicine*, 1967, 67, 1849–1853.
Bowers, M., Chipman, A., Schwartz, A., & Dann, O. T. Dynamics of psychedelic drug

abuse. *Archives of General Psychiatry*, 1967, 16, 560–566.

Brill, N. Q., Compton, E., & Grayson, H. M. Personality factors in marijuana use. *Archives of General Psychiatry*, 1971, 24, 163–165.

Brooks, H. B. Teaching teachers to teach about drugs. *National Association of Secondary School Principals Bulletin*, 1971, 55, 127–134.

Cameron, D. C. Addiction: Current issues. *American Journal of Psychiatry*, 1963, 120, 313–319.

Carey, J. T., & Mandel, J. A San Francisco Bay Area "speed scene." *Journal of Health and Social Behavior*, 1968, 9, 164–174.

Chein, I. The status of sociological and social psychological knowledge concerning narcotics. In, *Narcotic drug addiction problems*. Washington, D.C.: United States Department of Health, Education, and Welfare, 1959.

Chein, I. Psychological function of drug use. In H. Sternberg (Ed.), *Scientific basis of drug dependence*. London: Churchill, 1969.

Chein, I., Gerard, D., Lee, R., & Rosenfeld, E. *The road to H.* New York: Basic Books, 1964.

Clark, J. A. The prognosis in drug addiction. *Journal of Mental Science*, 1962, 108, 411–418.

Cockett, R., & Marks, V. Amphetamine taking among young offenders. *British Journal of Psychiatry*, 1969, 115, 1203–1204.

Cohen, M., & Klein, D. F. Drug abuse in a young psychiatric population. *American Journal of Orthopsychiatry*, 1970, 40, 448–455.

Cooper, M. Differences in self-perception among physically dependent drug addicts, alcohol addicts and controls. *Dissertation Abstracts*, 1959, 19, 2672.

Davis, F., & Munoz, L. Heads and freaks: Patterns and meanings of drug use among hippies. *Journal of Health and Social Behavior*, 1968, 9, 156–164.

Davis, G. C., & Brehm, M. L. Juvenile prisoners: Motivational factors in drug use. *Proceedings of the Annual Convention of the American Psychological Association*, 1971, 6 (Pt. 1), 333–334.

Dearden, M. H., & Jekel, T. F. Pilot program in high school drug education utilizing nondirective techniques and sensitivity training. *Journal of School Health*, 1971, 41, 118–124.

Edwards, A. E., Bloom, M. H., & Cohen, S. The psychedelics: Love or hostility potion? *Psychological Reports*, 1969, 24, 843–846.

Flynn, W. R. The pursuit of purity: A defensive use of drug abuse in adolescents. *Adolescence*, 1970, 5, 141–150.

Freedman, D. S. On the uses and abuses of LSD. *Archives of General Psychiatry*, 1968, 18, 330–347.

Frosch, W., Robbins, E., & Stern, M. Untoward reactions to LSD resulting in hospitalization. *New England Journal of Medicine*, 1965, 273, 1235–1239.

Gamso, R. R., & Mason, P. A. A hospital for adolescent drug addicts. *Psychiatric Quarterly Supplement*, 1958, 32, 99–109.

Gerard, D., & Kornetsky, C. A social and psychiatric study of adolescent opiate addicts. *Psychiatric Quarterly*, 1954, 28, 113–125.

Gilbert, J. G., & Lombardi, D. N. Personality characteristics of young male narcotic addicts. *Journal of Consulting Psychology*, 1967, 31, 536–538.

Gillie, O. Drug addiction: Facts and folklore. *Science Journal*, 1969, 5A, 75–80.

Gold, L. Toward an understanding of adolescent drug addictions. *Federal Probation*, 1957, 22, 42–48.

Green, M. G., Blake, B. F., Carboy, G. J., & Zenhausenn, R. T. Personality characteristics of the middle class high school drug user. *Proceedings of the Annual Convention of the American Psychological Association*, 1971, 6 (Pt. 2), 559–560.

Gusfield, J. The structural context of college drinking. In G. L. Maddox (Ed.), *The domesticated drug: Drinking among collegians*. New Haven: Conn.: College and University Press, 1970.

Hager, D. L., Verner, A. M., & Stewart, C. S. Patterns of adolescent drug use in middle America. *Journal of Counseling Psychology*, 1971, 18, 292–297.

Harris, E. M. Measurement of alienation in college students: Marijuana users and nonusers. *Journal of School Health*, 1971, 41, 130–133.

Hekimian, L. J., & Glershon, S. Characteristics of drug abusers admitted to a psychiatric hospital. *Journal of American Medical Association*, 1968, 205, 125–130.

Hensala, J., Epstein, L., & Blacker, L. LSD and psychiatric inpatients. *Archives of General Psychiatry*, 1967, 16, 554–559.

Hill, H. E., How to help the addict. *Contemporary Psychology*, 1957, 2, 113–114.

Hill, H. E., Haertzen, D. A., & Glaser, R. Personality characteristics of narcotic addicts as indicated by the MMPI. *The Journal of General Psychology*, 1960, 62, 127–139.

Hirsh, R. Group therapy with parents of adolescent drug addicts. *Psychiatric Quarterly*, 1961, 35, 702–710.

Hogan, R., Mankin, D., Conway, J., & Fox, S. Personality correlates of undergraduate marijuana use. *Journal of Consulting and Clinical Psychology*, 1970, 35, 58–63.

Holmberg, M. B., & Jansson, B. Experiences from an outpatient department for drug addiction in Goteberg. *Acta Psychiatrica Scandinavica*, 1968, 44, 172–189.

Janowitz, J. D. There's no hiding place down there. *American Journal of Orthopsychiatry*, 1967, 37, 296.

Jessor, R., Carman, R., & Grossman, P. Expectations of need satisfaction and drinking patterns of college students. *Quarterly Journal of Studies on Alcohol*, 1968, 29, 101–116.

Jessor, R., Collins, M. I., & Jessor, S. L. On becoming a drinker: Social-psychological aspects of an adolescent transition. *Annals of the New York Academy of Sciences*, 1972, 197, 199–213.

Jessor, R., Graves, T. D., Hanson, R. C., & Jessor, S. L. *Society, personality, and deviant behavior: A study of a tri-ethnic community*. New York: Holt, Rinehart & Winston, 1968.

Jones, M. C. Personality correlates and antecedents of drinking patterns in adult males. *Journal of Consulting and Clinical Psychology*, 1968, 32, 2–12.

Jones, M. C. Personality antecedents and correlates of drinking patterns in women. *Journal of Consulting and Clinical Psychology*, 1971, 36, 61–69.

Keeler, M. H. Motivation for marijuana use: A correlate of adverse reaction. *American Journal of Psychiatry*, 1968, 125, 386–390.

Keniston, K. *The uncommitted*. New York: Delta, 1965.

Kleber, H. K. Student use of hallucinogens. *Journal of American College Health Association*, 1965, 14, 109–117.

Klein, J., & Phillips, D. From hard to soft drugs: Temporal and substantive changes in drug usage among gangs in a working class community. *Journal of Health and Social Behavior*, 1968, 9, 139–145.

Knight, R. C., & Prout, C. T. A study of results in hospital treatment of drug addicts. *American Journal of Psychiatry*, 1951, 108, 303–308.

Kuehn, J. L. Student drug user and his family. *Journal of College Student Personnel*, 1970, 1, 404–413.

Laskowitz, D. The adolescent drug addict: An Adlerian view. *Journal of Individual Psychology*, 1961, 17, 68–79.

Leary, T., Metzmer, R., & Alpert, R. *The psychedelic experience: A manual based upon the Tibetan Book of the Dead*. New Hyde Park, N.Y.: University Books, 1964.

Leeds, D. P. Personality patterns and modes of behavior of male adolescent narcotic addicts and their mothers. *Dissertation Abstracts*, 1965, 26, 2861.

Lewis, J. M., & Osberg, J. W. Treatment of narcotic addicts: Observations on institutional treatment of character disorder. *American Journal of Orthopsychiatry*, 1958, 28, 730–749.

Liebert, R. S. Drug use: Symptom disease or adolescent experimentation: The task of therapy. *College Health*, 1967, 16, 25–29.

Little, R. B., & Pearson, M. M. The management of pathologic interdependence in drug addiction. *American Journal of Psychiatry*, 1966, 123, 554–560.

Ludwig, A., & Levine, J. Patterns of hallucinogenic drug abuse. *Journal of the American Medical Association*, 1965, 191, 92–96.

MacKay, J. Clinical observations on adolescent problem drinkers. *Quarterly Journal of Studies on Alcohol*, 1961, 22, 124–134.

Maddox, G. L. Drinking prior to college. In G. L. Maddox (Ed.), *The domesticated drug: Drinking among collegians*. New Haven, Conn.: College and University Press, 1970.

Malcolm, A. I. Drug abuse and social alienation. *Today's Education*, 1970, 59, 28–31.

Mamlet, L. N. Consciousness-limiting side effects of consciousness-expanding drugs. *American Journal of Orthopsychiatry*, 1967, 37, 296–297.

Mason, P. The mother of the addict. *Psychiatric Quarterly Supplement*, 1958, 32, 189–199.

McAree, C. P., Steffenhagen, R. A., & Zheutlin, L. S. Personality factors in college drug users. *International Journal of Social Psychiatry*, 1969, 15, 102–106.

McClelland, D. C. The power of positive drinking. *Psychology Today*, 1971, 4, 40–41, 78–79.

McGlothlin, W. H., & Cohen, S. Use of hallucinogenic drugs among college students. *American Journal of Psychiatry*, 1965, 122, 572–574.

Mitchell, K. R., Kirkby, R. J., & Mitchell, D. M. Notes on sex differences in student drug usage. *Psychological Reports*, 1970, 27, 116.

Mizner, G. L., Barter, J. T., & Werme, P. H. Patterns of drug use among college students: A preliminary report. *American Journal of Psychiatry*, 1970, 127, 15–24.

Mizruchi, E. H., & Perrucci, R. Prescription, proscription and permissiveness: Aspects of norms and deviant drinking behavior. In G. L. Maddox (Ed.), *The domesticated drug: Drinking among collegians*. New Haven, Conn.: College and University Press, 1970.

Modlin, H. C., & Montes, A. Narcotic addiction in physicians. *American Journal of Psychiatry*, 1964, 121, 358.

Monroe, J. J., Miller, J., & Lyle, W. The extension of psychopathic deviancy scales for the screening of addict patients. *Educational and Psychological Measurement*, 1964, 2, 47–56.

Murray, J. B. Drug addiction. *Journal of General Psychology*, 1967, 77, 41–68.

Norton, W. A. The marijuana habit: Some observations of a small group of users. *Canadian Psychiatric Association Journal*, 1968, 13, 163–173.

Nyswander, M. *The drug addict as a patient*. New York: Grune & Stratton, 1956.

Parker, F. Self-role strain and drinking disposition at a prealcoholic age level. *Journal of Social Psychology*, 1969, 78, 55–61.

Pearce, J. The role of education in combatting drug abuse. *Journal of School Health*, 1971, 41, 83–88.

Pearlman, S. Drug use and experience in an urban college population. *American Journal of Orthopsychiatry*, 1968, 38, 503–514.

Rettig, S., & Pasamanick, B. Subcultural identification of hospitalized male drug addicts: A further examination. *Journal of Nervous and Mental Disease*, 1964, 139, 83–86.

Robins, L. N. *Deviant children grown up*. Boston: Williams & Wilkins, 1966.

Rogers, E. Group influence on student drinking behavior. In G. L. Maddox (Ed.), *The domesticated drug: Drinking among collegians*. New Haven, Conn.: College and University Press, 1970.

Rosenberg, C. M. Young drug addicts: Addiction and its consequences. *Medical Journal of Australia*, 1968, 1, 1031–1033.

Rosenberg, C. M. Determinants of psychiatric illness in young people. *British Journal of Psychiatry*, 1969, 15, 907–915.

Rosenbloom, J. R. Notes on Jewish drug addicts. *Psychological Reports*, 1969, 5, 769–772.

Sadava, S. W. *College student drug use: A social-psychological study*. (Doctoral dissertation, University of Colorado) Boulder, Colorado: University Microfilms, 1970, No. 70-23749.

Savitt, R. A. Psychoanalytic studies on addiction. *Psychoanalytic Quarterly*, 1963, 32, 43–57.

Scher, J. Patterns and profiles of addiction and drug abuse. *Archives of General Psychiatry*, 1966, 15, 539–551.

Skolnick, J. H. Religious affiliation and drinking behavior, *Quarterly Journal of Studies on Alcohol*, 1958, 19, 452–470.

Smart, R. G., & Fejer, D. Illicit drug users: Their social backgrounds, drug use and psychopathology. *Journal of Health and Social Behavior*, 1969, 10, 297–308.

Snyder, C. R. *Alcohol and the Jews*. Glencoe, Ill.: The Free Press, 1958.

Sorio, J. Vice as a psychiatric infirmity. *Actas Lusa Espanoles de Neurologia y Psiquiatria*, 1967, 26, 171–181.

Steffenhagen, R. A., McAree, C. P., & Zheutlin, L. S. Social and acdemic factors associated with drug use on the University of Vermont campus. *International Journal of Social Psychiatry*, 1969, 15, 92–96.

Suchman, E. A. The hang-loose ethic and the

spirit of drug use. *Journal of Health and Social Behavior*, 1968, 9, 146—155.

Vaillant, G. E. Parent-child cultural disparity and drug addiction. *The Journal of Nervous and Mental Disease*, 1966, 142, 534—539. (a)

Vaillant, G. E. A twelve-year follow-up of New York narcotic addicts: Some social and psychiatric characteristics. *Archives of General Psychiatry*, 1966, 15, 599—609. (b)

Vogel, V., Isbell, H., & Chapman, K. Present status of narcotic addiction. *Journal of the American Medical Association*, 1948, 138, 1019—1026.

Wakefield, D. (Ed.) *The addict.* Greenwich, Conn.: Fawcett, 1963.

Welpton, D. F. Psychodynamics of chronic LSD use. *Journal of Nervous and Mental Disease*, 1968, 147, 377—385.

Williams, A. Social drinking, anxiety and depression. *Journal of Personality and Social Psychology*, 1966, 3, 689—693.

Williams, A. Psychological needs and social drinking among college students.. *Quarterly Journal of Studies on Alcohol*, 1968, 29, 355—363.

Williams, A. College problem drinkers: A personality profile. In G. Maddox (Ed.), *The domesticated drug: Drinking among collegians.* New Haven, Conn.: College and University Press, 1970.

Zimmering, P. Drug addiction in relation to problems of adolescence. *American Journal of Psychiatry*, 1952, 109, 272—278.

Zucker, R. Sex-role identity patterns and drinking behavior among adolescents. *Quarterly Journal of Studies on Alcohol*, 1968, 22, 868—884.

The Use of Methadone in a Representative Group of Heroin Addicts

ROBERT T. DALE and FARLEY ROSS DALE

This paper is to report the early results of a study using methadone maintenance in a representative group of hard-core heroin addicts. It includes a detailed report of the preliminary data obtained during the admission evaluation of the patients and second, third, and eighth month follow-up reports describing their progress. A random sample of urine reports obtained during the twelfth month of the program is also included.

PROCEDURE

A total of 814 patients were admitted into a methadone maintenance treatment program in accord with the Federal regulations for the investigational use of methadone. The admission criteria were: a history of physiological dependence on one or more opiate drugs, one or more failures of treatment for physiologic dependence on opiates, and evidence of current dependence on opiates. Although patients under 18 were excluded, no attempt was made to further screen out patients on the basis of ethnic background, evidence of employability, level of education, degree of motivation, or any other factor which would seem to bias this study.

It was our purpose to determine as closely as possible the general effectiveness of methadone with the addict population at large.

The admission work-up on each patient was in accord with the Federal protocol (*Federal Register*, 1971). Patients accepted into the program were started on a low dose of methadone, i.e., 20 mg, and the dose was built gradually as tolerated so that, by the end of the second month of treatment, a stabilization dose for the majority of patients was in the accepted blocking range of 80–120 mg per day. Only 3% of the patients were being successfully maintained below 80 mg per day by the end of the second month. At intervals not exceeding one week, each patient's urine was analyzed by thin-layer chromatography for methadone, morphine, quinine, barbiturates, and amphetamines. The thin-layer chromatography was carried out by Long Island Laboratories, a division of Cybertek, Inc., Plainview, Long Island, New York. All urine specimens were obtained under close supervision.

Patients were referred for rehabilitative measures as indicated. Group and individual psychotherapy and job counseling were made available at the clinic where the

From R. Dale, & F. Dale. The use of methadone in a representative group of heroin addicts. *International Journal of the Addictions*, 1973, *8*, 293–308. Reprinted by courtesy of Marcel Dekker, Inc.

341

metahdone was dispensed. However, patients were not required to make use of the available rehabilitative resources in order to be retained on the program.

Patients failing a total of four appointments for medication without verifiable medical or legal excuse, even if these failures were not consecutive, were required to begin the program again by reporting daily for their medication for two weeks. Any additional failed appointments (greater than four) without medical or legal excuse led to dismissal from the program without the possibility of readmission. Such patients were categorized as discharged because of "failed appointments." The other specific categories for being discharged from the program were as follows: abuse of other drugs such as alcohol, amphetamines, or barbiturates; behavioral disturbance, including criminal behavior; and failure to show methadone in the urine on testing with thin-layer chromatography. Patients failing to show methadone in their urine on either a total of four nonconsecutive reports or three consecutive reports were discharged from the program.

For the purpose of this paper, results of drug urinalyses during the second, fourth, and eight month of treatment are reported and compared. The results, from the standpoint of heroin use, are reported on the basis of frequency of "perfect urine" during each of these months. The term "perfect urine" is defined here as urine showing methadone but no morphine (heroin) or quinine. Since methadone is being used exclusively in this study as an antiopiate agent, a urine could then include other drugs such as barbiturates and amphetamines and still be termed a "perfect urine" by this definition—as long as the urine revealed methadone but no morphine (heroin) or quinine. The abuse of other drugs such as barbiturates and amphetamines is described separately.

In addition, during the third month of treatment, a detailed follow-up questionnaire was administered to a random sample of 390 of the active patients. The questionnaire obtained specific information regarding each patient's employment record both before and after entering the program, including proof of employment; the arrest record since joining the program compared with the year just prior to this; and each patient's attitude as to whether methadone was regarded as a lifetime treatment program. A patient's report of his arrest record on the questionnaire was checked against his chart for accuracy to see if any absences from the program were accounted for by an arrest the patient had denied or not mentioned when the questionnaire was administered. Also, during the eighth month of treatment, a random sample of 100 patients was similarly studied as to employment and arrest record.

RESULTS

Of the original 814 patients accepted into the program, 199 were inactive at the end of two months treatment. Of these 199, 9 (5%) had transferred to other methadone programs and 190 (23%) had been discharged. By the end of eight months, 322 had become inactive. Of these 322, 18 (2%) had transferred to other programs and 304 (37%) had been discharged. Whether all of these discharges should properly be considered "treatment failures" is a matter of interpretation since the majority (75%) had been discharged *in absentia* for failed appointments. The category of "failed appointments" includes patients who came for only one visit as well as patients who reappeared after being discharged, expecting to continue the program. Thus far readmission of such patients has not been allowed. The various reasons for discharge and their percentages are summarized in Table 1.

The preliminary data obtained as a part of the admission evaluation and work-up on each patient have been divided for comparative purposes into that which was obtained from those patients who remained active for the first two months and those who became inactive during the first two months of their treatment (Tables 2 and 3).

Table 1. Discharged Patients

Reason	By end of two months N	By end of two months %	By end of eight months N	By end of eight months %
Failed appointments	165	87	227	75
No methadone in urine	14	7	52	17
Abuse of other drugs	8	4	18	6
Behavioral problems	3	2	7	2
Totals	190	100	304	100

In both our active and inactive groups, the older aged, hard-core street ghetto addict with a criminal record is most frequently represented. This is of importance since these patients would be expected to represent the nucleus of the heroin epidemic. It is noted that a comparison of the percentage of active to inactive for each ethnic group indicates a somewhat different success rate by ethnic group on the basis of the first two months of the study. Also, our active pa-

Table 2. Personal and Family Histories of Active and Inactive Patients (at Two Months)

	Active N	Active %	Inactive N	Inactive %
Sex				
Male	447	73	149	75
Female	168	27	50	25
Ethnic Group				
Black	341	55	123	62
Puerto Rican	157	26	34	17
White	117	19	42	21
Mean Age	36.9		30.1	
Place of Birth				
New York City	305	50	104	52
New York State	7	1	6	3
Southern states	110	18	33	17
Other states	72	12	25	13
Puerto Rico	112	18	28	14
Other countries	9	1	3	2
Stated occupation				
Professional	2	0.3	0	0
Managerial	82	13	45	23
Skilled labor	199	32	52	26
Unskilled labor	263	43	87	44
Student	15	3	3	2
Never employed	53	9	12	6
Criminal	1	0.1	0	0
Employed at time of admission				
Males	89	20	36	24
Females	27	16	9	17
Total	116	19	45	23
Previous military service	132	21	30	15
Used drugs in service	70	53 (of 132)	19	63 (of 30)
Education				
High school graduate	184	30	55	28
College	48	8	15	8
College graduate	7	1	2	1

Table 2—*Continued*

	Active		Inactive	
	N	%	N	%
Family history				
Single	298	48	81	41
Married	132	21	48	24
Divorced	317 { 51	8	118 { 12	6
Separated	134	22	58	29
Living alone	324	53	81	41
Living with spouse	126	20	39	20
Spouse or ex-spouse				
addicted	86	27	44	37
		(of 317)		(of 118)
Parents living together	333	54	90	45
Parents separated	222	36	73	37
Parents divorced	60	10	36	18
Other addicts in family	126	20	42	21
Spouse or ex-spouse				
knows of addiction	249	79	67	57
		(of 317)		(of 118)
At least one parent				
knows of addiction				
Welfare status				
Welfare	554	90	177	89
Nonwelfare	61	10	22	11

tients had a higher mean age than our inactive. Further, a much greater percentage of the inactive patients described support from other persons for their habit. This suggests that addicts receiving outside support for their habits may be less well motivated for methadone maintenance, perhaps because they are not forced into criminal behavior to get money for drugs. Also, nearly twice the percentage of inactives as opposed to actives were under some legal compulsion such as parole or probation to enter the methadone program. Also, it should be noted that the active patients had a significantly higher number of spontaneous remissions in their histories, suggesting that a history of spontaneous remission may indicate a more highly motivated patient. The most common "reasons" given for these remissions were such statements as, "Got tired of it," or statements indicating a change of environment such as, "Moved out of the City."

In terms of other drug use, alcohol is, as expected, the most frequently abused substance which can be legally obtained (Table 3). On the other hand, of the illegal drugs used by these heroin addicts, apart from heroin itself, cocaine is by far the most important quantitatively and economically. For example, 73% of our active and 57% of our inactive patients admitted to regular use of cocaine at some time in their life, usually concomitant with heroin use.

While it is a frequent clinical impression among those working in drug addiction that barbiturate addiction is more troublesome among females, this has never been, to our knowledge, well documented. This impression is generally confirmed by our admission data showing that, among the active patients, approximately the same percentage of males abused barbiturates as females (whereas in the case of all other drugs, the males exceeded females) and in the case of

Table 3. Addiction History and Criminal Record of Active and Inactive Patients (at Two Months)

	Active		Inactive	
	N	%	N	%
Years on heroin				
Less than 1 yr	8	1	3	2
1–5 yr	151	25	54	27
6–10 yr	126	20	69	35
10 yr	330	54	73	37
Pattern of development of drug use				
Marijuana, heroin	220	36	65	33
Marijuana, amphetamines, heroin	12	2	5	3
Marijuana, cocaine, heroin	38	6	12	6
Amphetamines, heroin	8	1	2	1
Cocaine, heroin	8	1	0	0
Began with heroin	300	49	94	47
Marijuana, barbiturates, heroin	20	3	17	9
Other	9	1	4	2
Use of heroin ($ per day)				
Less than 15$				
Males	3	0.6	0	0
Females	3	0.6	0	0
Totals	5	0.8	0	0
$15–30				
Males	51	11	26	17
Females	29	17	4	8
Totals	80	13	30	18
$31–60				
Males	166	37	47	32
Females	52	30	10	20
Totals	218	35	57	29
$61–100				
Males	140	31	38	26
Females	51	30	23	46
Totals	191	31	61	31
Greater than $100				
Males	87	19	38	26
Females	34	20	13	26
Totals	121	20	51	26
Current and/or past use of other opiates				
Males	117	26	34	23
Females	35	21	10	20
Totals	152	25	44	22
Current and/or past use of cocaine				
Males	344	77	89	60
Females	107	64	25	50
Totals	451	73	114	57
Current and/or past use of marijuana				
Males	190	43	65	44
Females	56	33	17	34
Totals	246	40	82	41
Current and/or past use of amphetamines				
Males	74	17	30	20
Females	14	8	6	12
Totals	88	14	36	18

Table 3—*Continued*

	Active		Inactive	
	N	%	N	%
Current and/or past use of barbiturates				
Males	130	29	38	26
Females	51	30	16	32
Totals	181	29	54	27
Current and/or past use of LSD hallucinogens				
Males	50	11	15	10
Females	9	5	3	6
Totals	59	10	18	9
Daily use of alcohol (current only)				
Males	270	60	120	81
Females	91	54	23	46
Totals	361	59	143	71
Detoxification				
1 time	167	27	49	25
More than 1	233	38	68	34
Psychotherapy	225	37	61	31
Spontaneous remissions	452	73	113	57
Other methadone maintenance programs	107	17	32	16
Number of arrests				
None	73	12	61	31
1	62	10	18	9
2–4	187	30	43	22
5	293	48	77	39
Years in prison				
Less than 1 yr	75	12	33	17
1–2 yr	87	14	30	15
3–8 yr	167	27	19	10
More than 8 yr	96	15	22	11
Legal cases pending	48	8	29	15
Methods of supporting habit				
Petty thieving	359	58	100	50
Prostitution	93	15	26	13
	(49% of females)		(48% of females)	
Pimping	96	16	32	16
Selling drugs	369	60	119	60
Breaking and entering	171	28	44	22
Armed robbery	103	17	32	16
Support from other persons	174	28	93	47
Working	191	31	63	32

inactive patients, an even greater percentage of females abused barbiturates. Thin-layer chromatography also revealed a greater frequency of barbiturate abuse among females (see Table 7).

Our preliminary evaluation data on abuse of other drugs also shed some light on the much disputed pattern of development of drug use in heroin addiction. Approximately one-half of the heroin addict population in this study began their illegal drug use with marijuana. On the other hand, approximately one-half of our patients began their illegal drug use with heroin itself (Table 3).

Table 4. Frequency of "Perfect Urine" Reports (Methadone Without Heroin or Quinine) During Second, Fourth, and Eighth Months

Number of "perfect urine" reports during month	Second month N = 615 (total patient pop.)		Fourth month N = 100 (random sample)		Eighth month N = 100 (random sample)	
	N	%	N	%	N	%
All four "perfect"						
Black	32	9	9	16	19	35
Puerto Rican	43	27	10	42	12	50
White	35	30	12	60	19	86
Totals	110	18	31	31	50	50
Three-out-of-four "perfect"						
Black	51	14	8	14	7	13
Puerto Rican	30	19	5	21	5	21
White	30	26	2	10	2	9
Totals	111	18	15	15	14	14
Two-out-of-four "perfect"						
Black	80	23	11	20	6	11
Puerto Rican	39	25	4	17	2	8
White	28	24	2	10	0	0
Totals	147	24	17	17	8	8
One-out-of-four "perfect"						
Black	40	12	12	21	9	16
Puerto Rican	28	28	3	13	2	8
White	12	10	2	10	1	5
Totals	80	13	17	17	12	12
None "perfect"						
Black	138	40	16	29	13	24
Puerto Rican	17	11	2	8	3	13
White	12	10	2	10	0	0
Totals	167	27	20	20	16	16

A detailed analysis of the urine reports of the entire active patient population for the second month of treatment was made, and a random sample was analyzed for the fourth and eighth months of treatment (Table 4). In addition, during the first week of the twelfth month of program operation, a sample of 100 urine reports taken at random from the entire patient population was analyzed without regard to length of time any patient had been in treatment (Table 5).

In overview, the most striking feature of these urine reports is the improvement that is shown the longer the patients are under treatment. Although an active discharge policy removed those who were abusing the program from the standpoint of not taking the methadone as directed, it still can be said, because of the relatively small number of such discharges, that there was a definite tendency for spontaneous improvement from the standpoint of urine reports during the early weeks and months of the program. For example, during the second month, only 18% of the patients had all urine reports "perfect." This increased to 31% by the fourth month and to 50% by the eighth month. Also, the random sample of 100 urine reports during the first week of the twelfth month of the program indicates that this improvement continued since, in this sample, 75% of the urine reports were "perfect."

An additional feature noted in comparing the urine reports during the second, fourth, and eighth months was a persistent ethnic difference. The frequency of "perfect urine" was significantly lower during all of these months among Black patients than among Puerto Rican or White. In this regard, it is of

Table 5. Random Sample of 100 Urine Reports Showing Frequency of "Perfect Urine" During the First Week of the Twelfth Month of Program[a]

Ethnic group	"Perfect urine"[b]	
	N	%
Black (N = 50)	36	72
Puerto Rican (N = 34)	25	74
White (N = 16)	14	88
Total (N = 100)	75	75

[a]Patients included in this table were unselected as to length of time on the program. Duration of treatment varied from several days to one year.

[b]Urine reports showing methadone without heroin or quinine.

Table 6. Patients Looking on Methadone as a Lifetime Treatment Program (Third Month)

Category	N	%
Black (N = 215)	39	18
Puerto Rican (N = 97)	44	45
White (N = 78)	29	37
Under 30 (N = 124)	33	27
30 and over (N = 266)	79	30
Males (N = 286)	75	26
Females (N = 104)	37	35
Total (N = 390)	112	29

interest that when asked during the third month whether they felt methadone maintenance would have to be a lifetime treatment program, only 18% of the Black patients indicated this. On the other hand, 45% of the Puerto Ricans and 37% of the Whites felt they would require methadone as a lifetime program (Table 6).

Urine reports also indicated improvement in terms of abuse of other drugs (Table 7). (Here, however, the discharge of those patients severely abusing such drugs as amphetamines and barbiturates undoubtedly contributed to the overall improvement.) In the second month, thin-layer chromatography revealed that 21% of the total number of active patients abused barbiturates, while during the eighth month only 10% showed this abuse. Abuse of amphetamines decreased to a lesser extent, from 6% during the second month to 4% during the eighth month. Also, it is of interest that White patients showed more frequent amphetamine abuse than other ethnic groups (Table 7).

In terms of employment, 20% of the males had some form of employment or were attending school before joining the program. By the end of the third month, 34% of the males were employed or in school and by the end of the eighth month, 44% of the males were thus occupied (Table 8). Since total, sustained abstinence from heroin was not attained by all patients during the early

Table 7. Barbiturate and Amphetamine Abuse among Methadone Patients: Frequency of Patients with Positive Urine Reports During Second, Fourth, and Eighth Months

	Second month N = 615 (total patient pop.)		Fourth month N = 100 (random sample)		Eighth month N = 100 (random sample)	
	N	%	N	%	N	%
Barbiturates						
Black	82	24	3	5	7	13
Puerto Rican	17	11	3	13	1	4
White	32	27	3	15	2	9
Male	87	19	5	7	7	9
Female	44	26	4	16	3	12
Totals	121	21	9	9	10	10
Amphetamines						
Black	15	4	0	0	0	0
Puerto Rican	13	8	1	4	1	4
White	11	9	2	10	3	14
Male	27	6	2	3	4	5
Female	12	7	1	4	0	0
Totals	39	6	3	3	4	4

months of therapy, an attempt was made to determine the relationship between total, sustained abstinence from heroin as shown by a "perfect urine" and social rehabilitation in terms of a job and or schooling. In other words: Could a quantitative reduction in

Table 8. Success Rate at Obtaining and Retaining a Job or Schooling

	Third month N = 390 (random sample)		Eighth month N = 100 (random sample)	
Category	N	%	N	%
Black	63	29	16	30
Puerto Rican	24	25	8	33
White	27	35	14	64
Under 30	41	33	13	43
30 and Over	73	27	25	38
Males	98	34	33	44
Females	16	15	5	25
Totals	114	29	38	38

heroin use be as helpful to some patients as total abstinence was to others? In answer to this, during the fourth month, 27% of the working and/or school group had either no urines "perfect" or only one-out-of-four "perfect." In this group of 27% working and/ or school patients who usually had "dirty" urines, it is quite possible—and we feel likely—that a quantitative reduction in the use of heroin contributed significantly to their social rehabilitation.

By the end of the first three months of treatment, 6% of the patients had been arrested and 13% had been arrested by the end of the eighth month (Table 9). The 13% figure at the end of eight months should be contrasted with a 25% arrest rate in a group of patients admitted to the detoxification unit at Morris Bernstein Institute in New York City and followed over a period of three to five months without methadone maintenance (Committee Report, 1968). Also, it should be noted that 36% of our patients had been arrested during the 12 months prior to joining the program.

DISCUSSION

The early results of this study have thus far confirmed the work of Dole, Nyswander, and others showing that methadone is effective as an antiheroin agent (Dole et al., 1965, 1966, 1967, 1968, 1969). Thus, from the standpoint of the current heroin epidemic, it can be said that methadone, when administered to a representative sample of the hard-core addict population (rather than to a highly selected group of patients) still has definite value in decreasing antisocial behavior and contributing to the initial steps toward social rehabilitation (i.e., job or school). Indeed, in terms of these criteria, our success rate is very similar to Dole and Nyswander as reported by the Methadone Maintenance Evaluation Committee (Committee Report, 1968).

It was also encouraging to note that longitudinal analysis of the urine reports indicates a tendency for spontaneous improvement

Table 9. Arrest Record

Category	Arrested 12 mo. before methadone (N = 390)		Arrested 3 mo. after methadone (N = 390)		Arrested 8 mo. after methadone (N = 100)	
	N	%	N	%	N	%
Black	74	34	13	6	8	15
Puerto Rican	36	37	6	6	3	13
White	31	40	5	6	2	9
Under 30	48	39	11	9	5	16
30 and Over	93	35	13	5	8	11
Males	116	58	22	8	12	16
Females	25	24	2	2	1	4
Totals	141	36	24	6	13	13

from the standpoint of heroin abuse with increased time on methadone maintenance. However, as we have pointed out, a continuously "perfect urine" is not required for a patient to show some degree of social rehabilitation. A quantitative reduction in use of heroin may be nearly as significant or helpful to certain patients as total abstinence shown by "perfect urine." As such, methadone maintenance should, perhaps, more properly be considered an effective *palliative* measure against heroin addiction and, quite obviously, not a curative one, not only because the drug itself is addictive, but because it does not produce total, sustained abstinence from heroin in *all* patients. For example, Dole (1969) and Taylor (1971) have also reported some intermittent heroin use among methadone patients. However, until an agent is introduced which will produce the desired total abstinence, we feel methadone maintenance should not be condemned for this. Moreover, patients who intermittently show abuse of heroin by having "dirty" urine should likewise not be condemned and ultimately discharged from methadone maintenance programs since, as this study demonstrates, a definite degree of social rehabilitation can occur in such patients. Also, improvement in urine reports may occur with time.

It should be noted that our discharge rate of 23% during the first two months of treatment is similar to that reported by Jaffe et al. (1969) in a small study carried out on a random sample of patients who were, as ours, not highly selected and who were, therefore, more representative of the addict population at large. By comparison, the Methadone Maintenance Evaluation Committee described only 13% treatment failures after four years of follow-up in the Dole-Nyswander study (Committee Report, 1968). This figure, we note became higher as their program expanded and as their patient population was less closely selected (Gearing, 1971). It is believed that a comparison of the characteristics of our group of patients and those in the early Dole-Nyswander study will reveal why our treatment failure rate, and possibly Jaffe's, was higher. First, it will be noted that most of our discharges were on the basis of missed appointments. None of these discharged patients has been allowed readmission into the program. In the Dole-Nyswander program as described by the Methadone Maintenance Evaluation Committee, readmissions were apparently accepted in some cases but not counted as treatment failures (Gearing, 1971).

Second, it should be noted that initially 90% of our patients were receiving welfare support whereas only 40% of the Dole-Nyswander patients were on welfare at the outset. (At the end of one year, 72% of our entire patient population was receiving welfare.) At the time this study was carried out, in order for a known narcotic addict to qualify for welfare in New York City, the addict had to provide evidence he was in some form of narcotic addiction treatment program. Some of our poorest patients were sent to us by welfare under this form of compulsion. The difficulty seems to arise when welfare compels heroin addicts to seek methadone maintenance or, for that matter, other forms of treatment as a condition for receiving welfare payments.

Third, on the basis of our early findings, success with methadone maintenance appears to be somewhat related to ethnic background. During the early weeks and months of treatment, the Black street-ghetto addict does not appear to do as well with methadone maintenance as does his White or Puerto Rican counterpart. Generally speaking, he has the poorest urine reports and makes up the greatest percentage of treatment failures. In the Dole-Nyswander group of patients, 48% of the patients were White as opposed to only 33% Black and 18% Puerto Rican (Committee Report, 1968). Presumably, the use of various motivational criteria in the selection of their patients resulted in this unrepresentative ethnic distribution. According to the City of New York's Narcotic Registry Statistical Report (1969), only 43.9% of the City's population of addicts are Black. In our original group of 814 patients, 57% were Black.

Since Black patients make up the largest proportion of the addict population, it is admittedly disappointing that they appear to do less well on methadone maintenance than other groups—at least in these early studies. This, together with a lesser degree of acceptance of methadone as a lifetime treatment program, may reveal a tendency toward rejection of methadone as a treatment modality by many Black patients. This will bear close scrutiny in future follow-ups. On the other hand, it should be pointed out that the long years of social, economic, and political neglect of the Black ghettos have led to narcotic addiction becoming an almost accepted way of life there, with little more social stigma than that associated with the use of alcohol in most other communities. Since the disease has obvious socioeconomic roots, it may simply be that the disorder is most difficult to treat in patients coming from communities where the conditions causing it are more pervasive and of longer duration.

Summary

A total of 814 patients were admitted into a methadone maintenance treatment program in accord with the Federal regulations for the investigational use of methadone. Although patients under 18 were excluded, patients were unselected as to ethnic background, evidence of employability, level of education, degree of motivation, or any other factor which would seem to bias the study. Our purpose was to determine as closely as possible the general effectiveness of methadone with the addict population at large.

By the end of the second month, 23% of our patients had been discharged and, by the end of the eighth month, 37%. Whether all of these discharges should be considered treatment failures is a matter of interpretation, since the majority (75%) had been discharged *in absentia* for failed appointments, and many of these patients have reappeared expecting to continue the program. Thus far, however, they have not been permitted to do so. An extensive comparison is made between the characteristics of the active and inactive patients at two months to better determine the features of patients who are successful and unsuccessful with methadone maintenance therapy.

The arrest rate for our patients for a three-month period of observation was 6% and for an eight-month period, 13%. This is contrasted with a 25% arrest rate for a group of untreated narcotic users followed over a period of three to five months. The employment rate for males in the program increased from 20% at the time of admission to 44% by the end of the eighth month. Further, there was a tendency for urine reports indicating heroin abuse to become less frequent with duration of time on methadone maintenance therapy. We conclude that methadone maintenance therapy can be effective when applied to a representative group of hard-core heroin addicts.

REFERENCES

Committee Report. Progress report of evaluation of methadone maintenance treatment program as of March 31, 1968. *JAMA* 208: 2712–2714, 1968.

Dole, V. P., and Nyswander, M. A medical treatment for diacetylmorphine (heroin) addiction. *JAMA* 193: 646–650, 1965.

Dole, V. P., Nyswander, M., and Kreek, M. J. Narcotics blockade. *Arch. Internal Med.* 118: 304–309, 1966.

Dole, V. P., et al. Heroin addiction–a metabolic disease. *Arch. Internal Med.* 120: 19–24, 1967.

Dole, V. P., Nyswander, M. E., and Warner, A. Successful treatment of 750 criminal addicts. *JAMA* 206: 2708–2711, 1968.

Dole, V. P., et al. Methadone treatment of randomly selected criminal addicts. *New Engl. J. Med.* 280: 1372–1375, 1969.

Dupont, R. L. Profile of a heroin-addiction epidemic. *New Engl. J. Med.* 285: 321–324, 1971.

Eli Lilly Co., *Information Concerning the Investigational Use of Methadone Hydrochloride.* November 1970.

Federal Register. Conditions for investigational use of methadone for maintenance programs for narcotic addicts. *Federal Register,* April 2, 1971.

Gearing, F. R. *Successes and Failures in Methadone Maintenance Treatment of Heroin Addiction in New York City.* Presented at the Third National Conference on Methadone Treatment, New York City, November 14, 1970.

Gearing, F. R. *Methadone Maintenance Program.* Progress report through March 31, 1971–A five-year evaluation submitted to New York State Narcotics Control Commission in compliance with terms of contract Number c-49432, 1971.

Jaffe, J. H., Zaks, M. S., and Washington, E. N. Experience with the use of methadone in a multimodality program for the treatment of narcotics users. *Intern. J. Addictions* 4: 481–490, 1969.

Narcotics Register Statistical Report–1969. Department of Health, Research, and Professional Training, 125 Worth Street, N.Y., N.Y. 10013.

Taylor, W. J. R. *Report to American Medical Association Annual Meeting.* June, 1971.

6

CRIME

Introduction

A distressingly large number of people in cities are the victims of serious crimes. For example, police records indicate that nearly 435,000 violent crimes (murder, forcible rape, robbery, and aggravated assault) and about 2,420,000 property crimes (burglary, larceny/theft, and auto theft) were committed in large cities[1] in 1973 (Federal Bureau of Investigation, 1974). While these numbers are disturbing, interviews with representative samples of residents of 13 major cities suggest that the actual number of serious crimes is two to three times the officially reported number in many cities (Law Enforcement Assistance Administration, 1974).

The individual and social costs of violent crimes and property crimes are also considerable. The President's Commission on Law Enforcement and Administration of Justice (1967) estimated that medical expenses and the loss of earnings due to violent crimes were about $815,000,000 a year, that property crimes cost the public about $3,932,000,000 a year, and that the cost of apprehending, trying, and incarcerating offenders in all criminal cases was about $4,212,000,000 a year. Although the economic costs of organized crime and white collar crime are also substantial, only serious crimes against persons and property appear to worry and intimidate large numbers of urban dwellers (Gallup, 1973; Hindelang, 1974). Accordingly, we will examine the research findings in an attempt to identify some of the factors that cause people to commit violent crimes and property crimes, and to assess the effectiveness of strategies designed to reduce the incidence of these crimes.

---

1. Cities with more than 250,000 inhabitants.

CORRELATES OF CRIMINAL BEHAVIOR

The behavior of people who commit crimes has been subjected to considerable inquiry. Unfortunately, much of that inquiry is flawed in important ways. First, most of the studies have tried to identify the *correlates* of juvenile delinquency.[2] The relative availability of samples of presumed delinquents, the paucity of available samples of adult offenders, and the difficulty of conducting causal studies of juvenile or adult crime make this bias understandable. Regrettably, the findings tell us only that a number of psychological and sociocultural characteristics appear more often in groups considered delinquent than in groups considered nondelinquent; they do not tell us if these characteristics are important determinants of criminal behavior. Second, many of the studies used official records or the subjects' own reports to identify delinquents. Unfortunately, both measures have serious weaknesses. Official records do not contain the delinquent acts of many adolescents; that is, many of the adolescents who commit crimes are not caught or not arrested (Black & Reiss, 1970). As a result, samples labeled "nondelinquent" may actually contain sizable numbers of people who committed crimes. While self-reported delinquency should permit the researcher to identify adolescents who have committed crimes but who have no official records, this technique is also vulnerable to distortion; that is, subjects may not remember every delinquent act they committed, may omit some or all delinquent acts, and/or may fabricate delinquent acts. Third, the definitions of official delinquency and self-reported delinquency include an assortment of minor offenses. Since many of the studies did not analyze separately adolescents who committed violent crimes or property crimes, the reported correlates may be correlates of misconduct and misdemeanors rather than correlates of serious crimes against persons and/or property.

Despite the prevalence of these shortcomings, several studies have used more rigorous definitions of criminal behavior than official records or self-report and several studies have examined separately the correlates of violent crime. Moreover, the arrest rates indicate that youthful offenders warrant our attention; that is, more than 50% of the people arrested for violent crimes and 75% of the people arrested for property crimes are between 15 and 25 (Federal Bureau of Investigation, 1971). Accordingly, let us look at the research findings in an attempt to identify some of the factors that may be responsible for serious crimes against persons and property.

Groups of adolescents defined as delinquent and groups of adolescents defined as nondelinquent appear to differ on a variety of psychological and sociocultural

2. Although the legal definition of juvenile delinquency is not the same in every state, juvenile delinquency usually refers to crimes committed by those under the age of 18. These crimes characteristically include all adult crimes plus offenses such as incorrigibility and running away from home.

dimensions.[3] Those dimensions include personality characteristics, family relationships, friendships, feelings about school, and scholastic performance.

The findings suggest that adolescents defined as delinquent have lower self-esteem (Jensen, 1973; Sumpter, 1972), less self-control (Hindelang, 1972; Jensen, 1973), and weaker social values (Bandura & Walters, 1959; Hackler, 1970; Hindelang, 1972; Jaffe, 1969; Jensen, 1972, 1973; Liska, 1973) than adolescents defined as nondelinquent. For example, Jensen (1973) analyzed the responses of nearly 2,600 junior and senior high school students and found that self-esteem, self-control, and acceptance of the law as morally binding were negatively related to delinquent behavior for both white and black adolescents. In a study of personality and self-reported delinquent behavior among 582 high school students, Hindelang (1972) found that adolescents who were relatively stubborn, undependable, and deceitful in dealing with others, who were relatively immature, moody, and undercontrolled, and who were comparatively shallow and unconcerned with social mores were more likely to get into fights using weapons, to damage property, and to steal goods worth more than ten dollars. Using age, intelligence, father's occupational status, and area of residence to match 26 boys with histories of aggressive, antisocial behavior and 26 boys who school counselors felt were neither noticeably aggressive nor noticeably withdrawn, Bandura and Walters (1959) interviewed each of the boys and their parents. The results indicate that aggressive boys expressed weaker feelings of guilt about behaving in antisocial ways than control boys.

The relationship between adolescents and parents also appears to be related to delinquent behavior. The data suggest that adolescents defined as nondelinquent receive more emotional support from parents (Bandura & Walters, 1959; Jensen, 1972; Piliavin, Vadum, & Hardyck, 1969; Walberg, 1972) and have closer relationships with their fathers (Bandura & Walters, 1959; Gold & Mann, 1972; Piliavin et al., 1969) than adolescents defined as delinquent. For example, Jensen (1972) found that paternal support was negatively related to delinquent behavior in a sample of nearly 1,600 students, and Bandura and Walters (1959) indicated that the fathers of aggressive boys reportedly gave their sons less affection in early childhood and were more hostile, rejecting, and punitive than the fathers of control boys. Bandura and Walters also found that aggressive boys felt less warmth for their fathers, were more hostile toward their fathers, and identified less with their fathers than control boys.

The hypothesized relationship between broken homes and delinquent behavior has attracted considerable attention (see Wilkinson, 1974). For example, Chilton and Markle (1972) analyzed the records of 8,944 children who were referred to Florida juvenile courts. The results indicate that black children charged with of-

3. Since most of the people charged with committing serious crimes against persons and/or property are male (Federal Bureau of Investigation, 1974), we will confine our review to the characteristics of male offenders.

fenses lived in broken homes somewhat more often than black children in the general population (58% versus 43%), that white children charged with offenses came from broken homes considerably more often than white children in the general population (29% versus 13%), and that black children (69%) and white children (50%) charged with violent crimes came from broken homes much more often than black children and white children in the general population. Using the self-reports of about 1,700 adolescents from lower- and working-class homes, Berger and Simon (1974) found that family organization (intact versus broken home) was unrelated to property crimes and violent crimes among lower-class white and black adolescents. Among working-class adolescents, whites from broken homes were somewhat more likely to commit property crimes and violent crimes than whites from intact homes, whereas blacks from broken homes were somewhat more likely to be involved in property crimes than blacks from intact homes. Herzog (1970) noted that it "may or may not be true that father-less boys are overrepresented among those who engage in behavior defined as delinquent. However, evidence suggests that: (1) if they are, it is not specifically father absence which caused the delinquency, but rather the frequent precursors, concomitants, and consequences of father absence; (2) the presence of some fathers might be more conducive than their absence to delinquent behavior; (3) the difference in frequency, if it exists, is relatively minor and is dwarfed by other factors far more strongly associated with delinquency—including depressed income and community factors" (p. 113).

While a disproportionately large number of arrested juveniles come from low-income homes (Wolfgang, Figlio, & Sellin, 1972), studies of self-reported delinquency suggest that middle-class adolescents commit as many delinquent acts as lower-class adolescents. For example, Williams and Gold (1972) analyzed the responses of a national probability sample of 456 13- to 16-year-olds. The data provide no evidence for a relationship between lower- or middle-class member-ship and the frequency and seriousness of delinquent acts. Berger and Simon (1974) compared 3,112 lower-, working-, middle-, and upper-class adolescents. The results indicate that social class and the incidence of violent acts were unre-lated. If the results of these studies are valid, they imply that law enforcement agencies act in ways that permit sizable numbers of middle-class juvenile offend-ers to avoid formal arrest.

Official records also indicate that a disproportionately large number of arrested juveniles are black (e.g., Wolfgang et al., 1972); however, most studies of self-reported delinquency have found little or no difference in the number or seriousness of delinquent acts committed by blacks and whites (e.g., Gould, 1969b; Hindelang, 1972; Williams & Gold, 1972). Studies by Berger and Simon (1974) and Walberg, Yeh, and Paton (1974) are exceptions. Berger and Simon found that a larger proportion of blacks were in fights, carried weapons, used weapons, and/or committed robbery, though they did not find any difference between blacks and whites in the commission of property crimes. In contrast, Walberg *et al.* found that a larger percentage of white high school students, compared to black high school students, engaged in theft and participated in gang fights.

Not surprisingly, adolescents defined as delinquent are more likely to have delinquent friends than adolescents defined as nondelinquent (Frease, 1973; Gold & Mann, 1972; Gould, 1969a; Hackler, 1970; Jensen, 1972; Liska, 1973). Using interviews with a nationally representative sample of 456 adolescents, Gold and Mann (1972) found that the number of delinquent acts committed by the adolescents correlated highly with the perceived delinquency of their friends. Gould (1969a) compared 119 high school students with juvenile court records and 98 with no records. The data reveal that adolescents with records were much more likely to associate with delinquents. Hackler (1970) analyzed the responses of 211 ninth-grade boys and found that self-reported delinquency was strongly related to the delinquent behavior of close friends.[4]

Adolescents labeled as delinquent also differ from adolescents labeled as nondelinquent on a number of school-related dimensions. Delinquents have less favorable attitudes toward school (Piliavin *et al.*, 1969), lower grades (Hackler, 1970; Palmore & Hammond, 1964; Wolfgang *et al.*, 1972), stronger feelings of failure (Frease, 1973; Walberg, 1972), and would like to acquire considerably more education than they expect to acquire (Quicker, 1974). For example, Piliavin *et al.* (1969) found that attitudes toward school and teachers were negatively related to delinquent activity, apprehension by the police, and official arrest in a sample of 693 white and black adolescents. In an attempt to assess the effects of educational goal discrepancies on delinquent behavior, Quicker (1974) examined the responses of 1,338 students to a questionnaire administered during their first and fourth years of high school. Among ninth graders with no reported delinquency, 35% who reported large differences between their educational aspirations and expectations, compared to 3% who reported small differences between aspirations and expectations, committed at least one serious crime by the twelfth grade.

While these findings suggest that juvenile delinquency is related to a number of psychological and sociocultural variables, they do not establish a causal sequence; for example, low self-esteem and little parental support may be outcomes of delinquent behavior rather than determinants. Nevertheless, there may be a causal relationship between some or all of these variables and

---

4. There is a great deal of sociological literature on gang behavior. Many of these studies examine the role that gang leadership or followership plays for the individual; some of these studies describe the interactions within gangs and their influence on the individual. While this material is valuable, it is essentially descriptive and does not suit our attempt to present the results of experimental or correlational studies. Accordingly, it has been omitted.

delinquent behavior. In other words, the probability of an adolescent committing delinquent acts may increase as the number of unfavorable psychological
and sociocultural characteristics increases. In turn, delinquent behavior may have
an adverse effect on self-esteem and social values, parental support, relations
with certain peers, attitudes toward school, and/or scholastic performance.
Longitudinal research is obviously needed to clarify the nature of these proposed
relationships.

Studies of violent criminal offenders yield several insights and implications.
Some studies suggest that people who commit violent crimes tend to be overcontrolled; that is, they respond to feelings of resentment and frustration by
rigidly controlling their impulses until their inhibitions to react aggressively are
overwhelmed (Megargee, 1966; Megargee & Mendelsohn, 1965; Molof, 1967a;
Tupin, Mahar, & Smith, 1973). Other studies imply that some violent offenders
are undercontrolled; that is, they respond to resentment and frustration by
behaving aggressively (Peterson, Pittman, & O'Neal, 1962; Sarbin, Wenk, & Sherwood, 1968; Tupin et al., 1973). Despite these findings, studies of incarcerated
offenders have failed to predict which offenders would commit violent crimes
after they were released and which offenders would not (Monahan & Cummings, 1975, reading 6.1).

In an attempt to test the hypothesis that extremely assaultive offenders are
overcontrolled, Megargee (1966) compared four groups of juvenile offenders: 9
extremely assaultive offenders, 21 moderately assaultive offenders, 26 property
offenders, and 20 juveniles detained for incorrigibility. Neither property offenders nor incorrigibles had any known records of assaultive crimes. The four groups
were compared on three groups of measures: predetention behavior, behavior
while incarcerated, and interview and test scores.

The measures of predetention behavior and behavior while incarcerated provide considerable support for Megargee's hypothesis; the interview data and test
scores provide less support. The interviews reveal that extremely assaultive
offenders reported less physical aggression against authorities; on those tests that
were difficult to fake, they also had lower scores on measures of impulsiveness
than other offenders.

Megargee and Mendelsohn (1965) and Molof (1967a) also reported findings
consistent with the hypothesis that extremely assaultive offenders are overcontrolled. Megargee and Mendelsohn found that extremely assaultive offenders
scored higher than moderately assaultive offenders, nonviolent offenders, and
people defined as noncriminal on an assault scale. The scale correlated positively
with measures of conformity, control, and repression, and negatively with
measures of acting out and hostility. Molof compared 300 adolescents who
committed homicide, forcible rape, or aggravated assault and 5,815 adolescents

who committed nonviolent crimes. The results indicate that assaultive offenders were less likely to have records of serious school behavior problems before the age of 12, police contacts, prior court commitments, prior escapes from incarceration, and histories of psychiatric or psychological observation, evaluation, or therapy. Based on retrospective reports of fighting in childhood, Tupin *et al.* (1973) found that murderers with little or no histories of violent crime fought less often than nonviolent offenders. In contrast, murderers with histories of recurrent violent crime fought more often than nonviolent offenders. Similarly, Peterson *et al.* (1962) found that violent offenders were less tolerant of frustration than nonviolent offenders, and Sarbin *et al.* (1968) reported that adolescents who committed violent crimes were more aggressive than adolescents who committed nonviolent crimes. These studies shed light on the personality dynamics of some extremely assaultive offenders. They also indicate, at least in part, why it is so difficult to predict who will behave violently. To wit, extremely assaultive offenders are not marked by one distinctive set of personality traits. Moreover, most people who are undercontrolled or overcontrolled will never commit extremely violent acts.

The inability to predict who will behave violently is carefully documented by Monahan and Cummings (1975, reading 6.1). In a review of the literature, they noted that "the conclusion to emerge most strikingly from these studies is the great degree to which violence is overpredicted. Of those predicted to be dangerous, between 65% and 99% are false positives—people who will not, in fact, commit a dangerous act" (Monahan & Cummings, 1975, p. 157). As a result, Monahan and Cummings argued that there is no empirical justification for a variety of purportedly preventive strategies; for example, preventive detention, civil commitment, indeterminate sentencing, and early intervention programs.

Drug use, televised violence, and genetic endowment have also been accused of contributing to violent crime. Although the findings are fragmentary, studies of drug use and crime imply that the cost of heroin causes many users to commit violent crimes. Studies of heroin addiction suggest that heroin addicts, in an attempt to obtain the large amounts of money they need to purchase heroin, tend to commit more serious crimes after becoming dependent on heroin (Blum, 1967; Friedman & Friedman, 1973; Jacoby, Weiner, & Wolfgang, 1973). Studies that compared offenders who used drugs—primarily heroin—and offenders for whom there was no evidence of drug use also indicate that larger proportions of drug users were charged with robbery, though smaller proportions of drug users were charged with aggravated assault (Swezey & Chambers, 1974).

There are several anecdotal reports of crimes being modeled directly after television performances (*Time,* 1975). However, we were unable to find any studies of the relationship between exposure to violent programs and violent criminal behavior, though a number of studies did indicate that a preference for violent programs and aggressive behavior were related (e.g., Eron, Huesmann, Lefkowitz, & Walder, 1974).

While a number of biological explanations of violent criminal behavior have been proposed, they have failed to receive empirical support (Gibbons, 1973). For example, the most recent biological explanation, the XYY chromosomal pattern, has been linked theoretically to aggressive antisocial behavior. However, the existing data indicate that "XYY males in an institutional setting are *less* violent or aggressive when compared to matched chromosomally normal fellow inmates; and their criminal histories involve crimes against property rather than persons" (Fox, 1971, p. 72).

Many studies have been conducted in an attempt to identify the processes that result in aggressive behavior. Though most of these studies have been carried out in laboratory rather than field settings and have dealt with relatively mild forms of aggression, the findings are still instructive. Those findings indicate that if aggression is rewarded, it is more likely to recur; that aggression is a likely response to frustration, particularly if the frustrating events are seen as arbitrary; that people usually behave aggressively when they feel that their social roles require aggressive behavior; and that the probability of aggressive behavior increases when models who behave aggressively, on television or elsewhere, are observed (Costello & Zalkind, 1970).

REDUCING CRIME

A number of strategies designed to reduce crime have been subjected to empirical test. We have placed these strategies in three categories: strategies directed at prospective offenders, strategies directed at actual offenders, and strategies directed at incarcerated offenders.

Prospective Offenders

In an attempt to determine if prospective offenders are deterred by the likelihood and/or severity of punishment, a number of investigators correlated the certainty and severity of punishment and the rates for serious crimes (Antunes & Hunt, 1973; Bailey, Martin, & Gray, 1974; Chiricos & Waldo, 1970; Ehrlich, 1972; Tittle, 1969).[5] The results reveal sizable inverse relationships between the certainty of punishment and the rates of assault, robbery, burglary, and theft.

5. Certainty of punishment for a given offense was usually defined by the number of offenders who entered prison in each state divided by the number of offenses in each state known to the police during a given period of time. Severity of punishment for a given offense was usually defined by the average number of months that offenders who were released from prison during a given period of time had spent in prison. The rate for a given offense was usually defined by the number of offenses known to the police per 100,000 inhabitants during a given period of time.

The results, with one exception, also show negligible relationships between the severity of punishment and the incidence of serious crimes other than homicide. For example, Tittle (1969) found that certainty of punishment correlated −.46 with assault, −.36 with robbery, −.31 with burglary, and −.37 with theft. Tittle also found that severity of punishment correlated .18 with assault, .05 with robbery, .14 with burglary, and .14 with theft. While these findings suggest that the certainty of punishment has some deterring effect, the results of a subsequent study (Tittle & Rowe, 1974) imply that "there is a critical level that certainty of punishment must reach before there is a noticeable change in volume of crime" (p. 458). Using arrest clearance rates[6] and crime rates in Florida cities, Tittle and Rowe found that the correlation between certainty of arrest and the crime rate was −.48 for those cities in which the certainty of arrest was greater than 30%, and .19 for those cities in which the certainty of arrest was less than 30%. Tittle and Rowe also found that the correlation between certainty of arrest and the crime rate did not diminish when the percentage of each city's population that was poor, the percentage that was black, and city size were statistically controlled.

Studies of murder and capital punishment show that the death penalty does not have a deterring effect (Bailey, 1974; Savitz, 1958; Schuessler, 1952; Sellin, 1967). For example, Bailey compared the rates for 1967 and 1968 of first degree murder, second degree murder, total murder, and homicide in states that had capital punishment and in neighboring states that had abolished it. The data indicate that the rates for each type of offense were *higher* in states with capital punishment in about 60% of the comparisons. Bailey also correlated the execution rates during 1962−67 and the four offense rates for 1967 and 1968 in the capital punishment states and found, with one exception, only slight inverse relationships. Apparently, the death penalty is not a more effective deterrent than long-term imprisonment.

In an attempt to increase the certainty of punishment, a number of strategies designed to increase the risk of apprehension have been tried; for example, changes in police training, more patrol cars in high crime areas, high intensity street lamps, citizen patrols, methadone clinics for heroin users, and the design of public housing. Unfortunately, only a few of these strategies have been systematically evaluated. Among those that have, Newman's (1973, reading 3.3) study of public housing projects indicated that public housing can be designed in ways that reduce considerably the incidence of crime and studies by Gearing (1970), Dale and Dale (1973, reading 5.4), and Brown *et al.* (1973) suggest that methadone maintenance can lower substantially the number of crimes committed by program participants.

6. Arrest clearance means that the police believe that they have arrested the person who committed the crime.

In an attempt to lessen the impact of poverty and the incidence of crime, job programs for youths from poor families have been created. For example, the in-school Neighborhood Youth Corps provided hundreds of thousands of high school students 16 to 21 years of age from poor families with jobs. Participants were allowed to work up to 15 hours a week during the school year and up to 32 hours a week during the summer. While they worked, the students met periodically with Neighborhood Youth Corps counselors to talk about their problems, their progress in the program, the role and value of education, and the importance of finishing high school. In an attempt to determine the impact of the Neighborhood Youth Corps on delinquency, Robin (1969, reading 6.2) compared the police records of 82 males who enrolled as school year and summer program participants and who averaged 11.5 months of work, 50 males who were accepted into the summer program only and who averaged 8.3 weeks of work, and 54 males who were not accepted into the program. Subjects in the latter two groups were randomly assigned to those groups from a pool of eligible applicants.

Analysis of police records provide no evidence that participation in the Neighborhood Youth Corps in Cincinnati reduced the incidence of serious crimes. For example, before applying or enrolling, 38% of the year-round participants and 63% of the controls had records of serious offenses. During the period that participants worked, 17% of the participants and 20% of the controls were found guilty of committing serious offenses. Among subjects who had records of serious offenses before applying or enrolling, 25% of the year-round participants and 25% of the controls added serious offenses to their records in the period that participants worked. Among subjects who did not have records of serious offenses before applying or enrolling, 12% of the year-round participants and 10% of the controls acquired records for serious offenses during the time participants worked. Robin also noted that a study of the Neighborhood Youth Corps in Detroit yielded similar findings. These results do not support the hypothesis that short-term employment of adolescents from poor families reduces crime; the results of a recent study (Odell, 1974, reading 6.4) suggest that the kinds of jobs the program provided—jobs that paid the minimum wage and that probably offered little or no opportunity for advancement—may have been responsible for the program's apparent failure to reduce the incidence of serious crimes.

Actual Offenders

Proposals for stringent gun control laws have aroused much controversy; however, the data imply that laws restricting the sale of guns would reduce considerably the number of homicides. Zimring (1968) analyzed the records of homicides and serious assaults reported to the Chicago police during 1965–67. He found that "the rate of homicide per 100 police reported attacks is about five times as great for firearms as for knives, the second most dangerous weapon available" (p. 735). He also found that about two-thirds of the homicides resulted from altercations between people who knew each other, that the reasons for killing with a gun were the same as the reasons for killing with a knife, and that similar proportions of knife attacks and gun attacks were apparently meant to injure seriously or kill. Taken together, these findings suggest that stringent gun control laws would reduce considerably the number of murders. Despite the ongoing controversy generated by proposals for such laws, the results of several surveys (e.g., Erskine, 1972; Hindelang, 1974) indicate that there is considerable public support for stricter laws. For example, Hindelang reported that 70% of the respondents in a national survey said they would favor a law requiring a person to obtain a police permit before that person could buy a gun.

A variety of strategies have been tried in an attempt to increase the ability of the police to apprehend people who commit serious crimes. Unfortunately, the research findings tend to show that most strategies have little or no effect (*Time*, 1975). For example, a study of squad car cruising in Kansas City, Missouri yielded no evidence of a relationship between the number of squad cars patrolling experimental areas and the incidence of crime. Although some strategies do seem to work, the absence of control groups limits the conclusions that can be drawn. To illustrate, the use of taxis by New York City policemen in stakeouts and streets patrols appears to have resulted in an unusually large number of arrests.

The Supreme Court decisions requiring policemen to follow constitutionally-based procedures when interrogating defendants have been blamed by some for the increase in the rate of crime. The data, however, do not support this contention. In a recent study, Witt (1973) found that while policemen felt handicapped, there was no evidence that protection of defendants' civil liberties reduced the percentage of convictions.

Every person taken into custody and charged with a crime has the constitutional right to a fair trial. Unfortunately, the number of people who are apprehended and charged with crimes far exceeds the capacity of most criminal courts. As a result, most cases are settled by plea bargaining; that is, the prosecutor offers the defendant a reduced sentence in exchange for a plea of guilty to a lesser charge. How well does plea bargaining work? While it may prevent court dockets from becoming hopelessly backlogged, it metes out little or no punishment to thousands of defendants who have allegedly committed serious crimes and who plead guilty to reduced charges. For example, there were 94,000 felony arrests in New York City in 1970, but only 3,000 defendants were sentenced to prison for a year or more (Zimroth, 1972). For defendants who cannot raise bail, the alternative to plea bargaining is remaining in jail for many months while awaiting trial. As a result, many of these defendants accept the prosecutor's offer, even if they are innocent.

In an attempt to solve the problems created by plea bargaining, Zimroth advocates "not only a dramatic increase in the amount and productivity of court resources, but more fundamentally, a reduction in the number of cases the system must handle" (p. 44). There seem to be a number of ways to reduce that caseload. One, eliminate drunkenness, gambling, prostitution, and homosexuality as criminal offenses. Two, establish clinics that would legally provide doses of heroin to addicts. Together, these offenses presently account for about 30% of the reported arrests.

Incarcerated Offenders

What effects do penal institutions have on inmates? What are the effects of treatment in institutions and in community settings? How useful are strategies designed to integrate released offenders into the community? In an attempt to answer these questions, we will look at the research findings that focus on the impact of incarceration, the effects of different types of treatment, and the usefulness of halfway houses and job programs.

In an attempt to determine the relationship between the amount of time spent in prison and the extent to which inmates feel that resuming their careers as criminals would be rewarding, Harris (1975) administered a questionnaire to 129 black and 105 white inmates of a prison for youthful offenders. Each subject had a record of previous imprisonment. The inmates' responses reveal that time spent in prison prior to their present sentences and the expected value of criminal behavior were curvilinearly related. As a result, Harris analyzed separately the data on inmates who had spent little time in prison (six months for blacks and twelve months for whites) and inmates who had spent considerable time in prison. Among inmates who had spent little time in prison, length of imprisonment and the expected value of criminal behavior were negatively related. Among inmates who had spent considerable time in prison, the relationship was positive. One interpretation of these findings is that short prison terms may have a rehabilitative effect while extended imprisonment may have a criminalizing effect.

Studies of the amount of time served and the rate of recidivism provide support for the interpretation that extended imprisonment may have a criminalizing effect. Jaman (1968) compared the parole performances of first offenders who had committed robbery and who had served either less than or more than the median time in prison for that offense. In an attempt to create comparable groups, Jaman matched subjects on age, ethnic status, and type of parole supervision received. During follow-up periods of 6, 12, and 24 months, offenders who served less than the median time in prison were less likely than offenders who served more than the median time to violate parole or to return to prison for committing another crime. Among 1,252 prisoners that the state of Florida was forced to release because they were convicted unconstitutionally, the recidivism rate was 13.6% after thirty months. Among a group of prisoners who served their sentences, the recidivism rate was 25.4% (Wicker, 1972). Although Wicker's report did not indicate if the two groups of prisoners were similar in ways that might cause them to return to prison, the rate for the prisoners who were released because they were convicted unconstitutionally was much lower than the rates reported elsewhere (Babst & Mannering, 1965; Glaser, 1964; Scarpitti & Stephenson, 1968; Vasoli & Fahey, 1970).

A provocative study that employed college students as guards or as prisoners in a simulated prison purportedly shows that the characteristics of prisons brutalize guards, who in turn torment and dehumanize prisoners (Haney, Banks, & Zimbardo, 1973). However, Banuazizi and Mohavedi (1975) noted that the demand characteristics of the experimental situation were considerable, that most guards said they were role playing a tough guard, and that the behavior predicted by a sample of college students who were given a description of the prison experiment was quite similar to the behavior of the student guards and prisoners. As a result, Banuazizi and Mohavedi argued that "the subjects responded to a number of demand characteristics in the experimental situation, acting out their stereotypic images of a prison guard and, to a lesser extent, of a prisoner. To the extent that such confounding variables were operative, the subjects' behavior cannot be explained as strategic, coping responses to an asymmetrical power situation analogous to that of a real prison" (p. 159). Of course, real guards may also act out their stereotypic images of a prison guard, particularly if training is inadequate and peer group pressures to engage in abuses of power are considerable.

Various treatments have been employed in institutional and community settings in an attempt to help offenders and reduce recidivism. These treatments include individual therapy, group counseling, behavior modification, and milieu therapy.

Only a handful of well designed evaluations of individual therapy have been reported. Adams (1962) assigned prisoners aged 17 to 23 to two groups: those who received psychotherapy several times a week for about nine months and those who did not. Each of the prisoners was also rated as amenable to treatment or not amenable to treatment. Analysis of parole violations indicates that the treated amenables had the lowest percentage of violations. The data also indicate that inmates who were considered not amenable to treatment and who received treatment had the highest percentage of violations. These findings suggest that individual therapy can have beneficial effects when offenders who are likely to respond favorably can be identified. They also imply that the indiscriminate use of individual therapy is likely to have adverse effects on some recipients.

Guttmann (1963) compared adolescents at two training schools who received about nine months of intensive individual therapy and adolescents who received ordinary institutional care. The results indicate that treated offenders at one school had a lower parole violation rate than controls. In the second school, the difference was reversed. In an attempt to explain these findings, Guttmann noted that different kinds of therapy were used in the two schools. In the first school, therapists joined patients in many activities and emphasized personal responsibility for one's behavior. In the second school, therapists apparently used psychoanalytic therapy. Since psychoanalysis usually takes years, participants were probably released by the school before analysis was completed. Shireman, Mann, Larsen, and Young (1972, reading 6.3) suggested that this experience may have been more damaging than ordinary institutional care.

A small number of studies have tried to evaluate group counseling in institutional settings (Harrison, 1964; Kassebaum, Ward, & Wilner, 1971; Robison & Kevorkian, 1967; Sarason & Ganzer, 1973; Seckel, 1965). The results indicate that counseling appears to succeed in some settings and fail in others. For example, Sarason and Ganzer (1973) randomly assigned 192 adolescent offenders to discussion groups, to groups in which modeling was used to teach appropriate behaviors, or to standard institutional care. The group discussions dealt with various situations that adolescent offenders had trouble handling: for example, applying for a job, resisting peer pressure to engage in delinquent acts, and working toward future goals rather than seeking immediate gratification. Sixteen discussions were held during a four-week period. A three-year follow-up indicated that adolescents who participated in group discussions were much less likely to be recidivists than adolescents who received standard institutional care. Kassebaum et al. (1971) compared four groups of imprisoned felons: 171 who were randomly assigned to small counseling groups, 269 who were randomly designated as a control group, 274 who volunteered for small group counseling, and 173 who chose not to volunteer. Inmates who received counseling participated in approximately 40 sessions. Analysis of recidivism rates after 6, 12, 24, and 36 months yielded no differences between either assigned or volunteer experimental and control groups. Robison and Kevorkian (1967) evaluated the impact of social-therapy groups in a California prison. Each group contained about 12 men and met five times a week. Although therapists were recruited initially from the civilian population, inmates who were members of groups for some time and who displayed favorable changes in behavior were also permitted to function as therapists. Follow-up data indicate that participants had a lower parole violation rate than controls a year after being released. Moreover, the rate of violation was particularly favorable among participants whose groups were led by inmate therapists. Unfortunately, the difference between experimental and control groups was no longer statistically significant after two years. It is suggested that occasional counseling after participants were released from prison might have helped to maintain the lower parole violation rate.

There are probably several reasons why group counseling succeeds in some settings and fails in others; for example, the charcteristics of the inmates, the characteristics of the therapists, the intent and duration of counseling, and the support that released offenders receive from the community. However, research designed to determine the roles that these variables play needs to be carried out before any conclusions can be legitimately drawn.

While numerous studies of behavior modification and juvenile delinquency have been conducted (see Davidson & Seidman, 1974), only a handful have used control groups and measured recidivism (Alexander & Parsons, 1973; Cohen & Filipczak, 1971; Phillips, Phillips, Fixsen, & Wolf, 1973; Schwitzgebel, 1964). One of the most instructive is the evaluation by Phillips *et al.* of a community-based treatment home. Phillips *et al.* wanted to teach delinquent youths the social, academic, self-help, and pre-vocational skills that would help them avoid trouble with their families, their teachers, and the police. Toward that end, they created Achievement Place, a family-style treatment home located in the community and staffed by two professional teaching-parents; that is, a husband and wife who were trained to teach delinquent boys. A token economy system was used to help motivate the boys in the home to learn new behaviors. In other words, points were awarded for appropriate behaviors and deducted for inappropriate behaviors. Initially, points could be exchanged each day for an assortment of privileges. After a short time, the daily schedule was changed to a weekly exchange schedule. When the teaching-parents felt that a boy was ready, the point system was replaced by the merit system; that is, all privileges were free. Once a boy was able to handle the merit system, he was returned to his own home. During their stay at Achievement Place, boys attended school in the community where teachers evaluated their behavior by filling out report cards each day. After dinner, teaching-parents and boys met to discuss the events of the day, modify or establish rules, and decide on penalties for any violations of the rules.

Phillips *et al.* compared 16 juvenile offenders who were committed to Achievement Place, 15 juvenile offenders who were sent to a state training school, and 13 juvenile offenders who were placed on probation. Although offenders were not randomly assigned to treatments, "all were potential candidates for Achievement Place when they were adjudicated" (Phillips *et al.*, 1973, p. 76). During the year preceding treatment, adolescents in the three groups had similar records of police and court contacts. Two years after treatment began, a much smaller percentage of Achievement Place boys were recidivists; that is, 54% of the boys placed on probation, 53% of the boys sent to training school, and 19% of the boys assigned to Achievement Place had been placed in state institutions for committing delinquent acts. Of those who had not been institutionalized, Achievement Place boys were far more likely to stay in school and get satisfactory grades.

When an attempt to replicate the Achievement Place experience failed, Phillips *et al.* realized that the success of Achievement Place depended on the character of the interactions between teaching-parents and boys. To wit, "there were three essential differences between the successful and the unsuccessful teaching-parents. One was in the social-teaching component—the way they gave instructions and feedback. Successful teaching-parents teach in a nonconfronting, straightforward, enthusiastic way that gives a positive atmosphere to the whole house. The second difference was in the social-skill-training component—the teaching of social skills that make the youths more reinforcing and less aversive in interpersonal relationships. The third was the self-government component—teaching the youths how to negotiate and criticize constructively and always including the youths in any decisions about the program" (pp. 78–79).

Milieu therapy tries to treat offenders by creating a therapeutic environment or milieu. That milieu characteristically includes fewer imposed controls than standard correctional settings, supportive group supervisors, small group counseling, and carefully planned work activities. For example, Molof (1967b) randomly assigned 469 juvenile offenders to a small forestry camp or to regular juvenile institutions. The camp provided a supportive staff and the chance to work with adults to preserve the environment. Fifteen months after being released, 36% of the adolescents who were sent to the camp and 35% of the adolescents who were committed to regular institutions had violated parole.

The Fremont experiment (Seckel, 1967) provided wards with school classes, part-time jobs, small group therapy, field trips, visits home, and a relatively short period of confinement. In an attempt to evaluate Fremont, 16- to 19-year-old offenders were randomly assigned to Fremont or to standard correctional facilities. Although a two year follow-up yielded no evidence of a difference in the parole violation rates of experimental and control groups, youths who were committed to Fremont when the program began were less likely to violate parole than youths who were sent to Fremont at a later time. Since offenders in the control group did not display a similar pattern, Seckel proposed that this difference may have been due to the high staff turnover that took place after Fremont had been operating for some time. These findings imply that facilities like Fremont may reduce recidivism when there is little staff turnover.

The Fricot Ranch study (Jesness, 1965) tried to create closer relationships between group supervisors and juvenile wards by establishing an experimental unit of two supervisors and 20 boys. Boys were randomly assigned to the experimental unit or the regular unit of two supervisors and 50 boys. Jesness also sought to heighten the experimental supervisors' "therapeutic concern and to personalize the relationships between staff members and wards" (Shireman *et al.*, 1972, p. 45). The boys' responses indicate that the experimental unit produced a more favorable climate and more favorable attitudes than the regular unit. A one year follow-up revealed that 32% of the experimental wards and 48% of the control wards violated parole. Analysis of violation rates also reveals that the difference between experimental and control wards who were rated as neurotic and anxious or as immature and aggressive was especially marked. Unfortunately, the experimental wards caught up to the control wards after three years; that is, about 80% of the boys in each group had violated parole.

Preliminary data from the radically altered Massachusetts youth correctional system (Ohlin, Coates, & Miller, 1975) imply that the failure of milieu therapy to reduce recidivism may be due to the difference between the milieu created by the therapeutic community and the milieu that the adolescent encounters when released. The Massachusetts program sought to establish therapeutic communities characterized by high staff-ward involvement and participation by wards in the decision-making process. The program also encouraged participation by the surrounding community so as to generate the support needed to reintegrate juvenile offenders successfully into that community. So far, a six-month follow-up has revealed a dramatic decline in the rate of recidivism.

Halfway houses and job programs have been created in an attempt to help released offenders adjust to community life. The halfway house is a transitional facility that characteristically offers professional assistance with personal and vocational problems, and room and board at little or no cost to people who have just been released from prison. In a review of the research, Sullivan, Seigel, and Clear (1974) found that few well designed studies of the effectiveness of halfway houses had been carried out. They also found that the existing data provide no support for the hypothesis that released offenders who stay at halfway houses are less likely to be recidivists than released offenders who are placed on parole. However, Sullivan *et al.* suggested that this apparent failure may be due to the way halfway houses are organized and administered; for example, while a house may espouse an open and permissive philosophy, staff members may engage in intensive surveillance of residents. Before conclusions about the usefulness of halfway houses are drawn, research designed to test this hypothesis needs to be carried out.

Although the findings are fragmentary, they suggest that good jobs reduce the rate of recidivism. They also suggest that the rate of recidivism is unaffected by jobs that are onerous and/or very low paying (Evans, 1968; Odell, 1974, reading 6.4; Robin, 1969, reading 6.2; Vasoli & Fahey, 1970). For example, Odell compared 60 juvenile offenders who came from lower-class homes, who were high school dropouts, who displayed elementary or junior high school level academic skills, and who averaged nearly 11 adjudicated offenses. Subjects were randomly assigned to four groups. The first group was given normal supervision by caseworkers. The second group received three months of intensive individual and group counseling, as well as normal caseworker supervision. Members of the third, or experimental group were placed in a three-month high school equivalency diploma program that featured interesting subject matter, programmed learning, and individual instruction. When they completed the program, subjects were placed by juvenile court personnel in jobs provided by local employers. If they wished to acquire more education, court personnel helped them enroll in local vocational schools or junior colleges. The fourth group was placed in the same high school equivalency diploma program, but was not helped to find jobs or to acquire additional education.

The results indicate that the experimental treatment—the high school equivalency diploma program and placement in jobs or in school—had very favorable effects. After nine months, nearly all the experimental subjects were employed or in school, those who worked averaged $86.00 a week, and the mean recidivism rate was only 5% for three three-month periods. Subjects who pursued equivalency diplomas, but were not helped to find jobs, also had a very low mean recidivism rate; however, only 64% were employed or in school and those who worked averaged only $61.00 a week. The performance of subjects who received normal caseworker supervision or intensive individual and group counseling was distressing. Only 10% were working or in school and the mean recidivism rate was about 30% in each group. In related studies, Evans (1968) found that working steadily, earning decent wages, and obtaining at least one job that required some skill were related to completing parole, and Robin (1969, reading 6.2) found that jobs which paid the minimum wage and which apparently offered little or no opportunity for advancement had no effect on the incidence of serious crimes committed by 16- to 21-year-old high school students from poor families. While these findings are not conclusive, they suggest that providing juvenile and adult offenders with satisfactory jobs may be an effective way to reduce the rate of recidivism.

REFERENCES

Adams, S. The PICO project. In N. Johnston, L. Savitz, & M. Wolfgang (Eds.), *The sociology of punishment and correction.* New York: Wiley, 1962, pp. 213–224.

Alexander, J., & Parsons, B. Short-term behavioral intervention with delinquent families: Impact on family process and recidivism. *Journal of Abnormal Psychology*, 1973, 81, 219–225.

Antunes, G., & Hunt, L. The impact of certainty and severity of punishment on levels of crime in American states: An extended analysis. *Journal of Criminal Law and Criminology*, 1973, 64, 486–493.

Babst, D., & Mannering, J. Probation versus imprisonment for similar types of offenders: A comparison by subsequent violations. *Journal of Research in Crime and Delinquency*, 1965, 2, 60–71.

Bailey, W. Murder and the death penalty. *Journal of Criminal Law & Criminology*, 1974, 65, 416–423.

Bailey, W., Martin, J., & Gray, L. Crime and deterrence: A correlation analysis. *Journal of Research in Crime and Delinquency*, 1974, 11, 124–143.

Bandura, A., & Walters, R. *Adolescent aggression*. New York: Ronald Press, 1959.

Banuazizi, A., & Mohavedi, S. Interpersonal dynamics in a simulated prison: A methodological anlysis. *American Psychologist*, 1975, 30, 152–160.

Berger, A., & Simon, W. Black families and the Moynihan report: A research evaluation. *Social Problems*, 1974, 22, 145–161.

Black, D., & Reiss, Jr., A. Police control of juveniles. *American Sociological Review*, 1970, 35, 63–77.

Blum, R. Drugs, behavior and crime. *Annals of the American Academy of Political and Social Sciences*, 1967, 374, 135–146.

Brown, B., DuPont, R., Bass, U., Brewster, G., Glendinning, S., Kozel, N., & Meyers, M. Impact of a large-scale narcotics treatment program: A six month experience. *International Journal of the Addictions*, 1973, 8, 49–57.

Chilton, R., & Markle, G. Family disruption, delinquent conduct and the effect of subclassification. *American Sociological Review*, 1972, 37, 93–99.

Chiricos, T., & Waldo, G. Punishment and crime: An examination of some empirical evidence. *Social Problems*, 1970, 18, 200–217.

Cohen, H., & Filipczak, J. *A new learning environment*. San Francisco: Jossey-Bass, 1971.

Costello, T., & Zalkind, S. Cities, behavioral research and community mental health. In D. Adelson & B. Kalis (Eds.), *Community psychology and mental health*. San Francisco: Chandler, 1970, pp. 177–207.

Dale, R., & Dale, F. The use of methadone in a representative group of heroin addicts.

International Journal of the Addictions, 1973, 8, 293–308.

Davidson, W., & Seidman, E. Studies of behavior modification and juvenile delinquency: A review, methodological critique, and social perspective. *Psychological Bulletin*, 1974, 81, 998–1011.

Ehrlich, I. The deterrent effect of criminal law enforcement. *Journal of Legal Studies*, 1972, 1, 259–276.

Eron, L., Huesmann, L., Lefkowtiz, M., & Walder, L. How learning conditions in early childhood—including mass media—relate to aggression in late adolescence. *American Journal of Orthopsychiatry*, 1974, 44, 412–423.

Erskine, H. The polls: Gun control. *Public Opinion Quarterly*, 1972, 36, 455–469.

Evans, R. The labor market and parole success. *Journal of Human Resources*, 1968, 3, 201–212.

Federal Bureau of Investigation. *Crime in the United States: Uniform crime reports, 1970*. Washington, D.C.: U.S. Government Printing Office, 1971.

Federal Bureau of Investigation. *Crime in the United States: Uniform crime reports, 1973*. Washington, D.C.: U.S. Government Printing Office, 1974.

Fox, R. The XYY offender: A modern myth? *Journal of Criminal Law, Criminology and Police Science*, 1971, 62, 59–73.

Frease, D. Schools and delinquency: Some intervening processes. *Pacific Sociological Review*, 1973, 16, 426–448.

Friedman, C., & Friedman, A. *Drug abuse and delinquency*. Paper prepared for the National Commission on Marihuana and Drug Abuse, 1973.

Gallup, G. *The Gallup Opinion Index*, report no. 91. Princeton, N.J.: The Gallup Opinion Index, 1973.

Gearing, F. Evaluation of methadone maintenance treatment program. *International Journal of the Addictions*, 1970, 5, 517–543.

Gibbons, D. *Society, crime, and criminal careers*, second edition. Englewood Cliffs, N.J.: Prentice-Hall, 1973.

Glaser, D. *The effectiveness of a prison and parole system*. Indianapolis: Bobbs-Merrill, 1964.

Gold, M., & Mann, D. Delinquency as defense. *American Journal of Orthopsychiatry*, 1972, 42, 463–479.

Gould, L. Juvenile entrepreneurs. *American Journal of Sociology*, 1969, 74, 710–719. (a)

Gould, L. Who defines delinquency: A comparison of self-reported and officially-reported indices of delinquency for three racial groups. *Social Problems*, 1969, 16, 325–336. (b)

Guttmann, E. *Effects of short-term psychiatric treatment on boys in two California Youth Authority institutions.* Sacramento: State of California, Department of the Youth Authority, 1963.

Hackler, J. Testing a causal model of delinquency. *Sociological Quarterly,* 1970, 11, 511–523.

Haney, C., Banks, W., & Zimbardo, P. Interpersonal dynamics in a simulated prison. *International Journal of Criminology and Penology*, 1973, 1, 69–97.

Harris, A. Imprisonment and the expected value of criminal choice: A specification and test of aspects of the labeling perspective. *American Sociological Review*, 1975, 40, 71–87.

Harrison, R. Model for group counseling. In R. Harrison & P. Mueller, *Clue hunting about group counseling and parole outcome.* Research report no. 11. Sacramento: Department of Corrections, California Youth and Adult Corrections Agency, 1964.

Herzog, E. Social stereotypes and social research. *Journal of Social Issues*, 1970, 26 (3), 109–125.

Hindelang, M. The relationship of self-reported delinquency to scales of the CPI and MMPI. *Journal of Criminal Law, Criminology and Police Science*, 1972, 63, 75–81.

Hindelang, M. Public opinion regarding crime, criminal justice, and related topics. *Journal of Research in Crime and Delinquency*, 1974, 11, 101–116.

Jacoby, J., Weiner, N., & Wolfgang, M. *Drug use and criminality in a birth cohort.* Paper prepared for the National Commission on Marihuana and Drug Abuse, 1973.

Jaffe, E. Family anomie and delinquency: Development of the concept and some empirical findings. *British Journal of Criminology*, 1969, 9, 376–388.

Jaman, D. *Parole outcome and time served by first releases committed for robbery and burglary, 1965 releases.* Sacramento: California Department of Corrections, Measurement Unit, 1968.

Jensen, G. Parents, peers, and delinquent action: A test of the differential association perspective. *American Journal of Sociology*, 1972, 78, 562–575.

Jensen, G. Inner containment and delinquency. *Journal of Criminal Law and Criminology.* 1973, 64, 464–470.

Jesness, C. *The Fricot Ranch study: Outcomes with small vs. large living groups in rehabilitation of delinquents.* Research report no. 47. Sacramento: Department of the Youth Authority, California Youth and Adult Corrections Agency, 1965.

Kassebaum, G., Ward, D., & Wilner, D. *Prison treatment and parole survival: An empirical assessment.* New York: Wiley, 1971.

Law Enforcement Assistance Administration. *Crime in the nation's five largest cities: National crime panel surveys of Chicago, Detroit, Los Angeles, New York, and Philadelphia.* Washington, D.C.: U.S. Government Printing Office, 1974.

Liska, A. Causal structures underlying the relationship between delinquent involvement and delinquent peers. *Sociology and Social Research*, 1973, 58, 23–36.

Megargee, E. Undercontrolled and overcontrolled personality types in extreme antisocial aggression. *Psychological Monographs*, 1966, 80, Whole No. 611.

Megargee, E., & Mendelsohn, G. The assessment of the chronically overcontrolled assaultive offender. Mimeographed manuscript, 1965.

Molof, M. *Differences between assaultive and non-assaultive juvenile offenders in the California Youth Authority.* Sacramento: Division of Research, Department of the Youth Authority, State of California, 1967. (a)

Molof, M. Forestry camp study: *Comparison of recidivism rates of camp-eligible boys randomly assigned to camp and institutional programs.* Research report no. 53. Sacramento: Department of the Youth Authority, California Youth and Adult Corrections Agency, 1967. (b)

Monahan, J., & Cummings, L. Social police implications of the inability to predict violence. *Journal of Social Issues*, 1975,

31, (2), 153–164.

Newman, O. Defensible space: Crime prevention through urban design. *Ekistics*, 1973, 36, 325–332.

Odell, B. Accelerating entry into the opportunity structure: A sociologically based treatment for delinquent youth. *Sociology and Social Research*, 1974, 58, 312–317.

Ohlin, L., Coates, R., & Miller, A. Evaluating the reform of youth correction in Massachusetts. *Journal of Research in Crime and Delinquency*, 1975, 12, 3–16.

Peterson, R., Pittman, D., & O'Neal, P. Stabilities in deviance: A study of assaultive and non-assaultive offenders. *Journal of Criminal Law, Criminology and Police Science*, 1962, 53, 44–48.

Phillips, E., Phillips, E., Fixsen, D., & Wolf, M. Behavior shaping works for delinquents. *Psychology Today*, 1973, 7 (1), 75–79.

Piliavin, I., Vadum, A., & Hardyck, J. Delinquency, personal costs and parental treatment: A test of the reward-cost model of juvenile criminality. *Journal of Criminal Law, Criminology and Police Science*, 1969, 60, 165–172.

President's Commission on Law Enforcement and Administration of Justice. *The challenge of crime in a free society*. Washington, D.C.: U.S. Government Printing Office, 1967.

Quicker, J. The effect of goal discrepancy on delinquency. *Social Problems*, 1974, 22, 76–86.

Robin, G. Anti-poverty programs and delinquency. *Journal of Criminal Law, Criminology and Police Science*, 1969, 60, 323–331.

Robison, J., & Kevorkian, M. *Intensive treatment project: Phase II. Parole outcome: Interim report*. Research report no. 27. Sacramento: Department of Corrections, California Youth and Adult Corrections Agency, 1967.

Sarason, I., & Ganzer, V. Modeling and group discussion in the rehabilitation of juvenile delinquents. *Journal of Counseling Psychology*, 1973, 20, 442–449.

Sarbin, T., Wenk, E., & Sherwood, D. An effort to identify assault-prone offenders. *Journal of Research in Crime and Delinquency*, 1968, 5, 66–71.

Savitz, L. A study of capital punishment.

Journal of Criminal Law, Criminology and Police Science, 1958, 49, 338–341.

Scarpitti, F., & Stephenson, R. A study of probation effectiveness. *Journal of Criminal Law, Criminology and Police Science*, 1968, 59, 361–369.

Schuessler, K. The deterrent influence of the death penalty. *Annals of the American Academy of Political and Social Science*, 1952, 284, 54–62.

Schwitzgebel, R. *Streetcorner research*. Cambridge: Harvard University Press, 1964.

Seckel, J. *Experiments in group counseling at two Youth Authority institutions*. Sacramento: Department of the Youth Authority, California Youth and Adult Corrections Agency, 1965.

Seckel, J. *The Fremont experiment: Assessment of residential treatment at a Youth Authority reception center*. Sacramento: Department of the Youth Authority, California Youth and Adult Corrections Agency, 1967.

Sellin, T. Homicides in retentionist and abolitionist states. In T. Sellin (ed.), *Capital punishment*. New York: Harper & Row, 1967, pp. 135–138.

Shireman, C., Mann, K., Larsen, C., & Young, T. Findings from experiments in treatment in the correctional institution. *Social Service Review*, 1972, 46, 38–59.

Sullivan, D., Seigel, L., & Clear, T. The halfway house, ten years later: Reappraisal of correctional innovation. *Canadian Journal of Criminology and Corrections*, 1974, 16, 188–197.

Sumpter, G. The youthful offender: A descriptive analysis. *Canadian Journal of Criminology and Corrections*, 1972, 14, 282–296.

Swezey, R., & Chambers, A. Drug use and criminal activity: Some relationship indices. *Drug Forum*, 1974, 3, 161–171.

Time, 1975 (June 30), 105 (27), 10–24.

Tittle, C. Crime rates and legal sanctions. *Social Problems*, 1969, 16, 409–423.

Tittle, C., & Rowe, A. Certainty of arrest and crime rates: A further test of the deterrence hypothesis. *Social Forces*, 1974, 52, 455–462.

Tupin, J., Mahar, D., & Smith, D. Two types of violent offenders with psychosocial descriptors. *Diseases of the Nervous System*, 1973, 34, 356–363.

Vasoli, R., & Fahey, F. Halfway house for reformatory releases. *Crime and Delinquency*, 1970, 16, 292–304.

Walberg, H. Urban schooling and delinquency: Toward an integrative theory. *American Educational Research Journal*, 1972, 9, 285–300.

Walberg, H., Yeh, E., & Paton, S. Family background, ethnicity, and urban delinquency. *Journal of Research in Crime and Delinquency*. 1974, 11, 80–87.

Wicker, T. The wrong model. *The New York Times*, July 27, 1972, p. 31.

Wilkinson, K. The broken family and juvenile delinquency: Scientific explanation or ideology? *Social Problems*, 1974, 21, 726–739.

Williams, J., & Gold, M. From delinquent behavior to official delinquency. *Social Problems*, 1972, 20, 209–229.

Witt, J. Non-coercive interrogation and the administration of criminal justice: The impact of Miranda on police effectuality. *Journal of Criminal Law and Criminology*, 1973, 64, 320–332.

Wolfgang, M., Figlio, R., & Sellin, T. *Delinquency in a birth cohort*. Chicago: University of Chicago Press, 1972.

Zimring, F. Is gun control likely to reduce violent killings? *University of Chicago Law Review*, 1968, 35, 721–737.

Zimroth, P. 101,000 defendants were convicted of misdemeanors last year. 98,000 of them had pleaded guilty—to get reduced sentences. *The New York Times Magazine, The New York Times*, May 28, 1972.

6.1
Social Policy Implications
of the Inability to Predict Violence

JOHN MONAHAN and LESLEY CUMMINGS

Among the most theoretically intriguing and pragmatically significant areas in which behavioral science affects social policy is in the prediction by psychologists and psychiatrists of violence in society. Fear of violence has become such a fact of life in urban America that the possibility of preventing violence by identifying its perpetrators before they strike is bound to have substantial political attraction. We wish here to briefly review current social policy based on the prediction of violence, as well as the empirical literature on the validity of such predictions, and to focus upon several social policy changes implied by our findings.

Current Social Policy

The task of identifying the violence-prone rests primarily with the mental health and criminal justice systems. At least seventeen states include a prediction of dangerousness as part of their civil commitment criteria (Kittrie, 1971), resulting in approximately 50,000 persons each year involuntarily detained for society's protection and their own treatment (Rubin, 1972). Of the 600,000 persons who will be apprehended and accused of index crimes against persons (homicide, aggravated assault, rape and robbery) in a year, 5% to 10% will be given a mental health examination to advise the court about their potential for dangerous behavior, and an additional 10,000 persons will annually be confined as dangerous "mentally ill offenders," including "sexual psychopaths" and those found not guilty by reason of insanity (Rubin, 1972). In addition, the judicial choice of probation or prison for "normal offenders" can be heavily swayed by formal or informal assessments of dangerousness, as can decisions about suitability for community rehabilitation programs or fitness for granting bail (Foote, 1970; Dershowitz, 1970). Predictions of violence likewise play a crucial role in deciding the transfer of a case from juvenile to adult court (Fox, 1972).

While predictions of violence are often critical in deciding who will be detained for the protection of society, they are equally essential in deciding when that detention will end. The indeterminate sentence is perhaps the most extreme example of reliance

From J. Monahan & L. Cummings. Social policy implications of the inability to predict violence. *Journal of Social Issues*, 1975, *31*, (2), 153–164. Reprinted by permission.

on predictions of violence in determining length of incarceration. The individual is incarcerated for an unspecified or vaguely specified amount of time, e.g., 1 to 15 years, on the basis of his assumed dangerousness, and released when authorities predict that he is no longer dangerous. Parole decisions in more determinate sentences also rely heavily upon predictions of violence (Wenk, Robison & Smith, 1972). In general, whenever a form of correctional or mental health treatment is applied to an assumed dangerous person, his release from the treatment institution (prison, civil mental hospital, or hospital for the criminally insane) is predicated on a negative prediction of dangerousness. The only way to know when the treatment of a dangerous person is over is to know when he is no longer dangerous.

A persistent problem confronting those who would frame social policy concerning violence is the definition of the subject matter. Some define violence to include only injury or death to persons (Rubin, 1972), while others include the destruction of property. Violent *thoughts* are considered dangerous by some (Ervin & Lion, 1969). In the District of Columbia, dangerousness is defined in terms of acts "which result in harm to others, or cause *trouble* or *inconvenience* to others" (Comment, 1965). A federal court once ruled that writing a bad check was a sufficiently "dangerous" behavior to justify commitment (Overholser v. Russell, 1960). It is no wonder that the President of the National Council on Crime and Delinquency recently called the identification of dangerous persons "the greatest unresolved problem the criminal justice system faces" (Rector, 1973, p. 186). Violence, as Skolnick (1969, p. 4) points out, "is an ambiguous term whose meaning is established through political processes." Etymology may reveal more about its nature than can be found in legal statutes or psychiatric reports: "dangerousness" derives from a 13th century word meaning "difficult to deal with or please" (Steadman, 1973).

The Validity of Violence Prediction

Despite the ubiquity of violence prediction in current mental health and criminal justice practice, there has been amazingly little empirical research on its validity. The studies which do exist, however, lead to very consistent conclusions (Monahan, 1975a, 1975b, in press).

Wenk, Robison and Smith (1972) report three massive studies on the prediction of violence undertaken in the California Department of Corrections. In the first study, a "violence prediction scale," including variables such as commitment offense, number of prior commitments, opiate use and length of imprisonment, was able to isolate a small group of offenders who were three times more likely to commit a violent act than parolees in general. However, eighty-six percent of those identified as violent did not, in fact, commit a violent act while on parole.

In the second study, over seven thousand parolees were assigned to various categories keyed to their potential aggressiveness on the basis of their case histories and psychiatric reports. One in five parolees was assigned to a "potentially aggressive" category, and the rest to a "less aggressive" category. During a one-year follow-up, however, the rate of crimes involving actual violence for the potentially aggressive group was only 3.1 per thousand compared with 2.8 per thousand among the less aggressive group. Thus, for every correct identification of a potentially aggressive individual, there were 326 incorrect ones.

The final study reported by Wenk *et al.* (1972) sampled over four thousand California Youth Authority wards. Attention was directed to the record of violence in the youth's past, and an extensive background investigation was conducted, including psychiatric diagnoses and a psychological test battery. Subjects were followed for 15 months after release, and data on 100 variables were analyzed retrospectively to see which items predicted a violent act of recidivism. The authors concluded that the parole decision-maker who used a history of actual violence as his sole predictor of future violence would have 19 false positives in every 20 predictions, and yet "there is no other form of simple classification available thus far that would enable him to improve on this level of efficiency" (p. 399). Several multivariate regression equations were developed from the data, but none was even hypothetically capable of doing better than attaining an eight to one false positive to true positive ratio.

Kozol, Boucher and Garofalo (1972) have reported a 10-year study involving almost six hundred offenders. Each offender was examined independently by at least two psychiatrists, two psychologists and a social worker. A full psychological test battery was administered and a complete case history compiled. During a five-year follow-up period in the community, 8% of those predicted not to be dangerous became recidivists by committing a serious assaultive act, and 34.7% of those predicted to be dangerous committed such an act.

While the assessment of dangerousness by Kozol and his colleagues appears to have some validity, the problem of false positives stands out. Sixty-five percent of the individuals identified as dangerous did not, in fact, commit a dangerous act. Despite the extensive examining, testing and data gathering they undertook, Kozol *et al.* were wrong in 2 out of every 3 predictions of dangerousness. (For an analysis of the methodological flaws of this study, see Monahan (1973b) and the rejoinder by Kozol, Boucher, & Garofalo (1973). Data very similar to that of Kozol *et al.* has recently been released by the Patuxent Institution.[1]

Finally, in 1966, the U.S. Supreme Court held that Johnnie Baxstrom had been denied equal protection of the law by being detained beyond his maximum sentence in an institution for the criminally insane without

the benefit of a new hearing to determine his current dangerousness (Baxstrom v. Herold, 1966). The ruling resulted in the transfer of nearly 1,000 persons "reputed to be some of the most dangerous mental patients in the state (of New York)" (Steadman, 1972) from hospitals for the criminally insane to civil mental hospitals. It also provided an excellent opportunity for naturalistic research on the validity of the psychiatric predictions of dangerousness upon which the extended detention was based.

There has been an extensive follow-up program on the Baxstrom patients (Steadman & Cocozza, 1974). Researchers find that the level of violence experienced in the civil mental hospitals was much less than had been feared, that the civil hospitals adapted well to the massive transfer of patients and that the Baxstrom patients were being treated the same as the civil patients. The precautions that the civil hospitals had undertaken in anticipation of the supposedly dangerous patients—the setting up of secure wards and provision of judo training to the staff—were largely for naught (Rappeport, 1973). Only twenty percent of the Baxstrom patients were assaultive to persons in the civil hospital or community at any time during a four-year follow-up of their transfer. Further, only 3% of Baxstrom patients were sufficiently dangerous to be returned to a hospital for the criminally insane during 4 years after the decision (Steadman and Halfon, 1971). Steadman and Keveles (1972) followed 121 Baxstrom patients who had been released into the community (i.e., discharged from both the criminal and civil mental hospitals). During an average of 2 1/2 years of freedom, only 9 of the 121 patients (8%) were convicted of a crime, and only *one* of those convictions was for a violent act.

The conclusion to emerge most strikingly from these studies is the great degree to which violence is overpredicted. Of those predicted to be dangerous, between 65% and 99% are false positives—people who will not, in fact, commit a dangerous act. Indeed, the

---

1. State of Maryland. *Maryland's defective delinquency statute.* Baltimore, Maryland: Department of Public Safety and Correctional Services, 1973.

literature has been consistent on this point ever since Pinel took the chains off the supposedly dangerous mental patients at La Bicetre in 1792, and the resulting lack of violence gave lie to the psychiatric predictions which had justified their restraint. Violence is vastly overpredicted whether simple behavioral indicators are used or sophisticated multivariate analyses are employed, and whether psychological tests are administered or thorough psychiatric examinations are performed.

We are left with the stark moral issue: how many false positives—how many innocent men and women—are we willing to sacrifice to protect ourselves from one violent individual? "What represents an acceptable trade-off between the values of public safety and individual liberty?" (Wenk et al., 1972, p. 401). No one insists that prediction be perfect. We do not, after all, require absolute certainty for convicting the guilty, only proof "beyond a reasonable doubt." That means that we are willing to tolerate the conviction of some innocent persons to assure the confinement of a much larger number of guilty criminals (Dershowitz, 1970). But we insist on a process that minimizes erroneous confinement. How can this prized principle of our jurisprudence be squared with the fact that, where the prediction of dangerousness is concerned, we are willing to lock up many to save ourselves from a few?

SOME SOCIAL POLICY CHANGES SUGGESTED BY THE LITERATURE ON THE VALIDITY OF VIOLENCE PREDICTION

While the consistent finding that behavioral scientists are unable to predict violence at even a minimal level of accuracy has numerous implications for the modification of current social policy, we shall limit our discussion to four areas: (a) preventive detention; (b) civil commitment; (c) indeterminate sentencing; and (d) early intervention programs.

Preventive Detention

The debate over pre-trial preventive detention—the confinement of an individual who has been charged with, but not convicted of, an offense—is a recurrent one which has taken on increased importance in recent years (Foote, 1970). Charges of unconstitutionality weigh against claims that the streets are not safe due to the release of dangerous offenders on bail.

The data on the prediction of violence address themselves significantly to this policy issue. The fact that dangerousness is greatly overpredicted even by behavioral scientists (who are in the business of predicting behavior) suggests grave caution in relying upon the predictions of untrained judges as the principal means for deciding who should be detained. Dershowitz (1970) accurately refers to pre-trial detention as "imprisonment by judicial hunch."

While the research implies that relying upon predictions of violence will result in a great many persons incarcerated until proven innocent, that result may not be apparent to the public. Dershowitz (1970) notes that "the most serious danger in any system of preventive confinement is that it always seems to be working well, even when it is performing dismally. This is so because it is in the nature of any system of preventive detention to display its successes in reducing crime while it hides its frequent errors" (p. 18). (See Monahan, in press, for a full discussion of the factors leading to the over-prediction of violence, and possible strategies for improving predictive accuracy.)

Given that past behavior tends to be the best single predictor of future behavior (Mischel, 1968; 1973), perhaps evidence of past violence (i.e., previous violent felony convictions) might weigh more heavily than psychiatric or judicial predictions in making decisions about pre-trial detention (cf. Speiser, 1970).

Civil Commitment

While a general policy of preventive detention is a highly controversial issue, there is one group in society for which preventive detention, in the absence of a conviction or even an allegation of crime, is readily tolerated—the "mentally ill" (Dershowitz, 1970). This is no doubt due to the widespread public belief that the psychologically disturbed are intrinsically more violence-prone than the rest of society (Rabkin, 1972). This belief is frequently reinforced by the media, which takes great pains to report when an offender is an ex-mental patient, or has even seen a private psychiatrist or psychologist, but which never notes it when a criminal does not have a previous psychiatric history.

The research literature on violence and psychological disorder, however, does not support public opinion. The most extensive review of the area, citing scores of studies, concluded that "an individual with a label of mental illness is quite capable of committing any act of violence known to man, but probably does not do so with any greater frequency than his neighbor in the general population" (Gulevich and Bourne, 1970, p. 323).

The lack of ability to predict dangerousness, combined with the similar base-rates for violence among the psychologically disturbed and "normals," suggests that there is no empirical basis to support the preventive detention of those psychologically disturbed persons who have not committed a violent act (Monahan, 1974a, 1974b). A similar conclusion was reached by Pennsylvania's Task Force in Commitment Procedures studying revisions of that state's mental health laws: "since the capacity to predict dangerous conduct is no greater in the case of mentally ill persons than others, preventive detention is no more justified in the case of mental illness than elsewhere."[2] Likewise, one can-

2. Commonwealth of Pennsylvania. *Report of the Task Force on commitment procedures.* Philadelphia, Penna.: Department of Public Welfare, 1972.

not argue for the preventive detention of the mentally ill on the therapeutic grounds that they can be helped by psychiatric or psychological treatment, since no form of treatment has yet been demonstrated to have an enduring effect on reducing violent behavior (Geis & Monahan, 1976; Monahan, 1973a; Monahan & Cummings, 1974).

Indeterminate Sentencing

Indeterminate sentencing, according to Ramsey Clark (1970), "affords the public the protection of potentially long confinement without the necessity that long sentences be served. It gives the best of both worlds—long protection for the public, yet a fully flexible opportunity for the convict's rehabilitation" (p. 224). The assumption is that behavioral scientists on the parole board can determine when an offender is no longer a threat to society (when he is "rehabilitated") and release him.

The data on the validity of violence prediction, however, belie this assumption. There is no non-arbitrary method of determining when an offender is no longer dangerous.

The inaccuracy of violence prediction, in itself, might not be enough reason to abolish indeterminate sentences. If indeterminate sentences were more humane than determinate ones, there might be reason to maintain them. Community treatment programs, for example, have not been demonstrated to reduce recidivism compared with a prison sentence, but they have been shown to be more humane than prison and much more economical. If a similar humanitarian benefit could be shown to accrue to indeterminate sentencing, it might be justified.

Just the opposite of humaneness, however, appears to be the case. "There is considerable evidence, mainly in the form of testimony from prisoners and ex-prisoners of various California prisons (where indeterminate sentences are the rule), that indefinite sentences are one of the most painful aspects of prison life" (American Friends Service Committee, 1971, p. 93). One inmate commented on "the total waste of time spent while here and the constant mental torture of never really knowing how long you'll be here. The indeterminate sentence structure gives you no peace of mind and absolutely nothing to work for" (p. 94). Note, too, that the mean time spent in prison in those jurisdictions which have adopted the indeterminate sentence is substantially longer than that served in jurisdictions where the judge fixes the sentence (American Friends Service Committee, 1971).

There appears to us to be no empirical or moral justification for continued experimentation with indeterminate sentencing. Based partially on the prediction research as it has been reviewed in this paper, the California Senate recently and overwhelmingly voted to return to judicially—rather than psychologically—determined sentences.[3] There is reason to believe that other states may soon follow suit (Morris, 1974).

Early Intervention

While the gross inaccuracy of violence prediction has serious ramifications for the confinement and treatment of alleged offenders, convicted offenders, and the "mentally ill," it has even more important implications for the confinement and treatment of those who have not committed a deviant act.

Former President Nixon, in 1970, asked the Department of Health, Education and Welfare to study the proposals of Arnold Hutschnecker, a psychiatric consultant to the National Commission on the Causes and Prevention of Violence. Hutschnecker suggested that psychological tests such as the Rorschach be administered to all six-year-olds in the United States to determine their potential for criminal behavior, followed by "massive psychological and psychiatric treatment for those children found to be crim-

inally inclined." Such a program, Hutschnecker said, was "a better short-term solution to the crime problem that urban reconstruction. Teenage boys later found to be persisting in incorrigible behavior would be remanded to camps . . . " (Maynard, 1970).

Perhaps even more amazingly, Hutschnecker has more recently recommended a psychiatric overseer for the President. "I cannot help think if an American President had a staff psychiatrist, perhaps a case such as Watergate might not have had a chance to develop. A President has a personal physician to watch over his physical health. Why could a man of outstanding leadership not have a physician watching over his and his staff's mental health?" (1973). Like Juvenal, one wonders who will guard the guardians (see Szasz's retort to Hutschnecker, 1973).

Hutschnecker is not alone in his advocacy of coerced intervention. Bellak (1971) states that "a psychiatric examination of children at school entrance time should be required, like vaccination. If a child is found to be in a markedly disturbed environment, school attendance should be denied unless parents are willing to have the child or themselves treated or advised . . . In those who are already dangerously disturbed, enforced treatment might prevent many future Oswalds (whose mother was able to remove him from treatment)" (p. 120). It is precisely this assessment of dangerousness, however, which is beyond the ability of behavioral scientists. How many normal children will we label and stigmatize as "dangerously disturbed" in order to isolate a future assassin? In an attempt to quell opposition with a right-wing smear, Bellak (1971) states: "Not unlike the fluoridation of water, excessive alarm over mental health legislation is likely to disappear eventually, quietly" (p. 121). That hollow silence might also be a requiem for human autonomy.

Conclusion

Current social policy on the prediction of violence is infused with well-meaning inten-

---

3. Monahan, J. *Abolishing the indeterminate sentence.* Testimony before the California Senate Select Committee on Penal Institutions, Sacramento, April 1975.

tions. We detain people without trial, commit them, sentence them indefinitely, and intervene in their lives in various other ways for "their own good," as well as for our own protection. The empirical fact of the invalidity of violence prediction suggests that neither the interests of society nor the interests of the identified individual are being served by social policies based on the prediction of violence. We must once again pay heed to the admonition of Justice Brandeis:

Experience should teach us to be most on our guard to protect liberty when the government's purposes are beneficent. Men born to freedom are naturally alert to repel invasion of their liberty by evil-minded rulers. The greatest dangers to liberty lurk in insidious encroachment by men of zeal, well-meaning but without understanding [Olmstead v. United States, 1928].

REFERENCES

American Friends Service Committee, *Struggle for justice*, New York: Hill and Wang, 1971.

Baxstrom, v. Herold, *U.S. Reports*, 1966, 383, 107.

Bellak, L. The need for public health laws for psychiatric illness. *American Journal of Public Health*, 1971, 61, 119–121.

Brandeis, L. D. (1928) *Olmstead v. United States*, 277 U.S. 438, 479 (dissenting).

Clark, R. *Crime in America*. New York: Simon and Schuster, 1970.

Comment, Liberty and required mental health treatment. *University of Pennsylvania Law Review*, 1963, 14, 1067–1070.

Dershowitz, A. Imprisonment by judicial hunch: the case against pretrial preventive detention. *The Prison Journal*, 1970, L, 12–22.

Ervin, F. & Lion, J. Clinical evaluation of the violent patient. In D. Mulvihill and M. Tumin (Eds.) *Crimes of Violence*. U.S. Government Printing Office, 1969, Vol. 13, pp. 1163–1188.

Foote, C. Preventive detention—what is the issue? *The Prison Journal*, 1970, L, 3–11.

Fox, S. Predictive devices and the reform of juvenile justice. In S. Glueck and E.

Glueck (Eds.) *Identification of predelinquents*. New York: Intercontinental Medical Book Corporation, 1972, 107–114.

Geis, G. & Monahan, J. The social ecology of violence. In T. Lickona (Ed.) *Morality: Theory, research, and social issues*. New York: Holt, Rinehart, and Winston, 1976.

Gulevich, G. & Bourne, P. Mental illness and violence. In D. Daniels, M. Gilula and F. Ochberg, (Eds.) *Violence and the Struggle for Existence*. Boston: Little, Brown and Company, 1970, 309–326.

Hutschnecker, A. The stigma of seeing a psychiatrist. *The New York Times*, July 4, 1973, P. E-15.

Kittrie, N. *The right to be different*. Baltimore: John Hopkins University Press, 1971.

Kozol, H., Boucher, R. & Garofalo, R. The diagnosis and treatment of dangerousness. *Crime and Delinquency*, 1972, 18, 371–392.

Kozol, H., Boucher, R. & Garofalo, R. Dangerousness. *Crime and Delinquency*, 1973, 19, 554–555.

Maynard, R. Doctor would test children to curb crime. *Los Angeles Times*, April 5, 1970, Sect. A, p. 9.

Mischel, W. *Personality and Assessment*. New York: Wiley, 1968.

Mischel, W. Toward a cognitive social learning reconceptualization of personality. *Psychological Review*, 1973, 80, 252–283.

Monahan, J. Abolish the insanity defense?— Not yet. *Rutgers Law Review*, 1973, 26, 719–741 (a).

Monahan, J. Dangerous offenders: a critique of Kozol, *et al. Crime and Delinquency*, 1973, 19, 418–420 (b).

Monahan, J. The psychiatrization of criminal behavior. In A. Brooks (Ed.) *Law, Psychiatry, and the mental health system*. Boston: Little, Brown, & Co., 1974, 696–699 (a).

Monahan, J. Dangerousness and civil commitment. In United States Senate, Committee on the Judiciary (Eds.) *Reform of the federal criminal laws*. Washington, D.C.: Government Printing Office, 1974, 7083–7093 (b).

Monahan, J. The prediction of violence. In D. Chappell and J. Monahan (Eds.) *Violence and criminal justice*. Lexington, Mass.: Lexington Books, 1975, 15–31 (a).

Monahan, J. The prevention of violence. In J. Monahan (Ed.) *Community mental health and the criminal justice system.* New York: Pergamon Press, 1975, 13–34 (b).

Monahan, J. Improving predictions of violence. *American Journal of Psychiatry*, in press.

Monahan, J. & Cummings, L. The prediction of violence as a function of its perceived consequences. *Journal of Criminal Justice*, 1974, 2, 239–242.

Morris, N. *The future of imprisonment.* Chicago: University of Chicago Press, 1974.

Olmstead v. U.S. *U.S. Reports*, 1928, 277, 438–479.

Overholser, V. Russell, *Federal Reporter*, (2nd. ed.), 1960, 282, 195.

Rabkin, J. Opinions about mental illness: a review of the literature. *Psychological Bulletin*, 1972, 78, 153–171.

Rappeport, J. A response to "Implications from the Baxstrom experience." *Bulletin of the American Academy of Psychiatry and the Law*, 1973, 1, 197–198.

Rector, M. Who are the dangerous? *Bulletin of the American Academy of Psychiatry and the Law*, 1973, 1, 186–188.

Rubin, B. Prediction of dangerousness in mentally ill criminals. *Archives of General Psychiatry*, 1972, 27, 397–407.

Shah, S. Dangerousness and civil commitment of the mentally ill: Some public policy considerations. *American Journal of Psychiatry*, 1975, 132, 501–505.

Skolnick, J. *The politics of protest.* New York: Simon & Schuster, 1969.

Speiser, L. Preventive detention: the position of the American Civil Liberties Union. *The Prison Journal*, 1970, L, 49–52.

Steadman, H. Implications from the Baxstrom experience. *Bulletin of the American Academy of Psychiatry and the Law*, 1973, 1, 189–196 (a).

Steadman, H. The psychiatrist as a conservative agent of social control. *Social Problems*, 1972, 20, 263–271.

Steadman, H. & Cocozza, J. *Careers of the criminally insane.* Lexington, Mass.: Lexington, Books, 1974.

Steadman, H. & Halfon, A. The Baxstrom patients: backgrounds and outcome, *Seminars in Psychiatry*, 1971, 3, 376–386.

Steadman, H. & Keveles, G. The community adjustment and criminal activity of the Baxstrom patients: 1966–1970. *American Journal of Psychiatry*, 1972, 129, 304–310.

Szasz, T. The dominion of psychiatry. The *New York Times*, August 5, 1973, P. E-15.

Wenk, E., Robison, J. & Smith, G. Can violence be predicted?, *Crime and Delinquency*, 1972, 18, 393–402.

Anti-Poverty Programs and Delinquency

GERALD D. ROBIN

The provision of jobs, training, or work experience is an important component in many anti-poverty programs, frequently being the base around which the entire program is structured and developed. Within this work-oriented milieu the program participants are offered services in the form of counseling, remedial education, and job supervision. The dialogue supporting such programs has increasingly emphasized their contribution toward reducing delinquency and youth crime by inculcating more positive and socially acceptable attitudes and values in the youths and by constructively occupying leisure time through employment activities, thereby reducing the inclination and opportunity of its recipients to engage in behavior which would make them the objects of law enforcement attention. Examples of serious scientific attempts to explore empirically the hypothesis that such programs reduce delinquency are not only isolated but virtually nonexistent in the literature. Because of this, because the anti-poverty program evaluated in the present study was the in-school Neighborhood Youth Corps—one of the largest and best known federally created and subsidized pro-

grams, reaching hundreds of thousands of ghetto youths in their natural milieu and at a time when they are highly susceptible to contacts with the police—and because it was possible to establish a control group of unassailable quality, the findings presented in this paper are particularly relevant.

The in-school Neighborhood Youth Corps (NYC) program provides jobs to students 16 through 21 years of age who come from poor families.[1] During the school term these students are permitted to work as many as fifteen hours a week and up to thirty-two hours a week during the summer, at a standard rate of $1.25 per hour; a majority of the in-school NYC projects are operated (sponsored) by school boards and educational institutions.[2] At their employment sites the student "enrollees" are under the

1. The *out-of-school* Neighborhood Youth Corps program provides "full time" employment to youths who have dropped out of school; one of the out-of-school program's main objectives is to encourage the enrollees to return to school in order to complete their high school education.
2. These conditions were in effect at the time the present study was conducted. More recently, there have been efforts to lower the entrance age to 14 years and to provide for a pay *scale* rather than a fixed rate of compensation.

From G. Robin. Anti-poverty programs and delinquency. *Journal of Criminal Law, Criminology and Police Science.*, 1969, *60*, 323–331. Copyright © 1969 by Northwestern University School of Law. Reprinted by special permission of the Journal of Criminal Law, Criminology and Police Science.

direction of a work supervisor and are also assigned NYC counselors who periodically meet with them to discuss their problems, progress in the program, the role and value of education, and the need to complete high school.

THE GROUPS STUDIED

Exploration of the hypothesis that participation in anti-poverty programs reduces delinquency is explored here by an analysis of the police records of random samples of Negro youths interviewed in the summer of 1966 who, as of the time of sample selection (1) were actively enrolled and working in the in-school Neighborhood Youth Corps program operated by the Public Board of Education in Cincinnati—hereafter referred to as *year-round* enrollees, (2) were about to enter the Cincinnati NYC program for the first time—hereafter referred to as *summer-only* enrollees, and (3) had applied for enrollment and been found eligible but were not accepted into the program in order that they might be used as a control group. The larger study of which the police contact analysis is but a part was a longitudinal survey that involved interviewing NYC and control youths three times over a one-year period, with the first phase of interviewing conducted at the start of the 1966 summer and the last wave in March 1967, a month after the collection of the police contact data. The fact that the police record analysis is based upon those youths who were originally interviewed rather than upon the entire sample of names selected from the NYC records is not a serious limitation because at least four-fifths of the youths in each sample of names selected were in fact interviewed; in addition, virtually all of the non-respondents were uninterviewed because they could not be located within the time available rather than because of refusals or other more substantial factors associated with self-selection.

On June 2, 1966, two-hundred names stratified by sex within school were ran-domly selected from the active NYC files containing the names of all youths (723) who were enrolled in the program at that point, of which 167 (84%) were interviewed. Because this group had worked in the Neighborhood Youth Corps for at least some part of that school year, they are referred to, for convenience and in order to distinguish them from the second experimental sample to be described below, as *year-round* enrollees. This does not mean that, as of the time their names were drawn from the active files, they were enrolled in the program for an entire school year, school term or for a total of one year overall. The *summer-only* group consisted of youths who were to enter the NYC for the first time in the 1966 summer program and who were to be terminated at its conclusion, because of a reduction in the number of authorized jobs which would be available in the fall of 1967—this in contrast to the year-round youths who were not summarily terminated from the NYC at a particular point but rather were permitted to remain in the program and were subject to voluntary and involuntary departure for any number of reasons over a long period of time; in fact, fully half of this group were still working in the NYC when the police record data were collected in February 1967. The summer-only enrollees, on the other hand, were exposed to the NYC for a maximum period of 8 to 11 weeks, depending upon their summer assignment; many of them had assignments that lasted 6 to 8 weeks or may have left the project before its completion. While the utilization of two treatment groups, the year-round and summer-only enrollees, with which to compare the controls has certain advantages which will become apparent in the analysis, one which may be mentioned at this point is the variation in the length of program participation which they introduce: the summer-only youths were in the NYC for an average of 8 weeks, while the average length of participation for the year-round enrollees, at the time of the police record determination, was 14 months. Findings based upon the year-round sample may suggest that there is a critical minimal period of program exposure which must obtain before the program's effect on reducing delinquency becomes manifest and that such exposure is not satisfied by a summer's experience in the program.

The summer-only and control groups were established from the 351 names of youths who, as of June 1966, were on the "waiting list" for entrance into the summer program; that is, there were 351 youths in Cincinnati who had applied for admission to the NYC prior to June 1966, had been screened and found eligible, and who had never worked in the program before. These "waiting list" names were arranged alphabetically and randomly assigned to the summer-only or control groups. This procedure led to the creation of an eligible universe of 136 summer-only names (130 of whom were interviewed) and 173 control names (136 of whom were interviewed). As part of their cooperation and participation in the study, the NYC administrators agreed not to accept any of the controls into the program until all field phases of the investigation were completed, and to terminate all new summer-only (SO) enrollees at the end of the 1966 summer program, this latter group also to be excluded from re-entering until all field phases were completed. It is singularly important to note that the control and summer-only groups were experimentally created specifically for research purposes and were established by a chance termination of *which* "waiting list" youths were to be admitted to the program. This random assignment of youths to the control or treatment (SO) group eliminated bias associated with self-selection, a serious shortcoming in some recent anti-poverty studies which have utilized "no shows"—applicants who do not enroll in programs after being accepted—as a control group.[3] Those who *reject* program participation are likely to be considerably

different from enrollees, particularly with respect to motivation and associated variables that may be criteria for measuring program effectiveness. No such compromise was required to identify and utilize a control group in the present study in Cincinnati: their exclusion from the Neighborhood Youth Corps was determined by fortuitous circumstances in which the youths themselves played no part and by a methodologically unassailable procedure which could not have resulted in systematic differences between the control and summer-only, or indeed year-round (YR) enrollees.[4]

Because almost all of the youths in the samples were Negroes, cases of white youths were excluded from the study. Thus, the number of Negro youths who were interviewed in each sample and who therefore constitute the groups on which the police record analysis is based is 138 year-round enrollees (82 males, 56 females), 109 summer-only enrollees (50 males, 59 females), and 119 controls (54 males, 65 females).

SOURCE OF POLICE CONTACT DATA

Identification on all of the youths originally interviewed and accompanying data collection forms were submitted to law enforcement authorities in Cincinnati in order to ascertain whether they had any juvenile or adult record of police contacts, and if so, to record the date and charges entered against the youths for each police contact. After the Master Record File—the central register from which juvenile police contacts were abstracted—had been inspected for this pur-

---

3. Peterson, *An Evaluation of the Concept of Trainee Camps for Unemployed Youth.*

4. Despite the random distribution of waiting list youths into control and summer-only subjects, this procedure did not in any way affect the *total* number of youths who worked in the program, since the 1966 Cincinnati summer program quota could not accommodate all eligible applicants. Thus, while the specific individuals on the waiting list who were admitted to the program were guided and determined by research considerations, the *sum total of services* offered in the 1966 summer program was completely unaffected by the study design.

pose, the forms were sent to the Adult Division of the police department, since at the time of offense record determination many of the "youths" were officially adults, and all *criminal* charges against them were entered on the forms. The Master Record File in the Juvenile Division contained all recorded police contacts which a youth had with the law, regardless of the precinct of origination. Thus, despite the nature of the police contact—of its severity or triviality, and of the location of the offense and the original jurisdiction of police administration over the case—if the police contact was recorded at any level it was routinely processed and entered into the juvenile Master Record File. Furthermore, the Master Record File had been maintained for a sufficiently long period such that it was in operation before any of the youths in the present study were seven years of age, so that it contained all of the ever-recorded delinquencies committed by the youths. Thus, the complete history of recorded juvenile, as well as adult, police contacts was collected. Because a majority of the youths in each sample were 16 years old when they enrolled in or applied to the program, and because approximately nine-tenths of them were between 16 and 18 years of age at the time the police contact data were collected, youths with offense records will frequently be referred to as delinquents, although it is recognized that technically individuals who incur their first police contact after juvenile status are considered criminals.

THE FINDINGS

Delinquency patterns and prevalence are primarily an expression of, or at least largely predictable from, socioeconomic status, sex, race and age; because all of the subjects in the study were Negroes of approximately the same age who were living in poverty and because the police record analysis was of course performed separately for males and females, in both experimental groups the distribution and *interaction* of these and other variables associated with Negro poverty were very closely matched with that of the controls. The serious limitation in the summer-only sample in the present analysis is the very brief period of their participation in the Neighborhood Youth Corps, thus constituting a severe restriction on one of the most important "follow-up" police contact exposure periods—the reader will recall that the average duration in the program for the summer-only group was 8 weeks, while that for the year-round enrollees at the time that the delinquency data were collected was approximately 14 months. Obviously, the greater the interval, the more likely that offenses will be committed which result in officially reported police contacts. This variable, however, has been "equated" in the year-round and control groups through natural conditions resulting from the fact that these two groups of youths tended to apply for admission and to enroll in the program over essentially the same time period, and were therefore characterized by the same police contact exposure intervals, *e.g.*, the average length of NYC participation for the year-round youths, at the time the offense data were collected, was 13.6 months while the functionally and analytically equivalent follow-up period for the controls—the interval between their application to the program and the date the offense records were checked—was 12.8 months.

The analysis which follows is based upon the identification of carefully constructed and meaningful time periods in relation to program enrollment and program participation for the year-round and summer-only youths, and the date of application for the controls.[5] Thus, the police contact profile for the experimental youths has been delineated, inspected, and calculated for the periods *before* they enrolled in the Neighborhood Youth Corps, *while* they were working in the program, and from the point of *enrollment to the date of the offense*

5. The dates on which the year-round youths *applied* to the program were not available.

record check. The second time period mentioned—*while* the youths were actively enrolled in the program—constitutes perhaps the most relevant temporal base for testing the relationship between NYC participation and delinquency—whereas the last period alluded to combines the *in-program* (*while* the youths were active in the NYC) with the *after program* period (the interval between termination from the NYC and the date of the offense record check) in order to ascertain whether there was any *overall* change in the enrollees' delinquency proneness prior to entering the NYC as contrasted with that which obtained from the time they joined until the offense record data were collected. In the case of the controls, the temporal frame of reference was dichotomized into *before application* (equivalent to the pre-enrollment period of the experimental youths) and *after application, i.e.,* from the point of application to the date of the offense record check (approximating the interval between enrollment and the offense record check for both experimental groups and equivalent to the time *while* the YR enrollees were working in the program). The terms "prior" or "previous" will refer to the period before enrollment or application, and the term "subsequent" to the period after enrollment or application to the date of the offense record check. With the preceding comments by way of introduction, the findings may now be presented.

Prior to enrollment/application among the males, a significantly[6] larger proportion of the controls (63%) than of the experimental samples (38% YR, 34% SO) had committed serious offenses, the latter defined as acts against the person or property violations and hereafter referred to interchangeably as felonies, personal/property offenses, or serious offenses; 37% of the year-round and 39% of the control youths had incurred minor or nonserious police contacts of the misdemeanor variety, while 49% YR, 54%

6. The term "significant" refers to statistically significant differences in proportions at at least .05 level of confidence.

SO and two-thirds of the controls had an offense record of some kind. Among the females in this time period, twice as many controls (19%) as year-round youths (7%), and the same proportion of summer-only youths (19%) had committed serious offenses, twice as many controls (23%) as year-round or summer-only enrollees (10–11%) had incurred minor police contacts, and 37% of the control females had an offense record before applying to the program, compared with only 16% of the year-round and one-fifth of the summer-only females before enrolling, significant differences which place the control females at a "disadvantage" in relation to the year-round females.

Moreover, the average number of felonies, misdemeanors, or any offenses committed by all of the controls before application and by all of the experimental youths before enrollment was either virtually identical, or greater among the controls than the enrollees; the same was true concerning the number of offenses of a given typology committed by those who had such charges against them. For example, among all males, the mean number of felony police contacts incurred by the controls before application to the NYC was 1.2, compared with 0.7 for each of the year-round and summer-only groups. Among the male youths who were charged with felonies before enrollment/application to the program, the average number of such charges for this subgroup of control youths was 1.9 compared with 2.0 for the year-round enrollees and 2.2 for the summer-only enrollees. Similarly, the mean number of total police contacts prior to application was 3.3 for the male controls, 3.0 for the male year-round youths, and 3.5 for the male summer-only enrollees. The same trend of results obtained for the females and for the distribution of misdemeanors in the "before" period. Furthermore, because differences in the average number of felony charges, misdemeanor charges, or any police contacts incurred by the total group of control and experimental youths, as well as by those specific subgroups of youths who committed the respective kinds of offenses, generally approached zero and rarely exceeded .3 in all of the tables generated for the delinquency analysis, continued reference to the number of acts or offenses will be avoided, since these differences could hardly be more inconsequential.

Thus, both the control males and females in Cincinnati were noticeably more delinquent in their police contact typology in the pre-application period than were the corresponding experimental youths, and this difference was greatest between the controls and the year-round sample—the experimental group which offered the most critical opportunity for testing the effect of NYC participation on delinquency and youth crime.

While they were in the NYC the proportion of year-round males who incurred police contacts represented a 33% reduction from the proportion who had an offense record prior to joining the program (from 49% to 33%), but the proportion of control males who committed offenses after applying for admission—encompassing a follow-up exposure period which was equivalent to that of the year-round males—was 39% less than the proportion who were offenders prior to trying to join the NYC (from 67% to 41%). Similarly, the male YRs charged with serious offenses decreased from 38% before enrollment to 17% *while* in the program—a 55% reduction in those who committed felonies while working in the NYC—whereas the proportion of control males with offenses against the person/property decreased by 68% (from 63% before to 20% after application). Thus, despite the fact that the control males were more serious offenders prior to application than were the year-round males prior to enrollment, the latter were equally as likely to commit serious offenses while they were active in the NYC program as were the control males after application; nor were there any significant differences in the proportion of the year-round versus control males in this same time period who committed misdemeanors or who had

any offenses charged to their record. *Accordingly, there is no evidence that NYC participation reduced delinquency among its enrollees while they were working in the program, a somewhat unexpected finding if for no reason other than that the program utilized approximately 1,000 hours of what would otherwise have been leisure time and therefore opportunity for misbehavior.* Nor was program participation related to delinquency prevention after termination from the NYC: the YR males had worked in the NYC fully six times as long as the SO males (11.5 months versus 8.3 weeks), and the exposure period after termination was shorter for the year-round (3.6 months) than for the SO males (5.3 months); yet, the proportion of both groups who committed offenses after leaving the program was the same (23% YR and 20% SO). In the interval between enrollment/application and the offense record check—which was twice as long for the controls (13 months) as for the summer-only enrollees (7 months)—there were no significant differences between the male controls and either of the experimental samples in the proportion of youths who were charged with serious, minor, or any offenses; indeed, with one exception, the proportions were virtually identical: 21% YR, 20% C and 12% SO were charged with felonies, 29% YR, 28% C and 26% SO with misdemeanors, and 39% YR, 41% C and 36% SO with any offenses.

The above analysis is based upon the *gross* effects of the program in reducing anti-social behavior without identifying specific subgroups of youths with records and determining whether these individuals benefited from program participation as reflected in their police contact profiles in appropriate follow-up periods. The crucial test of the NYC's effect on youth crime is its ability to insulate those youths who were delinquent prior to enrollment from continuing to commit offenses *while* they are working in the program, as well as from the point of entrance to the program throughout the subsequent exposure period (*i.e.,* up to the point of the offense record check)—thus yielding the program's *net* rather than *gross* effects on delinquency; exclusive focus on the latter approach has serious shortcomings, not noted by the author of a recent study of the effects of the out-of-school Neighborhood Youth Corps program on police contacts, which purported to demonstrate that *that* program reduced delinquency among the female enrollees.[7]

Among the youths who had serious police

contacts prior to enrollment/application, the proportion of year-round males who committed serious offenses while they were working in the NYC was identical to that of the male controls charged with offenses against person/property subsequent to application (one-quarter). Similarly, among those with misdemeanor offenses or any record previously, there were no significant differences in the proportion of year-round versus control males who had minor or any police contacts charged against them *while* in the NYC and *after* application, respectively. Finally, holding constant police contact typology prior to enrollment/application, there were no significant differences subsequently between the control and the experimental males: (1) of those with serious previous offenses, 29% YR, 24% SO and 25% C incurred serious police contacts subsequently, (2) of those with minor offenses previously, 37% YR, 33% SO and 35% C continued to commit such offenses subsequently, and (3) of those with any previous offense record, 48% YR, 48% SO and 50% C were offenders subsequently. As indicated earlier, the difference in the *number* of police contacts which characterized the individual samples was so small that a routine presentation of this information is unwarranted. Illustrative of this point is that among those with felony charges prior to enrollment/application, the average number of serious charges incurred subsequently was 0.3 for the year-round, 0.3 for the controls and 0.4 for the summer-only males; similarly, disregarding previous records, the average number of felonies committed by those charged with such acts in the subsequent period was 1.3 for the year-round, 1.3 for the controls and 1.7 for the summer-only males; this same pattern of differences in the number of police contacts approaching zero obtained for the remaining typological subgroups (number of misdemeanors and number of any police contacts) of youths.

Up to this point the analysis has been concerned with whether NYC participation tended to insulate youths who prior to en-

7. Walther & Magnusson, *A Retrospective Study of the Effectiveness of Out-of-School Neighborhood Youth Corps Programs in Four Urban Sites* 116–124. In addition, these authors utilize a highly questionable approach in inferring program effects on youth crime, one based upon changes in the number of police contacts and changes in the proportion of total police contacts which were serious. For example, Walther and Magnusson report that before application to the program the 115 experimental youths had a total of 294 police contacts compared with only 15 police contacts after application; these figures compare with 250 police contacts incurred by the 115 controls before application and 23 police contacts after application, and apparently take some consolation in the "greater" reduction in the police contacts of the enrollees. Stated somewhat differently, these figures indicate that the experimental youths were charged with an average of 2.6 police contacts before applying to the NYC and 0.1 after application; in the same time periods the average number of police contacts for the controls went from 2.2 to 0.2. Similarly, the authors make much of the "finding" that before application 49% of all police contacts incurred by the enrollees were serious ones (*143 out of 294*) and that after application only 20% (*3 out of 15*) were. By contrast, so the authors reason, before application 38% of the total police charges against the controls were serious ones (96 out of 250), which increased to 48% after application (*11 out of 23*). Thus, Walther and Magnusson infer positive program effect on the basis that the proportion of serious charges in relation to total police contacts decreased from 49% to 20% among the NYC participants and increased from 38% to 48% among the controls. This approach is open to serious criticism on the basis of its logic and meaningfulness alone, not to mention that by using a measure of central tendency, the same figures reveal that the average number of serious offenses committed by the experimental youths before application was 1.2 compared with 0.0 after application, while among the controls the mean reduction in serious police contacts was from 0.8 to 0.1. What these statistics on serious police contacts suggest much more strongly than program effect is that after applying to the out-of-school Neighborhood Youth Corps virtually none of the youths in either group were charged with serious offenses.

rollment had committed serious offenses from continuing to do so once they started to work in the program, those who were minor offenders previously from continuing to commit or engage in misdemeanant behavior, and youths who had known records of previous contacts from incurring subsequent police contacts. Another related aspect of this analysis, however, is whether NYC participation prevented youths who prior to enrollment had no serious charges against them from committing felonies after they entered the program, as well as those who had no previous misdemeanors from incurring minor police contacts subsequently. On both of these criteria, NYC participation continued to demonstrate no effect on reducing criminality: of the 51 year-round males who had no felony charges prior to enrollment, 12% were charged with serious offenses while they were working in the NYC, while in the functionally equivalent time period 10% of the control males who had no serious offense records prior to application acquired one after application; similarly, 19% of the year-round and 23% of the control males who had no misdemeanor police contacts before enrollment/application were charged with minor offenses while in the NYC and after they applied to the program. Moreover, when the interval between enrollment and the date of the offense record check is used for the enrollees—a period directly comparable with the subsequent time period for the controls—the proportion of the year-round males who committed their first serious offense during this time was 16% (12% did so in the shorter exposure period *while* in the program) and the proportion who committed their first minor offense was 25% (19% did so *while* in the program), compared with the same statistics reported above for the control males of 10% and 23% who, after application to the program, committed their first serious and minor offenses, respectively.

Of perhaps equal importance as the indices of "delinquency reduction" utilized above in

studying the relationship between NYC participation and police contacts is the program's effect on discouraging youths who were *non-delinquent* prior to enrolling from *becoming* delinquent after entering. That is, it may be more reasonable to expect that NYC participation would be more successful in *preventing* delinquency than in *reducing* it. While it is obviously a less demanding and more modest task to prevent youths who have not become the objects of police action and attention from doing so than it is to discourage already delinquent youths from persisting in their misconduct, the former accomplishment would nonetheless be substantial. Unfortunately, however, there was no evidence that this occurred as a result of the Neighborhood Youth Corps: of the year-round males without an offense record prior to enrollment, 24% acquired one, *i.e., became* delinquent *while* working in the NYC, the very same proportion as the previously non-delinquent control males who became delinquent after applying to the program. With respect to the previously non-delinquent females, 98% of the year-round enrollees continued to be non-delinquent while in the NYC as did 98% of the control females after application. Finally, among both males and females who were non-delinquent prior to enrollment/application, there were no significant differences in the proportion who became delinquent subsequently: among the males, one-third YR (31%), 24% C and 22% SO did so, while among the females less than 3% of any sample subsequently became delinquent.

THE DETROIT DATA

An analysis of the police records similar to the above was performed for the same typology of random samples of interviewed Negroes (after excluding a small number of white cases) who were enrolled in and applied to the Detroit in-public school Neighborhood Youth Corps program: 161 year-round enrollees (51 males, 110 females), 239 summer-only enrollees (132 males, 107 females),[8] and 124 controls (38 males, 86 females). There are three reasons that less confidence should be placed in the Detroit than in the Cincinnati data, two of which deal with the control group and the other with the Master Record File, discussed below.

First, because a sample of financially eligible applicants not admitted to the NYC was not available in Detroit, applicants who, prior to the date of sample selection in the summer of 1966, had been rejected because of over-income were utilized as the control subjects. It was desirable to use the smallest possible over-income cutoff point that would identify an adequate sample size of controls in order to minimize serious poverty status differences between them and the experimental (YR and SO) youths, who of course had met the financial eligibility criteria. A family over-income of $1,500 as the cutoff point yielded 245 names of applicants who were utilized as the control sample in Detroit. While the control group in Detroit represents a slight compromise, the average family income by which they exceeded the financial eligibility requirements of the Neighborhood Youth Corps was only $648, confirming that the financial background of the two experimental groups—year-round and summer-only enrollees—was not substantially less than that of the control group in Detroit. Family income differentials would only be serious if they were such as to identify distinct social class categories, because of the known and documented class-related variation in behavior patterns. It is submitted that discrepancies in financial background of what amounts to a few hundred dollars annually are not likely to cause or account for differentials in the present criterion and that, therefore, no injury has been done by accepting the minimally over-income Detroit youths as valid controls. It would indeed be difficult to argue, for example, that the Detroit controls from 6-member households whose annual family income exceeded the eligibility requirement by $673 were, in their behavior, attitudes, motivation, values, etc., discernably different and presumably "better" than those from even less fortunate families. Even when the average family over-income of the Detroit controls was related to size of household, it never reached as much as $1,000.

Secondly, out of the population of 245 controls, only 140, or 57%, were interviewed.[9] While the completion rate for the Detroit control group is admittedly low, it should be noted that it represents the entire eligible universe rather than a sample proper selected from a larger population; thus the interview-to-universe ratio is quite high for the controls in Detroit: 1 out of less than every 2 controls in the population was interviewed. In addition, almost without exception the reason for not obtaining interviews with the Detroit controls was that they could not be located in time or had moved and were therefore physically inaccessible—reasons which, a priori, would not distinguish the uninterviewed controls from those who were. Thus, despite a low completion *rate*, a high interview/ population ratio and the absence of self-selection factors served to maximize the representativeness of those controls in Detroit who were interviewed.

Finally, the charges listed in the juvenile Master Record File in Detroit did not contain all known recorded police contacts but only those—presumably representing the more serious offenses—which were filtered through the individual police precincts after

8. The summer-only sample consisted of Negroes who worked in the 1966 summer program operated by Total Action against Poverty, rather than by the Detroit Public Board of Education, because the latter sponsor did not anticipate a reduction in their Fall 1967 quota which would make it necessary to terminate a substantial number of the enrollees who worked in the NYC during their 1966 summer program.

9. All of the eligible summer-only enrollees and 70% of the sample of year-round names selected were interviewed.

they had been recorded in the latter's record. Thus, in Detroit all of the charges recorded at the precinct level, for one reason or another, were not routinely made known to and incorporated into the Master Record File, which was the source of data collection in the present study. However, the structure of the present analysis is less concerned with the absolute number of police contacts or delinquency typology than it is with the comparative profile of police contacts among the controls and experimental youths, to which the same procedural limitations were applicable. Thus, since there is no reason to believe that the underrecording of the number of juvenile police contacts and their typology is not randomly distributed among the experimental and control groups, *i.e.,* since there is no systematic bias in recording juvenile police contacts among the youth samples, the utilization of this data in Detroit is not viewed as problematic. With the preceding remarks by way of introduction and qualification, the Detroit findings may now be summarized below.

Because the number of youths in each group type in Detroit who had a known offense record was initially restricted because of this last mentioned procedural consideration, segmentation of data—holding constant offense status and typology prior to enrollment/application in order to measure change in subsequent periods—was limited. *The gross effects in Detroit, however, are the same as those in Cincinnati, revealing no effect of program participation on reducing or preventing delinquency.* Among the males, prior to enrolling in the Neighborhood Youth Corps 17% YR, 21% SO and 21% C had been charged with felonies, 2% YR, 10% SO and 18% C with misdemeanors, and 17% YR, 24% SO and 29% C had an offense record. In other words, in the pre-enrollment/application period the controls were equally as, if not more, delinquent than the experimental youths. Yet, the proportion of control males who committed felonies (11%), misdemeanors (5%) or any offenses (13%) after

application was no different from that of the year-round males who committed the same offenses *while* working in the NYC, or from the proportion of summer-only males who incurred this typology of offenses after enrolling in the program.

Among the females in Detroit, there were no significant differences in the proportion who previously were charged with serious offenses (7% YR, 17% SO, 9% C), with misdemeanors (5% YR, 18% SO, 7% C) or with any offenses (10% YR, 26% SO, 14% C). Nor were there any salient differences in the proportion of controls who subsequently committed felonies (4%), misdemeanors (none) or any offenses (4%) compared with year-round females who were charged with felonies (2%), misdemeanors (2%), or any offenses (4%) *while* working in the NYC, or compared with summer-only females (5% felonies, 8% misdemeanors, 11% any offenses) after entering the program. Among both male and female youths in Detroit who were non-delinquent prior to enrollment/application, almost all of them continued to remain free of an offense record subsequently: among the males, 92% YR *while* in the program and in the entire subsequent period, 93% controls and 92% of the summer-only after joining the program did so; and among the females 97% while in the program, 99% controls and 90% of the summer-only after joining the program continued to remain non-delinquent.

SUMMARY

Separate analyses of the police records of year-round and summer-only enrollees who worked in the in-school Neighborhood Youth Corps programs in Cincinnati and Detroit compared with those of control youths who applied to the program revealed that NYC participation, among both males and females, was unrelated to delinquency prevention or reduction. Examination of the gross and net effects of program participation disclosed no evidence that working in the program made enrollees with a previous offense record less likely to continue to commit offenses while they were working in the program, in any way had a positive effect on particular types of offenders, or reduced overall the number of police contacts or specific kinds of offensive behavior. Nor, among enrollees who had no previous offense record prior to enrollment, did the program dissuade them from entering the ranks of delinquency more so than was the case with the controls in the absence of program dissuade them from entering the there any indication that NYC participation had an effect on reducing criminality on the part of enrollees while the youths were working in the program or after they left it.

Assuming that police contacts are a valid index of variation in illegal behavior, then the putative importance of anti-poverty programs that consist largely of the creation of work opportunities in reducing criminality among juveniles and young people may be more illusive than real.

Findings from Experiments in Treatment in the Correctional Institution

CHARLES H. SHIREMAN, KATHARINE BAIRD MANN,
CHARLES LARSEN, and THOMAS YOUNG

In a small but remarkably penetrating volume of essays on the law and criminality, Francis A. Allen referred to the recent few decades in the history of society's treatment of the criminal offender as the "era of the rehabilitative ideal" (1:26ff). The ideal rests upon assumptions to the effect that the age-old themes of retribution, deterrence, and incapacitation no longer wholly prescribe the goals of correctional practice. Instead, treatment of the offender should have a therapeutic function designed to serve the interest of both the offender and society.

In keeping with the rehabilitative ideal, modern corrections very generally emphasizes its helping and treatment mission. However, dedication to a lofty purpose does not, alone, assure its accomplishment. Thus, in recent years we have also become increasingly aware of the necessity for testing and expanding the knowledge and theory base available for the task of rehabilitation. Such awareness has led to the implementation of a number of evaluative research projects in corrections.

The present paper represents an effort to collect, examine, collate, and assess the find-ings of some of these projects having to do with treatment in correctional institutions, juvenile and adult. The task is a difficult one. Correctional research has not proceeded in orderly, incremental patterns. Individual researchers, practitioners, and agencies have designed different programs calculated to test a wide variety of treatment theories under varying conditions. Not all the factors exerting impact upon these tests can even be perceived, much less defined and measured. The sort of replication necessary to the verification of preliminary findings of individual projects is almost impossible under such conditions.

In addition to these inherent difficulties, certain further limitations of the data herein presented must be kept in mind. The list of projects considered was limited in several ways. It included only endeavors that (a) had been completed within the ten years prior to the winter of 1968–69, when the authors' data collection was terminated; (b) produced reports generally available to interested scholars; (c) were carried out in the United States; and (d) sought to test methods of treating institutionalized offend-

From C. Shireman, K. Mann, C. Larsen, & T. Young. Findings from experiments in treatment in the correctional institution. *Social Service Review*, 1972, *46*, 38–59. Copyright © 1972 by The University of Chicago. Printed in U.S.A. Reprinted by permission.

ers, juvenile or adult. All projects in early prevention or in the treatment of individuals thought to be potential offenders were omitted as falling outside the focus on delinquents in institutions. Projects directed specifically at the treatment of addiction were also ruled out as being of an order difficult to compare with studies of other correctional programs.

A further consideration ruling out much of the literature describing current correctional programs was the limitation of the study to the examination of treatment modalities that had been subjected to research employing some form of evaluative experimental design. The reasons for this tactic are obvious. Readily available in considerable numbers are annual reports and other descriptions of many programs claiming various rates of "success." All too often, little consideration is given the relationship between such programs and offenders' successful adjustment, or lack of it. Do offenders "adjust" because of treatment efforts, or might success rates have been just as high or higher if they had simply been left alone? Such questions can be answered only by some form of experimental design that designates the target treatment group; draws from it experimental treatment and control groups on the basis of sound sampling techniques; applies a described technique to the experimental while withholding it from the control group; and develops meaningful measures upon the basis of which treatment outcomes may be compared for two groups. Thus, this paper focuses upon reported experimental research, although note is taken of some reports of descriptive research that complements the findings of the experimental projects described.

Insistence upon some form of experimental design results in the omission of comment upon many creative correctional programs. For example, very regrettably, the authors could find no reports upon experimentally designed research projects testing the numerous current approaches to the application to correctional practice of "be-havior modification" theory—the "token economy" or other efforts based upon immediate and direct reward or sanction. This seems surprising, in view of the number of such programs and of their apparent promise for the field of corrections.[1]

Evaluative research necessitates, of course, a criterion by which "success" can be measured. While it is true that the correctional institution is thought by many to have a variety of social functions, including social protection through incapacitation of the offender and maintenance of the deterrent power of the law, the basic criterion used in this report is that employed by most of the projects cited: postrelease behavioral change as measured by the presence or absence of recidivism. However, at some points reference is made to other, proximate goals, such as the production of positive attitudinal change on the part of the institutional inmate. Indices of success or failure in the achievement of such proximate goals may shed light upon or provide some support for claims that behavioral change has been produced.

The inadequacy of officially reported recidivism as a measure of behavior in the community is recognized, but in the reports here analyzed there appears no reason to indicate that such inadequacy is not randomly distributed between experimental and control groups. Thus, the recidivism criterion should provide at least a rough comparison of the incidence of violative or nonviolative behavior on the part of the members of two groups.

The institutional treatment modalities upon which adequate reports were found may be categorized into four groups: milieu therapy, group counseling, short-term individual psychiatric treatment, and plastic surgery.

1. For a review of such reports as are available upon the application to corrections of behavior-modification theory, see U.S. Department of Health, Education, and Welfare (19).

MILIEU THERAPY

In corrections, the therapeutic-milieu concept has been subjected to research evaluation almost exclusively in juvenile correctional institutions. However, any attempt to summarize the findings of projects employing milieu therapy as a primary treatment method in such institutions encounters one of the major dilemmas of correctional research: the operational definition of the treatment variable. The phrases "milieu therapy" or "therapeutic milieu/community" are spoken and written with ease. Abstract definitions can readily be given them. But how does one construct and apply a milieu? How is the degree to which one has been successful in doing so to be determined? How does one go about measuring an "administrative philosophy" or an "atmosphere conducive to the development of a nondelinquent value system"?

To some degree, each of the projects reviewed attempts to solve this problem differently. Still, common themes do run through them. An approximate "ideal model" of such milieus does appear discernible. As operationalized, the therapeutic milieu seems to revolve around determined administrative and staff dedication to the use of the institutional experience as part of a coherent philosophy of treatment. This is opposed to the more usual correctional institutional dependence upon custody, control, and power to compel conforming behavior. The milieu-treatment goal is to work with the individual, rather than to do to or for him. To the greatest extent possible, his total institutional life is to be pervaded by positive interpersonal relationships with staff and peers. Rather than being remote authoritarian figures, staff members are to be persons who are involved with, committed to, and approachable by wards. Efforts are made to decrease the degree of imposed control and to increase personal responsibility for one's own behavior. Such controls as are necessary are maintained to the extent possible by positive reward rather than by the application of negative sanction. Planned provision for inmate-group participation in decision-making is common.

An effort is usually made to implement these goals through having wards live and function in smaller groups and with lower ward-to-staff ratios than in most correctional institutional settings. Living groups of twenty-four or less are usual, and, during the active part of the day, the group for whom one staff member is responsible frequently ranges around ten members.

Three of the milieu-therapy inquiries reported in this section arise from studies of existing programs and endeavor to define and isolate certain milieu factors and determine individual reactions to them (12, 14, 18). This series of studies appears to demonstrate the capacity of the therapeutically oriented milieu to produce more positive inmate attitudes and institutional behavior than does an orientation to custody and control. Such an outcome is shown, first, in the scholarly study by Street, Vinter, and Perrow (18). Their work identified three types of institutional milieu orientations, ranging along a custody-treatment continuum:

a) Obedience-conformity, emphasizing conditioning through training in respect for authority and conformity;

b) Re-education—development, or seeking to bring about changes in attitudes and values, acquisition of skills, and new social behaviors through training and education; and

c) Treatment, attempting varying degrees of psychological reconstitution of the individual through individual, group, or milieu approaches.

The authors report a study of six institutions, two of each of the above types. Differing organizational goals were found to be clearly related to differing patterns of staff organization and perceptions, staff-inmate relationships, and inmate perceptions and attitudes. Inmates of the obedience-conformity institutions demonstrated relatively negative perceptions of the institution and staff. However, they tended to manifest behavior that was overtly consistent with institutional goals, but that contained strong elements of covert opposition partially masked by a sort of "playing it cool." Residents of the treatment institutions were more likely to develop positive orientations, improved personal and social controls, skills in problem-solving, and self-understanding. Wards in the re-education-development institutions fell somewhere between the other two, but seemed to show some improvement in personal skill and emotional control (18:250).

This ability of differing orientations toward the institutional mission to produce differing attitudinal reactions seems confirmed by the Roberts study (12). Here, differences were found between two California Youth Authority forestry camps in administrative and staff perceptions of the camps' missions and methods. One was oriented toward control-guidance and work-training, the other toward a more permissive-interpersonal and therapeutic-community program. Ward reactions to the two types of milieu clearly differed, and the permissive-therapeutic milieu more frequently produced predominantly positive attitudes. Some further confirmation of these findings appears in the Eynon and Simpson study undertaken in Ohio (4), in which boys' reactions to care in small, low-security forestry camps were compared with reactions to the large, conventional state juvenile correctional institution. (This study was also notable in its finding that, in both the low-security camps and the larger institution, inmate attitudes toward the institution, its staff, and its program were apparently much more favorable than those often expected on the part of institutionalized youngsters.)

It does appear, then, that it is not true that "an institution is an institution" and that all institutions can be depended upon to produce predominantly criminalizing inmate responses. Improved therapeutic milieus may result in improved and less delinquency-ori-

ented inmate perceptions and attitudes. But do such attitudes carry over to the extent that the graduates of the therapeutic-milieu institution demonstrate superior postrelease behavior? This does not seem to be conclusively demonstrated. For example, the report upon the Youth Authority forestry-camp study cited above notes:

Despite the apparent effect of such differences in staff philosophy and practice upon wards and camps, there is no indication that the factors studied had any lasting postrelease effect upon the wards in terms of their tendency to violate or not to violate parole (4:81).

Apparently, two milieus differing widely along theoretically very significant dimensions were identified. These differences were perceived by wards, who reacted to them differentially, in line with theoretical expectations. But, disappointingly, such differential ward reactions were not shown to have been carried over into parole performance.

A further experimentally designed California Youth Authority Study seems to confirm the absence of differential impact upon recidivism rates (11). This study, by Martin J. Molof, sought to compare the effectiveness of the forestry camp with the larger, more rigid juvenile correctional institution. The forestry camp has in recent years become a widely accepted method of treating delinquent youth. Generally, such camps are employed for the selected youth deemed able to fit safely into and benefit from an outdoor program in a minimum-security setting. The camp is thought to provide a milieu quite different from that of the usual institution. Its major aspects include helpful and satisfying interpersonal relationships made possible by smaller numbers; engagement with functioning adults in productive work; and, in general, the avoidance of the negative aspects of institutional incarceration. In addition, of course, such a camp serves conservation, forestry, and other public interests.

The Molof study was designed as at least a

preliminary test of the presumed greater treatment effectiveness of the forestry camp. The study population was composed of 469 male offenders aged sixteen and over who had been committed to the Youth Authority and been found by the usual Authority classification procedures to be eligible for either the camp or the regular institutional programs. Of these, 315 were randomly selected for camp assignment, and 154 went to other institutions. Four Authority camps were used. Most institution boys went to one of three standard, large-scale youth-correctional institutions.

The project found that, for boys randomly assigned to one facility or the other and not transferred for more than thirty days, recidivism rates were 35.3 percent for institution and 36.4 percent for camp assignees. (The measure of recidivism used was suspension of parole within fifteen months.)

The findings of these two forestry-camp studies appear to cast a new and somewhat pessimistic light upon previous California Youth Authority observations that graduates of forestry camps generally demonstrated lower recidivism rates than youths released from the state's general youth-correctional facilities. Failure rates of forestry-camp graduates had also been found to be lower than those predicted by "base expectancy scores" made up from wards' classificiations on certain weighted background variables previously shown to be statistically related to recidivism (11:36).[2] These previously found differences in parole success rates may well result from the fact that offenders normally selected for camp are different from those assigned to regular institutions, even though these differences are apparently too subtle to appear in the studies leading to the framing of the base expectancy scores. Classification personnel evidently do employ perceptions of subtle factors beyond those making up actuarially based expectancy scores. Thus, they select from similar base

2. For a listing of such variables see Molof (11:36).

expectancy groups persons best able to use the camp experience.

Results generally negative in terms of impact upon recidivism are reported from two other sophisticated California Youth Authority therapeutic milieu projects, the Fremont experiment (15) and the Marshall program (8). These were short-term-therapy programs, the first based upon five-month and the second upon ninety-day periods of institutionalization, as opposed to the usual programs that last approximately nine months. Therapeutic communities provided individual and small-group counseling, frequent community meetings of the entire living group, carefully planned school and religious programs, and, in the case of the Marshall project, weekly group meetings with parents.

The subjects of these projects were fifteen- to seventeen-year-old delinquent boys committed to the Youth Authority. In both instances, experimental-group recidivism rates were compared with those of control groups committed for the usual longer Youth Authority programs. Carefully controlled random selection was used in order to assure the comparability of the two groups. In neither instance were statistically significant differences in parole performance revealed. However, the data from the Fremont experiment give some indication that boys released during the early stage of the program violated parole less frequently than did later releasees. It seems possible that this result may have stemmed from reported high staff turnover and lower staff morale in the later stages of the program. Similarly, the data from the Marshall program provide some hints that that program may have been particularly effective with older boys who had been involved in group offenses and were more "sociable," in that they tended to participate more in group activities with minimum conflict. Further, more important than the findings of overall failure to produce reduced recidivism rates may be the fact that these two experiments, using greatly reduced periods of confinement, produced success rates comparable to those of the regular institutional program, with its much longer institutionalization. If confirmed by further inquiry, this apparent finding to the effect that short institutional stays can be made just as productive as long ones may be of major importance to social-policy-makers in the field of corrections.

Still another California Youth Authority project, the Fricot Ranch study, which dealt with somewhat younger boys, presents data at least suggesting possible explanations for the apparent failure of the above-cited projects to reduce overall recidivism rates (7). Perhaps the most significant product of this study was the development and testing of a typology or classification scheme through which the boys were grouped into eight different types upon the basis of statistical analysis of their performance on a battery of diagnostic tests. The resultant typology seems to emphasize personality factors, with nature of offense, offense history, and socioeconomic status and its correlates only tangentially employed. It is remarkably similar to the maturity-level classification system developed by the Youth Authority's Community Treatment Project—an often-cited landmark in community-based treatment (2:2–4). The eight types are: (a) socialized, conformist; (b) immature, passive; (c) neurotic, anxious; (d) immature, aggressive; (e) cultural delinquent; (f) manipulator; (g) neurotic, acting-out; and (h) neurotic, depressed.

The Fricot experimental program, experienced by boys of all the designated types, was based on the observation that in the institution's normal program, with groups of fifty or more boys in a living unit, there was little opportunity for the development of close relationships between ward and staff. In such a situation, the first concern of staff necessarily becomes the maintenance of control. Thus, the project reduced the living unit size to twenty and increased the day-time staff-ward ratio to one to ten (versus the one to twenty-five ratio in the control or regular program). Further careful efforts were made to heighten the staff's therapeutic concern and to personalize the relationships between staff members and wards. These efforts apparently were successful in creating an institutional experience markedly different from that in the standard program. Sociometric tests administered to wards in the experimental and the control units showed that differences in emotional climate and ward attitudes existed between the two, presumably as a product of the differing institutional environments experienced. It seems clear that the concept of the "therapeutic milieu" can be made viable operationally and that it does have measurable impact upon ward attitudes. However, in the Fricot project, in contrast to the projects noted previously, the striven-for differential impact upon attitudes was associated with differences in parole performance. After a twelve-month parole exposure, only 32 percent of the Fricot experimental group boys had violated parole, compared with the 48 percent of the control group members who had violated.

Of perhaps even greater importance is the finding concerning apparent differential treatment impact upon different individuals. The author reports that "the more intensive, internally oriented experimental . . . program was most successful with the neurotic and immature subjects" (7:157). Considering only the three neurotic types together (types c, g, and h above), the violation rate of the control group exceeded that of the experimental group by 48 percentage points (7:158–159).

Together, then, this cluster of projects seems to indicate that the concept of a "therapeutic milieu" can be operationalized and its effects measured. It appears that it can be especially effective with certain types of delinquents. The precise "package" making up a therapeutic milieu varies from program to program. A conglomerate of treatment methods under one roof does not make a therapeutic milieu, but milieus can and have been constructed that seem to exert favorable impact upon ward attitudes toward self and toward the correctional program. In some instances, these attitudes seem to carry over strongly enough to influence postinstitutional behavior.

GROUP COUNSELING

The use of groups in treatment takes many forms.[3] Groups are used for psychotherapy, socialization, and problem-solving, but the term "group counseling" is frequently applied to a somewhat amorphous but probably identifiable treatment method that has been widely used and subjected to some experimentation, particularly in California's adult penal system. One of its proponents describes it as follows:

Group counseling is a form of supportive treatment. It is focused on past and present conscious reality experiences and problems, as well as future goals. It builds on the strengths of the members and modifies attitudes and feelings which have contributed to criminal behavior. Basic personality change is not the objective of group counseling. The goal is to improve the attitudes and social adjustments of inmates and parolees [6:3].

Group counseling is distinguished from group psychotherapy in the California system both theoretically and operationally, as follows:

Group psychotherapy performed by psychiatrists, psychologists, and social workers in psychiatric hospitals, clinics, and offices is generally a deeper form of group treatment than group counseling, having as an objective the resolution of intra-psychic conflicts by bringing them into consciousness. . . . Group counseling is provided by career correctional employees from personnel classes which

have the most sustained contact with inmates. These include correctional officers, vocational and academic teachers, work foremen in prison industry . . . correctional counselors, and others [6:3].

Thus, group counseling is operationally defined as a treatment method which seeks to change attitudes and produce socialization through group interaction and discussion. It is promoted through group sessions with correctional staff members who have not had clinical training. In the California system this method was operationalized by training "basic employees" to be leaders. These leaders meet once a week for an hour or an hour and one-half with groups of eight to fifteen inmates. It is assumed that these meetings result in changes in communication patterns, relationships, roles, and group structure within the prison. It is also assumed that if the group is well led the members will gradually take on some of the norms and values of the leader. Further, it is expected that in these meetings offenders will gradually develop their own self-governing miniature social system. The focus is not on the individual's personal attitudes or behavior, but on living-unit policy. Theoretically, such a plan shifts the issue of controls and sanctions from a "stand-off" situation of staff versus inmates to one consisting of self-regulation arrived at through community discussion and consensus.

The second important aspect of the program is confidentiality. In an attempt to promote meaningful inmate participation, it is stipulated that group leaders are not to report the content of group-counseling sessions to higher authorities, or to anyone outside the group.

Unfortunately, the reports available about this treatment modality do not provide recorded examples of group sessions. Obviously, the process must vary with group composition and peer-group pressures, the personal style of the leader, and a variety of other factors. Group counseling is a far from uniform experimental variable.

3. Guided Group Interaction is a currently widely employed treatment form based upon the building of a cultural climate in which the group becomes an instrument requiring its members to examine the utility of delinquent behavior. While it was developed in the small-institution setting, the major research reports upon it published during the time-span of this study deal with its application in community-based, nonresidential treatment centers. See Weeks (20), Empey (3), and Stephenson and Scarpitti (17).

Three reports on the application of this technique are examined here, all from the California correctional system. The first is Harrison and Mueller's retrospective analysis of the parole outcomes of 8,112 inmates released from five institutions for men (6:3). Each subject had been engaged in small-group counseling once a week for an hour to an hour and one-half. Those participating in the same group with the same leader for one year or more were said to have belonged to stable groups. Those who received group counseling, but did not meet the stable-group criterion, were said to belong to un-stable groups. In addition, a control group whose members received no group counseling was identified.

This study found that men with group counseling did significantly better after twelve months on parole and somewhat better, although not statistically significantly so, after twenty-four months than those with no group counseling. Those with stable group counseling did significantly better on parole at both twelve and twenty-four months than those with unstable counseling (6:3, 33 [Table 10]). One group that had a community-living program, plus group counseling (small groups meeting four times a week and living-unit meetings once a week), achieved a success rate of 75.9 percent after one year on parole, compared with a 61.1 percent figure for the control group, a difference statistically significant at the .02 level (6:22).

Findings such as these are heartening, as they provide some data to be used cautiously in decision-making. However, they are far from definitive. The method used in selecting treatment and comparison groups provides no assurance of their comparability. As far as can be determined from the report, favorable differences in outcome may be a product of the fact that project staff were skilled in selecting inmates who might respond well to the program. The same inmates might also respond well to any program. Data were incomplete at important points, and data collection was done by in-mate clerks whose work varied in accuracy (6:12–13). Furthermore, the retrospective nature of the study does not permit certainty that small-group counseling, as it is defined, was actually employed. Finally, the results of this project find some confirmation in one but none at all in another of two further projects, herein reported, which employed more refined research design.

The second group-counseling project, reported by Seckel, directed its effort to male teen-agers and young adults (14). All were repeated offenders. In one institution housing boys with a median age of 16.7, three forms of experimental group-programming were employed: (a) small groups (six to eight boys) participating in group-counseling sessions once a week; (b) larger community meetings four times weekly; and (c) combinations of small groups and community meetings. A control group received no treatment other than standard institutional care. In a second institution, working with boys with a median age of nineteen, a small-group meeting for group counseling once a week constituted the experimental treatment. In each setting, treatment lasted for six months. The experimental programs often seemed successful in producing changes in the direction of less delinquent orientation, as measured by attitudinal inventories (14: 9–26). However, fifteen- and thirty-month parole follow-ups revealed no statistically significant differences in success rates for any of the three treatment groups, when compared to controls, and no statistically significant difference between the three treatment methods (14:9–19, 56–57 [tables]).

A third project in group counseling, reported by Robison and Kevorkian, had as its subjects young adult, aggressive first offenders (13). This project also employed a combined small-group/community meeting format as its treatment variable. After one year in the community 79 percent of the 319 experimental subjects were maintaining a favorable adjustment, as compared to 71 percent of 142 controls, a difference statistically significant at the 4.66 level. After two years the difference in parole performance between the two groups was no longer statistically significant (13:5–9).

What conclusions can be drawn from this trio of projects? First, there is some indication that with some offenders small-group counseling and the community-meeting treatment formats do exert a positive effect on postrelease behavior in the community. This effect is difficult to measure, and we do not know precisely in which offenders or under what conditions it is produced. The fact that positive results seem to have been secured by the two projects with adults and not in the one with juveniles may not be coincidence. Are older subjects more socialized and thus more responsive to this treatment form? In these, as in the other projects reported, the treatment effect is obviously obscured by unknown variations in postinstitutional care, but such variations remain unstudied. In sum, it is evident that in this area of correctional research we are still confronted by a confusing picture that calls for more systematically derived hard data. It is also apparent from the above that "group counseling," when carried out in forms representing its logical extension, comes to resemble "milieu therapy." It may be that increased experimentation with the small-group counseling/community-meeting format will lead to more precise definitions and to new forms of milieu treatment.

SHORT-TERM INDIVIDUAL PSYCHIATRIC TREATMENT IN THE JUVENILE INSTITUTION

The California Youth Authority also provides the major reported project testing the effectiveness of short-term psychotherapy in the juvenile correctional institution (5). In this experiment, teams of psychiatrists, psychologists, and social workers were employed in two Youth Authority institutions for delinquent adolescents, the Fred C. Nelles School and the Preston School of Industry. At each institution experimental

and control groups were selected on a random basis from populations of boys, all of whom had been diagnosed as being in need of and probably amenable to psychotherapy. Experimental-group members were given individual interview therapy, in most cases for one hour twice a week. Treatment was short-term only by comparison with much other analytically oriented, intensive psychotherapy. The average length of stay of wards in the treatment program was slightly less than nine months. Analysis of the parole-violation rates achieved by the project groups revealed that at Nelles boys in the experimental group had done measurably better than their controls, who had undergone more usual custody-oriented institutional programs. At Preston, on the other hand, the psychiatrically treated group showed a higher violation rate than did controls.

Such results reveal the complexity of measuring and holding constant the numerous variables involved in research in correctional effectiveness. Data analysis indicates that the median age of the Nelles boys was 15.1 years and that of the Preston group 17.5 years. Is this the factor that created the differential result? Perhaps more importantly, the experimental treatment variable—psychotherapy—took on one aspect as it was implemented at Nelles and another at Preston. At Nelles staff morale was retrospectively reported as having been high. Clinical staff members at least attempted to implement a philosophy that they should help make the total institutional impact a correctional one. Boys and therapists were engaged together in numerous activities. Attempts at improved communication with custody staff were made. Treatment was seemingly reality-based; it emphasized personal responsibility for behavior rather than psychodynamic etiology. By contrast, the Preston clinical staff reportedly attempted more traditional insight-producing and transference therapy. Time may not have been sufficient to do this, it is speculated, and premature discontinuance of therapy may have left some patients more vulnerable than if treatment had not been attempted. Furthermore, the older Preston boys may have responded more negatively to jibes from peers occasioned by their being in psychotherapy ("You got to be nuts to see a head shrinker!").

In sum, for neither the Nelles nor the Preston groups do we know the precise nature of the treatment rendered or the complex of intervening variables that may have affected treatment response. Even so, there is indication that, at least in work with younger institutionalized delinquents, short-term, reality-oriented psychotherapy interwoven with the attempted construction of a therapeutic community may exert a strong enough continuing influence over some wards to influence their parole performance significantly. We cannot tell from the data which wards might be so positively influenced, which might fail to respond, or which, if any, might respond negatively.

PLASTIC SURGERY

Shakespeare echoed an ancient belief when he wrote: "It is hard for the face to conceal the thoughts of the heart—the true character of the soul. The look without is an index of what is within." The old belief is probably largely myth, but many practitioners and scholars do hold that gross ugliness or disfigurement may contribute to the individual's turning to antisocial behavior. The unattractive person may find employment more difficult to obtain. If he finds work he probably has a lesser chance of rising to a managerial level. His appearance may contribute to both a private self-concept and a negative societal reaction, which may reinforce any tendencies toward violative behavior.

The incidence of disfigurement among imprisoned offenders is reported to be surprisingly large. One survey of 450 consecutive admissions to the New York City Department of Corrections Reception and Diagnostic Center revealed that 47 percent

had at least moderate disfigurement, not including needle marks from heroin injection (9:45). Such observations as these have led to the undertaking of a number of plastic surgery programs in correctional facilities. However, most of these have been neither so designed nor so reported as to provide tests of their effectiveness, though some reports do cite data that at least suggest that they may be of considerable value (16).

One carefully designed and well-reported experimental study is available—that made at the Montefiore Hospital in New York City (10). While the greater part of the intervention efforts were carried out during the postinstitutional period, the program actually began while the offender was in confinement.

Inmates of the New York City jail system serving time at Riker's Island were advised of the possible availability of plastic surgery. From a total of 1,424 applicants 425 successfully completed qualifying physical and psychological examinations. Almost all had been arrested many times. Thirty-two percent had been convicted six or more times. Nearly half of the subjects were black, 30 percent were white, and 20 percent were Puerto Rican. Sixty-seven percent were heroin addicts. The most frequently requested types of surgery were those for the repair of developmental and traumatically acquired deformities, removal of tattoos, and removal of needle marks from heroin usage.

Accepted applicants were assigned on a random basis to four groups, which were balanced for narcotic addiction and ethnicity. Group I was given the required plastic surgery, plus fairly extensive vocational and social services, including drug rehabilitation and detoxification, vocational counseling and placement, and referral for public assistance, health, and legal services as needed. Group II received surgery alone; Group III received only vocational and social services (comparable to those given Group I members); and Group IV served as a control group given no treatment. After extensive

Table 1. Recidivism Rates, by Groups

Group	Recidivism Rate
Group I (Surgery and services) .	44 percent
Group II (Surgery alone)	55 percent
Group III (Services alone)	58 percent
Group IV (Controls— no treatment)	72 percent

losses due to failure to accept final referral for service and inaccessibility at follow-up, the total sample was reduced to 168.[4]

At a one-year follow-up after release, recidivism rates, defined as arrests for new offenses, were those shown in Table 1.

Differences in success rates between all treatment groups and the controls were statistically significant. Further analysis revealed that:

1. The incidence of recidivism was 49 percent for persons receiving surgery, compared with 66 percent for those not receiving surgery.

2. In general, the nonaddicts' records were largely responsible for the more favorable performance of the groups receiving surgery. Recidivism was 36 percentage points lower

4. The degree to which the groups finally given surgical and/or social services treatment were truly comparable to the control group remains a matter of speculation. The original assignment to the four groups was on a random basis. This should have produced comparable groups. But there were a considerable number of dropouts from the group to be given service; e.g., from the "surgery only" group 54 out of 95 refused surgery after the original screening and acceptance. There is a possibility that the group finally given surgery may have contained a higher proportion of men determined to "do something about their problems" than did the control group. The experimenters were confronted with a research problem for which there is no satisfactory answer although they did run tests showing that the various groups did not differ significantly on a series of selected, theoretically important, background variables (addiction, ethnicity, prior conviction, education, age, mental status, etc.). They also found that those undergoing and those refusing surgery did not generally differ along these same background variables. Such tests, though reassuring, do not entirely dispel the possibility of more subtle differences along motivational lines.

among surgically treated nonaddicts than among nonaddict controls. Addicts, on the other hand, apparently benefited little from surgery, as there were no statistically significant differences between the recidivism rates of surgically treated and control addicts.

3. Addicts did respond favorably to the social and vocational services program. Based upon comparisons with the addict controls, social and vocational services without surgery provided a reduction of 31 percentage points and such services with surgery a reduction of 29 percentage points in recidivism rates.

4. Nonaddicts receiving social and vocational services only (no surgery) recidivated at a rate 33 percentage points higher than controls: 89 percent vs. 56 percent.

5. When the length of time subjects remained out of prison was studied, it was found that both addict and nonaddict subjects receiving surgery stayed out of prison longer than did those not receiving surgery.

It appears, then, that the use of plastic surgery, under proper controls and with careful screening, can be of value in the rehabilitation of nonaddict, disfigured, adult repeated offenders. The particular constellation of social and vocational services offered at Montefiore seemed helpful to addicts, but did not appear to help—and may even have harmed—nonaddict offenders.

EXPERIMENTS IN INSTITUTIONAL REHABILITATION: AN OVERVIEW

What does a review of the past several years' experimental research in institutional rehabilitation teach us? First, a note of caution must be interjected. None of the studies herein reviewed speaks to the effectiveness of institutional versus noninstitutional care. All have dealt with comparisons among different kinds of care within the institution. It remains theoretically possible that large proportions of the subjects of all the programs reviewed might have achieved either better or worse adjustments if permitted to remain in the free community. However, during the entire professional careers of correctional practitioners now on the scene, large numbers of offenders are going to be institutionalized. Thus the endeavor to determine which types of institutional programs might provide the greatest rehabilitative potential remains enormously important—even though strife over the relative value of institutional versus community treatment remains unresolved.

It must further be admitted that research to date has not finally demonstrated the superior effectiveness of any of the forms of institutional treatment subjected to examination. Nonetheless, certain still-tentative learnings do emerge for cautious application to practice and for further testing:

1. The data suggest that certain forms of institutional treatment may have impact sufficiently powerful to influence postrelease parole performance positively. This appears true of:

a) Milieu therapy, offered on a short-term basis, during a period of high staff morale and dedication (Fremont project), or with older "sociable" delinquents (Marshall project), or longer periods of intensive milieu therapy with younger boys, with neurotic delinquents appearing to respond especially favorably (Fricot Ranch project);

b) Group counseling with young adult first offenders (California Intensive Treatment Project);

c) Short-term individual psychiatric therapy combined with attempts at total institutional impact, in work with younger adolescents (California Youth Authority Short-Term Psychiatric Treatment Project at Nelles School); and

d) Provision of plastic surgery to disfigured or deformed, nonaddicted, adult repeated offenders (Montefiore project).

It is true that in most of these treatment forms there have been many projects that have failed—usually more than have succeeded. It is also true that perceivable impact upon postrelease performance may disappear with time. No type of treatment can pretend to immunize permanently against the vicissitudes of a deleterious environment. (It may also be important to future planning of correctional programs to note that none of the projects in imaginative and intensive institutional care described above was accompanied by efforts to provide to the subjects equally imaginative after-care.) Measurements of parole adjustment taken after considerable periods in the community have, at least in some instances, shown that experimentally treated subjects have "gotten off to a better start" in the free world than have releasees from standard institutional programs. Thus some experimenters, working under some conditions, have demonstrated that treatment can be effective with considerable proportions of subject groups. This has been true of some projects in most of the treatment forms considered.

This finding is crucial. It outweighs in significance the observations that there have been numerous failing projects. The central fact remains: it apparently is possible to so shape institutional programs as to positively influence the behavior of human beings.

The findings concerning parole success are reinforced by those based upon different outcome criteria. Some of the experimental programs have clearly shown that they can produce more positive personal self-concepts, more favorable perceptions of the nature of the treatment program, and less delinquency-prone attitudes. The shaping of the fundamental attitudes and perceptions of human beings is no small achievement.

2. While there is thus encouraging indication that achieving treatment goals is not forever impossible, knowledge of precisely how and for whom they may best be achieved remains rudimentary. In spite of serious endeavors, treatment programs are often not described precisely enough that they can be exactly replicated elsewhere. Available reports deal with treatment as administered by particular human beings, under conditions not all of which are perceived, to subjects about whom a limited range of information is available. We do not

know which subjects may respond favorably and which unfavorably. We know of even the best programs only that proportions of favorable outcomes of their "graduates" exceed those achieved by untreated controls by a margin greater than would be expected by chance.

Under such conditions, the true power of the experimental treatment program may not be accurately indicated. For example, a slight preponderance of positive outcomes for experimental as compared to control subjects may mean that the experimental program is generally slightly more effective than the standard institutional program undergone by the control group. On the other hand, it may mean that it exerts a strong positive impact upon some subjects, but is quite harmful to others. In reporting the overall proportions of favorable to unfavorable outcomes, such variations in impact are lost.

As an obvious implication of these manifold uncertainties, it appears that the massive intervention that institutionalization represents should be used with care. If we do not know precisely what "treatment" is, and who is "treatable," we should be hesitant indeed about committing a person to the institution solely in order to provide treatment. A presumption in favor of less massive intervention—various forms of care within the community—may well be the sounder social policy. Thus, institutionalization would be employed only when recourse to other treatment forms has been exhausted, and when it remains necessary for social protection or similar purposes.

3. Intriguing possibilities suggest themselves when the attempt is made to discern the common elements of the programs which have apparently produced positive results. One such element seems to be an intensive experience with decency in human relationships. Thus, one does not gain the impression that the central helpful factor in any project has been a simple, unitary change in program. Single rooms rather than dormitories, reduced staff-inmate ratios,

therapeutic interviews each week, participatory decision-making, the offer of plastic surgery—all those factors may be helpful in themselves, but it is at least possible that they are equally important as they represent changes in the basic nature of the relationships between human beings involved. The decency of which we speak has many aspects. It involves depth of concern for the individual and respect for him as a human being of worth. It involves honesty, and it involves understanding of him and of his feelings, including those that may be negative. In fact, there may operate in many of the projects discussed a sort of "placebo effect." Thus, the very fact of involvement in a program known to be something new and experimental, something receiving a great deal of attention and considered highly important, may in itself represent to the subject a sort of recognition of his importance and worth and may thus help in drawing forth his favorable response.

This emphasis upon the possible basic importance of "simple" decency does not mean that treatment can best be undertaken by a "bunch of good fellows." Truly decent treatment involves, for example, clear perception of subjects' behavior and understanding both of its probable causes and, above all, of the feelings associated with it and with treatment. This necessitates, in turn, true insight into our own feelings and emotional responses, particularly to negative reactions to us as persons and as authority figures. Some few "naturals" possess these understandings to a relatively high degree. But such understandings are, for the great majority of us, not easy to come by. From this fact comes the necessity for pertinent education, for in-service training, and for the guided and carefully analyzed experience that should constitute the core of continuing staff development.

It is evident from the above that the past decade of correctional research has produced some constructive clues to the design of improved institutional treatment programs, but such clues remain tentative in nature and they are all too few. True, reports of correctional research are elusive, and it is probable that some that might have been included in this report were missed. Even if due allowance is made for this fact, it is patently evident that research-based inquiry into the effectiveness of correctional treatment remains at a depressing minimum. As a result, the knowledge base necessary to sound correctional policy-making simply does not exist.

Sir Winston Churchill is said to have observed that "true genius resides in the capacity for evaluation of uncertain, hazardous, and conflicting information." Such is the nature of the information available to correctional policy-makers. But relatively few of us can lay claim to genius. As a result, correctional programs are too frequently inaugurated, preserved, altered, or replaced on the basis of untested assumptions, emotional attitudes toward offenders, the search for panaceas, or the impassioned—if not necessarily informed—advocacy of zealots. The observation that similar situations also exist in most other branches of the behavioral sciences gives little comfort. The fact remains that long dedication to strategies of action, to the exclusion of strategies of inquiry, has rendered corrections particularly liable to the attacks of legislators, news media, and members of the supporting public. Firm answers cannot be given to questions about what the tax dollar devoted to corrections actually buys in the way of social utility. Much more serious, no wholly convincing assurance can be given that the awesome power the correctional institution is given over the offender, juvenile or adult, is wielded constructively and responsibly. The real and disturbing possibility thus exists that for the great majority of those confined in the correctional institution the era of the "rehabilitative ideal" may well consist more of illusion than of substance— the conclusion that was also reached by Francis Allen in the well-known essay referred to in the opening passage of this paper.

REFERENCES

1. Allen, Francis A. *The Borderland of Criminal Justice: Essays in Law and Criminology.* Chicago and London: University of Chicago Press, 1964.
2. California Department of the Youth Authority. California Youth and Adult Corrections Agency. *The Community Treatment Project after Five Years.* Sacramento, 1966.
3. Empey, LaMar T. *The Provo Experiment: A Brief Review.* Los Angeles: Youth Studies Center, University of Southern California, 1966.
4. Eynon, Thomas G., and Simpson, Jon E. "The Boy's Perception of Himself in a State Training School for Delinquents." *Social Service Review* 39 (March 1965): 31–37.
5. Guttmann, Evelyn S. *Effects of Short-Term Psychiatric Treatment on Boys in Two California Youth Authority Institutions.* Sacramento: Department of the Youth Authority, California Youth and Adult Corrections Agency, 1963.
6. Harrison, Robert M. "Model for Group Counseling." In *Clue-hunting about Group Counseling and Parole Outcome,* by Robert M. Harrison and Paul F. C. Mueller. Research Report No. 11. Sacramento: Department of Corrections, California Youth and Adult Corrections Agency, 1964.
7. Jesness, Carl F. *The Fricot Ranch Study: Outcomes with Small vs. Large Living Groups in Rehabilitation of Delinquents.* Research Report No. 47. Sacramento: Department of the Youth Authority, California Youth and Adult Corrections Agency, 1965.
8. Knight, Doug. *The Marshall Program: Assessment of a Short-Term Institutional Treatment Program. Part I: Parole Outcome and Background Characteristics.* Research Report No. 56. Sacramento: Department of the Youth Authority, California Youth and Adult Corrections Agency, 1969.
9. Kurtzberg, Richard; Safar, Howard; and Mandell, Wallace. "Plastic Surgery in Corrections." *Federal Probation* 33 (September 1969): 45.

10. Mandell, Wallace; Lewin, Michael; Kurtzberg, Richard L.; Safar, Howard; and Shuster, Marvin. *Surgical and Social Rehabilitation of Adult Offenders, Final Report, Part I.* New York: Montefiore Hospital and Medical Center, Staten Island Mental Health Society, and New York City Department of Corrections, 1967.

11. Molof, Martin J. *Forestry Camp Study: Comparison of Recidivism Rates of Camp-Eligible Boys Randomly Assigned to Camp and Institutional Programs.* Research Report No. 53. Sacramento: Department of the Youth Authority, California Youth and Adult Corrections Agency, 1967.

12. Roberts, Chester F. *Rehabilitative Influences in California Youth Conservation Camps. Phase II: Staff Policies and Ward Reactions.* Research Report No. 54. Sacramento: Department of the Youth Authority, California Youth and Adult Corrections Agency, 1968.

13. Robison, James, and Kevorkian, Marinette. *Intensive Treatment Project. Phase II, Parole Outcome: Interim Report.* Research Report No. 27. Sacramento: Department of Corrections. California Youth and Adult Corrections Agency, 1967.

14. Seckel, Joachim P. *Experiments in Group Counseling at Two Youth Authority Institutions.* Research Report No. 46. Sacramento: Department of the Youth Authority, California Youth and Adult Corrections Agency, 1965.

15. ____. *The Fremont Experiment: Assessment of Residential Treatment at a Youth Authority Reception Center.* Research Report No. 50. Sacramento: Department of the Youth Authority, California Youth and Adult Corrections Agency, 1969.

16. Spira, M.; Chaizen, J. H.; Gerrow, F. J.; and Hardy, S. B. "Plastic Surgery in the Texas Prison System." *British Journal of Plastic Surgery* 19 (October 1966): 364–71.

17. Stephenson, Richard, and Scarpitti, Frank R. *The Rehabilitation of Delinquent Boys.* New Brunswick, N.J.: Rutgers University, 1967.

18. Street, David; Vinter, Robert D.; and Perrow, Charles. *Organization for Treatment: A Comparative Study of Institutions for Delinquents.* New York: Free Press, 1966.

19. United States Department of Health, Education, and Welfare, National Institute of Mental Health, Center for Studies of Crime and Delinquency. *Development and Legal Regulation of Co-ercive Behavior Modification Techniques with Offenders.* Public Health Service Publication No. 2067. Washington, D.C.: Government Printing Office, 1970.

20. Weeks, H. Ashley. *Youthful Offenders at Highfields.* Ann Arbor: University of Michigan Press, 1958.

Accelerating Entry into the Opportunity Structure:

A Sociologically-Based Treatment for Delinquent Youth

BRIAN NEAL ODELL

Traditionally, juvenile court treatment programs have been based upon psychological or psychiatric interpretations of behavior. In such programs, delinquency is viewed as a symptom of the client's emotional or personality problems; the social situation of the youth draws relatively little attention except as it contributes to the child's purported emotional problems.

In recent years, sociological explanations of delinquency have been advanced which argue that the delinquent's anti-social behavior results not from his personality problems and emotional inadequacies, but from failures within the social system.[1] Prominent among these formulations has been Cloward and Ohlin's (1960) theory of differential access to opportunity. Combining the anomie theory of Merton (1957:146) and the "Chicago school" concept of differentials in access to illegitimate means (Shaw 1930 and 1931; Shaw and McKay, 1942; Shaw et al, 1929), Cloward and Ohlin concluded that individuals become delinquent because they are denied access to the legitimate opportunity structure. All people, Cloward and Ohlin argue, aspire initially toward the traditional indices of success (e.g., wealth and material possessions); but some people—particularly lower-class individuals—are denied access to the legitimate means to achieve such success (e.g., education and vocational training). Blocked from entry into the legitimate opportunity structure, they are forced to turn to illegal means to achieve their success-goals. It is at this point that they become delinquent.[2]

Cloward and Ohlin's opportunity theory introduces several concepts which are of critical importance in explaining lower-class delinquency. First, it is argued that the lower-class individual aspires to the same success-goals as the middle-class individual. Second, it is pointed out that the legitimate means to achieve these goals are less available to the lower-class individual. Third, the

1. Matza (1964) provides a cogent assessment of both the individual and social structure causation theories.

2. Empirical tests of Cloward and Ohlin's opportunity theory include Short et al (1965), Fredericks and Molnar (1969), Landis and Scarpitti (1965), Landis et al (1964), and Elliott (1962). Theoretical treatments of the opportunity theory include Bordua (1961) and Himelhock (1965).

From B. Odell. Accelerating entry into the opportunity structure: A sociologically-based treatment for delinquent youth. *Sociology and Social Research*, 1974, *58*, 312–317. Reprinted by permission.

lack of importance attributed by lower-class persons to education is shown to represent not a devaluing of education, but rather a realistic perception of their lack of access to educational opportunity. And fourth, lower-class delinquency is depicted as a problem of the individual only to the extent that the individual is denied access to the means of legitimate success.

What are the implications of this theory for juvenile court treatment programs? Would not a program which prepares the individual to enter the opportunity structure be more effective than a program which ministers to emotional or personality problems? In an attempt to answer this question an analysis was made of an "opportunity theory" treatment program at a Midwestern juvenile court. This program prepares delinquents to enter the opportunity structure by providing both a high school equivalency diploma course and assistance in securing employment. It was hypothesized that completion of the program would lead to a position in the opportunity structure and that this position, in turn, would lead to a decrease in delinquency. The results indicate that: (1) Completion of the high school equivalency program did indeed permit the delinquent youth to enter the legitimate opportunity structure. (2) The opportunity theory treatment program was significantly more effective than the traditional psychologically-based "casework" programs in reducing recidivism. (3) The impressive drop in recidivism among the delinquents who entered the opportunity structure may have been due as much to their changed self-concepts and reference groups as it was to their new position in the opportunity structure.

THE RESEARCH DESIGN

Sixty boys under the jurisdiction of the St. Louis County juvenile court in Clayton and under the supervision of juvenile court caseworkers were included in the study. The youths were high school dropouts, ages 15 years and 10 months to 16 years and 3 months, with "serious and persistent" patterns of juvenile offenses. The number of adjudicated offenses committed by each boy ranged from 6 to 19 with a mean of 10.7. All boys were lower class when measured against the traditional indices; of the 60 boys, 44 were nonwhite and 16 were white. The boys as a group evidenced massive educational retardation; demonstrated skill level was 4.1 years behind the last grade placement. The boys' case histories revealed sporadic and short-lived attempts to secure and retain employment. Most had help part-time jobs at some time, but none had a work pattern which yielded even a subsistence level of income.

Through a random process, the original sample of 60 boys was divided into four groups of 15; measurement of the boys' intelligence and level of educational impairment revealed not significant differences between the groups. Racial composition of the groups was controlled to insure an equal white—non-white ratio. The groups were:

Group I—*Traditional Casework*—This was a control group. These boys continued under the supervision of their caseworkers and were entered in no experimental program. In this and all groups, both the subjects and their caseworkers were unaware of the nature of the research design. Throughout the duration of the project, caseworkers had complete latitude to take any action they felt necessary to serve the needs of the client and the community. This was true for all groups.

Group II—*Intensive Casework*—To control for the fact that the boys in the experimental groups might sense that they were participating in "something special" and thus respond to the special attention rather than the independent variable, Group II was provided with a "special" program. This group participated in a three-month program of intensive counseling involving both the boys and their parents. Group and individual sessions were held in addition to the boys' regular conferences with their caseworkers.

Group III—*Education and Employment*—

This was an experimental group. Fifteen boys were enrolled in the juvenile court's high school equivalency diploma program. This program is based upon high interest subject matter, programmed learning, and a tutorial system in which each youth proceeds at his own pace. Tutors were area college students and community volunteers. The duration of the program ranges from four to twelve weeks during which time the youth is prepared to pass the Graduate Equivalency Test which yields the G.E.D. high school equivalency diploma.

After completion of the program, youths were placed by court personnel in jobs provided by local employers. Each job provided a minimum work week of thirty hours and an hourly pay rate of at least $1.40. Graduates of the program who desired further education were enrolled, with the assistance of court personnel, in local vocational schools or junior colleges.

Group IV—*Education Only*—This group was also enrolled in the G.E.D. high school equivalency program. After completion of the program, however, they were not given assistance in securing jobs or further education. This group had its tutoring sessions at a different time than Group III and was unaware of the additional assistance provided that group.

RESULTS

Evaluations of the youths were made at three-month intervals for a period of nine months following the completion of the initial three-month experimental period. As expected, Groups III and IV, the two groups participating in the G.E.D. diploma program, demonstrated significantly greater entry into the opportunity structure (conceptualized as regular employment or participation in post-high school education or training programs); and, furthermore, these results were maintained throughout the period of evaluation. In Group III, 13 of the 15 youths completed their G.E.D. programs within three months; two youths dropped out after three weeks.

Table 1. Participation in the Opportunity Structure

(School or Employment)

Groups	3 months	6 months	9 months
I*	1 (n = 13)	2 (n = 12)	1 (n = 10)
IIa	2 (n = 14)	3 (n = 13)	1 (n = 11)
IIIb	13 (n = 15)	13 (n = 15)	13 (n = 15)
IVc	7 (n = 14)	8 (n = 14)	9 (n = 14)
	$X^2 = 23.479$	$X^2 = 17.403$	$X^2 = 17.510$
	$p < .001$	$p < .011$	$p < .011$

*During the twelve-month program, contact was lost with five boys in this group. One moved out of town, and four were placed by their caseworkers in institutional settings.

aCommunication was lost with four boys in this group. Two moved outside the court's jurisdiction, one could not be located, and one was placed in an institution.

bCommunication was broken with no one in this group.

cOne boy in this group was placed in an institution.

In Group IV, again, 13 of the 15 boys completed the program within the allotted time; one dropped out after a month, and one was placed by his caseworker in an out-of-town institution a week before the inception of the program. Table 1 reveals the participation of the boys in jobs or training programs for a nine-month period following completion of the three-month experimental project.

In a second test of the boys' entry into the opportunity structure, the mean weekly income of those boys who secured jobs was computed. Table 2 depicts these findings. Apparently the G.E.D. high school equivalency program permitted a significant number of chronic juvenile offenders to enter the opportunity structure. The G.E.D. program participants (Groups III and IV) had more employment and higher income than either Group I, which received the standard counseling services of the court, or Group II, which participated in an intensive counseling program. Furthermore, the employment gained by Groups III and IV, especially Group III, was of a less menial nature and

Table 2. Mean Weekly Income for Those Working

(Gross Income)

Time	Group I	r	Group II	r	Group III	r	Group IV	r
Period								
3 months	$22.50 (n = 1)	1.0	$34.20 (n = 2)	3.5	$56.90 (n = 9)	29.0	$42.30 (n = 7)	13.0
6 months	$34.20 (n = 2)	3.5	$36.70 (n = 3)	8.0	$65.10 (n = 11)	46.0	$48.70 (n = 7)	21.0
9 months	$35.60 (n = 1)	6.0	$43.40 (n = 1)	17.0	$86.00 (n = 11)	57.0	$60.90 (n = 7)	37.0

Mann—Whitney U
n_1 (10) = groups I and II
n_2 (52) = groups III and IV
a = .0001; c.v. = 3.76
z = 4.855, p < .0001; r = ranking

promised occupational advancement and some sense of security.

It was hypothesized earlier that juvenile offenses among lower-class youth represent the use of illegal means to secure societally-approved goals such as wealth and material possessions. Further, it was argued that youths who enter the legitimate opportunity structure through training and employment would be less likely to commit further delinquency. The results of this study support these conclusions.

Table 3 depicts the percentage of boys in each group who were re-referred to the juvenile court during each three-month period. Recidivism was markedly higher among Groups I and II, the casework groups, than among Groups III and IV, the G.E.D. groups.[3] Not only was the percentage of offenses lower among Groups III and IV, but the nature of their referrals differed from Groups I and II. Only one offense among Groups III and IV was a property offense (shoplifting), the remainder were minor authority offenses. Among Groups I and II, however, there were serious property offenses including two burglaries and three larcenies. The entry of Groups III and IV into the opportunity structure appears to

have led to a decrease in their adjudicated delinquency. Thus, Cloward and Ohlin's hypotheses are tentatively supported.

Interviews were conducted with the boys in the four groups at the inception and the completion of the project. The interview procedures were loosely structured and the results not subject to empirical verification. However, it was our impression that the boys in Groups I and II retained their negative self-images and anti-social reference groups while Groups III and IV developed more positive self-images and more "traditional" reference groups. Indeed, the boys in the G.E.D. high school equivalency groups seemed to identify with their former tutors, court personnel, and their employers. They defined themselves as on the way to a "good life."

Table 3. Recidivism by 3-Month Periods*

(In Percentages, Non-Cumulative)

Groups	3 months	6 months	9 months
I	38.5%	33.4%	20.0%
II	35.7%	23.0%	27.3%
III	6.7%	0.0%	6.7%
IV	7.2%	0.0%	7.2%
	$X^2 = 7.518$	$X^2 = 10.454$	$X^2 = 3.124$
	p < .05	p < .02	p < .30

*These percentages represent only adjudicated offenses.

3. The poor performance of the casework groups confirms previous studies of casework ineffectiveness. See, for example, Powers and Witmer (1951), Meyer et al (1965), and Fisher (1973).

Whether this transformation occurred as a result of the relationship with the tutors, positive reenforcement from significant others, their experiences in earning an income, or some other factor cannot be determined at this time. It does appear, however, that entry into the opportunity structure carries with it changes in self-image and reference group.

Furthermore, these changes may have insulated the boys from further delinquency as much as did their new status in the opportunity structure (cf. Reckless, 1961; Reckless and Dinitz, 1967; Reckless et al, 1956). Thus, complete support of Cloward and Ohlin's theory has not been demonstrated. The experimental groups did evidence a dramatic decrease in delinquency. But it is not yet determined whether this resulted from the change in self-image and reference group or the entry into the opportunity structure. It is hypothesized, however, that these two phenomena parallel each other and access to the opportunity structure brings about an improvement in self-image and reference group.

CONCLUSIONS

It is acknowledged that this study was restricted by a small sample and a limited period of evaluation. Nevertheless, several general conclusions may be offered:

(1) Juvenile court treatment programs based upon sociological (opportunity structure) or social-psychological (self-image and reference group) constructs seem to decrease recidivism among lower-class, persistently-offending boys more dramatically than do more traditional treatment programs based upon psychiatric or psychological formulations of behavior.

(2) A high school equivalency program coupled with a job placement program is effective in curtailing delinquency among lower-class boys who have dropped out of school. Such a program is more effective than a high school equivalency program unsupported by a job-placement program.

Either program is more effective than a traditional casework approach.

(3) Cloward and Ohlin's theory of differential access to the opportunity structure is tentatively supported.

(4) Increased access to the opportunity structure seems accompanied by a more positive self-image and allegiance to more 'approved' reference groups.

(5) Additional research is necessary to define the independent and/or dependent effects of these factors in controlling delinquency.

REFERENCES

Bordua, D. J. 1961 "A Critique of Sociological Interpretations of Gang Delinquency." The Annals of the American Academy of Political and Social Science 338 (November):120—36.

Cloward, Richard A., and Lloyd E. Ohlin. 1960 Delinquency and Opportunity: A Theory of Delinquent Gangs. New York: Free Press.

Elliott, D. S. 1962 "Delinquency and Perceived Opportunity." Sociological Inquiry 32 (Spring):216—27.

Fischer, J. 1973 "Is Casework Effective? A Review." Social Work 18 (January):5—20.

Fredericks, Marcel A., and Martin Molnar. 1969 "Relative Occupational Anticipations and Aspirations of Delinquents and Non-delinquents." Journal of Research in Crime and Delinquency 6:1—7.

Himelhoch, J. 1965 "Delinquency and Opportunity: An End and a Beginning of Theory." Pp. 189—207 in Alvin Gouldner and S. M. Miller (eds.), Applied Sociology. New York: Free Press.

Landis, Judson R., and Frank R. Scarpitti. 1965 "Perceptions Regarding Value Orientation and Legitimate Opportunity: Delinquents and Non-Delinquents." Social Forces 44:83—91.

Landis, Judson R., Simon Dinitz, and Walter C. Reckless. 1964 "Differential Perceptions of Life Chances: A Research Note." Sociological Inquiry 34 (Winter):60—6.

Matza, D. 1964 Delinquency and Drift. New York: Wiley.

Merton, R. K. 1957 Social Theory and

Social Structure. Glencoe, Ill.: Free Press. Revised and enlarged edition.

Meyer, Henry J., Edgar Borgatta, and Wyatt Jones. 1965 Girls at Vocational High: An Experiment in Social Work Intervention. New York: Russell Sage Foundation.

Powers, Edwin, and Helen Witmer. 1951 An Experiment in the Prevention of Delinquency: The Cambridge-Somerville Youth Study. New York: Columbia University Press.

Reckless, W. C. 1961 "A New Theory of Delinquency and Crime." Federal Probation 25 (December):42–6.

Reckless, Walter C., and Simon Dinitz. 1967 "Pioneering with Self-Concept as a Vulnerability Factor in Delinquency." Journal of Criminal Law, Criminology and Police Science 58:515–23.

Reckless, Walter C., Simon Dinitz, and Ellen Murray. 1956 "Self Concept as an In-

sulator against Delinquency." American Sociological Review 21:744–6.

Shaw, C. R. 1930 The Jack-Roller. Chicago: University of Chicago Press.

———. 1931 The Natural History of a Delinquent Career. Chicago: University of Chicago Press.

Shaw, Clifford R., and Henry D. McKay. 1942 Juvenile Delinquency and Urban Areas. Chicago: University of Chicago Press.

Shaw, Clifford R., Frederick M. Zorbaugh, Henry D. McKay, and Leonard S. Cottrell. 1929 Delinquency Areas. Chicago: University of Chicago Press.

Short, James F., Jr., Ramon Rivera, and Ray A. Tennyson. 1965 "Perceived Opportunities, Gang Membership and Delinquency." American Sociological Review 30 (February):56–67.

7

GHETTO RIOTS

Introduction

During the 1960's, riots broke out in the black ghettos of many cities. Some people were killed, many were injured, and property damage was extensive. In an attempt to find out who rioted, why the riots occurred, and what might be done to prevent riots, a large number of studies were carried out. Many of these studies were guided by two theories whose explanations of riot participation and implications for riot prevention differ markedly: riffraff theory and relative deprivation theory. Riffraff theory contains three propositions: only an infinitesimal proportion of the black community participated in the riots; participants were largely uprooted, unskilled, unemployed, unattached, and/or criminal; and almost all blacks opposed and deplored the riots. According to those who espoused the theory, the key to riot prevention is more vigorous police action. Relative deprivation theory argues that blacks, compared to whites, have been deprived of a variety of educational, occupational, residential, and recreational opportunities. Awareness of this difference in opportunities generates feelings of frustration, which motivate blacks to riot in response to a precipitating event, for example, the arrest of a member of the black community. The implication for riot prevention is clear: equalize the opportunities available to blacks and whites.

Within white communities many people expressed beliefs that were consistent with riffraff or with relative deprivation theories (Campbell & Shuman, 1968, reading 7.1). Twenty-nine percent felt the riots were mainly a way of looting, while 43% thought they were principally a protest against unfair conditions. In response to a question about riot prevention, 47% first recommended more police control, whereas 20% suggested social and economic improvements. Within black communities, a different pattern of beliefs emerged. Ten percent saw the riots primarily as a vehicle for looting, while 58% felt the riots were mainly a protest against unfair conditions. Similarly, 9% favored more police control as a way of preventing riots, while 54% first proposed social and economic change.

How valid are these theories? Do they enable us to distinguish between people who participate in riots and people who don't? Do they increase our understanding of why people riot? A review of the research findings provides no support for riffraff theory. Using data from Los Angeles, Newark, and Detroit to arrive at a probable ratio of black rioters to black arrestees, Fogelson (1971, reading 7.2) estimated that 4% of the blacks living in areas in which the riot occurred participated in the riot in Cincinnati, 11% participated in Detroit, 15% in Newark, 16% in Grand Rapids, 26% in Dayton, and 35% in New Haven. With the exception of Cincinnati, these estimates, though speculative, are hardly infinitesimal proportions of the black communities.

Among those who reportedly participated in a riot, their socioeconomic and demographic characteristics suggest that they are not largely uprooted, unskilled, unemployed, unattached, and/or criminal. For example, Geschwender and Singer (1970) interviewed 499 black males who were arrested for participating in the Detroit riot. They found that 87% were reportedly employed. Among these arrestees, 49% said they held white collar, skilled, or semi-skilled positions, and 60% reported weekly incomes of $100 or more. Unfortunately, two methodological weaknesses make these findings tentative rather than conclusive. One, it's plausible that a number of arrestees were not rioters, but were caught by police tactics designed to clear the streets. Two, no attempt was made to check the veracity of the arrestees' verbal reports. Fogelson (1971, reading 7.2) reported that sizable percentages of arrestees—ranging from 40% in Buffalo to 92% in Dayton—had criminal records; however, he argued that these figures do not prove that a majority of arrestees were criminals. For example, one acquires a criminal record simply by being arrested—in many cases, simply by being picked up for suspicious conduct and later released. Since close police surveillance of the black community results in a disproportionately high number of arrests among black males, the sizable percentage of criminal records among riot arrestees—many of whom were young black males—is not unexpected. (Police discrimination against young black males is also discussed in the introduction to the readings on prejudice and racism and in reading 1.3.)

Concerning the proposition that an overwhelming majority of blacks opposed and deplored the riots, Campbell and Schuman found that 34% thought the riots helped the cause of black rights, 23% thought they hurt, and 25% felt they made no difference. In Los Angeles, 38% of the blacks interviewed referred to the disorders as a revolt, revolution, or insurrection; 64% thought the targets that were attacked deserved to be; and 58% felt the effects of the riot would be favorable (Sears & Tomlinson, 1968).

In an attempt to assess the adequacy of relative deprivation theory, McPhail (1970, reading 7.3) examined the findings of a number of studies conducted after the riots in Watts, Omaha, Detroit, Milwaukee, and Newark (Caplan & Paige, 1968a, 1968b; Flaming, 1968; Geschwender, Singer, & Harrington, 1969; Geschwender, Singer & Osborn, 1969; Murphy & Watson, 1967; Raine, 1967; Reynolds, 1968; Sears & McConahay, 1967a, 1967b; Tomlinson, 1967). Since these studies looked at many possible correlates of riot participation, McPhail assigned these correlates to 24 specific categories: for example, attitudes and expectations about jobs and housing, blacks' social contact with whites, occupational level, and opinions about police malpractice. These categories were in turn assigned to six more general categories: namely, attitude statements, social relations and interactions, socioeconomic attributes, experience and/or opinions of discrimination, demographic attributes, and political participation. There were 173 correlations—between an attitude, attribute, or behavior and participation in a riot—bearing on the deprivation-frustration-aggression hypothesis; 32% were not statistically significant, 61% yielded significant correlation coefficients less than .30, 7% produced coefficients between .30 and .39, and 1% generated coefficients of .40 or more. In short, while two-thirds of the associations were statistically significant, all but 8% accounted for negligible proportions of the variance in riot participation.*

Given these findings, McPhail concluded that individual attributes, attitudes, and experiences were relatively unimportant determinants of participation in a riot. As an alternative, he proposed that studies of the availability of people for riot participation, of the settings and times in which large numbers of available people are near one another, and of the process of assembling are much more likely to lead to an understanding of civil disorder participation.

While studies of availability, proximity, and the assembling process may be instructive, McPhail's conclusion that individual attributes, attitudes, and experiences were relatively unimportant determinants of riot participation is only one of several plausible interpretations of the data. For one, the data were gathered after the riots had taken place. As a result, the attitudes of the people interviewed may have been influenced by the riots and/or the coverage by the media. Two, the ways in which participation in a riot was defined may have resulted in the misclassification of substantial numbers of people. Whether a person participated in a riot was usually determined by self-report. Accordingly, it's conceivable that a number of people who didn't participate claimed they did, and vice versa. A second measure of participation in some studies was "arrest." Unfortunately, it's plausible that a sizable number of people were not rioters,

*Note that these proportions of explained variance are not unrepresentative of the results of much psychological research.

but were caught by police tactics designed to clear the streets. Even when people were correctly identified as participants, few attempts were made to distinguish among degrees of participation: for example, the person who threw a brick through a window versus the person who spent much time looting and setting fires. Given these shortcomings, modest relationships are all that could be expected. As a result, we still don't know how useful relative deprivation theory is. Three, the validity of many of the measures of frustration is suspect. Consequently, the small correlation coefficients may have been due to inadequate measures rather than to a negligible relationship between frustration and riot participation. Four, whether people participate in a riot may be determined by a constellation of psychological and situational factors. Accordingly, analysis of the possible determinants, one at a time, is bound to yield many small correlation coefficients. In order to determine the utility of the deprivation-frustration-aggression hypothesis, then, multivariate analyses of the data need to be carried out. Five, there may be no one comprehensive explanation of why people riot. In other words, different groups of ghetto residents may have participated in riots for different reasons. As a result, no one explanation, such as relative deprivation theory, can account for the behavior of all of the participants.

In a study that tested the validity of the last two interpretations, Moinat, Raine, Burbeck, and Davison (1972) asked 586 black residents in the Los Angeles riot area questions covering a broad range of areas: for example, socio-economic and demographic characteristics; level of political awareness and involvement; social distance from whites; perception of police brutality; discrimination in housing, jobs, stores, schools, and other community agencies; and attitudes toward the riot. Each respondent was also asked whether he/she was very active, somewhat active, or not at all active in the disorder.

In a multivariate analysis of the relationship between 80 representative variables and degree of riot participation, the many and varied correlates each accounted for very little independent variance. Taken together, they explained only 36% of the variance. As a result, the sample was divided into four groups—males over 27, males aged 27 or younger, females over 27, and females aged 27 or younger—and a second set of analyses was performed. The results indicate that the first ten variables within each group explained a substantial proportion of variance—ranging from 42% for older females to 78% for young males. Among the strongest correlates were salience and experience of police brutality, a belief that most of the people in the area supported the riot, and reports of specific forms of discrimination. Accordingly, the authors' conclusion that "one cannot predict who will riot" (Moinat *et al.*, p. 58) does not appear warranted, although the failure of the research to indicate whether specific forms of perceived police brutality occurred prior to or during the riot makes interpretation difficult.

Support for Moinat, Raine, Burbeck, and Davison's finding that police brutality was a major correlate, and perhaps a precipitant, of participation in a riot is provided by several studies. For example, Hahn and Feagin (1970) reported that sizable minorities of ghetto dwellers in Detroit, Watts, and Bedford-Stuyvesant felt that police brutality was a major cause of the riots in these areas. Moreover, Mendelsohn's study of the Detroit police conducted shortly after the 1967 riot (1970, reading 7.4) suggests that many policemen harbor beliefs which seem likely to engender acts of mistreatment. The findings indicate that:

> ... the typical white officer (below the rank of inspector) views the black community as a privileged minority, unsatisfied with its already privileged position and prepared to use violence to attain still further advantage over the white community. The community is perceived, further, as susceptible to the influence of agitators capable of galvanizing into action a people without real grievances. Finally, the black community is viewed as deficient in respect for law and order. Implicit in this view is a conception of the black community as primitive, emotional, and easily aroused to antisocial action, and with an ultimate goal of domination over whites rather than a goal of equality. [pp. 752-53]

Given these beliefs, and the profound need for an effective working relationship between police and ghetto communities, Mendelsohn recommended that the police role be redefined in terms of the public services police provide, that officers who establish good relations with ghetto communities be rewarded, that university and in-service training for police officers be increased, and that police-community relations programs be rigorously evaluated.

The relative infrequency of riots over a long period of time makes it exceedingly difficult to predict when they will occur. However, it is easy to predict where they will occur—in urban ghettos. There are many reasons for improving conditions in the ghettos; riots simply underscore the need.

REFERENCES

Campbell, A., & Schuman, H. Racial attitudes in fifteen American cities. In *Supplemental studies for the National Advisory Commission on Civil Disorders*. Washington, D.C.: Government Printing Office, 1968.

Caplan, N., & Paige, J. Data on Newark and Detroit residents. In National Advisory Commission on Civil Disorders, *Report of the National Advisory Commission on Civil Disorders*. Washington, D.C.: Government Printing Office, 1968a, pp. 171–178.

Caplan, N., & Paige, J. A study of ghetto rioters. *Scientific American*, 1968b, 219, 15–21.

Fleming, K. *Who riots and why?: Black and white perspectives in Milwaukee*. Milwaukee: Milwaukee Urban League, 1968.

Fogelson, R. *Violence as protest: A study of riots and ghettos*. New York: Doubleday & Company, 1971.

Geschwender, J., Singer, B., & Harrington, J. *Status inconsistency, deprivation and the Detroit riot*. Paper presented at the annual meetings of the American Sociological Association, San Francisco, California, 1969.

Geschwender, J., Singer, B., & Osborn, R. *Social isolation and riot participation.* Paper presented at the annual meetings of the American Sociological Association, San Francisco, California, 1969.

Geschwender, J., & Singer, B. Deprivation and the Detroit riot. *Social Problems,* 1970, 17 (4), 457–463.

Hahn, H., & Feagin, J. Riot-precipitating police practices: Attitudes in urban ghettos. *Phylon,* 1970, 31, 183–193.

McPhail, C. Civil disorder participation: A critical examination of recent research. *American Sociological Review,* 1971, 36, 1058–1073.

Mendelsohn, R. Police-community relations: A need in search of police support. *American Behavioral Scientist,* 1970, 13, 745–760.

Moinat, S., Raine, W., Burbeck, S., & Davison, K. Black ghetto residents as rioters. *Journal of Social Issues,* 1972, 28 (4), 45–62.

Murphy, R., & Watson, J. *The structure of discontent: The relationship between social structure, grievance and support for the Los Angeles riot.* Los Angeles: University of California Institute of Govern-ment and Public Affairs, 1967.

Raine, W. *The perception of police brutality in south central Los Angeles.* Los Angeles: University of California Institute of Gov-ernment and Public Affairs, 1967.

Reynolds, H. Black power, community power and jobs. In L. Masotti & D. Bowen (Eds.), *Riots and rebellion: Civil violence in the urban community.* Beverly Hills: Sage Publications, 1968, pp. 237–260.

Sears, D., & McConahay, J. *Riot participation.* Los Angeles: University of California Institute of Government and Public Af-fairs, 1967a.

Sears, D., & McConahay, J. *The politics of discontent.* Los Angeles: University of California Institute of Government and Public Affairs, 1967b.

Sears, D., & Tomlinson, T. Riot ideology in Los Angeles: A study of Negro attitudes. *Social Science Quarterly,* 1968, 49, 485–503.

Tomlinson, T. *Ideological foundation for Negro action: A comparative analysis of militant and non-militant views of the Los Angeles riot.* Los Angeles: University of California Institute of Government and Public Affairs, 1967.

The Uses of Violence

ANGUS CAMPBELL and HOWARD SCHUMAN

This chapter deals with Negro and white beliefs about, and involvement in, the riots that have occurred in Detroit, Newark, and many other American cities. We begin with a comparison of Negro and white perceptions of the causes and character of the riots. Identical questions were asked both Negroes and whites and the results reveal a number of differences between the two samples. We next attempt to describe those respondents who indicate a willingness to participate in rioting or other related forms of violence. This second section replicates findings of earlier studies carried out by other investigators in Los Angeles, Detroit and Newark, with some extensions made possible by additional questions, a comparative framework, and larger sample sizes. The chapter ends with a brief look at advocacy of violence within the white population.

THE NATURE OF THE RIOTS

The differences between Negro and white definitions of the riots, perceptions of cause, and prescriptions for prevention are shown in the series of questions presented in Tables 1 to 5. The first question asked each respondent to characterize the riots as "mainly a protest by Negroes against unfair conditions" or "mainly a way of looting and things like that." White men are fairly evenly split between viewing the riots as a protest and viewing them as largely criminal in nature, while white women choose protest rather than looting by two to one. Negroes were *not* so split: 58 percent regard the riots

Table 1. "Some people say these disturbances are mainly a protest by Negroes against unfair conditions. Others say they are mainly a way of looting and things like that. Which of these seems more correct to you?"

[In percent]

	Negro		White	
	Men	Women	Men	Women
Mainly protest	56	59	38	48
Mainly looting	9	10	33	24
50/50 mixture	30	25	25	24
Don't know ..	5	6	4	4
	100	100	100	100

From A. Campbell, & H. Schuman. Racial attitudes in fifteen American cities. In *Supplemental Studies for the National Advisory Commission on Civil Disorders*. Washington, D.C.: U.S. Government Printing Office, 1968, pp. 47–51.

Table 2. "What do you think was the main cause of these disturbances?"

[In percent]

Most frequent types of spontaneous response*	Negro		White	
	Men	Women	Men	Women
Discrimination unfair treatment	49	48	22	27
Unemployment ..	23	22	13	13
Inferior jobs	13	10	5	5
Bad housing	23	20	15	15
Poor education ..	10	9	7	7
Poverty	10	8	11	9
Police brutality ..	10	4	2	1
Black Power or other "radicals"	4	5	26	21
Looters and other undesirables ...	11	11	34	34
Communists	0	0	8	5

*Each mention to this question was coded separately, and since some people mentioned more than one cause, the percentages do not add to 100. Only reasons mentioned by at least 10 percent of a group are presented here, except for the response "Communist" which is slightly under this limit.

as mainly a protest and another 28 percent characterize them as partly a protest. Only 10 percent of the Negro sample saw the riots as mainly a matter of looting and similar offenses.

The main *cause* of the riots (see Table 2) according to spontaneous responses by nearly half the black sample lies in, or is associated with, unfair treatment of Negroes by whites. For example:

"Want to be treated like a human being."

"Unfairness to the Negro. The Negro has been pushed back for years. They are tired of being pushed around. They want better things in life just like the whites."

"Mostly Negroes want more in life and want to be treated the same as whites. Some of them have just as much sense and education as whites and want to be respected just as much as they [whites] respect another one of their own. . . ."

Table 3. "Do you think the large disturbances like those in Detroit and Newark were planned in advance, or that there was some planning but not much, or weren't they planned at all?"

[In percent]

	Negro		White	
	Men	Women	Men	Women
Planned in advance	16	20	47	50
Some planning but not much	37	34	37	34
Not planned at all .	38	30	12	10
Don't know	9	16	4	6
	100	100	100	100

Specific grievances often follow responses such as the above, particularly in the areas of employment and housing, but it is worth noting that they are frequently linked to words like "unjust" and "unfair" and sometimes to mention of "lack of respect." The phrases "want to be treated like anyone else" and "want to be treated the same as whites" recur frequently. A number of other specific grievance-type causes are also mentioned, such as police brutality, but in each instance by a relatively small part of the sample.*

Whites offer the same causes of the riots as do Negroes, but with only about half the frequency. On the other hand, while few Negroes perceive the riots as caused by "leaders"—black nationalist, Communist, or any other type—nearly a quarter of the white sample cite radical leaders as a major cause. Similarly, only one out of ten Negroes lay blame for the riots on criminal or other

*We have shown earlier (Chapter 4) that direct questions on police practices indicate considerable resentment by Negroes and it is probable that specific questions relating police actions to the riots would have elicited more frequent perceptions of a causal link. But it seems clear that when Negroes are asked to think of the *main* cause of rioting, they more often think of general white treatment of Negroes and of specific economic areas.

Table 4. "What do you think is the most important thing the city government in (Central City) could do to keep a disturbance like the one in Detroit from breaking out here?"

[In percent]

First type of response mentioned	Negro		White	
	Men	Women	Men	Women
Better employment	26	24	11	9
End discrmination	14	15	2	3
Better housing	8	8	4	4
Other social and economic improvements	7	5	4	3
Better police treatment	6	1	0	1
Improve communications between Negroes and whites; show Negroes whites care	12	13	10	13
More black control of institutions	0	0	0	0
More police control	9	8	51	42
Can't do anything, have already tried everything	3	5	8	8
Don't know	15	21	10	17
	100	100	100	100

undesirable elements, but one of out of three whites see this factor as important.

Since whites emphasize the role of radical leaders and of criminally inclined participants, it is not surprising that many believe the riots were "planned in advance" (Table 3): nearly half hold unequivocally to this belief and another third believe there was *some* planning. A much smaller proportion of Negroes (18 percent) see the riots as generally planned in advance, another third see some planning, but a third believe there was no planning at all.

A general "open-ended" question shown in Table 4 on the most important means to prevent future riots suggests a clear difference in focus by race. More than half of the Negro sample spontaneously mention improvement of social and economic conditions as the first solution, with more and better jobs the most frequently offered specific recommendation. Only one-fifth of the white sample think immediately in terms of such social and economic changes. On the other hand, nearly half the white sample call first for stronger police control, as against only one out of ten Negroes in the sample who mention police control as their first answer. As shown earlier, . . . when the long-term alternatives of police control *versus* improvement of Negro conditions are posed bluntly, a majority of white respondents choose the latter and another quarter say that *both* are needed. Likewise, some white respondents qualify their spontaneous first mention of police control shown in Table 4 by indicating support for economic improvements as well. The difference between races seems more one of salience and focus of attention than absolute opposition.

Finally, the long-term effects of the riots are viewed in very different ways by Negroes and whites (Table 5). Most whites (64 percent) believe the riots have hurt the cause of Negro rights and few believe they have helped. But a third of the black sample think that the riots have aided the Negro cause in America, while only a quarter think the riots have been mainly harmful in effect.

The reasons offered by Negroes for the belief that riots *help* are primarily in terms of tangible gains in the very same areas mentioned in response to questions about causes and prevention. About 20 percent of the Negro sample believe that in one way or another the riots have stimulated action to

Table 5. "On the whole, do you think the disturbances have helped or hurt the cause of Negro rights, or would you say they haven't made much difference?"

	[In percent]		[In percent]	
	Negro		White	
	Men	Women	Men	Women
Helped	37	30	13	14
Hurt	22	24	69	59
Helped and hurt equally	12	11	7	7
Made no difference	21	28	9	17
Don't know	8	7	2	3
	100	100	100	100

"Why do you feel that way?"

	[In percent]			
	Negro		White	
	Men	Women	Men	Women
First reason given:				
Helped:				
Tangible gains (e.g., more jobs)	19	20	8	8
Whites understand Negroes' problems better ...	14	10	8	8
Show of Negro power	9	5	2	1
Hurt:				
Destruction, injury	8	8	2	3
Increased anti-Negro sentiments	16	19	64	54
Made no difference:				
No tangible gain	19	23	5	12
Negroes are still not satisfied	0	1	7	10
Don't know	15	14	4	4
	100	100	100	100

solve the major problems confronting Negroes. For example:

"They are making attempts to give us better jobs and respect."

". . . they are trying to make it so it won't occur again . . . helping Negro to start up retail business . . . trying to get more Negro national guardsmen."

"They are getting better jobs and better housing and better schools. That's what they were fighting for."

A smaller proportion of Negro respondents (11 percent) believe that the riots have awakened the average white person to an understanding of Negro problems in America, a perception shared by almost the same proportion of white respondents. Finally, a small number of Negro respondents (7 percent) evince special pride in the demonstration of black courage and power that they see in the riots.

Negroes who see harm in the riots speak primarily in terms of the destruction and violence. White respondents, on the other hand, give overwhelming emphasis to anti-Negro sentiments aroused or stimulated by the riots. For example, white respondents reply in such terms as:

". . . it hurt because they got more people bitter . . . it's getting us a little more scared . . . Everyone is scared, you're scared to open your door now."

". . . they are doing harm to their real cause, as people forget the real thing and remember the wrong things they have done and stop helping them."

"Because of the vandalism and taking other people's property. This hurt them very much . . . People have bad opinions of them when they read about these things."

Sixty percent of the white sample report the rise in such anti-Negro sentiments, but only 18% of the Negroes mention this as an unfavorable consequence of the riots. Indeed, nearly as many black respondents perceive an increase in white understanding of Negro problems because of the riots as perceive an increase in white hostility.

Suburban white results have not been presented in Tables 1 to 5 but in general they are very similar to white city results. For example, where 33 percent of white city males see the riots as "mainly a way of looting and things like that," 35 percent of white suburban males choose that response; comparable figures for white females are 24 percent and 27 percent. As another example, more police control is mentioned first as the most important way to prevent riots by 51 percent of white city males as against 54 percent of suburban males, and by 42 percent of white city females as against 43 percent of suburban females. From a descriptive standpoint, city whites and suburban whites seem to perceive the riots in very much the same terms.

The findings presented thus far in this section add up to quite different—although not opposite—Negro and white perspectives on the causes, consequences, and prevention of urban riots in America. A solid, and at points overwhelming, majority of Negroes in these 15 cities see the riots as largely spontaneous black protests against unfair treatment, economic deprivation, or a combination of the two. The main way to prevent future riots is, in this view, to remove the underlying causes. Moreover, more Negroes think the riots helped in this direction than

think the riots were harmful, although the division is close.

Only about 10 percent of the Negro sample dissent clearly from this viewpoint and consider the riots criminal activity to be suppressed primarily by police control. Tables 1 to 5 indicate little sex difference for Negroes in this respect. The tables presented below allow analysis by age and education of three questions already discussed. Table 6 does not indicate any clear educational different among Negroes with regard to perception of the riots as mainly protest or mainly looting, but does suggest a generally consistent trend by age, with a greater proportion of younger people than of older people seeing the riot as a form of protest. The age trend is supported by the results in Table 7, which deals with whether the riots helped or hurt the cause of Negro rights. In this case there also appears to be a slight relation to education, with the *more* educated tending to perceive good coming out of the riots, especially among Negroes in their 20's and 30's. These results taken together suggest that, for the present at least, Negroes who take a wholly negative view of the riots represent the viewpoint of an older generation.

The white sample as a whole differs considerably from the black sample on the riots, but it does *not* present simply a mirror image of the nearly universal Negro definition. If that were the case, the white sample would hold an almost unanimous view of the riots as conspiratorial or criminal in nature, and as responding only to police control. Instead, we find white respondents distributed over a range of positions and outlooks. This makes it more difficult, however, to describe them in summary fashion in this report. About a third of the white sample seem committed to a view of the riots close to that of most Negroes, namely, as protests against real economic and social grievances, protests that should be met by constructive attempts to remove these grievances. About a third see the riots as largely unjustified but conspiratorial assaults on law and order led by criminal, demagogic, or other undesirable

Table 6. "Some people say these disturbances are mainly a protest by Negroes against unfair conditions. Others say they are mainly a way of looting and things like that. Which of these seems more correct to you?"

BY NEGRO AGE AND EDUCATION CATEGORIES (RESULTS FOR MEN AND WOMEN AVERAGED) In percent

	Age 16-19*	Age 20-39					Age 40-69				
		8th grade or less	9-11 grades	12 grades	Some college	College graduate	8th grade or less	9-11 grades	12 grades	Some college	College graduate
Mainly protest	60	65	56	65	69	61	43	56	61	60	33
Mainly looting	11	5	10	5	4	4	12	10	13	9	13
50/50 mixture	25	21	26	27	24	35	30	27	23	30	54
Don't know	4	9	8	3	3	0	15	7	3	1	0
	100	100	100	100	100	100	100	100	100	100	100

*This group combines all education categories.

Table 7. "On the whole, do you think the disturbances have helped or hurt the cause of Negro rights, or would you say they haven't made much difference?"

BY NEGRO AGE AND EDUCATION CATEGORIES (RESULTS FOR MEN AND WOMEN AVERAGED) In percent

	Age 16-19*	Age 20-39					Age 40-69				
		8th grade or less	9-11 grades	12 grades	Some college	College graduate	8th grade or less	9-11 grades	12 grades	Some college	College graduate
Helped	36	33	33	39	40	67	24	24	34	36	28
Hurt	24	28	21	19	14	9	28	27	31	19	24
Helped and hurt equally	9	8	9	14	17	1	10	10	10	19	37
Haven't made much difference	25	25	29	23	16	18	24	31	19	24	9
Don't know	6	6	8	5	13	5	14	8	6	2	2
	100	100	100	100	100	100	100	100	100	100	100

*This group combines all educational categories.

Table 8. "Some people say these disturbances are mainly a protest by Negroes against unfair conditions. Others say they are mainly a way of looting and things like that. Which of these seems more correct to you?"

BY WHITE AGE AND EDUCATION CATEGORIES (RESULTS FOR MEN AND WOMEN AVERAGED) In Percent

	Age 16–19*	Age 20–39					Age 40–69				
		8th grade or less	9–11 grades	12 grades	Some college	College graduate	8th grade or less	9–11 grades	12 grades	Some college	College graduate
Mainly protest	62	30	32	48	56	60	32	36	35	41	49
Mainly looting	17	44	33	25	16	13	38	37	36	30	15
50/50 mixture	18	22	34	26	28	21	21	23	27	22	26
Don't know	3	4	1	1	0	6	9	4	2	7	10
	100	100	100	100	100	100	100	100	100	100	100

*This group combines all educational categories.

elements, assaults that should be met first of all by firm police action. The remaining third or so of the white sample consists of people who combine both views more or less equally, as well as people who have no clear opinions on the matter.

A major purpose of later reports will be to describe and understand better these white divisions in perception. For the present, we can note from Tables 1 to 5 that men appear slightly more inclined than women to regard the riots as mainly "looting" and to favor primarily police control. Table 8 below indicates a strong trend, especially among younger persons, for the *more* educated to perceive the riots as mainly protests rather than as mainly looting. Age differences are somewhat less consistent and strong, but youth apparently has the same effect as greater education in making the riots seem to be purposive protests rather than simply episodes of mass criminal activity. Thus age trends for white city respondents are similar to those for Negroes. Indeed, a comparison of Tables 6 and 8 reveals that among teenagers and also among college graduates at older age levels, about the same proportion of whites and Negroes perceive the riots as protests. The young and the better educated of both races converge in their perceptions of the basic character of the riots.

Where white perceptions of the riots are in wholly negative terms, this is most obviously interpretable as opposition to violence, looting, and destruction. This is no doubt correct, but it is well to recognize also that a substantial proportion of the white sample is opposed to *non*-violent protest actions by Negroes as well as to violence. More than a quarter of the white sample (23 percent of the men, 32 percent of the women) believe Negroes are not justified in using "*orderly marches* to protest against racial discrimination" and more than two-thirds believe that "sit-in" protests are unjustified (tables not shown). Thus a substantial proportion of the white sample is against *any* active protest by Negroes.

Indeed, to a rather large segment of the white population the attempt to distinguish

Table 9. "Some Negro leaders are talking about having nonviolent marches and demonstrations in several cities in 1968 to protest lack of opportunities for Negroes. Do you think such demonstrations are different from the riots, or that there is no real difference?"

[In percent]

	White		
	Men	Women	Total
Nonviolent demonstrations differ from riots	63	56	60
No real difference	32	38	35
Don't know	5	6	5
	100	100	100

"violent" from "nonviolent" demonstration is not very meaningful, as Table 9 indicates. Thus a third of the white population is so repelled by the idea of active Negro protest that it cannot or does not wish to distinguish between nonviolent demonstrations and riots. The response "no real difference" is explained by white respondents in terms such as the following:

"They're still just looking for aggravation. They're *looking* for trouble. They're just out looking to see what they can stir up, just hoping to aggravate people on the opposite side. That's all."

"Even the peaceful ones get into big fights usually and a bunch go to jail before it is over."

"Just plotting up a riot."

"All I know is it's a mess. They are troublemakers."

In general, then, fully a third of the white population sees riots as simply the inevitable consequence of, if not the same as, the type of protests Negroes have engaged in from the late 1950's onwards. This helps explain why, not infrequently, white respondents join the names of Martin Luther King and H. Rap Brown as though they stood for exactly the same thing. . . .

Who Riots? An Evaluation of Riffraff Theory

ROBERT FOGELSON

... It is not hard to challenge the first point of the riffraff theory—that an infinitesimal fraction of the black population, no more than 1 or 2 per cent, actively participated in the riots. If only 1 or 2 per cent of the blacks rioted in Detroit or Newark, then, in view of the large number of persons arrested there, the police must have apprehended almost all the rioters,[1] a conclusion contradicted by the eyewitness accounts of these riots. Also, according to the University of Michigan's Survey Research Center, 11 per cent of the blacks fifteen years and older rioted in Detroit, and 45 per cent of the black males between the ages of fifteen and thirty-five rioted in Newark.[2] It is, however, much harder to reach a more precise estimate of how large a segment of the black population actively participated in the riots. For an estimate depends on the answers to two difficult questions: how many blacks might have joined in the riots? and how many blacks did join in the riots? Fortunately, the survey research and arrest data provide tentative answers to these questions and rough estimates of riot participation.

To determine how many blacks might have joined in the riots, it is incorrect to use the total number of blacks in the community. The reason why is illustrated by a brief discussion of the McCone Commission Report, which based its estimate of riot participation on all of Los Angeles County's 650,000 blacks.[3] This figure is wrong for two main reasons. First, the 1965 riots occurred principally in south-central Los Angeles, and not in Los Angeles County's small and dispersed black enclaves. Blacks from these communities should not have been counted any more than blacks from Chicago's South Side should be counted to determine how many might have joined in the West Side riots of 1966. Second, south-central Los Angeles contains a sizable number of residents who, for a variety of reasons, could not possibly have participated in the 1965 riots. Neither the infants and elderly, the lame, halt, and blind, nor the residents in prison, hospitals, and the armed forces should have been counted. Thus to

---

1. In Detroit the black arrestees were 1.2 per cent of the nonwhite population; in Newark they were 1.0 per cent of the nonwhite population.
2. *Kerner Commission Report*, 172.

3. See Scoble, "The McCone Commission," 11; and Fogelson, "White on Black," 345.

determine how many blacks might have joined in the riots, it is essential to compute the number of potential rioters in the community.

The potential rioters are, to begin with, the residents of the riot area, not the metropolis, not the city, and not necessarily even the poverty area, but rather the neighborhood which experienced the rioting. To chart the riot area—or, in effect, to fix boundaries of the rioting, looting, arson, and assault—is an overwhelming task, one well beyond the scope of this brief essay. Fortunately, the Kerner Commission mapped the riot areas for Detroit, Newark, and several other cities in the course of its investigation.[4] And on the basis of the commission's maps the number of blacks living in the riot areas was computed. But, to continue, only some of the blacks living in the riot areas— namely, males and females between the ages of ten and fifty-nine inclusive—are the potential rioters. This definition is a broad one. It excludes children under ten and adults over fifty-nine not only for reasons of common sense, but also because they were only 1 per cent of the arrestees. And it includes the handicapped and the institutionalized, who are admittedly few in number, and women, even though they were less likely than men to join in the riots.[5]

The definition of potential rioters as all blacks living in the riot areas between the ages of ten and fifty-nine inclusive maximizes the base of the population and thereby minimizes the extent of participation. It is, if anything, biased in favor of the riffraff theory. And if this definition is applied to the dozen riots in which more than two hundred persons were arrested (and for which the arrest sheets were collected and the riot areas mapped) the numbers of blacks who might have joined in the riots are 166,400 in Los Angeles (August 1965),

149,000 in Detroit (July 1967), 90,700 in Philadelphia (August 1964), 46,500 in Newark (July 1967), 42,000 in Cincinnati (June 1967), 38,900 in Harlem (July 1964), 29,700 in Bedford-Stuyvesant (July 1964), 22,900 in Atlanta (June 1967), 13,700 in Chicago (July 1966), 15,300 in Rochester (July 1964), 12,600 in Cleveland (June 1966), and 5200 in New Haven (August 1967). It should be noted, however, that these figures, which are based on 1960 Census Tract data, probably underestimate the number of potential rioters.[6]

To determine how many blacks did join in the riots in these communities is much harder. The only data available are the U.C.L.A. survey of the Los Angeles riots and the University of Michigan surveys of the Newark and Detroit riots. About the other nine riots there is no information whatsoever. What is more, for the purpose of measuring riot participation among blacks between the ages of ten and fifty-nine even the available surveys are not particularly illuminating. The Newark survey included only black males between the ages of fifteen and thirty-five; the Detroit survey included only blacks above the age of fifteen; and the Los Angeles survey did not make explicit its age limits.[7] Notwithstanding these limitations, there is a way, albeit a highly speculative way, to derive estimates of riot participation from the survey research and arrest data. It requires two fairly simple, though not totally reliable, calculations. First, to find the ratio between the number of rioters in a given age group in Los Angeles, Newark, and Detroit and the number of arrestees in the same age groups in these cities. And second, to apply this ratio to these and the other nine cities— or, in effect, to multiply the number of arrestees by this ratio—and thereby estimate the number of rioters.

If this approach is applied, the results are as follows: of the 33,500 or so blacks in the

4. *Kerner Commission Report*, 113.
5. For another definition of potential rioters, see Jay Schulman, "Ghetto Residence, Political Alienation, and Riot Orientation," in L. Masotti, ed., *Urban Disorders, Violence, and Urban Victimization* (Beverly Hills, Calif., 1968).

6. U.S. Bureau of the Census, *U.S. Censuses of Population and Housing: 1960. Census Tracts* (Washington, D.C., 1962).
7. Sears, "Riot Activity"; *Kerner Commission Report*, 171–78.

Los Angeles ghetto between the ages of twenty-five and thirty-four, approximately 1200 were arrested in the 1965 riots, and, according to the Sears survey, roughly 22 per cent, or 7200, were active in the riots. Hence the ratio of rioters to arrestees in Los Angeles was about six to one. Of the 9800 or so black males in the Newark riot area between the ages of fifteen and thirty-five, approximately 900 were arrested in the 1967 riots, and, according to the Caplan survey, roughly 45 per cent, or 4400, partici- pated in the riots. Hence the ratio of rioters to arrestees in Newark was about five to one. Of the 147,000 or so blacks in the Detroit riot area fifteen years and older, approxi- mately 5400 were arrested in the 1967 riots, and, again according to the Caplan survey, roughly 11 per cent, or 16,200, joined in the riots. Hence the ratio of rioters to arrestees in Detroit was about three to one.

Whether the ratios which hold for Los Angeles, Newark, and Detroit would hold for the other cities is impossible to say. But if the ratio of six to one is applied to Los Angeles, the ratio of three to one in Detroit, and the ratio of five to one in Newark and the other cities, the numbers of blacks who participated in the riots are 23,200 in Los Angeles, 16,900 in Detroit, 1900 in Phila- delphia, 6900 in Newark, 1800 in Cincin- nati, 1100 in Harlem, 1800 in Bedford- Stuyvesant, 800 in Atlanta, 3900 in Rochester, 1900 in Chicago, 1600 in Cleve- land, and 1800 in New Haven. And if these estimates are reasonably accurate, the pro- portions of blacks who participated in these riots are 14 per cent in Los Angeles, 11 per cent in Detroit, 2 per cent in Philadelphia, 15 per cent in Newark, 4 per cent in Cincin- nati, 3 per cent in Harlem, 6 per cent in Bedford-Stuyvesant, 3 per cent in Atlanta, 25 per cent in Rochester, 14 per cent in Chicago, 13 per cent in Cleveland, and 35 per cent in New Haven.[8]

These estimates are highly speculative: riot areas have imprecise boundaries, ghetto resi- dents are constantly moving, survey research is an inexact science, and police practices differ from one city to another. But these estimates are no more speculative than the personal impressions of courageous, but terribly harried, newspaper reporters or the official statements of concerned, but hardly dispassionate, public figures. These estimates also vary considerably from one city to the next, and, for reasons which are unclear,[9] they are lower in Detroit and Newark than in smaller communities which suffered much less serious rioting. But these estimates far exceed the riffraff theory's estimates; and, even more noteworthy, nowhere except in Philadelphia are they as low as 2 per cent of the black population. Hence the rioters were a minority, but a substantial minority—and, in view of the historic efficacy of the cus- tomary restraints on rioting in the United States, a significant minority too.[10] And to characterize them otherwise is not only to confuse the historical record but also to mis- lead the American public.

The second point of the riffraff theory— that the rioters, far from being repre- sentative of the ghetto community, were mainly the riffraff and outside agitators—has a certain plausibility. According to the arrest data, as the McCone Commission and other official agencies have noted, many rioters were young, unattached, unskilled, unem- ployed, uprooted, and, broadly defined, criminals.[11] But according to the census and other data, many blacks, rioters or non-riot- ers, are juveniles or young adults; many are single (or separated, divorced, and wi- dowed), many unskilled and unemployed, and many recent immigrants; many have criminal records, too.[12] Hence to test the

8. For an attempt to apply this approach to the Washington, D.C., riots of 1968, see Ben W. Gilbert et al., *Ten Blocks from the White House* (New York, 1968), 224–25.

9. See Fogelson and Hill, "Who Riots?" 231.
10. See chapter 5.
11. *McCone Commission Report*, 24–25; *N.J. Riot Report*, 129–33.
12. U.S. Bureau of the Census; *U.S. Censuses of Population and Housing: 1960. Census Tracts*; President's Commission on Law Enforcement and Administration of Justice, *The Challenge of Crime in a Free Society* (Washington, D.C., 1967), 75.

second point of the riffraff theory it is not enough just to ask whether many of the rioters fit into these categories; obviously they do. It is also necessary to ask whether a greater proportion of the actual rioters than the potential rioters fit into these categories. And to this question the arrest sheets from a dozen riots[13] over the past four years in which two hundred or more persons were arrested provide fairly reliable answers.

Although a majority of the arrestees (ranging from 68 per cent in the Cincinnati riots to 92 per cent in the New Haven riots) were adults, the rioters were a good deal younger than the potential rioters.[14] The difference was not manifested among the juveniles (defined, for the sake of consistency, as youths between the ages of ten and seventeen), who were a higher proportion of the arrestees than the residents in only four cities. Rather, the difference was manifested among the teen-agers and young adults from fifteen to twenty-four years of age. In four riots they were a majority (ranging from 52 per cent in the Bedford-Stuyvesant riots to 73 per cent in the Cincinnati riots); and only in the Rochester riots were they less than 40 per cent. The difference was also manifested among the young adults between the ages of twenty-five and thirty-four, who were considerably overrepresented in all but one riot where the fifteen to twenty-four age group was not a majority. Needless to say, the middle-aged and elderly from thirty-five to fifty-nine years of age (as well as the children from ten to fourteen years of age) were underrepresented in the riots. In sum, the teen-agers and young adults between the ages of

fifteen and thirty-four, who are a minority of the potential rioters in every city except New Haven, were an overwhelming majority of the arrestees (ranging from 65 per cent in Harlem to 90 per cent in Atlanta) in all the riots.

At first glance the rioters also seem much more likely to be single, though much less likely to be separated, divorced, and widowed, than the potential rioters. In the seven riots for which information is available, single people were a majority (ranging from 57 per cent in the Atlanta riots to 76 per cent in the Cincinnati riots) in all except the Rochester and the Detroit riots.[15] By contrast, only about one in five of the potential rioters is single, though another one in five is separated, divorced, and widowed.[16] In view of the extremely heavy participation of the teen-agers and young adults, however, the difference is considerably less impressive. Indeed, if the arrestees in all the riots for which information is available are divided into two categories, one twenty-five years of age and under and the other twenty-six years of age and over, the difference virtually vanishes. Of the younger arrestees fully 78 per cent were single and only 20 per cent married; and of the older arrestees fully 54 per cent were married and only 31 per cent single. These proportions differ so little from the proportions for the ghetto residents that it is fair to say that, if age is held constant, the rioters were about as likely to be single as the potential rioters.

At first glance, too, the rioters seem much more likely to be unskilled and unemployed than the potential rioters. Although the unskilled are a minority (ranging from 28 per cent in Detroit to 48 per cent in Cincinnati) in every city save Atlanta, they were a majority (ranging from 50 per cent in the De-

13. Harlem (July 1964), Bedford-Stuyvesant (July 1964), Rochester (July 1964), Philadelphia (August 1964), Los Angeles (August 1965), Cleveland (June 1966), Chicago (July 1966), Atlanta (September 1966), Cincinnati (June 1967), Newark (July 1967), Detroit (July 1967), and New Haven (August 1967).
14. The potential rioters include all the nonwhite residents of the riot areas between the ages of ten and fifty-nine inclusive. Their numbers were obtained from U.S. Bureau of the Census, *U.S. Censuses of Population and Housing: 1960. Census Tracts.*

15. The findings for the Detroit rioters are based on Sheldon Lachman and Benjamin Singer, "The Detroit Riot of 1967" (Detroit, 1968), 19, a study of five hundred male arrestees prepared for the U.S. Department of Labor.
16. The findings for both arrestees and residents are based on males and females fourteen years of age and older.

troit riots to 76 per cent in the Cleveland riots) in the ten riots for which information is available.[17] And although the unemployed are a small minority (ranging from 8 per cent in Chicago to 12 per cent in Newark) in the cities, they were a large minority (ranging from 18 per cent in the Atlanta riots to 43 per cent in the Chicago riots) in the eight riots for which information is available.[18] At a second glance, however, these differences are a good deal less impressive. The occupational distributions of the arrestees and the residents are quite similar; and the disparities partly reflect the extremely heavy participation of teen-agers and young adults who are somewhat more likely to be unskilled. Also, the Department of Labor's figures sharply underestimate unemployment in the ghettos;[19] and the remaining disparities largely reflect the exceptionally high unemployment among black teen-agers and young adults. So, if age is again held constant, the rioters were about as likely to be unskilled and unemployed as the potential rioters.

A great many rioters were also born in the South.[20] They were a majority (ranging from 51 per cent in the Chicago riots to 66 per cent in the Los Angeles riots) in five of the eight riots for which information is available and a large minority (ranging from 19 per cent in the Cincinnati riots to 47 per cent in the Harlem riots) in the other three.

But a great many potential rioters were born in the South too. Indeed, the potential rioters were more likely to be born in the South in four of the eight cities; and in none of the other four were they less likely to be born there by much more than a few percentage points. Doubtless the extremely heavy participation of teen-agers and young adults, who were less likely to be born in the South, reduces the proportion of newcomers involved in the riots. But if the arrestees are again separated into two groups, with twenty-five years of age the dividing point, the difference, small to begin with, becomes negligible. Of the younger rioters 36 per cent were born in the South; and of the older rioters 62 per cent were born there; and these figures differ little from the figures for the ghetto residents of the same age. So, if age is held constant again, the rioters were about as likely to be born in the South as the potential rioters.

A majority of the arrestees (ranging from 57 per cent in the Detroit riots to 82 per cent in the Cleveland riots) also had prior criminal records in all but two of the eight riots for which information is available. But it is one thing to have a record and quite another to be a criminal; and there are a number of reasons why these figures do not prove that the arrestees were criminals. First, a criminal record in the United States simply means an arrest, as opposed to a conviction; probably no more than one half of the arrestees with a record had been convicted, and probably no more than one quarter for a major crime. Second, according to the President's Crime Commission, which has made the only estimate I know of, roughly 50 to 90 per cent of black males in the ghettos have criminal records.[21] And third, if the findings of the President's Commission on

17. The findings for the arrestees are based on black males eighteen years of age and older. The findings for the Newark arrestees come from *N.J. Riot Report*, 271, and the findings for the Detroit arrestees from Lachman and Singer, "The Detroit Riot of 1967," 14.
18. "Unemployment in 15 Metropolitan Areas," *Monthly Labor Review*, January 1968, 5–6; *N.J. Riot Report*, 271.
19. Especially because the Department only counts people actively seeking employment. See "New Jobless Count Ups the Figure," *Business Week*, December 10, 1966, 160–62, and *Kerner Commission Report*, 257. For further remarks, see Fogelson and Hill, "Who Riots?" 236.
20. The South as defined here includes Alabama, Arkansas, Florida, Georgia, Louisiana, Mississippi, North Carolina, South Carolina, Tennessee, Texas, and Virginia. For obvious reasons I have excluded Atlanta from this survey.

21. See President's Commission on Law Enforcement, *The Challenge of Crime*, 75, and Ronald Christensen, "Projected Percentage of U.S. Population with Criminal Arrest and Conviction Records," in the Commission's *Task Force Report: Science and Technology*, (Washington, D.C., 1967), 216–18.

Crime in the District of Columbia are applicable elsewhere, the arrestees were much more likely to be employed and much less likely to have criminal records (and especially major criminal records) than convicted felons.[22] Hence to label the rioters as criminals is simply to brand most blacks (or at any rate most black males) as criminals.

If the firsthand descriptions of the riots are reliable, a few left-wing radicals and black nationalists encouraged the rioters and exploited the rioting. It would have been surprising had they not done so. But according to the arrest sheets, the overwhelming majority of the rioters were not outsiders. In none of the twelve riots did the proportion of the arrestees who resided in the stricken cities fall below 90 per cent. It ranged from 92 per cent in Newark to 100 per cent in Cincinnati. According to the Kerner Commission, too, most rioters were long-term residents of their cities.[23] The arrest sheets do not of course reveal whether or not a few agitators conspired to bring about the riots. But a good deal of other evidence is available on this point. The F.B.I. issued a brief report on the 1964 riots; F.B.I. director J. Edgar Hoover and Attorney General Ramsey Clark released public statements on the 1967 riots; and the Kerner Commission made a thorough analysis of the federal, state, and municipal reports on the 1967 riots.[24] And on the basis of this information, it is quite clear that the agitators did not secretly organize or effectively control the riots.

Hence the second point of the riffraff theory is inaccurate too. Depending on the riot, roughly two thirds to nine tenths of the arrestees were teen-agers or young adults, one half to two thirds single or otherwise unattached, one half to three quarters unskilled, one fifth to two fifths unemployed,

and one third to two thirds uprooted; and one third to nine tenths had prior criminal records. But these figures do not sharply distinguish the rioters from the potential rioters; and to the extent that they do this reflects mainly the extremely heavy involvement of young adults who are more likely than their fathers to be single, unskilled, and unemployed (though not uprooted or previously arrested). That young men born and raised in the ghettos who reached maturity in the 1950s and 1960s participated so heavily in the riots is not surprising. What is surprising is that, in view of the historic efficacy of the restraints on rioting among blacks, fully one quarter to one half of the arrestees (again depending on the riot) were skilled or semiskilled, three fifths to four fifths were employed, and one third to two thirds were northern-born. Thus to claim that the rioters were mainly the riffraff and outside agitators rather than fairly typical young adult males is to seriously misinterpret the riots.

Before concluding the analysis of the second point of the riffraff theory, however, it is necessary to examine it from a somewhat different viewpoint. Even though the theory is disproved when the rioters are treated city by city, it may be confirmed if they are considered according to day of arrest, type of offense, year of the riot, or region of the country. In other words, even if the riffraff theory fails to account for the rioters as a whole, it might account for the rioters who were arrested on the first day or the second day, for looting or arson, in 1964 or 1967, or in the North or the South. It is impossible to tell whether there were differences from one region to another because not enough arrest sheets are on hand from the southern riots. But it is possible to say whether there were differences from one day to another, from one type of offense to the next, and from one year to another because day of arrest and criminal charge are included on the arrest sheets and the sheets are available from three or more riots in 1964,

22. See *Report of the President's Commission on Crime in the District of Columbia* (Washington, D.C., 1966), chapter 3.
23. *Kerner Commission Report*, 232.
24. Federal Bureau of Investigation, "Report on the 1964 Riots," September 1964; New York *Times*, August 2, 3, 1967; *Kerner Commission Report*, 201–2.

1966, and 1967.[25] By so doing it is possible to evaluate further this point of the riffraff theory and in the process to learn more about participation in the 1960s riots.

If the arrestees[26] are broken down into blacks arrested on the first day, second day, and third day and after, their profiles are extremely perplexing. The blacks arrested on the first day were most likely to be under twenty-five years of age, single, unskilled, and unemployed and next most likely to have a criminal record; but they were also least likely to be born in the South. The blacks arrested on the second day were most likely to have a criminal record and next most likely to be under twenty-five years of age, unskilled, unemployed, and born in the South; but they were also least likely to be single. And the blacks arrested on the third day were most likely to be born in the South and next most likely to be single; but they were also least likely to be under twenty-five years of age, unskilled, and unemployed and to have a criminal record. Hence the blacks arrested on the first day bear the closest resemblance to the riffraff. But they were not only the least likely to be born in the South but also the most likely to be white-collar workers. In view of these inconsistencies it is safe to conclude that the riffraff theory is not confirmed if the arrestees are classified according to day of arrest.

A few patterns do emerge, however. The relatively young, single, unskilled, and unemployed blacks were more active on the first day of the riots than on the second day and more active on the second day than on the third day. The opposite is true for the relatively old, married, skilled, and employed blacks. Perhaps even more revealing, this pattern is reversed if the rioters are classified according to birthplace. The blacks born in the North were more active on the first day of the riots than on the second day and

more active on the second day than on the third day. Again, the opposite is true for the blacks born in the South. If the arrest sheets are reliable, then, the upcoming (and presumably more militant)[27] generation of urban blacks started the rioting. And only later on did the current (and presumably less militant) generation of urban blacks overcome its inhibitions and join its children in the streets of the ghettos.

If the arrestees are broken down into rioters,[28] looters, arsonists, and assaulters,[29] their profiles are once again rather inconsistent. The rioters were most likely to be unskilled and born in the South; but they were also least likely to be under twenty-five years of age and unemployed. The looters were most likely to be unemployed and second most likely to be single, unskilled, and born in the South and to have a criminal record; but they were also least likely to be under twenty-five years of age. By contrast, the arsonists were most likely to be under twenty-five years of age and single and to have a criminal record; but they were also least likely to be unskilled, unemployed, and born in the South. The assaulters were second most likely to be under twenty-five years of age and unemployed; but they were also second least likely to be single, unskilled, and born in the South and to have a criminal record. Thus the rioters, looters, arsonists, and assaulters all differ enough from the riffraff that it is fair to say that the riffraff theory is not confirmed if the arrestees are classified according to criminal charges.

A few patterns also emerge here, however. Leaving aside the rioters arrested for curfew

25. In 1965 the sheets are available only for the Los Angeles riots.
26. I have excluded the Detroit and Los Angeles riots from this analysis because the great number of arrestees there might skew the findings.

27. Gary Marx, *Protest and Prejudice* (New York, 1967), 53–54; Angus Campbell and Howard Schuman, "Racial Attitudes in Fifteen American Cities," in *Supplemental Studies for the National Advisory Commission on Civil Disorders* (Washington, D.C., 1968), 17–19, 55–57.
28. The rioters were arrested mainly for disorderly conduct, curfew violations, and other minor offenses.
29. The assaulters were arrested mainly for throwing stones, obstructing policemen, and carrying weapons.

violation and the other relatively minor offenses lumped under rioting, the looters
were probably the least dangerous and disaffected of the participants. Hence it is noteworthy that, as the blacks least likely to be
under twenty-five years of age and second
most likely to be born in the South, they
bear the closest resemblance to the current
(or passing) generation of urban blacks. That
they were most likely to be unemployed and
the second most likely to be unskilled suggests that they looted out of an immediate
sense of economic deprivation rather than a
profound sense of racial exploitation.[30]
Also, leaving aside the snipers, whose involvement in the riots was greatly exag-
gerated and whose representation among the
arrestees was virtually nil, the arsonists were
the most dangerous and disaffected. It
should therefore be noted that, as the blacks
most likely to be under twenty-five years of
age and least likely to be born in the South,
they bear the closest resemblance to the
upcoming generation of urban blacks. That
they were least likely to be unskilled and, by
a wide margin, unemployed suggests that
intense racial militancy is not inconsistent
with relatively sound economic position.[31]

If the arrestees are broken down into the
blacks who rioted in 1964, 1966, and
1967,[32] their profiles are again quite perplexing. The 1964 rioters were most likely
to be unskilled and next most likely to be
under twenty-five years of age, single, and
unemployed. By contrast, the 1966 rioters
were most likely to be born in the South and
to have a criminal record, but only next
most likely to be under twenty-five years of
age, single, unskilled, and unemployed. And
the 1967 rioters were most likely to be
under twenty-five years of age, single, and
unemployed, but also least likely to be un-

skilled and born in the South and to have a
criminal record. Hence none of these
groups—nor, for that matter, the Los
Angeles rioters—consistently (or even re-
motely) resembles the riffraff. And it is reasonable to conclude that the riffraff theory
is not confirmed if the arrestees are classified
according to year of the riot either.

A few patterns also emerge here, however.
The young and single blacks were more
active in the 1967 riots than in the 1966
riots and more active in the 1966 riots than
in the 1964 riots. So were the unskilled
blacks. The opposite is true for the mature
and married blacks. It is also true for the
unemployed blacks. Perhaps even more noteworthy, the blacks born in the North were
more active in the 1967 riots than in the
1966 riots and more active in the 1966 riots
than in the 1964 riots. And the opposite is
true for the blacks born in the South. In
1964, 51 per cent of the rioters were born in
the South and 44 per cent in the North; in
1966, the year of the Atlanta riots[33] 52 per
cent were born in the South and 47 per cent
in the North; and in 1967, 33 per cent were
born in the South and 64 per cent in the
North. Leaving aside the inconsistency in
occupational and employment status, which
I cannot explain, the arrest sheets suggest
that the upcoming generation of urban
blacks has played an increasingly active role
in the riots.

To sum up, the arrest sheets do not confirm the second point of the riffraff theory if
the arrestees are classified according to day
of arrest, type of offense, or year of the riot.
But they do suggest a few patterns in the
riot process. Apparently the upcoming generation of urban blacks, the young and single
blacks born in the northern ghettos, joined
in the riots first; and it was particularly
active in the rioting and burning. The current generation of urban blacks, the mature
and married blacks born in the rural South,
joined in thereafter; and it was particularly

---

30. See chapter 4.
31. It should be noted, however, that the rsonists
were less than 1 per cent (65 out of about 7600) of
the arrestees.
32. I have excluded the Detroit rioters here because the great number of arrestees there might
skew the findings.

33. A total of 775 blacks, 95 per cent of whom
were born in the South, were arrested in Atlanta.

active in the rioting and looting. What is more, the upcoming (and presumably more militant) generation has increased its participation over time much more rapidly than the older generation. Hence the fairly typical young adults born and raised in the northern ghettos who reached maturity in the 1950s and 1960s were not just the main source of rioters. They were also the rioters who joined in at the beginning, who engaged in the most serious forms of violence, and who, in all likelihood, will predominate in future riots.[34]

The third point of the riffraff theory—that the overwhelming majority of the black population, the 98 or 99 per cent who did not join in the rioting, unequivocally opposed the riots—also has a certain plausibility. A sizable majority of the potential rioters refrained from rioting, and their restraint could be construed as a repudiation of the riots. In one city after another, too, many moderate black leaders—among them, James Farmer of New York, John A. Buggs of Los Angeles, James Threatt of Newark, and Nicholas Hood of Detroit—labored valiantly to restrain the rioters.[35] And many ordinary blacks registered sharp protest against the violence while the rioting was under way and expressed extreme dismay at the consequences when it was over. From Washington, too, a group of national black leaders, including Martin Luther King, Jr., A. Philip Randolph, Roy Wilkins, and Whitney Young criticized the riots as "ineffective, disruptive and highly damaging" and called on the blacks to "forego the temptation to disregard the law."[36] This evidence, it could be argued, proves that the overwhelming majority of the black population unequivocally opposed the riots.

And yet it could also be argued that this evidence proves nothing of the kind. About one out of five potential rioters did join in the riots, and the other four might have refrained from rioting more because they feared the local policemen and National Guardsmen than because they disapproved of the riots. Moreover, the moderate black leaders labored in vain to restrain the rioters: no matter how strongly committed to their race or how deeply concerned about their community, they had little impact on the course of the riots.[37] Also, many ordinary blacks objected to the violence not so much because they sympathized with the authorities as because they suspected that blacks, not whites, would suffer the worst losses. If Martin Luther King, Jr., and other moderates appealed for nonviolence, Stokely Carmichael and other militants did not; and by the end of the summer of 1967 it was not clear which, if either, of them spoke for the black people.[38] Hence the evidence proves nothing conclusively—except perhaps that to gauge community sentiment about the riots with any accuracy it is essential to raise more revealing questions, probe more relevant sources, and offer more tentative answers.

To begin with, it is not particularly enlightening simply to ask whther the black population supported or opposed the riots. To do so is to assume that the blacks felt clearly one way or another about the rioting, when, in all probability, they had mixed feelings, and that the blacks agreed basically about the rioting, when, in all likelihood, they had sharp disagreements. It is more illuminating to ask whether the blacks believed that the riots were beneficial or essential or, even if not, inevitable, and whether the blacks objected to the rioting mainly on principled or pragmatic grounds. It is also more illuminating to ask what proportion of blacks (and especially of blacks who did not participate as rioters or counter-rioters) and which groups of blacks considered the riot-

34. For a brief analysis of the Washington rioters of 1968, see Gilbert *et al., Ten Blocks from The White House,* 226—35.
35. F.B.I., "Report on the 1964 Riots," 5—6. See also chapter 5.
36. New York *Times,* July 27, 1967.

37. See chapter 6.
38. New York *Times,* July 14—18, 26—29, August 1, 2, 7, 10, 11, 16, 1967.

ing beneficial, essential, and inevitable. To phrase the questions in these ways is to allow for the ambiguities in the black positions and the differences among the ghetto residents which are at the core of the black community's attitudes toward the riots.

Unfortunately the information available is extremely scanty. The position of the moderate black leaders is well documented; so is the ideology of the militant black leaders. The activities of the rioters are also well known; and so are the efforts of the counter-rioters. But the leaders and the participants are a minority, even if a substantial one, of the ghetto population. And about the position and activities of the rank-and-file and uninvolved blacks, not much is known. Nor are the studies of arrest sheets particularly helpful. There are, however, a few local and national opinion surveys taken in the ghettos during the 1960s[39] as well as some firsthand descriptions of the riots and on-the-spot interviews with the ghetto residents made during or shortly after the rioting.[40] And these opinion surveys and impressionistic accounts convey with reasonable accuracy the black community's sentiments about the riots.

According to the opinion surveys, the black community's attitude is ambivalent. Of the blacks in Los Angeles interviewed by U.C.L.A.'s Institute of Government and Public Affairs in 1965, only one third favored the rioting, yet two thirds believed that it would increase the whites' awareness and sympathy and improve the blacks' position; only one eighth thought that violent protest was their most effective weapon, yet two thirds believed that the riots had a purpose and five sixths that the victims deserved their treatment; three

fourths preferred negotiation and nonviolent protest, yet only one fourth believed that there would be no more riots in Los Angeles.[41] Of the blacks interviewed across the nation by Louis Harris and Associates in 1966, 68 per cent felt that they stood to lose by the rioting; yet 64 per cent felt that it has helped their cause, 20 per cent that it has hurt, and 17 per cent that it has made no difference; 59 per cent were confident that they will win their rights without violence, but 21 per cent were convinced that violence will be necessary and 20 per cent were not certain; 61 per cent predicted that there will be further rioting, 31 per cent were not sure, and only 8 per cent predicted that there will be no rioting in the future.[42]

According to the Institute of Government and Public Affairs, moreover, the blacks in Los Angeles objected to the rioting mainly on pragmatic rather than principled grounds; they disapproved of the consequences of the riots rather than the riots themselves. Whereas 29 per cent disliked the burning and 19 per cent the looting, 21 per cent protested the shooting and the killing and 13 per cent the police action, and only 1 per cent objected to the rioting and 1 per cent to the assault.[43] According to the Institute of Government and Public Affairs, too, the relatively well-to-do and well-educated supported the Los Angeles riots as much as the less well-off and less well-educated, though in Detroit, according to the University of Michigan's Survey Research Center, the counter-rioters tended to be more affluent and better educated than the rioters. And according to the Harris organization, lower- and lower-middle-income blacks were a bit more likely to regard the riots favorably than middle- and upper-middle-income blacks; and blacks thirty-four years and younger were much more likely to do so than

39. William Brink and Louis Harris, *Black and White* (New York, 1967), 184–279; Hazel Erskine, "The Polls: Demonstrations and Race Riots," *Public Opinion Quarterly*, Winter 1967–68, 655–77; Sears, "Riot Activity"; Schulman, "Ghetto Residence."

40. Frank Besag, *The Anatomy of a Riot: Buffalo, 1967* (Buffalo, N.Y., 1967), 138–39, 180–81, 188–90.

41. Sears, "Riot Activity," table 35; Schulman, "Ghetto Residence," 23–24, tables 5, 5.1.

42. Brink and Harris, *Black and White*, 260–66; Erskine, "The Polls," 671.

43. Sears, "Riot Activity, table 17.

blacks fifty years and older and even more than blacks between the ages of thirty-five and forty-nine.[44]

These findings are consistent with the impressionistic accounts of the riots. Firsthand descriptions of the riots and on-the-spot interviews with ghetto residents reveal a great deal of tacit support for the rioters among the non-rioters. Apparently many of them also saw the rioting as a legitimate protest against ghetto grievances, a protest which, if need be, would be delivered again. Their feelings were well articulated by a middle-age black woman who ran an art gallery in south-central Los Angeles: "I will not take a Molotov cocktail," she said, "but I am as mad as they (the rioters) are."[45] These findings are also consistent with a common-sense approach to the riots. After all, is it conceivable that several hundred riots could have erupted in nearly every black ghetto in the United States over the past five years against the opposition of 98 to 99 per cent of the black community? And is it conceivable that militant young blacks would have ignored the customary restraints on rioting in the United States, including the commitment to orderly social change, unless they enjoyed the tacit support of at least a sizable minority of the black community?

If the survey research, arrest data, and impressionistic accounts are indicative, the rioters were a small but significant minority of the black population, fairly representative of the ghetto residents, and especially of the young adult males, and tacitly supported by at least a large minority of the black community. Hence the riots were a manifestation of race and racism in the United States, a reflection of the social problems of black ghettos, a protest against the essential conditions of life there, and an indicator of the necessity for fundamental changes in American society. If the riffraff theory has been inaccurate in the past, it will probably be invalid in the future too. The riots appear to be gaining support from many segments of the black community. Of the blacks asked by Louis Harris in 1966 if they would join in riots, 15 per cent replied that they would, 24 per cent that they were unsure, and 61 per cent that they would not. Moreover, the lower-middle-, middle-, and upper-middle-income blacks were more likely to respond affirmatively than the lower-income blacks. And of the blacks thirty-four years and younger, the upcoming generation, fully 19 per cent said that they would join a riot, 24 per cent that they were uncertain, and only 57 per cent that they would not. At the start of the 1970s these responses are anything but reassuring.[46]

44. Brink and Harris, *Black and White*, 264.
45. *McCone Commission Archives*, XV, interview 29; XVI, interview 90; Besag, *Anatomy of a Riot*, 138–39, 188–89.

46. Brink and Harris, *Black and White*, 266. For a more recent survey of black attitudes toward rioting, see Campbell and Schuman, "Racial Attitudes in Fifteen American Cities," 47–57.

Civil Disorder Participation:

A Critical Examination of Recent Research

CLARK McPHAIL

INTRODUCTION

Until recently, students of collective behavior were without the necessary empirical data to test many of their hypotheses concerning the occurrence of or participation in riots and civil disorders. This situation has been altered within the last decade by the secondary analysis of historical records (e.g., Rude, 1964), by the use of census data (e.g., Lieberson and Silverman, 1965) and most notably by the increased incidence of civil disorders in the United States during the 1960's and the consequent increase in civil disorder research.

Whether investigators have attempted to account for the occurrence of or individual participation in civil disorders, a single explanatory model has explicitly or implicitly guided or provided a basis for *ex post facto* interpretation of the majority of the findings.

The sociological and popular cliché is that "frustration" or "discontent" or "despair" is the root cause of rebellion. Cliché or not, the basic relationship appears to be as fundamental to understanding civil strife as the

law of gravity is to atmospheric physics: relative deprivation, the phrase I have used, is a necessary precondition for civil strife of any kind, and the more severe is relative deprivation, the more likely and severe is strife.

Underlying this relative deprivation approach to civil strife is a frustration-aggression mechanism, apparently a fundamental part of our psychological make-up. When we feel thwarted in an attempt to get something we want, we are likely to get angry, and when we get angry the most satisfying inherent response is to strike out at the source of frustration (Gurr, 1968:52–53).

A typical version of the "deprivation-frustration-aggression" (DFA) explanation of civil disorder goes something like the following. Minority group members have been deprived of a variety of educational, occupational, financial, residential, and recreational opportunities. These are typically referred to as "underlying causes" (Lieberson and Silverman, 1965) and may be conceptualized and measured as absolute or relative deprivations. For example, it has been argued that Black Americans can compare their condi-

From C. McPhail, Civil disorder participation: A critical examination of recent research. *American Sociological Review*, 1971, *36*, 1058–1073. Reprinted by permission of the American Sociological Association.

tion to that of the middle-class life style of white Americans as portrayed on television (Spilerman, 1970:640). Their "absolute" deprivation is set in sharp relief by the recognition that others in the society have what they are denied by virtue of their minority group status. As a consequence of this "relative" deprivation, it is argued, frustration increases. The DFA linkage is rendered complete by some salient action, typically referred to as a "precipitating event" (Lieberson and Silverman, 1965), in which a majority group member blatantly discriminates against a minority group member. This comes to the attention of other minority group members who criticize, challenge, or attack the discriminator. In response to this, (additional) social control agents are called to the scene to deal with the threat to law and order, property rights, etc. Their arrival and/or action attracts more minority group members, a confrontation develops and minority group members respond to their frustration with aggression in the form of violence against the property and persons of the majority group which the discriminator and/or social control agents represent. This scenario provides an oversimplified but essentially accurate illustration of the DFA explanation of civil disorder occurrence and participation.

This explanation has been examined on both aggregate and individual levels by a number of investigators over the past six years. Studies by Lieberson and Silverman (1965), Bloombaum (1968), Downes (1968), Wanderer (1969), and Spilerman (1970) have examined the relationship between the socioeconomic-political attributes of cities and the occurrence or intensity of civil disorders.[1] This research has provided data for an "aggregate" assessment of the DFA explanation. The general pattern in these data has been recently summarized by Spilerman: "In all instances, upon controlling for Negro population, the explanation

failed to account for the distribution of disorders. More generally, we conclude that differences in disorder-proneness cannot be explained in terms of variations in the objective situation of the Negro. Instead, an explanation which identifies disorder proneness as an attribute of the individual seems better to account for the findings" (Spilerman, 1970:645). He provides no evidence for this alternate explanation of civil disorders. His contention remains an empirical question. However, it is a question for which there are considerable available and relevant data, for his contention is one shared or anticipated by the majority of researchers studying individual participation in the civil disorders of the 1960's. The bulk of that research examined the association between individual attributes and civil disorder participation. The objectives of the present paper are to summarize the results of those studies, to assess the adequacy of the DFA explanation of individual participation in terms of those results, and, to critically evaluate the focus of these studies in terms of its utility for future research in this area.[2]

A SUMMARY OF THE RIOT PARTICIPATION DATA

This summary is based upon an examination of ten reports of research on individual participation in five different riots: Los Angeles (Watts), 1965; Omaha, 1966; Detriot, 1967; Milwaukee, 1967; and Newark, 1967. I will first describe the operational measures of riot participation employed in these studies and then describe and summarize the range of "independent variables" examined in association with riot participation. Finally, I will report the results of

---

1. My comments on "riot occurrence" research are restricted to studies of civil disorder in the U.S.

2. Admittedly, the comparison of different studies by different investigators with different samples, operational procedures, etc., is extremely problematic. I know of no way of resolving these problems of quality control. Nevertheless, in my judgment, it is time to attempt some overall summary and assessment of what we have learned about riot participation from the research done in the past six years.

secondary analysis of these data, indicating the magnitude of association which obtains between the various "independent variables" and the various measures of riot participation.

THE DEPENDENT VARIABLES IN RIOT PARTICIPATION STUDIES

What have researchers attempted to account for in their examination of riot participation?

Type I. Arrestee Status. The most frequently employed measure of participation has been the arrestee status of the respondent. Six studies compared a sample of respondents arrested on riot charges with a control sample of the nonarrestee community in which the disorder occurred (Sears and McConahay, 1967a; Tomlinson, 1967; Flaming, 1968; Reynolds, 1968; Geschwender *et al.,* 1969a; Geschwender *et al.,* 1969b).

Type II. Respondent's Reported Status. The next most frequent measure of participation has been that of the respondent's report of his participation status during the disorder; i.e., his report of whether or not, or the extent to which, he was "active" during the disorder. Four studies employed this measure (Murphy and Watson, 1967; Raine, 1967; Sears and McConahay, 1967b; Tomlinson, 1967).

Type III. Respondent's Witness of Others' Behavior(s). Two studies operationalized participation in terms of the respondent's reported witness of specific riot behaviors by others during the disorder, viz., shooting, stoning, burning, and crowds of people. In one study these witness-reports were combined into an index, and respondents were differentiated in terms of the relative frequency with which they reported witnessing the events (Sears and McConahay, 1967b). In the second study, respondents were simply differentiated in terms of whether they had observed each separate behavior (Tomlinson, 1967).

Type IV. Respondent's Reported Status and Witness of Others' Behavior(s). A single study combined respondents' reports of their own participation status (as in Type II, above) with reports of witnessing the riot behaviors of others (as in Type III, above) (Sears and McConahay, 1967a). Self-reported "active" witnesses to looting, burning and crowds were classified "Gladiators." Self-reported "not-active" witnesses to the same three phenomena were classified "Active Spectators." Self-reported "not-active" witnesses to two of the phenomena were classified "Distant Spectators." Self-reported "not active" non-witnesses were classified as "Saw-Nothings."

Type V. Respondent's Reported Status and Behavior(s). The Kerner Commission Studies (Caplan and Paige, 1968a, 1968b) combined respondents' reports of their "active/non-active" status with reports of some of their specific behaviors during the disorder. Respondents were classified as "rioters" if they reported they were active *or* reported breaking windows, looting, firebombing, or other "anti-social" [sic] behaviors. Respondents were classified as "Not-Involved" if they reported staying at home or merely observing the riot from in front of their homes. Respondents were classified as "Counter-rioters" if they reported trying to stop the riot, calling the fire department, or engaging in some other "pro-social" [sic] behavior, irrespective of their report of their active or not-active status.

THE INDEPENDENT VARIABLES IN RIOT PARTICIPATION STUDIES

The "independent" variables were identified by examining the various research reports for all cross-tabulations between the five measures of riot participation described above and all other variables.[3] The latter were designated "independent" variables by

3. I did not include that category of independent variables involving respondent's "explanations" of why they participated. These constitute a valuable source of data on "vocabularies of motives" and deserve separate examination and discussion.

virtue of the fact that the original investigators explicitly or implicitly treated them as factors producing or resulting in riot participation.

A large number of different independent variables were examined by the various investigators in relation to riot participation. A separate treatment of each would be prohibitive. I arbitrarily classified these different independent variables into 24 specific categories and then regrouped them into six more general categories.[4] A description of these categories and their proportionate use in the riot participation research is presented in the first two columns of Table 1.

Social science research has come to depend heavily upon attitudinal data to predict the occurrence of phenomena of interest (Tausky and Piedmont, 1968). The riot participation studies are no exception. Respondents' "Attitude Statements" constituted 28% of all independent variables examined in relation to riot participation measures. This category was followed by approximately equivalent use of "Social Relationships and Interaction Patterns" (20%),[5] "Socioeconomic Attributes" (19%),[6] and respondents' reported "Experiences of and/or Opinions about Discrimination Toward Blacks" (17%).[7] "Demographic Attributes" of respondents constituted about 10%, and measures of "Political

Participation" about 5% of the remaining independent variables examined in relation to riot participation.[8]

MAGNITUDE AND DIRECTION OF ASSOCIATION

The relationships between the different independent variables and measures of riot participation have been summarized and interpreted in a number of different scholarly and popular publications. Many of the relationships have been reported as statistically significant. Few of the accompanying discussions, however, have specified the magnitude of association. It is precisely the magnitude, and to a great extent the direction, of association that is critical for our assessment of the relationship between the different classes of independent variables and riot participation.

A total of 287 associations between the aforementioned 24 categories of independent variables and the five measures of participation were presented in the research reports that I examined.[9] All 287 associations were subjected to secondary analysis to determine the magnitude and direction of association involved. To determine the magnitude of association, I computed Cramer's V for each of the 287 contingency tables.[10] Each table was then examined by

---

4. A complete listing of the specific associations from which these classifications were constructed can be obtained by writing the author.

5. This included number of group memberships, type of group membership, interaction with neighbors, church attendance, living alone or with others, organization membership and a social isolation index which combines information on organizational membership, living alone or with others, marital status and length of residence in the riot city.

6. This included SES level of residential area of the respondent, condition of the respondent's residence, and respondent's judgment of his personal economic status during the past few years.

7. A large proportion of these associations involve "opinions about discrimination" and thus would be appropriately considered as attitudinal items. They are treated here under "discrimination" by virtue of their frequent combination with reported experience of discrimination on several multivariate indices.

8. Attitudinal data are typically characterized as individual attributes from which tendencies or predispositions to behave are inferred. If all attitudinal data, including opinions about discrimination, are lumped together with the data on socioeconomic and demographic attributes of individuals, 75% of all the independent variables examined in the riot participation studies were individual attributes.

9. One hundred and seventy-two (60%) involved bivariate associations and 115 (40%) involved bivariate associations with controls.

10. Cramer's V was used because it ranges from .00 to 1.00 and, by virtue of controlling for N and df, may be compared across different sized contingency tables. V is based on χ^2. Where χ^2 values were not reported by the original investigators, they were computed by the author. Where the data required for computing V were not reported, the original investigators' own judgment about the magnitude of association was accepted. This involved eleven associations, three described as "not significant" and eight as "low" by Caplan and Paige (1968b).

Table 1. Independent Variables—Frequency of Use and of Different Magnitudes of Association with Riot Participation

Independent Variables	f	%	n.s.	.00 .09	.10 .19	.20 .29	.30 .39	.40 +	Total
ATTITUDE STATEMENTS (I)		28%							
1. Political Attributes	42	15	9		21	10	2		42
2. Job/housing Atts. & Expects.	22	8	8	1	5	4	2	2	22
3. Blacks' Atts. re:whites	10	3	1		7	2			10
4. Blacks' Atts. re:blacks	5	2			3	2			5
SOCIAL RELATIONS & INTER-ACTIONS (II)		20%							
5. Blacks social contacts w/whites	25	9	17		6	2			25
6. Other relations & inter.*	23	8	6	2	12	2	1		23
7. Marital status	6	2	1		1	4			6
8. Structure-Family of Orientation	4	1	2		2				4
SOCIOECONOMIC ATTRIBUTES (III)		19%							
9. Attribute Consistency	23	8	11		5	7			23
10. Education level	10	3	1	1	3	4	1		10
11. Income level	8	3	5		2	1			8
12. Employment	7	2	2		3	2			7
13. Underemployment	3	1			2	1			3
14. Occupational level	3	1	1	1	1				3
15. Other SES Indicators**	3	1	2		1				3
EXPERIENCE/OPINION OF DIS-CRIMINATION (IV)		17%							
16. Exper./Opinion of Police Malpractice	40	14	13	1	17	4	5		40
17. Exper./Opinion of Discrmination	10	3	2	1	7				10
DEMOGRAPHIC ATTRIBUTES (V)		10%							
18. Age	9	3			4	2	1	2	9
19. Place of Birth/Length of Residence	8	3	2		4	1	1		8
20. Region of Socialization	6	2	1	1		4			6
21. Sex	5	2	2	1	1			1	5
22. Ethnicity	1	0						1	1
POLITICAL PARTICIPATION (VI)		5%							
23. Voting Behavior	12	4	5		5	2			12
24. Civil Rights Discussion/ Activities	2	1			1	1			2
TOTALS	287		91	9	113	55	13	6	287
		100%	32%	3%	39%	19%	5%	2%	100%

*See fn. 5; **see fn. 6.

inspection to determine the presence or absence of a monotonic distribution of cases consistent with the direction specified by the hypothesis. Finally, I examined each category of independent variables and each type of participation measure for salient patterns of relationship, and all associations with a magnitude of .30 or higher were sorted out for further consideration. The results of these analyses are presented below.

The frequency with which varying magnitudes of association obtained between the 24 specific categories of independent variables and all measures of riot participation is summarized in columns three through eight of Table 1. For convenience throughout my discussion, I have made the conventional division of the range of magnitudes of association into four categories: not significant;[11] low = less than .29; moderate = .30 to .59; and high = .60 and above.

Of the 287 associations examined, 91 (32%) were not significant at the .05 level. Of the remaining associations, 177 (61%) were low, and 17 associations (6%) were moderate. Only two of the 287 associations (1%) were of a magnitude of .60 or higher.[12] Seventy percent of the 287 associations exhibited monotonic distributions consistent with the direction specified by the hypothesis, while only 13% exhibited distributions opposite those specified. In 17% of the associations the distribution of cases and non-monotonic and therefore also inconsistent with the direction specified by the hypothesis. It may be noted that the majority of associations with riot participation are statistically significant and in a direction consistent with the hypotheses under examination. At the same time the over-

whelming majority of these associations are of a consistently low magnitude.

Three questions should be raised about these results. First, what are the implications of these data for the DFA explanation of individual riot participation? Second, how do the few moderate and high associations contribute to our understanding of the riot participation process? Third, what are the implications of these results for the foci of future studies of individual participation in civil disorders and related phenomena?

THE DEPRIVATION-FRUSTRATION-AGGRESSION EXPLANATION

The hypotheses which draw upon this explanation are seldom submitted to inclusive empirical test. More frequently than not, the relationship between deprivation *and* aggression, or frustration and aggression, is examined, and the function of the third variable is inferred. This is invariably the case with examinations of "absolute deprivation" in relation to riot participation; i.e., it is assumed that absolute deprivation produces frustration and in turn riot participation. Similarly, examinations of frustration and riot participation rest on a necessary inference of prior or concomitant deprivation. On the other hand, examinations of relationships between measures of relative deprivation and riot participation almost necessarily measure a discrepancy between actual deprivation and an alternative state (which by inference is more desirable) and thus constitute simultaneous measures of deprivation and frustration in relation to riot participation.

In the data reported above, 173 of the 287 associations have some bearing upon the DFA argument.[13] Of the 173 associations,

---

11. The .05 level was employed and, because the direction of the association was at issue, the one-tailed test was used.
12. Of the 172 bivariate associations, 11 (6%) were between .30 and 1.00. Of the 115 bivariate associations with controls, 8 (7%) were between .30 and 1.00. Thus, of the 19 moderate and high associations, 11 (58%) involved simple bivariate contingencies and 8 (42%) involved bivariate with control contingencies.

13. I acknowledge my arbitrary imposition of an interpretive scheme on the available data. However, the classification of these data into the deprivation, frustration, and deprivation-frustration categories is consistent with their classification by the original investigators and with the theoretical literature on civil disorder participation.

50 are between various measures of deprivation and riot participation; e.g., personal
experience of police malpractice, education
level, income level, employment, occupational level, other socioeconomic status
indicators, and one demographic attribute—
ethnicity. There are 84 associations between
various measures of frustration and riot
participation. These are essentially attitudinal measures,[14] e.g., attitudes about the
political system, an opinion index of police
malpractices, attitudes and expectations regarding whites.[15] There are 39 associations
between combined measures of deprivation
and frustration, and riot participation. These
include all the socioeconomic attribute consistency measures, measures combining experience of *and* opinion about police
malpractices, measures of job and housing
attitudes and expectations,[16] measures of
underemployment, and black attitudes regarding whites and blacks who are in better
financial conditions.[17] Table 2 summarizes

14. I prefer to take these data at face value as
statements of frustration made by the individual
respondent. This avoids making the problematic
inference from the "overt statement" to some underlying or latent tendency. For a similar treatment of attitude statements, see DeFleur and
Westie (1963).
15. The index of consumer discontent was employed by Murphy (1967) and was based on
whether the respondent had complaints often,
sometimes, or rarely about practices of stores and
merchants in six areas: credit policy, overcharging,
inferior goods, insulting remarks, check cashing
policy, and quick repossession. The one item involving black attitudes toward whites was the respondent's extent of agreement with the assertion:
"Sometimes I hate white people" (Caplan and
Paige, 1968a).
16. Seventeen of the 22 associations involving
statements of "job and housing expectations" were
classified as tests of the "frustration" hypothesis.
The remaining five were classified as tests of the
"deprivation-frustration" hypothesis. Four of these
examined attitudes toward the growth of job opportunities for blacks, controlling for different
levels of educational and occupational achievement. The fifth examined the extent of agreement
with the statement: "Do you feel your job is
appropriate considering the education you have?"
17. Black respondents were asked: "Is the gap in
income between Negroes and whites increasing,
decreasing, or not changing?" and "Is the gap between those Negroes who are better off and those
who are poorer, increasing, decreasing, or not
changing?" Both are reported by Caplan and Paige
(1968b).

the frequency of various magnitudes of associations between the three categories of
data bearing on the DFA explanation and
riot participation.

Of the 50 "tests" of the deprivation association with riot participation, only two
(4%) were of moderate magnitude. Of the 84
"tests" of the frustration association with
riot participation, ten (12%) were of a
moderate magnitude. Of the 39 tests of the
deprivation and frustration association with
riot participation, one (3%) was of high
magnitude. Of the total 173 associations
bearing on the DFA explanation, 32% were
not significant, 61% were of a low magnitude, 7% were of a moderate magnitude, and
less than 1% were of a high magnitude.
Again, the majority of these associations
were statistically significant and in the "predicted" direction but of a consistently low
magnitude.

The DFA explanation receives scant
empirical support when personal attributes
bearing on this argument are examined in
relation to individual riot participation. In
view of these results concerning individual
riot participation, and the results of Spilerman (1970) and others concerning the occurrence of riots, there is considerable
reason for rejecting the sociological and
popular cliché that absolute or relative
deprivation and the ensuing frustration or
discontent or despair is the root cause of
rebellion. These results require a careful reexamination of the assumption that the
DFA relationship is " . . . as fundamental to
understanding civil strife as the law of
gravity is to atmospheric physics . . ." (Gurr,
1968:52).

AN ANALYSIS OF THE MODERATE AND
HIGH ASSOCIATIONS

How do the moderate and high associations
which did obtain inform our understanding
of the riot participation process? To answer
this question we must ask: Are there general
patterns of relationship between the different categories of independent variables
and the various measures of riot participa-

Table 2. Categories of Deprivation-Frustration-Aggression Data by Frequency of Magnitude of Association with Riot Participation

	n.s.	.00 .09	.10 .19	.20 .29	.30 .39	.40 +	Total
DEPRIVATION							
Education	1	1	3	4	1		10
Income	5		2	1			8
Employment	2		3	2			7
Occupation level	1	1	1				3
Other SES Indicators	2		1				3
Exper. Police Malpract.	8		10				18
Ethnicity						1	1
Total	(19)	(2)	(20)	(7)	(1)	(1)	(50)
Percent	38%	4%	40%	14%	2%	2%	100%
FRUSTRATION							
Political Attitudes	9		19	10	2		40
Job/Housing Atts./Expect.*	5	1	4	4	2	1	17
Black Atts. re:whites**			1				1
Opinion of Police Malpract.	5	1	6	4	5		21
Opinion of Discrimination**		1	4				5
Total	(19)	(3)	(34)	(18)	(9)	(1)	(84)
Percent	23%	4%	40%	21%	11%	1%	100%
DEPRIVATION & FRUSTRATION							
Job/Housing Atts./Expect.*	3		1			1	5
Black Atts. re:whites***	1						1
Black Atts. re:blacks***			1				1
SES Attribute Consistency	11		5	7			23
Underemployment			2	1			3
Exper./Opinion Police Malpr.			1				1
Exper./Opinion Discrimination	2		3				5
Total	(17)		(13)	(8)		(1)	(39)
Percent	43%		33%	20%		3%	100%
TOTAL	(55)	(5)	(67)	(33)	(10)	(3)	(173)
PERCENT	32%	3%	39%	19%	6%	1%	100%

*See fn. 16; **See fn. 15; ***See fn. 17.

tion? What are the specific independent and dependent variables involved in the moderate and high associations? What interpretations can be placed on these findings?

General Patterns of Association

Are the new moderate and high relationships which did obtain associated with particular categories of independent variables and/or particular operational measures of riot participation? Of all the categories of independent variables, "Demographic Attri-butes" yielded the largest percentage of moderate and high associations (20%). This was followed by "Experience and Opinion of Discrimination Toward Blacks" (10%), "Attitude Statements" (7%), and "Socio-economic Attributes" (2%). "Political Participation" measures yielded no moderate or high associations with any of the measures of riot participation.

Of the different measures of riot participation, Type IV—"Respondent's Reported Participation Status and Witness of Others' Behavior(s)" yielded the largest proportion of moderate or high associations; one of four cross tabulations (25%) was of moderate strength. Type I–"Arrestee Status" yielded the next highest percentage of moderate and high associations (12%), followed by Type V–"Respondent's Reported Participation Status and Behavior(s)" (6%). Type II–"Respondent's Reported Participation Status," and Type III–"Respondent's Witness of Others' Behavior(s)" yielded no moderate or high associations with any of the independent variables examined.

Of the 287 associations examined, only 19 (7%) were of a magnitude of .30 or higher. Five of these were between "Attitude Statements" and I–"Arrestee Status"; five were between "Experience or Opinion of Discrimination Toward Blacks" and I–"Arrestee Status"; three between "Demographic Attributes" and I–"Arrestee Status"; two were between "Demographic Attributes" and V–"Reported Participation Status and Behaviors"; and one each between "Social Relationships and Interactions" and I–"Arrestee Status," "Demographic Attributes" and IV–"Reported Participation Status and Witness to Others' Behavior(s)," "Socio-economic Attributes" and V–"Reported Participation Status and Behaviors."

Specific Moderate and High Association

The specific independent variables, measures of riot participation, V values, df, N, and the civil disorder involved for the 19 moderate and high associations are listed in Table 3. The majority of moderate and high associations are between the "Arrestee Status" measure of participation and respondents' "Opinions About Discrimination" and their "Attitude Statements" about job and housing opportunities and the political system. There are several aspects of these moderate and high associations which warrant examination.

Opinions About Police Discrimination

The category of independent variables yielding the highest proportion of moderate and high associations–"Experience and Opinions of Discrimination"–involves associations between respondents' opinions about (not their personal experiences of) police malpractices toward blacks. Further, these associations hold for both black and white Milwaukee riots arrestees' opinions about police malpractices toward blacks.[18] A crucial aspect of these associations is that respondents' opinion statements about police malpractices were made after their arrest; i.e., after their "operational" participation in the civil disorder. By contrast, Raine's (1967) study of the Los Angeles (Watts) riot yielded no moderate or high associations between respondents' experience of, knowledge or opinions about, police malpractices and their reported riot participation status (Type II).

It was noted above that the "Arrestee Status" measure of participation, Type I, yielded a larger proportion of moderate and high associations (12%) than did any other measure of participation.[19] Further, "Experience or Opinion of Discrimination" and "Arrestee Status" yielded as large a proportion of the moderate and high associations (27%) as any other category of independent variable and any other measure of participation. A popular interpretation of the associa-

18. Opinions about physically violent police practices toward blacks–unnecessary force in arrest, and beatings in custody–were associated with participation for black but not white arrestees. Conversely, opinion about police harassment of blacks–unnecessary frisking and searching of homes–yielded moderate associations with participation for white but not black arrestees in the 1967 Milwaukee riot (Flaming, 1968).

19. Fogelson and Hill (1968) mention a number of problems with "Arrestee Status" measures of riot participation. Arrestees may falsify certain information regarding their place of residence and place of employment. The measures assume the arrest process is nonselective, when in fact police can only apprehend a small fraction of their target population and may likely single out those who are slow of foot, who have the appearance of "riff-raff," etc. Arrestee data are based on apprehensions and not convictions. All we can be certain of with the "arrestee status" measure of riot participation is that the person was in the area when and where the police were arresting people. The measure tells us almost nothing about the person's behavior.

Table 3. Independent Variables Showing Moderate and High Association with Civil Disorder Participation

	Control	D F A[a]	Particip.	V	df	N	Dis-order	Investigator
OPINION OF POLICE DISCRIMINATION AGAINST BLACKS								
1. Beating in custody	blacks	F	I/A-C[b]	+.36[c]	1	(131)	Mil.	Flaming (1968)
2. Unnec. force in arrests	blacks	F	I/A-C	+.30	1	(141)	Mil.	Flaming (1968)
3. Unnec. frisk in arrests	whites	F	I/A-C	+.33	1	(126)	Mil.	Flaming (1968)
4. Unnec. search of homes	whites	F	I/A-C	+.31[d]	1	(122)	Mil.	Flaming (1968)
5. Index police malpractice	whites	F	I/A-C	+.31[d]	2	(67)	Mil.	Flaming (1968)
ATTITUDES	blacks with							
6. Job opport. for blacks	lo.ed.lo.occup.	DF	I/A-C	+.62[d]	1	(41)	Mil.	Flaming (1968)
7. Job opport. for blacks		F	I/A-C	+.50	1	(269)	Mil.	Flaming (1968)
8. Job opport. for blacks		F	I/A-C	+.33	1	(143)	Mil.	Flaming (1968)
9. House opport. for blacks		F	I/A-C	+.30	1	(336)	Mil.	Flaming (1968)
10. Voting particip. in govt.[e]		F	I/A-C	+.39	1	(137)	Mil.	Flaming (1968)
11. U.S. not worth fighting for[f]		F	V/R-CR	+.35	1	(94)	Det.	Caplan-Paige (1968a)
DEMOGRAPHIC ATTRIBUTES								
12. Age		NA	I/A-C	+.60	1	(286)	Mil.	Flaming (1968)
13. Age		NA	I/A-C	+.40	2	(964)	Det.	Geschwender (1969a)
14. Age		NA	V/R-NI	+.34	3	(331)	Det.	Caplan-Paige (1968a)
15. Ethnicity		D	I/A-C	+.49	1	(286)	Mil.	Flaming (1968)
16. Sex		NA	IV/G-A-D-SN	?.40	3	(507)	Watts	Sears (1967a)
17. Born in riot city		NA	V/R-NI	-.32	1	(233)	Newark	Caplan-Paige (1968a)
SOCIOECONOMIC ATTRIBUTES								
18. Educational level		D	V/R-CR	?.33	3	(102)	Det.	Caplan-Paige (1968a)
SOCIAL RELATIONS/INTERACTIONS								
19. Social Isolation Index		NA	I/A-C	+.31	4	(890)	Det.	Geschwender (1967b)

[a]Indicates classification as deprivation-D, frustration-F, deprivation-frustration-DF, or not applicable-NA.

[b]I/A-C: Arrestee Status, Arrestee-Control; IV/G-A-D-SN: Respondent's Reported Participation Status and Witness of others' Behavior(s), Gladiator-Active Spectator-Distant Spectator-Saw Nothing; V/R-NI-CR: Respondent's Reported Participation Status and Behavior(s), Rioter-Not Involved-Counter Rioter.

[c]+ indicates a monotonic distribution consistent with and — indicates a distribution opposite the direction specified by the hypothesis; ? indicates a nonmonotonic distribution which is inconsistent with the direction specified by the hypothesis.

[d]These V values are probably inflated due to insufficient cell frequencies which inflate the χ value on which V is based.

[e]Arrestees agree with statement: "Voting is the only way people like me have any say about how government runs things."

[f]Rioters say country not worth fighting for in major world war.

tion between opinions about police malpractices toward blacks and participation in civil disorder is that the latter is the product of the former. An alternate interpretation, which is equally plausible, suggests that the arrest experience, for black and white respondents, may well result in the statement of a number of negative opinions about police malpractices.

Other Attitudes

But what of the remaining moderate and high associations between respondents' attitudes about job and housing opportunities, voting effectiveness, loyalty to the government, and participation in civil disorder? What interpretation can be placed on these findings? It is clear that a large segment of American society in general and black Americans in particular have consistently been denied the opportunity of full participation in the social, economic, and political arenas of their choosing. There is growing dissatisfaction on the part of these citizens with their treatment by the establishment and the more affluent white majority it represents. The denial of these citizens and their dissatisfaction are empirical facts. However, the connection between either or both of these facts and participation in civil disorder is another matter. As our previous discussion indicated, there is but scant support for this line of reasoning when we examine the available data. Only 13 (8%) of the total 173 "tests" bearing on the DFA explanation were of moderate or high magnitude. Of these 13, ten involved attitudinal measures and six of these involved the aforementioned relationships between "negative attitudes toward the police" and riot participation operationalized as "Arrestee Status." What of the remaining moderate and high associations between attitude statements and riot participation? On what basis can we assert a causal connection? There are at least three theoretical or methodological problems which caution against drawing a causal relation between attitude and behavior.

The first problem with attitude-participation data involves the chronological sequence in which they are ordinarily gathered. As the data on attitudes toward police and arrestee status participation have suggested, this is not a matter which can easily be dismissed. Too frequently a respondent's attitude or opinion statement after the disorder, at "time 3," is taken as an indicator of some cognitive state or predispositional set prior to the disorder, at "time 1," which presumably produced the individual's participation in the disorder at "time 2."[20] The attitude or opinion statement at "time 3" may well be a product of experiences of the respondent at or following the "time 2" event.

A second problem with the attitude-participation data has to do with the basis for assuming that a connection exists between attitudes and behavior even when time order is controlled. An increasing number of studies fail to yield consistent evidence that an attitude statement at "time 1" is followed at "time 2" by the behavior which the inferred attitude is supposed to produce (e.g., Wicker, 1969).

A third and perhaps most serious problem with the attitude-participation data is one that characterizes the connection between any attribute and the behavior it is assumed to produce. The theoretical schemes which have guided or followed most of the civil disorder participation research have attempted to account for participation in terms of attributes. Individual's attitude statements, as well as their ascribed or achieved attributes, e.g., age, sex, ethnicity or education, income, occupation, etc., have been treated as overt indicators of covert tendencies to behave, and riot participation has been viewed as a function of those tendencies. The problem arises when an attempt is made to specify the tendencies and the behaviors which are the products. Singu-

20. This problem has been noted by Rossi *et al.,* (1968); Sears (1966); Sears and McConahay (1967b); and Fogelson and Hill (1968).

lar and redundant behavior is rather easily interpreted as the product of a singular and continuing tendency. But what of the multiple and differentiated behaviors? To account for them in the same way requires positing multiple and differentiated tendencies plus some switching process which turns them on and off. This problem has not been acknowledged, let alone resolved, by riot participation researchers. This becomes evident upon examining the limitations of their operational measures of participation and, in turn, the attributes and inferred tendencies introduced to account for the participation.

As indicated earlier, the measures of participation differ considerably in terms of their operational criteria. However, they are similarly limited in their failure to sample directly and representatively the variation in respondents' behavior content across the time duration of the disorder. For example, Sears and McConahay suggested that "... the most active level of riot participation" involved "overt, aggressive (illegal) acts" (1967a:2). This position assumes that a person is an "active" participant when engaged in illegal acts, or in "anti-social" acts, to use the language of other investigators (e.g., Caplan and Paige, 1968a:331, fn. 111). The methodological strategy which follows from such a position is to determine at which point or points in time a person is engaged in illegal or "anti-social" activity. Only at those points would the person be considered a riot participant. Unfortunately, such differentiation is not found in the measures of riot participation employed in any of the studies under discussion here. Rather, a determination was made as to whether or not persons had engaged in any illegal or "anti-social" activity.[21] Those who

reported that they had not were classified as nonparticipants. Those who reported they had were classified as participants. The latter classification procedure is problematic in that it neither recognizes nor accommodates the person who intermittently engages in legal and illegal acts through the course of the civil disorder. He can hardly be designated "not involved" nor can he be classified a "counter rioter." He is necessarily an intermittent participant and nonparticipant. It is conceivable that many persons present for any period of time across the duration of a civil disorder are intermittently engaged in nonrioting and rioting and/or counter-rioting activities, if not in fact all three.[22] Consider the following hypothetical example:

Within a one-hour period of time, a person might walk from a bar or residence to the scene of a street arrest; chat with friends and acquaintances; curse the police; make a pass at a girl; throw a rock at a departing police car; light someone's cigarette; run down the street and join others in rocking and overturning a car; watch someone set the car on fire; drink a can of looted beer; assist firemen in extinguishing a fire as it spreads to an apartment house and so on.

Even if a person engages in the most extreme act of violence against person or property during a disorder, he is not likely to be continuously or exclusively so engaged.

---

21. The most frequently employed operational measure of participation was "Arrestee Status" (Type I), and it provides no description of variation in behavior content across time (See fn. 20 above). Of the remaining measures only Type V, "Respondent's Reported Participation Status and Behavior(s)," solicited reports of the respondent's behavior content, and it provides no specification of variation in behavior content across time.

22. Warren (1969) reports aggregate data on indices of rioting behavior (entering into broken stores, picking up goods and taking them home, breaking windows, making fire bombs, throwing fire bombs), counter-rioting behavior (trying to stop the riot, painting "soul brother" signs on buildings, helping to put out fires, giving help to people hurt or homeless, calling the fire department, giving sandwiches and coffee to soldiers), and withdrawal behavior (leaving the neighborhood during the disturbance, staying at home and not going out during the disturbance). Unfortunately, data are not yet available which would indicate whether or not individuals were engaged in more than one of these different sets of activity and/or routine activities as well. Conot's (1967) journalistic account of the Watts riot indicates that people in the area engaged in a variety of routine activities (e.g., talking, smoking, drinking, eating, making love, etc.) as well as "illegal" and "pro-legal" activities during the course of the disorder.

Rather, he is likely to be intermittently engaged in a wide range of routine and "illegal" activities during the course of his presence in the area of the disorder. Unfortunately, measures of civil disorder participation have failed to recognize, record, and attempt to account for this differentiation in behaviors through space and across time. Perhaps unwittingly, participation in civil disorder has been conceptualized as a monolithic phenomenon and measured accordingly.

Assuming my hypothetical characterization of participation variation is reasonably accurate, when might it be assumed that the individual's tendency to behave—inferred from his attitude statement or other attributes—is operating? Which tendency materializes prior to the person's cursing of the policemen? Does it disappear prior to his pass at the female, reappear when he assists others in overturning a car, and then vanish when he helps firemen put out the flames in the apartment house? Furthermore, as Blumer (1955) has noted, how can antecedent tendencies to behave presuppose and thereby incorporate the ongoing activities of others which inevitably impinge on the individual in any situation of social interaction?[23] How can the tendencies join the participant's activities with those of others in the "anti-social" coordinated behaviors of over-turning a car, or the "pro-social" coordinated behaviors of helping firemen extinguish some flames? There appears to be no way in which *a* tendency to behave, inferred from knowledge of an individual's attributes—before or after the event—can be

logically connected to the variation in riot participation behaviors of the individual.[24]

Demographic and Socioeconomic Attributes, and Social Relationships

The moderate and high associations between age, sex, ethnicity, educational level[25] and riot participation must be treated with caution for several reasons. As a brief re-examination of Table 1 will reveal, these particular attributes did not consistently yield moderate or high associations with riot participation. At the same time, the few moderate and high associations which did obtain warrant discussion. Age, sex, ethnicity, and education level are vulnerable to the same questions raised in the preceding section about the presumed connection between attributes, inferred tendencies to behave, and riot participation. There is no compelling reason to accept the inference that persons are more impetuous because of their youth, more daring because of their gender, more disenchanted because of their race, or less rational because of their educational level. An equally plausible interpretation of these data is that such persons are

23. The individual does bring a "response repertoire" into the situation. These responses can be viewed as "behavioral dispositions," and the actions of situational others can be viewed as discriminative stimuli which elicit a variety of different behaviors and behavior combinations toward different objects across time. However, such a view rests not on a repertoire of "predispositions" which impel the person to behave in the situation, but rather upon the relationship between the situated actions of the individual and others which call out responses the individual is capable of making.

24. Some proponents of "attitude" explanations recognize the complexity of the problem and the necessity for introducing between attitudes and behavior such intervening variables as "situational behaviors" and "social structural considerations" (e.g., Erhlich, 1969).
25. Only one of nine relationships between education level and riot participation yielded a moderate or high correlation, and the directionality in this one instance is not clear. This might be treated as a chance occurrence. On the other hand, there is a certain logic which connects young, black, males, without educational credentials and therefore unemployed, as maximally available for participation in a variety of street activities, rioting included (Liebow, 1967). Unfortunately, none of the riot researchers has as yet provided us with a sensitive multivariate analysis of this or any other package of socioeconomic and demographic attributes in relation to riot participation. It might be that multivariate indices would yield an impressive correlation with participation in civil disorders. Should that relationship obtain, however, it would still be necessary to connect the attributes to participation with some form of theoretical glue. Predispositions and availability are two possibilities. My own biases lean toward the latter.

simply more available for participation by virtue of the large amount of unscheduled or uncommitted time which results from being young, black, male, and without educational credentials in the urban ghettos of contemporary U.S. society.

A similar line of interpretation can be applied to the relationship between Geschwender *et al.'s* (1969b) "Social Isolation Index" and riot participation. The index included persons who were single, lived alone, had no organization memberships, and who had lived in the riot city fewer than ten years.[26] None of those variables, considered alone, yielded a moderate or high association with riot participation. Taken together, however, they yield a moderate association with riot participation. Geschwender *et al.'s* respondents—all of whom were black males—can be viewed as more available for participation by virtue of their minimal implication in scheduled social relationships and the competing claims and demands on time and behavior which those relationships entail.

AN ALTERNATE FOCUS

The predominant explanations of social behavior in the 20th century have focused on "what people carry within them from place to place" (Melbin, 1969:664). This traditional concern with determining what attributes people carry and the "tendencies within" inferred from those attributes have prevented giving attention to what people do with, and in relation to, one another. As Cohen has noted: ". . . the dominant bias in American sociology has been toward formu-

lating theory in terms of variables that describe initial states, on the one hand, and outcomes, on the other, rather than in terms of processes whereby acts and complex structures of action are built, elaborated, and transformed" (1965:9).

Civil disorders are complex and differentiated phenomena. Attempts to account for their occurrence and individual participation therein have failed to acknowledge this complexity, theoretically and operationally.[27] This shortcoming has been magnified by focusing on the "states" or attributes of communities and individuals as causal variables. Examinations of the most reliable data now available suggest that such a focus has not been empirically fruitful. Perhaps it is time to give serious attention to the possibility that the individual and the joined performances in which people engage are the products of the behaviors which they take toward and receive from others. The shortcomings of the recent civil disorder studies give rise to several questions about what people do with, and in relation to, one another prior to and during civil disorders. Answers to these questions would appear fundamental to an understanding of civil disorder participation.

First, a necessary condition for the initiation of civil disorder is a large number of persons with a period of unscheduled or uncommitted time at their disposal. The discussion of the preceding section suggested that some persons are more likely than others to be riot participants, but not because they are "riot-prone" or because we can infer other motivational tendencies from their attributes; rather, their attributes crudely describe the presence or absence of their contacts and relationships with others which decrease or increase their availability for riot participation by virtue of the behaviors others can address to them. It is importnat to recall in this connection that the

---

26. Although Geschwender *et al.'s* "Social Isolation Index" includes a measure of the respondent's short term residence in the riot city, the National Advisory Commission on Civil Disorders (1968) reported a negative relationship between being born outside the riot city and riot participation ($V=-.32$). In general, the relationships between being native born in the riot city, length of residence, age at arrival in the riot city, region of socialization, and riot participation yielded no consistent pattern.

27. Wanderer's (1968, 1969) and Warren's (1969) examinations of the patterns of variation in riot activities across different disorders represent important exceptions.

majority of disorders examined by the Kerner Commission began on weekends and/or in the evenings when the majority of people were free from the competing demands and claims of work obligations and commitments. A related finding was that the majoirty of the disorders began at or near major vehicular or pedestrian intersections in densely populated areas. A fundamental question, then, is: What settings at what points in time yield large numbers of available persons in general proximity to one another?[28]

The availability and general proximity of persons constitute but one necessary condition. This must be supplemented by a mobilization process. I do not refer here to a "motivational factor" but to a sequence of interpersonal exchanges[29] whereby people learn of an event transpiring at some alternate place in space and come to converge on that common place in time and space. [30] The "assembling process," which is essential to the explanation of all "collective behavioral" phenomena, has received almost no attention by theorists or researchers (Milgram and Toch, 1969:532).[31] The second fundamental question, then, is: What produces assemblages of persons in a common time-space frame?

An assemblage of persons in a common

place in time and space provides a platform from which a variety of individual and joined performances can be launched. Recent studies of civil disorder participation have neither recognized, recorded, nor attempted to account for this variation.

A monolithic conception of civil disorder participation is no longer tenable. The third and fourth questions to which students of participation must address themselves are: What are the variety of individual and joined performances in which people engage during the course of the disorder? And what produces, maintains, and alters these varied performances?

There is good reason to believe that answers to these questions about civil disorder participation will not come from continued attention to individual attributes and to "predispositions to behave" which are inferred therefrom. In view of the considerable effort expended in that direction and the scanty results, an alternate focus is long overdue. One such focus would seek to answer these questions by attending to what people do with, and in relation to, one another. Until we acquire more systematic knowledge of individuals' immediate interactional environments, ". . . we will not appreciate how powerfully and pervasively they work . . . (and) . . . the massive cues to conduct that are provided by immediate surroundings will remain slighted" (Melbin, 1969:665).

28. For other discussions of the relationship between setting, available populations and collective violence, see McCall (1970), Kerr and Siegel (1954), and Grimshaw (1960).
29. Smelser's "mobilization of motivation for organized action" gives minimal emphasis to the interpersonal communication of participants in civil disorders (1963:253–261; 1964:117–118).
30. Lachman and Singer's (1968) study of participants in the 1967 Detroit riot revealed that the majority were engaged in a variety of routine activities at disparate and distant locations when they learned "a riot was going on" and that there was considerable time lapse before they moved to the area in which the riot was occuring.
31. In a separate paper, McPhail and Miller, (1971) report the results of, so far as we know, the first systematic study of the assembling process. This study is based on a sample of an aggregate-assemblage of approximately 5,000 persons, some of whom were dispersed or arrested by the police for engaging in rioting behaviors.

REFERENCES

Bloombaum, Milton, 1968, "The conditions underlying race riots as portrayed by multidimensional scalogram analysis: A re-analysis of Lieberson and Silverman's data." American Sociological Review 33 (February):76–91.

Blumer, Herbert, 1955, "Attitudes and the social act." Social Problems 3 (Summer):59–65.

Caplan, Nathan S. and Jeffrey M. Paige, 1968a, Data on Newark and Detroit Residents. Pp. 171–178, fn. 111–143 in National Advisory Commission on Civil Disorders, Report of the National Advisory Commission on Civil Disorders. Washington, D.C.: U.S. Government Printing Office.

———, 1968b, "A study of ghetto rioters." Scientific American 219 (August):15–21.

Cohen, Albert K., 1965, "The sociology of the deviant act." American Sociological Review 30 (February):5–14.

Conot, Robert, 1967, Rivers of Blood, Years of Darkness. New York: Bantam Books.

DeFleur, Melvin and Frank Westie, 1963, "Attitude as a scientific concept." Social Forces 42 (September):17–31.

Downes, Bryan T., 1968, "Social and political characteristics of riot cities: A comparative study." Social Science Quarterly 49:504–520.

Erlich, Howard, 1969, "Attitudes, behavior and intervening variables." American Sociologist 4 (February):20–34.

Feierabend, Ivo K., Rosalind L. Feierabend, and B. A. Nesvold, 1969, "Social change and political violence: Cross national patterns." Pp. 606–665 in Hugh D. Graham and Ted R. Gurr (eds.), Violence in America. New York: New American Library.

Flaming, Karl H., 1968, Who Riots and Why?: Black and White Perspectives in Milwaukee. Milwaukee: Milwaukee Urban League.

Fogelson, Robert M. and Robert B. Hill, 1968, "Who riots?: A study of participation in the 1967 riots." Pp. 221–248 in National Advisory Commission on Civil Disorders, Supplementary Studies for the National Advisory Commission on Civil Disorders, Washington, D.C.: U.S. Government Printing Office.

Geschwender, James, Benjamin Singer, and J. Harrington, 1969a, "Status inconsistency, deprivation and the Detroit riot." Paper presented at the annual meetings of the American Sociological Association, San Francisco, California.

Geschwender, James, Benjamin Singer, and Richard Osborn, 1969b, "Social isolation and riot participation." Paper presented at the annual meetings of the American Sociological Association, San Francisco, California.

Grimshaw, Allen D., 1960, "Urban racial violence in the United States: Changing ecological considerations." American Journal of Sociology 66 (September):109–119.

Gurr, Ted R., 1968, "Urban disorder: Perspectives from the comparative study of civil strife." Pp. 51–67 in Louis H. Masotti and Don R. Bowen (eds.), Riots and Rebellion: Civil Violence in the Urban Community. Beverly Hills: Sage Publications.

Kerr, Clark and Abraham Siegel, 1954, "The inter-industry propensity to strike: An international comparison." In A. W. Kornhauser (ed.), Industrial Conflict, New York: McGraw-Hill.

Lachman, Sheldon and Benjamin Singer, 1968, The Detroit Riot of July 1967. Detroit: Behavior Research Institute.

Lieberson, Stanley and Arnold Silverman, 1965, "The precipitants and underlying conditions of race riots." American Sociological Review 30 (December):887–898.

Liebow, Elliot, 1967, Tally's Corner. Boston: Little, Brown.

McCall, Michel, 1970, "Some ecological aspects of Negro slum riots." Pp. 345–362 in Joseph Gusfield (ed.), Protest, Reform and Revolt. New York, John Wiley.

McPhail, Clark and David Miller, 1971, "The assembling process: A theoretical and empirical examination." Paper presented at the annual meetings of the American Sociological Association, Denver, Colorado.

Melbin, Murray, 1969, "Behavior rhythms in mental hospitals." American Journal of Sociology 74 (May): 650–665.

Milgram, Stanley and Hans Toch, 1969, "Collective behavior and social movements." Pp. 507–610 in Gardner Lindsey and Elliot Aronson (eds.), Handbook of Social Psychology, 2nd ed., Vol. IV. Reading, Massachusetts: Addison-Wesley.

Murphy, Raymond and James W. Watson, 1967, The Structure of Discontent: The Relationship Between Social Structure, Grievance and Support for the Los Angeles Riot. Los Angeles: University of California Institute of Government and Public Affairs.

National Advisory Commission on Civil Disorders, 1968, Report of the National Advisory Commission on Civil Disorders. New York: Bantam Books.

Raine, Walter, 1967, The Perception of Police Brutality in South Central Los

Angeles. Los Angeles: University of California Institute of Government and Public Affairs.

Reynolds, Harry W., 1968, "Black power, community power and jobs." Pp. 237–260 in Louis H. Masotti and Don R. Bowen (eds.), Riots and Rebellion: Civil Violence in the Urban Community. Beverly Hills: Sage Publications.

Robinson, W. S., 1950, "Ecological correlations and the behavior of individuals." American Sociological Review 15 (June):351–357.

Rossi, Peter, Richard A. Berk, David P. Boesel, et al., 1968, "Between white and black: The faces of American institutions in the ghetto." Pp. 71–215 in National Advisory Commission on Civil Disorders, Supplemental Studies for the National Advisory Commission on Civil Disorders. Washington, D.C.: U.S. Government Printing Office.

Rudé, George, 1964, The Crowd in History. New York: John Wiley.

Sears, David O., 1966, "Riot activity and evaluation: An overview of the Negro survey." Unpublished paper written for the U.S. Office of Economic Opportunity, and cited in Fogelson and Hill (1968).

Sears, David O. and John B. McConahay, 1967a, Riot Participation. Los Angeles: Univeristy of California Institute of Government and Public Affairs.

———, 1967b, The Politics of Discontent. Los Angeles; University of California Institute of Government and Public Affairs.

Smelser, Neil J., 1963, Theory of Collective Behavior. New York: Free Press of Glencoe.

———, 1964, "Theoretical issues of scope and problems." The Sociological Quarterly 5 (Spring):117–121.

Southwood, Kenneth, 1970, "Cultural and structural disequilibrium within nations and its relationship to political violence." Paper read at the annual meetings of the Ohio Valley Sociological Society, Akron, Ohio.

Spilerman, Seymour, 1970, "The causes of racial disturbances: A comparison of alternative explanations." American Sociological Review 35 (August):627–649.

Tausky, Curt and Eugene Piedmont, 1968, "The sampling of behavior." The American Sociologist 3 (February):49–51.

Tomlinson, T. M., 1967, Ideological Foundation for Negro Action: A Comparative Analysis of Militant and Nonmilitant Views of the Los Angeles Riot. Los Angeles: University of California Institute of Government and Public Affairs.

Wanderer, Jules, 1968, "1967 riots: A test of the congruity of events." Social Problems 16 (Fall):193–197.

———, 1969, "An index of riot severity and some correlates." American Journal of Sociology 74 (March):500–505.

Warren, Donald I., 1969, "Neighborhood structure and riot behavior in Detroit: Some exploratory findings." Social Problems 16 (Spring): 464–484.

Wicker, A. W., 1969, "Attitudes versus actions: The relationship of verbal and overt behavioral responses to attitude objects." Journal of Social Issues 25:41–78.

Police-Community Relations:

A Need in Search of Police Support

ROBERT A. MENDELSOHN

As the society responds to changes in technology, increased educational levels, redistribution of population centers, admission to civil society of previously excluded groups, and a host of other structural phenomena, so does the role and method of operation of the police. One major consequence of these trends for the police has been to place them under considerably more restraint than was true even a short time ago (Bordua, 1968; President's Commission on Law Enforcement and Administration of Justice, 1967b). Thus, it would be reasonable to assume that instances of "police brutality" are less frequent than in the past, and that police officers are less able to administer "street justice." Though officers may complain about the role of Supreme Court decisions and the activities of civil liberties groups in these changes, their real source lies in the far-ranging developments listed above. A second major result of these broad social changes has been an increasing demand, among the black citizenry, for improved police services combined with an increasing impatience and anger at police for real and imagined mistreatment of citizens. A third major consequence has been the impetus for increasing police professionalization. This in effect is an attempt to transfer the motivating forces on officers from control by a given subcommunity to internalized standards of conduct. These standards are presumably derived from the canons of effective and responsible police work.

POLICE-COMMUNITY NEGATIVISM

All these changes increase the stress on the police by disrupting traditional methods of operation or by requiring an increased degree of contact with, and understanding of, negatively viewed groups.

Yet it is reasonably clear that, unless a disastrous and panicky repression sets in, these are the trends of the future, if for no other reason than they are consistent with trends in the larger society.[1] In fact, more-

1. Bordua argues that there has been a relative shift from coercion as a method of social control. He cites human relations approaches to industrial management, child rearing techniques, and other evidence. He goes on to argue that social control is becoming more and more "distributive" in nature. Included in this latter category are economic sanctions, persuasion, and a vast array of welfare state programs.

From R. Mendelsohn. Police-community relations: A need in search of police support. *American Behavioral Scientist*, 1970, *13*, 745–760. Reprinted by permission of the Publisher, Sage Publications, Inc.

over, the potential for improving police work that resides in these trends is quite substantial. It is a truism that effective police work requires the support of he community. As the President's Commission (1967b:144) puts it:

Even if fairer treatment of minority groups were the sole consideration, police departments would have an obligation to attempt to achieve and maintain good police-community relations. In fact, however, much more is at stake. Police-community relationships have a direct bearing on the character of life in our cities, and on the community's ability to maintain stability and to solve its problems. At the same time, the police department's capacity to deal with crime depends to a large extent upon its relationship with the citizenry. Indeed, no lasting improvement in law enforcement is likely in this country unless police-community relations are substantially improved. . . . A dissatisfied public will not support the police enthusiastically . . . when the police and public are at odds, the police tend to become isolated from the public and become less capable of understanding and adapting to the community and its changing needs. . . . Poor police-community relations adversely affect the ability of the police to prevent crime and apprehend criminals.

While no one would be naive enough to believe that improved police-community relations will in themselves, given the multiple causes of crime and riots, eliminate these disruptive events, it is difficult to see how much can be done without a change in police attitudes toward the black community.

The truism, unfortunately, may be a truism for only a minority of officers. Within the department in Detroit, there was, following the riot, a most striking absence of concern with the importance of police-community relations as a riot deterrent.[2] There

was also a lack of appreciation of the role police play in contributing to riot etiology. Strikingly illustrative of this disinterest are the responses to the question, "What needs to be done to prevent future riots?"[3] although responses to other questions would perhaps do as well. As can be seen, until the inspector and above rank (labelled "inspectors")[4] is attained, there is no support whatever among white officers for improved police-community relations; indeed, far and away the most popular response calls for a better trained, better equipped, and larger

---

2. Although it may be argued that these responses occurred two years ago and in response to a cataclysmic event, it is the author's belief that the beliefs expressed in these responses are stable and have not changed markedly in two years. Probably some shifts in belief have occurred in this time span but whatever shifts have occurred are hardly commensurate with the need.

3. This question and all other data from Detroit referred to in this paper come from a survey on police attitudes, particularly about the riot of 1967, carried out from November 1967 through March 1968. A random sample, stratified by rank and race, were exhaustively questioned on riot interpretation, police response to the riot, police work in general, attitudes toward both blacks and whites, morale, and police-community relations. In addition, the usual demographic material was obtained along with a variety of responses to the officers' status and hopes. The white officers interviewed were fifty-seven inspectors and executives, thirty-three lieutenants, thirty-six sergeants, thirty-six detectives, and eighty-six patrolmen. The black officers interviewed included thirty-eight officers. In the tables, the thirty-six black officers of rank of lieutenant and below are not differentiated by rank. The number of black officers in each rank is too small for such a breakdown. The two black inspectors are included with the inspectors. For further details, see Mendelsohn (1969).

4. Inspectors include officers from the highest professional rank, the superintendent, to various executives and to those with the rank of "inspector." This group as a whole generally exercises command and executive functions. For example, an inspector will ordinarily be in command of a precinct. Lieutenants are superior to sergeants who, in turn, are superior to patrolmen, the lowest rank. If assigned to a precinct, a lieutenant may command a platoon. Detectives may be of various ranks but in the sample of this study, they do not carry additional rank such as detective sergeant. Those with ranks of detective sergeant or detective lieutenant were coded as sergeant and lieutenant respectively. This is the correct procedure for two reasons: (1) they are superior in rank to that of detective; (2) they were obtained, respectively, from the sergeant and lieutenant rosters provided by the Police Department. With a few exceptions, these ranks constitute all the ranks within the department.

Table 1. What needs to be done to prevent future riots?

(in percentages)

Race[a]	White					Black
Rank[b]	Insp. (n = 93)	Lt. (n = 41)	Sgt. (n = 52)	Det. (n = 60)	Ptr. (n = 113)	All Ranks (n = 54)
Program						
Law and/or more efficient police	21.5	43.9	55.8	66.7	65.5	18.5
Social action (e.g., education, better race relations)	37.7	31.7	25.0	20.0	25.6	46.3
Improve police-community relations	19.4	4.9	3.8	3.3	0.0	13.0
Other	21.5	19.5	15.4	10.0	8.8	22.2
TOTAL	100.1	100.0	100.0	100.0	99.9	100.0

[a]Although the views of black officers are not the main focus of this paper, it is instructive to examine the difference in views of white and black officers. Accordingly, the views of black officers are included in this and the other tables.

[b]The data in the table record the first two reasons mentioned by the respondents. Accordingly it is a table of responses rather than subjects. Those officers who responded with "don't know" or not applicable answers are not included. This was the case for four inspectors, five lieutenants, six sergeants, seven detectives, nineteen patrolmen, and two black officers.

force, and "stricter" law enforcement.[5] Certainly, there is little in this to suggest that there is any comprehension of, much less support for, the idea, which I will advocate, that the role of the police should include close ties with persons in the community, considerable openness to public scrutiny, increased community service, and a major advocacy role for the disadvantaged and oppressed.

The irony of this reaction is that the police, despite a self-conception that their role is one of apprehending law-breakers and keeping blacks in their place (Edwards, 1968), in fact, probably provide more essential services to lower-class residents than most other governmental service organiza-

5. Obviously, there is not that much support at the inspector level either. Evidence to be presented later, however, indicates that a need for improved police-community relations is recognized by a substantially larger group than shown in response to this question. How deep and insightful this support is will be discussed later.

tions. Intervention in family quarrels, running an "ambulance service" working with troubled youth, and a large variety of other responsibilities consume more police time than the apprehension of criminals. As can be seen even by this superficial recitation, many of these are among the most difficult or most undesirable to be found in large cities. Yet it is the police who perform these services, not the professionals who flee the city after daylight hours. Furthermore, even though many police officers think of themselves as functioning to control the black population, it is probably easier, as Bordua (1968) has pointed out, for a ghetto resident to obtain a needed service from the police than from a teacher, a social worker, a housing inspector, a psychiatrist, or a sanitation man. More specifically, then, the irony is that the police are already providing many of the services that potentially form the basis for an effective police-community interaction but cannot grasp its implications for improving their effectiveness in the area of crime control—the very area in which their conception of police work requires them to be effective.

The failure to make the connection between police-community relations and the perceived role of the police in crime prevention and control may be attributed to two main factors. First, the average officer is undereducated and the ability to perceive what is, after all, a complex connection requires analytical abilities that are distinctively functions of education. As Skolnick (1969) has pointed out, the average officer joining the force is less educated than his civilian peers, and the educational level of officers has actually been declining since the Depression.[6] It is this, rather than the assumed authoritarian character structure of the officer, that matters. In fact, while studies of police officers' personalities are rare, the available evidence (Niederhoffer, 1967)[7] would indicate that officers, on joining the force, are not particularly authoritarian. They are, however, certainly conventional and become authoritarian and cynical as they continue with the force.

The second main factor blocking improved police-community relations is the police attitude toward the people with whom they would have to frankly and intimately interact if they are to develop an effective program. Numerous studies presented or reviewed in Skolnick (1966, 1969) have clearly shown that many, indeed most,

police officers manifest considerable anti-black feeling and find it difficult to avoid viewing themselves, literally, as front line troops against the rebellious and uncivilized blacks. To be sure, white police officers are not particularly different from working-class whites in general in this anti-black feeling; rather perhaps, the average officer is more direct in his verbal utterances than the equivocating, but just as hostile, civilian.

The study in Detroit provides some of the dimensions of this dislike. The typical white officer, lieutenant and below, interprets the motives for the riot in predominantly negative terms. He clearly does not see it as a meaningless event but, rather, as a reflection of the undisciplined, hostile or morally corrupt nature of the black community. This is shown in Table 2. This interpretation is consistent with his general view of the black community. As Table 3 shows, he sees the black community as a privileged minority which, rather than rebelling against white authority, obviously ought to be grateful to that authority. Furthermore, he sees the lower-class black community as manifesting relatively little respect for law and order. This comparison takes on more significance when it is compared to his view of the white community. These data are presented in Table 4.[8] Finally, the officer's view of

6. This deficiency has been recognized by the Police Department in Detroit and is also a central point in the reforms suggested by Locke (1969), a former administrative assistant to the commissioner, in his recent book on the Detroit riot. Officers are encouraged to pursue college studies and are rewarded for this by reducing the time spans required to take promotional exams and by other rewards as well.

7. Niederhoffer (1967) notes that recruits to the New York Police Department score about average on the California F Scale. They seem reasonably idealistic about police work but rapidly change in the direction of the substantial cynicism that characterizes the veteran officer. Interestingly, this increase in cynicism occurs while they are still in the Academy and before they have any real street experience. Later in this paper, I will discuss the effects of street experience on police attitudes.

8. Most striking, of course, is the fact that the officers' chief differentiation is along class lines, even though all officers (including black ones) always rate whites as higher in respect for law and order than blacks. This class differentiation made by white officers is potentially of great value to an effective police-community relations program. It hardly needs to be said, however, that to most officers, a black is lower class unless the citizen proves otherwise. Then there may be a change in attitude toward him. By then, however, it is often too late. The seriousness of the officers' dislike of the lower-class black is compounded by the fact that, despite the increased entry of blacks into the middle class, proportionally larger numbers of blacks are lower class than are whites.

It should also be pointed out that black officers make the same differentiations as do white officers. They rate the middle class as higher than the slum group and, within class, evaluate white citizens as having more respect for law and order than black citizens. Black officers, however, assign higher respect for law and order, among blacks,

Table 2. What do you think was the long term cause of the riot?

(in percentages)

Race	White					Black
Rank[a]	Insp. (n = 94)	Lt. (n = 40)	Sgt. (n = 43)	Det. (n = 49)	Ptr. (n = 104)	All Ranks (n = 53)
Cause						
Persons (e.g., agitators, militants)	18.1	22.5	14.0	14.3	26.9	9.4
Undisciplined self-interest (e.g., something for nothing)	6.4	10.0	32.6	26.5	17.3	11.3
Protest (e.g., frustration, jobs, mistreatment)	43.6	17.5	20.9	20.4	22.1	54.7
Temper of the times (e.g., violence elsewhere, no respect for authority)	27.6	50.0	27.9	34.7	31.7	24.5
Other	4.2	0.0	4.6	4.1	1.9	0.0
TOTAL	99.9	100.0	100.0	100.0	99.9	99.9

[a]The data in the table record the first two reasons mentioned by the respondents. Accordingly, it is a table of responses rather than subjects. Those officers who responded with "don't know" or not applicable answers are not included. This was the case for five inspectors, nine sergeants, three detectives, fifteen patrolmen, and five black officers.

citizen hostility toward him as an officer shows a clear differentiation between white and black. He is not unsympathetic toward white hostility, as Table 5 shows, but he interprets black hostility (Table 6) in highly negative terms with relatively little insight into its likely causes or the police contribution. This interpretation is, of course, consistent with a warfare view of his relations with the black community and with his other views which have been presented above.

Summing up, the typical white officer (below the rank of inspector[9]) views the

black community as a privileged minority, unsatisfied with its already privileged position and prepared to use violence[10] to attain still further advantage over the white community. The community is perceived, further, as susceptible to the influence of agitators capable of galvanizing into action a people without real grievances. Finally, the

most understanding and sympathetic view of the black community as can be seen from the tables. This likely comes about from their increased sophistication, their contact with leaders and concerned citizens of the black community, and their removal from the confrontations of the street. It may also be a function of the kind of persons who become inspectors. The issue is discussed in Mendelsohn (1969).

10. The majority of white officers below the rank of inspector responded "yes" to the question "Do you believe the more that Negroes get the more they want and the more they will rely on force to get it?"

than all white officers (except inspectors). Most significantly, they do not assume that anger at the police by black citizens is a function of the antisocial nature of the black community but is rather due to real or perceived police mistreatment of black citizens.

9. Of all white officers, the inspectors present the

Table 3. Here is a list of areas in which some people say Negroes are not treated fairly. Do you think they are treated very unfairly, slightly unfairly, the same as whites, or that things are actually in their favor?

(in percentages)

Race	White					Black
Rank	Insp. (n = 59)	Lt. (n = 33)	Sgt. (n = 36)	Det. (n = 36)	Ptr. (n = 86)	All Ranks (n = 36)
Area Housing						
VU	24	12	22	6	12	67
U	34	39	39	28	29	25
S	30	33	25	56	37	3
F	10	12	14	11	19	3
DK, NA	2	3	0	0	3	3
Schools						
VU	3	0	0	0	0	47
U	7	6	3	3	0	33
S	44	45	31	33	40	14
F	41	48	67	64	59	3˙
DK, NA	5	0	0	0	1	3
Jobs						
VU	15	3	11	6	5	56
U	25	18	14	22	17	33
S	30	36	44	56	43	8
F	29	42	31	17	31	0
DK, NA	0	0	0	0	3	3
Welfare Agencies						
VU	0	0	0	0	0	8
U	2	0	0	0	0	19
S	25	15	14	11	10	39
F	64	79	83	86	86	28
DK, NA	8	6	3	3	3	6
Stores						
VU	12	3	8	0	1	22
U	5	9	8	8	13	33
S	71	76	72	86	70	36
F	5	9	8	6	13	3
DK, NA	7	3	3	0	3	6
Law Enforcement Agencies						
VU	2	0	6	0	0	56
U	14	15	14	3	7	31
S	68	55	53	72	57	6
F	14	30	28	25	34	3
DK, NA	3	0	0	0	2	6

black community is viewed as deficient in respect for law and order. Implicit in this view is a conception of the black community as primitive, emotional, and easily aroused to antisocial action, and with an ultimate goal of domination over whites rather than a goal of equality.[11]

11. Except for the emphasis on law and order and a disinclination among officers of ranks of detective and above to see the riot as planned, there is

Table 4. Mean Perceived Scores on Respect for Law and Order (at the present time) in Middle-Class and Slum Communities by Race

Race			White			Black
Rank	Insp.	Lt.	Sgt.	Det.	Ptr.	All Ranks
Group						
Black middle class	6.8	6.5	6.3	6.4	6.0	7.0
White middle class	8.0	7.6	7.6	7.8	7.6	7.4
Black slum	4.1	2.6	2.4	2.6	2.0	3.0
White slum	4.7	3.7	3.6	4.3	3.3	4.1

Table 5. Many people have noted that the average white citizen often has negative feelings toward the police. Why do you think they feel that way?

(in percentages)

Race		White			Black
Rank[a]	Lt. (n = 33)	Sgt. (n = 36)	Det. (n = 36)	Ptr. (n = 86)	All Ranks (n = 36)
Reason					
Antisocial nature of white community	12.1	2.8	5.6	8.1	11.1
Unpleasant experiences; everyone hates authority a little bit	57.6	69.4	52.8	48.8	41.7
Statement not true	15.2	8.3	11.1	18.6	11.1
Other	15.2	11.1	16.7	18.6	22.2
DK, NA	0.0	8.3	13.9	5.8	13.9
TOTAL	100.1	99.9	100.1	99.9	100.0

[a]Unfortunately, inspectors and above ranks were not asked this question.

nothing especially distinctive about white officers' interpretation of the riot or their views of the black community. The same may be said for black officers. White officers mirror the views of the white citizenry, particularly the working-class citizenry, and black officers mirror the views of the black community. Further, although persons in the community sample of the Detroit study were not asked about whether blacks suffer from discrimination, past and recent polls (Pettigrew, 1964; Newsweek, 1969b) show that police attitudes in this matter are quite similar to those of whites in general. It is clear that most of the variance in riot interpretation and view of the black community is a function of race and class. This suggests that there is little variance remaining to be influenced by the effects of experience as a police officer qua officer in these matters. This indeed turns out to be the state of affairs. Patrolmen who have served only in all white precincts are not differentiable in attitudes from those whose sole experience has been in all black precincts. Nor are officers (of

This is, of course, not to say that he acts on this conception in all his interactions while on duty. Quite the contrary—most of the time, as Skolnick (1966) has pointed out in his discussion of the warrant policeman,

ranks from lieutenant to patrolmen) whose major experience has been in white areas differentiable from officers whose major experience has been in black areas. Certainly the claim that officers' attitudes are understandable in the face of the dangers they face and the experiences they have with blacks is challenged by such data.

Since, as innumerable surveys (Herbers, 1968; Hedegard, 1969; Newsweek, 1969a) have shown, the goal of the overwhelming majority of black citizens is equality rather than domination, integration rather than separation, the potential for misunderstanding and conflict between white officers and black citizens is ominous.

Table 6. A recent survey in the *Free Press* found that a majority of Negroes in the riot areas felt that police behavior toward Negroes was a major cause of the riot. Why do you think they feel that way?

(in percentages)

Race	White					Black
Rank	Insp. (n = 59)	Lt. (n = 33)	Sgt. (n = 36)	Det. (n = 36)	Ptr. (n = 86)	All Ranks (n = 36)
Reason Police behavior or perception of police behavior by Negroes[a] (e.g., Negroes treated unfairly)	54.2[b]	27.3	19.4	19.4	19.8	69.4
Antisocial nature of black community (e.g., no respect for law and order; more Negroes are criminals)	0.0	33.3	55.6	50.0	39.5	5.6
Statement is not true	15.2	6.1	11.1	11.1	11.6	5.6
Other	23.7	18.2	8.3	8.3	19.8	19.4
DK, NA	6.8	15.2	5.6	11.1	9.3	0.0
TOTAL	99.9	100.1	100.0	99.9	100.0	100.0

[a]Very few white officers believe that police *in fact* discriminate against blacks with the exception of inspectors (see note b). Most of the officers responding within this category are saying that Negroes *feel* police discriminate. Black officers reverse the explanation. The majority responding in this category believe police in fact do discriminate.

[b]Half the inspectors responding in this category state blacks feel the way they do because the police represent the power structure. Only inspectors give this reason.

practical considerations play a major role. Further, the professional standards to which most officers strive to adhere are of great influence. But obviously an officer carrying around such a view of the black community is going to act on it at some points. For example, a view of blacks as hostile toward him predisposes an officer to use unnecessary force when he interprets the situation as threatening. In turn, what he decides to be threatening is a function, in part, of his generalized belief system about the black community. If he is wrong, or at times even when he is right, the resulting police-community tensions can have far-reaching and explosive consequences. In terms of the con-

cern of this paper, however, even if he is able to behave judiciously despite these views, they hardly would incline him toward concern with improving police-community relations, and that is, as I have been arguing, a critical need.

These beliefs, then, make such far-reaching programs for police-community relations, as proposed by the President's Commission (1967b) and Bordua (1968), most difficult, perhaps impossible, to attain. The following considerations complicate adequate solution still further: (1) the increasing crime rate [12]

12. The best evidence would suggest that, even accounting for more efficient methods of reporting crime, the rate has been rising (President's Commis-

with its demands for more vigorous police control despite the likely failure of such tactics to affect the crime rate in the long run (Menninger, 1968); (2) the pervasive feeling among officers that theirs is a disrespected profession[13] (Wilson, 1963; President's Commission, 1967b) with its concomitant and resulting reinforcement of in-group loyalties and alienation from the larger society; and (3) the reluctance of the police to add still another "disrespected" group to the list of police responsibilities. It thus becomes apparent that implementation of an effective and revolutionary program in police-community relations is highly problematical. Still, given the strategic importance of the police, an effort must be made.

Such an effort must begin where there are positive potentials at work. These may be identified as follows. First, from the black side, there is an increasing demand for better police services. Studies reported by the President's Commission (1967b) clearly indicate that a majority of blacks would support, indeed desperately want, a fair and effective police presence. This is hardly surprising since it is predominantly blacks who are the victims of crime.

Second, there is, among many—particularly higher echelon—officers, some recognition of the need for effective police-community relations and a corresponding realization that the police contribute, at least in some measure, to the problems in the community. For example, sixty-six percent of officers of the rank of inspector agree with the statement that "the behavior of the police has contributed to the tense situation that exists in the Negro areas of the city." Sixty-nine percent of inspectors favor increased police involvement with the com-

munity. Furthermore, these officers have a positive view of the purpose of police-community relations work. Twenty-nine percent of inspectors hope such programs will produce closer contact between police and community or open lines of communication, seventeen percent feel it would let people present their problems and complaints to the police, forty-nine percent believe it would promote better understanding of *each other's problems* and improve police relations with the black community, and seventeen percent think it would help in the pursuit of solutions to police and community problems that are mutually acceptable. By contrast, very few inspectors cite using such contacts as an intelligence source, to promote a positive police "image," or to get citizens to respect law and order. Finally, fully eighty-one percent of these executive officers thought the police should do more in the way of police-community relations. [14] Fifty-four percent of those who believed more should be done felt it should take the form of increased involvement in community affairs, many advocating more meetings with citizens' groups.[15]

14. Response to this question may be an over-estimate of the commitment of the inspectors to police-community relations. The question specified should police do more *if time and money were available.* Thus the question avoids the issue of priorities on police time and money.

15. Though these responses are correctly cited as positive potentials, it must be pointed out that there remains a large group of police executives who are not convinced of the importance of even these minimal programs. Perhaps more significant is the fact that only a handful of officers see improved police-community relations as functionally related to reducing crime. Finally, police executives more strongly support programs for crime reduction and riot avoidance which place the responsibility on other social forces or agencies. For example, the two most popular responses given by these officers on ways to prevent future riots is improvement in the socioeconomic and educational status of blacks and the imposition of stiffer penalties by the courts. Both kinds of social change are well beyond the power of the police to effect. It is undoubtedly true that improvement in the status and skills of the black community is a critical step to make in eliminating riots and reducing crime. It is also true that this police response attests to some sophistication and sympathy and is a realistic one.

sion, 1967a). Whether, however, it is in fact higher than in previous eras of our nation's history is open to question.

13. This is an incorrect belief particularly as it applies to the white community. The President's Commission (1967b) reviews the evidence of public reaction to the police, and, by and large, the police are positively viewed by whites.

Among lower-echelon officers, there is considerably less support but, even here, a majority of officers state that they favor a human relations approach toward the black community. It is doubtful that this support goes very deep but it may be something on which to build. In addition, there is some evidence from Niederhoffer that many officers begin their police careers with some idealism and desire to help others. While his data clearly show that most of this idealism is lost, it may be possible to recapture it. Suggestions for how this might be done are presented below.

RECAPTURING THE IDEALISM

Considering the balance of positive and negative forces, presented here, affecting the development of an effective police-community relations program, the conclusion must be that to date the negative forces predominate. If this situation is to change, a number of steps are required.

First, there must be an explicit redefinition of the police role, reinforced by strongly supported professional norms. This redefinition would conform with what police in fact do in providing public service. Explicit recognition must be given to the police responsibility for assisting citizens who lack resources or sufficient power to obtain such resources. Equally important, the redefinition of the police role must provide a rationale for the importance of this work from both a general humanitarian and a practical point of view. This is to say, the officer needs to learn the connection between good community relations and greater effectiveness in crime control. Given the attitudes of most officers, it is difficult to see how this redefinition can be accomplished without strong professional norms supporting such activity. Professional

norms would also shield the police, to some extent, from those groups in the community that reflect antipathy toward black Americans. Another way to put this last point is that so long as the police permit themselves to be used to carry out the mandate of large segments of the white population, they will always be cast in the role of victimizers and victimized. They will carry out the mandate of the white citizenry but unlike the citizenry cannot avoid that policy's implications. They thus become the visible representatives of the white power structure, a point not lost on a number of police administrators.[16]

There is good reason to believe that those professional norms which implicitly require officers to disengage themselves from a firmly held set of attitudes before they take action will not be easily inculcated. As Wilson has pointed out, police officers' conception of their roles is often at variance with idealized professional norms. For example, many officers regard violence as a way of instilling "respect" for police, a belief that most professionally oriented officers would reject. In addition, there are some professional norms that fly in the face of the hostility many officers feel toward blacks. Both impediments to the adoption of professional norms do not seem to be functions of specific police experience with black citizens.[17] Rather they come from attitudes learned from their primary reference groups in the process of growing up in a society that

---

The danger, however, is that, given this view, the police will be inclined to do less than they could. Of course, quite aside from the inspectors' views, there remains the problem of getting the cooperation and support of lower-echelon officers.

16. As Table 5 shows, twenty-seven percent of inspectors believe the reason blacks blame police for the riot is that police represent the white power structure. With second mentions included, this rises to thirty percent. This explanation is totally absent among officers below this echelon.

17. As indicated earlier, the specific assignment of officers (with the exception of those at the inspector level) does not seem related to attitudes. This suggests that police attitudes toward blacks (and indeed work norms) is a function of police tradition and attitudes, and primary reference group attitudes. These provide the "filtering system" through which experience is channeled. Thus, it is the filtering system that matters and which must be changed if officers are going to accept the changes being advocated.

discriminates against black Americans and from generalized police tradition and attitudes. Since police agencies have no control over the early socialization experiences of the men who become officers, it is they who must take primary responsibility for the education of their officers.

This discussion leads to the second and third recommendations. There must be increased university training for police officers and more effective in-service training programs. Such programs will provide the intellectual background for understanding the centrality of police-community relations. As indicated earlier, the need for increased education has been recognized by the Detroit Police Department. Third, it is absolutely essential that command and executive officers reward, through promotion and other positive reinforcements, officers who exemplify good relations with the community and who innovate new techniques for improved relations. Of all the steps that can be taken, none may be more potent than reward by superiors of officers who exemplify commitment to positive community attitudes.

A fourth recommendation is that a program of research must be vigorously undertaken to evaluate the effect of new (and old) programs pertaining to police-community relations. Nothing succeeds like demonstrated success. Research may provide that evidence of success. This means that close ties between the police and the academic community must be vigorously established.

Finally, innovation and willingness to try new ideas in the area of police-community relations must be strongly rewarded. Included must be a recognition that old solutions are not adequate. The following are several programs suggested by Bordua and briefly noted here. They really deserve complete discussion but are presented mainly to provide an idea as to what innovation might involve. Police must be willing to talk with all groups in the community, including militants. As the most visible representatives of law and order, they must make that role

more than a euphemism for repression by adopting an advocacy role in regard to the poor and disadvantaged. Police must expand and professionalize their Youth Bureaus. To earn the confidence of the community, they must develop a citizen observer program (with observers recruited from all political groups). They must know community mores and through careful program and operations analysis determine which police practices offend such mores without commensurate pay-off in crime reduction or decrease in police-community tensions.

The police are inevitably and inextricably involved in the black community. The sole question is how they will relate to that community. While obviously substantially improved police-community relations will be just one factor in reducing both urban crime and the likelihood of further riots, it is a certainty that the way the police handle their relations with the black community will play a major role in the direction that American cities take.

REFERENCES

Bordua, D. J. (1968) "Comments on police-community relations." Unpublished paper.

Edwards, G. (1968) The Police on the Urban Frontier: A Guide to Community Understanding. New York: Institute of Human Relations Press.

Hedegard, J. M. (1969) "Detroit community attitudes on race and urban rioting." Detroit Riot Study, unpublished paper.

Herbers, J. (1968) "Study says Negro justifies rioting as social protest." New York Times 118 (July 28): 1 ff.

Locke, H. G. (1969) The Detroit Riot of 1967. Detroit: Wayne State Univ. Press.

Mendelsohn, R. A. (1969) "The police interpretation of the Detroit riot of 1967: an examination of the dimensions and determinants of the interpretation." Detroit Riot Study, unpublished paper.

Menninger, K. (1968) The Crime of Punishment. New York: Viking Press.

Newsweek Editors (1969a) "Report from black America." Newsweek 73 (June 30): 17–35.

—— (1969b) "The troubled American: a special report on the white majority." Newsweek 74 (October 6): 28–68.

Niederhoffer, A. (1967) Behind the Shield. New York: Doubleday.

Pettigrew, T. F. (1964) A Profile of the Negro American. Princeton: D. Von Nostrand.

President's Commission on Law Enforcement and Administration of Justice (1967a) The Challenge of Crime in a Free Society. Washington, D.C.: U.S. Government Printing Office.

—— (1967b) Task Force Report: The Police. Washington, D.C.: U.S. Government Printing Office.

Skolnick, J. H. (1969) The Politics of Protest. New York: Ballantine Books.

—— (1966) Justice Without Trial. New York: John Wiley.

Wilson, J. Q. (1963) "The police and their problems: a theory." Public Policy 12: 189–216.

8

EFFECTS OF THE URBAN ENVIRONMENT

Introduction

There are many features of large cities that people seem to like: for example, plays, concerts, museums, restaurants, and the abundance of goods and services. There are also a number of features that many people seem to dislike: for example, crowds, noxious odors, noise, littered streets, polluted air, and congested roads and highways. Although the data are fragmentary, they suggest that heavy automobile traffic, the carbon monoxide emitted at peak levels of traffic, and unpredictably paced loud noise are not only unpleasant to urban dwellers, but can interfere with psychological processes as well as physical ones. The data also suggest that the effects of population density in public places and in housing are moderated by a number of variables.

TRAFFIC, POLLUTION, AND NOISE

In a preliminary investigation designed to assess the impact of traffic on the residents of city streets, Appleyard and Lintell (1972, reading 8.1) interviewed equal numbers of young, middle-aged, and elderly residents of three adjacent streets in San Francisco. Although the streets contained similar housing, there were considerable differences in the amount of traffic. The first street averaged 15,750 vehicles every 24 hours, the second street 8,700 vehicles, and the third street 2,000 vehicles. The findings suggest that these differences in traffic were responsible for an assortment of differences in perception and behavior. Residents of the heavily trafficked street were bothered by the noise, vibrations, and automotive exhaust. They rarely used the street to socialize and their sense of personal territory seldom extended beyond the confines of their apartments. In contrast, residents of the lightly trafficked street were seldom bothered by noise and automotive exhaust, they socialized extensively in front of their homes and at the corner grocery, and their sense of personal territory usually included the entire block.

Studies by Lewis, Baddeley, Bonham, and Lovett (1970) and Horvath, Dahms, and O'Hanlon (1971, reading 8.2) indicate that the automotive exhaust produced by heavy traffic also has deleterious effects on seeing and hearing. Lewis *et al.* (1970) measured the performance of 16 subjects on a variety of tests in two experimental sessions separated by one week. During one session, half the subjects breathed pure air from medical cylinders and half breathed air comparable to that breathed by drivers on a road traversed by about 830 cars an hour. During the second session, the sources of air for each subject were reversed. The results indicate that subjects detected fewer signals on a test of auditory vigilance and took more time to complete tests of addition and sentence comprehension while breathing polluted air. On a test of digit copying, the average digit height did not differ over conditions. Horvath, Dahms, and O'Hanlon (1971, reading 8.2) tried to find out if carbon monoxide gas, a component of polluted air, was a factor responsible for the deterioration of vigilance. Ten male volunteers participated in three weekly experimental sessions. During the first hour of each session, subjects were exposed to one of three gas mixtures containing carbon monoxide concentrations of 0 ppm (parts per million), 26 ppm, or 111 ppm. The concentrations of 26 ppm and 111 ppm were representative of the average and peak levels of Los Angeles traffic. During the second hour, subjects continued to breathe the same gas mixture while performing a visual monitoring task. The data indicate that exposure to 111 ppm of carbon monoxide accelerated the deterioration of vigilance; that is, while the proportion of signals correctly identified under each condition declined over time, the decline was considerably more precipitous when subjects were exposed to 111 ppm of carbon monoxide. These findings, then, suggest that the exhaust generated by heavy traffic may have damaging, and perhaps dangerous, effects on both the people living in heavily trafficked areas and the people in the cars.

The findings of several laboratory investigations of the behavioral aftereffects of exposure to loud, unpredictably paced, uncontrollable noise (Glass & Singer, 1972a, reading 8.3; 1972b) are consistent with the reported impact of heavy traffic on residents:

> The steady drone of traffic was certainly bad, but the random deep-throated roar of a bus or large truck, with the accompanying shudder that rattled every window, unnerved the most hardened resident, especially when it continued day and night. The screeching of brakes at the intersections added to the distress. [Appleyard & Lintell, 1972, p. 89]

For example, Glass and Singer found that subjects who were exposed to loud aperiodic noise for 23 minutes were much less tolerant of post-noise frustration and made more mistakes on a task requiring care and attention than subjects who were exposed to loud periodic noise. In a second experiment, they found that subjects who were given the option to terminate loud aperiodic noise displayed considerably more tolerance for post-noise frustration and made fewer mistakes on a task requiring care and attention than subjects who were given no option, even though most subjects who were given the option did not exercise it. In an attempt to explain these findings, Glass and Singer (1972a) suggested that subjects who are not given the option to terminate the noise "experience not only the aversiveness of unpredictable noise but also the 'anxiety' connected with their felt inability to do anything about it. Perceived-control subjects, on the other hand, are exposed only to the stress of the noise itself; they do not experience additional anxiety produced by feelings of helplessness" (p. 462). The observations of Appleyard and Lintell provide support for the hypothesized importance of perceived and actual control:

> The intensive traffic conditions . . . led to both stress and withdrawal. Those people who found the traffic conditions intolerable, especially those with children, had moved elsewhere, and the people who lived there at the time of the survey . . . only used [the street] when they had to. . . . If they could, they lived at the backs of their houses. For those who treated [the street] as a transient residence, this condition was tolerable. Those who had to treat it as a permanent residence . . . suffered [pp. 96–97].

The results of these studies have a number of implications. The observed effects of automotive exhaust underscore the need for effective antipollution devices in automobiles. The investigations of the impact of noise provide persuasive reasons for locating noisy factories far from residential areas, constructing walls in ways that effectively damp noise, and routing highways and jet flights beyond the earshot of residential and work environments (Glass & Singer, 1972b). Appleyard and Lintell's inquiry into the effects of traffic suggests that reducing traffic in residential areas would improve the quality of life. Toward that end, Appleyard and Lintell proposed improving public transit, increasing the capacity of the city's main arteries, and using a variety of devices to discourage traffic on residential streets. On streets where the flow and speed of traffic cannot be reduced, they suggested planting trees and hedges, constructing low walls, and providing alternative play areas for children.

POPULATION DENSITY

The behavior of people in large cities often seems hurried and insensitive; for example, people push one another in an attempt to board a crowded subway car, bump into one another on the street without apologizing, and bypass presumed drunks lying on sidewalks without a backward glance. In an attempt to explain these behaviors, Milgram (1970) suggested that since large cities contain large numbers of people, a high population density, and a heterogeneous populace, the city dweller is confronted with more sensory inputs than he can process. As a result, he experiences stimulus overload. In an attempt to reduce this overload, the individual engages in a variety of adaptive responses; for example, he allots less time to each input, he ignores low priority inputs, and he behaves in ways that permit only weak and superficial forms of involvement with others. Perhaps the most disturbing consequence of these responses to overload is the presumed unwillingness of many city dwellers to respond to the plight of a stranger.

A small number of studies designed to test some of these assumptions have been carried out in urban settings. Although these studies did not include comparable non-urban settings, the findings suggest that many city dwellers would *not* refuse to offer help to a stranger, and that helping behavior is affected by a number of variables. In a series of laboratory experiments, Latané and Darley (1969) found that people who overheard in the presence of others an ambiguous emergency—such as hearing someone fall and cry out—were less likely to offer help than people who overheard an ambiguous emergency by themselves. In an attempt to explain this difference, Latané and Darley suggested that two processes lessen the likelihood of intervention when others are present. One, each bystander may be "led by the *apparent* lack of concern of the others to interpret the situation as being less serious than he would if alone" (p. 265). Two, when other people are present, "the responsibility for action is diffused and each may feel less necessity to help" (p. 265).

In an attempt to test the diffusion of responsibility hypothesis under field conditions, Piliavin, Rodin, and Piliavin (1969) carried out a study in a New York subway. Shortly after the train left the station, the "victim"—a casually dressed white or black male who either was carrying a cane or who smelled of liquor and carried a liquor bottle—staggered forward and collapsed. If the victim was not helped after 70 seconds passed, an accomplice provided assistance. The results fail to provide support for the diffusion of responsibility hypothesis; that is, the time that elapsed before a bystander helped the victim did not increase as the number of males—who provided most of the help—in the immediate area increased. The results also indicate that one or more passengers helped the victim within 70 seconds on 78% of the trials, that the victim with the cane was helped more frequently (on 95% of the trials) than the drunk (on 50% of the trials), and that passengers displayed a slight tendency to help victims of their own race.

The effects of race on helping behavior in urban settings have also been examined in non-emergency situations. For example, approximately 550 black and 550 white residents of Brooklyn, New York received phone calls from someone whose car had broken down on a local parkway and who was trying to call a garage (Gaertner & Bickman, 1971). The caller, a black male who spoke with a "modified 'southern Negro' dialect" (p. 219) or a white male whose speech was "typical of whites in New York" (p. 219), apologized for disturbing the subject, told the subject that he had no more change, and asked the subject if he/she would please call the garage and let them know where he was stranded. The findings indicate that 54% of the people who were contacted called the garage; that white males, white females, and black females notified the garage slightly more often when the caller was white; and that a somewhat larger proportion of males, compared to females, provided assistance. In a study conducted in a major railroad terminal in New York (Thayer, 1973), an ostensibly deaf student—a white male, a white female, a black male, or a black female—approached equal numbers of white and black males and females who were walking alone, held out a dime, and displayed the following handwritten message: "I am *deaf*. Could you please help me? Dial (phone number) and just ask if Harold will pick me (Carol, or John) up at school. Thank you" (p. 9). Fifty-five percent of the people who were approached helped the student. Although similar numbers of calls were made by white males, white females, black males, and black females, black students were helped more often than white students (64% versus 46%). This difference was due to the unwillingness of every white male who was approached to help the white male student, and the refusal of most of the females, black and white, to help the white female student.

Although the generalizability of the findings is limited by the small number of field studies and the use of just one major city, the data suggest that a substantial proportion of city dwellers are responsive to the plight of another person. However, we do not know if a larger or perhaps a smaller proportion of non-city dwellers may respond similarly. The data also suggest that helping behavior is moderated by the nature of the victim's plight, the difficulty of escaping from the situation, and the race and sex of the victim and the bystander.

Only a handful of studies have examined the presumed effects of densely populated urban housing in the United States.* While the findings are fragmentary (Lawrence, 1974, reading 8.4), they indicate that density is a multidimensional variable, and they imply that the impact of density is moderated by the amount of personal living space residents have and by their attitudes toward extensive interpersonal contact. These findings also imply that the relationship between densely populated low-income housing and the fertility and public assistance rates may be due to the extremely limited monetary resources of lower-class families rather than to the effects of density, and that densely populated

---

*Although several laboratory investigations of the effects of population density on human beings have been carried out (e.g., Freedman, Klevansky, & Ehrlich, 1971; Griffit & Veitch, 1971; Stokols, Rall, Pinner, & Schopler, 1973), subjects were exposed to high-density conditions for relatively short periods of time, for example, 70 minutes. Since it seems likely that the psychological effects of living in densely populated housing for years differ markedly from the effects of participating briefly in a crowded experimental setting, we have omitted these studies from consideration.

high-rise low-income housing may create conditions that generate acts of delinquency.

Although many of the dwellings and streets in Boston's West End were densely
populated, most residents expressed a great deal of satisfaction with their apartments and the neighborhood (Hartman, 1963, reading 3.1). In an attempt to
explain these findings, Hartman indicated that friendships with many neighbors
and extensive social interaction were integral, highly desirable facets of life in
the West End. For example, residents were in and out of one another's apartments, sat on stoops, congregated on street corners, leaned out of windows,
talked with shopkeepers, and strolled in the local area. As a result, the personal
living space of most residents extended well beyond the bounds of their own
apartments. These observations led Hartman to conclude that the "measures and
standards of residential density must be revised to include a realistic assessment
of available living space as well as consideration of the preferred pattern and
intensity of interpersonal contact" (p. 129).

The results of Kasl and Harburg's (1972) study of the perceptions and attitudes of people living in a black high stress tract, a white high stress tract, a
black low stress tract, and a white low stress tract in Detroit indicate that persons
per room and dissatisfaction with one's dwelling correlated .30 and .27 in the
high stress areas and .10 and .12 in the low stress areas. While these coefficients
are fairly modest, we may infer that, among other factors, large middle-class
families are more likely to have the resources to cope with family size than large
lower-class families. For example, middle-class homes are likely to have larger
rooms, a more workable layout, and walls that damp sound reasonably well.

Galle, Gove, and McPherson (1972) sought to determine the relationship
between four components of density—persons per room, rooms per housing unit,
housing units per structure, and structures per acre—and each of five archival
measures that presumably reflected social pathology in 74 Chicago communities.
These measures included the mortality rate, the fertility rate, the rate of public
assistance to children, the juvenile delinquency rate, and the rate of admissions to
mental hospitals. In an attempt to remove the effects of social class and of
ethnic status, Galle et al. chose three measures of class and three measures of
ethnicity. Each set of measures was combined into an index in a way that maximized the relationship between each index and the several measures of social
pathology. These indexes were then used to try to partial out the effects of
social class and of ethnic status.

The results indicate that the relationship between the four components of
density and each measure of social pathology still was considerable; that is, the
multiple correlation coefficients ranged from .37 to .58. Additional analyses
indicate that persons per room and housing units per structure were the two
most powerful correlates of the mortality rate, fertility rate, public assistance

rate, and juvenile delinquency rate. One interpretation of these findings is that the relationship between density and the measures of social pathology is considerable within lower-class communities and negligible within other communities. It also seems likely that density is largely a correlate, rather than a cause, of the high fertility rate and public assistance rate in lower-class communities. In other words, it seems plausible to argue that the relationship between persons per room and the fertility rate is due primarily to the inability of larger lower-class families to obtain housing appropriate to their size. As families increase in size, it becomes more difficult, given these families' limited monetary resources, to purchase minimally adequate necessities. As a result, large families are more likely than small families to receive public aid for dependent children. As regards the relationship between the measures of density and the incidence of juvenile delinquency, Galle *et al.* suggested that children in overcrowded apartments are likely to be confronted with irritable parents, constant noise, and no opportunities for privacy. In an attempt to seek relief, these children leave their apartments whenever they can. The presence of many housing units per structure brings large numbers of these children together under conditions that make it exceedingly difficult for parents to monitor and control their behavior.

While these findings are suggestive, Galle *et al.* pointed out that a number of factors limit the conclusions that may be drawn. One, relationships that appear when archival data are analyzed may not appear when individual families are studied. Two, the measures of density and of social pathology were correlated. As a result, the findings may be interpreted in a number of ways.

The results of a study of the apparent effects of building height and project size on the incidence of crime in New York City's public housing projects (Newman, 1972) suggest that the impact of persons per room and housing units per structure on the juvenile delinquency rate may be moderated by the height and number of buildings in a project. Newman compared the crime rate in four types of housing projects: six stories or less and 1,000 units or less, six stories or less and more than 1,000 units, more than six stories and 1,000 units or less, and more than six stories and more than 1,000 units. He found that the crime rate in large high-rise projects—projects that were more than six stories and contained more than 1,000 units—was considerably higher than the crime rates in the other three types of projects. However, Newman's findings also indicate that a high crime rate is not an inevitable feature of large high-rise projects. Rather, the incidence of crime is reduced considerably when these projects contain three interacting features of design. One, the space outside the individual apartment units should be designed in ways that cause tenants and outsiders to perceive that the public spaces comprising the project are part of the tenants' personal territory. Two, the grounds of the project and the building interiors should be designed in ways that provide residents and formal authorities with natural opportunities to observe all public and semi-private spaces and paths. Three, perception of the project as unique, isolated, and stigmatized.

The results of these studies indicate that high density does not necessarily result in individual and social deterioration. Rather, the findings suggest that the effects of density are moderated by cultural, economic, and design variables.

REFERENCES

Appleyard, D., & Lintell, M. The environmental quality of city streets: The residents' viewpoint. *Journal of the American Institute of Planners*, 1972, 38, 84–101.

Freedman, J., Klevansky, S., & Ehrlich, P. The effects of crowding on human task performance. *Journal of Applied Social Psychology*, 1971, 1, 7–25.

Gaertner, S., & Bickman, L. Effects of race on the elicitation of helping behavior: The wrong number technique. *Journal of Personality and Social Psychology*, 1971, 20, 218–222.

Galle, O., Gove, W., & McPherson, J. Population density and pathology: What are the relations for man? *Science*, 1972, 176 (4030), 23–30.

Glass, D., & Singer, J. Behavioral aftereffects of unpredictable and uncontrollable aversive events. *American Scientist*, 1972, 60, 457–465. (a)

Glass, D., & Singer, J. *Urban stress: Experiments on noise and social stressors.* New York: Academic Press, 1972. (b)

Griffitt, W., & Veitch, R. Hot and crowded: Influences of population density and temperature on interpersonal affective behavior. *Journal of Personality and Social Psychology*, 1971, 17, 92–98.

Hartman, C. Social values and housing orientations. *Journal of Social Issues,* 1963, 19 (2), 113–131.

Horvath, S., Dahms, T., & O'Hanlon, J. Carbon monoxide and human vigilance: A deleterious effect of present urban concentrations. *Archives of Environmental Health*, 1971, 23, 343–347.

Kasl, S., & Harburg, E. Perceptions of the neighborhood and the desire to move out. *Journal of the American Institute of Planners*, 1972, 38, 318–324.

Latané, B., & Darley, J. Bystander "apathy." *American Scientist,* 1969, 57, 244–268.

Lawrence, J. Science and sentiment: Overview of research on crowding and human behavior. *Psychological Bulletin*, 1974, 81, 712–720.

Lewis, J., Baddeley, A., Bonham, K., & Lovett, D. Traffic pollution and mental efficiency. *Nature,* 1970, 225(5227), 95–97.

Milgram, S. The experience of living in cities: A psychological analysis. *Science*, 1970, 167 (3924), 1461–1468.

Newman, O. *Defensible space.* New York: Macmillan, 1972.

Piliavin, I., Rodin, J., & Piliavin, J. Good samaritanism: An underground phenomenon? *Journal of Personality and Social Psychology*, 1969, 13, 289–299.

Stokols, D., Rall, M., Pinner, B., & Schopler, J. Physical, social, and personal determinants of the perception of crowding. *Environment and Behavior*, 1973, 5, 87–115.

Thayer, S. Lend me your ears: Racial and sexual factors in helping the deaf. *Journal of Personality and Social Psychology*, 1973, 28, 8–11.

The Environmental Quality of City Streets:

The Residents' Viewpoint

DONALD APPLEYARD and MARK LINTELL

Protests and research about the environmental and social impact of transportation systems have paid most attention to the problems created by new freeways through urban areas. But while these are the more dramatic instances of traffic impacts, the rapid growth of vehicular traffic has swamped residential streets in cities across the United States and in other countries. Traffic on city streets may affect as many, if not more, people than traffic on freeways. In San Francisco, approximately 60 percent of the city's major streets (those with a daily traffic volume of over 10,000 vehicles) are lined with residences.[1]

Studies of urban streets (such as the current TOPICS program of the Federal Highway Administration) have concentrated almost exclusively on increasing their traffic capacity, through devices such as street widening, signalization, and one-way streets, with no parallel accounting of the environmental and social costs of these alternatives. Wilfred Owen (1969) recently directed attention to the role that city streets play in the

environmental quality of cities as "the main corridors and front parlors" of the city, but even he did not point out that people also have to live along city streets. To our knowledge, the only empirical studies of life on city streets, apart from some studies of traffic noise and a Michigan study of the economic and environmental effects of one-way streets (Michigan, 1969), have been those carried out in Britain since the Buchanan Report (Her Majesty's Stationary Office, 1963 and Chu, 1971).[2]

The investigation reported here is a small-scale attempt to identify the environmental concerns of those who live on city streets in San Francisco. It is a pilot study using observation and open response interview techniques, and does not pretend to statistical significance. The results however are suggestive. The project grew out of the San Francisco City Planning Department's concern over increasing traffic on the city's streets and the side effects of street widen-

2. For example, the Barnsbury Environmental Study (Great Britain, Ministry of Housing and Local Government, 1968) and the Pimlico Precinct Study (City of Westminster, 1968).

1. Estimated from Report no. 4, San Francisco City Planning Department (1969–70).

Abridged from D. Appleyard & M. Lintell. The environmental quality of city streets: The residents' viewpoint. *Journal of the American Institute of Planners*, 1972, *38*, 84–101. Reprinted by permission.

ings and other proposed changes in the street system. It was one of a series of studies of environmental conditions made in San Francisco during 1969 and 1970 (San Francisco City Planning Department, 1969–70).

Study Streets

Of the street blocks selected for a general study of street living three streets are reported upon here to serve as a model of the research approach and because they contrast the effects of traffic on similar types of streets. The street blocks chosen were adjacent north-south residential streets in the northern part of the city.

Traffic

The major environmental differences between the streets were their traffic levels. The first street, which we shall call HEAVY STREET, was a one-way street which synchronized stop lights and a peak hour traffic volume (at the evening rush hour of 900 vehicles per hour (average 15,750 vehicles over twenty-four hours). The second street, MODERATE STREET, was a two-way street with a peak traffic flow of 550 vehicles per hour (average 8,700 vehicles over twenty-four hours); the third street, LIGHT STREET, had a volume of only 200 vehicles at peak hour (average 2,000 vehicles over twenty-four hours).[3]

Speeds on all streets could rise to forty-five miles an hour or more but only on HEAVY STREET was the speed controlled by the synchronized lights. Traffic volumes had increased on HEAVY and MODERATE STREETS ten years earlier when they were connected to a freeway at their southern terminal. Through traffic was dominant on MODERATE and HEAVY STREETS, and traffic composition included more trucks and buses on HEAVY STREET than on the others.

3. All traffic statistics were obtained from the San Francisco Department of Public Works, Traffic Engineering Section.

Population

The three study blocks were part of a residual Italian neighborhood that also included other white residents and a small but growing Oriental minority. By social class, education, and income the streets were relatively homogeneous. Contrasts, however, occurred in age, family composition, ownership, and length of residence.

LIGHT STREET was predominantly a family street with many children. Grownup children were even returning to bring up their own children there. One-half of the people interviewed were homeowners, and the average length of residence was 16.3 years. HEAVY STREET, at the other extreme, had almost no children on its block. It was inhabited mostly by single persons of all ages from 20 years upward, with many old people, especially single elderly women. The average length of residence on HEAVY STREET was 8.0 years, and people were nearly all renters. Rents were also somewhat higher on HEAVY STREET, averaging $140 a month among our respondents, whereas those on LIGHT STREET averaged $103. MODERATE STREET stood in between. Average length of residence here was 9.2 years and the average rent was $120. (See table 1.)

Environment

The three streets were typical San Francisco streets, with terrace houses or apartments built up to the building-line, very few front-yards and very few gaps between the houses. The architectural style ranged from Victorian to modern. The buildings were finished in either wood, stucco, or brick and were of white or light colors. They were pleasant-looking blocks. The streets were each fairly level, with a slight gradient to the south. They were close to various shopping and community facilities.

Study Design

Two sources of information were used in the study. Detailed interviews lasting about an

Table 1. Street Profiles

Street Characteristics:	Heavy Street	Moderate Street	Light Street
Peak hour traffic flow (vehicles/hour)	900	550	200
Average daily traffic flow (vehicles)	15,750	8,700	2,000
Traffic flow direction	one-way	two-way	two-way
Vehicle speed range (mph)	30–50	10–45	10–35
Noise levels (percentage of time above 65 decibels at the sidewalk)	45%	25%	5%
Accidents (per annum over a 4 block length)	17	12	. . .
Land uses	Residential (apartment blocks, apartments)	Residential (apartment blocks, apartments, single family homes), corner store	Residential (apartments, single family homes), corner store, small business
Street width (feet)	69	69	69
Pavement width (feet)	52	41	39
Sidewalk width (feet)	8.5	14	15
Average building height (no. of storeys)	3.5	3.0	2.5
Interview sample:	HEAVY STREET	MODERATE STREET	LIGHT STREET
Mean household size (no. of people)	1.5	2.6	2.7
Percentage renters	92%	67%	50%
Mean household income ($1,000's)	6.6	8.1	10.0
Mean income/member of household	4.4	3.1	3.7
Mean number of school years completed	14	13	15
Mean length of residence (years)	8.0	9.2	16.3
Mean rents ($ per month)	140.00	120.00	103.00

Source: Traffic statistics and accident counts were obtained from the San Francisco Department of Public Works, Traffic Engineering Section. All other information came from interviews, summer 1969.

hour were held with twelve residents on each block, composed of three equal age categories, the young (under twenty-five), the middle-aged (twenty-five to fifty-five), and the elderly (over fifty-five). This was not a very large sample but since they represented about 30 percent of the households on each block, their attitudes were probably representative of those on the three blocks. Second, systematic observations and, where possible, objective measurements of pedestrian and traffic activity on the streets were carried out.

The study design stemmed from earlier papers by Appleyard and others (Appleyard and Lynch, 1967; Appleyard and Okamoto, 1968) which proposed environmental criteria to be used in transportation system design. The criteria identified in the earlier studies were hypothetical in nature and for this investigation were slightly modified to cover the probable concerns of those living on urban streets. Five major criteria categories were employed to describe the character and day-to-day use of the street and the concerns and satisfactions of the residents. The interview was introduced as a survey of what the resident thought of his street, inviting suggestions for its improvement. The residents were not told that we were primarily interested in the effects of traffic.

The criteria categories were:

Traffic hazard: concerns for safety in the street associated with traffic activity.

Stress, noise, and pollution: dissatisfaction with noise, vibration, fumes, dust, and feelings of anxiety concerning traffic.

Social interaction: the degree to which residents had friends and acquaintances on the block, and the degree to which the street was a community.

Privacy and home territory: the residents' responses to intrusion from outside their homes, and the extent of their sensed personal territory or turf.

Environmental awareness: the degree to which the respondents were aware of their physical surroundings and were concerned for the external appearance of the buildings and the street.

Each question in the interview was related to one of the above categories, though some answers had relevance to more than one. The answers were independently rated on a five-point scale as "environmental quality" ratings by the interviewer and another member of the study team according to a general description of each criterion. Disparate judgments were discussed and a consensus rating was eventually recorded. No attempt was made to weight the responses in terms of their overall importance to the residents although this report emphasizes the main points of concern for the residents as expressed in the interviews. . . .

So far, a public report on the study has met with considerable response in San Francisco. The general concerns of the study, and many of the individual conclusions, have been featured in the local press and on television. Furthermore the officially adopted San Francisco "Urban Design Plan" (San Francisco, City Planning Department, 1971) incorporates many of the recommendations for limiting through traffic on residential streets and creating "protected residential areas."

Traffic Hazard

Accident counts were equally high on HEAVY and MODERATE STREETS (means of seventeen and twelve accidents per year over a four-block length).

The danger of traffic was of concern to inhabitants on all three streets, but especially so on HEAVY STREET (ratings 3.7, 3.8). (See table 2.) These findings are not surprising, since the need for "safe intersections" was the most repeated concern in a concurrent citywide survey of city residents (Kaplan et al., 1969).

HEAVY STREET is a one-way street with synchronized stoplights which enable bunches of vehicles, already with momentum from traveling downhill, to travel through at speeds of up to fifty miles an hour. The fast speeds were frequently mentioned in the responses. The very heavy traffic volumes on HEAVY STREET made it unsafe for children, and even for people washing their cars. For residents trying to manoeuver out of their garages, a one-way street has advantages over a two-way street, since the driver only has to look one way, but getting a car into a garage can be more difficult since the driver either has to swing across the traffic flow or pull to one side and wait for a lull. Excessive speed was the cause of most of the perceived traffic safety problems, especially on HEAVY STREET. Residents, seeing a large number of cars speeding down the hill, would wait for someone to make a false move or would listen for the screeching of brakes. Several residents wanted the speed limit on HEAVY STREET reduced.

LIGHT STREET, with only a small amount of through traffic, had problems of a different nature. It tended to attract the occasional hotrodder who was, in some instances, a greater menace than the steady stream of traffic on HEAVY STREET. He appeared without warning, often jumping the stop signs at intersections, and was extremely dangerous for children playing in the street. Another problem on LIGHT STREET was the temptation to park where it was immediately convenient. Delivery trucks often parked on the corner when making deliveries to the grocery and blocked the view down the cross street for motorists approaching the intersection.

Table 2. Mean Ratings of Traffic Hazard (Low traffic hazard ratings were given to responses indicating feelings of safety and security from traffic and other related incidents. Rating: 1 = very safe, 5 = very unsafe.)

Question	Heavy Street	Moderate Street	Light Street
What is traffic like on this street, how would you describe it? Does it bother you at all?	3.7	3.2	2.2
Is it ever dangerous on your street and around your home? (traffic accidents; incidents, etc.)	3.8	3.0	2.5

The traffic is very dangerous.—Traffic accidents are frequent at both intersections, especially at rush hours.—Traffic is fast, the signals are set fast.—It's dangerous for children because of traffic. You can't wash your car on the street for fear of being knocked down and if water is sprayed on passing cars, they get very angry.—I think it is a highly accident-prone area. I often hear screeching brakes.—This street is murder; I like European streets better. (HEAVY STREET)

It's a busy street, I don't trust the children on the sidewalk.—Hear brakes screeching at corners at night.—It's difficult backing out of the garage because of traffic.—Accidents and near-accidents frequently at (intersection).—Sometimes dangerous with commuter traffic between 5:00–6:00, especially round grocery on corner.—There's something deadly about the street. (MODERATE STREET)

Sidewalks are fine; kids can play, buggies or strollers get round cars very comfortably.—Children have to be taught care in crossing the street.—Traffic is getting worse. (LIGHT STREET)

Residents of MODERATE STREET perceived less safety problems arising from traffic than did the residents of HEAVY STREET. However, they were concerned about traffic dangers. As one respondent put it, "There have been some accidents and I am taking precautions."

Apart from the direct effects of traffic on the feelings of safety, there were some indirect effects. The continuous presence of strangers on HEAVY STREET, even though they were in automobiles, evinced some feelings of fear. One young housewife had frequently been "hassled" from passing cars, and some of the older ladies on HEAVY STREET were "afraid to stop and chat."

As can be seen from the aggregated ratings, there was a consistent trend through all age groups to consider LIGHT STREET as being safe, MODERATE STREET as being neither safe nor unsafe, and HEAVY STREET as being unsafe.

Stress, Noise, and Pollution

Measurements of noise levels were made on all three streets. The sound levels were determined through the use of Sound Survey Meters, utilized at four periods during a weekday; early morning (6:30 to 8:30 a.m.), late morning (11:00 a.m. to 12:30 p.m.), late afternoon (5:00 to 6:00 p.m.), and early evening (7:00 to 8:00 p.m.). In each measurement period, fifty consecutive measurements were made at fifteen second intervals at corner and midblock locations on each street. To translate these measurements into a useful measure of average conditions, the percentages of time that the noise exceeded certain A-weighted decibel levels [dB(A)] were calculated. From these we computed a traffic noise index,[4] a recognized measure of

4. The traffic noise index is a function of the 50 percent noise level and the difference between the 10 percent and 90 percent levels.

noise problems, which can be used to predict probable dissatisfaction due to noise. (Griffiths and Langdon, 1968).

On HEAVY STREET, noise levels were above sixty-five decibels 45 percent of the time and did not fall below fifty-five decibels more than 10 percent of the time except in the early morning. These noise levels were so high that the traffic noise index read right off the scale. . . .

On MODERATE STREET, sound levels were above sixty-five decibels 25 percent of the time. By the traffic noise index, the noise level (6.5) would be rated as "definitely unsatisfactory." On LIGHT STREET, the quietest of the three, sound levels rose above sixty-five decibels only 5 percent of the time, meaning that one-half of the residents would consider the noise level "unsatisfactory and one-half "satisfactory."

The two-minute sample sound level recordings on MODERATE STREET show that the noise levels tended to be more variable than on HEAVY STREET but in the same range, whereas the sound level chart on LIGHT STREET shows an ambient noise level much lower than the other two streets.

After the danger of traffic itself, traffic noise, vibrations, fumes, soot, and trash were considered to be the most stressful aspects of the environment on these three streets. (See table 3.) On HEAVY STREET, the noise was so severe that one elderly couple was forced to try to catch up on sleep in the daytime. Many, especially the older people, were unable to be objective about the other characteristics of their street because these stresses totally colored their perceptions of their environment. Adjectives such as "unbearable," or "too much" or "vulnerable" were typical of the responses.

$$TNI = L_{50} + 4(L_{10} - L_{90}) - 30$$

This figure has been shown to correlate with expressions of annoyance. Our budget did not allow us to take the customary hourly samplings over the full twenty-four-hour period.

As with traffic hazard, the large mass of vehicles was not always the major problem. It was often the lone individual or the unusual vehicle that disturbed the situation. This was certainly true of HEAVY STREET where the large majority of cars were reasonably quiet and passed by at a smooth even flow. The real offenders were sports cars, buses, and trucks. The steady drone of traffic was certainly bad, but the random deep-throated roar of a bus or large truck, with the accompanying shudder that rattled every window, unnerved the most hardened resident, especially when it continued day and night. The screeching of brakes at the intersections added to the distress.

Residents on HEAVY STREET had petitioned for a sign prohibiting trucks and buses. The sign was installed, but it did not mention buses. It was small, the same color as the background, and was seldom seen. In any case, the law was not enforced, so truck drivers had learned to continue on their way with impunity. Noise problems were not so acute on MODERATE STREET, where people were more bothered by the fumes, dust, and soot which penetrated into their living rooms and bedrooms. LIGHT STREET had a few complaints of occasional noise.

Other Forms of Pollution The condition and cleanliness of the buildings on the three streets was generally high. Maintenance and clean appearance were clearly important to all the inhabitants. HEAVY STREET was constantly on show to outsiders who were traveling through it, and the owners of the buildings were careful to maintain a high standard of cleanliness despite the "disgusting amount of litter." The *appearance* of a quality environment was therefore maintained—and paid for through higher rents—but because the street did not encourage people to be outgoing, tenants were reluctant to accept responsibility for the street itself. Therefore, they avoided picking up trash and were slow to defend the street against vandalism and abuse.

Table 3. Mean Ratings of Stress, Noise, and Pollution (Low stress, noise, and pollution ratings were given to responses indicating lack of nuisance, adequacy and suitability of street lighting, local services, road and sidewalk width, and good street maintenance. Rating: 1 = low stress, 5 = high stress.)

Question	Heavy Street	Moderate Street	Light Street
Is there anything that bothers you or causes you nuisance on and around this street?	4.5	3.3	2.6
Are you ever troubled by noise and/or vibration?	3.7	2.5	2.4
Are you bothered at all by dirt, pollution, smells, glare? Does it to your knowledge cause any ill health?	3.4	2.9	2.0
Is there adequate street lighting?	1.4	2.0	2.4
Is the street too wide or too narrow?	2.1	1.9	1.7
Are the sidewalks too wide or too narrow?	2.5	1.8	1.3
Do you have adequate local services: garbage collection, street cleaning?	2.2	2.1	2.1
Is your street well maintained, are front yards, planting, sidewalks, etc., well kept up?	1.5	1.8	1.9

Traffic noise bothers me, mostly during the day, but it's heavy at night, also.—I am bothered by the exhaust from traffic and noise. Lately the trucks have been returning to this street, even though they are banned.—Troubled by traffic noise, mostly trucks and motorbikes. The street acts like an echo chamber, especially for sirens. It continues day and night.—Bothered by noise and vibration. I have to straighten pictures frequently.—Noise is terrible from traffic. I can feel vibration even up on the fourth floor, especially from buses.—Have to take a nap during the day as don't get enough sleep at night because of the traffic.—The street is well maintained by old ladies washing down front steps once a week.—Other than traffic, it has a very nice appearance.— It's absolutely disgusting the amount of litter there is.—It's terribly dirty and we often have traffic fumes. I sometimes leave only the rear window open. (HEAVY STREET)

The car gets dirty because it is parked on the street.—Smells from big trucks, not very often.—Bothered by vibration from trucks sometimes, and by noise of hotrodders revving up.—Feel helpless as far as traffic is concerned, I can never finish cleaning.—It's a dirty street, I have to be a janitor and sweep the street. People in cars dump cigar ash and beer cans in the gutter.—It's getting worse because of traffic; getting dirtier. The rot has set in. (MODERATE STREET)

Sometimes bothered by noise of the occasional big truck which will wake the baby.—Motorbikes occasionally make a noise.—At night sounds of hotrodders frequently.—Street well maintained. Usually someone sweeping, my mother or people next door.—A very relaxed family neighborhood, perfect. It makes me very happy.—There are parking conflicts, parking is a pain because outside people put their cars in the driveways. (LIGHT STREET)

On MODERATE STREET, concerns for trash, dust, and soot, where specifically referred to, were more pronounced than on HEAVY STREET. This street was going through a difficult stage. Traffic and traffic problems were increasing, and there was no clear demarcation between public territory, which was the responsibility of the city, and local territory, which might have been the responsibility of the residents. People in parked cars had been observed dumping the contents of ash trays and beer cans into the gutter. Even so, it was still seen as a "good respectable place to live" and sidewalk maintenance by the local inhabitants helped to keep up the appearance of the street.

LIGHT STREET was very seldom seen by outsiders and so the issue of maintenance was a local matter. This street was also seen to be changing and residents had noticed signs of deterioration. As one resident put it, "The quality of [LIGHT STREET] is getting better in that people take great care of their properties, but worse in that there is more traffic and more cars on the street." Indeed, the responses showed that many inhabitants took an interest in looking after the cleanliness of the street, and some had planted their own trees.

The only other inconvenience mentioned was the crowded parking conditions. Many suburban commuters and users of the nearby shopping center were parking on all three streets and taking up parking spaces of the residents. In response to questions concerning the adequacy of street lighting, garbage collection, and street cleaning, respondents considered the three streets to be without serious problems.

In reaction to all these issues, each age group found HEAVY STREET more severe, and the old and middle-aged groups found MODERATE STREET worse than LIGHT STREET. The only exceptions were residents under twenty-five, who were more critical of LIGHT STREET. People on LIGHT STREET tended in many cases to be more aware and more critical of their street,

while those on MODERATE STREET were more apathetic.

Social Interaction

Residents were asked a series of questions about the friendliness of the street, the numbers of friends and acquaintances they possessed, and the places where people met. Each respondent was shown a photograph of the buildings on the street and asked to point out where any friends, relatives, or acquaintances lived.

On LIGHT STREET, inhabitants were found to have three times as many friends and twice as many acquaintances on the street itself (9.3 friends and acquaintances per person) as those on HEAVY STREET (4 per person). The diagrammatic network of social contacts . . . shows clearly that contact *across* the street was much less frequent on HEAVY STREET than on LIGHT STREET. The friendliness on LIGHT STREET was no doubt related to the small amount of traffic, but also to the larger number of children on the street and the longer length of residence of the inhabitants. The statements of the inhabitants corroborate this.

On HEAVY STREET, there was very little social interaction. With few if any friends (0.9 per respondent) the residents did not consider it a friendly street. Although it might be argued that this was primarily a consequence of the life style of those living on HEAVY STREET (Keller, 1969), the sense of loneliness came out very clearly, especially in the responses of the elderly. As for MODERATE STREET, residents felt that the old community was on the point of extinction. "It used to be friendly; what was outside has now withdrawn into the buildings. People are preoccupied with their own lives." Some of the families had been there a long time, but the number of longtime residents was diminishing. As other respondents put it, "It is half-way from here to there,"

"An in-between street with no real sense of community." There was still a core of original Italian residents lamenting that "There are no longer any friends around here." The average number of friends and acquaintances per respondent was only a little higher (total 5.4 per person) than on HEAVY STREET.

There were sharp differences between age groups. The middle-aged residents on the three streets possessed a similar number of friends, although those on LIGHT STREET had more acquaintances. This age group was probably more mobile and better equipped to make friends than the other groups. The young and old, on the other hand, who had many less social contacts on HEAVY STREET than on LIGHT STREET, appeared to be more affected by the amount of traffic, especially in establishing casual acquaintanceship with neighbors in the street.

From the notations of street activities drawn by the subjects on the map of the streets, it can be seen that LIGHT STREET had the heaviest use, mostly by teenagers and children. MODERATE STREET had lighter use, more by adults than by children, and HEAVY STREET had little or no use, even by adults. The few reported activities on HEAVY STREET consisted of middle-aged and elderly people walking on the sidewalks but seldom stopping to pass the time of day with a neighbor or friend. Reports on MODERATE STREET indicated that the sidewalks were more heavily used by adults, especially by a group of old men who frequently gathered outside the corner store. Children and some teenagers played on the sidewalks, mostly on the eastern side of the street (probably because most of their homes were on the eastern side and they didn't like to cross the road except at the crossings). On LIGHT STREET, people used the sidewalks more than any other part of the street, but children and teenagers often played games in the middle of the street. Children also used the sidewalks extensively because of their gentle gradient and their

width. Again, a corner store acted as a magnet for middle-aged and elderly people, and a tennis store across the road attracted a small group of young adults. Front porches and steps on LIGHT STREET, and to a certain extent on MODERATE STREET, were used for sitting, chatting with friends, and, by children, for play. The residents of HEAVY STREET regretted their lack of porches.

In conclusion, there was a marked difference in the way these three streets were seen and used, especially by the young and elderly. On the one hand, LIGHT STREET was a lively close-knit community whose residents made full use of their street. The street had been divided into different use zones by the residents. Front steps were used for sitting and chatting, sidewalks by children for playing, and by adults for standing and passing the time of day (especially round the corner store), and the roadway by children and teenagers for playing more active games like football. However, the street was seen as a whole and no part was out of bounds. This full use of the street was paralleled by an acute awareness of the physical environment (as will be described in the section on environmental awareness).

HEAVY STREET, on the other hand, had little or no sidewalk activity and was used solely as a corridor between the sanctuary of individual homes and the outside world. Residents kept very much to themselves so that there was no feeling of community at all, and they failed to notice and remember the detailed physical environment around them. MODERATE STREET again seemed to fall somewhere between the two extremes. It was still quite an active social street, although there was no strong feeling of community. Most activity was confined to the sidewalks, where a finely sensed boundary separated pedestrians from traffic. The ratings in table 4 reflect these differences between the three streets, particularly the perceived lack of meeting places for old people and play places for children on

Table 4. Mean Ratings of Social Interaction (Ratings of high social interaction were given to responses indicating friendliness and community feeling, a wide variety of friends, relatives and acquaintances, and intensive use of the street space. Rating: 1 = high, 5 = low.)

Question	Heavy Street	Moderate Street	Light Street
Do you think this is a friendly street? Do you think there is a feeling of community on this street?	3.2	2.0	2.0
Where do people congregate on the street if at all?	4.4	3.2	1.4
Where do children play if at all?	4.5	3.0	1.7
Where do teenagers gather if at all?	4.7	4.1	3.0
Where do adults casually meet and chat outside if at all?	4.1	2.5	2.7
Do you have any friends and relatives who live on this street?	4.2	3.2	2.8
Which people on this street do you know by sight?	3.5	2.8	1.8

It's getting worse. There are very few children, even less than before.—The only people I have noticed on the street are an older couple in this building who stand outside every night, otherwise there are only people walking on their way somewhere.—Everybody on (HEAVY STREET) is going somewhere else, not in this neighborhood.—Friendly neighbors, we talk over garden fences.—It's not a friendly street as people are afraid to go into the street because of the traffic. (HEAVY STREET)

Friendly street, many people related.—Friendly street, several families have lived here a long time.—There are no longer any of my friends around here any more. Dislike most about street? I don't know neighbors any more. I feel helpless not knowing anyone in case of emergency.—Doesn't feel that there is any community any more. However, many say hello.—There's nobody around. (MODERATE STREET)

Friendly street, people chatting washing cars, people on their way somewhere always drop in.—The corner grocery is the social center. I get a kick to go up there and spend an hour talking.—All family people, very friendly.—Kids used to play in the street all the time, but now with a car every two minutes, they have to go to the park.—Everybody knows each other. (LIGHT STREET)

HEAVY STREET, where mean response ratings usually exceeded 4.0.

Privacy and Home Territory

A number of questions were asked to gauge whether inhabitants felt they had sufficient privacy, and whether they had any feelings of stewardship over their streets.

In their responses, residents of LIGHT and MODERATE STREETS, especially middle-aged residents, evidenced great pride in their homes and streets. (See table 5.) On HEAVY STREET there was little peace and seclusion, even within the home, and residents struggled to retain some feeling of personal identity in their surroundings.

Perception of individual privacy was high throughout this area, perhaps because of the feeling of "privacy and seclusion that exists in any middle class area," as one respondent put it. Inevitably, in a tightknit community like the one that existed on LIGHT STREET, life on the street tended to intrude

Table 5. Mean Ratings of Privacy and Home Territory (High ratings of privacy and home territory were given to responses indicating seclusion, lack of intrusion or invasion, extended personal territories, and a sense of belonging and responsibility. Rating: 1 = high; 5 = low.)

Question	Heavy Street	Moderate Street	Light Street
Do you think that your street is relatively secluded?	3.4	2.1	2.4
Do you feel that your street is overcrowded or cramped?	3.3	1.6	2.0
Do you find that street life intrudes into your home at all?	2.9	1.2	1.8
Do you feel that your privacy is invaded by neighbors or from the street in any way while you are in and around your home?	2.5	1.6	2.2
Where do you feel that your "home" extends to; in other words, what do you see as your personal territory or turf?	3.0	2.3	1.2
Do you think of this street as your real home, where you really belong?	2.9	1.9	2.1
Do you feel any sense of responsibility for the way the street looks and for what happens on it?	2.6	2.8	1.3
If an outsider criticized your street would you defend it?	3.0	2.2	1.6

Do you think of this street as your real home where you belong?—Definitely not. It's hard to say where we feel our home is.—Where do you feel your home extends to?—Just this apartment, not even that.—There is a raging war between the residents and those terrible commuters from Marin. The residents want to dynamite patches of the road to slow traffic.—My outdoor space is the roof or the fire escape where I may have plants. (HEAVY STREET)

I am out there with a broom from one end of the block to the other. I am known as the "woman with the broom." (MODERATE STREET)

I tend the sidewalk trees outside the house and the rose bushes in the front.—I like our little street, even though I am not a home owner.—I keep it clean of debris, pick up broken bottles, notify people of anything wrong.—I feel my home extends to the whole block [very emphatic].—I always clean the street, take in dirt off the street, pick up nails, broken glass and paper. At least ten people take care of the street. (LIGHT STREET)

more into a person's home than it would on a less friendly street, but the residents had achieved a good balance wherein they maintained their own household privacy and yet contributed to the sense of community. As one woman enthusiastically put it, "Only happiness enters in." Children and young people often preferred the lack of seclusion because they liked to be part of things. On LIGHT STREET a satisfactory balance had been achieved between a feeling of privacy and contact with the outside world. Even on HEAVY STREET residents occasionally enjoyed the street activity. ("I feel it's alive, busy, and invigorating.") However, for the majority, the constant noise and vibration were a persistent intrusion into the home and ruined any feeling of peace and solitude. .

. . Even though legally a householder's responsibilities extend to the maintenance of the sidewalk immediately outside his building, residents on MODERATE and LIGHT STREETS considered part of all of the street as their territory. However, the HEAVY STREET resident's sense of personal territory did not extend into the street, and for some, mostly renters in the large apartment blocks, it was confined to their own apartment and no further. This pattern of territorial space corresponds to the pattern of social use of each street. The contrast between the territorial restrictions of those living on HEAVY STREET and the territorial expansiveness of those on LIGHT STREET is one of the more salient findings of the study. The residents on LIGHT STREET are quite similar in this respect to those West End Italians in Boston who considered the boundaries between house and street space to be quite permeable (Fried and Gleicher, 1961). In sum, HEAVY STREET was seen as considerably less private than the other two streets, especially for those most confined to the street, the young and the old.

Environmental Awareness

Street dwellers were each asked to recall all important features of their street, to judge whether their street was in any way different from surrounding streets, and to draw a map of their street. . . .

The responses to the questions were much richer in content—and more critical in character—on LIGHT STREET than on the other two streets. This can be partly explained by the greater differentiation of frontyards and smaller houses but it clearly stemmed from an increased awareness of the street environment by the residents themselves.

Interest in the street as evidenced by the maps drawn varied by age group. LIGHT STREET had tremendous appeal for children, who recalled individual buildings, frontyards, steps, particular parked cars, manhole covers, telegraph poles, and even the brickwork setting around the base of a tree. Many of these detailed elements were obviously encountered during their play on the street. On MODERATE STREET, where there was less street activity, the maps of children and young people were accordingly less rich.

Middle-aged people on the other hand seemed to have a more complete impression of their street. Their recollections included combinations of buildings, sidewalks, the roadway, and the traffic itself. For them, LIGHT STREET was seen as a collection of individual buildings with differences in frontyards and porches. MODERATE STREET was much more straight-walled. Residents had accurate memories of driveways, pedestrian crossings, and road markings (possibly because it was seen as a traffic route with finely defined boundaries).

HEAVY STREET was seen overwhelmingly as a continuous traffic corridor, straight-sided without a break for cross streets, and packed with cars. The traffic itself was an easily identified characteristic of the busier street.

As for the responsiveness of the street environment to the needs of the street dwellers, LIGHT STREET once more showed up well. (See table 6.) Two trees had been planted in the sidewalk, other plants were thriving in the occasional frontyards and flower boxes were prevalent. On HEAVY STREET, the sidewalks were too narrow to allow anything to grow except the very small bushes that flanked the doors of one or two apartment buildings.

Study Conclusions

1. The intensive traffic conditions on HEAVY STREET led to both stress and withdrawal. Those people who found the traffic conditions intolerable, especially those with children, had moved elsewhere, and the people who lived there at the time of the survey had either withdrawn from the street or had never become engaged in it. They only used it when they had to, they had few local

Table 6. Mean Ratings of Environmental Awareness (Ratings of high environmental awareness were given to responses that described the street as having a distinct sense of being a particular place and different from other streets, and that were full of rich, varied, and affectionate detail. Rating: 1 = high, 5 = low.)

Questions	Heavy Street	Moderate Street	Light Street
Do you find your street and the life that goes on there interesting? Do you get bored by life on this street, do you find it monotonous?	3.3	2.9	2.3
What parts of the street do you like most? What parts do you find least attractive?	3.1	2.6	2.1
What first comes to mind when you think of your street?	2.3	3.1	2.5
Could you please try to draw a map of what you think of as this street showing all the features of the street and the buildings that stick in your mind no matter how trivial they seem to be.	2.7	2.5	2.1
Do you think this street is different from surrounding streets, is it special or unique in any way?	2.2	3.6	2.1
Do you think there are many different kinds of people on this street? Can you describe them?	3.4	2.1	1.8

I dislike the sterility of the surroundings.—I don't like the fact that there is no greenery.—The first thing that comes to mind are apartment buildings, small apartments, five to six units. This wasn't so until ten years ago when they made the street one-way, before that there was a feeling of neighborhood.—Physically it feels as if you are looking over a void, the street is nonexistent.—The street facade is extremely unmemorable, dull brick or bland plaster. The surfaces are flat and static.—First thing that comes to mind, fast traffic.—It's absolutely dead, not even any night life, nothing. (HEAVY STREET)

Different from other streets in that it has a yellow line down the middle, others don't.—It's all dull, which is what I seek.—First thing that comes to mind, cars especially. (MODERATE STREET)

The houses are not overbearing, they are all different with varigated in-and-out facade.—It's like living in the heart of the city, my wife is constantly looking out of the window. There is a lot of activity—men standing talking outside their houses, the kids playing, etc.—Variety of people, all ages. People sit on front steps and chat, visit other people. It's a comforting block, very cheerful.—I like the set backs, they give individuality. (LIGHT STREET)

friends and acquaintances, and they had become oblivious to the street as a living environment. If they could, they lived at the backs of their houses. For those who treated HEAVY STREET as a transient residence, this condition was tolerable. Those who had

to treat it as a permanent residence because they were too old or too poor to leave suffered.

In contrast, those who lived on LIGHT STREET were very much engaged with their street. They saw it as their own territory.

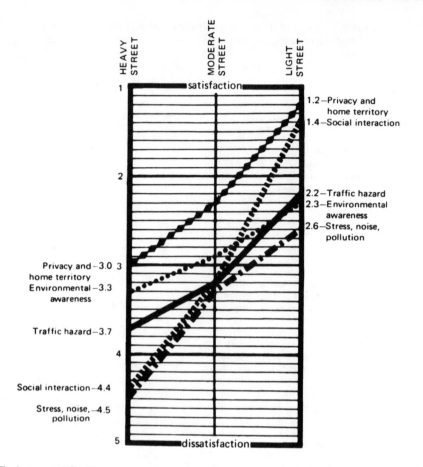

Fig. 1. Environmental Quality.

Note: The following interview questions were chosen to represent the "environmental quality" criteria illustrated in this figure.

Traffic hazard: What is traffic like on this street, how would you describe it? Does it bother you at all?

Stress, noise, and pollution: Is there anything that bothers you or causes you nuisance on and around this street?

Social interaction: Where do people congregate on the street, if at all?

Privacy and home territory: Where do you feel that your "home" extends to; in other words what do you see as your personal territory or turf?

Environmental awareness: Do you find your street and the life that goes on there interesting? Do you get bored by life on this street, do you find it monotonous?

Their children played on the sidewalk and in the street. They had many friends and acquaintances (over twice as many on the average as those on HEAVY STREET), they noted many more features of the street when they were asked to make a drawing of it, and they were generally much more aware of their street. Despite all this, the rents on HEAVY STREET were higher. Perhaps the apartments on that street, because of their higher exposure and turnover, were more available to a transient population.

The living conditions of those who lived on MODERATE STREET lay somewhere in between the other two, but the residents' levels of satisfaction were lower than their middle position might suggest.

From our results we can state some hypotheses about the apparent effects of traffic on the environmental and social quality of these streets (see figure 1). These hypotheses should be tested in later studies.

a. Heavy traffic activity is associated with more apartment renters and less owner-occupants and families with children. The income levels of the residents are in a similar range.

b. Heavy traffic is associated with much less social interaction and street activity. Conversely, a street with little traffic, and many families, promotes a rich social climate and a strong sense of community.

c. Heavy traffic is associated with a withdrawal from the physical environment. Conversely, residents of the street with low traffic show an acute, critical, and appreciative awareness of and care for the physical environment.

2. There are some exceptions to the above conclusions. Many respondents on MODERATE STREET had chosen that street for its livable environment. MODERATE STREET, however, was changing from a quiet residential street into a major traffic corridor. Therefore, the residents there were often more dissatisfied than those on HEAVY STREET. Their original expectations for the environment were higher and their disappointment was therefore greater.

On LIGHT STREET some respondents perceived the occasional hot-rodder as worse than the traffic on HEAVY STREET for similar reasons. When people expect traffic to be heavy, their behavior adapts to the situation and traffic is tolerated. When they expect it to be light, a hot-rodder is especially intrusive. In conclusion, people were dissatisfied with the streets with lighter traffic when their environmental expectations were not realized either through an environmental decline from a previously higher quality or from deviant traffic behavior.

3. The appearance of environmental quality was found to be quite different from the environmental quality as revealed by the comments of the residents. HEAVY STREET was well maintained and appeared to be of high quality to the outsider (for example, to the city urban design staff in earlier field surveys of the area). The residents were aware of its high status, yet the presence of heavy traffic lowered its quality below that of more modest-looking streets.

4. The pattern of interview responses suggested that the issues of safety, stress, condition, pollution, privacy, and territoriality, followed closely by neighborliness, were of primary concern to the inhabitants of all the streets. Issues such as sense of identity, environmental interest, appropriateness, and individual self-expression were not considered important if the other issues were seen as problems.

5. The general trend was toward increased traffic on each of the three streets, with the prospect that the environment of each street would decline further.

Discussion of Conclusions

Objective observations of environmental quality through traffic flow and noise counts, showed that environmental conditions on HEAVY STREET were particularly severe. Though complaints were numerous, however, they were not so strong as one might reasonably expect. There had been very little public complaint or protest by any group. Why was this?

One major reason appears to be that the erosion of environmental quality had been subtle and slow, taking place over a period of ten years or more. During this time the workings of *environmental selection*, and *environmental adaptation* had been allowed to operate. These are important phenomena to consider in measurements of response to environmental quality.

1. The workings of *environmental selection* may be stated as follows: an environment tends to be selected by those groups who find it most amenable, and to be re-

jected by those who find it least amenable. Hence when traffic increased on HEAVY STREET, families with children moved away, and single people and couples whose local environmental needs were less but who valued accessibility tended to replace them. The principle does not work perfectly, however. Those who are unable to select their preferred environment through lack of financial, informational, or psychological resources become "locked in" to certain environments, and are therefore likely to suffer the most from changing environmental quality. On HEAVY STREET the older people, finding it too costly and too much effort to move, experienced severe discomforts, and the families who had to remain on MODERATE STREET experienced the loss of friends. Similar predicaments face lower income populations.

People may select a less than ideal environment for reasons other than lack of resources. Many make a *compromise*, sacrificing amenity for the benefits of, for example, an easily available apartment or accessibility to other parts of the city. The apartments on LIGHT STREET had less turnover so they were seldom on the market. Others make *errors of judgment*. Visually HEAVY STREET is a well-maintained high quality street. Therefore, an apartment hunter might be deceived. Another kind of error is the *inability to predict future deterioration*. When many of the present inhabitants moved in to HEAVY and MODERATE STREETS conditions were good. Since then they have worsened.

2. By *environmental adaptation* we mean that those who remain in one environment for a length of time will become adapted (or resigned) to it whether or not it is or has been pleasant, especially if they see no future change in sight. Evidence for this phenomenon can be found in this study, especially in some of the more indifferent responses on HEAVY STREET. (Such evidence can also be found in the research literature in this field [Sonnenfeld, 1966; Wohlwill, 1968].) Those with low expecta-

tions or aspirations may be content with any environment.

Besides private adaptation, there appears to be a more publicly oriented defensive kind of adaptation. Most people are stuck with the choices they have made. When an interviewer arrives at the door and asks if there is anything they dislike about their environment, people may not wish to complain even though they may privately acknowledge that their environment is unsatisfactory. They may refuse to complain in order to keep up their social image and the sales value of their property, or through reluctance to admit that they have limited resources or have made an error of judgment.

Individual and family adjustments to a deteriorating environment were further muted because there was no clear public target for resentment, only the individual automobiles and trucks. No particular agency was threatening the environment or initiating changes. This worked both ways; residents' hopes were not raised that anything would be done about their problem, but neither were their frustrations focused sufficiently for them to band together in protest.

Despite the private nature of the adjustments and the slowness of the deterioration, a majority of the inhabitants were still well aware of their plight, as their comments tell.

One final and more positive finding of this study was what it told us of life on a "good" residential street, namely LIGHT STREET. Since we cannot hope to improve urban environments without some positive goals to work toward, LIGHT STREET performs a critical function.

Environmental Proposals

1. Policy usually has to be made without the benefit of adequate research, and this study is no exception. The strongest proposal resulting from the study was the designation in the adopted Urban Design Plan (San Francisco City Planning Department, 1971) of

"protected residential areas" throughout San Francisco. These are areas which will be protected from through traffic by policies such as the improvement of public transit; the concentration of traffic on the city's main arteries by increasing their capacity through separated grades, selective widening, parking controls, and so on; and the blocking of through traffic by devices such as rough pavement surfaces, "necking down" entrances, bending alignments, landscaping, lighting and sidewalk treatment, all of which would slow traffic down to a residential pace (and incidentally provide more street recreation space).

2. On streets where traffic flows and speeds could not be reduced, ways of ameliorating conditions were proposed. These included sidewalk protection by means of trees, low walls, hedges, and so on; the provision of alternative play spaces to divert children's activities away from the dangerous street; the protection of residences from glaring street lights, car lamps, and the view of passing vehicles through the planting of trees; the clear definition of parking spaces; and the encouragement of inhabitants to exercise some interest in their own frontyards and sidewalks through provisions and subsidies for private planting, benches, and the like.

Environmental Standards

Environmental conditions on residential streets will not be improved unless means of determining acceptable and unacceptable conditions are available. Present planning thought is running against the formulation of standards, as planners have come to realize the variability of population needs and situations and the difficulties of scaling environmental conditions. Yet without standards or specific guidelines, planning controls will remain amorphous and ineffectual. There is an urgent need at the very least to articulate unacceptable environmental conditions for particular groups. These conditions might be couched in the form of environmental performance standards.

The field of noise abatement, which has progressed quite far in trying to set environmental standards related to behavioral response, has encountered some difficulties. Simple decibel ratings (for example, forty-five decibels as a tolerable level inside residences) have to be modified by the "duration, frequency, substantive content of the sound and individual differences" (U.S., Department of Housing and Urban Development, 1969). The Traffic Noise Index (Griffiths and Langdon, 1968), developed in Britain, attempts to take a few of these factors into account. The Buchanan Report (Her Majesty's Stationary Office, 1964) identified "vulnerable" populations. But what about standards which will allow people to feel comfortable on sidewalks, or to cross the street, which encourage neighborliness, allow privacy and an ample sense of personal territory, or which promote care and interest for the physical environment of the street? These are even more difficult measures to scale. The effort to measure pedestrian crossing delay times as an indicator of residential quality, which was used in the *Kensington Environmental Management Study* (Greater London Council, 1966), was an interesting attempt in this direction. The work reported here is not substantial enough to develop such indicators, but this is the direction of our research.[5]

Research Implications

The results of this study are suggestive but obviously unrepresentative. Our a priori groupings of issues under criteria headings proved a useful way of organizing the interviews and observations. More studies examining larger numbers of street conditions and types of population are clearly required.

5. A study of a larger residential area in Oakland, California, is now under way supported by small grants from the U.S. Department of Transportation and the National Institute of Mental Health.

Such studies should use more structured questionnaires that would allow subjects to make their own ratings and selections from adjective and other check lists (Craik, 1967; Shaffer, 1967). They should also use a more comprehensive set of observable environmental indicators (such as pedestrian delay times, counts of street activity, closed windows, drawn blinds, parked cars, trash, flower boxes, and other signs of personal care) and a finer assessment of traffic variables (including flows at different times of day and night, speed levels, traffic composition, traffic control signals, and so on.

Multivariate analyses of interviews, traffic composition, and environmental indicators would then allow us to understand the ways in which factors tend to cluster, and to develop predictive models from regression analyses of response to various conditions. With such models, indices (similar to the traffic noise index) could be established to predict subjective responses to environmental phenomena such as levels of privacy, neighborliness, street identity, stress, and sense of safety for residential streets. The ability to predict the flow and speed of traffic from environmental conditions, given the desire lines operating in an area, would allow the control of speeds and flows at environmentally acceptable levels. We know that signs alone do not control speed. What are the effects of rough surfaces, trees, "necking down" streets, and street bends on these traffic variables?

Finally, more extensive surveys to assess the numbers of people who actually live under the deteriorated environmental conditions of streets with heavy traffic are needed. In a recent book, J. M. Thompson (1970) calculated that one million people in London would be living within 200 yards of the proposed motorway system. The implication was that one million people would be suffering from a deteriorated environment. Such accounts of conditions in a U.S. metropolitan area might have a significant impact on the allocation of investment to environmental improvements.

REFERENCES

Appleyard, D., and K. Lynch (1967) "Sensuous Criteria for Highway Design." In J. L. Shofer and E. N. Thomas, "Strategies for the Evaluation of Alternative Transportation Plans" (Research Report, The Transportation Center, Northwestern University, Evanston, Illinois).

Appleyard, D., and R. Okamoto (1968) "Environmental Criteria for Ideal Transportation Systems," in Barton Aschman Associates (ed.,), *Guidelines for New Transportation Systems* (U.S. Department of Housing and Urban Development, Washington, D.C.).

Chu, V. (1971) *Urban Road Traffic/Environmental Research and Studies: A Selective Annotated Bibliography* (Centre for Environmental Studies, London).

City of Westminster (1968) *The Pimlico Precinct Study* (London).

Craik, K. H. (1968) "The Comprehension of the Everyday Physical Environment," *Journal of the American Institute of Planners*, 34 (January): 29–37.

Fried, M., and P. Gleicher (1961) "Some Residential Satisfactions in an Urban Slum," *Journal of the American Institute of Planners*, 27 (November): 305–315.

Great Britain, Ministry of Housing and Local Government (1968) *The Barnsbury Environmental Study* (Islington, London).

Great Britain, Ministry of Housing and Local Government (1969) *General Improvement Areas.*

Greater London Council (1969) *Kensington Environmental Management Study*, publication 39 (London).

Griffiths, I. D., and F. J. Langdon (1968) "Subjective Response to Road Traffic Noise," *Journal of Sound and Vibration*, 8 (1): 16–32.

Her Majesty's Stationary Office (1963) *Traffic in Towns* (The Buchanan Report) (London).

Kaplan, M., S. Gans, and K. Kahn (1969) "Social Reconnaissance Survey, Part 2," San Francisco Urban Design Study, San Francisco City Planning Department.

Michigan, Department of State Highways (1969) "The Economic and Environmental Effects of One-way Streets in Residential Areas."

Owen, W. "Transport: Key to the Future of Cities." In H. Perloff (ed.), *The Quality of the Urban Environment* (Baltimore: Johns Hopkins Press).

San Francisco City Planning Department (1969–70) "Preliminary Reports," nos. 1 to 8, San Francisco Urban Design Study.

San Francisco City Planning Department (1971) "The Urban Design Plan for the Comprehensive Plan of San Francisco."

Shaffer, M. T. (1967) "Attitudes, Community Values, and Highway Planning," *Highway Research Record*, 187.

Sonnenfeld, J. (1966) "Variable Values in Space Landscape." *Journal of Social Issues*, 22 (January): 71–82.

Thompson, J. M. (1970) *Motorways in London* (London: Andworth and Co., Ltd.).

United States, Department of Housing and Urban Development (1969) "Noise Abatement and Control: Departmental Policy, Implementation Responsibilities, and Standards," unpublished circular (September).

Wohlwill, J. F. (1966) "The Psychology of Stimulation." In R. Kates and J. F. Wohlwill (ed.), *Journal of Social Issues* 22 (January): 127–136.

Carbon Monoxide and Human Vigilance:

A Deleterious Effect of Present Urban Concentrations

STEVEN M. HORVATH,

THOMAS E. DAHMS, and JAMES F. O'HANLON

Recently, national attention was focused on the possibility that present urban concentrations of carbon monoxide may impair human vigilance.[1] This is a disquieting possibility since the successful completion of many practical tasks (eg, automobile driving) apparently requires a high level of vigilance. However, little is known of how vigilance, the general responsivity of the central nervous system to incoming sensory information,[2] is affected by exposure to CO. Lewis et al[3] administered a test of auditory vigilance to subjects being exposed to roadway air polluted by 830 vehicles per hour. Those subjects detected significantly fewer signals breathing the polluted air than they had while breathing uncontaminated air. Lewis et al[3] made no attempt to define the factors responsible for that decline in performance. The work of other investigators strongly implicates CO as an agent capable of impairing complex psychophysiological functions. For example, CO exposures resulting in blood carboxyhemoglobin (COHb) levels of less than 5% were found associated with deterioration in various sensory, perceptual, and cognitive functions in man.[4,5] Similarly,

Beard and Wertheim[6] demonstrated that exposures to a graded series of CO concentrations between 50 and 250 ppm caused a progressive deterioration in subjects' abilities to estimate the passage of time. Beard and Wertheim did not measure COHb directly but rather estimated those levels from standard reference tables.[7] They suggested that time perception began to be affected at COHb levels below 2%.

Thus, previous investigations have shown that vigilance declined in men breathing polluted air and that CO, a component of polluted air, was capable of impairing various complex psychophysiological functions. The study reported here was undertaken to show whether CO concentrations presently found in the urban atmosphere can impair human vigilance.

METHODS AND MATERIALS

Fifteen healthy male volunteers responded to a call for subjects. They were medically examined, and interviewed in an effort to determine their usual daily exposures to CO including cigarette smoking. Five of these subjects were eliminated from the study when basal measurements of blood COHb levels indicated that they had been exposed to atmospheric CO or had been smoking cigarettes. Upon being told of the blood data, these subjects confirmed that they were indeed smokers but felt that this fact was not important despite the emphasis in the preliminary screening that smokers were not being used as subjects. The ten remaining subjects were between 21 and 32 years of age.

Each subject arrived at the laboratory at the same time of day (beginning at either 0830 or 0930 hours) for three test sessions, a week apart. The subject inspired a different gas mixture in each session. The mixtures were obtained from a commercial source and an aliquot from each mixture was assayed to determine its respective CO concentrations exactly. The gas mixtures contained CO concentrations of 0 (i.e., < 0.5), 26, and 111 ppm. The two higher concentrations were selected beforehand as being representative of the average and peak levels found in Los Angeles driving by Haagen-Smit.[8]

To begin each session, the subject rested for one hour while breathing the appropriate gas mixture through a supported mouthpiece attached by tubing to a demand valve regulator on the gas cylinder. Gas mixtures were administered in a single-blind, partially counterbalanced manner, ie, no more than two subjects, nor less than one, received the gas mixture in the same order. After the rest period, the subject immediately walked to a nearby room where he was seated within a specially constructed chamber and resumed breathing the same gas mixture through apparatus similar to that described previously.

The chamber was air-conditioned, double-walled with interior dimensions of 4 × 4 × 6¼ feet. It contained a chair for the subject. Mounted on an interior wall opposite the subject was a small box displaying a 1-inch circular aperture. Behind that aperture was a ground-glass diffusing screen and behind that

a 50-w projection lamp. Voltage across the lamp was controlled by apparatus described elsewhere.[9] Between the display and the subject was a bench which served as an armrest and contained conveniently located response buttons. Button-press responses were recorded on a recorder located outside the chamber.

While seated within the chamber the subject performed a monitoring task in two parts. In both, the task consisted of judging and responding to each in a series of one-second light pulses which appeared on the display every three seconds. The pulses could be either "nonsignals" (dimmer) or "signals" (brighter). The nonsignal brightness was constant for all subjects, but the signal brightnesses were determined individually in a preliminary psychophysical test (ie, each subject's signal brightness was set at a level that produced 90% detections under alerted conditions). The subject responded by pressing a button after each pulse to indicate whether he judged it to be a signal or nonsignal.

In the first or alerted test, the subject was shown ten signals randomly, though not successively, interspersed among 50 nonsignals. Then he rested for a minute before undertaking a 60-minute vigilance test. In the latter, he was shown ten signals similarly interspersed among 290 nonsignals in each successive, 15-minute period. Throughout the test, each subject's heart rate was monitored and recorded on the electrocardiogram channel of a polygraph. The electronic analog output of a dry gas meter was similarly recorded for later determining the subject's expired minute ventilatory volume ($\dot{V}_e$)....

RESULTS

The COHb levels that were measured before exposure to CO (0 minute), and after 60 to 65 and 135 to 140 minutes of exposure are given in the Table. The Figure shows the mean percentage of signals correctly identified by the subjects during the alerted tests

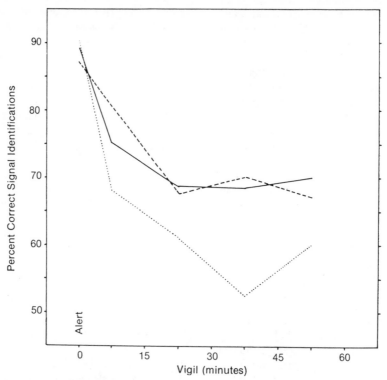

Fig. 1. Percent Correct Signal Identifications for the Nonsmokers in the Alerted Test and as a Function of Time in the Vigil for Each of the Three Levels of Inspired Carbon Monoxide (0 [solid line], 26 [dashed line], and 111 [dotted line] ppm).

and during successive 15-minute periods in the vigilance tests. There were no significant differences between the alerted levels of performance in different conditions. However, during the vigilance test, the subjects identified fewer signals while breathing 111 ppm CO than while breathing either of the other gas mixtures. The mean difference in correct signal identifications between conditions wherein the subjects breathed 111 and 0 ppm of CO was tested using Dunnett's test.[10] That difference was significant (t = 2.31; k = 3; df = 18; $P < 0.05$). The mean difference in that respect between conditions wherein they breathed 26 and 0 ppm of CO was tested in the same manner and found not significant. The general decline in the mean percentage of signals correctly

identified over successive 15-minute periods in the vigilance test was tested by analysis of variance for all conditions combined; it was also significant (F = 6.25; df = 3, 27; $P < 0.01$). The percentage of nonsignals incorrectly identified (ie, as signals) did not exceed 5% for any individual and did not appear to be differentially affected by the different gas mixtures for the groups as a whole. No further analysis was performed on those data.

Heart rate and $\dot{V}_e$ were computed from data collected and averaged over the 60-minute vigilance tests. The subjects' mean heart rate was 71, 72, and 74 beats per minute, and their mean $\dot{V}_e$ was 8.50, 8.54, and 8.51 liters (body temperature, pressure, saturation) in the 0, 26, and 111 ppm of CO

Carboxyhemoglobin Levels After Various Exposures

Carbon Monoxide Inhaled (ppm)	Percent Saturation		
	0 Minute	60 to 65 Minutes	135 to 140 Minutes
0	0.8 ± 0.35 (0.4–1.6)	0.8 ± 0.23 (0.5–1.3)	0.8 ± 0.21 (0.6–1.2)
26	0.8 ± 0.57 (0.4–1.2)	1.6 ± 0.60 (1.1–1.9)	2.3 ± 0.55 (1.9–2.4)
111	0.9 ± 0.46 (0.5–1.8)	4.2 ± 1.15 (3.3–6.7)	6.6 ± 1.27 (5.7–9.8)

conditions, respectively. No difference between conditions in either heart rate or V_e was significant.

COMMENT

It is well known that humans experience great difficulty in maintaining high vigilance in monotonous tasks.[11] In the present study, the subjects' signal identification performance generally deteriorated during the vigilance tests. However, the two-hour plus exposure to 111 ppm of CO seemed to potentiate the effect of monotony on vigilance. The subjects apparently lost vigilance more rapidly than normal, as their average COHb level rose to 6.6%. Since similar CO exposures are not uncommon in certain driving and industrial situations, we feel that these results have an important practical implication. Persons who sustain increases in COHb saturation of more than about 2% or 3% may become less effective in coping effectively with unexpected events and more liable to perform routine tasks in an inefficient manner. The danger this could pose to drivers or operators of heavy machinery need not be elaborated. . . .

A final methodological point should be made. The data presented in the Table indicate the importance of directly measuring the COHb levels in subjects participating in studies similar to that reported here. The subjects' COHb levels did not approach equilibrium during the 2¼-hour exposure period. At no time was it possible to accurately predict those levels from standard reference tables, such as those of Forbes et al.[7] Furthermore, the wide range of individual differences in COHb levels measured prior to experimental CO exposures seemed to indicate the subjects' unwillingness or inability to control their preexperimental CO exposure. Large individual differences in the rate of CO uptake were also evident as the subjects were exposed to 111 ppm of CO. All of these findings lead to the conclusion that it would be very difficult to assess the true relationship between the low concentrations of inspired CO and most psychophysiological variables without directly measuring blood COHb levels during exposure. Merely to predict those levels (assuming that accurate data exist for doing so) would be to ignore potential sources of error from individual differences in prior exposure to CO, ventilatory volume, pulmonary diffusing capacity, and competitive equilibrium rates between oxygen and CO for hemoglobin at lung and tissue levels.

REFERENCES

1. *Effects of Chronic Exposure to Low Levels of Carbon Monoxide on Human Health, Behavior, and Performance*, Committee on Effects of Atmospheric Contaminants on Human Health and Welfare. Washington, DC, National Research Council, National Academy of Sciences, 1969.
2. Head H: The conception of nervous and mental energy: Vigilance, a physiological state of the central nervous system. *Brit J Psychol* 14:126–146, 1923.
3. Lewis, J, Baddeley AO, Bonham KG, et al: Traffic pollution and mental efficiency. *Nature* 225:95, 1969.

4. Schulte JH: Effects of mild carbon monoxide intoxication. *Arch Environ Health* 7:524—530, 1963.

5. McFarland RA, Roughton FJW, Hulperin MH, et al: The effects of carbon monoxide and altitude on visual thresholds. *J Aviat Med* 15:381—394, 1944.

6. Beard RR, Wertheim GA: Behavioral impairment associated with small doses of carbon monoxide. *Amer J Public Health* 57:2012—2022, 1967.

7. Forbes WH, Sargent F, Roughton FJW: The rate of carbon monoxide uptake by normal men. *Amer J Physiol* 143:594—625, 1945.

8. Haagen-Smit AJ: Carbon monoxide levels of city driving. *Arch Environ Health* 12:548—551, 1966.

9. Baker CH, O'Hanlon JF: *The Use of Reference Signals in a Visual Vigilance Task: I. Reference Signals Continuously Displayed*, technical report 750-1. Human Factors Research, Inc, 1963.

10. Winer BJ: *Statistical Principles in Experimental Design.* New York, McGraw-Hill Book Co Inc, 1962.

11. Davies DR, Tune GS: *Human Vigilance Performance.* London, Staples Press Ltd, 1970.

Behavioral Aftereffects of Unpredictable and Uncontrollable Aversive Events

DAVID C. GLASS and JEROME E. SINGER

Several years ago, we happened to read the following account in a *Fortune* magazine article:

In the Bronx borough of New York City one evening last spring, four boys were at play, shouting and racing in and out of an apartment building. Suddenly, from a second-floor window, came the crack of a pistol. One of the boys sprawled dead on the pavement. . . . The killer . . . confessed to police that he was a night worker who had lost control of himself because the noise from the boys prevented him from sleeping [Mecklin 1969].

This incident may be an extreme example of the impact of noise on man, but it does highlight potential consequences of the increasing deterioration of our "sound environment." The research we describe in this paper does not attempt to document such dramatic effects; rather, it is confined to an examination of the influence of noise and related stressors on more mundane behavioral and psychophysiological processes. And even these effects are difficult to demonstrate, for, in time, people simply learn to ignore noise. However, the proposition that

man is adaptable has an important corollary: namely, man pays a price for adaptation that is observable in behavior (Selye 1956; Dubos 1965; Wohlwill 1970).

Our research was initially undertaken as a test of the hypothesis that adaptation is costly to the organism. But, as we shall see later, the results suggest a somewhat different interpretation. The original idea was to allow subjects to adapt to repeatedly presented high-intensity sound and then to determine whether the process of adaptation or habituation left subjects less able to cope with subsequent environmental demands. (We use the terms habituation and adaptation interchangeably throughout this paper; the convention is adopted with full knowledge that not all forms of adaptation necessarily involve the same basic processes [cf. Thompson and Spencer 1966; Lazarus 1968].)

The basic notion was that mental effort entailed in the adaptive process affects subsequent behavior adversely. Following Lazarus (e.g. 1968), we assumed that adaptation is a cognitive process involving re-evaluation of the noise stressor as benign or the use of more direct action strategies for

From D. Glass & J. Singer. Behavioral aftereffects of unpredictable and uncontrollable aversive events. *American Scientist*, 1972, *60*, 457–465. Reprinted by permission.

coping with noise—e.g. "filtering" noise out of awareness by becoming engrossed in some task. We did not attempt to measure various adaptive strategies; instead, we assumed that subjects would use one or another strategy, resulting in a decrement of autonomic response to noise. This decrement was, in effect, our principal index of adaptation.

NOISE AND TASK PERFORMANCE

Before describing behavioral aftereffects of noise adaptation, we will first consider noise effects occurring during the process of acoustic stimulation. Noise may be defined as any sound that is physiologically arousing and stressful, subjectively annoying, or disruptive of performance (Anastasi 1964). But do we have any evidence that noise is in fact a stressor with measurable consequences resulting from its repeated application? There are dozens of newspaper accounts and magazine stories that suggest an affirmative answer. However, psycho-acousticians are not at all convinced that noise has deleterious effects on man. Comprehensive reviews of systematic research on noise (e.g. Broadbent 1957; Kryter 1970) conclude that there is no compelling evidence of adverse effects of high-intensity noise per se on human task performance. Laboratory-produced noise does not affect a subject's ability to do mental and psychomotor tasks ranging from the boringly simple to the interesting and challenging. Other than as a damaging agent to the ear, or as a source of interference with tasks requiring communication, or an indirect effect from interference with sleep and thus lowered task efficiency, noise does not seem to impair human performance.

Data from our own research provide support for this conclusion. On relatively simple mental tasks—arithmetic addition, number comparison, verbal skills—there appears to be little evidence of task impairment during noise stimulation, even when sound approaches levels of 110 dbA. (The abbreviation dbA refers to the decibel measurement made on the A-scale of a sound-level meter,

where higher frequencies are weighted more heavily because they are more annoying to the human ear. A sound of 110 dbA is about what one would hear if one were operating a riveting machine.) We have tested well over 200 subjects in our laboratories, and a typical set of results is presented in Table 1. The test—number comparison—required the subject to indicate whether successive sets of multiple digits were the same or different (French, Ekstrom, and Price 1963). There are obviously no differences in average number of errors between noise conditions during the first part of the testing session (about 12 minutes), but whatever errors do appear tend to decline during the second 12-minute period. We interpret these error decrements as behavioral evidence of noise adaptation. As we shall see later, physiological indicators of adaptation were also obtained in these studies.

Our research has customarily used broadband noise consisting of a specially prepared tape recording of the following sounds superimposed upon one another: (1) two people speaking Spanish; (2) one person speaking Armenian; (3) a mimeograph machine; (4) a desk calculator; (5) a typewriter. We selected this particular concatenation of sounds as an analogue of the spectrum of complex noise often present in the urban environment. A sound-spectrographic analysis of the noise recording showed that energy did indeed range broadly from 500 Hz to 7,000 Hz, with the mode at about 700 Hz. Free field stimulation was used throughout most of the research, with the noise delivered over a speaker mounted on the wall directly behind the seated subject.

We have suggested that noise per se has minimal effects on task performance. There are, however, several exceptions to this generalization. In particular, performance is impaired when (1) long-term vigilance demands are placed on the subject; (2) the task is otherwise complex; (3) noise is intermittent. Evidence for vigilance-task impairments has been extensively documented elsewhere (e.g. Broadbent 1971) and does

Table 1. Average Number of Errors on Part 1 and Average Decrements in Errors from Part 1 to Part 2 of the Number Comparison Test

	Experimental condition		
	Loud noise (108 dbA) (n = 18)	Soft noise (56 dbA) (n = 20)	No noise control (n = 10)
Part 1 errors	3.28	3.30	2.80
Decrement in errors from Part 1 to Part 2	−1.85	−1.48	−0.20

not need to be repeated at this time. Evidence of intermittency effects has also been reported by other investigators (Broadbent 1957), but a word or two is needed here. Briefly, this research has shown that intermittent noise is experienced as more aversive than continuous noise, and if the intermittency is aperiodic (i.e. unpredictable), felt aversiveness is still greater. Other studies have reported corresponding effects for task efficiency; for example, aperiodic noise degrades performance more than does continuous or periodic noise (e.g. Sanders 1961). The tasks used in most of this research were relatively simple verbal and numerical tests.

We have not been able to replicate the aperiodicity effect in our own laboratories. Our results for periodic and aperiodic noise, on tasks like number comparison and addition, are presented in Table 2. It is clear from even casual examination of the table

that aperiodic noise does not produce more task deficits than periodic noise, even when both are at 108 dbA levels of intensity. It should also be noted that unsignaled noise does not result in greater performance errors than signaled noise. Signaling and periodicity are each a form of predictability, and we have studied the influence of both variables in our research.

Though unpredictable noise does not degrade *simple* task performance, it does exert a greater impact on *complex* task performance than predictable noise. In two of our experiments, deterioration of performance was observed if excessive demands were placed on the subject's information-processing capacities—as when he was working on two tasks simultaneously or maintaining continual vigilance on a tracking task (Finkelman and Glass 1970; Glass and Singer 1972). It would appear that unpredictable noise directly affects performance only

Table 2. Average Number of Errors on Part 1 and Average Decrements in Errors from Part 1 to Part 2 of the Addition Test

	Experimental condition		
	Aperiodic noise (n = 18)	Periodic noise (n = 20)	No noise control (n = 10)
Part 1 errors	5.28	5.79	2.20
Decrement in errors from Part 1 to Part 2	−0.54	−1.78	−0.08

when the subject is working at maximum capacity.

There is one general consistency in these exceptions to the earlier conclusion that noise itself does not have adverse effects on performance. All three appear to reflect the operation, not of noise alone, but of noise mediated by cognitive processes. Two are presumably situations in which the organism becomes overloaded; that is, task inputs are so numerous that they inhibit adequate information processing, and noise becomes still another input for the organism to monitor. The noise continually overloads the subject and in such situations produces performance deficits that do not wane with repeated exposure. The deleterious effects of aperiodic noise probably reflect the fact that unpredictable stressors have a more aversive impact on behavior than predictable stressors (e.g. Berlyne 1960). These observations underscore the importance of cognitive factors in mediating the effects of noise on behavior. For unpredictability is an extra-stimulus variable, and task complexity and vigilance may be viewed as instances of cognitive overload.

AFTEREFFECTS OF UNPREDICTABLE NOISE

At the outset, we stated that the principal rationale for our research was the notion that adaptation to noise results in adverse behavioral aftereffects. Our implicit assumption has been that the individual expends "psychic energy" in the course of the adaptive process, and this leaves him less able to cope with subsequent environmental demands and frustrations (cf. Selye 1956). Since there is some evidence to suggest that unpredictable noise is more aversive than predictable noise, we anticipated that adaptation to the former type of stimulation would be more costly to the individual. Specifically, we hypothesized that unpredictable noise, in contrast to predictable noise, would lead to greater reductions in tolerance for post-noise frustration and

greater impairments of performance on a task requiring care and attention.

The prototypic procedure used to test this hypothesis is as follows. Upon entering the laboratory, the subject was told that the purpose of the study was to investigate "the effects of noise levels on task performance and physiological processes." The use of skin electrodes was then explained, and leads were attached to the subject's fingers and arm. After a brief resting period, the experimenter outlined the tasks the subject would be working on during noise exposure—usually verbal and numerical tests.

Following the task instructions, the noise session proper began. Sound was delivered intermittently—at either random or fixed intervals—throughout a 23-, 24-, or 25-minute period, depending on the particular experiment being conducted. In fixed or predictable conditions, the noise was presented at the end of every minute for about 9 seconds. In random, or unpredictable, conditions, delivery of noise was randomized with respect to both length of the bursts and intervals between them. In some studies, the intensity of each type of noise was varied so that half the subjects in the unpredictable and predictable conditions heard 108 dbA sound, whereas the other half heard 56 dbA sound. The total time of exposure was identical in all conditions—about 3½ to 5 minutes, depending on the particular study. Following termination of the noise, the experimenter re-entered the chamber and administered the tasks designed to measure aftereffects of adaptation. Subjects assigned to no-noise control conditions were treated identically to experimental subjects, except for the absence of the noise stimuli.

Let us now consider illustrative results from the first of these noise experiments (Glass, Singer, and Friedman 1969, Experiment 1). We begin with evidence pertaining to noise adaptation. Phasic skin conductance (GSR) was monitored throughout the noise session, and, as noted earlier, the decrement in reactivity on this measure was taken as an index of adaptation. Figure 1 shows these

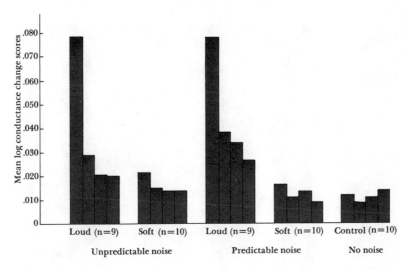

Fig. 1. Mean Log Conductance Change Scores for Four Successive Blocks of Noise Bursts.

adaptation data as mean log conductance change scores within each of four successive blocks of noise bursts (Montagu and Coles 1966). There is a clear decline in GSR response on successive blocks of trials in each noise condition. Since initial reactions to loud noise (108 dbA) were greater than to soft noise (56 dbA), the magnitude of GSR decline is understandably greater in the former condition. However, the magnitude and rate of adaptation is virtually identical in predictable and unpredictable conditions within each noise-intensity treatment: that is, subjects were equally reactive at the beginning of the noise session and equally unreactive at the end.

It would appear that phasic skin conductance responses to noise occur during initial exposure and wane with repeated stimulation. Assuming that physiological stress reactions interfere with performance efficiency, we may also expect initial task errors to decline over the course of noise exposure. Recall that the task results presented earlier generally conformed to such expectations (see Tables 1 and 2). This phenomenon of adaptation is indeed pervasive; it characterized almost every subject in each of our experiments, and it appeared on several different autonomic channels—GSR, vasoconstriction of peripheral blood vessels, muscle-action potentials. We may thus conclude that there is a generalized stress response to noise which habituates with repeated stimulation.

Our major hypothesis stated that noise adaptation would lead to deleterious behavioral aftereffects, and this expectation was in fact confirmed. Exposure to unpredictable noise, in contrast to predictable noise, was followed by impaired task performance and lowered tolerance for post-noise frustrations. Even though noise adaptation took place to an equivalent degree under both predictable and unpredictable conditions, the magnitude of adverse aftereffects was greater under unpredictable conditions. Before presenting results in support of this general conclusion, we must first explain how frustration tolerance was measured.

Following noise termination, four line diagrams (Fig. 2) printed on 5 × 7 inch cards were arranged in four piles in front of the subject (Feather 1961; Glass and Singer 1972). Each pile consisted of cards with the same diagram on them. The subject's task was to trace over all the lines of a given diagram, or puzzle, without tracing any line

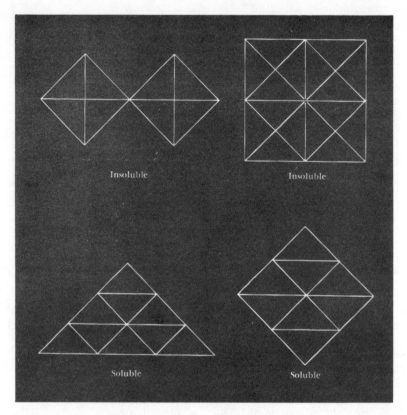

Fig. 2. Insoluble and Soluble Puzzles.

twice and without lifting his pencil from the figure. He was told that he could take as many trials at a given puzzle as he wished but that there was a time limit on how long he could work on a particular trial, and the experimenter would inform him when his time was up. At the end of that time, he had to decide whether to take another card from the same pile and try that puzzle again or move on to the puzzle in the next pile. If he decided to move on, he could not go back to the previous puzzle.

Two of the line diagrams were in fact insoluble, but very few subjects were able to see this. The insoluble puzzles were presumed to lead to failure and frustration. Indeed, we repeatedly observed outward signs of exasperation as subjects attempted over and over again to solve the insoluble.

While this was going on in the experimental chamber, the experimenter was in the control room observing and recording the number of trials taken by a subject on each puzzle. These data provided us with a measure of his persistence on the insoluble puzzles: namely, the fewer the number of trials, the less the persistence, and, by interpretation, the lower the subject's tolerance for an inherently frustrating task.

Typical results on this task are shown in Figure 3. As can be seen, subjects took significantly fewer trials following exposure to loud unpredictable noise than to the loud and soft predictable noise, and this effect was true for both of the insoluble puzzles. Almost all subjects solved the soluble puzzles within 4 or 5 trials. It would appear, then, that lowered tolerance for frustration

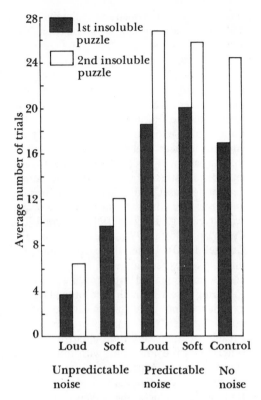

Fig. 3. Average Number of Trials on the First and Second Insoluble Puzzles.

is an adverse consequence of exposure to the presumably more aversive unpredictable noise. There is also an unexpected tendency for this effect to appear even when the unpredictable noise is not particularly loud. Soft unpredictable noise was associated with lower tolerance of frustration than loud predictable noise. Unpredictability is indeed a potent factor in the production of noise aftereffects.

It should be noted, however, that our measure of frustration tolerance could be regarded as an index of adaptive lack of persistence on an insoluble task. Put somewhat differently, it may be that taking fewer trials on the insoluble puzzles was an adaptive rather than maladaptive response. Such an interpretation is theoretically possible, but we find it difficult to understand why

unpredictable noise would lead to more adaptive responses to insoluble problems than predictable noise. Unpredictable stressors have been shown by others to exert a more aversive impact on behavior than predictable stressors (e.g. Berlyne 1960), and thus we might expect maladaptive consequences after exposure to the former type of stimulation.

The alternative interpretation of our frustration-tolerance measure is also difficult to maintain in the face of results obtained in another post-noise task. It was expected that unpredictable noise, in contrast to predictable noise, would impair quality of performance on a task requiring care and attention. Subjects were therefore given a proofreading test immediately following completion of the insoluble puzzle test. They were asked to correct errors, such as transpositions and misspellings, that had been deliberately introduced into a 7-page passage. Each subject was given 15 minutes on this task, and quality of performance was measured as the percentage of "errors not found" of the total number of errors that could have been detected at the point the subject was told to stop work.

There were no significant differences between noise conditions in the total amount read by subjects. However, Figure 4 shows the predicted differences in average percentage of errors missed in the completed part of the proofreading task. Loud unpredictable noise is associated with a greater percentage of proofreading errors than either loud or soft predictable noise. Although soft unpredictable noise leads to greater impairment of proofreading accuracy than loud predictable noise, the difference is not statistically significant, as in the case of the frustration-tolerance measure.

Taken together, our findings suggest that people adapt to noise but show behavioral deficits after noise termination. We cannot say that these deficits are the direct result of noise adaptation; it is just as likely that they occur in spite of adaptation. Later, we will refer to data which in fact support the

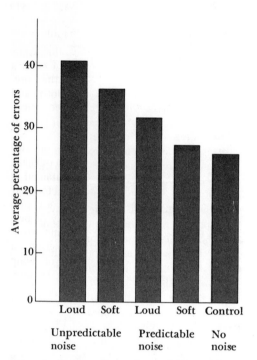

Fig. 4. Average Percentage of Errors Missed in the Proofreading Task.

second interpretation. For the moment, however, we have simply shown that exposure to unpredictable noise leads to more adverse aftereffects than exposure to predictable noise. A psychological factor, unpredictability, appears to be more important than physical parameters of noise (e.g. intensity), in producing post-noise deficits. The case for the existence of this phenomenon is strengthened by the range of conditions over which it has been found in various replications (see Glass and Singer 1972). These include: (1) different ways of manipulating unpredictability, (2) different levels of physical noise intensity, (3) different male and female subject populations, and (4) different laboratory locations.

PERCEIVED CONTROL OVER NOISE

The research described thus far does not provide precise theoretical understanding of

the relationship between unpredictable noise and adverse aftereffects. It is not enough to assume that unpredictable noise is more aversive than predictable noise; we still need to specify why it is more aversive and, indeed, why negative effects appear primarily after noise termination. A possible answer to the first question is based on the notion that exposure to an unpredictable stressor induces feelings in the individual that he cannot control his environment—or at least certain stressful aspects of it. He cannot determine onset and offset of the stressor, and he is even unable to anticipate its occurrence (see, e.g., Haggard 1946; Pervin 1963; Corah and Boffa 1970; Geer, Davison, and Gatchel 1970). Under these conditions, we might well expect lowered frustration tolerance and impaired proofreading accuracy following stress arousal. The individual has experienced not only the aversiveness of the noise but also the "anxiety" of being incapable of doing anything about it. On the other hand, providing him with information about when to expect the noise affords a measure of cognitive control over the situation, which reduces the adverse effects of unpredictability. The validity of this line of reasoning was tested in a series of 8 experiments, but we will present only one illustrative study here. Additional data can be found in a monograph summarizing our research (Glass and Singer 1972).

The prototypic experiment involved two groups of subjects who listened to the unpredictable noise tape played at 108 dbA. One group (perceived control) was given control over the noise, whereas the other (no perceived control) did not receive this option. At the beginning of the experiment, subjects in the perceived-control condition were shown a microswitch attached to the side of their chair and told that they could at any time terminate the noise for the remainder of the session by pressing the switch. They were further informed that the experimenter preferred that they not press the switch, but the choice was entirely up to them. The latter instruction was given particular emphasis in order to induce forces against pressing the switch, while at the same time giving subjects a feeling that they could press it if they so desired. In fact, few subjects used the switch throughout noise exposure. All other details of procedure and measurement in this experiment were virtually identical to those used in the unpredictability experiments.

In order to determine whether or not the manipulations were successful in inducing the perception of control, all subjects were asked in a postexperimental questionnaire: "To what extent did you feel that you really could have had the noise stopped during today's session?" The rating scale on the questionnaire was from 1 = "No control at all" to 9 = "Complete control." The mean for the 9 subjects in the perceived-control

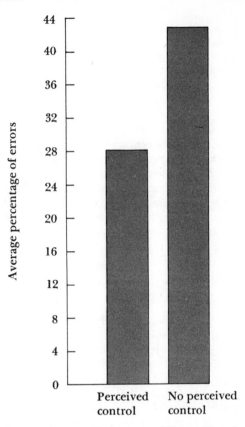

Fig. 6. Average Percentage of Errors Missed in the Proofreading Task.

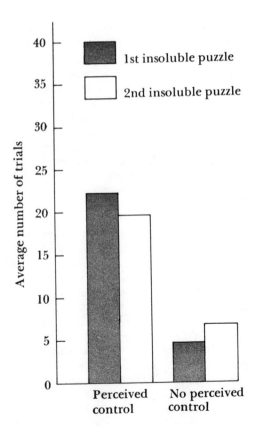

Fig. 5. Average Number of Trials on the First and Second Insoluble Puzzles.

condition was 7.4 and for the 9 subjects in the no-perceived-control condition, 3.0. The difference was statistically significant at better than the .01 level.

Subjects in both conditions adapted to the noise as measured by phasic skin conductance decrements and decline in task errors. The aftereffect results present a somewhat different picture, however. Figures 5 and 6 show these data. It is immediately obvious that perception of control over noise termination had a dramatic impact on the aftereffect measures. Tolerance for postnoise frustration was appreciably increased and proofreading errors substantially declined.

These ameliorative effects have been obtained with a number of experimental variations of perceived control, including the induction of a perceived contingency between instrumental responding and avoidance of noise (see Glass and Singer 1972). Other data from these studies indicate a tendency toward reduced physiological reactions to initial noise bursts when subjects believed they could escape or avoid the noise. The results of our research thus suggest that perception of control reduces the aversive impact of unpredictable noise and, hence, deleterious aftereffects of exposure to such stimulation. To reiterate our earlier conclusion, psychological (i.e. cognitive) factors, not simply physical parameters of noise, are the important elements in the production of noise aftereffects.

PERCEIVED CONTROL AND HELPLESSNESS

The perception of control appears to reduce negative aftereffects of unpredictable noise—but why? What specific stress-reducing mechanisms are aroused by the manipulation of controllability? In answering this question, we reasoned that inescapable and unpredictable noise confronts the individual with a situation in which he is at the mercy of his environment. As we noted earlier, he is powerless to affect the occurrence of the stressor and he certainly cannot anticipate its onset. We may describe his psychological state under these circumstances as one of helplessness.

The notion that uncontrollable stress results in a sense of helplessness has been developed in several previous studies (e.g. Grinker and Spiegel 1945; Janis 1962; Mandler and Watson 1966; Lazarus 1966), and even in animal research there have been a number of treatments of helplessness and the closely related theme of hopelessness (Mowrer 1960; Richter 1957). More recently, Seligman, and his colleagues (e.g. Seligman, Maier, and Solomon 1971) have proposed a theory of "learned helplessness," the basic premises of which are as follows: (1) when aversive stimuli are uncontrollable, the organism learns that his responses are

independent of his outcomes; (2) the acquisition of this relationship interferes with the learning of a subsequent relationship in which the organism's responses would in fact control and thereby ameliorate the aversive stimulus. In other words, it is not the stressful event itself that causes interference but the individual's lack of control over the event. This lack of control induces a state of helplessness in which there is an absence of incentives for initiating actions aimed at avoiding or escaping from the aversive stimulus. If, on the other hand, the individual has learned that he can control the stimulus, escape and avoidance behaviors will be facilitated in subsequent exposures to the same and similar stressors.

Seligman explicitly states that his definition of control is in terms of the experimenter's arrangement of experimental events, not in terms of the individual's perception of them. Our primary concern, by contrast, has been with perceived control—that is, the belief that control over aversive stimulation is possible even though the individual does not actually exert control. This difference in definition does not necessarily imply an inconsistency, and, for our purposes, we may consider Seligman's theory as one version of a more general helplessness hypothesis which deals with a wide gamut of consequences resulting from uncontrollable stressful events.

The helplessness hypothesis provides a nice explanation of the relationship between unpredictable and uncontrollable noise and deleterious aftereffects. If the impact of a repeatedly presented aversive event is greatest where feelings of helplessness are maximal, it follows that adverse aftereffects will also be maximal. Our working thesis is, then, that exposure to uncontrollable noise produces feelings of helplessness which interfere with later functioning. Perceived-control subjects learn to label their situation as one in which they are not helpless. By contrast, no-perceived-control subjects do not develop such expectations.

Subsequent performance after noise

stimulation is affected in a way that is consistent with prior experience, when control was or was not perceived as available. Presumably, the helpless group experience not only the aversiveness of unpredictable noise but also the "anxiety" connected with their felt inability to do anything about it. Perceived-control subjects, on the other hand, are exposed only to the stress of the noise itself; they do not experience additional anxiety produced by feelings of helplessness. We tentatively conclude, therefore, that unpredictable noise produces adverse aftereffects because it is more aversive than predictable noise, its greater aversiveness being a function of the sense of helplessness induced in an individual who is unable to control and/or predict its onset and offset.

OTHER COGNITIVE FACTORS

The importance of unpredictability and uncontrollability in determining noise aftereffects led us to examine other cognitive factors that might be expected, on a priori grounds, to interact with noise (cf. Zimbardo 1969). These additional studies illustrate the extension of our cognitive approach while, at the same time, delimiting the scope of our effects; it is as important to know which cognitive variables do not affect noise as to know which do. In the first of these experiments, we considered the extent to which "relative deprivation" would, under certain circumstances, modify the consequences of a noise stressor (cf. Pettigrew 1967).

An individual exposed to noise will experience a certain amount of discomfort and incur a certain measure of negative aftereffects. If that same individual is exposed to the noise under identical physical conditions but with knowledge that someone else is being exposed to less intense noise, his resulting feelings of relative deprivation should increase the aversiveness of the noise and its consequent negative aftereffects. This prediction assumes that frustration stemming from relative deprivation generalizes to the

stressful event itself and makes for a more generally aversive experience. In those instances where a subject finds himself better off relative to a comparison person, there should be an arousal of relative satisfaction rather than relative deprivation. This satisfaction will lower the total aversiveness of the noise situation by a similar process of generalization and, therefore, reduce adverse post-noise consequences.

An experiment designed to test these propositions was conducted by two of our students, Brett Silverstein and Ilene Staff. The results were unequivocal. When subjects were relatively deprived with respect to noise—when they thought another person (i.e. a confederate of the experimenter) was undergoing less noise—they showed greater impairment on a somewhat modified version of the proofreading task and on the Stroop Color Word Test (aftereffect measures used in this study). Conversely, when they believed that the confederate was undergoing more severe noise, subjects showed few aftereffect deficits. (The Stroop test, widely used in psychology [Jensen and Rohwer 1966], consists of a series of color names, each of which is printed in incongruent colors. The subject's task, in this version of the test, is to write the letter of the appropriate color under each color name. For example, if the word "red" is printed in blue, the subject should write "b" for "blue" under the word. This moderately stressful test requires that a subject be alert in order to resolve competition between opposing response tendencies.)

The results of the proofreading and Stroop tests, based on 10 cases in each condition, are shown in Figures 7 and 8. The no-relative-deprivation subjects (those who were ostensibly exposed to the same noise as the confederate) provide a bench mark for comparison purposes. They were told they would receive moderately intense noise, and they behaved as though this is what they did hear, though the sound was actually an intense 108 dbA. The high-relative-deprivation subjects underwent the same promised

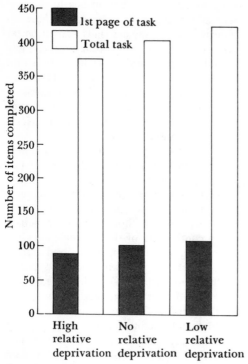

Fig. 7. Number of Items Completed on the Stroop Test.

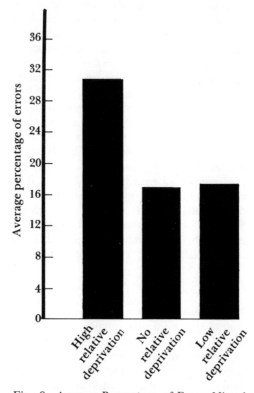

Fig. 8. Average Percentage of Errors Missed in the Proofreading Task.

level of noise, but they were informed that the confederate would receive a less intense set of stimuli. They did significantly less well on the aftertasks than the no-relative-deprivation subjects. As expected, the low-relative-deprivation subjects behaved like the no-deprivation controls. It should be noted that questionnaire data confirmed the success of the deprivation manipulation. Subjects in the high-relative deprivation category felt they had received more intense noise than the confederate; subjects in the low-relative-deprivation group felt they had received less noise; and the no-relative-deprivation subjects perceived no difference.

This experiment underscores the importance of still another cognitive factor in reactivity to noise. It is both fascinating and ironic to note that stress aftereffects decline

when others are perceived to be in more stressful circumstances and increase when others are ostensibly experiencing less stress. There are at least two ways in which these effects can be explained. First, exposure to the relative deprivation condition amounts to victimization by an arbitrary and unfair experimenter, which should evoke anger in addition to stress. The experience of anger could directly impair task performance or lower the subject's motivation to do well as a means of expressing anger against the experimenter. In either case, we would expect impaired performance on the proofreading and Stroop tests among the relative-deprivation group compared to the no-deprivation controls. Subjects in the low-relative deprivation condition should show superior performance compared to the controls. Knowing that they had received favored treatment from the experimenter may have evoked positive feelings which directly counteracted the effects of the noise stress or motivated them to do well on the tasks as a way of thanking the experimenter. The results reported in Figs. 7 and 8 are, of course, consistent with these explanations.

Alternatively, we might interpret the effects of the relative deprivation manipulation in a manner similar to that which was used to explain the effects of perceived control. Although this approach is somewhat less compelling than the explanation given above, it does have the advantage of being coordinate with our previous theorizing about controllability and its impact on stress aftereffects. Thus, we assume that the noxiousness of a stress depends, in part, on the person's evaluation of the stress in relation to his ability to cope with it. The more overwhelming it seems and the fewer his adaptive resources, the more likely he is to label the situation as one in which he is helpless. Perceived control would reduce the stressor's effects primarily by increasing the person's evaluation of his coping resources, thereby leading him to label the situation as one in which he is not helpless.

In analogous fashion, relative deprivation may exert its effects by providing the individual with additional information about his helplessness. If others are less deprived with respect to a stressor, and if there seems to be little opportunity to change this state of affairs, the individual may well conclude that he is relatively powerless to cope with the resultant stress. This labeling process may cause him to reassess the stressor's magnitude, hence increasing negative aftereffects. By contrast, the person in a state of low relative deprivation realizes that there are others who are in even worse circumstances. This will enable him to revise his assessment of his coping resources and reduce perceived aversiveness of the stressor and, therefore, the severity of the aftereffects.

The relative deprivation experiment was one of a series aimed at exploring the impact of various cognitive factors (other than controllability and predictability) upon noise effects and aftereffects. Thus, a choice of whether or not to experience noise was also found to influence the severity of aftereffects. When people were required to work under noisy conditions, they suffered aftereffects of a given level of severity; if, however, people worked under noisy circumstances as a consequence of a free and informed decision on their part, the aftereffects of noise were mitigated. The necessity of the noise, whether defined as an unavoidable concomitant of an important activity or as gratuitous, was also investigated in our research. It is presently equivocal whether this factor affects noise-produced aftereffect performance; however, there are indications that an adequate test has yet to be made of the effects of the necessity variable. We intend to examine this and related cognitive factors in future stress research in our laboratories.

NON-NOISE STRESSORS

While noise was the stressor used in the studies described up to this point, we do not believe our findings and interpretations hinge upon its unique characteristics. The pattern of results obtained with noise—almost universal adaptation followed by adverse aftereffects as a function of cognitive factors surrounding noise exposure—has been obtained with other stressors (Glass and Singer 1972). For example, data from experiments using electric shock demonstrate that adverse behavioral consequences are reduced if this form of stimulation is both predictable and controllable. Still other research in our laboratories has indicated that these two cognitive variables produce similar effects with social stressors, such as bureaucratic frustration and arbitrary discrimination.

The bureaucracy experiment is a good illustration. Subjects who were exposed to a contrived experience with bureaucratic red tape showed adverse aftereffects, both general and specific. The general aftereffect was a drop in efficiency of cognitive functioning as measured by proofreading. The specific effects were that subjects who attributed their bureaucratic troubles to an immutable system over which they felt little control became docile and compliant; subjects who attributed their bureaucratic troubles to the people involved (presumably over whom control was more likely) became reactive and negative. Although subjects who were exposed to the stress of bureaucratic harassment showed adverse aftereffects, they demonstrated them in different ways, as a function of what they learned about the controllability of their environment. Subjects who were harassed by a bureaucratic official learned of their potential control of the system, had this control rendered ineffectual, and then attempted to reduce their sense of helplessness by exercising control over those with whom they subsequently interacted. Subjects who were harassed by bureaucratic regulations, rather than by the bureaucrat, learned that they were in a system in which they could not exercise control—there was no point of leverage—and, in subsequent exchanges, they quickly acceded to the other's control rather than expend useless effort in a chimerical quest to establish their own control.

The electric-shock experiments allowed us to generalize the effects of unpredictability and perceived uncontrollability. We realize that a somewhat liberal interpretation is required to assume that the bureaucracy experiment manipulated perceived control, and it is certainly not reasonable to argue that it varied the predictability of stressful stimulation. However, broadness of application is perhaps more important in new areas of research than point-by-point comparability between two or more similar types of variables. The strategy of testing for aftereffects over a number of physical and social stressors was part of the general rationale underlying our program of research. A strong case can now be made that exposure to a variety of aversive events leads to negative aftereffects.

PSYCHIC COSTS OF STRESS

Analogues of urban stress, whether physical or social, have few direct effects; people adapt to stress. But, stressors do have disruptive aftereffects, and these are more a function of the cognitive circumstances in which stimulation takes place than of the sheer magnitude or intensity of stimulation. These conclusions do not mean that aftereffect phenomena are the "psychic price" paid by the individual for his adaptation to noxious stimulation. Such a hypothesis was indeed the original basis for our research, but the results presented thus far do not provide confirmation. It is entirely possible that aftereffects are as much post-stressor phenomena as post-adaptation phenomena. The designs and findings of our research do not indicate whether aftereffects occurred in spite of adaptation or because of the effort entailed in the adaptive process. Further analysis and experimentation with the noise stressor enabled us to reach a partial adjudication of this rather nice theoretical issue.

As we noted earlier, adaptation is a cognitive process involving one or another mechanism designed to filter out of awareness certain aspects of the aversive agent or, in some other way, reappraise it as benign. We assumed that physiological adaptation is one index of this process and that the effort entailed in achieving adaptation is reflected in the magnitude of decline of physiological response to the stressor. Given these assumptions, we were able to conclude that greater amounts of adaptation are not systematically related to greater post-noise deficits. We inferred this lack of association from two analyses (see Glass and Singer 1972).

First, there was a very low correlation $(-.20)$ between aftereffect scores (i.e. proofreading) and indices of adaptation magnitude for subjects in various unpredictable and uncontrollable noise conditions. Second, we conducted still another noise experiment in which we failed to find differences in adverse aftereffects in two unpredictable conditions—one in which the usual autonomic adaptation took place and one in which GSR decrements were inhibited by using long intervals between noise bursts. On the basis of these and related data, we tentatively suggest that aftereffect phenomena represent behavioral consequences of cumulative exposure to noxious stimulation. It is not the adaptive process itself that causes deleterious aftereffects but the fact of mere exposure in spite of adaptation.

Stress aftereffects, whether caused by noise or by some other aversive event, may be viewed as an instance of the "delayed reaction" effect observed in a number of field studies of psychological stress (e.g. Grinker and Spiegel 1945; Basowitz et al. 1955). They may be observed relatively soon after termination of the aversive event, as in the case of increased anxiety among army personnel in the period immediately following graduation from airborne training school. On the other hand, they may not become evident for several months, as in the case of soldiers who are relatively calm during combat but manifest severe attacks of anxiety months later and miles removed from the scene of battle. The fact that adaptation takes place during the stress period suggests that reactivity is being minimized and that the individual is learning to work in spite of stress.

Continued exposure to the stressor, however, may produce cumulative effects which appear only after stimulation is terminated. It is as if the person does not experience maximal stress until he is no longer required to cope with the stressor; only then do the behavioral consequences of the event become evident. Korchin (1965) has nicely summarized the dynamics of delayed reaction in the following terms: "This [the delayed reaction] might represent a release phenomenon from the control of feelings and associated stress behaviors which had been necessary for adaptive behavior [during stress exposure]." In other words, aftereffects of the kind observed in our research may well represent residues of cumulative stress which appear only after maintenance of effective functioning is no longer required. The adaptive process may not be directly implicated in the production of stress aftereffects, but it would still seem important to question the validity of the simplistic idea that man's adaptability is of unqualified benefit to his subsequent functioning.

REFERENCES

Anastasi, A. 1964. *Fields of Applied Psychology*. New York: McGraw-Hill.

Basowitz, H., H. Persky, S. J. Korchin, and R. R. Grinker. 1955. *Anxiety and Stress*. New York: McGraw-Hill.

Berlyne, D. E. 1960. *Conflict, Arousal, and Curiosity*. New York: McGraw-Hill.

Broadbent, D. E. 1957. Effects of noise on behavior. In C. M. Harris, Ed., *Handbook of Noise Control*. New York: McGraw-Hill.

Broadbent, D. E. 1971. *Decision and Stress*. New York: Academic Press.

Corah, N. L., and J. Boffa. 1970. Perceived control, self-observation, and response to aversive stimulation. *Journal of Personality and Social Psychology* 16:1–14.

Dubos, E. 1965. *Man Adapting*. New Haven: Yale University Press.

Feather, N. T. 1961. The relationship of persistence at a task to expectation of success and achievement related motives. *Journal of Abnormal and Social Psychology* 63:552–61.

Finkelman, J. M., and D. C. Glass. 1970. Reappraisal of the relationship between noise and human performance by means of a subsidiary task measure. *Journal of Applied Psychology* 54:211–13.

French, J. W., R. B. Ekstrom, and L. A. Price. 1963. *Manual for Kit of Reference Tests for Cognitive Factors*. Princeton, N.J.: Educational Testing Service.

Geer, J. H., G. C. Davison, and R. I. Gatchel. 1970. Reduction of stress in humans through nonveridical perceived control of aversive stimulation. *Journal of Personality and Social Psychology* 16:731–38.

Glass, D. C., J. E. Singer, and Lucy N. Friedman. 1969. Psychic cost of adaptation to an environmental stressor. *Journal of Personality and Social Psychology* 12:200–10.

Glass, D. C., and J. E. Singer. 1972. *Urban Stress: Experiments in Noise and Social Stressors.* New York: Academic Press.

Grinker, R. R., and J. P. Spiegel. 1945. *Men under Stress.* New York: McGraw-Hill.

Haggard, E. A. Some conditions determining adjustment during and readjustment following experimentally induced stress. In S. S. Tomkins, Ed., *Contemporary Psychopathology.* Cambridge: Harvard University Press.

Janis, I. L. 1962. Psychological effects of warnings. In G. W. Baker and D. W. Chapman, Eds., *Man and Society in Disaster.* New York: Basic Books.

Jensen, A. R., and W. D. Rohwer, Jr. 1966. The Stroop color-word test: A review. *Acta psychologica* 25:36–93.

Korchin, S. J. 1965. Some psychological determinants of stress behavior. In S. Z. Klausner, Ed., *The Quest for Self-Control.* New York: Free Press, p. 260.

Lazarus, R. S. 1966. *Psychological Stress and the Coping Process.* New York: McGraw-Hill.

Lazarus, R. S. 1968. Emotions and adaptation: Conceptual and empirical relations. In W. J. Arnold, Ed., *Nebraska Symposium on Motivation.* Lincoln: University of Nebraska Press.

Mandler, G., and D. L. Watson. 1966. Anxiety and the interruption of behavior. In C. D. Spielberger, Ed., *Anxiety and Behavior.* New York: Academic Press.

Mecklin, J. M. It's time to turn down all that noise. *Fortune.* October 1969, p. 130.

Montagu, J. D., and E. M. Coles. 1966. Mechanism and measurement of the galvanic skin response. *Psychological Bulletin* 65:261–79.

Mowrer, O. H. 1960. *Learning Theory and Behavior.* New York: Wiley.

Pervin, L. A. 1963. The need to predict and control under conditions of threat. *Journal of Personality* 31:570–87.

Pettigrew, T. F. 1967. Social evaluation theory: Convergences and applications. In D. Levine, Ed., *Nebraska Symposium on Motivation.* Lincoln: University of Nebraska Press.

Richter, C. P. 1957. On the phenomenon of sudden death in animals and man. *Psychosomatic Medicine* 19:191–98.

Sanders, A. F. 1961. The influence of noise on two discrimination tasks. *Ergonomics* 4:253–58.

Seligman, M. E. P., S. F. Maier, and R. L. Solomon. 1971. Unpredictable and uncontrollable aversive events. In F. R. Brush, Ed., *Aversive Conditioning and Learning.* New York: Academic Press.

Selye, H. 1956. *The Stress of Life.* New York: McGraw-Hill.

Thompson, R. F., and W. A. Spencer. 1966. Habituation: A model phenomenon for the study of neural substrates of behavior. *Psychological Review* 73:16–43.

Wohlwill, J. F. 1970. The emerging discipline of environmental psychology. *American Psychologist* 25:303–12.

Zimbardo, P. G. 1969. *The Cognitive Control of Motivation.* Glenview, Ill.: Scott, Foresman.

8.4
Science and Sentiment:
Overview of Research on Crowding and Human Behavior

JOHN E. S. LAWRENCE

Recent awareness of the world population growth rate has generated considerable academic and popular interest in the social significance of population density and crowding. Widely publicized national commissions on civil disorders, in 1968, and violence, in 1969, related urban congestion to rioting (Report, 1968, p. 325) and overcrowding to aggression (Carstairs, 1969, p. 730).

The behavioral sciences seem for some reason to have been slow to react. In 1970, an article by Bartz appeared in the *American Psychologist* entitled, "While Psychologists Doze On." The author admitted to feeling like "an impotent observer . . . on the deck of the Titanic." Referring to the borrowed time for America's way of life, he indicted the discipline for inattention to the anabatic onslaught of population-growth-related problems. Noting that it might prove difficult for psychologists to divert their gaze from "nude marathons, chicken pecks, subjective probability, and preference for body products," he urged them to awaken and respond to the "dark predictions" of population polemicists.

Three years later, a search of current journals still yields little in the way of consolidated research in this direction, certainly rather less than seems warranted. Such population-related literature as there exists in psychology contains remarkably few studies on the effects of population density (expressed as a relationship between numbers of individuals and units of available space) on human behavior. Yet there is a persistent body of opinion that holds "overcrowding," generally associated with high population and little space, to be a purveyor of social malaise. (For a summary of some of those views, see Schorr, 1964.)

It is the purpose of this brief article to review some of the extant psychological evidence and demonstrate that arguments which attribute various forms of psycho- and socio-pathology simply to overcrowding are presently based, at least, on shaky foundations.

ANIMAL STUDIES

Conclusions drawn from the study of non-human populations may be largely re-

Abridged from J. Lawrence. Science and sentiment: Overview of research on crowding and human behavior. *Psychological Bulletin*, 1974, *81*, 712–720. Copyright 1974 by the American Psychological Association. Reprinted by permission.

sponsible for the awe with which exponential rises in human population are regarded. A large body of research has accumulated on the effects of density and spatial limitation on animals, not all of which is consistent (Deevey, 1972). However, there is enough evidence of a disturbing nature to prompt careful investigation among humans.

Cybernetic regulatory mechanisms appear to moderate population growth specifically as a function of density in microorganisms, insects, and animals (Hoagland, 1963). This means that critical population densities result in sociopathological behaviors, at which point the growth curve asymptotes and responses return to normal. Classic research by Calhoun (1962) details such behavioral abnormalities in laboratory rats. He allowed groups of rats to breed naturally and with adequate resources. Growth rates increased sharply until inhibited by breakdowns in social behaviors that included catatonia, hyperactivity, and indiscriminate aggression. The reproductive organs of both sexes regressed and normally meticulous maternal care reverted to cannibalism, even to the marauding of others' nests.

Corroborative evidence can be found for the effects of density on aggression and other asocial behaviors in cats (Leyhausen, 1965) and monkeys (Southwick, 1967). (For an extensive review of this literature, see Snyder, 1968, and Freedman, 1973.)

Possibly the best known field study concerning density and animal behavior was conducted on a small herd of sika deer on an island in the Chesapeake Bay (Christian, Flyger, & Davis, 1960). Released and left free to breed uninterrupted and with adequate resources, the herd increased in numbers until density reached a ratio of approximately one deer per acre. At this point the mortality rate soared unaccountably. Food and water were abundant, and there was no evidence of exogenous disease. Subsequent examination of the carcasses revealed a variety of endocrinological disorders, apparently resulting from extreme stress brought on as a reaction to overcrowd-

ing. Symptoms included greatly enlarged adrenal glands (by almost 50%) and reproductive dysfunctions. Deevey (1960) related similar evidence of cyclical mortality increases in lemmings and the snowshoe hare.

The results of the previous studies have achieved considerable prominence in the existing social literature on crowding. The degree of generalization to human populations, however, is strongly contested. Those arguing *for* generalization point out the similarities in endocrine functioning between human and animal species in response to stress (Deevey, 1972; Hartley, 1972). Others dispute the simplicity of such comparison. Hawley (1972), for example, suggested that since reputable biologists have discovered no useful application of the findings to relevant human situations, the social scientist should be excused "for his inability to appreciate [for instance] Calhoun's contribution [p. 522]," and Calhoun himself is extremely cautious in considering the possibility of an approximation to some common biological heritage (1970, p. 202).

Whatever one's bias in the longstanding argument between comparative and social scientists, experimental findings on animals stand in this case as a provocative reminder of the need for further research among humans. Despite strong evidence for the influence of social factors on human perceptions of stress and hence on their levels of adreno-cortical secretion (Mason & Brady, 1964), little if any research has yet explored the effects, for instance, of some measure of crowding on endocrine functioning in humans.

CITIES

As a result of the constant juxtaposition of the animal studies already surveyed with research on human populations, there has been a simplistic tendency to extrapolate from the former with an eye to the large urban centers and their associated social problems. Some of the more prominent statements of this philosophy include: "That overcrowding increases the propensity to aggressive behavior has long been known and demonstrated experimentally by sociological research" as asserted without reference by Lorenz (1966, p. 244). Leyhausen (1965) saw "the ill effects on the individual of living in overcrowded communities" as constituting an "imminent danger to human survival." The lack of "adequate space" can lead to "neuroses, delinquency and violence [Holford, 1970, p. 550] ."

It is important to understand the personal and deep conviction with which these ideas are propagated:

Nearly five years in prisoner-of-war camps taught me that overcrowded human societies reflect the symptoms of overcrowded wolf, cat, goat, mouse, rat or rabbit communities to the last detail, and that all differences are merely species-specific; the basic forces of social interaction and of organization are *in principle* identical and there is true homology between Man and Animal throughout the whole range of vertebrates [Leyhausen, 1965, p. 31].

Impressive though they may be, these assertions are polemical, largely without scientific support, and seem only to confuse the issue further. A more cautious, but still uncheerful, view holds that "overcrowding may have a serious impact on human behavior, and that social scientists should consider [it] when attempting to explain a wide range of pathological behaviors [Galle, Gove, & McPherson, 1972] ."

The preceding sample of pessimistic predictions is by no means exhaustive. The Kerner Commission (Report, 1968) identified crowded ghetto conditions as one of five interacting causal factors in the riots of 1967. Furthermore, Freedman et al. (1972) referred to the results of investigating press reports which associated crowding with a formidable list of disorders including physical malfunction, drug addiction, and war. There is, however, in the evidence to date

little corroboration for these somber assessments.

Investigations of demographic data have been conducted on city populations in Hong Kong (Schmitt, 1963), Honolulu (Schmitt, 1966), and Chicago (Galle et al., 1972; Winsborough, 1965). Although there was some indication of a relationship between, for example, higher crime rates with increased population density as variously defined, no simple or even consistent pattern exists. It has been suggested (Hall, 1965, p. 191) that "culture is possibly the most significant single variable in determining what constitutes stressful density." Hall's theory of proxemics addresses this aspect of man's perceptions and use of space primarily from an anthropological viewpoint (Hall, 1970). While the precise dimensions of the differences in perceptions of stressful density have yet to be defined, it does appear that comparison of crowding effects may be difficult between and across the multicultures of contemporary cities. Thus, initially significant correlations between density and sociopathology tend to vanish when attempts are made to control for ethnic and other relevant socioeconomic variables (Pressman & Carol, 1971; Winsborough, 1965). Galle et al. (1972) developed indexes of sociopathology in Chicago to match as closely as possible the disorders exhibited in the behaviors of Calhoun's rats. Employing correlational analysis, they found a significant relationship between density and pathology, which disappeared when they controlled for class and ethnicity. When finer definitions of density were used, a significant relationship was again established between their measures of density and each of the pathologies; moreover, these positive correlations remained when class and ethnicity were controlled. The authors, however, stressed that not only may conclusions as to causality clearly not be inferred from this kind of analysis but also that cross-sectional correlations may not necessarily be replicated at the level of the individual. Furthermore it seems difficult, even with precise definitions, to identify the independent effects of density as opposed to those of other relevant socioeconomic variables.

Schmitt's (1963, 1966) two studies present conflicting results: Significant positive relationships between density and various sociopathologies obtained from Honolulu census tract data (1966) contradict earlier research in Hong Kong (1963) by the same author. The reason that the correlations still held in this case (1966) when education and income were controlled, may be detected in the width of these socioeconomic categories as defined by Schmitt (p. 38).

While at best there seems inconsistent support for the proposed relationship, it is important to note that *density* and *overcrowding*, as terms, are neither synonymous nor used consistently across studies. Schmitt, for example, adopted Jacobs's (1961) differentiation between density (population per net area) and overcrowding (persons per room) and concluded that population per net area is "the more significant variable [Schmitt, 1966, p. 39]." Galle et al., on the other hand, found "persons per acre" an insufficient definition. They introduced the concept of "interpersonal press" as two distinct factors: "persons per room" and "persons per housing unit [1972, p. 26]." They further included two other structural measures of density and reasoned that "the number of persons per room is the most important determinant of the effect of density on pathology [p. 27]."

The association between population density and infectious disease was reviewed extensively by Cassell (1971), who concluded that as of then there was no evidence of causation in the relationship. The incidence of suicide is also inconsistently related to population density. Carstairs (1969) reported that while suicide is related to social isolation, attempted suicide is associated with high-density conditions. In a study in Edinburgh, Scotland, suicide was found to be more frequent in the overcrowded area of the city; in Buffalo, New York, no such relationship was established (Lester, 1970).

Positive correlations were found between completed suicide and crowded conditions in Santiago, Chile (Chuaqui, Lemkau, Legarreta, & Contresas, 1966) but not in London, England (Sainsbury, 1955). Again, measures of density differed: The Santiago study referred to thousands per square kilometer, in Buffalo it was persons per acre, and in Edinburgh, persons per room.

Although psychology has traditionally explored the effects of varying stimulus impacts upon the individual, the interaction between man and his physical environment has only recently begun to be investigated. Kates and Wohlwill (1966) and Proshansky, Ittelson, and Rivlin (1970) documented much of the genesis of this field of inquiry. Reconnaisance over preliminary directions for research, on the influences specifically of urban environments on the individual, has revealed wide differences of opinion. Parr (1966), for example, has emphasized the regularity of structure and excessive constriction characteristic of the city landscape. Citing sensory deprivation studies, he suggested that monotony and the lack of visual interest or stimulus variety should be explored for possible harmful effects upon the individual. Milgram (1970), however, argued practically the opposite. In the development also of some theoretical statements for experimental inquiry, he invoked the general systems concept of "overload" and proposed that adaptive mechanisms in the individual might lead to withdrawal and a sense of anonymity in response to the frenetic atmosphere of urban life.

In the absence of any substantial or cohesive body of empirical evidence, all firm statements are to be treated with caution. The cities are, nevertheless, not without their defenders. Terming the "supposed correlation between high densities and trouble" as "simply incorrect," Jacobs (1961) argued for the "exuberant diversity" of the city as a necessarily creative force in modern life. But perhaps the most important and neglected observation is that the centrifugal movement of urban populations has resulted in a steady decline in population density both within and across metropolitan areas (Guest, 1973; Hawley, 1972). This is not to say that people appear to be moving away from cities but from city centers. In parenthesis, it further seems to be worth investigating whether the resulting "spreading disease of interior [city] space [Hawley, 1972, p. 528]" may be more conducive to higher crime rates and to rises in other socio-pathological indexes (e.g., disease) than the conditions of density it appears to be replacing.

DEFINITIONS

Methodological difficulties aside, perhaps the critical deficiency in most accounts has been the semantic confusion generated by the interchangeability of terms such as crowding, overpopulation, and density. In 1963, Biderman proposed that "density is not regarded as a fruitful unitary concept for use in scientific study." Except in extreme cases in which the press of crowding approaches "physical displacement of the human body, density of occupancy has significance only in interdependent relationships with many other variables of the situation, environmental, structural, temporal, psychological and social [p. 40]." So even when specifically defined, density as a demographic variable is of dubious psychological value.

Recent attempts to clarify this imprecision have generally labeled crowding as the dependent variable, being varied as a function of (a) space and (b) number of people. The psychological phenomenon of crowding is, however, "only indirectly related to mere numbers of densities of people [Proshansky et al., 1970, p. 182]" if it is assumed that individuals will differ in their reactions to their immediate social environment and, therefore, that one may feel crowded among a few people or not crowded among many. Closely related to the concepts of *privacy* and *territoriality*, crowding is understood to be a social factor relating the number of people present to the individual's freedom of choice. Increased density of course may be operationally defined as an increase in numbers, holding space constant, or a decrease in space, holding numbers of people constant.

The necessary psychological distinction between crowding as the independent or dependent variable was made by Stokols (1972b). As a *stressor situation* the term *crowding* refers to the interaction of those variables which give rise to the experience of being crowded. As a *syndrome of stress* it is associated with the psychological experience itself.

This distinction may be made at the individual or the societal level. Environmental or social restrictions will interact with individual predispositional variables to produce the sensation of crowding. Thus, crowding may be seen as a motivational state directed toward minimization of the unpleasant consequences of perceived constraints (Stokols, 1972a).

It was necessary to make these distinctions in order to perform experimental manipulations of some of the variables that might cause the feeling of being crowded. Using these definitions, the term *overcrowding* has no significance, the extent of the restriction imposed on the subject being measured only in units of social or spatial density. . . .

. . . Crowding has also been defined as a subjective experience resulting from overstimulation of the nervous system (Esser, 1971). A recent and independent experimental definition is somewhat similar, proposing that "being crowded" is receiving excessive stimulation from social sources (Desor, 1971).

It is obvious from the exploratory range of these definitions that simple causal statements about urban crowding have little validity. It is also apparent that crowding as a psychological concept is still in its infancy. . . .*

*Editors' note. The author's review of experimental research with humans has been omitted.

CONCLUSIONS

The preceding is a brief, but fairly broad, coverage of some of the main themes in the psychological literature on crowding. Important peripheral areas not covered here include such concepts as territoriality, privacy, and proxemics (see Proshansky et al., 1970) and the theory of undermanning and overmanning (Barker, 1968). A recent and comprehensive bibliography of the crowding literature may be found in Choldin and McGinty (1972).

The field is confused—by definitions, by conflicting data, and, as psychology often is, by popular conjecture. The animal data are most easily interpreted and possibly of least use to man. The urban findings are inconclusive, demonstrating no unequivocal relationship between population density and social ills. Finally, clinical and experimental models are at odds, and the results of experiments are again inconclusive.

Perhaps the only certain conclusion that can be drawn at this time is that there is no clear demonstrable linear relationship between high density and aberrant human behaviors, or between the social crowding of the individual and aggression. It is impossible to do more than speculate further.

If it is assumed that the psychological experience of crowding causes stress and therefore motivates the individual to alleviate that stress, it is possible to invoke a number of psychological theories to predict his behavior (cf. Stokols, 1972b, pp. 80 ff.). In short, these may involve various cognitive or behavioral adjustments directed toward alleviation of reactance, dissonance reduction, or the restoring of cognitive consistency. Roughly speaking, there are three courses of action open: a change in self, a change in the environment (spatial or social), or a departure from the situation. In the absence of satisfaction resulting from any one of these alternatives, if for any reason of coercion or dysfunction the individual may not leave the field, then frustration, anxiety, and the physiological symptoms of stress may ensue.

There is abundant evidence that prolonged stress is associated with physical and psychiatric disorder. There is also evidence that frustration may in some cases lead to aggression. The circumstances under which this chain is triggered and whether or not the process is completed up to prolonged stress remain the questions at issue.

. . . It seems inconceivable that research has not already somewhere examined the effects of experimentally induced sensations of crowding on the physiological indicators of stress. If the psychological experience of crowding, as a function of social or spatial density were reliably to produce physiological stress, then there would be genuine grounds for concern. Researchers might then follow up more closely on the urban studies in search of postmortem data on endocrinological dysfunction in areas of high density.

In the absence of such hard evidence and based on the preceding review of the current literature, one is led to conclude that such a relationship probably does not exist . . . Individuals occasionally seek more populous conditions than housing project designers prescribe for them (Schorr, 1964, p. 12). Furthermore, although controlled experiments are difficult in extreme conditions of confinement, and such conditions are almost impossible to simulate (Altman, 1961, p. 23), the majority of people experiencing cramped living in the Antarctic, for example, appear to remain in good health (Gunderson, 1968; Law, 1960). Thus, it should be determined whether or not some individuals may seek, even prefer, crowded situations. In passing, it is interesting to note that the relatively densely populated existence in college dormitories is often superficially referred to as a worthwhile experience by both those who impose it and those who have suffered it.

Finally, psychological theories of emotional labeling would predict that the subjective experience of social crowding might be mediated by the subjects' perceptions of the way *others* reacted to the situation, an important and as yet unexplored factor.

In summary, therefore, there is not yet any sizable body of consistent evidence to relate high densities with "trouble." Density itself is a troublesome concept. Prognoses of future civil conflict as a direct result of overcrowding, urban or otherwise, are premature and have no firm basis of empirical support in the psychological literature to date.

Rather, conflict may be an indirect result. If, for instance, increased population implies increased government, which in turn implies greater regulation of individual behavior (Choucri, 1972), then the probability of social conflict may be increased, particularly if the changes are rapid. There is a steadily increasing emphasis on planning, and consequences in the psychological realm include those proposed by Skinner (1971), which are profoundly challenging.

Population growth amidst waning resources has forced an awareness of the environment and its impact/constraint upon human life. Reaction to the imagined horrors of overcrowding by a nation that has traditionally expanded limits without bound is probably only a small and preliminary part of that awareness. In general system-theoretical terms, the subsystem is sensing the constraints of the larger system in which it is embedded, that is, symptoms of the initial phase of either adaptation or breakdown. As to which of the two it turns out to be, only time or possibly timely intervention will tell.

REFERENCES

Altman, J. W. Space psychology: Some considerations in the study of astronauts' behavior. Pittsburgh, Penn.: American Institute for Research, 1961.

Austin, F. H. A review of stress and fatigue monitoring of naval aviators during aircraft carrier operation: Blood and urine biochemical study. In P. G. Bourne, The psychology and physiology of stress. New York: Academic Press, 1969.

Barker, R. G. Ecological psychology: Con-cepts and methods for studying the environment of human behavior. Stanford: Stanford University Press, 1968.

Bartz, W. R. While psychologists doze on. American Psychologist, 1970, 25, 500–503.

Biderman, A. D., Louria, M., & Bacchus, J. Historical incidents of extreme overcrowding. Washington, D.C.: Bureau of Social Science Research, 1963.

Calhoun, J. B. Population density and social pathology. Scientific American, 1962, 206, 139–150.

Calhoun, J. B. The role of space in animal sociology. In H. Proshansky, W. Ittelson, & L. Rivlin (Eds.), Environmental psychology. New York: Holt, Rinehart & Winston, 1970.

Carstairs, G. M. Overcrowding and human aggression. In H. D. Graham & T. D. Gurr. Violence in America: Staff report to the National Commission on the Causes and Prevention of Violence. New York: Signet Books, 1969.

Cassell, J. Health consequences of population density and crowding. In National Academy of Sciences, Rapid population growth: Consequences and policy implications. Baltimore: Johns Hopkins Press, 1971.

Choldin, H. M., & McGinty, M. J. Bibliography: Population density, crowding, and social relations. Man-Environment Systems, 1972, 2, 131–158.

Choucri, N. Population resources and technology. In D. A. Kay & E. B. Skolnikoff (Eds.), World ecocrisis: International organizations in response. Madison, Wis.: University of Wisconsin Press, 1972.

Chuaqui, C., Lemkau, P. V., Legarreta, A., & Contresas, M. A. Suicide in Santiago, Chile. Public Health Reports, 1966, 81, 1109–1117.

Christian, J., Flyger, V., & Davis, D. Factors in the mass mortality of a herd of sika deer (cervus nippon). Chesapeake Science, 1960, 1, 79–95.

Deevey, E. S. The hare and the haruspex: A cautionary tale. The Yale Review, 1960, 49, 161–179.

Deevey, E. S. The equilibrium population. In W. Petersen (Ed.), Readings in population. New York: Macmillan, 1972.

Desor, J. A. Toward a psychological theory

of crowding. *Journal of Personality and Social Psychology*, 1972, 21, 79–83.

Esser, A. H. The psychopathology of crowding in institutions for the mentally ill and retarded. *Man-Environment Systems*, September 1971, S 66.

Esser, A. H. Experiences of crowding: Illustration of a paradigm for man-environment relations. *Representative Research in Social Psychology*, 1973, 4, 207–218.

Freedman, J. L., Levy, A. S., Buchanan, R. W., & Price, J. Crowding and human aggressiveness. *Journal of Experimental Social Psychology*, 1972, 8, 528–548.

Freedman, J. L. The effects of population density on humans. In J. T. Fawcett (Ed.), *Psychological perspectives on population.* New York: Basic Books, 1973.

Galle, O. R., Gove, W. R., & McPherson, J. M. Population density and pathology: What are the relationships for man? *Science*, 1972, 176, 23–30.

Griffit, W., & Veitch, R. Hot and crowded: Influences of population density and temperature on interpersonal affective behavior. *Journal of Personality and Social Psychology*, 1971, 17, 92–98.

Guest, A. M. Urban growth and population densities. *Demography*, 1973, 10, 53–69.

Gunderson, E. K. E. Mental health problems in Antarctica. *Archives of Environmental Health*, 1968, 17, 558–564.

Hall, E. T. Human adaptability to high density. *Ekistics*, 1965, 20, 191–193.

Hall, E. T. The anthropology of space: An organizing model. In H. Proshansky, W. Ittelson, & L. Rivlin (Eds.), *Environmental psychology.* New York: Holt, Rinehart & Winston, 1970.

Harris, E. G., & Paluck, R. J. The effects of crowding in an educational setting. *Man-Environment Systems*, May 1971, S 55.

Hartley, S. F. *Population: Quantity vs. quality.* Englewood Cliffs, N.J.: Prentice-Hall, 1972.

Hawley, A. H. Population density and the city. *Demography*, 1972, 9, 521–529.

Hoagland, H. Cybernetics of population control. In R. O. Greep (Ed.), *Human fertility and population problems.* Cambridge, Mass.: Schenckman Publishing, 1963.

Holford, Sir W. The built environment: Its creations, motivations and control. In H.

Proshansky, W. Ittelson, & L. Rivlin (Eds.), *Environmental psychology.* New York: Holt, Rinehart & Winston, 1970.

Hutt, C., & Vaizey, M. J. Differential effects of group density on social behavior. *Nature*, 1966, 209, 1371–1372.

Jacobs, J. *The death and life of great American cities.* New York: Random House, 1961.

Kates, R. W., & Wohlwill, J. F. (Eds.) Man's response to the physical environment. *Journal of Social Issues*, 1966, 22(4).

Law, P. Some psychological aspects of life at an Antarctic station. *Discovery*, 1960, 21, 431–437.

Lester, D. Social disorganization and completed suicide. *Social Psychiatry*, 1970, 5, 175–176.

Leyhausen, P. The sane community—A density problem? *Discovery*, 1965, 26, 27–33.

Loo, C. M. The effects of spatial density on the social behavior of children. *Journal of Applied Social Psychology*, 1972, 2, 372–381.

Lorenz, K. *On aggression.* New York: Bantam Books, 1966.

Ludwig, A. M. Psychedelic effects produced by sensory overload. *American Journal of Psychiatry*, 1972, 128, 114–117.

Mason, J. W., & Brady, J. V. The sensitivity of psychoendocrine systems to social and physical environment. In P. H. Leiderman & D. Shapiro (Eds.), *Psychobiological approaches to social behavior.* Palo Alto, Calif.: Stanford University Press, 1964.

Milgram, S. The experience of living in cities. *Science*, 1970, 167, 1461–1468.

Parr, A. E. Psychological aspects of urbanology. *Journal of Social Issues*, 1966, 22, 39–45.

Pressman, I., & Carol, A. Crime as a diseconomy of scale. *Review of Social Economy*, 1971, 29, 227–236.

Proshansky, H., Ittelson, W., & Rivlin, L. Freedom of choice and behavior in a physical setting. In H. Proshansky, W. Ittelson, & L. Rivlin (Eds.), *Environmental Psychology.* New York: Holt, Rinehart & Winston, 1970.

Report of the National Advisory Commission on Civil Disorders. New York: Bantam Books, 1968.

Sainsbury, P. *Suicide in London.* London: Chapman and Hall, 1955.

Schmitt, R. C. Implications of density in Hong Kong. *Journal of the American Institute of Planners,* 1963, 29, 210–217.

Schmitt, R. C. Density, health and social disorganization. *Journal of the American Institute of Planners,* 1966, 32, 38–40.

Schorr, A. L. *Slums and social insecurity.* London: Thomas Nelson, 1964.

Skinner, B. F. *Beyond freedom and dignity.* New York: Knopf, 1971.

Snyder, R. L. Reproduction and population pressures. In E. Stellar & J. M. Sprague (Eds.), *Progress in physiological psychology.* (Vol. 2) New York: Academic Press, 1968.

Solomon, P. (Ed.) *Sensory deprivation.* Cambridge, Mass.: Harvard University Press, 1961.

Southwick, C. H. An experimental study of intragroup agonistic behavior in rhesus monkeys. *Behavior,* 1967, 28, 182–209.

Stokols, D. On the distinction between density and crowding: Some implications for future research. *Psychological Review,* 1972, 79, 275–277. (a)

Stokols, D. A social-psychological model of human crowding phenomena. *Journal of the American Institute of Planners,* 1972, 38, 72–83. (b)

Stokols, D., Rall, M., Pinner B., & Schopler, J. Physical, social and personal determinants of the perception of crowding. *Environment and Behavior,* 1973, 5, 87–115.

Winsborough, H. H. The social consequences of high population density. *Law and Contemporary Problems,* 1965, 30, 120–126.

Author Index

(Citations for Introductions only)

Subject Index

(Citations for Introductions only)